EIGHTH EDITION

EXPLORING CORPORATE STRATEGY

Gerry Johnson
University of Strathclyde

Kevan Scholes
Sheffield Hallam University

Richard Whittington
Saïd Business School, University of Oxford

 Prentice Hall
FINANCIAL TIMES

An imprint of **Pearson Education**
Harlow, England • London • New York • Boston • San Francisco • Toronto
Sydney • Tokyo • Singapore • Hong Kong • Seoul • Taipei • New Delhi
Cape Town • Madrid • Mexico City • Amsterdam • Munich • Paris • Milan

Pearson Education Limited
Edinburgh Gate
Harlow
Essex CM20 2JE
England

and Associated Companies throughout the world

Visit us on the World Wide Web at:
www.pearsoned.co.uk

Fifth edition published under the Prentice Hall imprint 1998
Sixth edition published under the Financial Times Prentice Hall imprint 2002
Seventh edition 2005
Eighth edition published 2008

ISBN: 978-0-273-71191-9 (text only)
ISBN: 978-0-273-71192-6 (text and cases)

British Library Cataloguing-in-Publication Data
A catalogue record for this book is available from the British Library

10 9 8 7 6 5 4 3 2 1
11 10 09 08 07

Typeset in 9.5/13pt Linoletter by 35
Printed and bound by Rotolito Lombarda, Italy

The publisher's policy is to use paper manufactured from sustainable forests.

Brief Contents

Detailed Contents

Supporting resources

Visit the *Exploring Corporate Strategy, eighth edition* Companion Website at **www.pearsoned.co.uk/ecs**.

Register to create your own personal account using the access code supplied with the copy of the book. Access the following teaching and learning resources:

Resources for students

- **Key concepts: audio downloads, video clips, animations** and **quick tests** to reinforce your understanding
- **Chapter audio summaries** that you can download or listen to online
- **Self assessment questions** and a **personal gradebook** so you can test your learning and track your progress
- **Revision flashcards** to help you prepare for your exams
- A **multi-lingual online glossary** to explain key concepts
- Guidance on **how to analyse a case study**
- **Links** to relevant sites on the web so you can explore more about the organisations featured in the case examples and case studies

Also: The student Companion Website with Grade Tracker provides the following features:

- Enables students to save their scores from self assessment questions, and lecturers to monitor the scores of their class
- Search tool to help locate specific items of content
- Online help and support to assist with website usage and troubleshooting

Resources for instructors

- **Instructor's manual**, including extensive teaching notes for cases and suggested teaching plans
- Media-rich downloadable **PowerPoint slides**, including animations, video clips and key exhibits from the book
- **Classic cases** – over 60 case studies from previous editions of the book
- **Secure testbank** containing over 600 questions

Also: the following instructor resources are available off-line:

- Instructor's manual in hard copy, with CD containing PowerPoint slides and classic cases
- Video resources on DVD

For more information please contact your local Pearson Education sales representative or visit **www.pearsoned.co.uk/ecs**

List of Illustrations

List of Exhibits

Preface

We are delighted to offer this eighth edition of *Exploring Corporate Strategy*. With sales of previous editions approaching 800,000, we know that we have many loyal readers. At the same time, the strategy field is constantly changing. For this edition, therefore, we have consulted our users to introduce several new features, while taking care to retain features that have been well proven with many students and tutors from all over the world. Here we will highlight the key innovations of this edition, and then recap some of the classic features of the book.

The principal innovation of the eighth edition is to reorganise existing materials and introduce new materials to create four new chapters. These new chapters reflect advances in academic research, changes in practice and course developments in many universities around the world. These chapters are:

- Chapter 5 Culture and Strategy, incorporating a strong historical theme, with the growing appreciation of phenomena such as path dependency and institutionalised patterns of behaviour.

- Chapter 8 International Strategy, reflecting of course the growing internationalisation of business, but also the international ambitions of students in many universities.

- Chapter 9 Innovation and Entrepreneurship, responding to the increasing pace of innovation in many industries and the growing interest amongst many students in establishing their own enterprises.

- Chapter 15 The Practice of Strategy, emerging in part from a new research domain in which two of the authors are active, but also the need for students to have insight into the practical details of who gets involved in strategy, what they do and the methodologies they use.

While adding these chapters, we have been very aware of the need to offer students manageable amounts of reading. Accordingly we have slimmed down the text, so that students now have more, but shorter chapters than in previous editions. Overall, the eighth edition is shorter than the seventh.

A second significant development for this edition is the extension of the strategy lenses from three to four. We believe strongly that a strategy textbook should not encourage a narrow orthodoxy with regard to strategic issues. The strategy lenses are one of the ways in which we try to help students see strategy in different ways. As well as the analytically orientated design lens, the gradualist style of the experience lens and the innovative ideas lens, we introduce a discourse lens. This discourse lens reflects both the growth of academic research on the role of language in strategy and the practical importance of mastering this language in the 'strategic conversation' of organisations. At the same time as adding this fourth lens, we have adopted a new format for the lens-inspired 'commentaries' that follow each of the three parts of the book. This format is designed to be concise and user-friendly.

As well as these innovations, the eighth edition builds on established strengths of the book:

● *Outstanding pedagogical features*. Each chapter has clear learning outcomes, definitions of key concepts in the margins, practical questions associated with real-life illustrations, and concise end-of-chapter case examples through which students can easily apply what they have learnt. The website (www.pearsoned.co.uk/ecs) has a wealth of resources for students and tutors, including audio summaries, flashcards, a glossary, self-assessment questions, assignments, additional cases and PowerPoint slides.

● *Up-to-date materials*. As well as the new chapters, we have thoroughly revised the other chapters, updating the references so students and teachers can easily access the latest research. The majority of the 86 illustrations and 15 end-of-chapter case examples are entirely new to this edition. The Text and Cases version has 17 new cases and 19 fully revised ones. We have incorporated new theoretical perspectives, such as complexity theory, discourse theory and strategy-as-practice.

● *Encouraging critical thinking*. As well as the four strategy lenses, we encourage critical thinking by ending each chapter with a 'key debate', introducing students to research evidence and theory on key issues of the chapter and encouraging students to take a view. Our 'three circles' model – depicting the overlapping issues of strategic position, strategic choices and strategy in action – challenges a simple linear, sequential view of the strategy process.

● *Range of examples*. This edition maintains the wide range of examples used in the text, illustrations and cases. We draw from all over the world, and from a wide range of type and size of organisation. An important distinctive feature of *Exploring Corporate Strategy* is the use of examples from the public and voluntary sectors, where many students will be employed.

● *Attractive text layout and design*. We continue to use colours and photographic materials to improve clarity and ease of 'navigation' through the text. Reading the text should be an enjoyable and straightforward process.

A guide to how to get the most from all the features and learning materials of *Exploring Corporate Strategy* follows this preface.

Many people have helped us with the development of this new edition. Another innovation for this edition has been the introduction of an Advisory Board of 20 experienced users of the book. Their guidance has been immensely useful as we have undertaken the substantial revisions of this edition, and we hope to be able to develop the Advisory Board and its role in the future. But many other adopters of the book provide more informal advice and suggestions – many of whom we have had the pleasure of meeting at our annual teachers' workshops. This kind of feedback is invaluable. Also, our students and clients at Sheffield, Strathclyde, Lancaster and Oxford and the many other places where we teach are a constant source of ideas and challenge and it would be impossible to write a book of this type without this direct feedback. Our own work and contacts have expanded considerably as a result of our book and we now all have important links across the world who have been a source of stimulation to us.

Our contacts in Ireland, The Netherlands, Denmark, Sweden, France, Canada, Australia, New Zealand, Singapore and the USA are especially valued.

We would like to thank those who have contributed directly to the book by providing case studies, and those organisations that have been brave enough to be written up as case studies. The growing popularity of *Exploring Corporate Strategy* has often presented these case study companies with practical problems in coping with direct enquiries from tutors and students. We hope that those using the book will respect the wishes of the case study companies and *not* contact them directly for further information. There are many colleagues that we need to thank for assisting us in improving our understanding of particular aspects of the subject or related area. Strategy is such a vast domain that this assistance is essential if the book is to remain up to date. So thank you to Julia Balogun, John Barbour, Nic Beech, George Burt, Mark Gilmartin, Stéphane Girod, Royston Greenwood, Paula Jarzabkowski, Phyl Johnson, John Kind, Aidan McQuade, Michael Mayer, Thomas Powell, Ian Sayers, Jill Shepherd, Angela Sutherland, Catherine Walker and Basak Yakis. Special thanks are due to all those who provided and helped develop illustrations and cases – their assistance is acknowledged at the foot of those illustrations. Thanks are also due to Christine Reid at Strathclyde for her valuable assistance with references. Our thanks are also due to those who have had a part in preparing the manuscript for the book, in particular Lorna Carlaw at Strathclyde and Kate Goodman at Oxford.

Gerry Johnson
Kevan Scholes
Richard Whittington

November 2007

Getting the Most from *Exploring Corporate Strategy*

Through the various editions of *Exploring Corporate Strategy* we have tried to respond to the continuing demand for more material whilst keeping the size of the text manageable for readers. These demands have included more depth in topics, more coverage of particular sectors or simply more examples and tasks for students. We have already produced additional materials and publications and improved the cross-referencing to other material where it is relevant to a particular section of the text. With the launch of the *Enhanced Media Edition* of the seventh edition in 2006 our range of *web-based materials* for tutors and students was considerably extended. This note gives some practical advice on how you might gain most advantage from this wide and varied range of materials.

Using *Exploring Corporate Strategy*

To get the most from *Exploring Corporate Strategy* and related materials the broad advice to students and managers is to ensure that you have achieved three things:

● you understand the concepts;

● you can apply these concepts to practical situations – if you are a manager it is particularly important to apply the concepts to your own work context;

● you read more widely than *Exploring Corporate Strategy*.

Features of the text

● *Learning outcomes* are included at the beginning of each chapter which show what you should have achieved on completing the chapter. Check that you have understood all of these.

● *Key terms* are highlighted in the text and explained in the margins.

● *Illustration* boxes appear throughout the chapter and include questions so they can be used as 'mini' cases. Make sure that you read and answer these to check that you understand the theory/practice connection. If you are a manager, always ask yourself an additional question: 'what are the lessons for me and my organisation from this example?' Do this for the case examples and case studies too, if you can. The best strategic managers are those who can transfer learning from one situation to another.

● *Chapter summaries* help you to recap and review the main points of the chapter.

● *Work assignments* are organised in two levels of difficulty. Your tutors may have set some of these as course tests. In any case, you should treat these in the way you would previous examination papers – as a means of testing your own learning of both concepts and applications. If you are a manager, take the opportunity to work through these assignments for your own organisation and involve other members of your team if you can.

- *Recommended key readings* are listed at the end of each chapter. Make sure that you are familiar with those that are relevant to your course of study. There are extensive references for more detailed study and in-depth research.

- *A case example* is included at the end of each chapter to help you consolidate your learning of the major themes. Answer the questions at the end of the example.

- A *part commentary* appears at the end of each major section of the book. Use the commentaries to ensure that you can see connections between issues in different chapters of that part and that you can see the part theme in more than one way (through the strategy lenses as described in Chapter 1).

- If you are using the Text and Cases version try to read the cases relevant to the topics on your course – even if they are not set as class work or assessments. The *Guide to Using Case Studies* on page 599 indicates the main focus of each case and the relevant chapter. Case study introductions highlight which key learning points are covered by the case. Also look for relevant classic cases on the website (see below). Their relevance to topics in the book is indicated in the table on pages 602–603.

Check the companion website (see below) regularly for updates and additional material and ask if your tutor has a copy of the *Exploring Corporate Strategy* video material (see details below).

Teaching and learning resources

A wide range of material has been developed to support and enhance your use of this book. Students can access the companion website by redeeming the unique registration code provided with each new copy of the book. Tutors should contact their local Pearson Education representative to enable access to the instructor resources. Details of your local representative can be found at www.pearsoned.co.uk/replocator.

Exploring Corporate Strategy website (www.pearsoned.co.uk/ecs)

Material for students and tutors is added and updated on a regular basis.

For students:

- Revision aids (flashcards, key concepts and glossary in six languages).
- Audio summaries of chapters and important concepts.
- Self-assessment questions, work assignments and grade book.
- Help with case studies (weblinks, FT articles and advice on analysing cases).

For tutors:

- Extensive instructor's Manual (with case study teaching notes and work assignment debriefs).

- PowerPoint slides.
- Secure test bank of assessment questions.

Exploring Corporate Strategy – video resources DVD

The DVD contains mini briefings on selected topics from the authors and material to support some of the case studies.

1 With the Experts (the authors explain key concepts for use in class):
  - Strategy in different contexts
  - Porter's five forces
  - Core competences
  - Strategic drift and the cultural web
2 Case study organisations (supplementary material to use in class):
  - SABMiller (international development)
  - eBay (success and sustainability)
  - Amazon.com (business-level strategy)
  - Eurotunnel (a clash of national cultures)
  - Manchester United (football club or business?)
  - easyJet (competitive strategy)
  - Marks & Spencer (two CEOs on managing turnaround)

The Exploring Strategic Management series

This series from FT/Prentice Hall builds on readers' knowledge of *Exploring Corporate Strategy* and provides more depth by topic or sector. All these books have been written in conjunction with Gerry Johnson and Kevan Scholes. Books available are:

- V. Ambrosini with G. Johnson and K. Scholes, *Exploring Techniques of Analysis and Evaluation in Strategic Management*, 1998; ISBN: 0-13-570680-7
- T. Grundy with G. Johnson and K. Scholes, *Exploring Strategic Financial Management*, 1998; ISBN: 0-13-570102-3
- J. Balogun and V. Hope-Hailey with G. Johnson and K. Scholes, *Exploring Strategic Change*, 3rd edition, 2008; ISBN: 0-273-70802-3
- G. Johnson and K. Scholes (editors), *Exploring Public Sector Strategy*, FT/Prentice Hall, 2001; ISBN: 0-273-64687-7

A note for tutors

Instructor's manual

A comprehensive set of supporting material for tutors including:

- how to plan programmes using the text;
- using the case studies;
- teaching notes for case studies;
- tutor briefs for end-of-chapter work assignments and questions linked to illustrations;

- a CD containing PowerPoint slides for all chapters in the book (including all the Exhibits from the book) and a test bank of assessment questions;

Since the first publication of the book we have always been concerned that good-quality practical support and advice to tutors is provided. This has been one of the driving forces behind the growth of the support material. The advice above for students and managers is also likely to be relevant to tutors.

Since 1989 we have run annual one-day workshops for tutors (also in Scotland since 1995). These have proved to be very popular with both experienced tutors and those who are new to the subject.

Details of forthcoming workshops are posted on our website. We hope that the exploitation of our website will make this support more comprehensive, more universal in coverage and more consistent in terms of the support tutors can expect, irrespective of their location.

We are always happy to receive feedback from users of the book. Contact us at:

KScholes@scholes.u-net.com
gerry.johnson@lancaster.ac.uk
richard.whittington@said-business-school.oxford.ac.uk

Guided Tour

→ Navigation and setting the scene

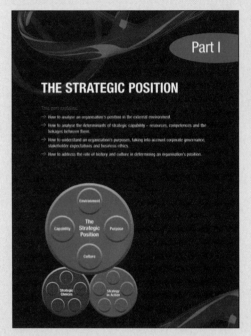

Learning outcomes enable you to check that you have understood all the major areas by the end of the chapter.

Part opening page identifies the chapters and topics covered within each part.

The **'three circles' navigational diagram** shows where you are in the three-part structure that underpins the book.

→ Strategy in context

Illustrations showcase the application of specific strategic issues in the real world so you can identify and relate theory and practice.

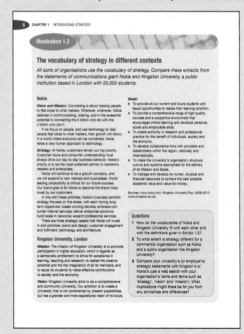

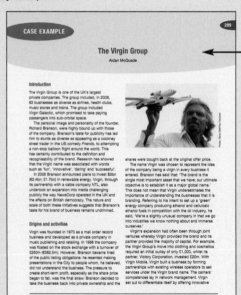

The **Case example** at the end of each chapter provides a broad view of the topic of the chapter in the context of a wide range of global organisations and in a variety of sectors.

→ Critical thinking and further study

Key debate – the final illustration in each chapter invites you to reflect on topical and contentious questions of strategy.

Work assignments are organised into two levels of difficulty, and provide interesting and stimulating questions to test your learning of key concepts and applications.

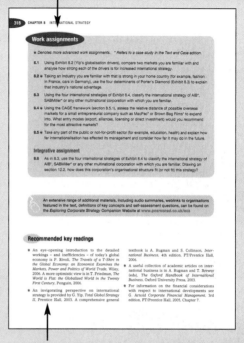

Recommended key readings direct you to other relevant sources so that you can read and research further into the key topics discussed in the chapter.

Commentaries appear at the end of each Part, presenting a view of strategy through four different 'lenses' to help you to see strategy in different ways and widen your perspectives.

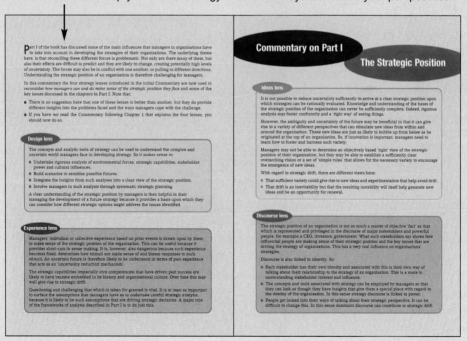

→ Checking your understanding

Key concept icons in the text direct you to audio and other resources on the companion website where you can check and reinforce your understanding of key concepts.

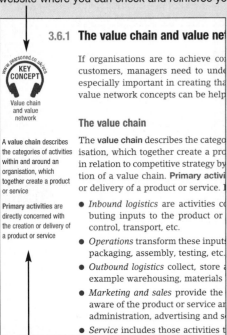

3.6.1 The value chain and value ne...

If organisations are to achieve co... customers, managers need to unde... especially important in creating tha... value network concepts can be help...

The value chain

A **value chain** describes the categories of activities within and around an organisation, which together create a product or service

The **value chain** describes the catego... isation, which together create a pro... in relation to competitive strategy by... tion of a value chain. **Primary activi**... or delivery of a product or service. **I**...

Primary activities are directly concerned with the creation or delivery of a product or service

● *Inbound logistics* are activities c... buting inputs to the product or... control, transport, etc.

● *Operations* transform these input... packaging, assembly, testing, etc.

● *Outbound logistics* collect, store a... example warehousing, materials

● *Marketing and sales* provide the... aware of the product or service a... administration, advertising and s...

● *Service* includes those activities t...

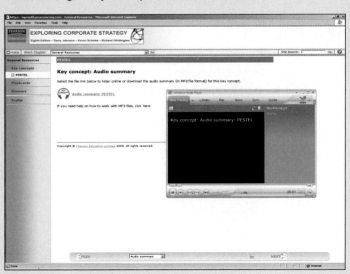

Key terms are highlighted in the text with a brief explanation in the margin when they first appear. These terms are also included in the **Glossary** at the end of the book and on the companion website where you can find them in six languages. You can test your understanding of these key terms using **flashcards** on the website.

Watch and listen to short **video clips** that focus on key concepts in strategic management on the companion website.

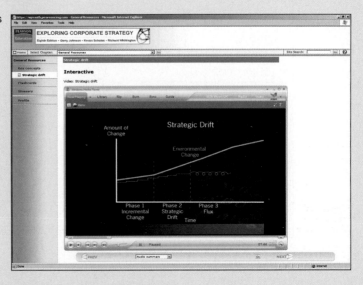

→ Checking your understanding (continued)

Use the **Self-assessment questions** on the companion website to test your knowledge.
Save your score in a personal gradebook and track your progress.

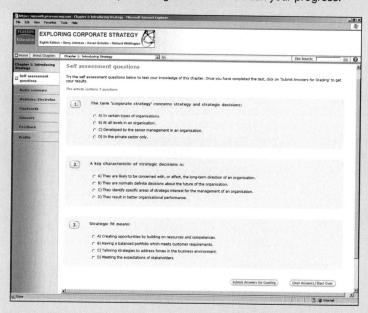

Chapter summaries recap and reinforce the key points to take away from the chapter.
Download or listen online to the **audio summaries** on the companion website.

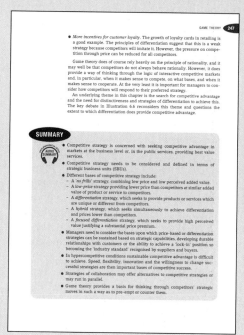

Acknowledgements

The Advisory Board for *Exploring Corporate Strategy* 8th edition

Special thanks are due to the following advisory board members for their valued insightful and constructive comments, which have helped shape the contents of this present edition:

Antony Beckett, University of the West of England
James Cunningham, NUI, Galway
Mike Danilovic, Jonkoping Business School
Erik Dirksen, Universiteit Van Amsterdam
Sarah Dixon, Kingston University
Frederic Fréry, ESCP-EAP
Keld Harbo, Aarhus School of Business
Mary Klemm, Bradford University
Ron Livingstone, Glasgow Caledonian University
Tina McGuiness, Sheffield University
Ian McKeown, University of Wolverhampton
Bruce Millett, University of Southern Queensland
Robert Morgan, Cardiff University
Jesper Norus, Copenhagen Business School (F)
Hans Roosendaal, University of Twente
Jill Shepherd, Simon Fraser University
Anders Soderholm, Umea Universiteit
John Toth, Leeds Metropolitan University
Rehan Ul Haq, University of Birmingham
Jamie Weatherston, University of Northumbria

It is with sadness that we have learned of the death of Jesper Norus in summer 2006. We take this opportunity to express our sincere condolences to his family and friends, colleagues and students by whom he will be much missed.

Publisher's acknowledgements

We are grateful to the following for permission to reproduce copyright material:

Illustration 2.2 Figure adapted from *The Future of BioSciences: Four Scenarios for 2020 and Their Implications for Human Healthcare*, edited by Paul J.H. Schoemaker and Michael S. Tomczyk, Copyright © 2006 by the Mack Center for Technological Innovation and Decision Strategies International. All rights reserved. (Schoemaker, P.J.H. and Tomcyzk, M.S. 2006); Exhibit 2.2 adapted from *Competitive Strategy: Techniques for Analyzing Industries and Competitors*, The Free Press, a Division of Simon & Schuster Adult Publishing Group (Porter, M.E. 1980); Exhibit 2.4 adapted from *Hypercompetitive Rivalries: Competing in Highly Dynamic Environments*, The Free Press, a Division of Simon & Schuster Adult Publishing Group (D'Aveni, R.A. and Gunther, R. 1995); Exhibit 2.8 adapted from Charting your company's future from *Harvard Business Review*, Vol. 80, No. 6, reprinted by permission of *Harvard Business Review* (Kim, C. and Mauborgne, R. 2002); Chapter 2 Case Example, Table 3 from Euromonitor International, *The World Brewing Industry*, reprinted by permission of Euromonitor International; Exhibits 3.6 and 3.7 adapted from *Competitive Advantage: Creating and Sustaining Superior Performance*, The Free Press, a Division of Simon & Schuster Adult Publishing Group (Porter, M.E. 1985); Exhibit 4.2 adapted from David-Pitt Watson, Hermes; Exhibit 4.11 adapted from Strategy as simple rules in *Harvard Business Review*, January, reprinted by permission of *Harvard Business Review* (Eisenhardt, K.M. and Sull, D.N. 2001); Illustrations 5.4 and 14.2 courtesy of Anne McCann; Exhibit 5.6 adapted from *Turnaround: Managerial Recipes for Strategic Success*, pub Associated Business Press, reprinted by permission of Peter H. Grinyer and J.-C. Spender (Grinyer, P.H. and Spender, J.-C. 1979); Exhibit 6.4 from Strategies to fight low-cost rivals in *Harvard Business Review*, Vol. 84, Issue 12, December 2006, reprinted by permission of *Harvard Business Review* (Kumar, N. 2006); Illustration 6.5, Figure 1 adapted from *Thinking Strategically: The Competitive Edge in Business, Politics, and Everyday Life*, W.W. Norton & Company, Inc. (Dixit, A.K. and Nalebuff, B.J. 1991); Exhibit 7.2 adapted from *Corporate Strategy*, pub Penguin, reprinted with permission of the Ansoff Family Trust (Ansoff, H. 1988); Illustration 7.4, Figure 1 reproduced with the permission of Dow Jones & Company, Inc., from www.bigcharts.com, 2007; permission conveyed through Copyright Clearance Center, Inc.; Exhibits 7.5 and 7.10 adapted from *Corporate Level Strategy*, Copyright © 1994 John Wiley & Sons, Inc., reprinted with permission of John Wiley & Sons, Inc. (Goold, M. *et al.* 1994); Chapter 7 References, p. 294 Figure from *The New Corporate Strategy*, Copyright © 1988, reprinted with permission of John Wiley & Sons, Inc. and the Ansoff Family Trust (Ansoff, H. 1988); Exhibit 8.3 adapted from Michael E.

Porter, *The Competitive Advantage of Nations*, 1990, Palgrave Macmillan, reproduced with permission of Palgrave Macmillan and The Free Press, a Division of Simon & Schuster Adult Publishing Group (Porter, M.E. 1990); Exhibit 8.4 adapted from Changing patterns of international competition in *California Management Review*, Vol. 28, No. 2, by permission of The Regents of the University of California (Porter, M.E. 1987); Exhibit 8.5 adapted from Global gamesmanship in *Harvard Business Review*, May 2003, reprinted by permission of *Harvard Business Review* (Macmillan, I. *et al*. 2003); Exhibit 8.7 from *Managing Across Borders: The Transnational Solution*, Harvard Business School Press (Bartlett, C.A. and Ghoshal, S. 1989); Chapter 8 Case Example, Figure 1 reproduced with the permission of Dow Jones & Company, Inc., from www.bigcharts.com, 11 October 2006; permission conveyed through Copyright Clearance Center, Inc.; Exhibit 9.2 reprinted from *Omega*, Vol. 3, No. 6, W.J. Abernathy and J.M. Utterback, A dynamic model of process and product innovation, pp. 639-56, Copyright © 1975, with permission from Elsevier (Abernathy, W.J. and Utterback, J.M. 1975); Illustration 9.3, Figure 1 from Alexa.com, reprinted by permission of Alexa Internet; Exhibit 9.4 adapted from *The Innovator's Solution*, Harvard Business School Press (Christensen, C. and Raynor, M.E. 2003); Exhibit 9.5 from *The Entrepreneurial Mindset*, Harvard Business School Press (Macmillan, I. and McGrath, R.G. 2000); Exhibit 10.2 from All aboard the M&A express in *Sunday Times Business Focus*, 31 December 2006, © NI Syndication Ltd., 31.12.06; Exhibit 10.9 adapted from Strategy as a portfolio of real options in *Harvard Business Review*, September-October, reprinted by permission of *Harvard Business Review* (Luehrman, T.A. 1998); Exhibit 12.5 adapted from *Managing Across Borders: The Transnational Solution, 2nd Edition*, Harvard Business School Press (Bartlett, C.A. and Ghoshal, S. 1998); Exhibit 13.3 adapted from *Strategic Human Resource Management*, Oxford University Press (Gratton, L. *et al*. 1999); Exhibit 13.5 adapted from *Electronic Commerce*, Copyright 2000 © John Wiley & Sons Ltd., reproduced with permission (Timmers, P. 2000); Exhibit 13.10 from *Managing Innovation: Integrating technological, market and organisational change, 3rd edition*, Copyright 2005 © John Wiley & Sons Ltd., reproduced with permission (Tidd, J. *et al*. 2005); Exhibits 13.11 and 13.12 adapted from *Managing Innovation: Integrating technological, market and organisational change, 2nd edition*, Copyright 2001 © John Wiley & Sons Ltd., reproduced with permission (Tidd, J. *et al*. 2001); Exhibit 14.2 adapted from *Exploring Strategic Change, 2nd Edition*, Pearson Education Ltd. (Balogun, J. and Hope Hailey, V. 1999); Exhibit 15.4 reprinted from *Advances in Strategic Management*, Vol. 22, W. Ocasio and J. Joseph, An attention-based theory of strategy formulation: linking micro- and macroperspectives in strategy processes, pp. 39-62, Copyright 2005, with permission from Elsevier (Ocasio, W. and Joseph, J. 2005); Chapter 15 Case Example, Figure p. 609 reproduced with the permission of MSNBC Interactive News, LLC, from www.msnbc.com, 2006; permission conveyed through Copyright Clearance Center, Inc.

Illustration 1.2 extract from Kingston University Plan, 2006–2010, www.kingston.ac.uk, reprinted by permission of Kingston University; Chapter 1 Case Example extracts from Electrolux *Annual Report 2005* and www.electrolux.com reprinted by permission of AB Electrolux; Illustration 2.5 updated from Global influences on the public sector in *Exploring Public Sector Strategy* edited by G. Johnson and K. Scholes, pub FT/Prentice Hall, reprinted by permission of D.J. Eppink and S. de Waal (Eppink, D.J. and de Waal, S. 2001); Illustration 3.1 extract © *Freeport-McMoRan Copper and Gold, Inc. Annual Report 2006*. All Rights Reserved; Illustration 3.1 extract from *Royal Opera House Annual Review 2005/6*, reprinted by permission of Royal Opera House; Illustration 4.5 The Metropolitan Police mission and values statements, reprinted by permission of Metropolitan Police Service; Illustration 4.5 Villeroy & Boch vision and values statements, reprinted by permission of Villeroy & Boch AG; Chapter 4 Case Example extracts from The Big Question: Does the RED campaign help big Eastern brands more than Africa? in *The Independent*, 9 March, Copyright The Independent 9.3.07 (Vallely, P. 2007); Chapter 4 Case Example extracts from Mind the Gap – with this attack on globalization in *The Times*, 24 October, © Gerard Baker. NI Syndication Ltd., 24.10.06 (Baker, G. 2006); Illustration 5.2 extracts from When in China . . . in *Management Today*, May, Haymarket Business Publications Ltd. (Slater, D. 2006); Illustration 5.3 adapted from Institutional theory and strategic management in *Strategic Management: A Multiple-Perspective Approach* edited by M. Jenkins and V. Ambrosini, Palgrave Macmillan (Johnson, G. and Greenwood, R. 2007); Illustration 6.4 extracts from Response from the AHRC to the Lambert Review of Business-University Collaboration, http://www.ahrc.ac.uk, reprinted by permission of Arts and Humanities Research Council (AHRC 2003); Illustration 7.3 extracts from *Annual Report 2002* reprinted by permission of Berkshire Hathaway, Inc. and Warren E. Buffett; Chapter 10 Case Example, extracts from *Tesco Annual Report 2006*, www.tesco.com/Investor Relations, reprinted by permission of Tesco Stores Ltd.; Illustration 13.3 abridged from New Power Generation in *Management Today*, December, Haymarket Business Publications Ltd. (Wylie, I. 2005); Illustration 13.5 extracts from www.together.gov.uk, reproduced under the terms of the Click-Use Licence; Illustration 14.3 extract from Sir Terry Leahy in *Management Today*, February, Haymarket Business Publications Ltd. (Blackhurst, C. 2004);

Illustration 14.6 extract reprinted by permission, H. Tsoukas and R. Chia, On organizational becoming: Rethinking organizational change, *Organization Science*, Vol. 13, No. 5, 2002. Copyright 2002, the Institute for Operations Research and the Management Sciences (INFORMS), 7240 Parkway Drive, Suite 310, Hanover, MD 21076 USA (Tsoukas, H. and Chia, R. 2002); Chapter 14 Case Example courtesy of John Howie; Illustration 15.1 extracts from Strategy Unit Job Description for a Team Member: Band A, from http://www.cabinetoffice.gov.uk/strategy/jobs/band_a.asp. Reproduced under the terms of the Click-Use Licence.

We are grateful to the Financial Times Limited for permission to reprint the following material:

Illustration 10.1 Reach verses risk, © *Financial Times*, 14 December 2006; Illustration 13.2 The DIY craze extends to loans, © *Financial Times*, 26 November 2005; Illustration 13.4 Psion chief's warning to tech wannabees, © *Financial Times*, 26 December 2005; Chapter 13 Case example All to play for: Microsoft and Sony take video games battle to next level, © *Financial Times (US edition)*, 11 May 2005.

Photographs: AB Electrolux, p. 25; Action Plus Sports Images: Glyn Kirk, p. 93; Alamy Images: p. 89; 1Apix p. 433; David Ball p. 131; Dominic Burke p. 53; John Crum p. 355; DIOMEDIA p. 399; Tracey Fahy p. 323; Horizon International Images Limited p. 473; Superstock p. 514, p. 557; BAA Aviation Photo Library: p. 221; Britain on View: Grant Pritchard p. 177; Corbis: Claro Cortes IV/Reuters p. 128; Getty Images: Charles Hewitt/Picture Post p. 208; Robert Harding World Imagery: Panoramic Images p. 517; Intel Corporation, p. 429; PA Photos: Associated Press p. 175, p. 320, p. 589; DPA p. 251; Reuters: Robert Galbraith p. 470; Rex Features: Steve Bell p. 289; Steve Forrest p. 352; Richard Jones p. 388; STILL Pictures The Whole Earth Photo Library: (FREELENS Pool) Tack p. 293; View Pictures Ltd: Dennis Gilbert p. 1.

In some instances we have been unable to trace the owners of copyright material, and we would appreciate any information that would enable us to do so.

The Strategic Position

Strategic Choices

Strategy in Action

1

Introducing Strategy

LEARNING OUTCOMES

After reading this chapter you should be able to:

→ Understand the characteristics of strategic decisions and what is meant by strategy and strategic management, distinguishing them from operational management.

→ Understand how strategic priorities vary by level: corporate, business and operational.

→ Understand the basic vocabulary of strategy, as used in different contexts.

→ Understand the three key elements of the *Exploring Corporate Strategy* strategic management model.

→ Understand the kinds of people involved in strategy – managers, in-house specialists and strategy consultants – and the work they do.

1.1 INTRODUCTION

In November 2006 Yahoo! manager Brad Garlinghouse issued a memo that directly challenged the senior management of the Internet giant. Leaked to the media as 'The Peanut Butter Manifesto', his memo accused Yahoo!'s leadership of lacking strategic direction. Growth had slowed, Google had overtaken Yahoo! in terms of online advertising revenues, and the share price had fallen by nearly a third since the start of the year. According to Brad Garlinghouse, Yahoo! was spread too thin, like peanut butter. It was time for strategic change.

All organisations are faced with the challenges of strategic direction: some from a desire to grasp new opportunities, others to overcome significant problems, as at Yahoo!. This book deals with why changes in strategic direction take place in organisations, why they are important, how such decisions are taken, and the concepts that can be useful in understanding these issues. This introductory chapter addresses particularly the meaning of 'strategy' and 'strategic management', why they are so important and what distinguishes them from other organisational challenges, tasks and decisions. It also introduces the kind of work that different types of managers involved in strategy may do, whether as general managers, in-house specialists or as strategy consultants. The chapter will draw on the Yahoo! example in Illustration 1.1 to illustrate its points.

This book uses the term 'corporate' strategy for two main reasons. First, because the book is concerned with strategy and strategic decisions in all types of organisation – small and large, commercial enterprises as well as public services – and the word 'corporate' embraces them all. Second, because, as the term is used in this book (discussed more fully in section 1.2.2), 'corporate strategy' denotes the most general level of strategy in an organisation and in this sense embraces other levels of strategy. Readers will probably come across other terms, such as 'strategic management', 'business policy' and 'organisational strategy', but these are all used to describe the same general topic.

1.2 WHAT IS STRATEGY?

KEY CONCEPT
Strategy

Why were the issues facing Yahoo! described as 'strategic'?[1] What types of issues are strategic and what distinguishes them from operational issues in organisations?

1.2.1 The characteristics of strategic decisions

The words 'strategy' and 'strategic decisions' are typically associated with issues like these:

- *The long-term direction* of an organisation. Brad Garlinghouse explicitly recognised that strategic change in Yahoo! would require a 'marathon and not a sprint'. Strategy at Yahoo! involved long-term decisions about what sort of company it should be, and realising these decisions would take plenty of time.

- *The scope of an organisation's activities*. For example, should the organisation concentrate on one area of activity, or should it have many? Brad Garlinghouse believed that Yahoo! was spread too thinly over too many different activities.

- *Advantage* for the organisation over competition. The problem at Yahoo! was that it was losing its advantage to faster-growing companies such as Google. Advantage may be achieved in different ways and may also mean different things. For example, in the public sector, strategic advantage could be thought of as providing better value services than other providers, thus attracting support and funding from government.

- *Strategic fit with the business environment*. Organisations need appropriate *positioning* in their environment, for example in terms of the extent to which products or services meet clearly identified market needs. This might take the form of a small business trying to find a particular niche in a market, or a multinational corporation seeking to buy up businesses that have already found successful market positions. According to Brad Garlinghouse, Yahoo! was trying to succeed in too many environments.

- *The organisation's resources and competences*.[2] Following 'the resource-based view' of strategy, strategy is about exploiting the strategic capability of an organisation, in terms of its resources and competences, to provide competitive advantage and/or yield new opportunities. For example, an organisation might try to leverage resources such as technology skills or strong brands. Yahoo! claims a brand 'synonymous with the Internet', theoretically giving it clear advantage in that environment.

- *The values and expectations* of powerful actors in and around the organisation. These actors – individuals, groups or even other organisations – can drive fundamental issues such as whether an organisation is expansionist or more concerned with consolidation, or where the boundaries are drawn for the organisation's activities. At Yahoo!, the senior managers may have pursued growth in too many directions and been too reluctant to hold themselves accountable. But lower-level managers, ordinary employees, suppliers, customers and Internet users all have a stake in the future of Yahoo! too. The beliefs and values of these *stakeholders* will have a greater or lesser influence on the strategy development of an organisation, depending on the power of each. Certainly, Brad Garlinghouse was making a bold bid for influence over what seemed to be a failing strategy.

Overall, the most basic definition of strategy might be 'the long-term direction of an organisation'. However, the characteristics described above can provide the basis for a fuller definition:

Strategy is the direction and scope of an organisation over the long term, which achieves *advantage* in a changing *environment* through its configuration of *resources and competences* with the aim of fulfilling *stakeholder* expectations.

Exhibit 1.1 summarises these characteristics of strategic decisions and also highlights some of the implications:

- *Complexity* is a defining feature of strategy and strategic decisions and is especially so in organisations with wide geographical scope, such as multinational

Strategy is the *direction* and *scope* of an organisation over the *long term*, which achieves *advantage* in a changing *environment* through its configuration of *resources and competences* with the aim of fulfilling *stakeholder expectations*

Illustration 1.1

Yahoo!'s peanut butter manifesto

Strategy can involve hard decisions about the scope of the business, its management and its organisation structure.

In November 2006, Brad Garlinghouse, MBA graduate and a Yahoo! senior vice president, wrote a memo to his top managers arguing that Yahoo!, the diversified Internet company, was spreading its resources too thinly, like peanut butter on a slice of bread. Edited extracts from the memo follow:

Three and half years ago, I enthusiastically joined Yahoo!. The magnitude of the opportunity was only matched by the magnitude of the assets. And an amazing team has been responsible for rebuilding Yahoo!. . . .

But all is not well. . . .

I imagine there's much discussion amongst the Company's senior-most leadership around the challenges we face. At the risk of being redundant, I wanted to share my take on our current situation and offer a recommended path forward, an attempt to be part of the solution rather than part of the problem.

RECOGNIZING OUR PROBLEMS

We lack a focused, cohesive vision for our company. We want to do everything and be everything – to everyone. We've known this for years, talk about it incessantly, but do nothing to fundamentally address it. We are scared to be left out. We are reactive instead of charting an unwavering course. We are separated into silos that far too frequently don't talk to each other. And when we do talk, it isn't to collaborate on a clearly focused strategy, but rather to argue and fight about ownership, strategies and tactics. . . .

I've heard our strategy described as spreading peanut butter across the myriad opportunities that continue to evolve in the online world. The result: a thin layer of investment spread across everything we do and thus we focus on nothing in particular.

I hate peanut butter. We all should.

We lack clarity of ownership and accountability. The most painful manifestation of this is the massive redundancy that exists throughout the organization. We now operate in an organizational structure – admittedly created with the best of intentions – that has become overly bureaucratic. For far too many employees, there is another person with dramatically similar and overlapping responsibilities. This slows us down and burdens the company with unnecessary costs.

There's a reason why a centerfielder and a left fielder have clear areas of ownership. Pursuing the same ball repeatedly results in either collisions or dropped balls. Knowing that someone else is pursuing the ball and hoping to avoid that collision – we have become timid in our pursuit. Again, the ball drops.

We lack decisiveness. Combine a lack of focus with unclear ownership, and the result is that decisions are either not made or are made when it is already too late. Without a clear and focused vision, and without complete clarity of ownership, we lack a macro perspective to guide our decisions and visibility into who should make those decisions. We are repeatedly stymied by challenging and hairy decisions. We are held hostage by our analysis paralysis.

We end up with competing (or redundant) initiatives and synergistic opportunities living in the different silos of our company. . . .

SOLVING OUR PROBLEMS

We have awesome assets. Nearly every media and communications company is painfully jealous of our

firms, or wide ranges of products or services. For example, Yahoo! faces the complexity both of a fast-moving market environment and poorly organised internal businesses.

● *Uncertainty* is inherent in strategy, because nobody can be sure about the future. For Yahoo!, the Internet environment is one of constant and unforeseeable innovation.

position. We have the largest audience, they are highly engaged and our brand is synonymous with the Internet.

If we get back up, embrace dramatic change, we will win.

I don't pretend there is only one path forward available to us. However, at a minimum, I want to be part of the solution and thus have outlined a plan here that I believe can work. It is my strong belief that we need to act very quickly or risk going further down a slippery slope. The plan here is not perfect; it is, however, FAR better than no action at all.

There are three pillars to my plan:

1 Focus the vision.
2 Restore accountability and clarity of ownership.
3 Execute a radical reorganization.

1 Focus the vision
a) We need to boldly and definitively declare what we are and what we are not.
b) We need to exit (sell?) non core businesses and eliminate duplicative projects and businesses.

My belief is that the smoothly spread peanut butter needs to turn into a deliberately sculpted strategy – that is narrowly focused. . . .

2 Restore accountability and clarity of ownership
a) Existing business owners must be held accountable for where we find ourselves today – heads must roll,
b) We must thoughtfully create senior roles that have holistic accountability for a particular line of business. . . .
c) We must redesign our performance and incentive systems.

I believe there are too many BU [Business Unit] leaders who have gotten away with unacceptable results and worse – unacceptable leadership. Too often they (we!) are the worst offenders of the problems outlined here. We must signal to both the employees and to our shareholders that we will hold these leaders (ourselves) accountable and implement change. . . .

3 Execute a radical reorganization
a) The current business unit structure must go away.
b) We must dramatically decentralize and eliminate as much of the matrix as possible.
c) We must reduce our headcount by 15–20%.

I emphatically believe we simply must eliminate the redundancies we have created and the first step in doing this is by restructuring our organization. We can be more efficient with fewer people and we can get more done, more quickly. We need to return more decision making to a new set of business units and their leadership. But we can't achieve this with baby step changes. We need to fundamentally rethink how we organize to win. . . .

I love Yahoo!. I'm proud to admit that I bleed purple and yellow. I'm proud to admit that I shaved a Y in the back of my head.

My motivation for this memo is the adamant belief that, as before, we have a tremendous opportunity ahead. I don't pretend that I have the only available answers, but we need to get the discussion going; change is needed and it is needed soon. We can be a stronger and faster company – a company with a clearer vision and clearer ownership and clearer accountability.

We may have fallen down, but the race is a marathon and not a sprint. I don't pretend that this will be easy. It will take courage, conviction, insight and tremendous commitment. I very much look forward to the challenge.

So let's get back up.

Catch the balls.

And stop eating peanut butter.

Source: Extracts from Brad Garlinghouse's memo to Yahoo! managers, November 2006. Reprinted in *Wall Street Journal*, 16 November 2006.

Questions

1 Why were the issues facing Yahoo! described as strategic? Refer to Exhibit 1.1.

2 Identify examples of issues that fit each of the circles of the model in Exhibit 1.3.

● *Operational decisions* are linked to strategy. For example, any attempt to co-ordinate Yahoo!'s business units more closely will have knock-on effects on web-page designs and links, career development and advertiser relationships. This link between overall strategy and operational aspects of the organisation is important for two other reasons. First, if the operational aspects of the organisation are not in line with the strategy, then, no matter how well

---

Exhibit 1.1   **Strategic decisions**

Strategic decisions are about:

- The **long-term** direction of an organisation
- The **scope** of an organisation's activities
- Gaining **advantage** over competitors
- Addressing changes in the **business environment**
- Building on resources and competences (**capability**)
- **Values and expectations** of stakeholders

Therefore they are likely to:

- Be **complex** in nature
- Be made in situations of **uncertainty**
- Affect **operational** decisions
- Require an **integrated** approach (both inside and outside an organisation)
- Involve considerable **change**

---

considered the strategy is, it will not succeed. Second, it is at the operational level that real strategic advantage can be achieved. Indeed, competence in particular operational activities might determine which strategic developments might make most sense.

- *Integration* is required for effective strategy. Managers have to cross functional and operational boundaries to deal with strategic problems and come to agreements with other managers who, inevitably, have different interests and perhaps different priorities. Yahoo! for example needs an integrated approach to powerful advertisers such as Sony and Vodafone from across all its businesses.

- *Relationships and networks* outside the organisation are important in strategy, for example with suppliers, distributors and customers. For Yahoo!, advertisers and users are crucial sets of relationships.

- *Change* is typically a crucial component of strategy. Change is often difficult because of the heritage of resources and because of organisational culture. According to Brad Garlinghouse at least, Yahoo!'s barriers to change seem to include a top management that is afraid of taking hard decisions and a lack of clear accountability amongst lower-level management.

1.2.2 Levels of strategy

Corporate-level strategy is concerned with the overall purpose and scope of an organisation and how value will be added to the different parts (business units) of the organisation

Strategies exist at a number of levels in an organisation. Taking Yahoo! again as an example, it is possible to distinguish at least three different levels of strategy. The top level is **corporate-level strategy**, concerned with the overall scope of an organisation and how value will be added to the different parts (business units) of the organisation. This could include issues of geographical coverage, diversity of products/services or business units, and how resources are to be allocated between the different parts of the organisation. For Yahoo!, whether to sell some of its existing businesses is clearly a crucial corporate-level decision. In general, corporate-level strategy is also likely to be concerned with the expectations of owners – the shareholders and the stock market. It may well take form in an explicit or implicit statement of 'mission' that reflects such expectations. Being clear about corporate-level strategy is important: determining the range of business to include is the *basis* of other strategic decisions.

Business-level strategy is about how to compete successfully in particular markets

The second level is **business-level strategy**, which is about how the various businesses included in the corporate strategy should compete in their particular markets (for this reason, business-level strategy is sometimes called 'competitive strategy'). In the public sector, the equivalent of business-level strategy is decisions about how units should provide best value services. This typically concerns issues such as pricing strategy, innovation or differentiation, for instance by better quality or a distinctive distribution channel. So, whereas corporate-level strategy involves decisions about the organisation as a whole, strategic decisions relate to particular strategic business units (SBUs) within the overall organisation. A **strategic business unit** is a part of an organisation for which there is a distinct external market for goods or services that is different from another SBU. Yahoo!'s strategic business units include businesses such as Yahoo! Photos and Yahoo! Music.

A strategic business unit is a part of an organisation for which there is a distinct external market for goods or services that is different from another SBU

Of course, in very simple organisations with only one business, the corporate strategy and the business-level strategy are nearly identical. None the less, even here, it is useful to distinguish a corporate-level strategy, because this provides the framework for whether and under what conditions other business opportunities might be added or rejected. Where the corporate strategy does include several businesses, there should be a clear link between strategies at an SBU level and the corporate level. In the case of Yahoo!, relationships with online advertisers stretch across different business units, and using, protecting and enhancing the Yahoo! brand is vital for all. The corporate strategy with regard to the brand should support the SBUs, but at the same time the SBUs have to make sure their business-level strategies do not damage the corporate whole or other SBUs in the group.

Operational strategies are concerned with how the component parts of an organisation deliver effectively the corporate- and business-level strategies in terms of resources, processes and people

The third level of strategy is at the operating end of an organisation. Here there are **operational strategies**, which are concerned with how the component parts of an organisation deliver effectively the corporate- and business-level strategies in terms of resources, processes and people. For example, Yahoo! has web-page designers in each of its businesses, for whom there are appropriate operational strategies in terms of design, layout and renewal. Indeed, in most businesses, successful business strategies depend to a large extent on decisions that are taken, or activities that occur, at the operational level. The integration of operational decisions and strategy is therefore of great importance, as mentioned earlier.

Illustration 1.2

The vocabulary of strategy in different contexts

All sorts of organisations use the vocabulary of strategy. Compare these extracts from the statements of communications giant Nokia and Kingston University, a public institution based in London with 20,000 students.

Nokia

Vision and Mission: Connecting is about helping people to feel close to what matters. Wherever, whenever, Nokia believes in communicating, sharing, and in the awesome potential in connecting the 2 billion who do with the 4 billion who don't.

If we focus on people, and use technology to help people feel close to what matters, then growth will follow. In a world where everyone can be connected, Nokia takes a very human approach to technology.

Strategy: At Nokia, customers remain our top priority. Customer focus and consumer understanding must always drive our day-to-day business behavior. Nokia's priority is to be the most preferred partner to operators, retailers and enterprises.

Nokia will continue to be a growth company, and we will expand to new markets and businesses. World leading productivity is critical for our future success. Our brand goal is for Nokia to become the brand most loved by our customers.

In line with these priorities, Nokia's business portfolio strategy focuses on five areas, with each having long-term objectives: create winning devices; embrace consumer Internet services; deliver enterprise solutions; build scale in networks; expand professional services.

There are three strategic assets that Nokia will invest in and prioritize: brand and design; customer engagement and fulfilment; technology and architecture.

Kingston University, London

Mission: The mission of Kingston University is to promote participation in higher education, which it regards as a democratic entitlement; to strive for excellence in learning, teaching and research; to realise the creative potential and fire the imagination of all its members; and to equip its students to make effective contributions to society and the economy.

Vision: Kingston University aims to be a comprehensive and community University. Our ambition is to create a University that is not constrained by present possibilities, but has a grander and more aspirational vision of its future.

Goals:

- To provide all our current and future students with equal opportunities to realise their learning ambition.
- To provide a comprehensive range of high-quality courses and a supportive environment that encourages critical learning and develops personal, social and employable skills.
- To create authority in research and professional practice for the benefit of individuals, society and the economy.
- To develop collaborative links with providers and stakeholders within the region, nationally and internationally.
- To make the University's organisation, structure, culture and systems appropriate for the delivery of its Mission and Goals.
- To manage and develop its human, physical and financial resources to achieve the best possible academic value and value-for-money.

Sources: www.nokia.com; Kingston University Plan, 2006–2010 (www.kingston.ac.uk).

Questions

1 How do the vocabularies of Nokia and Kingston University fit with each other and with the definitions given in Exhibit 1.2?

2 To what extent is strategy different for a commercial organisation such as Nokia and a public organisation like Kingston University?

3 Compare your university's (or employer's) strategic statements with Kingston's or Nokia's (use a web search with your organisation's name and terms such as 'strategy', 'vision' and 'mission'). What implications might there be for you from any similarities and differences?

1.2.3 The vocabulary of strategy

Although a definition of strategy was given at the end of section 1.2.1, in practice you will encounter many different definitions from different authors. You will also find a variety of terms used in relation to strategy, so it is worth devoting a little space to clarifying some of these. Exhibit 1.2 and Illustration 1.2 employ some of the terms that you will come across in this and other books on strategy and in everyday business usage. Exhibit 1.2 explains these in relation to a personal strategy readers may have followed themselves – improving physical fitness.

Exhibit 1.2   The vocabulary of strategy

Term	Definition	A personal example
Mission	Overriding purpose in line with the values or expectations of stakeholders	Be healthy and fit
Vision or strategic intent	Desired future state: the aspiration of the organisation	To run the London Marathon
Goal	General statement of aim or purpose	Lose weight and strengthen muscles
Objective	Quantification (if possible) or more precise statement of the goal	Lose 5 kilos by 1 September and run the marathon next year
Strategic capability	Resources, activities and processes. Some will be unique and provide 'competitive advantage'	Proximity to a fitness centre, a successful diet
Strategies	Long-term direction	Exercise regularly, compete in marathons locally, stick to appropriate diet
Business model	How product, service and information 'flow' between participating parties	Associate with a collaborative network (e.g. join running club)
Control	The monitoring of action steps to: ● assess effectiveness of strategies and actions ● modify as necessary strategies and/or actions	Monitor weight, kilometres run and measure times: if progress satisfactory, do nothing; if not, consider other strategies and actions

---

Not all these terms are always used in organisations or in strategy books: indeed, in this book the word 'goal' is rarely used. It will also be seen, through the many examples in this book, that terminology is not used consistently across organisations (see also Illustration 1.2). Managers and students of strategy need to be aware of this. Moreover, it may or may not be that mission, goals, objectives, strategies and so on are written down precisely. In some organisations this is done very formally; in others a mission or strategy might be implicit and, therefore, must be deduced from what an organisation is doing. However, as a general guideline the following terms are often used:

- A *mission* is a general expression of the overall purpose of the organisation, which, ideally, is in line with the values and expectations of major stakeholders and concerned with the scope and boundaries of the organisation. It is sometimes referred to in terms of the apparently simple but challenging question: *'What business are we in?'*

- A *vision* or *strategic intent* is the desired future state of the organisation. It is an aspiration around which a strategist, perhaps a chief executive, might seek to focus the attention and energies of members of the organisation.

- If the word *goal* is used, it usually means a general aim in line with the mission. It may well be qualitative in nature.

- On the other hand, an *objective* is more likely to be quantified, or at least to be a more precise aim in line with the goal. In this book the word 'objective' is used whether or not there is quantification.

- *Strategic capability* is concerned with the *resources and competences* that an organisation can use to provide value to customers or clients. *Unique resources* and *core competences* are the bases upon which an organisation achieves strategic advantage and is distinguished from competitors.

- The concept of *strategy* has already been defined. It is the long-term direction of the organisation. It is likely to be expressed in broad statements both about the direction that the organisation should be taking and the types of action required to achieve objectives. For example, it may be stated in terms of market entry, new products or services, or ways of operating.

- A *business model* describes the structure of product, service and information flows and the roles of the participating parties. For example, a traditional model for manufactured products is a linear flow of product from component manufacturers to product manufacturers to distributor to retailers to consumers. But information may flow directly between the product manufacturer and the final consumer (advertising and market research).

- *Strategic control* involves monitoring the extent to which the strategy is achieving the objectives and suggesting corrective action (or a reconsideration of the objectives).

As the book develops, many other terms will be introduced and explained. These are the basics with which to begin.

Illustration 1.2 compares strategy vocabulary from two organisations operating in very different *contexts*. Nokia is a private sector communications giant, competing against global corporations such as Motorola and Samsung. Profit is vital to Nokia, but still it sees its vision and mission in terms of connecting more people around the world. Kingston University, on the other hand, is a public university, with a commitment to increasing participation in higher education. But it too must earn revenues, and needs to make a surplus in order to be able to invest in the future. Kingston University is also competing for students and research funds, going head to head with similar universities in the United Kingdom and around the world. Corporate-level and business-level strategies are no less important for a public body such as Kingston University as a commercial one like Nokia.

Strategy vocabulary, therefore, is relevant to a wide range of contexts. A small entrepreneurial start-up will need a strategy statement to persuade investors and lenders of its viability. Public sector organisations need strategy statements not only to know what to do, but also to reassure their funders and regulators that what they do is what they should be doing. Voluntary organisations need to communicate exciting strategies in order to inspire volunteers and donors. If they are to prosper within the larger organisation, SBU managers need to propose clear strategies that are consistent with the objectives of their corporate owners and with the needs of other SBUs within the corporate whole. Even privately held organisations need persuasive strategy statements to motivate their employees and to build long-term relationships with their key customers or suppliers. Strategy vocabulary, therefore, is used in many different contexts, for many different purposes. Strategy is part of the everyday language of work.

1.3 STRATEGIC MANAGEMENT

The term *strategic management* underlines the importance of managers with regard to strategy. Strategies do not happen just by themselves. Strategy involves people, especially the managers who decide and implement strategy. Thus this book uses strategic management to emphasise the human element of strategy.

The strategic management role is different in nature from other aspects of management. An operational manager is most often required to deal with problems of operational control, such as the efficient production of goods, the management of a salesforce, the monitoring of financial performance or the design of some new system that will improve the level of customer service. These are all very important tasks, but they are essentially concerned with effectively managing resources already deployed, often in a limited part of the organisation within the context of an existing strategy. Operational control is what managers are involved in for most of their time. It is vital to the success of strategy, but it is not the same as strategic management.

For managers, strategic management involves a greater scope than that of any one area of operational management. Strategic management is concerned with complexity arising out of ambiguous and non-routine situations with organisation-wide rather than operation-specific implications. This is a major challenge for managers who are used to managing on a day-to-day basis the resources they control. It can be a particular problem because of the background of managers who may typically have been trained, perhaps over many years, to undertake operational tasks and to take operational responsibility. Accountants find that they still tend to see problems in financial terms, IT managers in IT terms, marketing managers in marketing terms, and so on. Of course, each of these aspects is important, but none is adequate alone. The manager who aspires to manage or influence strategy needs to develop a capability to take an overview, to conceive of the whole rather than just the parts of the situation facing an organisation. This is often referred to as the 'helicopter view'.

Because strategic management is characterised by its complexity, it is also necessary to make decisions and judgements based on the *conceptualisation* of difficult issues. Yet the early training and experience of managers is often about taking action, or about detailed *planning* or *analysis*. This book explains many analytical approaches to strategy, and it is concerned too with action related to the management of strategy. However, the major emphasis is on the importance of understanding the *strategic concepts* which inform this analysis and action.

Strategic management can be thought of as having three main elements within it, and it is these that provide the framework for the book. **Strategic management** includes understanding *the strategic position* of an organisation, making *strategic choices* for the future and managing *strategy in action*. Exhibit 1.3 shows these elements and defines the broad coverage of this book. The next sections of this chapter discuss each of these three elements of strategic management and identify the main issues that make up each element. But first it is important to understand why the exhibit has been drawn in this particular way.

Exhibit 1.3 could have shown the three elements in a linear sequence – first understanding the strategic position, then strategic choices and finally turning

Strategic management includes understanding *the strategic position* of an organisation, *strategic choices* for the future and managing *strategy in action*

Exhibit 1.3 The *Exploring Corporate Strategy* model

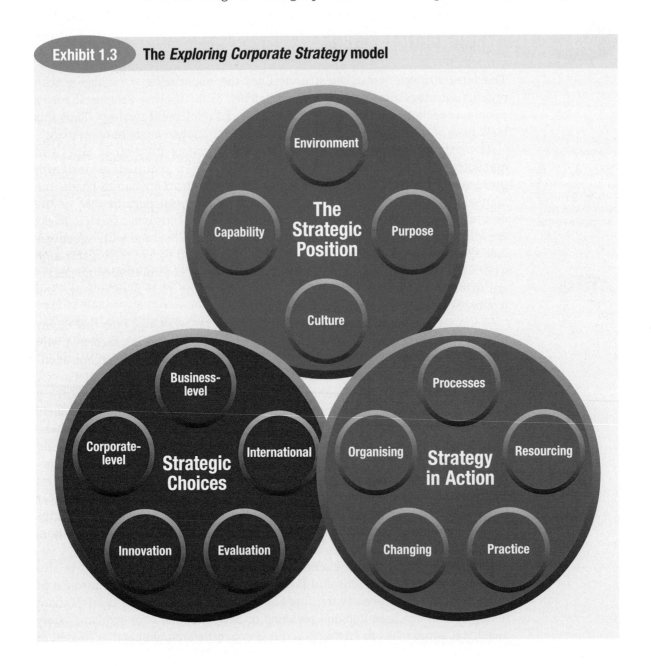

strategy into action. Indeed, many texts on the subject do just this. However, in practice, the elements of strategic management do not follow this linear sequence – they are interlinked and feed back on each other. For example, in some circumstances an understanding of the strategic position may best be built up from the experience of trying a strategy out in practice. Test marketing a prototype would be a good example. Here strategy in action informs understanding of the strategic position.

The interconnected circles of Exhibit 1.3 are designed to emphasise this non-linear nature of strategy. Position, choices and action should be seen as closely related, and in practice none has priority over another. It is only for structural convenience that the subject has been divided into sections in this book; the book's sequence is not meant to suggest that the process of strategic management must follow a neat and tidy path. Indeed, the evidence provided in Chapter 15 on how strategic management happens in practice suggests that it usually does not occur in tidy ways.

1.3.1 The strategic position

The strategic position is concerned with the impact on strategy of the external environment, an organisation's strategic capability (resources and competences) and the expectations and influence of stakeholders

KEY CONCEPT
www.pearsoned.co.uk/ecs

Strategic position

Understanding the **strategic position** is concerned with identifying the impact on strategy of the external environment, an organisation's strategic capability (resources and competences) and the expectations and influence of stakeholders. The sorts of questions this raises are central to future strategies and these issues are covered in the four chapters of Part I of this book:

● The *environment*. The organisation exists in the context of a complex political, economic, social, technological, environmental (i.e. green) and legal world. This environment changes and is more complex for some organisations than for others. How this affects the organisation could include an understanding of historical and environmental effects, as well as expected or potential changes in environmental variables. Many of those variables will give rise to *opportunities* and others will exert *threats* on the organisation – or both. A problem that has to be faced is that the range of variables is likely to be so great that it may not be possible or realistic to identify and understand each one. Therefore it is necessary to distil out of this complexity a view of the key environmental impacts on the organisation. Chapter 2 examines how this might be possible.

● The *strategic capability* of the organisation – made up of *resources and competences*. One way of thinking about the strategic capability of an organisation is to consider its *strengths* and *weaknesses* (for example, where it is at a competitive advantage or disadvantage). The aim is to form a view of the internal influences – and constraints – on strategic choices for the future. It is usually a combination of resources and high levels of competence in particular activities (in this book referred to as *core competences*) that provide advantages which competitors find difficult to imitate. Chapter 3 examines strategic capability in detail.

● Chapter 4 explores the major influences of *stakeholder expectations* on an organisation's *purposes*. Purpose is encapsulated in an organisation's *vision*, *mission* and *values*. Here the issue of *corporate governance* is important: who *should* the organisation primarily serve and how should managers be held responsible for this? This raises issues of *corporate social responsibility* and *ethics*. The chapter explores how both variations in international corporate governance systems and the *power* configurations within particular organisations can influence purpose.

● Chapter 5 examines how *cultural and historical influences* can also influence strategy. Cultural influences can be *organisational*, *sectoral* or *national*. Historical influences can create *lock-in* on particular strategic trajectories. The impact of these influences can be *strategic drift*, a failure to create necessary change. The chapter demonstrates how managers can analyse and challenge these historical and cultural influences on strategy.

These positioning issues were all important for Yahoo! as it faced its crisis in 2006. The external environment offered the threat of growing competition from Google. Its strong Internet brand and existing audience were key resources for defending its position. The company was struggling with its purposes, with top management apparently indecisive. The company none the less had inherited a strong culture, powerful enough to make Brad Garlinghouse shave a Y on his head and believe that his blood bled in the corporate colours of his employer.

1.3.2 Strategic choices

Strategic choices involve understanding the underlying bases for future strategy at both the business unit and corporate levels and the options for developing strategy in terms of both the directions and methods of development

Strategic choices involve the options for strategy in terms of both the directions in which strategy might move and the methods by which strategy might be pursued. For instance, an organisation might have to choose between alternative diversification moves, for example entering into new products and markets. As it diversifies, it has different methods available to it, for example developing a new product itself or acquiring an organisation already active in the area. Typical options and methods are covered in the five chapters that make up Part II of this book, as follows:

● There are strategic choices in terms of how the organisation seeks to compete at the *business level*. Typically these involve pricing and differentiation strategies, and decisions about how to compete or collaborate with competitors. These issues of business-level strategies will be discussed in Chapter 6.

● At the highest level in an organisation there are issues of *corporate-level strategy*, which are concerned with the scope, or breadth, of an organisation. These include *diversification* decisions about the portfolio of products and the spread of markets. For Yahoo!, being spread over too many businesses seems to be the major strategic problem. Corporate-level strategy is also concerned with the relationship between the separate parts of the business and how the corporate 'parent' adds value to these various parts. At Yahoo!, it is not clear how much the corporate parent is adding value to its constituent parts. These issues about the role of the centre and how it adds value are *parenting* issues and will be discussed in Chapter 7.

● *International strategy* is a form of diversification, into new geographical markets. It is often at least as challenging as diversification. Chapter 8 examines choices organisations have to make about which geographical markets to prioritise and how to enter them, by export, licensing, direct investment or acquisition.

- At the start of every organisation is an act of *entrepreneurship*. Most organisations have to *innovate* constantly simply to survive. Chapter 9 considers choices about innovation and entrepreneurship. Innovation choices involve issues such as being first-mover into a market, or simply a follower, and how much to listen to customers in developing new products or services. Entrepreneurship choices are many, but include choices of funding, building key external relationships, and timing of exit.

- Organisations have to make choices about the *methods* by which they pursue their strategies. Many organisations prefer to grow 'organically', in other words by building new businesses with their own resources. Other organisations might develop by mergers/acquisitions and/or strategic alliances with other organisations. These alternative methods are discussed in Chapter 10. Chapter 10 concludes with a discussion of the *success criteria* according to which different strategic choices can be evaluated.

1.3.3 Strategy in action

Strategy in action is concerned with ensuring that strategies are working in practice

Organising **strategy in action** is concerned with ensuring that chosen strategies are actually put into action. These issues are covered in the five chapters of Part III, and include the following:

- First of all, it is important to consider the *strategy development processes* of an organisation. The strategies that an organisation actually pursues are typically a mixture of the *intended* and the *emergent*. Intended strategies are the product of formal strategic planning and decision making, but the strategy that is actually pursued is typically somewhat emergent, including bottom-up initiatives, rapid responses to unanticipated opportunities and threats, and sheer chance. Chapter 11 considers the respective roles of intention and emergence in the overall strategy development of organisations.

- *Structuring* an organisation to support successful performance. This includes organisational *structures*, *processes* and *relationships* (and the interaction between these elements). According to Brad Garlinghouse, structural silos, matrix organisation and bureaucracy were all big problems for Yahoo!. These kinds of issue will be discussed in Chapter 12.

- *Resourcing* strategies in the separate resource areas (people, information, finance and technology) of an organisation in order to support overall strategies. The reverse is also important to success, that is the extent to which new strategies are built on the particular resource and competence strengths of an organisation. Chapter 13 considers this two-way relationship.

- Managing strategy very often involves *strategic change*, and Chapter 14 looks at the various issues involved in managing change. This will include the need to understand how the context of an organisation should influence the approach to change and the different types of *roles* for people in managing change. It also looks at the *styles* that can be adopted for managing change and the levers by which change can be effected.

- The final chapter of the book considers the actual *practice of strategy*. Thus Chapter 15 gets inside the overall processes of strategy development and change to look at the detailed activities involved – the *people* included in strategy, the *activities* they have to do and the kinds of *methodologies* they use to do it. These kinds of practicalities are a fitting end to the book and essential equipment for those who will have to go out and do strategy themselves.

1.4 STRATEGY AS A SUBJECT OF STUDY

Strategy as a subject of study has come a long way in the fifty or so years it has existed. In the beginning, strategy was to do with the *task of the general manager* and, perhaps most obviously, took form in the *business policy* courses run at universities such as Harvard going back to the 1960s. The continual question posed here was 'what would you do if you took over as chief executive of such and such an organisation?' The approach was based on the common-sense experience of executives and not so much on theory or research. Teaching was dominated by attempts to replicate real business situations in the classroom by the exposure of students to many case studies of strategic problems.[2]

In parallel there developed in the 1960s and 1970s the influence of books on *corporate planning*.[3] Here the emphasis was on trying to analyse the various influences on an organisation's well-being in such a way as to identify opportunities or threats to future development. It took the form of highly systematised approaches to planning – incorporating the mathematical techniques of operational research and economics. This analytic approach is a dominant legacy in the study of the subject. It assumes that managers can make optimal decisions for their organisations based on finding out all they possibly can about their organisational world and then making a rational analysis of alternatives. This was a highly influential approach and, for example, gave rise to specialist corporate planning departments in organisations in the private and public sectors, especially in the 1970s.

Both of these approaches came in for considerable criticism in the last decades of the twentieth century.[4] First, although the case study method is still a very important means of bringing 'real life' into the classroom, on its own the old business policy approach lacked a substantial research basis. There was little evidence to back up the common sense, and few theoretical frameworks to generalise beyond individual cases. Second, the analytical approach of specialised corporate planning departments proved poorly able to cope with the apparently more dynamic and competitive business world that emerged from the late 1970s. Three- or five-year strategic plans soon got overtaken by events. The response has been twofold.

On the one hand, academics have developed a growing body of research addressing the implications of different strategies for the financial performance of organisations. This body of research is known as the *content approach*, focused on the content (or nature) of different strategic options – such as innovation, diversification or internationalisation. For content researchers, the typical question is what sort of strategy performs best under what conditions. They argue that managers can benefit from lessons drawn from such research in order to make wiser strategic decisions. Strategic analysis and planning are more effective if underpinned by rigorous research evidence. The main academic discipline which inspires this research is economics, with the work of Michael Porter on industry structure in the 1980s and the resource-based theories of the 1990s particularly exemplary in this respect.[5]

On the other hand, a very different stream of research, led by such figures as Henry Mintzberg and Andrew Pettigrew, drew on sociology and psychology to argue that people were too imperfect and the world too complex for heavy reliance on analysis and planning, however rigorous the economics research.[6] From the 1970s, they and their followers developed a *process approach* to strategy, studying the realities of strategic decision making and strategic change processes.[7] These process researchers have shown again and again the real-world messiness of strategy formulation and implementation. The implication is that it is impossible to analyse everything up front and predict the future, and that the search for economically optimal decisions is futile. It is better to work with, rather than against, the messiness of organisations. This means accepting that managers make decisions which are as much to do with organisational politics and the history and culture of the organisation as they are to do with the economics of strategy, and that strategies will often get derailed in implementation. In this view, recognising imperfections and complexities is actually more effective than ignoring them, as in some purely economics approaches.

The twenty-first century has seen the emergence and growing acceptance of new streams of research that offer still more promising means of coping with organisational reality. This book highlights three:

- *Complexity theory*, drawn from the physical sciences, can be used to help manage the messy world of organisations. According to researchers such as Ralph Stacey and Kathy Eisenhardt, complexity theory principles can be used to achieve order and progress in the social world just as stable patterns of behaviour and well-adapted species seem to emerge in the natural world.[8] The hands-off methods of complexity theory, rather than the heavy-handed approaches of traditional management, are the best way to cope with real-world organisations. Complexity theory is one of the inspirations in the strategy as ideas lens (see section 1.6).

- *Discourse* researchers such as David Knights have drawn on sociological theories of language to point to how discourse – the way in which we talk about organisations – shapes what actually goes on.[9] The discourse perspective in particular highlights how mastery of strategy language and jargon can be a 'resource' for managers through which they gain influence and power and establish their legitimacy and identity as strategists. In this view, knowing how to 'talk strategy' is a key skill in organisational life. The insights of this view are encapsulated in the strategy as discourse lens (see below).

- *Strategy-as-practice* researchers have built on sociological and psychological traditions to examine more closely the actual practice of managers in strategy, developing a detailed understanding of the activities and techniques involved.[10] In some ways, these researchers are returning to the real case approach of the Harvard general manager perspective, but this time seeking to underpin it with systematic research. The promise of strategy-as-practice research is an enhanced capacity to design more practical strategy processes and train more skilled and reflective practitioners, allowing for the real complexities and unintended consequences of organisational life. Chapter 15 particularly draws on this new strategy-as-practice perspective.

Thus half a century of strategy research has produced many ways of approaching strategy. All can provide valuable insights and this book draws on them extensively. For example, while Chapters 2 and 3 rely heavily on economic approaches to analysing environments and resources, Chapters 4 and 5 adopt a strongly sociological and psychological sensitivity to organisational complexity and cultures. Subsequent chapters draw equally on economic, sociological and psychological perspectives. A strong theme in this book is that managers work best if open to different perspectives on the same problem, thereby enlarging their set of possible solutions. The importance of different perspectives is pursued through the strategy lenses (see section 1.6).

1.5 STRATEGY AS A JOB

Most readers of this book will have to engage with strategy to some extent or another. Strategy is not just the preserve of top management. Middle and lower-level managers have to work within their organisation's strategy, meeting the objectives set by the strategy and observing the constraints. Managers have to communicate strategy to their teams, and will achieve greater performance from them the more convincing they are in interpreting it. Indeed, middle and lower-level managers can increasingly play a part in shaping strategy. Brad Garlinghouse's attempt to influence strategy at Yahoo! is an extreme case, but involvement in strategy 'away-days' and various strategy consultation procedures is now a common experience for middle managers in many organisations (see Chapter 15). Being able to participate in an organisation's 'strategic conversation' – engaging with senior managers on the big issues facing them – is often part of what it takes to win promotion.[11]

Strategy, then, is part of many managers' ordinary jobs. However, there are specialist strategists as well, in both private and public sectors. Despite the disappointed hopes in analytical corporate planning of the 1960s and 1970s, there are many in-house strategic planning jobs available. Typically requiring a formal business education of some sort, strategic planning is a potential career route for many readers, especially after some operational experience. Strategy consulting has been a growth industry in the last decades, with the original leading firms such as McKinsey & Co., the Boston Consulting Group and Bain joined now by more generalist consultants such as Accenture, IBM Consulting and PwC, each with its own strategy consulting arm.[12] Again, business graduates are in demand for strategy consulting roles.[13]

The interviews in Illustration 1.3 give some insights into the different kinds of strategy work that managers and strategy specialists can do. Galina, the manager of an international subsidiary, Masoud, working in a governmental strategy unit, and Chantal, a strategy consultant, all have different experiences of strategy, but there are some common themes also. All find strategy work stimulating and rewarding. The two specialists, Masoud and Chantal, talk more than Galina of the analytical tools. Galina discovered directly the possible limits of a strategic plan, with the changes that were imposed in the first few years in the United Kingdom. She emphasises the importance of flexibility in strategy and the value of getting her managers to see the 'whole picture' through involving them in strategy making. But Masoud and Chantal too are concerned for much more than analysis. Chantal emphasises the importance of gaining 'traction' with clients, building consensus in order to ensure implementation. Masoud likewise does not take implementation for granted, continuing to work with departments after the delivery of recommendations. He sees strategy and delivery as intimately connected, with people involved in delivery needing an understanding of strategy to be effective, and strategists needing to understand delivery. For him, strategy is a valuable stepping stone in a career, something that will underpin his possible next move into a more operational role.

Strategy, then, is not just about abstract organisations: it is a job that people do. The task of this book is partly to equip readers to do this job better, and to work with others who have to do strategy too. Chapters 11 and 15 specifically discuss the various roles of middle and senior managers, strategic planners and strategy consultants in strategy work.

1.6 THE STRATEGY LENSES

The **strategy lenses** are four different ways of looking at the issues of strategy development for an organisation

This chapter has already highlighted the different perspectives on strategy that have emerged from strategy research. The practical value of different perspectives is explored in this book through the four **strategy lenses**. These lenses are introduced more fully immediately after this chapter and will provide the framework for separate *commentaries* on each of the three parts of this book. The important point of these lenses is to avoid approaching strategic problems from a single perspective. Looking at problems in different ways will raise new issues and new solutions. Thus, although the lenses are drawn from academic research on strategy, they should also be highly practical in the job of doing strategy.

In brief the four lenses see strategy as follows:

- *Strategy as design.* This takes the view that strategy development can be a logical process in which the forces and constraints on the organisation are weighed carefully through analytic and evaluative techniques to establish clear strategic direction. This creates conditions in which carefully planned strategy implementation should occur. The design lens usually grants top management the leadership role in strategy, with middle and lower management given supporting roles in implementation. This view is perhaps the most commonly held one about how strategy should be developed and what managing strategy is about. It is the traditional 'textbook' view.

- *Strategy as experience.* Here the view is that future strategies of organisations are heavily influenced by the experience of managers and others in the organisation based on their previous strategies. Strategies are driven not so much by clear-cut analysis as by the taken-for-granted assumptions and ways of doing things embedded in the culture of organisations. Insofar as different views and expectations within the organisation exist, they will be resolved not just through rational processes, as in the design lens, but through processes of

Illustration 1.3

Strategists

For Galina, Masoud and Chantal, strategy is a large part of their jobs.

Galina

After a start in marketing, Galina became managing director of the British subsidiary of a Russian information technology company at the age of 33. As well as developing the strategy for her local business, she has to interact regularly with the Moscow headquarters:

Moscow is interested in the big picture, not just the details. They are interested in the future of the business.

The original strategic plans for the subsidiary had had to be adapted heavily:

When we first came here, we had some ideas about strategy, but soon found the reality was very different to the plans. The strategy was not completely wrong, but in the second stage we had to change it a lot: we had to change techniques and adapt to the market. Now we are in the third stage, where we have the basics and need to focus on trends, to get ahead and be in the right place at the right time.

Galina works closely with her management team on strategy, taking them on an annual 'strategy away-day' (see Chapter 15):

Getting people together helps them see the whole picture, rather than just the bits they are responsible for. It is good to put all their separate realities together.

Galina is enthusiastic about working on strategy:

I like strategy work, definitely. The most exciting thing is to think about where we have come from and where we might be going. We started in a pub five years ago and we have somehow implemented what we were hoping for then. Strategy gives you a measure of success. It tells you how well you have done.

Her advice is:

Always have a strategy – have an ultimate idea in mind. But take feedback from the market and from your colleagues. Be ready to adjust the strategy: the adjustment is the most important.

Masoud

Aged 27, Masoud is a policy advisor in a central government strategy unit in the United Kingdom. He provides analysis and advice for ministers, often on a cross-departmental basis. He typically works on projects for several months at a time, continuing to work with responsible service departments after the delivery of recommendations. Projects involve talking to experts inside and outside government, statistical analysis, scenario analyses (see Chapter 2), sensitivity analyses (see Chapter 10), hypothesis testing (see Chapter 15) and writing reports and making presentations. As he has progressed, Masoud has become increasingly involved in the management of strategy projects, rather than the basic analysis itself.

Masoud explains what he likes most about strategy work in government:

bargaining and negotiation. Here, then, the view is that there is a tendency for the strategy to build on and continue what has gone on before.

- *Strategy as ideas.* Neither of the above lenses is especially helpful in explaining innovation. Design approaches risk being too rigid and top down; experience builds too much on the past. How then do new ideas come about? The ideas lens emphasises the importance of promoting diversity in and around organisations, which can potentially generate genuinely new ideas. Here strategy is seen as not so much planned from the top as emergent from within

I like most the challenge. It's working on issues that really matter, and often it's what you are reading about in the newspapers. They are really tough issues; these are problems facing the whole of society.

He thinks people should get involved in strategy:

I would encourage people to do strategy, because it gets to the heart of problems. In all organisations, having some experience of working on strategy is very valuable, even if it is not what you want to major on your whole career.

Masoud is considering moving into service delivery as the next step of his career, because he sees knowledge of strategy and knowledge of operations as so interconnected:

Part of doing strategy is you have to understand what can be delivered; and part of doing delivery is you have to understand the strategy.

Chantal

Chantal is in her early thirties and has worked in Paris for one of the top three international strategy consultancies since graduating in business. Consulting was attractive to her originally because she liked the idea of helping organisations improve. She chose her particular consultancy because

I had fun in the interview rounds and the people were inspiring. I pictured myself working with these kinds of topics and with these kinds of people.

She enjoys strategy consulting:

What I like is solving problems. It's a bit like working on a mystery case: you have a problem and then you have to find a solution to fit the company, and help it grow and to be better.

The work is intellectually challenging:

Time horizons are short. You have to solve your case in two to three months. There's lots of pressure. It pushes you and helps you to learn yourself. There are just three to four in a team, so you will make a significant contribution to the project even as a junior. You have a lot of autonomy and you're making a contribution right from the start, and at quite a high level.

The work can involve financial and market modelling (see Chapters 2 and 10), interviewing clients and customers, and working closely with the client's own teams. Chantal explains:

As a consultant, you spend a lot of time in building solid fact-based arguments that will help clients make business decisions. But as well as the facts, you have to have the ability to get traction. People have to agree, so you have to build consensus, to make sure that recommendations are supported and acted on.

Chantal summarises the appeal of strategy consulting:

I enjoy the learning, at a very high speed. There's the opportunity to increase your skills. One year in consulting is like two years in a normal business.

Source: interviews (interviewees anonymised).

Questions

1 Which of these strategy roles appeals to you most – manager of a business unit in a multinational, in-house strategy specialist or strategy consultant? Why?

2 What would you have to do to get such a role?

and around organisations as people respond to an uncertain and changing environment with a variety of initiatives. New ideas will emerge, but they are likely to have to battle for survival against other ideas and against the forces for conformity to past strategies (as the experience lens explains).

● *Strategy as discourse*. This lens sees strategy in terms of language. Managers spend most of their time communicating. Therefore command of strategy language becomes a resource for managers by which to shape 'objective' strategic analyses to their personal views and to gain influence, power and legitimacy. Approaching strategy as a discourse makes managers very attentive to the language in which they frame strategic problems, make strategy proposals, debate issues and then finally communicate strategic decisions. The language of strategy, and the concepts that underpin that language, can shape the strategy agenda in terms of what is discussed and how. Strategy 'talk' matters.

SUMMARY

www.pearsoned.co.uk/ecs
AUDIO SUMMARY

● Strategy is the *direction* and *scope* of an organisation over the *long term*, which achieves *advantage* in a changing *environment* through its configuration of *resources and competences* with the aim of fulfilling *stakeholder* expectations.

● Strategic decisions are made at a number of levels in organisations. *Corporate-level strategy* is concerned with an organisation's overall purpose and scope; *business-level (or competitive) strategy* with how to compete successfully in a market; and *operational strategies* with how resources, processes and people can effectively deliver corporate- and business-level strategies. Strategic management is distinguished from day-to-day operational management by the complexity of influences on decisions, the organisation-wide implications and their long-term implications.

● Strategic management has three major elements: understanding the *strategic position*, making *strategic choices* for the future and managing *strategy in action*. The strategic position of an organisation is influenced by the external environment, internal strategic capability and the expectations and influence of stakeholders. Strategic choices include the underlying bases of strategy at both the corporate and business levels and the directions and methods of development. Strategic management is also concerned with understanding which choices are likely to succeed or fail. Managing strategy in action is concerned with issues of structuring, resourcing to enable future strategies and managing change.

● The study of strategy has moved on from the original business policy and strategic planning traditions, to develop two main streams: strategy *content*, concerned with the nature of different strategic options; and strategy process, concerned with *processes* such as strategic decision making and strategic change. More approaches are currently developing, such as complexity theory, strategy discourse and strategy-as-practice.

● Strategy is also a kind of job. It is done full time by *strategic planners* and *strategy consultants*. Strategy is also an important part of the responsibilities of many managers: not just senior managers and managers responsible for strategic business units, but also those managers needing to influence their organisation's overall strategic direction.

● Organisations' strategic issues are best seen from a variety of perspectives, as suggested by the four *strategy lenses*. A *design* lens sees strategy in logical analytical ways. An *experience* lens sees strategy as the product of individual experience and organisational culture. The *ideas* lens sees strategy as emerging from ideas within and around an organisation. The *discourse* lens highlights the role of strategy language in shaping understandings within organisations, and points to the importance of being able to talk this language effectively.

Work assignments

✱ *Denotes more advanced work assignments.*   ** Refers to a case study in the Text and Cases edition.*

1.1 Drawing on Exhibit 1.2 and Illustration 1.2 as guides, note down and explain examples of the vocabulary of strategy used in the annual report or website of an organisation of your choice (for example, your university).

1.2 Using the *Exploring Corporate Strategy* model of Exhibit 1.3, map key issues relating to strategic position, strategic choices and strategy into action for either the Ministry of Sound* or an organisation with which you are familiar with (for example, your university).

1.3 ✱ Using annual reports, press articles and the Internet, write a brief case study (similar to that of Electrolux or Ministry of Sound*) that shows the strategic development and current strategic position of an organisation of your choice.

1.4 ✱ Using Exhibit 1.3 as a guide, show how the elements of strategic management differ in:

(a) a small business (e.g. MacPac*, Ekomate* or Brown Bag Films*)

(b) a large multinational business (e.g. Electrolux, SABMiller*, AIB*)

(c) a non-profit organisation (e.g. NHS Direct* or the Salvation Army*).

An extensive range of additional materials, including audio summaries, weblinks to organisations featured in the text, definitions of key concepts and self-assessment questions, can be found on the *Exploring Corporate Strategy* Companion Website at www.pearsoned.co.uk/ecs

Recommended key readings

It is always useful to read around a topic. As well as the specific references below, we particularly highlight:

- For general overviews of the evolving nature of the strategy discipline, R. Whittington, *What is strategy – and does it matter?*, 2nd edition, International Thompson, 2000; and H. Mintzberg, B. Ahlstrand and J. Lampel, *Strategy Safari: a Guided Tour through the Wilds of Strategic Management*, Simon & Schuster, 2000.

- Two classic and accessible articles on what strategy is, and might not be, are M. Porter, 'What is strategy?', *Harvard Business Review*, November–December (1996), pp. 61–78; and D. Hambrick and J. Fredrickson, 'Are you sure you have a strategy?', *Academy of Management Executive*, vol. 19, no. 4 (2005), pp. 51–62.

- For contemporary developments in strategy practice, business newspapers such as the *Financial Times*, *Les Echos* and the *Wall Street Journal* and business magazines such as *Business Week*, *The Economist*, *L'Expansion* and *Manager-Magazin*. See also the websites of the leading strategy consulting firms: www.mckinsey.com; www.bcg.com; www.bain.com.

References

1. The question 'What is strategy?' has been discussed in R. Whittington, *What is strategy – and does it matter?*, International Thomson, 1993/2000; M. Porter, 'What is strategy?', *Harvard Business Review*, November–December, 1996, pp. 61–78; and F. Fréry, 'The fundamental dimensions of strategy', *MIT Sloan Management Review*, vol. 48, no. 1 (2006), pp. 71–75.

2. The Harvard 'business policy' tradition is discussed in L. Greiner, A. Bhambri and T. Cummings, 'Searching for a strategy to teach strategy', *Academy of Management Learning and Education*, vol. 2, no. 4 (2003), pp. 401–420.

3. The classic book is H.I. Ansoff, *Corporate Strategy*, Penguin, 1965. For a summary of his work, see 'Obituary: Igor Ansoff, the father of strategic management', *Strategic Change*, vol. 11 (2002), pp. 437–438.

4. For reviews of the contemporary state of strategy as a discipline, see H. Volberda, 'Crisis in strategy: fragmentation, integration or synthesis', *European Management Review*, vol. 1, no. 1 (2004), pp. 35–42; and J. Mahoney and A. McGahan, 'The field of strategic management within the evolving science of strategic organization', *Strategic Organization*, vol. 5, no. 1 (2007), 79–99.

5. The classic statement of the industry structure view is M. Porter, *Competitive Strategy: Techniques for Analysing Industries and Firms*, Free Press, 1980. The classic statement of the resource-based view is J. Barney, 'Firm resources and sustained competitive advantage', *Journal of Management*, vol. 17, no. 1 (1991), pp. 91–120.

6. Henry Mintzberg's classic articles are collected in H. Mintzberg, *Mintzberg on Management: Inside our Strange World of Organizations*, Free Press, 1989. See also A. Pettigrew and R. Whipp, *Managing Change for Competitive Success*, Blackwell, 1991.

7. Two recent collections in the strategy process tradition are G. Szulanski, J. Porac and Y. Doz (eds), *Strategy Process: Advances in Strategic Management*, JAI Press, 2005; and S. Floyd, J. Roos, C. Jacobs and F. Kellermans (eds), *Innovating Strategy Process*, Blackwell, 2005.

8. See R. Stacey, *Managing Chaos: Dynamic business strategies in an unpredictable world*, Kogan Page, 1992; and S. Brown and K. Eisenhardt, *Competing on the Edge: Strategy as structured chaos*, HBR Press, 1998.

9. D. Knights, 'Changing spaces: the disruptive impact of a new epistemological location for the study of management', *Academy of Management Review*, vol. 17, no. 4 (1992), pp. 514–536; and R. Suddaby and R. Greenwood, 'Rhetorical strategies of legitimacy', *Administrative Science Quarterly*, vol. 50 (2005), pp. 35–67.

10. For recent samples of practice research, see G. Johnson, A. Langley, L. Melin and R. Whittington, *Strategy as Practice: Research Directions and Resources*, Cambridge University Press, 2007; and the special issue of P. Jarzabkowski, J. Balogun and D. Seidl, 'Strategizing: the challenge of a practice perspective', *Human Relations*, vol. 60, no. 1 (2007), pp. 5–27.

11. F. Westley, 'Middle managers and strategy: microdynamics of inclusion', *Strategic Management Journal*, vol. 11, no. 5 (1990), 337–351.

12. The major strategy consulting firms have a wealth of information on strategy careers and strategy in general: see www.mckinsey.com; www.bcg.com; www.bain.com.

13. University careers advisers can provide good advice on strategy consulting and strategic planning opportunities. See also www.vault.com.

Electrolux

By 2005 Sweden's Electrolux was the world's largest producer of domestic and professional appliances for the kitchen, cleaning and outdoor use. Its products included cookers, vacuum cleaners, washing machines, fridges, lawn mowers, chain saws and also tools for the construction and stone industries. It employed about 70,000 people and sold about 40 million products annually in about 150 countries. Its annual sales in 2005 were 129 billion Swedish krona (~€14bn; ~£10bn) and profits about 3.9bn krona (~€420m). But 2005 saw two changes that would push the company into second place in the industry – behind the US company *Whirlpool*. First, Whirlpool completed its acquisition of *Maytag* – which gave it about 47 per cent market share in the USA and global sales of some $US19bn (~€15bn). Second, Electrolux announced that it was to demerge its outdoor products division (mowers, chain saws, etc.) as *Husqvarna*. This left Electrolux to focus on the indoor products for both the home and professional cooking and cleaning organisations. So the 'new Electrolux' would have 57,000 employees and global sales of some SEK 104bn (~€11bn).

Photo: Electrolux

History

This was just the latest shift in strategy at Electrolux whose impressive growth and development started under the leadership of Alex Wenner-Gren in 1920s' Sweden. The early growth was built around an expertise in industrial design creating the leading products in refrigeration and vacuum cleaning. By the mid-1930s the company had also established production outside Sweden in Germany, UK, France, USA and Australia.

The period following the Second World War saw a major growth in demand for domestic appliances and Electrolux expanded its range into washing machines and dishwashers. In 1967 Hans Werthén took over as president and embarked on a series of acquisitions

that restructured the industry in Europe: 59 acquisitions were made in the 1970s alone followed by major acquisitions of Zanussi (Italy), White Consolidated Products (USA), the appliance division of Thorn EMI (UK) the outdoor products company Poulan/Weed Eater (USA) and AEG Hausgeräte (Germany). But the biggest acquisition of the 1980s was the Swedish Granges Group (this was a diversification into a metals conglomerate).

As a result of all these acquisitions, by 1990 75 per cent of Electrolux's sales were outside Sweden and this increased in the 1990s as Leif Johansson expanded into Eastern Europe, Asia (India and Thailand) and Central and South America (Mexico and Brazil). He then disposed of many of the 'non-core' industrial activities (particularly Granges). A major restructuring in the late 1990s created the shape of the group for the early 2000s – with about 85 per cent of sales in consumer durables and 15 per cent in related products for professional users (such as professional food service and laundry equipment).

The market

The 2005 annual report highlighted three critically important aspects of the company's markets that their strategies had to address:

Globalisation

'Electrolux operates in an industry with strong global competition. . . . Productivity within the industry has risen over the years, and consumers are offered increasingly better products at lower prices. More and more manufacturers are establishing plants in countries where production costs are considerably lower . . . and also purchasing more components there. In time, production costs for the major producers will essentially be at the same level. This will stimulate a shift of competitive focus to product development, marketing and brand-building.'

Market polarisation

'The combination of changing consumer preferences, the growth of global retail chains and greater global competition is leading to polarisation of the market. More consumers are demanding basic products. Companies that can improve efficiency in production and distribution will be able to achieve profitable growth in this segment. At the same time, demand for higher-price products is increasing.'

Consolidation of retailers

'The dealer structure in the household-appliances market [particularly in the USA] is being consolidated. Traditional dealers are losing market shares to large retail chains. The big chains benefit from high purchasing volumes and wide geographical coverage. This gives them greater opportunities to keep prices low. [But in turn, producers'] costs of serving large retailers is often lower than for traditional outlets, thanks to large volumes and efficient logistics.'

These three factors were also connected. For example, the rapid penetration of Asian producers (for example, LG and Samsung) into the US market was through securing big contracts with major US retailers (The Home Depot and Lowe's respectively).

Electrolux strategies

In the 2005 annual report the Chief Executive (Hans Stråberg) reflected on his first four years with the company and the challenges for the future:

Four years ago I took over as President and CEO of Electrolux. My goal was to accelerate the development of Electrolux as a market-driven company, based on greater understanding of customer needs. . . . We [said that we] would achieve [our goals] by:

- Continuing to cut costs and drive out complexity in all aspects of operations
- Increasing the rate of product renewal based on consumer insight
- Increasing our investment in marketing, and building the Electrolux brand as the global leader in our industry.

He continued by describing the major changes in strategy that had occurred over those four years whilst looking forward to the continuing and new challenges after the demerger in 2006:

Managing under-performers

We have divested or changed the business model for units that could be considered as non-core operations or in which profitability was too low. [For example], instead of continuing production of air-conditioners in the US, which was not profitable, we out-sourced these products to a manufacturer in China. Our operations in motors and compressors have been divested.

Moving production to low-cost countries

Maintaining competitive production costs is a prerequisite for survival in our markets. We will work on improving profitability either by divesting specific units or by changing the business model. It is also important to continue relocating production from high-cost to low-cost countries. . . . We have shut down plants where costs were much too high, and built new ones in countries with competitive cost levels. For example, we moved production of refrigerators from Greenville in the US to Juarez in Mexico. This has enabled us to cut costs and at the same time open a state-of-the-art production unit for serving the entire North American market. The goal is for these activities to be largely completed by late 2008.

More efficient production and logistics

We have put a good deal of time and effort into making production and logistics more efficient. This has involved reducing the number of product platforms, increasing productivity, reducing inventory levels and increasing delivery accuracy.

More efficient purchasing

Purchasing is another area where we have implemented changes in order to improve our cost position, mainly through better coordination at the global level. We have launched a project designed to drastically reduce the number of suppliers. We have also intensified our cooperation with suppliers in order to cut the costs of components. [But] there is a good deal still to be done. Among other things, we are increasing the share of purchases from low-cost countries.

Intensified product renewal

Our future depends on how well we can combine a continued focus on costs with intensified product renewal and systematic development of both our brands and our personnel. . . . Our process for product development based on consumer insight reduces the risk of incorrect investment decisions. Achieving better impact in development of new products has involved making global coordination more efficient, which has given us a number of new global products. The result of our investments in product development over the past years is clearly reflected in the number of product launches for core appliances, which rose from about 200 in 2002 to about 370 in 2005. . . . Investment in product development has risen by SEK 500 million (~€77m) over the past three years. Our goal is to invest at least 2% of sales in product development. We will continue to launch new products at a high rate.

Access to competence

Over the past years we have established [talent management] processes and tools that ensure the Group of access to competence in the future. Active leadership development, international career opportunities and a result-oriented corporate culture enable us to successfully develop our human resources. In order to lead development in our industry, we will have to act fast and dare to do things differently. [We will also need] a strong environmental commitment and good relations with our suppliers.

Starting to build a strong global brand

When I took over as President and CEO in 2002 I stressed that we had to prioritise building of the Electrolux brand, both globally and across all product categories. A strong brand enables a significant price premium in the market, which leads to a sustainable long-term increase in margin. Work on building a strong brand has been very comprehensive. The share of products sold under the Electrolux brand has risen from 16% of sales in 2002 to almost 50% in 2005. We will continue to work on building the Electrolux brand as the global leader in our industry. Our goal is for our investment in brand-building to correspond to at least 2% of sales.

Looking ahead to the near future

Hans Stråberg concluded his review of the business by a look forward to the following year:

We expect the Group to report higher profitability again in 2006. . . . In both North America and Europe we are going to launch a number of important new products. Professional Indoor Products will improve its position in the North American market in 2006 by developing new distribution channels for food-service equipment. The success of our floor-care operation in the higher price segments will continue, among other things on the basis of higher volumes for cyclone vacuum cleaners.

There will be no change in the rate of relocation of production to low-cost countries. During the second half of 2006 we will see the full effect of the cost-savings generated by moving production from Greenville in the US to Juarez in Mexico. We expect that sales will be adversely affected by the strike at our appliance plant in Nuremberg, Germany [planned to close in 2007]. Continued reduction of purchasing costs is a very important factor for increasing our profitability in 2006.

The strategy that has been effectively implemented in recent years by everyone in our organisation is paying off. In 2006 we will continue this important work on strengthening the Electrolux brand, launching new products and reducing costs.

Sources: Company website (www.electrolux.com); annual report 2005.

Questions

1 Refer to section 1.2.1 and explain why the issues facing Electrolux were strategic. Try to find examples of all of the items cited in that section.

2 What levels of strategy can you identify at Electrolux? (Refer to section 1.2.2.)

3 Identify the main factors about the strategic position of Electrolux. List these separately under environment, capability and expectations (see section 1.3.1). In your opinion which are the most important factors?

4 Think about strategic choices for the company in relation to the issues raised in section 1.3.2.

5 What are the main issues about strategy into action that might determine the success or failure of Electrolux's strategies? (Refer to section 1.3.3.)

Commentary

The Strategy Lenses

www.pearsoned.co.uk/ecs

KEY CONCEPT

Strategy lenses

Chapter 1 showed that the way strategy has been taught and researched has changed over the years. As this has happened different perspectives on the subject have arisen. The argument here is that these different perspectives are helpful in at least three ways:

- They provide *different insights* on strategy and the management of strategy. Think of everyday discussions you have. It is not unusual for people to say: 'But if you look at it this way. . . .' Taking one view can lead to a partial and perhaps biased understanding. A fuller picture, giving different insights, can be gained from multiple perspectives.

- These different insights can also prompt thinking about different *options or solutions* to strategic problems.

- They also flag up the *limitations and possible dangers* of one approach over another.

There is, therefore, both conceptual and practical value in taking a multi-perspective approach to strategy.

This commentary builds on the historically different perspectives on strategy to develop four *lenses* through which strategy in organisations can be viewed. They are:

- *Strategy as design*. The view that strategy development can be a logical process in which the forces and constraints on the organisation are weighed carefully through analytic and evaluative techniques to establish clear strategic direction and a basis for the carefully planned implementation of strategy. This is the most commonly held view about how strategy is developed and what managing strategy is about.

- *Strategy as experience*. The view that the strategies of organisations are substantially influenced by the experience of people (not least managers), taken-for-granted assumptions and ways of doing things in organisations. It is a perspective that helps account for the tendency for strategies to develop incrementally on the basis of the past and for them to be difficult to change. It also flags up the importance of understanding and challenging that which is taken for granted in organisations.

- *Strategy as ideas*. Emphasises the importance of variety and diversity in and around organisations that potentially helps generate new ideas. This perspective suggests that managing strategy is about creating the organisational context to foster the emergence of these ideas and developing them as they emerge. There is much less emphasis here on planned direction from the top.

- *Strategy as discourse*. Highlights the central importance of the language of strategy as a 'resource' for managers. Not only is this language the basis for communicating and explaining strategy, but also it is a basis for gaining influence and power and establishing the legitimacy and identity of the strategist.

The rest of this commentary explains the lenses in more detail. In so doing, the discussion addresses some key dimensions of strategic management. Amongst these are:

- *Rationality*. The extent to which the development of strategy is a rationally managed act. Of course the design lens assumes this is the case, but the other lenses raise questions about it.

- *Innovation* and change. The extent to which the management of strategy is likely to develop innovatory, change-oriented organisations; or conversely, consolidate strategies rooted in past experience and ways of doing things.

- *Legitimacy*. How strategy and the involvement in the management of strategy provide an identity for people – usually managers – of power, authority and influence in their organisations.

The lenses are then used in commentaries (on mauve pages) to interpret the content of the main chapters at the end of each part of the book and to encourage readers to reflect on the issues that have been raised in preceding chapters.

Strategy as design

The design lens views strategy development as a logical process in which the forces and constraints on the organisation are analysed and evaluated to establish clear strategic direction and a basis for the planned implementation of strategy

The design lens builds on two main principles. The first is that managers are, or should be, rational decision makers. The second is that they should be taking decisions about how to optimise economic performance of their organisations. Most managers would probably agree that that is what they are there to do. The principles of economics and the guidelines provided by the decision sciences support and feed the notion that this is what strategic management is all about.

Rational choice is based on the consideration of the consequences and therefore the 'anticipations of the future effects of possible actions'.[1] The implication is that managers can and should be able to weigh the benefits and disbenefits of different strategic options on the basis of evidence that informs them of likely outcomes of decisions they make. There are strong parallels here with the way strategic management is often explained in textbooks, by tutors and indeed by managers. Stated more fully, the assumptions typically underpinning a *design* view of strategy are as follows. First, in terms of *how strategic decisions are made*:

- *Systematic analysis*. Although the range of influences on an organisation's performance are many, careful analysis can identify those most likely to influence the organisation significantly. It may be possible to forecast, predict or build scenarios about future impacts so that managers can think through the conditions in which their organisation is likely to operate.

- *Strategic positioning*. This analysis provides a basis for the matching of organisational strengths and resources with changes in the environment so as to take advantage of opportunities and overcome or circumvent threats.

Arguably the strongest influence in providing ways of doing this has been the writings of Michael Porter[2] in the early 1980s (see Chapter 2).

- *Analytic thinking precedes and governs action*. Strategy making is often seen as a *linear process*. Decisions about what the strategy should be in terms of its content come first and are cascaded down through the organisation to those who have to make things happen. Decisions about what the strategy should be are therefore separate from and precede its implementation.

- *Objectives* are clear and explicit and the basis upon which *options are evaluated*. Given a thorough analysis of the factors internal and external to the organisation to inform management about the strategic position of the organisation, a range of options for future strategic direction are then considered and evaluated in terms of the objectives and that analysis. A strategic decision is then made on the basis of what is considered to be optimal, given all these considerations.

The design lens also makes assumptions about the *form and nature of organisations*:

- *Organisations are hierarchies*. It is the responsibility of top management to plan the destiny of the organisation. They make important decisions, and lower levels of management, and eventually the population of an organisation, carry out these decisions and implement the strategy decided at the top.

- *Organisations are rational systems*. Since the complexity organisations face can be understood analytically such that logical conclusions are reached, the associated assumption is that people in the organisation will adopt and accept such logic. The system can be controlled rationally too. *Control systems* (for example, budgets, targets, appraisals) provide the means by which top management can measure whether or not others in the organisation are meeting expected objectives and behaving in line with the strategy so that managers further up in the hierarchy can take corrective action.

- *Organisations are mechanisms* by which strategy can be put into effect. They are analogous to engineered systems or, perhaps, machines. So how an organisation is structured and controlled (see Chapter 12) needs to be suited to the strategy. There need to be internal mechanisms to ensure that strategy is, indeed, being considered rationally and dispassionately. For example, issues of corporate governance are largely concerned with the self-interest or wrong-doing of senior executives. However, the measures taken to address this problem have tended to focus on structured solutions, such as attempts to set up regulating committees and how boards of directors should be structured. The assumption has been that structures will, or should, affect behaviour.

Implications for management

Managers often talk as if strategy comes about in their organisations – or *should* come about – much as the design lens suggests: it is seen as valuable by managers. Arguably there are six reasons for this:

- *Dealing with complexity and uncertainty*. The design lens provides a means of coping with and talking about complex and uncertain issues in a rational, logical and structured way. Indeed there are *concepts*, *tools* and *techniques* that enable managers to help with this.

- Important *stakeholders may expect and value such an approach*. For example, banks, financial analysts, investors and employees, so it is an important means of gaining their support and confidence.

- *Management power and legitimacy*. Managers, particularly CEOs, face complex and often challenging situations. The assumptions, tools and techniques of design provide them with ways in which they can feel in control and exercise control in such circumstances.

- Rationality is *deeply rooted* in our way of thinking and in our systems of education. In this sense the design lens is embedded in our human psyche. For example, even when managers admit that strategy is not actually developed in ways the design lens suggests, they often think it should be.

- *A rational world*. Increasingly there seems to be evidence of an all-embracing rationality in our world. We live in a time of computer technology, global communication, space exploration, advanced medicine and so on: a world in which science and reasoned solutions to the problems we face seem to surround us and provide so many benefits.

- *The language of strategy*. In many respects the design lens, especially in its emphasis on analysis and control, is the orthodox approach to strategy development most commonly written about in books, taught at business schools and verbalised by management when they discuss the strategy of their organisations. So it is a useful language to know (see the discourse lens below).

Managers who see their role like this may be highly analytical and seen as credible, influential (and therefore legitimate) strategists, as Exhibit I.i shows. The associated assumption is that change and innovation can, or at least should be able to, be achieved through such rational and mechanistic approaches, though as the exhibit suggests, this may be less clearly so.

Exhibit I.i **Design lens**

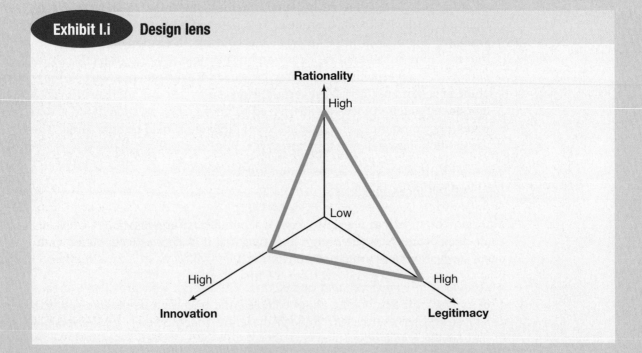

In summary, the design lens is useful in *thinking through and planning strategy* and as a way of managers positioning themselves as *credible strategists*. The question is whether this is an accurate or sufficient portrayal of strategic management. This book argues that the design lens is indeed useful but not sufficient. Other explanations help a fuller understanding of the practice of strategic management and provide insights into how the management of strategy can be approached.

Strategy as experience

Much of the evidence from research on how strategies actually develop gives a different picture than that seen through the design lens. As early as the 1950s, Herbert Simon and Charles Lindblom[3] pointed out that rational decision-making models were unrealistic. It is not possible to obtain the information necessary to achieve the sort of exhaustive analysis required; it is not possible to predict an uncertain future; there are limits in terms of cost and time in undertaking such analysis; organisations and environments are changing continually, so it is not possible for managers to take long-term decisions at a point in time. There are also psychological limitations on managers themselves which mean that they cannot be expected to weigh the consequences of all options or be the objective analysts such rationality would expect – a point which is discussed more fully below. The best that can be expected is what Simon termed 'bounded rationality' which results in managers *satisficing* rather than optimising: they do the best they can within the limits of their circumstances, knowledge and experience. The emphasis of the **experience lens** is, then, on the influence on strategy development of people's *individual and collective experience* and their *taken-for-granted assumptions*.

> The experience lens views strategy development as the outcome of individual and collective experience of individuals and their taken-for-granted assumptions

Individual experience and bias

Human beings function effectively not least because they have the cognitive capability to make sense of problems or issues they encounter. They recognise and make sense of these on the basis of past experience and what they come to believe to be true about the world. More formally, individual experience can be explained in terms of the mental (or cognitive) models people build over time to help make sense of their situation. Managers are no exception to this. When they face a problem they make sense of it in terms of the mental models that are the basis of their experience. This has major advantages. They are able to relate such problems to prior events and therefore have comparisons to draw upon. They can interpret one issue in the light of another. They therefore have bases for making decisions built on prior experience. If they did not have such mental models they could not function effectively; they would meet each situation as though they were experiencing it for the first time.

There are, however, downsides. Mental models simplify complexity. It is not possible for managers to operate in terms of 'perfect knowledge'. Understanding the effects of such *simplification processes* is important. Even if managers have a very rich understanding of their environment, they will not bring that complex understanding to bear for all situations and decisions. They will access part of that knowledge.[4] This is called *selective attention*: selecting from total understanding the parts of knowledge that seem most relevant. Managers also use *exemplars* and *prototypes*. For example, commonly competitors become prototypical. Television company executives came to see other television companies – even specific channels – as their competitors. They therefore readily accepted that satellite broadcasting could introduce new competition because it would introduce new television channels. However, they failed to see that the Internet and sites such as YouTube would become an alternative to watching television. There is also the risk that the 'chunk' of information most often used becomes the only information used and that stimuli from the environment are selected out to fit these dominant representations of reality. Information that squares with other television channels being the competitors is taken on board, whilst information counter to that is not. Sometimes this distortion can lead to severe errors as managers miss crucial indicators because they are, in effect, scanning the environment for issues and events that are familiar or readily recognisable.[5]

Whilst managers tend to see threats rather than opportunities in their environment,[6] they also often exaggerate and overestimate benefits[7] (known as 'attribution error'); for example, when it comes to investment decisions, forecasting the outcomes of risky projects and their own (or their organisation's) influence over events. They also tend to discount luck and inflate the capabilities of their organisation, whilst discounting or reducing the potential of competitors. As we all do, managers also typically make sense of new issues in the context of past issues; so when it comes to strategic decisions they are also likely to resolve a problem in much the same way as they dealt with a previous one seen as similar. Moreover, again, they are likely to search for evidence that supports those inclinations.

In summary, there are three important points:

- *Cognitive bias is inevitable*. The interpretation of events and issues in terms of prior experience is bound to occur. The idea that managers approach problems and issues of a strategic nature entirely dispassionately and objectively is unrealistic.

- *The future is likely to be made sense of in terms of the past*. Such interpretation and bias arise from experience of the past, not least in terms of what is seen to have worked or given rise to problems in the past. This is one explanation of why strategies tend to develop incrementally from prior strategy (see section 5.2.1).

- None the less, *experience may confer legitimacy and power*. Managers with extensive experience may well be seen as experts or have significant influence in an organisation.

There now exists a good deal of research that seeks to understand the strategy of organisations and the management of strategy in cognitive and sense-making terms, more fully explained by Gerard Hodgkinson and Paul Sparrow,[8] for example.

However, managers do not operate purely as individuals; they work and interact with others in organisations, and at this collective level there are also reasons to expect similar tendencies.

Collective experience and organisational culture

Meaning is not just a matter of individual cognition, but has a collective aspect to it. In this context cultural influences are important: indeed culture was defined by the anthropologist Clifford Geertz as 'socially established structures of meaning'.[9] It is an emphasis that Mats Alvesson, writing about organisational culture, agrees with.[10] How people, managers included, respond to and deal with issues is culturally informed. Central to the concept of culture is the importance of what is 'taken for granted' in terms of assumptions and in terms of activities or practices – 'the way we do things around here'. In everyday life, for example, there are assumptions such as the role of the family. However, these assumptions and associated ways of behaving differ between societies in different parts of the world. In organisational life, an equivalent example might be the different assumptions about the role of top managers in Western firms as compared with Japanese firms and the behaviours associated with such assumptions. However, taken-for-granted aspects of culture also exist at different levels: for example, within a managerial function such as marketing or finance; an organisational unit such as a business; or more widely a professional grouping, such as accountants, an industry sector or even a national culture. The links between culture and strategy are therefore important. They are discussed more fully in Chapter 5, but are also explored in the commentary sections in the book.

Implications for management

Viewed through the experience lens, strategies are seen to develop as managers try to relate their experience to the strategic issues that they face. There are four main implications:

● *Bargaining and negotiation* may take place between managers on the basis of different interpretations of events according to their past experience. This is the more likely, since managers' personal reputation and standing are likely to be based partly on such experience. This perspective is reflected in discussions of strategy development as political process (Chapters 4 and 14).

● There is a risk of *strategic drift* if managers are 'captured' by their own and their colleagues' experience. In such circumstances the strategy of the organisation gradually drifts away from the realities of its environment and towards an internally determined view of the world. This can lead to significant performance downturn and, potentially, the demise of the organisation (see section 5.2).

● *Strategic change* or *innovation is likely to be problematic*. It should not be assumed that the drawing up of a strategic plan laying out the logic of a strategic direction will of itself change that which is taken for granted. The notion that reasoned argument necessarily changes deeply embedded assumptions or ways of doing things is flawed; readers need only think of their own experience in trying to persuade others to rethink their religious beliefs or, indeed, allegiances to sports teams to realise this.

● *Surfacing, questioning and challenging* taken-for-granted experience and assumptions can therefore be of key importance in strategic management.

Exhibit I.ii **Experience lens**

This may be achieved by using the strategy tools and techniques, but can also be seen as part of the political process of organizations.

Exhibit I.ii summarises the discussion in relation to the three dimensions of strategy. The experience lens suggests that it is much more difficult to make strategic changes than the design lens might imply. And rationality, in the sense of the careful weighing of options in a search for optimal solutions, is not the emphasis, but rather people's individual and collective experience. Managers' experience may, however, be seen by colleagues as relevant and important and therefore bestow a degree of legitimacy.

Strategy as ideas

The extent to which the two lenses described so far explain innovation and the generation of new ideas is rather limited. The experience lens rather emphasises the tendency for organisations to conform to past ways of doing things. Notionally a design approach could promote innovation, but in fact tends to so emphasise control that it is also likely to result in conformity rather than innovation. So how to account for innovative strategies, processes and products? Moreover, how do organisations faced with fast-changing environments and short decision horizons, such as those in high-technology businesses or the fashion industries, cope with the speed of change and innovation required?

The ideas lens sees strategy as emergent from the ideas that bubble up from the variety and diversity in and around organisations

The **ideas lens** builds on complexity theory[11] and evolutionary theory[12] which, as Shona Brown and Kathy Eisenhardt[13] have shown, are helpful when it comes to explaining the sources of and conditions that help generate innovation. The basic tenets of evolutionary theory – variation, selection and retention – provide an understanding of how organisational context is important in relation to the generation of new ideas and how managers may help shape that context. The emphasis of complexity theory on how systems cope with uncertainty in non-linear ways adds to that understanding. Viewed through the ideas lens, top-down design and direction of strategy is de-emphasised. Rather, strategies are seen as emerging from ideas that bubble up from the variety and diversity in and around organisations.

The importance of variety

New ideas are generated in conditions of variety and diversity, whereas conditions of uniformity give rise to fewer new ideas. Whether the concern is with species, as in the natural world, people in societies or indeed ideas in organis-ations,[14] uniformity is not the norm; there exists *variety*. There is an ever-changing environment, different types of businesses, a variety of groups and individuals, a variety of their experience and ideas, and there are deviations from routine ways of doing things.[15] Evolution helps explain how any living system, including an organisation, evolves through natural selection acting upon such variation.

Variety is likely to be greatest where the environment is changing fastest. For example, in our biological world there has been the rapid development of new strains of viruses given the advances in modern medicine to fight them. There are parallels with regard to organisations. Organisations in industry sectors that are developing and fragmented tend to be more innovative than those in mature and concentrated industries,[16] because of the diversity of ideas that exist in such dynamic conditions. Take the example of the microelectronics industry. It is a fast-changing industry. This has spawned many different types of businesses, from hardware manufacturers through to software boutiques and firms engaged in applications of such technology. Within these organisations, in turn, there develop new ideas as people interpret opportunities and potential applications differently.

A good deal of this variety occurs naturally and quite likely outside managers' direct control. Since sensing of its environment takes place throughout an organ-isation, new ideas quite likely come from low down in an organisation, not just from the top.[17] Such ideas may not be well formed and will be more or less well informed and, at the individual level at least, they may be very diverse. Bill McKelvey refers to this as the 'distributed intelligence' of an organisation.[18] Moreover, innovation in large organisations often comes from outside their boundaries, perhaps from smaller businesses.[19]

People in organisations may seek to generate such variety and some of the ways they do this are discussed below. Variation may not, however, always be inten-tional. In the natural world, change and newness come about because of *imper-fections* – a mutation of a gene, for example – that may provide the basis for a 'fitter' organism in a changing environment. In organisations, ideas are also copied imperfectly between individuals, groups or organisations. Some of these will give rise to innovations better suited to the changing environment. A research chemist's idea may be taken up by a marketing executive but inter-preted differently from the original idea. Managers in one organisation may seek to copy the strategy of another, but will not do things in exactly the same way. Some of these imperfect copies will not be successful; but others may be. One famous example is Post-It, which originated in an 'imperfect' glue being applied to paper, but which resulted in a semi-adhesive for which the researcher saw market potential. There may also be surprises and unforeseen circumstances in the environment, the unexpected skills or views introduced by new appointees or unintended consequences arising from management initiatives.

Complexity theorists also point to the fact that all this differs markedly from the essentially linear view of the design lens. They refer to 'non-linearity' and show how, in such circumstances, apparently insignificant initial events can lead to major outcomes.

Of course, whilst organisations have the potential for huge variety, there may be intentional or non-intentional suppression of such variety. People's mental models and the culture of an organisation act as filters of ideas that do not 'fit'. Formal processes of control, planning and evaluation act to regularise what ideas will and will not go forward. The self-interest of powerful managers may block ideas counter to their own. So pressures for conformity may see off the potential novelty. Getting the appropriate balance between the need for sufficient control and a context that will stimulate new ideas becomes crucial.

Selection and retention

The implication of the design lens is that the selection of a strategy is a matter of deliberate choice to optimise some sort of outcome, for example competitive advantage leading to enhanced profits. Whilst deliberate acts of managers are not denied here, the ideas lens and evolutionary theory in particular suggest that selection is 'blind'[20] in the sense that outcomes cannot be known. Managers may exercise judgement and choice, but the strategies that develop are also the result of other processes of selection and retention. These include:

● *Functional benefit*. An idea may meet the needs of environmental and market forces. However many of these (from climate changes to competitor responses) can at best be partially known. There may, however, be other functions such as serving the *interests of individuals* within the organisation, for example in furthering career aspirations.

● *Alignment*. An idea is likely to be more successful if it *aligns with other successful ideas*, for example because it is what other organisations are doing or it fits the culture and experience of the organisation itself.

● *Attraction*. Some strategic ideas, by their very nature, are more or less attractive than others.[21] For example, ideas that are altruistic tend to spread and get adopted most.[22] In line with this, complexity theory emphasises the need for sufficient support or 'positive feedback', and some ideas are likely to attract this than others. For example, a new product idea in a science-based company received support because it addressed 'green' issues and its potential benefits interested colleagues in other divisions, friends and families of the managers developing it. The new product idea persisted despite strong evidence of its lack of commercial viability.

- *Retention*. As well as processes of selection, there are processes of retention. 'Retention occurs when selected variations are preserved, duplicated or otherwise reproduced'[23] leading to their future repetition. One key factor here is the extent to which ideas become routinised and thus retained. Routinisation varies from formal procedures (for example, job descriptions), accounting and control systems, management information systems, training, organisation structuring, to the formal or informal standardisation of work routines and the eventual embedding of such routines in the culture of the organisation.

The important point here is that managers cannot know the future and therefore cannot predict or control outcomes. None the less the internal and external context of the organisation will have a key impact on what new ideas are generated, selected and retained.

Implications for management[24]

A key message from the ideas lens is that managers need to be wary of assuming they can control the generation and adoption of new ideas. However, managers can foster new ideas and innovation by *creating the context* and conditions where they are more likely to emerge. First, they can do this by considering what the appropriate *boundaries* are for the organisation:

- The more the *boundaries between the organisation and its environment* are reduced, the more innovation is likely to occur. For some high-technology businesses it is difficult to see quite what their boundaries are. They are networks, intimately linked to their wider environment. As that environment changes, so do the ideas in the network. For example, in Formula One motor racing the different teams are intimately linked with the wider motor industry as well as other areas of advanced technology. As a result of this networking new ideas get imitated (but changed) very rapidly. In contrast an organisation where people are insulated from the environment, perhaps by relying on particular ways of doing things, as in a highly rule-based bureaucracy, will generate less variety of ideas and less innovation.

- *Interaction and cooperation* within organisations encourages variety and the spread of ideas.[25] However, there may be limits to this. Too many 'connections' may lead to an over-complex system.[26] There is also a danger that organisational structures become too established such that people's relationships become too predictable and ordered; rather, ideas tend to be generated more where there are 'weak ties' based on less established relationships.[27] All this may help explain why so much effort is spent by managers in changing organisational structures in the search for the most appropriate working environment (see Chapter 12).

Second, by promoting appropriate *behaviour* in an organisation. For example:

- *Questioning and challenge* is important. There are many organisations that have processes and procedures to foster new ideas. For example, large organisations often move executives across businesses or divisions with the specific intention of encouraging new ideas and challenging prevailing views.

Exhibit I.iii **Adaptive tensions**

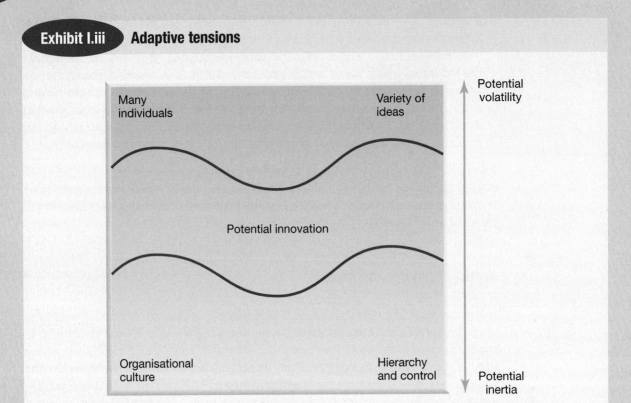

- *Experimentation* is important. This may take different forms. Some organisations have formal incentive programmes to encourage such experimentation. Others have established it as part of their culture. For example, Google gives staff 20 per cent of their time to pursue their own projects. Strategic experiments at an organisational level,[28] such as alliances and joint ventures, are also ways in which organisations may try out possible strategy developments and generate new ideas without overcommitment.

- Through *adaptive tension*. Since high levels of control and strict hierarchy are likely to encourage conformity and reduce variety, establishing appropriate levels of control therefore becomes crucial. Some complexity theorists argue that innovation and creativity emerge when there is sufficient order to make things happen but not when there is such rigidity of control as to prevent such innovation. This is the idea of 'adaptive tension' or 'edge of chaos'.[29] Innovation occurs most readily when the organisation never quite settles down into a steady state or equilibrium and volatility arising from variation is given sufficient rein (see Exhibit I.iii), though of course not to the extent that the organisation cannot function.

- *Order-generating rules*. There is no need for elaborate control to create sufficient order for an organisation to work effectively. Complexity theory suggests that ordered patterns of behaviour can come about through just a few 'order-generating rules'. Richard Pascale gives an example from the cement industry in Mexico. Cemex has done away with tight, planned scheduling for distributing its cement, because it has realised that the construction projects it is delivering to hardly ever proceed as scheduled:

> Cemex loads its fleets of cement trucks each morning and dispatches them with no preordained destination. The trick lies in how they make their rounds. Like ants scavenging a territory, they are guided to their destination by simple rules. . . . Cemex uses an algorithm based on *greed* (deliver as much cement as rapidly as possible to as many customers as possible) and *repulsion* (avoid duplication of effort by staying as far away from the other cement trucks as possible).[30]

- *Pattern recognition.* Ideas within the organisation are more likely to be developed by a reliance on 'pattern recognition' than formal analysis and planning. Strategy development is more about being able to discern promising ideas, monitor how they 'function' and 'fit' (see above) as they develop by being highly sensitive to their outcome and impact and mould the most promising into coherent strategies. Managers need to develop the competences to do this rather than being over-reliant on the formal tools and techniques of the design lens. In addition, since new ideas are unlikely to emerge fully formed – indeed they may be the result of 'imperfect copying', managers have to learn to tolerate such imperfection and allow for failures if they want innovation.

The ideas lens helps an understanding of where innovative strategies come from and how organisations cope with dynamic environments. It therefore de-emphasises the directive role of managers, their rationality and their power and therefore poses questions about whether or not top management really have control over strategic direction to the extent the design lens suggests. Exhibit I.iv summarises this.

Exhibit I.iv **Ideas lens**

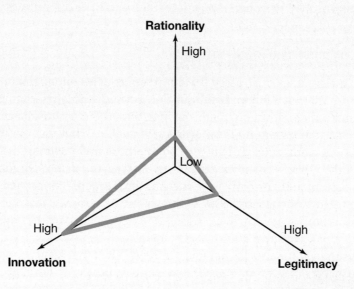

Strategy as discourse[31]

In many ways management is about discourse. Managers spend 75 per cent of their time communicating with others[32] in gathering information, persuading others of a course of action or following up decisions. In particular the management of strategy has a high discursive component. Managers and consultants talk about strategy and strategy is written as formal plans and mission statements, explained in annual reports and in newspaper releases. Efforts to get employees and other stakeholders to buy into strategy are also fundamentally discursive. Discourse is the language resource by which strategy is communicated, sustained and perpetuated. The ability to use discursive resources effectively can, then, be a distinct advantage and competence for an individual (see Chapter 15 on strategy practice which discusses strategy 'conversations'). Looking at strategy development in terms of **strategy as discourse** can also provide valuable insights. There are a number of linked concepts that help here.

Strategy as discourse sees strategy development in terms of language as a 'resource' for managers by which strategy is communicated, explained and sustained and through which managers gain influence, power and establish their legitimacy and identity as strategists.

Discourse and rationality

As discussion of the design lens pointed out, rationality is a central component of the orthodox language of strategy. From a management point of view, then, appearing rational is key to making strategy: 'To be rational is to make persuasive sense.'[33] Strategic management must seem more than just hunch and intuition; it is more like science and the models are like scientific models. As such, managers familiar with such logic can call on it and employ it to justify the 'rightness' of their arguments and views. Indeed David Knights[34] points out that even when managers find themselves unable to achieve the goals of strategy – unable, for example, to achieve competitive advantage – they do not deny the logic of the strategy, merely the ability of the organisation to achieve it. They may employ this language because they are themselves persuaded of the logic of a strategy, because they believe that by doing so their arguments will carry more weight with others, because it is the typical way in which strategy is communicated or because, by so doing, it positions themselves as an authority on the subject.

Discourse and influence

The language of strategy certainly seems to be convincing to others. David Barry and Michael Elmes[35] point out that strategy discourse has the characteristics to make it so. Strategy is not only written about in impressive documents – strategic plans or annual reports, for example – but also written about important phenomena such as markets, competitors and customers. It is often associated with 'heroic' chief executives or successful firms. Strategy discussions take place in important places such as boardrooms or strategy away-days. There is also evidence that the employment of strategy discourse works. Managers consciously employ the vocabulary and concepts of strategy to effect change,[36] to justify and legitimise strategies that are to be followed,[37] or to ensure conformity to the right ways to manage strategy.[38] In other words, managers draw on the concepts of strategy and the apparent 'rightness' of strategy concepts to convince others to comply.

Discourse, identity and legitimacy

How managers talk about strategy also positions them in relation to others, either by their own deliberate choice or as a result of how they are perceived. Discourse is therefore also related to the identity and legitimacy of managers. The common use of the language of rationality has been highlighted above. At other times or in other circumstances managers may also employ different discourse. For example, in trying to get a strategy implemented down the line drawing on the manager's previous experience as a 'hands-on worker' doing the job at an operational level might be useful. In other circumstances reference to prior experience in turning around an organisation may matter. In other contexts the language of the 'visionary leader' or the innovative entrepreneur may be employed.

As David Knights and Glenn Morgan[39] suggest, strategy discourse may be consciously or unconsciously employed by managers – particularly top managers – to provide for themselves certain benefits. It helps legitimise a manager as a knowledgeable strategist, employing the right concepts, using the right logic, doing the right thing and being at the forefront of management thinking. It also provides the sense of centrality, of 'making a difference' to the most centrally important aspects of organisational survival. Since over time different strategy discourses have been more or less the fashion, some elements of discourse are likely to be more effective than others at different times. In the 1960s and 1970s it was the language of corporate or strategic planning; in the 1980s there came to be more of an emphasis on organisational culture; and latterly strategy has become discussed and communicated more in terms of competences.

Discourse as power

In turn the discourse of strategy is linked to power and control. By understanding the concepts of strategy, or being seen to do so, it is top managers or strategy specialists who are positioned as having the knowledge about how to deal with the really difficult problems the organisation faces. The possession of such knowledge gives them power over others who do not have it. It 'allows managers to imagine themselves as controllers of . . . economic life'.[40]

Thus the discourse of strategy can also operate as social control. Groups may adopt particular ways of thinking, behaving and speaking about strategy. For example, some organisations, especially consultants, have developed their own discourse on strategy. Non-adherence to such approaches can bring about sanctions, as many strategy consultants have found! Or there may develop ways of approaching strategic issues that are embedded in particular discourse, for example a push to cut costs. In one sense the need to cut costs is indisputable. However, it can foster a mindset in which cutting becomes the norm and it is difficult to propose expansion or experimentation which would not lead to reduced costs. Indeed, such discourse may become part of a culture: taken for granted, difficult to recognise, difficult to question or change and therefore a powerful influence on behaviour. In this sense discourse is associated with power when it attracts followers and is self-reproducing and self-reinforcing.

Discourse and a critical perspective

A more extreme extension of these perspectives on strategy discourse is that the concepts and models of strategy are less to do with substance and more to do with image, identity and power: that the concepts of strategy are employed, developed and sustained as a basis for sustaining top management control and authority in league with a consultancy profession and academic profession that feeds it; that strategy is a convenient management myth.

Implications for managers

The fundamental lesson for managers is that the language of strategy they employ matters. The discourse lens provides a way of considering how this is so and, in turn, concepts and cues by which managers can manage more effectively:

- *Discourse and context*. It should be clear from the preceding discussion that different strategy discourses are likely to be more or less effective in different contexts and circumstances. How a strategy is explained and justified to a potential investor may call for a major emphasis on logic and reason under-pinning a financial case. A similarly rational approach may be needed to per-suade fellow managers, but perhaps with an additional component related to the benefits in terms of their own interests, future influence and standing. A similar explanation to the workforce of an organisation will have to address the implications for job security, but perhaps also needs to be expressed in ways that reinforce confidence in management. A press release on strategy will likely need to give thought to the main headlines or 'sound bites'. Careful thought needs to go into how strategy is explained and justified to whom.

- *Discourse and the management of strategic change*. Strategy discourse plays an especially important role in the diffusion of innovations, new management practices and the management of change.[41] In particular, different forms of language may be more or less useful in achieving the adoption and retention of new practices.[42] Language that appeals to emotion and self-interest may help adoption, but a reliance on this may lead to the early rejection of new practices. A more rational approach may mean that it takes longer to achieve adoption but will be less likely to result in early rejection. Language that appeals to or relates to accepted ways of doing things may, however, help ensure retention.

- *Common discourse*. It may be beneficial to seek to develop a common language of strategy in an organisation. This is a common reason for management development programmes in relation to strategy. The argued benefit is that managers can then communicate on the basis of a common set of generally understood concepts, terms and tools of strategy which makes strategy debate more effective. It is also a role management educators provide in the diffusion of strategy concepts and language of course.

- *A critical perspective for managers*. A less extreme and perhaps more con-structive view of a critical perspective on strategy is that the discourse lens should prompt managers and students alike to question just how substantial concepts and models to do with strategy really are. Are they really based on sound evidence and theory; do they really make a difference; or are they just

Exhibit I.v   **Discourse lens**

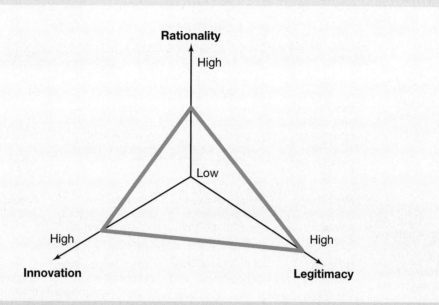

useful devices for managers to gain power and influence? In this sense, seeing strategy as discourse can prompt the healthy questioning of concepts, ideas and assumptions that might otherwise be taken for granted.

In summary, as shown in Exhibit I.v, the discourse lens emphasises that managers may well see the strategy arena as where power, identity, recognition (and therefore legitimacy) are sought. It raises the question of the extent to which managers rely on the appearance, if not the reality, of rational argument. The extent to which such discourse promotes change will depend on the motivations of the managers and the nature of the language used. However there is certainly evidence that language can play an important role in the management of change.

Conclusion

The core assumptions and underpinning theories of the four lenses of design, experience, ideas and discourse are summarised in Exhibit I.vi. They are not offered here as an exhaustive list. They are an attempt to encapsulate different approaches and insights into the complex concept of strategy. The suggestion is that you may usefully extend your exploration of different lenses yourself. It should be apparent in what you have read so far that the lenses presented here in fact each include several perspectives themselves. For example, the experience lens builds on explanations from cognition, sociology and cultural anthropology and the ideas lens builds on both evolutionary theory and complexity theory. So, within these lenses there are finer-grained insights that can be gained and the references and key readings should help with that. In addition there are whole books written that provide multiple perspectives on strategy, from the four that Richard Whittington[43] offers to the ten of Henry Mintzberg and his co-authors.[44]

Exhibit I.vi — A summary of the strategy lenses

Strategy as:

	Design	Experience	Ideas	Discourse
Overview/ summary	Deliberate positioning through rational processes to optimise economic performance	Incremental development as the outcome of individual and collective experience and the taken for granted	Emergence of order and innovation through variety, in and around the organisation	The language and concepts of strategy used as a basis for establishing identity and gaining influence, power and legitimacy
Assumptions about organisations	Mechanistic, hierarchical, rational systems	Cultures based on experience, legitimacy and past success	Complex and potentially diverse organic systems	Arenas of power and influence
Role of top management	Strategic decision makers	Enactors of their experience	'Coaches', creators of context and pattern recognisers	Exercising or gaining power and influence over others
Underpinning theories	Economics; decision sciences	Institutional theory; theories of culture; psychology	Complexity and evolutionary theories	Discourse theory; critical management theory

However, there are two overarching messages that come through consistently. The first is the one with which this commentary began: in considering a topic like strategy, it helps to take more than one perspective. The second is that, in so doing, there is a need to question the conventional wisdom of strategy encapsulated in the design lens. In particular the central tenet of managers at the top planning and directing strategy through machine-like organisations is too limited a view of what strategic management is about.

In the rest of the book the four lenses are employed in commentaries at the end of Parts I, II and III in particular to examine critically the coverage of each part and consider the management implications.

References

1. A useful review of the principles of rational decision making can be found in J.G. March, *A Primer on Decision Making: How Decisions Happen*, Simon & Schuster, 1994, Chapter 1, Limited Liability, pp. 1–35.
2. See M.E. Porter, *Competitive Strategy*, Free Press/Collier Macmillan, 1980, and *Competitive Advantage*, Free Press/Collier Macmillan, 1985.
3. See H.A. Simon, *The New Science of Management Decision*, Prentice Hall, 1960; and C.E. Lindblom, 'The science of muddling through', *Public Administration Review*, vol. 19 (1959), pp. 79–88.
4. For a review of these points see the introduction to J. Dutton, E. Walton and E. Abrahamson, 'Important dimensions of strategic issues: separating the wheat from the chaff', *Journal of Management Studies*, vol. 26, no. 4 (1989), pp. 380–395.

5. See A. Tversky and D. Kahnemann, 'Judgements under uncertainty: heuristics and biases', *Science*, vol. 185 (1975), pp. 1124–1131.

6. See J.E. Dutton and S.E. Jackson, 'Categorizing strategic issues: links to organizational action', *Academy of Management Review*, vol. 12 (1987), pp. 76–90. Also M.H. Anderson and M.L. Nicols, 'Information gathering and changes in threat and opportunity perceptions', *Journal of Management Studies*, vol. 44, no. 3 (2007), pp. 367–387.

7. See D. Lovallo and D. Kahneman, 'Delusions of success', *Harvard Business Review*, vol. 81, no. 7 (2003), pp. 56–64.

8. For a thorough explanation of the role of psychological processes in strategy see G.P. Hodgkinson and P.R. Sparrow, *The Competent Organization*, Open University Press, 2002.

9. See C. Geertz, *The Interpretation of Culture*, Basic Books, 1973, p. 12.

10. See M. Alvesson, *Understanding Organizational Culture*, Sage, 2002, p. 3.

11. For a fuller discussion of complexity theory in relation to strategy see R.D. Stacey, *Strategic Management and Organisational Dynamics: The Challenge of Complexity*, 3rd edition, Pearson Education, 2000.

12. For a systematic discussion of the implications of evolutionary theory on management see H. Aldrich, *Organizations Evolving*, Sage, 1999.

13. See S.L. Brown and K.M. Eisenhardt, *Competing on the Edge*, Harvard Business School Press, 1998.

14. An excellent discussion of the development of ideas (or what the authors refer to as 'memes') and the relationship of this to the role and nature of organisations can be found in J. Weeks and C. Galunic, 'A theory of the cultural evolution of the firm: the intra-organizational ecology of memes', *Organization Studies*, vol. 24, no. 8 (2003), pp. 1309–1352.

15. M.S. Feldman and B.T. Pentland, 'Reconceptualizing organizational routines as a source of flexibility and change', *Administrative Science Quarterly*, vol. 48, (2003), 94–118, show how 'performative' variations from standardised (they call them ostensive) routines may create variation which creates organisational change.

16. See Z.J. Acs and D.B. Audretsch, 'Innovation in large and small firms – an empirical analysis', *American Economic Review*, vol. 78, September (1988), pp. 678–690.

17. See G. Johnson and A.S. Huff, 'Everyday innovation/everyday strategy', in G. Hamel, G.K. Prahalad, H. Thomas and D. O'Neal (eds), *Strategic Flexibility – Managing in a Turbulent Environment*, Wiley, 1998, pp. 13–27. Patrick Regner also shows how new strategic directions can grow from the periphery of organisations in the face of opposition from the centre; see 'Strategy creation in the periphery: inductive versus deductive strategy making', *Journal of Management Studies*, vol. 40, no. 1 (2003), pp. 57–82.

18. Bill McKelvey, a complexity theorist, argues that the variety within this distributed intelligence is increased because individual managers seek to become better informed about their environment: see B. McKelvey, 'Simple rules for improving corporate IQ: basic lessons from complexity science', in P. Andriani and G. Passiante (eds), *Complexity, Theory and the Management of Networks*, Imperial College Press, 2004.

19. See E. von Hippel, *The Sources of Innovation*, Oxford University Press, 1988.

20. The concept of blind selection is explained more fully in the chapter by D. Barron on evolutionary theory in the *Oxford Handbook of Strategy*, ed. D. Faulkner and A. Campbell, Oxford University Press, 2003.

21. See Weeks and Galunic, reference 14.

22. The role of altruism and other bases of attraction is discussed by Susan Blackmore in *The Meme machine*, Oxford University Press, 1999.

23. See Aldrich, reference 12, p. 30.

24. For other imlications see some of the references above. In particular Brown and Eisenhardt, reference 13, McKelvey, reference 18 and Stacey, reference 11.

25. See M.S. Granovetter, 'The strength of weak ties', *American Journal of Sociology*, vol. 78, no. 6 (1973), pp. 1360–1380.

26. See McKelvey, reference 18.

27. M.S. Granovetter, (1973) 'The strength of weak ties', *American journal of Sociology*, vol. 78, no. 6, pp. 1360–1380.

28. Brown and Eisenhardt, reference 13, refer to 'low cost probes' as ways in which organisations carry out such experimentation.

29. This is the term used by Brown and Eisenhardt, reference 13, amongst others.

30. See R.T. Pascale, M. Millermann and L. Gioja, *Surfing the Edge of Chaos: The Laws of Nature and the New Laws of Business*, Texere, 2000, pp. 8–9.

31. We are grateful for the help of Nic Beech in the drafting of this section.

32. H. Mintzberg, *The Nature of Managerial Work*, Harper & Row, 1973.

33. This quote is from S.E. Green Jr, 'A Rhetorical theory of diffusion', *Academy of Management Review*, vol. 29, no. 4 (2004), pp. 653–669.

34. See D. Knights, 'Changing spaces: the disruptive impact of a new epistemological location for the study of management', *Academy of Management Review*, vol. 17, no. 3 (1992), pp. 514–536.

35. D. Barry and M. Elmes, 'Strategy retold: toward a narrative view of strategic discourse', *Academy of Management Review*, vol. 22, no. 2 (1997).

36. For example see C. Hardy, I. Palmer and N. Philips, 'Discourse as a strategic resource', *Human Relations*, vol. 53, no. 9 (2000); and L. Heracleous and M. Barrett, 'Organizational change as discourse: communicative actions and deep structures in the context of information technology implementation', *Academy of Management Journal*, vol. 44, no. 4 (2001), pp. 755–778.

37. See R. Suddaby and R. Greenwood, 'Rhetorical strategies of legitimacy', *Administrative Science Quarterly*, vol. 50 (2005), pp. 35–67. Also J. Sillence and F. Mueller, 'Switching strategic perspective: the reframing of accounts of responsibility', *Organization Studies*, vol. 28, no. 2 (2007), pp. 175–176.

38. See L. Oakes, B. Townley and D.J. Cooper, 'Business planning as pedagogy: language and institutions in a changing institutional field', *Administrative Science Quarterly*, vol. 43, no. 2 (1998), pp. 257–292.

39. D. Knights and G. Morgan 'Corporate strategy, organizations and subjectivity', *Organization Studies*, vol. 12, no. 2 (1991), pp. 251–273.

40. A. Spicer, 'Book review of *Recreating Strategy*', *Organization Studies*, vol. 25, no. 7 (2004), p. 1256.

41. See reference 36.

42. See references 37 and 38.

43. R. Whittington, *What is Strategy – and Does it Matter?*, 2nd edition, Thomson, 2000.

44. H. Mintzberg, B. Ahlstrand and J. Lampel, *Strategy Safari*, Prentice Hall, 1998.

Part I

THE STRATEGIC POSITION

This part explains:

→ How to analyse an organisation's position in the external environment.

→ How to analyse the determinants of strategic capability – resources, competences and the linkages between them.

→ How to understand an organisation's purposes, taking into account corporate governance, stakeholder expectations and business ethics.

→ How to address the role of history and culture in determining an organisation's position.

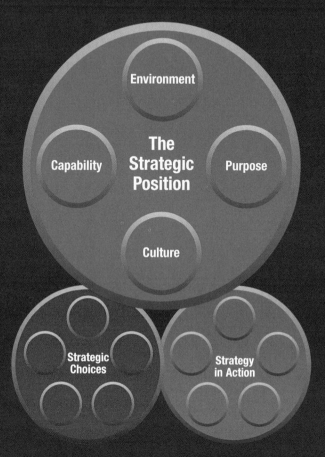

Introduction to Part I

This part of the book is concerned with understanding the strategic position of the organisation. By this is meant the factors that have to be taken into account at the outset of strategy development. There are two basic views here: one stresses external factors in the organisation's strategic position; the other emphasises internal factors. On the external side, many argue that environmental factors are what matters most to success: strategy development should be primarily about seeking attractive opportunities in the marketplace. Those favouring a more internal approach, on the other hand, argue that an organisation's specific strategic capabilities, resources or cultures should drive strategy. It is from these internal characteristics that distinctive strategies and superior performance can be built. In this view, organisations should focus on those environmental opportunities for which they start with a distinctive advantage in terms of internal characteristics.

It is important not to take too static or unified a view of either the environment or the organisation's inherited internal position. Environments change, and internal capabilities and resources need to develop, or 'stretch', in order to match such change.* Also, organisations are rarely simple, homogeneous units. There are different stakeholders, different cultures and different kinds of purpose within most organisations. These various internal drivers and constraints need to be understood as part of the internal position of an organisation.

Accordingly, Part I has four chapters, starting with analysis of the external position, and then developing an internal perspective incorporating dynamics and differences within the organisation:

- The overall theme of Chapter 2 is how managers can analyse the uncertain and increasingly complex world around them. This is addressed by considering various layers of influence from macro-environmental issues to specific forces affecting the competitive position. However, simply identifying particular influences is not sufficient. The challenge for a strategist is to understand the interaction of these different forces and how these impact on the organisation.

- Chapter 3 is concerned with understanding an organisation's strategic capability and how this underpins the competitive advantage of the organisation or sustains excellence in providing value-for-money products or services. This is explained by considering four main issues: what is meant by 'strategic

---

* The notion of strategy as 'stretch', rather than a static 'fit' to the environment, was introduced by G. Hamel and C.K. Prahalad, *Competing for the Future*, Harvard Business School Press, 1994. See also D.J. Teece, G. Pisano and A. Shuen, 'Dynamic capabilities and strategic management', *Strategic Management Journal*, vol. 18, no. 3 (1997), pp. 509–534.

capability'; how this might provide competitive advantage for organisations; how managers might analyse capabilities; and how they might manage the development of such capabilities.

- Chapter 4 is about how expectations 'shape' organisational purposes and strategies. This is considered within four main themes. Corporate governance is concerned with understanding whom the organisation is there to serve. Stakeholder influence raises the important issue of power relationships in organisations. A discussion of corporate social responsibility raises the question of what organisations should and should not be doing strategically, with implications for individuals' ethics. All of this is brought together in considering how strategists might express and explain the strategic purpose of their organisations.

- Chapter 5 takes an historical and cultural perspective on strategy. The business environment, the capabilities of an organisation and the expectations of stakeholders have historical roots. The theme of the chapter is that understanding history and culture helps managers develop the future strategy of their organisations. The chapter begins by explaining the phenomenon of strategic drift that highlights the importance of history and culture in relation to strategy development and the challenges of managing strategic change. The chapter then examines the influence of the history of an organisation on its current and future strategy and goes on to consider how that history can be analysed. It then explains how cultural influences at the national, institutional and organisational levels influence current and future strategy. It then explains the cultural web as a means of analysing culture and its influence on strategy.

Although this part of the book addresses the various topics in separate chapters, it should be stressed that there are strong links between these different influences on strategy. In practice, the external and internal views need to be reconciled. Environmental pressures for change will be constrained by the capabilities available to make changes, or by organisational cultures which may lead to resistance to change. Internal capabilities will be valuable only if the environment offers profitable opportunities to use them. Also, placing the analysis of position in a separate part, distinct from Parts II and III considering strategic choices and putting strategy into action, does not mean that these are distinct issues in practice. As the overlapping circles of Exhibit 1.3 in Chapter 1 underline, strategy is not a sequential process and strategic choices and strategic action feed back directly into both the understanding and the reality of strategic position.

Nevertheless, by providing for an analysis of the starting position, Part I is the foundation for approaching the kinds of strategic choices that an organisation typically has to make. For example, the nature of the environment and capabilities it has together help shape how an organisation should compete and the range of products and services it should offer. Similarly they inform the methods managers can choose between in order to pursue strategies, whether by building on internal resources, or by acquiring other organisations, or by partnering with others. These choices are pursued further in Part II.

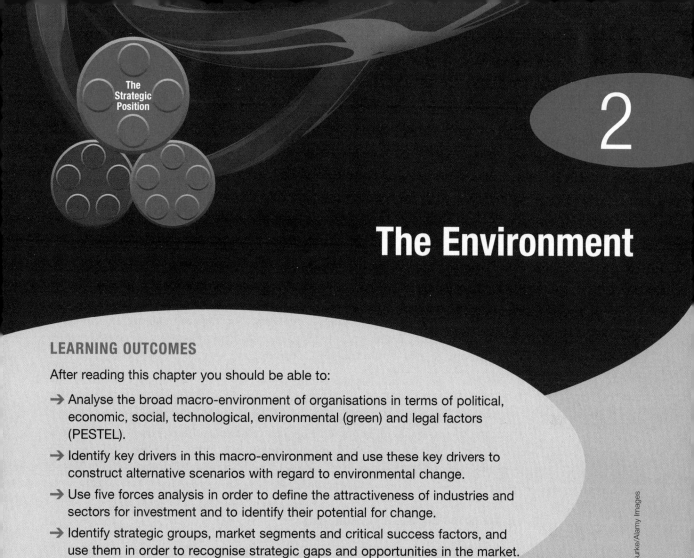

2

The Environment

LEARNING OUTCOMES

After reading this chapter you should be able to:

→ Analyse the broad macro-environment of organisations in terms of political, economic, social, technological, environmental (green) and legal factors (PESTEL).

→ Identify key drivers in this macro-environment and use these key drivers to construct alternative scenarios with regard to environmental change.

→ Use five forces analysis in order to define the attractiveness of industries and sectors for investment and to identify their potential for change.

→ Identify strategic groups, market segments and critical success factors, and use them in order to recognise strategic gaps and opportunities in the market.

Photo: Dominic Burke/Alamy Images

2.1　INTRODUCTION

The environment is what gives organisations their means of survival. In the private sector, satisfied customers are what keep an organisation in business; in the public sector, it is government, clients, patients or students that typically play the same role. However, the environment is also the source of threats: for example, hostile shifts in market demand, new regulatory requirements, revolutionary technologies or the entry of new competitors. Environmental change can be fatal for organisations. To take one example, after 200 years of prosperity, print publisher Encyclopedia Britannica was nearly swept out of existence by the rise of electronic information sources, such as Microsoft's Encarta and the online Wikipedia. It is vital that managers analyse their environments carefully in order to anticipate and – if possible – influence environmental change.

This chapter therefore provides frameworks for analysing changing and complex environments. These frameworks are organised in a series of 'layers' briefly introduced here and summarised in Exhibit 2.1:

● *The macro-environment* is the highest-level layer. This consists of broad environmental factors that impact to a greater or lesser extent on almost all organisations. Here, the PESTEL framework can be used to identify how future trends in the *political, economic, social, technological, environmental ('green') and legal* environments might impinge on organisations. This PESTEL analysis provides the broad 'data' from which to identify *key drivers of change*. These

Exhibit 2.1　Layers of the business environment

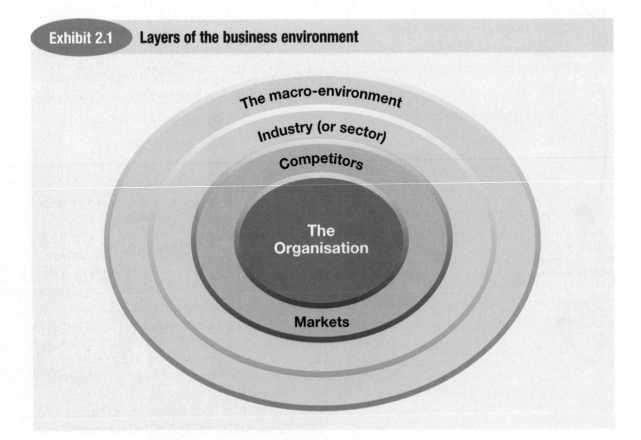

key drivers can be used to construct *scenarios* of possible futures. Scenarios consider how strategies might need to change depending on the different ways in which the business environment *might* change.

● *Industry*, or *sector*, forms the next layer with this broad general environment. This is made up of organisations producing the same products or services. Here the *five forces* framework is particularly useful in understanding the attractiveness of particular industries or sectors and potential threats from outside the present set of competitors. This chapter's key debate (Illustration 2.6) addresses the importance of industry factors, rather than business-specific factors, in determining success.

● *Competitors and markets* are the most immediate layer surrounding organisations. Within most industries or sectors there will be many different organisations with different characteristics and competing on different bases, some closer to a particular organisation, some more remote. The concept of *strategic groups* can help identify close and more remote competitors. Similarly, in the marketplace, customers' expectations are not all the same. They have a range of different requirements the importance of which can be understood through the concepts of *market segments* and *critical success factors*.

This chapter works through these three layers in turn, starting with the macro-environment.

2.2 THE MACRO-ENVIRONMENT

The three concepts in this section – PESTEL, key drivers and scenarios – are interrelated tools for analysing the broad macro-environment of an organisation. PESTEL provides a wide overview; key drivers help focus on what is most important; and scenarios build on key drivers to explore different ways in which the macro-environment might change.

2.2.1 The PESTEL framework

The PESTEL framework categorises environmental influences into six main types: political, economic, social, technological, environmental and legal

KEY CONCEPT
www.pearsoned.co.uk/ecs
PESTEL

The **PESTEL framework** (Illustration 2.1) provides a comprehensive list of influences on the possible success or failure of particular strategies. PESTEL stands for Political, Economic, Social, Technological, Environmental and Legal.[1] Politics highlights the role of governments; Economics refers to macro-economic factors such as exchange rates, business cycles and differential economic growth rates around the world; Social influences include changing cultures and demographics, for example ageing populations in many Western societies; Technological influences refer to innovations such as the Internet, nanotechnology or the rise of new composite materials; Environmental stands specifically for 'green' issues, such as pollution and waste; and finally Legal embraces legislative constraints or changes, such as health and safety legislation or restrictions on company mergers and acquisitions.

For managers, it is important to analyse how these factors are changing now and how they are likely to change in the future, drawing out implications for the

Illustration 2.1

PESTEL analysis of the airline industry

Environmental influences on organisations can be summarised within six categories.
For the airline industry, an initial list of influences under the six PESTEL analysis
categories might include the following:

Political

- Government support for national carriers
- Security controls
- Restrictions on migration

Economic

- National growth rates
- Fuel prices

Social

- Rise in travel by elderly
- Student international study exchanges

Technological

- Fuel-efficient engines and airframes
- Security check technologies
- Teleconferencing for business

Environmental

- Noise pollution controls
- Energy consumption controls
- Land for growing airports

Legal

- Restrictions on mergers
- Preferential airport rights for some carriers

Questions

1 What additional environmental influences would you add to this initial list for the airline industry?

2 From your more comprehensive list, which of these influences would you highlight as likely to be the 'key drivers for change' for airlines in the coming five years?

organisation. Many of these factors are linked together. For example, technology developments may simultaneously change economic factors (for example, creating new jobs), social factors (facilitating more leisure) and environmental factors (reducing pollution). As can be imagined, analysing these factors and their interrelationships can produce long and complex lists.

Rather than getting overwhelmed by a multitude of details, therefore, it is necessary to step back eventually to identify the **key drivers for change**. Key drivers for change are the high-impact factors likely to affect significantly the success or failure of strategy. Typical key drivers will vary by industry or sector. For example, a clothing retailer may be primarily concerned with social changes driving customer tastes and behaviour, for example forces encouraging out-of-town shopping. A computer manufacturer is likely to be concerned with technological

The **key drivers for change** are environmental factors that are likely to have a high impact on the success or failure of strategy change, for example increases in microprocessor speeds. Public sector managers are likely to be especially concerned with social change (for example, an ageing population), political change (changing government funding and policies) and legislative change (introducing new requirements). Identifying key drivers for change helps managers to focus on the PESTEL factors that are most important and which must be addressed as the highest priority. Many other changes will depend on these key drivers anyway (for example, an ageing population will drive changes in public policy and funding). Without a clear sense of the key drivers for change, managers will not be able to take the decisions that allow for effective action.

2.2.2 Building scenarios

When the business environment has high levels of uncertainty arising from either complexity or rapid change (or both), it is impossible to develop a single view of how environment influences might affect an organisation's strategies and indeed it would be dangerous to do so. Scenario analyses are carried out to allow for different possibilities and help prevent managers from closing their minds to alternatives. Thus **scenarios** offer plausible alternative views of how the business environment of an organisation might develop in the future.[2] They typically build on PESTEL analyses and the key drivers for change, but do not offer a single forecast of how the environment will change.

Scenarios typically start from the key drivers with the greatest uncertainty. Such key drivers could create radically different views of the future according to how they turn out. For example, in the oil business, key drivers might be technological change, oil reserves, economic growth and international political stability. It might be assumed that technological change and oil reserves are relatively certain, while economic growth and political stability are not. Scenarios could be constructed around different views about future political stability and economic growth. These key drivers are of course interrelated: high political instability and low economic growth are likely to go together. Constructing plausible alternative views of how the business environment might develop in the future therefore depends on knitting together interrelated drivers into internally consistent scenarios. In this analysis so far, therefore, two internally consistent and plausible scenarios could be proposed: one based on low growth and high instability, the other based on high growth and low instability.

Note that scenario planning does not attempt to predict the unpredictable: the point is to consider plausible alternative futures. Sharing and debating alternative scenarios improves organisational learning by making managers more perceptive about the forces in the business environment and what is really important. Managers should also evaluate and develop strategies (or contingency plans) for each scenario. They should then monitor the environment to see how it is actually unfolding and adjust strategies accordingly.

Because debating and learning are so valuable in the scenario building process, and scenarios deal with such high uncertainty, some scenario experts advise managers to avoid producing just three scenarios. Three scenarios tend to fall into a range of 'optimistic', 'middling' and 'pessimistic'. Managers naturally focus on the middling scenario and neglect the other two, reducing the amount

Scenarios are detailed and plausible views of how the business environment of an organisation might develop in the future based on key drivers for change about which there is a high level of uncertainty

Illustration 2.2

Scenarios for the biosciences in 2020

Nobody knows the future, but they can prepare for possible alternatives.

In 2006, researchers at the Wharton Business School collaborated with leading companies such as Hewlett Packard, Johnson & Johnson and Procter & Gamble to produce four scenarios for the future of biosciences in 2020. Biosciences include exciting high-tech industries such as genomics, stem cell therapy, cloning and regenerative medicine. The aim was to provide a broad framework for governments, business, researchers and doctors to work within as they considered the future for their particular specialities. The Wharton team were mindful that previous high-tech domains had failed to deliver on their initial promise: nuclear power for example fell radically out of favour from the late 1970s. The future for the biosciences is far from certain.

The Wharton team identified two fundamental but uncertain drivers for change: technological advance and public acceptance. On the first, the uncertainty was about the success of the technologies: after all, nuclear power had not deliverd the cheap energy originally hoped for. With regard to the second, public opinion regarding the biosciences is in the balance, with many calling for an end to stem cell research and cloning. The possibilities of technological success or failure, and public acceptance or rejection, define a matrix with four basic scenarios.

Where's the beef proposes a world in which large corporate and government research initiatives has failed to deliver hoped-for cures for diseases such as Alzheimer's and AIDS, but the public still has high expectations. Companies would be under fire and at risk of political intervention. The *Much ado about nothing* scenario is a world in which the public becomes sceptical after many technological disappointments. The result is that government funding for company and university research dries up. *The Biosciences held hostage* scenario is a very different one, in which technological successes actually frighten the public into a reaction against technology, ethical and safety concerns driving tight restrictions on research, testing and marketing. Finally, the *New age of medicine* offers the prospect of both success and acceptance, a world in which private corporations and university research labs would prosper together as they delivered breakthrough innovations to a grateful public.

The point of the four scenarios is not to say that one is more likely than the others. The Wharton team show that all four scenarios are perfectly possible. Whereas bioscience companies might easily become too focused on the positive *New age* scenario, they need to bear in mind the other possibilities. The implication is that they should be cautious in their expectations of technological breakthroughs and manage public opinion skillfully, otherwise biosciences could become the nuclear industry of the twenty-first century.

Source: http://mackcenter.wharton.upenn.edu/biosciences.

	Technology fails	Technology succeeds
Public acceptance	**Where's the beef?**	**New age of medicine**
Public rejection	**Much ado about nothing**	**Biosciences held hostage**

Source: Adapted from P.J.H. Schoemaker and M.S. Tomczyk (eds) *The Future of Biosciences*, The Mack Center, 2006.

Question

Over which of the two drivers – technological advance and public acceptance – do companies have the most influence? How should they exercise this influence?

of organisational learning and contingency planning. It is therefore typically better to have two or four scenarios, avoiding an easy mid-point. It does not matter if the scenarios do not come to pass: the value lies in the process of exploration and contingency planning that the scenarios set off.

Illustration 2.2 shows an example of scenario planning for the biosciences to 2020. Rather than incorporating a multitude of factors, the authors focus on two key drivers which (i) have high potential impact and (ii) are uncertain: technological advance and public acceptance. Both of these drivers may have different futures, which can be combined to create four internally consistent scenarios of the future. These four scenarios are each given memorable titles, to facilitate communication and debate. The authors do not predict that one will prevail over the others, nor do they allocate relative probabilities. Prediction would close down debate and learning, while probabilities would imply a spurious kind of accuracy.

Scenarios are especially useful where there are a limited number of key drivers influencing the success of strategy; where there is a high level of uncertainty about such influences; where outcomes could be radically different; and where organisations have to make substantial commitments into the future that may be highly inflexible and hard to reverse in adverse circumstances. The oil industry, where companies must invest in exploring oilfields which may have lives of 20 years or more, has traditionally been a leader in the use of scenarios because it faces a combination of all four of these conditions.[3]

2.3 INDUSTRIES AND SECTORS

The previous section looked at how forces in the macro-environment might influence the success or failure of an organisation's strategies. But the impact of these general factors tends to surface in the more immediate environment through changes in the competitive forces surrounding organisations. An important aspect of this for most organisations will be competition within their industry or sector. Economic theory defines an **industry** as 'a group of firms producing the same principal product'[4] or, more broadly, 'a group of firms producing products that are close substitutes for each other'.[5] This concept of an industry can be extended into the public services through the idea of a *sector*. Social services, health care or education also have many producers of the same kinds of services, which are effectively competing for resources. From a strategic management perspective it is useful for managers in any organisation to understand the competitive forces in their industry or sector since these will determine the attractiveness of that industry and the likely success or failure of particular organisations within it.

This section looks first at Michael Porter's *five forces framework* for industry analysis and then introduces techniques for analysing the *dynamics* of industries or sectors.

*An **industry** is a group of firms producing the same principal product or service*

*The **five forces framework** helps identify the attractiveness of an industry or sector in terms of competitive forces*

2.3.1 Competitive forces – the five forces framework

Porter's **five forces framework**[6] was originally developed as a way of assessing the attractiveness (profit potential) of different industries. The five forces constitute

Exhibit 2.2 **The five forces framework**

Potential entrants

Threat of entry

Suppliers

Bargaining power

Competitive rivalry

Buyers

Bargaining power

Threat of substitutes

Substitutes

Source: Adapted with the permission of The Free Press, a Division of Simon & Schuster Adult Publishing Group, from *Competitive Strategy: Techniques for Analyzing Industries and Competitors* by Michael E. Porter. Copyright © 1980, 1998 by The Free Press. All rights reserved.

KEY CONCEPT

www.pearsoned.co.uk/ecs

Porter's five forces

an industry's 'structure' (see Exhibit 2.2). Although initially developed with businesses in mind, industry structure analysis with the five forces framework is of value to most organisations. It can provide a useful starting point for strategic analysis even where profit criteria may not apply: in most parts of the public sector, each of the five forces has its equivalents. As well as assessing the attractiveness of an industry or sector, the five forces can help set an agenda for action on the various 'pinch-points' that they identify.

The five forces are: the *threat of entry* into an industry; the *threat of substitutes* to the industry's products or services; the *power of buyers* of the industry's products or services; the *power of suppliers* into the industry; and *the extent of rivalry* between competitors in the industry. Porter's essential message is that where these five forces are high, then industries are not attractive to compete in. There will be too much competition, and too much pressure, to allow reasonable profits. The rest of this section will introduce each of the five forces in more detail.

The threat of entry

Barriers to entry are factors that need to be overcome by new entrants if they are to compete successfully

How easy it is to enter the industry obviously influences the degree of competition. Threat of entry depends on the extent and height of **barriers to entry**. Barriers are the factors that need to be overcome by new entrants if they are to compete successfully. High barriers to entry are good for incumbents (existing competitors), because they protect them from new competitors coming in. Typical barriers are as follows:

- *Scale and experience*. In some industries, *economies of scale* are extremely important: for example, in the production of automobiles or the advertising of fast-moving consumer goods. Once incumbents have reached large-scale production, it will be very expensive for new entrants to match them and until they reach a similar volume they will have higher unit costs. This scale effect is accentuated where there are high *investment requirements* for entry, for example research costs in pharmaceuticals or capital equipment costs in automobiles. Barriers to entry also come from *experience curve* effects that give incumbents a cost advantage because they have learnt how to do things more efficiently than an inexperienced new entrant could possibly do (see Chapter 3). Until the new entrant has built up equivalent experience over time, it will tend to produce at higher cost. Of course, changing 'business models' can alter scale effects or make certain kinds of experience redundant. For example, Internet banking requires only 10,000 customers to be viable (particularly if they are from a profitable niche) and makes experience in running branches much less important.

- *Access to supply or distribution channels*. In many industries manufacturers have had control over supply and/or distribution channels. Sometimes this has been through direct ownership (vertical integration), sometimes just through customer or supplier loyalty. In some industries this barrier has been overcome by new entrants who have bypassed retail distributors and sold directly to consumers through e-commerce (for example, Dell Computers and Amazon).

- *Expected retaliation*. If an organisation considering entering an industry believes that the retaliation of an existing firm will be so great as to prevent entry, or mean that entry would be too costly, this is also a barrier. Retaliation could take the form of a price war or a marketing blitz. Just the knowledge that incumbents are prepared to retaliate is often sufficiently discouraging to act as a barrier. This dynamic interaction between incumbents and potential new entrants will be discussed more fully in section 2.3.2 In global markets this retaliation can take place at many different 'points' or locations (see Chapter 8).

- *Legislation or government action*. Legal restraints on new entry vary from patent protection (for example, pharmaceuticals), to regulation of markets (for example, pension selling), through to direct government action (for example, tariffs). Of course, organisations are vulnerable to new entrants if governments remove such protection, as has happened with deregulation of the airline industry.

- *Differentiation*. Differentiation means providing a product or service with higher perceived value than the competition; its importance will be discussed more fully in Chapter 6. Cars are differentiated, for example, by quality and branding. Steel, by contrast, is by and large a commodity, undifferentiated and therefore sold by the tonne. Steel buyers will simply buy the cheapest. Differentiation reduces the threat of entry because it increases customer loyalty.

The threat of substitutes

Substitutes can reduce demand for a particular 'class' of products as customers switch to the alternatives

Substitutes are products or services that offer a similar benefit to an industry's products or services, but by a different process. For example, aluminium is a substitute for steel in automobiles; trains are a substitute for cars; films and theatre are substitutes for each other. Managers often focus on their competitors in their own industry, and neglect the threat posed by substitutes. Substitutes can reduce demand for a particular 'class' of products as customers switch to alternatives – even to the extent that this class of products or services becomes obsolete. However, there does not have to be much actual switching for the substitute threat to have an effect. The simple risk of substitution puts a cap on the prices that can be charged in an industry. Thus, although Eurostar has no direct competitors in terms of train services from Paris to London, the prices it can charge are ultimately limited by the cost of flights between the two cities.

There are two important points to bear in mind about substitutes:

- *The price/performance ratio* is critical to substitution threats. A substitute is still an effective threat even if more expensive, so long as it offers performance advantages that customers value. Thus aluminium is more expensive than steel, but its relative lightness and its resistance to corrosion give it an advantage in some automobile manufacturing applications. It is the ratio of price to performance that matters, rather than simple price.

- *Extra-industry effects* are the core of the substitution concept. Substitutes come from outside the incumbents' industry and should not be confused with competitors' threats from within the industry. The value of the substitution concept is to force managers to look outside their own industry to consider more distant threats and constraints. The more threats of substitution there are, the less attractive the industry is likely to be.

The power of buyers

Buyers are the organisation's immediate customers, not necessarily the ultimate consumers

Customers, of course, are essential for the survival of any business. But sometimes customers – here **buyers** – can have such high bargaining power that their suppliers are hard pressed to make any profits at all.

Buyer power is likely to be high when some of the following conditions prevail:

- *Concentrated buyers*. Where a few large customers account for the majority of sales, buyer power is increased. This is the case on items such as milk in the grocery sector in many European countries, where just a few retailers dominate the market. If a product or service accounts for a high percentage of the buyers' total purchases their power is also likely to increase as they are more likely to 'shop around' to get the best price and therefore 'squeeze' suppliers than they would for more trivial purchases.

- *Low switching costs*. Where buyers can easily switch between one supplier or another, they have a strong negotiating position and can squeeze suppliers who are desperate for their business. Switching costs are typically low for weakly differentiated commodities such as steel.

- *Buyer competition threat*. If the buyer has some facilities to supply itself, or if it has the possibility of acquiring such facilities, it tends to be powerful. In negotiation with its suppliers, it can raise the threat of doing the suppliers' job themselves. This is called *backward vertical integration*, moving back to sources of supply, and might occur if satisfactory prices or quality from suppliers cannot be obtained. For example, glass manufacturers have lost power against their buyers as some large window manufacturers have decided to produce some of their own glass.

It is very important that *buyers* are distinguished from *ultimate consumers*. Thus for companies like Nestlé or Unilever, their buyers are retailers such as Carrefour or Tesco, not ordinary consumers (see discussion of the 'strategic customer' in section 2.4.3). Carrefour and Tesco have much more negotiating power than an ordinary consumer would have. The high buying power of such supermarkets has become a major source of pressure for the companies supplying them.

The power of suppliers

Suppliers supply the organisation with what is required to produce the product or service, and include labour and sources of finance

Suppliers are those who supply the organisation with what it needs to produce the product or service. As well as fuel, raw materials and equipment, this can include labour and sources of finance. The factors increasing supplier power are the converse to those for buyer power. Thus *supplier power* is likely to be high where there are:

- *Concentrated suppliers*. Where just a few producers dominate supply, suppliers have more power over buyers. The iron ore industry is now concentrated in the hands of three main producers, leaving the steel companies, relatively fragmented, in a very weak negotiating position for this essential raw material.

- *High switching cost*. If it is expensive or disruptive to move from one supplier to another, then the buyer becomes relatively dependent and correspondingly weak. Microsoft is a powerful supplier because of the high switching costs of moving from one operating system to another. Buyers are prepared to pay a premium to avoid the trouble, and Microsoft knows it.

- *Supplier competition threat*. Suppliers have increased power where they are able to cut out buyers who are acting as intermediaries. Thus airlines have been able to negotiate tough contracts with travel agencies as the rise of online booking has allowed them to create a direct route to customers. This is called *forward vertical integration*, moving up closer to the ultimate customer.

Most organisations have many suppliers, so it is necessary to concentrate the analysis on the most important ones or types. If their power is high, suppliers can capture all their buyers' own potential profits simply by raising their prices. Star football players have succeeded in raising their rewards to astronomical levels, while even the leading football clubs – their 'buyers' – struggle to make money.

Competitive rivalry

These wider competitive forces (the four arrows in the model) all impinge on the direct competitive rivalry between an organisation and its most immediate rivals. Thus low barriers to entry increase the number of rivals; powerful buyers with low switching costs force their suppliers to high rivalry in order to offer the best deals. The more competitive rivalry there is, the worse it is for incumbents within the industry.

Competitive rivals are organisations with similar products and services aimed at the same customer group (that is, not substitutes). In the European transport industry, Air France and British Airways are rivals; trains are a substitute. As well as the influence of the four previous forces, there are a number of additional factors directly affecting the degree of competitive rivalry in an industry or sector:

> **Competitive rivals** are organisations with similar products and services aimed at the same customer group

- *Competitor balance*. Where competitors are of roughly equal size there is the danger of intense competition as one competitor attempts to gain dominance over others. Conversely, less rivalrous industries tend to have one or two dominant organisations, with the smaller players reluctant to challenge the larger ones directly (for example, by focusing on niches to avoid the 'attention' of the dominant companies).

- *Industry growth rate*. In situations of strong growth, an organisation can grow with the market, but in situations of low growth or decline, any growth is likely to be at the expense of a rival, and meet with fierce resistance. Low-growth markets are therefore often associated with price competition and low profitability. The *industry life cycle* influences growth rates, and hence competitive conditions: see section 2.3.2.

- *High fixed costs*. Industries with high fixed costs, perhaps because they require high investments in capital equipment or initial research, tend to be highly rivalrous. Companies will seek to reduce unit costs by increasing their volumes: to do so, they typically cut their prices, prompting competitors to do the same and thereby triggering price wars in which everyone in the industry suffers. Similarly, if extra capacity can only be added in large increments (as in many manufacturing sectors, for example a chemical or glass factory), the competitor making such an addition is likely to create short-term overcapacity in the industry, leading to increased competition to use capacity.

- *High exit barriers*. The existence of high barriers to exit – in other words, closure or disinvestment – tends to increase rivalry, especially in declining industries. Excess capacity persists and consequently incumbents fight to maintain market share. Exit barriers might be high for a variety of reasons: for example, high redundancy costs or high investment in specific assets such as plant and equipment that others would not buy.

- *Low differentiation*. In a commodity market, where products or services are poorly differentiated, rivalry is increased because there is little to stop customers switching between competitors and the only way to compete is on price.

Implications of five forces analysis

The five forces framework provides useful insights into the forces at work in the industry or sector environment of an organisation. Illustration 2.3 describes the

Illustration 2.3

The consolidating steel industry

Five forces analysis helps understand the changing attractiveness of an industry.

For a long time, the steel industry was seen as a static and unprofitable one. Producers were nationally based, often state owned and frequently unprofitable – between the late 1990s and 2003, more than 50 independent steel producers went into bankruptcy in the USA. The twenty-first century has seen a revolution. For example, during 2006, Mittal Steel paid $35bn (£19.6bn; €28bn) to buy European steel giant Arcelor, creating the world's largest steel company. The following year, Indian conglomerate Tata bought Anglo-Dutch steel company Corus for $13bn. These high prices indicated considerable confidence in being able to turn the industry round.

New entrants

In the last 10 years, two powerful groups have entered world steel markets. First, after a period of privatisation and reorganisation, large Russian producers such as Severstal and Evraz entered export markets, exporting 30 million tonnes of steel by 2005. At the same time, Chinese producers have been investing in new production facilities, in the period 2003–2005 increasing capacity at a rate of 30 per cent a year. Since the 1990s, Chinese share of world capacity has increased more than two times, to 25 per cent in 2006, and Chinese producers have become the world's third largest exporter just behind Japan and Russia.

Substitutes

Steel is a nineteenth-century technology, increasingly substituted for by other materials such as aluminium in cars, plastics and aluminium in packaging and ceramics and composites in many high-tech applications. Steel's own technological advances sometimes work to reduce need: thus steel cans have become about one-third thinner over the last few decades.

Buyer power

Key buyers for steel include the global car manufacturers, such as Ford, Toyota and Volkswagen, and leading can producers such as Crown Holdings, which makes one-third of all food cans produced in North America and Europe. Such companies buy in volume, coordinating purchases around the world. Car manufacturers are sophisticated users, often leading in the technological development of their materials.

Supplier power

The key raw material for steel producers is iron ore. The big three ore producers – CVRD, Rio Tinto and BHP Billiton – control 70 per cent of the international market. In 2005, iron ore producers exploited surging demand by increasing prices by 72 per cent; in 2006 they increased prices by 19 per cent.

Competitive rivalry

The industry has traditionally been very fragmented: in 2000, the world's top five producers accounted for only 14 per cent of production. Most steel is sold on a commodity basis, by the tonne. Prices are highly cyclical, as stocks do not deteriorate and tend to flood the market when demand slows. In the late twentieth century demand growth averaged a moderate 2 per cent per annum. The start of the twenty-first century saw a boom in demand, driven particularly by Chinese growth. Between 2003 and 2005, prices of sheet steel for cars and fridges trebled to $600 (£336; €480) a tonne. Companies such as Nucor in the USA, Thyssen-Krupp in Germany as well as Mittal and Tata responded by buying up weaker players internationally. New steel giant Mittal accounted for about 10 per cent of world production in 2007. Mittal actually reduced capacity in some of its Western production centres.

Questions

1 In recent years, which of the five forces has become more positive for steel producers, which less so?

2 Explain the acquisition strategies of players such as Mittal, Tata and Nucor.

3 In the future, what might change to make the steel industry less attractive or more attractive?

five forces in the changing steel industry. It is important, however, to use the framework for more than simply listing the forces. The bottom line is an assessment of the attractiveness of the industry. The analysis should conclude with a judgement about whether the industry is a good one to compete in or not.

The analysis should next prompt investigation of the *implications* of these forces. For example:

- *Which industries to enter (or leave)?* The fundamental purpose of the five forces model is to identify the relative attractiveness of different industries: industries are attractive when the forces are weak. Managers should invest in industries where the five forces work in their favour and avoid or disinvest from markets where they are strongly against.

- *What influence can be exerted?* Industry structures are not necessarily fixed, but can be influenced by deliberate managerial strategies. For example, organisations can build barriers to entry by increasing advertising spend to improve customer loyalty. They can buy up competitors to reduce rivalry and increase power over suppliers or buyers. Influencing industry structure involves many issues relating to *competitive strategy* and will be a major concern of Chapter 6.

- *How are competitors differently affected?* Not all competitors will be affected equally by changes in industry structure, deliberate or spontaneous. If barriers are rising because of increased R&D or advertising spending, smaller players in the industry may not be able to keep up with the larger players, and be squeezed out. Similarly, growing buyer power is likely to hurt small competitors most. Strategic group analysis is helpful here (see section 2.4.1).

Although originating in the private sector, five forces analysis can have important implications for organisations in the public sector too. For example, the forces can be used to adjust the service offer or focus on key issues. Thus it might be worth switching managerial initiative from an arena with many crowded and overlapping services (for example, social work, probation services and education) to one that is less rivalrous and where the organisation can do something more distinctive. Similarly, strategies could be launched to reduce dependence on particularly powerful and expensive suppliers, for example energy sources or high-shortage skills.

Key issues in using the five forces framework

The five forces framework has to be used carefully and is not necessarily complete, even at the industry level. When using this framework, it is important to bear the following three issues in mind:

- *Defining the 'right' industry.* Most industries can be analysed at different levels. For example, the airline industry has several different segments such as domestic and long haul and different customer groups such as leisure, business and freight (see section 2.4.2 below). The competitive forces are likely to be different for each of these segments and can be analysed separately. It is often useful to conduct industry analysis at a disaggregated level, for each distinct segment. The overall picture for the industry as a whole can then be assembled.

- *Converging industries.* Industry definition is often difficult too because industry boundaries are continuously changing. For example, many industries, especially in high-tech arenas, are undergoing **convergence**, where previously separate industries begin to overlap or merge in terms of activities, technologies, products and customers.[7] Technological change has brought convergence between the telephone and photographic industries, for example, as mobile phones increasingly include camera and video functions. For a camera company like Kodak, phones are increasingly a substitute and the prospect of facing Nokia or Samsung as direct competitors is not remote.

> **Convergence** is where previously separate industries begin to overlap in terms of activities, technologies, products and customers

- *Complementary products.* Some analysts argue for a 'sixth force', organisations supplying complementary products or services. These **complementors** are players from whom customers buy complementary products that are worth more together than separately. Thus Dell and Microsoft are complementors insofar as computers and software are complementary products for buyers. Microsoft needs Dell to produce powerful machines to run its latest-generation software. Dell needs Microsoft to work its machines. Likewise, television programme makers and television guide producers are complements. Complementors raise two issues. The first is that complementors have opportunities for *cooperation*. It makes sense for Dell and Microsoft to keep each other in touch with their technological developments, for example. This implies a significant shift in perspective. While Porter's five forces sees organisations as battling against each other for share of industry value, complementors may cooperate to increase the value of the whole cake.[8] The second issue, however, is the potential for some complementors to demand a high share of the available value for themselves. Microsoft has been much more profitable than the manufacturers of complementary computer products and its high margins may have depressed the sales and margins available to companies like Dell. The potential for cooperation or antagonism with such a complementary 'sixth force' needs to be included in industry analyses.[9]

> **Complementors** are products or services for which customers are prepared to pay more if together than if they stand alone

2.3.2 The dynamics of industry structure

Industry structure analysis can easily become too static: after all, structure implies stability.[10] However, the previous sections have raised the issue of how competitive forces change *over time*. The key drivers for change are likely to alter industry structures and scenario analyses can be used to understand possible impacts. This section examines three additional approaches to understanding change in industry structure: the *industry life-cycle* concept; the notion of *hypercompetitive cycles of competition*; and *comparative five forces analyses*.

The industry life cycle

The power of the five forces typically varies with the stages of the industry life cycle. The industry life-cycle concept proposes that industries start small in their development stage, then go through a period of rapid growth (the equivalent to 'adolescence' in the human life cycle), culminating in a period of 'shake-out'. The final two stages are first a period of slow or even zero growth ('maturity'), before the final stage of decline ('old age'). Each of these stages has implications for the five forces.[11]

The *development stage* is an experimental one, typically with few players exercising little direct rivalry and highly differentiated products. The five forces are likely to be weak, therefore, though profits may actually be scarce because of high investment requirements. The next stage is one of high growth, with rivalry low as there is plenty of market opportunity for everybody. Buyers may be keen to secure supplies and lack sophistication about what they are buying, so diminishing their power. One downside of the growth stage is that barriers to entry may be low, as existing competitors have not built up much scale, experience or customer loyalty. Another potential downside is the power of suppliers if there is a shortage of components or materials that fast-growing businesses need for expansion. The *shake-out stage* begins as the growth rate starts to decline, so that increased rivalry forces the weakest of the new entrants out of the business. In the *maturity stage*, barriers to entry tend to increase, as control over distribution is established and economies of scale and experience curve benefits come into play. Products or service tend to standardise. Buyers may become more powerful as they become less avid for the industry's products or services and more confident in switching between suppliers. For major players, market share is typically key to survival, providing leverage against buyers and competitive advantage in terms of cost. Finally, the *decline stage* can be a period of extreme rivalry, especially where there are high exit barriers, as falling sales force remaining competitors into dog-eat-dog competition. Exhibit 2.3 summarises some of the conditions that can be expected at different stages in the life cycle.

It is important to avoid putting too much faith in the inevitability of life-cycle stages. One stage does not follow predictably after another: industries vary widely in the length of their growth stages, and others can rapidly 'de-mature' through radical innovation. The telephony industry, based for nearly a century on fixed-line telephones, de-matured rapidly with the introduction of mobile and

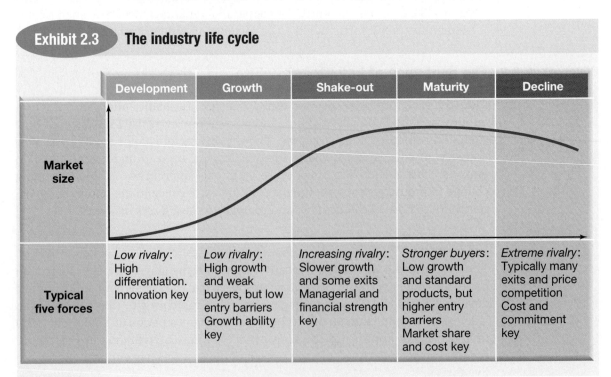

Exhibit 2.3   **The industry life cycle**

	Development	Growth	Shake-out	Maturity	Decline
Market size					
Typical five forces	*Low rivalry*: High differentiation. Innovation key	*Low rivalry*: High growth and weak buyers, but low entry barriers Growth ability key	*Increasing rivalry*: Slower growth and some exits Managerial and financial strength key	*Stronger buyers*: Low growth and standard products, but higher entry barriers Market share and cost key	*Extreme rivalry*: Typically many exits and price competition Cost and commitment key

Internet telephony. Anita McGahan warns of the 'maturity mindset', which can leave many managers complacent and slow to respond to new competition.[12] Managing in mature industries is not necessarily just about waiting for decline. Although steady progress through the stages is not inevitable, the life-cycle concept does none the less remind managers that conditions will change over time. Especially in fast-moving industries, five forces analyses need to be reviewed quite regularly.

Hypercompetition and competitive cycles[13]

Competitors constantly interact in terms of competitive moves: price cuts are matched and innovations imitated. These sequences of move and counter-move are called *cycles of competition*. In some industries, these interactions become so intense and fast that industry structures are constantly undermined. Such industries are *hypercompetitive* (intensely competitive), trapped by the aggressive interactions of competitors into negative downward cycles for all concerned. Competitors attack and counter-attack each other in a way that precludes stability and makes sustainable profits impossible. The cycle of competition concept underlines the fact that industry structures are not 'natural', but are often created and reshaped by the deliberate strategies of competitors. Exhibit 2.4 shows a theoretical cycle of competition, and an empirical example is given in Illustration 2.4.

Exhibit 2.4   Cycles of competition

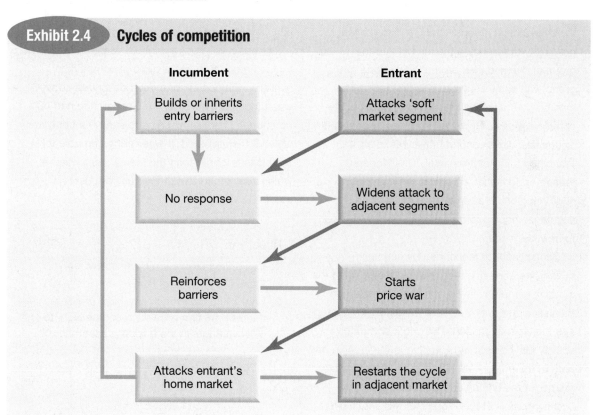

Source: Adapted with the permission of The Free Press, a Division of Simon & Schuster Adult. Publishing Group, from *Hypercompetitive Rivalries: Competing in Highly Dynamic Environments* by Richard A. D'Aveni with Robert Gunther. Copyright © 1994, 1995 by Richard A. D'Aveni. All rights reserved.

Illustration 2.4

Cycles of competition

Changes in the business environment and moves by competitors erode the competitive position of organisations which, in turn, respond by counter-moves. Competition moves through cycles and any competitive advantage is temporary.

Consider the interactions between Francotop, the highly profitable dominant player in a French consumer goods niche, and Deutschespitze, a German company with a similar product that was wishing to become a significant European-wide player.

Deutschespitze's first competitive move was to target a consumer age group where consumption and brand awareness in France were both low. Francotop had limited its marketing efforts to the over-25 age groups – the Germans saw a possibility of extending the market into the 18–25 group and aimed their promotional efforts at the group with some success. This first move was ignored by Francotop as it did not impact on its current business. However, from this bridgehead Deutschespitze's second move was to attack Francotop's key older market. This triggered Francotop to launch an advertising campaign reinforcing brand awareness in its traditional segments, hoping to confine the German company to its initial niche.

Deutschespitze responded by counter-advertising and price reductions – undermining the margins earned by its French rival. Competition then escalated with a counter-attack by Francotop into the German market. This wider competitive activity played itself out resulting in the erosion of both of the original strongholds and a progressive merger of the French and German markets.

It is possible at this stage that this whole cycle of competition could have repeated itself in an adjacent market, such as the UK. However, what happened was that Deutschespitze saw an opportunity to move away from this *cost/quality* basis of competition by adapting the product for use by businesses. Its core competences in R&D allowed it to get the adapted product to market faster than its French rival. It then consolidated these first-mover advantages by building and defending barriers. For example, it appointed key account salespeople and gave special offers for early adoption and three-year contracts.

Nevertheless, this stronghold came under attack by the French firm and a cycle of competition similar to the consumer market described above was triggered. However, the German firm had built up enough financial reserves to survive a price war, which it then initiated. It was willing and able to fund losses longer than the French competitor – which was forced to exit the business user market.

Questions

1 Could the French firm have slowed down the cycle of competition?

2 How could the French firm have prevented the German firm escalating competition, to its advantage, in the business user market?

Exhibit 2.4 shows a cycle of competition involving various moves and counter-moves between competitors over time. The starting point is a new entrant attacking an incumbent's established market, apparently protected by inherited entry barriers. The new entrant sensibly attacks a particularly 'soft' (unprotected) segment of the overall market. If receiving no strong competitive response from the incumbent (that is, no retaliation), the new entrant widens its attack to adjacent segments of the incumbent's market. There is a danger of increased industry rivalry and rapidly falling industry profits. In Exhibit 2.4, the incumbent finally responds by increasing entry barriers, perhaps by reinforcing customers' loyalty through increased differentiation. The new entrant counters with a price war. The final resort of the incumbent is to attack the new entrant's home market, hoping to do enough damage there to persuade the new entrant to back off. Thus rivalry increases in that home industry as well. The incumbent meanwhile does its best to raise its barriers to entry.

Illustration 2.4 demonstrates a similar cycle of competition in an international context. Here moves and counter-moves by organisations and their competitors take place simultaneously in several locations. So a competitive move in one arena, the German company's aggressive move into France, did not trigger off a counter-move in that arena (France), but in its competitor's home territory (Germany).

The competitive dynamics between organisations competing in different product or geographical markets (as in Illustration 2.4) is known as *multi-point competition*, in other words competition at multiple points in a business's portfolio of businesses. The possibility of multi-point competition does not necessarily increase competitive rivalry. Indeed, it can reduce competitive rivalry by raising the costs and risks of aggressive moves and counter-moves.[14] For an incumbent, having a small presence in the main market of a potential competitor can discourage any aggressive move by the competitor, because the competitor knows it risks prompt retaliation in its own most valuable market, where it will hurt most.

Hypercompetition
occurs where the
frequency, boldness
and aggressiveness of
dynamic movements by
competitors accelerate
to create a condition of
constant disequilibrium
and change

Hypercompetition occurs where the frequency, boldness and aggressiveness of competitor interactions accelerate to create a condition of constant disequilibrium and change.[15] Industry structures are permanently unstable and no industry can be judged securely attractive for any substantial period of time. In hypercompetitive conditions, it may not be worth investing heavily in building up barriers to entry or trying to reduce rivalry, perhaps by acquisition of competitor companies. Competitor moves will inevitably undermine attractive industry structures. The sustainability of competitive advantage is discussed further in Chapter 3, with competitive moves under conditions of hypercompetition returned to in Chapter 6. Some analysts claim that industries in general are becoming more hypercompetitive, because of international competition or technological change. However, the research evidence is divided on the trend to hypercompetition and it is wise not to be panicked into unduly hypercompetitive behaviour.[16] Aggressive cycles have a reinforcing character that are hard to stop once begun.

Comparative industry structure analyses

The industry life cycle and cycles of competition notions underline the need to make industry structure analysis dynamic. One effective means of doing this is to compare the five forces over time in a simple 'radar plot'.

Exhibit 2.5	Comparative industry structure analysis

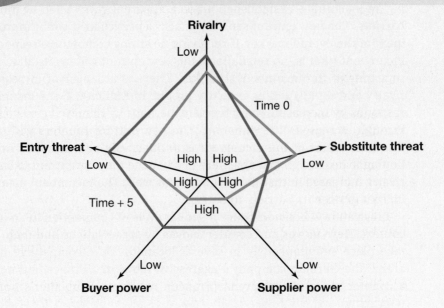

Source: Adapted from V. Lerville-Anger, F. Fréry, A. Gazengel and A. Ollivier, *Conduire le diagnostic global d'une unité industrielle*, Editions d'Organisation, Paris, 2001.

Exhibit 2.5 provides a framework for summarising the power of each of the five forces on five axes. Power diminishes as the axes go outwards. Where the forces are low, the total area enclosed by the lines between the axes is large; where the forces are high, the total area enclosed by the lines is small. The larger the enclosed area, therefore, the greater is the profit potential. In Exhibit 2.5, the industry at Time 0 (represented by the bright blue lines) has relatively low rivalry (just a few competitors) and faces low substitution threats. The threat of entry is moderate, but both buyer power and supplier power are relatively high. Overall, this looks like only a moderately attractive industry to invest in.

However, given the dynamic nature of industries, managers need to look forward: here five years represented by the dark blue lines in Exhibit 2.5. Managers are predicting in this case some rise in the threat of substitutes (perhaps new technologies will be developed). On the other hand, they predict a falling entry threat, while both buyer power and supplier power will be easing. Rivalry will reduce still further. This looks like a classic case of an industry in which a few players emerge with overall dominance. The area enclosed by the dark blue lines is large, suggesting a relatively attractive industry. For a firm confident of becoming one of the dominant players, this might be an industry well worth investing in.

Comparing the five forces over time on a radar plot thus helps to give industry structure analysis a dynamic aspect. Similar plots can be made to aid diversification decisions (see Chapter 7), where possible new industries to enter can be compared in terms of attractiveness. The lines are only approximate, of course, because they aggregate the many individual elements that make up each of the forces into a simple composite measure. Notice too that if one of the forces is very adverse, then this might nullify positive assessments on the other four axes: for example, an industry with low rivalry, low substitution, low entry barriers and low supplier power might still be unattractive if powerful buyers were able to demand highly discounted prices. With these warnings in mind, such radar plots can none the less be both a useful device for initial analysis and an effective summary of a final, more refined analysis.

2.4 COMPETITORS AND MARKETS

An industry or sector may be too high a level to provide for a detailed understanding of competition. The five forces can impact differently on different kinds of players. For example, Ford and Porsche may be in the same broad industry (automobiles), but they are positioned differently: they face different kinds of buyer power and supplier power at the very least. It is often useful to disaggregate. Many industries contain a range of companies, each of which has different capabilities and competes on different bases. These competitor differences are captured by the concept of *strategic groups*. Customers too can differ significantly. Such customer differences can be captured by distinguishing between *strategic customers* and ultimate consumers and between different *market segments*. Underpinning strategic groups and market segments is recognition of what *customers value* and *critical success factors*. These various concepts will now be discussed.

2.4.1 Strategic groups[17]

Strategic groups are organisations within an industry with similar strategic characteristics, following similar strategies or competing on similar bases

Strategic groups

Strategic groups are organisations within an industry or sector with similar strategic characteristics, following similar strategies or competing on similar bases. These characteristics are different from those in other strategic groups in the same industry or sector. For example, in the grocery retailing industry, supermarkets, convenience stores and corner shops each form different strategic groups. There are many different characteristics that distinguish between strategic groups but these can be grouped into two major categories (see Exhibit 2.6):[18] first, the *scope* of an organisation's activities (such as product range, geographical coverage and range of distribution channels used); second, the *resource commitment* (such as brands, marketing spend and extent of vertical integration). Which of these characteristics are especially relevant in terms of a given industry needs to be understood in terms of the history and development of that industry and the forces at work in the environment.

Strategic groups can be mapped onto two-dimensional charts – for example, one axis might be the extent of product range and the other axis the size of marketing spend. One method for establishing key dimensions by which to map strategic groups is to identify top performers (by growth or profitability) in an industry and to compare them with low performers. Characteristics that are shared by top performers, but not by low performers, are likely to be particularly relevant for mapping strategic groups. For example, the most profitable firms in an industry might all be narrow in terms of product range and lavish in terms of marketing spend, while the less profitable firms might be more widely spread in terms of products and restrained in their marketing. Here the two dimensions for mapping would be product range and marketing spend. A potential recommendation for the less profitable firms would be to cut back their product range and boost their marketing. In Illustration 2.5, Figure 1 shows a strategic group map of the major providers of MBAs in The Netherlands in 2007.

Illustration 2.5

Strategic groups in Dutch MBA education

Mapping of strategic groups can provide insights into the competitive structures of industries or sectors and the opportunities and constraints for development.

In the mid-2000s there were three kinds of institutions offering MBA courses in The Netherlands: traditional universities, for-profit business schools (FPBSs) and polytechnics:

- Traditional universities offered a wide range of subjects, carried out research, and attracted students both nationally and internationally. Their programmes were more academic than vocational. A university degree was generally valued more highly than that of a polytechnic.

- FPBSs were relatively new, and provided MBA degrees only. Some of the FPBS now offer a DBA course as well. Usually they were located close to the centre or capital of the country. MBA education at FPBSs was generally more of the action learning type, which made it attractive for practising managers. Many students already had diplomas from a university or polytechnic. Several of these schools received accreditation from the Dutch Validation Council. In 2005 the Dutch minister of education and culture recognised NIMBAS, an FPBS, as an official 'universiteit'. NIMBAS later merged with TIAS, the business school of Universiteit Tilburg.

- Polytechnics (in The Netherlands named HogeScholen) often attracted students from the region and provided education aimed more at application of theory than at developing conceptual thinking. Some of the polytechnics provided MBA degrees, in some cases in cooperation with universities in the UK.

Figure 1 gives an indication of how these three types of institution were positioned in terms of geographical coverage and 'orientation'. Figure 2 shows the barriers confronting organisations who wished to move from one group to another (they show the barriers *into* a group). For example, if the FPBSs tried to 'enter' the strategic group of traditional universities they would need to build up a reputation in research or innovation. They may not be interested in doing research, since there would be high costs and little pay-off for their effort. In reverse, for traditional universities to move in the direction of the FPBSs may be difficult since the faculty may not have skills in action learning and may be inexperienced at working with older students.

Figure 3 shows where 'strategic space' might exist. These spaces are created by changes in the macro-

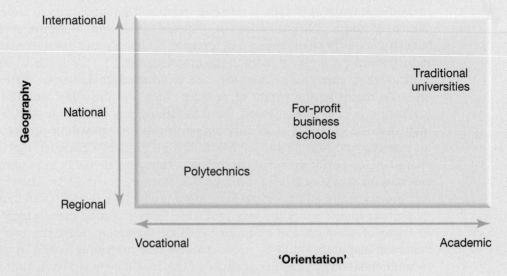

Figure 1 Strategic groups in MBA education in The Netherlands

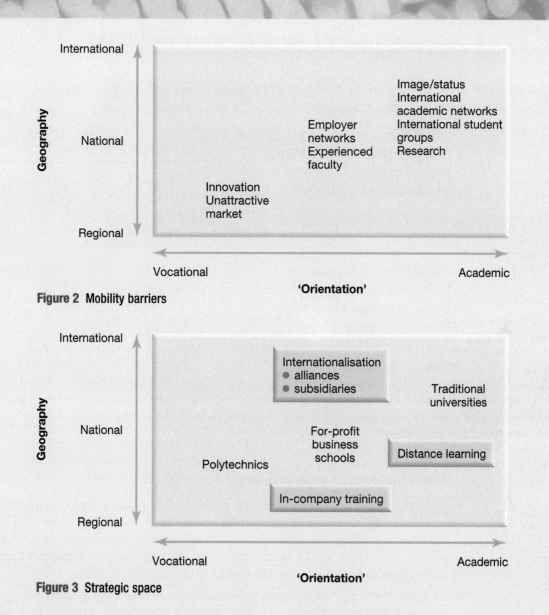

Figure 2 Mobility barriers

Figure 3 Strategic space

environment – particularly globalisation and information technology. This could provide opportunities for Dutch business schools to seek more international business. However, the reverse threat of international competitors entering the Dutch market was a major concern. Information and communication technology helps students study at their own place of work or at home, and also enables them to tap into an international network. So an American or British school could provide content over the Internet and local student support through partnerships with Dutch institutions. Indeed the University of Phoenix had already made efforts to do just this.

Source: This is an updated version of D.J. Eppink and S. de Waal, 'Global influences on the public sector', in G. Johnson and K. Scholes (eds), *Exploring Public Sector Strategy*, FT/Prentice Hall, 2001, chapter 3.

Question

How might this analysis influence the next strategic moves by each of the three types of institution?

Exhibit 2.6   **Some characteristics for identifying strategic groups**

It is useful to consider the extent to which organisations *differ* in terms of **characteristics** such as:

Scope of activities

- Extent of product (or service) diversity
- Extent of geographical coverage
- Number of market segments served
- Distribution channels used

Resource commitment

- Extent (number) of **branding**
- **Marketing effort** (e.g. advertising spread, size of salesforce)
- Extent of **vertical integration**
- Product or service **quality**
- **Technological leadership** (a leader or follower)
- **Size** of organisation

Sources: Based on M.E. Porter, *Competitive Strategy*, Free Press, 1980; and J. McGee and H. Thomas, 'Strategic groups: theory, research and taxonomy', *Strategic Management Journal*, vol. 7, no. 2 (1986), pp. 141–160.

This strategic group concept is useful in at least three ways:

- *Understanding competition.* Managers can focus on their direct competitors within their particular strategic group, rather than the whole industry. They can also establish the dimensions that distinguish them most from other groups, and which might be the basis for relative success or failure. These dimensions can then become the focus of their action.

- *Analysis of strategic opportunities.* Strategic group maps can identify the most attractive 'strategic spaces' within an industry. Some spaces on the map may be 'white spaces', relatively under-occupied. In the Dutch MBA market, for instance, examples are vocational degrees for the international market and semi-academic education for the regional in-company training market. Such white spaces might be unexploited opportunities. On the other hand, they could turn out to be 'black holes', impossible to exploit and likely to damage any entrant. A strategic group map is only the first stage of the analysis. Strategic spaces need to tested carefully.

- *Analysis of mobility barriers.* Of course, moving across the map to take advantage of opportunities is not costless. Often it will require difficult decisions and rare resources. Strategic groups are therefore characterised by 'mobility barriers', obstacles to movement from one strategic group to another. These are similar to barriers to entry in five forces analysis. In Illustration 2.5, Figure 2 shows examples of mobility barriers for the groupings identified in the industry. These may be substantial: to enter the international academic strategic group, a regional, vocational competitor would have to establish the appropriate image, mobilise networks, change its teaching methods and improve its remuneration levels. As with barriers to entry, it is good to be in a successful strategic group for which there are strong mobility barriers, to impede imitation.

2.4.2 Market segments

The concept of strategic groups discussed above helps with understanding the similarities and differences in the characteristics of 'producers' – those organisations that are actual or potential competitors. The concept of market segment focuses attention on differences in customer needs. A **market segment**[19] is a group of customers who have similar needs that are different from customer needs in other parts of the market. It will be seen in Chapter 3 that this understanding of what customers (and other stakeholders) value and how an organisation and its competitors are positioned to meet these needs are critical to understanding strategic capability.

The concept of market segments should remind managers of several important issues:

- *Customer needs* may vary for a whole variety of reasons – some of which are identified in Exhibit 2.7. Theoretically, any of these factors could be used to identify market segments. However, in practical terms it is important to consider which bases of segmentation are most important in any particular

> A **market segment** is a group of customers who have similar needs that are different from customer needs in other parts of the market

---

Exhibit 2.7 **Some bases of market segmentation**

Type of factor	Consumer markets	Industrial/ organisational markets
Characteristics of people/ organisations	Age, sex, race Income Family size Life-cycle stage Location Lifestyle	Industry Location Size Technology Profitability Management
Purchase/use situation	Size of purchase Brand loyalty Purpose of use Purchasing behaviour Importance of purchase Choice criteria	Application Importance of purchase Volume Frequency of purchase Purchasing procedure Choice criteria Distribution channel
Users' needs and preferences for product characteristics	Product similarity Price preference Brand preferences Desired features Quality	Performance requirements Assistance from suppliers Brand preferences Desired features Quality Service requirements

market. For example, in industrial markets, segmentation is often thought of in terms of industrial classification of buyers – such as 'we sell to the domestic appliance industry'. However, it may be that this is not the most relevant basis of segmentation when thinking about the future. Segmentation by buyer behaviour (for example, direct buying versus those users who buy through third parties such as contractors) or purchase value (for example, high-value bulk purchasers versus frequent low-value purchasers) might be more appropriate in some markets. Indeed, it is often useful to consider different bases of segmentation in the same market to help understand the dynamics of that market and how these are changing.

● *Relative market share* (that is, share in relation to that of competitors) within a market segment is an important consideration. Organisations that have built up most experience in servicing a particular market segment should not only have lower costs in so doing, but also have built relationships which may be difficult for others to break down. What customers value will vary by market segment and therefore 'producers' are likely to achieve advantage in segments that are especially suited to their particular strengths. They may find it very difficult to compete on a broader basis. For example, a small local brewery competing against the big brands on the basis of its low prices underpinned by low costs of distribution and marketing is confined to that segment of the local market that values low price.

● How market segments can be *identified and 'serviced'*[20] is influenced by a number of trends in the business environment already discussed in this chapter. For example, the wide availability of consumer data and the ability to process it electronically combined with increased flexibility of companies' operations allow segmentation to be undertaken at a micro-level – even down to individual consumers (so-called 'markets of one'). So Internet shopping selectively targets consumers with special offers based on their past purchasing patterns. The emergence of more affluent, mobile consumers means that geographical segmentation may be much less effective than lifestyle segmentation (across national boundaries).

2.4.3 Identifying the strategic customer

Bringing goods and services to market usually involves a range of organisations performing different roles. In Chapter 3 this will be discussed in more detail through the concept of the value network. For example, most consumers purchase goods through retail outlets. So the manufacturers must attend to two sorts of customers – the shops, their direct customers, and the shops' customers, the ultimate consumers of the product. Although both customers influence demand, usually one of these will be more influential than the others – this is the strategic customer. The **strategic customer** is the person(s) at whom the strategy is primarily addressed because they have the most influence over which goods or services are purchased. Unless there is clarity on who the strategic customer is, managers can end up analysing and targeting the wrong people. It is the desires of the strategic customer that provide the starting point for strategy. The requirements of the other customers are not unimportant – they have to be met – but the requirements of the strategic customer are paramount. Returning to the

The strategic customer is the person(s) at whom the strategy is primarily addressed because they have the most influence over which goods or services are purchased

example, it should be clear that for many consumer goods the retail outlet is the strategic customer as the way it displays, promotes and supports products in store is hugely influential on the final consumer preferences. In the public sector the strategic customer is very often the 'body' which controls the funds or authorises use rather than the user of the service. So family doctors are the strategic customers of pharmaceutical companies and so on.

2.4.4 Understanding what customers value – critical success factors

Although the concept of market segments is useful, managers may fail to be realistic about how markets are segmented and the strategic implications of that segmentation. It will be seen in the next chapter that an understanding of customer needs and how they differ between segments is crucial to developing the appropriate strategic capability in an organisation. However, customers will value many product/service features to a greater or lesser degree. From the potential providers' viewpoint it is valuable to understand which features are of particular importance to a group of customers (market segment). These are known as the critical success factors. **Critical success factors** (CSFs) are those product features that are particularly valued by a group of customers and, therefore, where the organisation must excel to outperform competition.

The extent to which the offerings of different providers address the factors valued by customers can be visualised by creating a strategy canvas[21] (see Exhibit 2.8). The canvas is a simple but useful way of comparing competitors' positions in a market and potential in different segments. The exhibit relates to one segment of the electrical engineering industry – company-based buyers of electrical engineering equipment – and illustrates the following:

Critical success factors (CSFs) are those product features that are particularly valued by a group of customers and, therefore, where the organisation must excel to outperform competition

- Five *critical success factors* are identified in Exhibit 2.8 as particularly important to customers on average (in rank order, the producer's reputation, after-sales service, delivery reliability, testing facilities and technical quality). They are the factors which would determine which provider was preferred, given similar prices.

- Three *competitor profiles* are drawn on the canvas against these factors. It is clear that the particular strengths that company A possesses are not the factors *most* valued by the average customer, whereas company B's strengths appear to have a better match. But nobody is doing particularly well with regard to testing and technical quality.

- *Segment choice* is the next issue. Company A could try to improve on the most highly valued factors. But companies B and C are already strong there, and their customers are highly satisfied. An alternative for company A is to focus on a particular market segment, those for whom testing and quality happen to be much more important than for the average customer. There is less competition there and greater room for improvement. This segment might be relatively small, but targeting this specifically could be much more profitable than tackling companies B and C head on in their areas of strength. Company A might focus on raising its profile at the right-hand end of the canvas.

The key messages from this example are that it is important to see value through the eyes of the customer and to be clear about relative strengths.

Exhibit 2.8 **A strategy canvas – perceived value by customers in the electrical engineering industry**

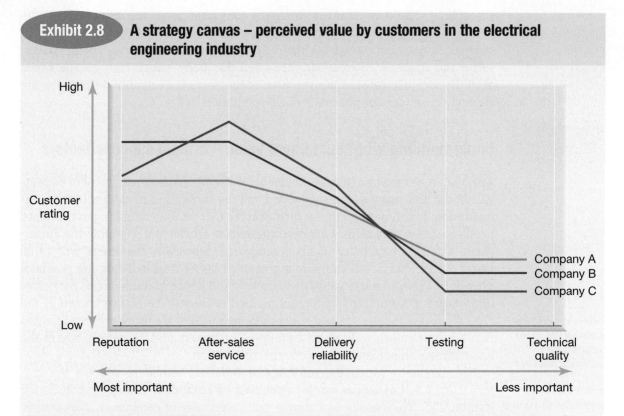

Although this might appear self-evident, a customer viewpoint and clarity about strengths may not be easy to achieve for several reasons:

● *Sense making*. Managers may not be able to *make sense* of the complex and varied behaviours they experience in their markets. Often they will have vast amounts of raw data about customer preferences and competitor moves, but they lack the capability to draw useful conclusions from these data (for example, to spot trends or connections). Market researchers and marketing consultants may be able to supply a clearer view from outside.

● *Distance from the ultimate customer*. Component and raw material suppliers, for example, may be distanced from the final users by several intermediaries – other manufacturers and distributors. Although these direct customers may be the strategic customers there is a danger that what value means to the final consumer is not understood. In other words, companies may be out of touch with what is ultimately driving demand for their product or service.

● *Internal biases*. Managers are prone to assume that their particular strengths are valued by customers, and that somehow their competitors are necessarily inferior. For example, professional groups in many public services have tended to assume that what they think best for the client automatically is the best, while being sceptical of private sector providers' ability to look after the 'true' needs of clients.

● *Changes over time*. Customers' values typically evolve, either because they become more experienced (through repeat purchase) or because competitive offerings become available which offer better value. Managers, however, are often trapped by their historical experience of the market (see Chapter 5).

2.5   OPPORTUNITIES AND THREATS

The concepts and frameworks discussed above should be helpful in understanding the factors in the macro-, industry and competitor/market environments of an organisation (Illustration 2.6 outlines a key debate: just how much do such industry and market factors affect successful strategic outcomes?). However, the critical issue is the *implications* that are drawn from this understanding in guiding strategic decisions and choices. The crucial next stage, therefore, is to draw from the environmental analysis specific strategic opportunities and threats for the organisation. Identifying these opportunities and threats is extremely valuable when thinking about strategic choices for the future (the subject of Chapters 6 to 9). Opportunities and threats forms one half of the strengths, weaknesses, opportunities and threats (SWOT) analyses that shape many companies' strategy formulation (see Chapter 3).[22] In responding strategically to the environment, the goal is to reduce identified threats and take advantage of the best opportunities.

A **strategic gap** is an opportunity in the competitive environment that is not being fully exploited by competitors

Taking advantage of a **strategic gap** is an effective way of managing threats and opportunities. W. Chan Kim and Renée Mauborgne have argued that if organisations simply concentrate on competing head to head with competitive rivals this will lead to competitive convergence where all 'players' find the environment tough and threatening.[23] They describe this as a 'red ocean' strategy – red because of the bloodiness of the competition and the red ink caused by financial losses. They urge instead that managers attempt 'blue ocean' strategies – searching for, or creating, wide open spaces, free from existing competition. Blue oceans are strategic gaps in the market, opportunities that are not being fully exploited by competitors. One such blue ocean strategy was the creation by Australian wine producers of fun, easy-to-understand and easy-to-drink wines. A red ocean strategy would have been to compete against the established French producers with fancy labels, wine jargon and complex tastes.

Strategic gaps can be identified with the help of the techniques in this chapter. In terms of Porter's five forces, strategic gaps are where rivalry is low. In terms of strategic group maps, gaps typically lie in the under-occupied 'white spaces'. In terms of the strategy canvas, potential strategic gaps are where a big difference can be established with the position of most companies on the various factors valued by customers.

With the concept of strategic gaps, six types of opportunity are particularly important, as follows.

Opportunities in substitute industries

Organisations face competition from industries that are producing substitutes, as discussed in section 2.3.1. But substitution also provides opportunities. In order to identify gaps a *realistic* assessment has to be made of the relative merits of the products/technologies (incumbent and potential substitutes) *in the eyes of the customer*. An example would be software companies substituting electronic versions of reference books and atlases for the traditional paper versions. From the customers' point of view, electronic versions have easier search facilities and are more likely to be up to date.

Opportunities in other strategic groups or strategic spaces

It is also possible to identify opportunities by looking across strategic groups – particularly if changes in the macro-environment make new market spaces economically viable. For example, deregulation of markets (say in electricity generation and distribution) and advances in IT (say with educational study programmes) could both create new market gaps. In the first case, the locally based smaller-scale generation of electricity becomes viable – possibly linked to waste incineration plants. In the latter case, geography can be 'shrunk' and educational programmes delivered across continents through the Internet and teleconferencing (together with local tutorial support). New strategic groups emerge in these industries/sectors.

Opportunities in targeting buyers

Sections 2.4.3 and 2.4.4 emphasised that the nature of the buyers can be complex, with the strategic customer critically important. It was also noted that there may be several people involved in the overall purchase decision. There may be opportunities in targeting neglected strategic customers or neglected influencers of purchasing decisions. It might, for instance, be worth targeting health and safety executives at a customer organisation: they might be willing to pay more for a safe product or service than the usual buyers in the purchasing department, typically more focused on cost.

Opportunities for complementary products and services

This involves a consideration of the potential value of complementary products and services. For example, in book retailing the overall 'book-buying experience' requires much more than just stocking the right books. It also includes providing an ambience conducive to browsing; the provision of a coffee bar might be seen as a complementary service.

Opportunities in new market segments

Looking for new market segments may provide opportunities but product/service features may need to change. If the emphasis is on selling emotional appeal, the alternative may be to provide a no-frills model that costs less and would appeal to another potential market. For example, the Body Shop, operating in the highly emotional cosmetics industry, challenged the accepted viewpoint. This was achieved by the production of purely functional products, noted for their lack of elaborate packaging or heavy advertising. This created new market space by attracting the consumer who wanted quality skin-care products without the added frills.

Opportunities over time

When predicting the impact of changes in the macro- or competitive environments it is important to consider how they are going to affect the consumer. Organisations can gain first-mover advantages that way. Cisco Systems realised that the future was going to create a significant need for high-speed data exchange and was at the forefront of producing equipment to address this future need. It identified new market space because no one else had assessed the likely implications of the Internet boom. This meant that it could offer specially designed products well ahead of its rivals, giving it an important competitive edge.

SUMMARY

www.pearsoned.co.uk/ecs
AUDIO SUMMARY

- Environmental influences can be thought of as layers around an organisation, with the outer layer making up the *macro-environment*, the middle layer making up the *industry or sector* and the inner layer *strategic groups* and *market segments*.

- The macro-environment can be analysed in terms of the *PESTEL factors*, from which *key drivers of change* can be identified. Alternative *scenarios* about the future can be constructed according to how the key drivers develop.

- Industries and sectors can be analysed in terms of *Porter's Five Forces* – barriers to entry, substitutes, buyer power, supplier power and rivalry. Together, these determine industry or sector attractiveness. Together, these determine industry or sector attractiveness, and can be influential for overall performance (see Key Debate, Illustration 2.6).

- Industries and sectors are dynamic, and their changes can be analysed in terms of the *industry life cycle, hypercompetitive cycles of competition* and *comparative five forces radar plots*.

- In the inner layer of the environment, *strategic group* analysis, *market segment* analysis and the *strategy canvas* can help identify strategic gaps or opportunities.

- *Blue ocean* strategies characterised by low rivalry are likely to be better opportunities than *red ocean* strategies with many rivals.

Illustration 2.6

How much does industry matter?

A good start in strategy must be to choose a profitable industry to compete in. But does simply being in the right industry matter more than having the right kinds of skills and resources?

This chapter has focused on the role of the environment in strategy making, with particular regard to industries. But the importance of industries in determining organisational performance has been challenged in recent years. This has led to a debate about whether strategy making should be externally orientated, starting with the environment, or internally orientated, starting with the organisation's own skills and resources (the focus of Chapter 3).[1]

Managers favouring an external approach look primarily *outside* the organisation, for example building market share in their industries through mergers and acquisitions or aggressive marketing. Managers favouring an internal approach concentrate their attention *inside* the organisation, fostering the skills of their people or nurturing technologies, for example. Because managerial time is limited, there is a real trade off to be made between external and internal approaches.

The chief advocate of the external approach is Michael Porter, Professor at Harvard Business School and founder of the Monitor Consulting Group. An influential sceptic of this approach is Richard Rumelt, a student at Harvard Business School but now at University of California Los Angeles. Porter, Rumelt and others have done a series of empirical studies examining the relative importance of industries in explaining organisations' performance.

Typically, these studies take a large sample of firms and compare the extent to which variance in profitability is due to firms or industries (controlling for other effects such as size). If firms within the same industry tend to bunch together in terms of profitability, it is industry that is accounting for the greater proportion of profitability: an external approach to strategy is supported. If firms within the same industry vary widely in terms of profitability, it is the specific skills and resources of the firms that matter most: an internal approach is most appropriate.

The two most important studies in fact find that more of the variance in profitability is due to firms rather than industries – firms account for 47 per cent in Rumelt's study of manufacturing (see the figure).[2] However, when Porter and McGahan included service industries as well as manufacturing, they found a larger industry effect (19 per cent).[3]

The implication from this work is that firm-specific factors generally influence profitability more than industry factors. Firms need to attend carefully to their

Per cent of variance in profitability due to:

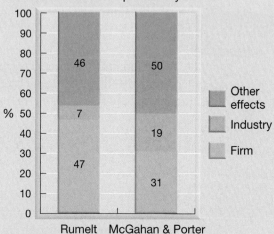

own skills and resources. However, the greater industry effect found in Porter and McGahan's study of both manufacturing and services suggests that industry's importance varies strongly by industry. External influences can matter more in some industries than others.

Notes

1. E.H. Bowman and C.E. Helfat, 'Does corporate strategy matter?', *Strategic Management Journal*, vol. 22, no. 1 (2001), pp. 1–14.
2. R.P. Rumelt, 'How much does industry matter?', *Strategic Management Journal*, vol. 12, no. 2 (1991), pp. 167–185.
3. M.E. Porter and A.M. McGahan, 'How much does industry matter really?', *Strategic Management Journal*, vol. 18, Summer Special Issue (1997), pp. 15–30; M.E. Porter and A.M. McGahan, 'The emergence and sustainability of abnormal profits', *Strategic Organization*, vol. 1, no. 1 (2003), pp. 79–108.

Question

Porter and McGahan's study suggests that some industries influence member firms' profitabilities more than others: in other words, their profitabilities bunch together. Why might some industries have a larger influence on their members' profitability than others?

Work assignments

✳ *Denotes more advanced work assignments.*   * *Refers to a case study in the Text and Cases edition.*

2.1 For an organisation of your choice, and using Illustration 2.1 as a model, carry out a PESTEL analysis and identify key drivers for change.

2.2 ✳ For the same organisation as in 2.1, and using Illustration 2.2 as a model, construct four scenarios for the evolution of its environment. What implications are there for the organisation's strategy?

2.3 Drawing on section 2.3, carry out a five forces analysis of the pharmaceutical industry* or the hifi industry*. What do you conclude about that industry's attractiveness?

2.4 ✳ Drawing on section 2.3, and particularly using the radar plot technique of Exhibit 2.5, choose two industries or sectors and compare their attractiveness in terms of the five forces (a) today; (b) in approximately three to five years' time. Justify your assessment of each of the five forces' strength. Which industry or sector would you invest in?

2.5 With regard to section 2.4.1 and Illustration 2.5, identify an industry (for example, the motor industry or clothing retailers) and, by comparing competitors, map out the main strategic groups in the industry according to key strategic dimensions. Try more than one set of key strategic dimensions to map the industry. Do the resulting maps identify any under-exploited opportunities in the industry?

2.6 ✳ Drawing on section 2.4.4, and particularly on Exhibit 2.8, identify critical success factors for an industry with which you and your peers are familiar (for example, clothing retailers or mobile phone companies). Using your own estimates (or those of your peers), construct a strategy canvas comparing the main competitors, as in Exhibit 2.8. What implications does your strategy canvas have for the strategies of these competitors?

2.7 To what extent are the models discussed in this chapter appropriate for analysing the environments of a public sector or not-for-profit organisation? Give examples to support your arguments.

Integrative assignment

2.8 Carry out a full analysis of an industry or sector of your choice (using for example PESTEL, Scenarios, Five Forces and Strategic Groups). Consider explicitly how the industry or sector is affected by globalisation (see Chapter 8, particularly Exhibit 8.2 on drivers) and innovation (see Chapter 9, particularly Exhibit 9.2 on product and process innovation).

An extensive range of additional materials, including audio summaries, weblinks to organisations featured in the text, definitions of key concepts and self-assessment questions, can be found on the *Exploring Corporate Strategy* Companion Website at **www.pearsoned.co.uk/ecs**

Recommended key readings

- The classic book on the analysis of industries is M.E. Porter, *Competitive Strategy*, Free Press, 1980. An updated view is available in M.E. Porter, 'Strategy and the Internet', *Harvard Business Review*, March (2001), pp. 2–19. An influential adaptation of Porter's basic ideas is W.C. Kim and R. Mauborgne, *Blue Ocean Strategy: How to Create Uncontested Market Space and Make Competition Irrelevant*, Harvard Business School Press, 2005.

- For approaches to how environments change, see K. van der Heijden, *Scenarios: the art of strategic conversation*, 2nd edition, Wiley, 2005, and the work of Michael Porter's colleague, A. McGahan, *How Industries Evolve*, Harvard Business School Press, 2004.

- A collection of academic articles on the latest views on PEST, scenarios and similar is the special issue of *International Studies of Management and Organization*, vol. 36, no. 3 (2006), edited by Peter McKiernan.

References

1. PESTEL is an extension of PEST (Politics, Economics, Social and Technology) analysis, taking more account of environmental ('green') and legal issues. For an application of PEST analysis to the world of business schools, relevant also to PESTEL, see H. Thomas, 'An analysis of the environment and competitive dynamics of management education', *Journal of Management Development*, vol. 26, no. 1 (2007), pp. 9–21.

2. For a discussion of scenario planning in practice, see K. van der Heijden, *Scenarios: the art of strategic conversation*, 2nd edition, Wiley, 2005. For how scenario planning fits with other forms of environmental analysis such as PESTEL, see P. Walsh, 'Dealing with the uncertainties of environmental change by adding scenario planning to the strategy reformulation equation', *Management Decision*, vol. 1, no. 43 (2005), pp. 113–122; and G. Burt, G. Wright, R. Bradfield and K. van der Heijden, 'The role of scenario planning in exploring the environment in view of the limitations of PEST and its derivatives', *International Studies of Management and Organization*, vol. 36, no. 3 (2006), pp. 50–76. For an extension of scenario analysis using causal fields, with a case study on the Iraq War, see B. MacKay and P. McKiernan, 'Back to the future: history and the diagnosis of environmental context', *International Studies of Management and Organization*, vol. 36, no. 3 (2006), pp. 93–110.

3. For the evolution of scenario practice at the Shell oil company, one of the most influential practitioners, see P. Cornelius, A. van de Putte and M. Romani, 'Three decades of scenario planning in Shell', *California Management Review*, vol. 49, no. 1 (2005), pp. 92–109.

4. D. Rutherford, *Routledge Dictionary of Economics*, 2nd edition, Routledge, 1995.

5. See M.E. Porter, *Competitive Strategy: Techniques for analysing industries and competitors*, Free Press, 1980, p. 5.

6. Porter, reference 5, chapter 1. C. Christensen, 'The past and future of competitive advantage', *Sloan Management Review*, vol. 42, no. 2 (2001), pp. 105–109 provides an interesting critique and update of some of the factors underlying Porter's five forces.

7. See L. Van den Berghe and K. Verweire, 'Convergence in the financial services industry', *Geneva Papers on Risk and Insurance*, vol. 25, no. 2 (2000), pp. 262–272; and A. Malhotra and A. Gupta, 'An investigation of firms' responses to industry convergence', *Academy of Management Proceedings*, 2001, pp. G1–6.

8. For discussions of the need for a collaborative as well as Porterian competitive approach to industry analysis, see J. Burton, 'Composite strategy: the combination of collaboration and competition', *Journal of General Management*, vol. 21, no. 1 (1995), pp. 3–28; and R. ul-Haq, *Alliances and Co-evolution: Insights from the Banking Sector*, Palgrave Macmillan, 2005.

9. The classic discussion is A. Brandenburger and B. Nalebuff, 'The right game: use game theory to shape strategy', *Harvard Business Review*, vol. 73, no. 4 (1995), pp. 57–71. On the dangers of 'complementors', see D. Yoffie and M. Kwak, 'With friends like these', *Harvard Business Review*, vol. 84, no. 9 (2006), pp. 88–98.

10. There is a good discussion of the static nature of the Porter model, and other limitations, in M. Grundy, 'Rethinking and reinventing Michael Porter's five forces model', *Strategic Change*, vol. 15 (2006), pp. 213–229.

11. A classic academic overview of the industry life cycle is S. Klepper, 'Industry life cycles', *Industrial and Corporate Change*, vol. 6, no. 1 (1996), pp. 119–143. See also A. McGahan, 'How industries evolve', *Business Strategy Review*, vol. 11, no. 3 (2000), pp. 1–16.

12. A. McGahan, 'How industries evolve', *Business Strategy Review*, vol. 11, no. 3 (2000), pp. 1–16.

13. For a full discussion of the dynamics of competition see R. D'Aveni (with R. Gunther), *Hypercompetitive Rivalries*, Free Press, 1995. For a critical overview of various recent perspectives on hypercompetition and turbulence, plus cases, see J. Slesky, J. Goes and O. Babüroglu, 'Contrasting perspectives of strategy making: applications in hyper environments', *Organization Studies*, vol. 28, no. 1 (2007), pp. 71–94.

14. J. Gimeno and C. Woo, 'Hypercompetition in a multi-market environment: the role of strategic similarity and

multi-market contact on competition de-escalation', *Organisation Science*, vol. 7, no. 3 (1996), pp. 323–341.

15. This definition is from D'Aveni, reference 12, p. 2. In his later book, R. D'Aveni, *Strategic Supremacy: How industry leaders create spheres of influence*, Simon & Schuster International, 2002, he gives examples of strategies that can help defend a strong position in conditions of hyper-competition.

16. G. McNamara, P. Vaaler and C. Devers, 'Same as ever it was: the search for evidence of increasing hypercom-petition', *Strategic Management Journal*, vol. 24 (2003), pp. 261–268; and R. Wiggins and T. Ruefli, 'Schumpeter's ghost: is hypercompetition making the best of times shorter?', *Strategic Management Journal*, vol. 26, no. 10 (2005), pp. 887–911.

17. For a review of the research on strategic groups see J. McGee, H. Thomas and M. Pruett, 'Strategic groups and the analysis of market structure and industry dynamics', *British Journal of Management*, vol. 6, no. 4 (1995), pp. 257–270. For an example of the use of strategic group analysis see C. Flavian, A. Haberberg and Y. Polo, 'Subtle strategic insights from strategic group analysis', *Journal of Strategic Marketing*, vol. 7, no. 2 (1999), pp. 89–106. A recent example is J. Pandian, J. Rajendran, H. Thomas and O. Furrer, 'Performance differences across strategic groups: an examination of financial market-based per-formance measures', *Strategic Change*, vol. 15, nos 7/8 (2006), pp. 373–383.

18. These characteristics are based on Porter, reference 5.

19. A useful discussion of segmentation in relation to competitive strategy is provided in M.E. Porter, *Com-petitive Advantage*, Free Press, 1985, chapter 7. See also the discussion on market segmentation in P. Kotler, G. Armstrong, J. Saunders and V. Wong, *Principles of Marketing*, 3rd European edition, FT/Prentice Hall, 2002, chapter 9. For a more detailed review of segmenta-tion methods see M. Wedel and W. Kamakura, *Market Segmentation: Conceptual and methodological foundations*, 2nd edition, Kluwer Academic, 1999.

20. M. Wedel, 'Is segmentation history?', *Marketing Research*, vol. 13, no. 4 (2001), pp. 26–29.

21. The term 'strategy canvas' was introduced by C. Kim and R. Maubourgne, 'Charting your company's future', *Harvard Business Review*, vol. 80, no. 6 (2002), pp. 76–82. There is similar discussion in G. Johnson, C. Bowman and P. Rudd's chapter, 'Competitor analysis', in V. Ambrosini with G. Johnson and K. Scholes (eds), *Exploring Techniques of Analysis and Evaluation in Strategic Management*, Prentice Hall, 1998.

22. The idea of SWOT as a common-sense checklist has been used for many years: for example, S. Tilles, 'Making strategy explicit', in I. Ansoff (ed.), *Business Strategy*, Penguin, 1968. See also T. Jacobs, J. Shepherd and G. Johnson's chapter on SWOT analysis in V. Ambrosini with G. Johnson and K. Scholes (see reference 21); and E. Valentin, 'SWOT analysis from a resource-based view', *Journal of Marketing Theory and Practice*, vol. 9, no. 2 (2001), pp. 54–69. SWOT will be discussed more fully in section 3.6.4 and Illustration 3.5.

23. W.C. Kim and R. Mauborgne, 'Value innovation: a leap into the blue ocean', *Journal of Business Strategy*, vol. 26, no. 4 (2005), pp. 22–28; and W.C. Kim and R. Mauborgne, *Blue Ocean Strategy: How to Create Uncontested Market Space and Make Competition Irrelevant*, Harvard Business School Press, 2005.

Global forces and the European brewing industry

Mike Blee and Richard Whittington

This case is centred on the European brewing industry and examines how the increasingly competitive pressure of operating within global markets is causing consolidation through acquisitions, alliances and closures within the industry. This has resulted in the growth of the brewers' reliance upon super brands.

In the first decade of the twenty-first century, European brewers faced a surprising paradox. The traditional centre of the beer industry worldwide, and still the largest regional market, Europe, was turning off beer. Beer consumption was falling in the largest markets of Germany and the United Kingdom, while burgeoning in emerging markets around the world. China, with 7 per cent annual growth, had become the largest single market by volume, while Brazilian volumes had overtaken Germany in 2005 (Euromonitor, 2006).

Photo: Picturesbyrob/Alamy

Table 1 details the overall decline of European beer consumption. Decline in traditional key markets is due to several factors. Governments are campaigning strongly against drunken driving, affecting the propensity to drink beer in restaurants, pubs and bars. There is increasing awareness of the effects of alcohol on health and fitness. Particularly In the United Kingdom, there is growing hostility towards so-called 'binge drinking', excessive alcohol consumption in pubs and clubs. Wines have also become increasingly popular in Northern European markets. However, beer consumption per capita varies widely between countries, being four times higher in Germany than in Italy, for example. Some traditionally low-consumption European markets have been showing good growth.

The drive against drunken driving and binge drinking has helped shift sales from the 'on-trade' (beer consumed on the premises, as in pubs or restaurants) to the off-trade (retail). Worldwide, the off-trade increased from 63 per cent of volume in 2000 to 66 per cent in 2005. The off-trade is increasingly dominated by large supermarket chains such as Tesco or Carrefour, which often use cut-price offers on beer in order to lure people into their shops. More than one-fifth of beer volume is now sold through supermarkets. German retailers such as Aldi and Lidl have had considerable success with their own 'private-label' (rather than brewery-branded) beers. However, although on-trade volumes are falling in Europe, the sales values are rising, as brewers introduce higher-priced premium products such as extra-cold lagers or fruit-flavoured beers. On the other hand, a good deal of this increasing demand for premium products is being satisfied by the import of apparently exotic beers from overseas (see Table 2).

Brewers' main purchasing costs are packaging (accounting for around half of non-labour costs), raw material such as barley, and energy. The European packaging industry is highly concentrated, dominated by international companies such as Crown in cans and Owens-Illinois in glass bottles. During 2006, Dutch brewer Heineken complained of an 11 per cent rise in packaging costs.

Table 1 European beer consumption by country and year (000 hectolitres)

Country	1980	2000	2001	2002	2003	2004	2005
Austria	7651	8762	8627	8734	8979	8881	8970
Belgium	12945	10064	9986	9901	9935	9703	N/A
Denmark	6698	5452	5282	5202	5181	4862	N/A
Finland	2738	4024	4085	4136	4179	4370	N/A
France	23745	21420	21331	20629	21168	20200	N/A
Germany†	89820	103105	100904	100385	97107	95639	94994
Greece	N/A	4288	4181	4247	3905	N/A	N/A
Ireland	4174	5594	5625	5536	5315	5206	N/A
Italy	9539	16289	16694	16340	17452	17194	17340
Luxembourg	417	472	445	440	373	N/A	N/A
Netherlands	12213	13129	12922	11985	12771	12687	12747
Norway*	7651	2327	2290	2420	2270	2490	N/A
Portugal	3534	6453	6276	5948	6008	6266	6224
Spain	20065	29151	31126	30715	33451	N/A	N/A
Sweden	3935	5011	4932	4998	4969	4635	4566
Switzerland*	4433	4194	4141	4127	4334	4262	N/A
UK	65490	57007	58234	59384	60302	59195	N/A

* Non-EU countries; †1980 excludes GDR. Figures adjusted.

Source: www.Brewersofeurope.org.

Table 2 Imports of beer by country

Country	Imports 2002 (% of consumption or production*)	Imports 2004 (% of consumption or production)
Austria	5.1	6.4
Belgium	4.74	10.2
Denmark	2.6	N/A
Finland	2.3	7.3
France	23	31
Germany	3.1	4
Greece	4.1	N/A
Ireland	N/A	N/A
Italy	27.15	37
Luxembourg	N/A	38.4
Netherlands	3.2	14.4
Norway	5.4	N/A
Portugal	1.1	N/A
Spain	11.7	N/A
Sweden	N/A	18
Switzerland	15.4	15.6
UK	10.9	12.3

* Import figures do not include beers brewed under licence in home country; countries vary in measuring % of production or consumption.

Source: www.brewersofeurope.org.

Acquisition, licensing and strategic alliances have all occurred as the leading brewers battle to control the market. There are global pressures for consolidation due to overcapacity within the industry, the need to contain costs and benefits of leveraging strong brands. For example, Belgian brewer Interbrew purchased parts of the old Bass Empire, Becks and Whitbread in 2001 and in 2004 announced a merger with Am Bev, the Brazilian brewery group, to create the largest brewer in the world, InBev. The second largest brewer, the American Anheuser-Busch, has been investing in China, Mexico and Europe. In 2002, South African Breweries acquired the Miller Group (USA) and Pilsner Urquell in the Czech Republic, becoming SABMiller. Smaller players in fast-growing Chinese and South American markets are being snapped up by the large international brewers too. Medium-sized Australian brewer Fosters is withdrawing from direct participation in many international markets, for example selling its European brand-rights to Scottish & Newcastle. Table 3 lists the world's top 10 brewing companies, which accounted for around half of world beer volumes. There remain many small specialist and regional

Table 3 The world's top 10 brewery companies by volume: 2005

Company	Share global volume (%)	Country of origin
InBev	10.8	Brazil–Belgium
Anheuser-Busch	9.4	USA
SABMiller	7.3	South Africa (relocated to UK)
Heineken	5.7	Netherlands
Morelo	2.9	Mexico
Carlsberg	2.9	Denmark
Coors	2.6	USA
TsingTao	2.4	China
Baltic Brewery Holdings	2.2	Denmark/UK
Asahi	2.1	Japan

Source: Euromonitor International, *The World Brewing Industry*.

brewers, such as the Dutch company Grolsch (see below) or the British Cobra Beer, originating in the Indian restaurant market.

Four brewing companies

Heineken (The Netherlands)

Heineken is the biggest of the European brewery businesses, and has three-quarters of its sales in the region. Total sales in 2006 were €11.8bn (£8bn). About 5 per cent of sales are in Asia–Pacific and 17 per cent of sales are in the Americas. The company's biggest brands are Heineken itself and Amstel. The company remains a family-controlled business, which it claims gives it the stability and independence to pursue steady growth internationally.

Heineken's strategy overseas is to use locally acquired companies as a means of introducing the Heineken brand to new markets. It aims to strengthen local companies by transferring expertise and technology. The result is to create economies of scale for both the local beers and Heineken. Heineken's four priorities for action are to accelerate revenue growth, to improve efficiency and cost reduction, to speed up strategy implementation and to focus on those markets where the company believes it can win.

Grolsch (The Netherlands)

Royal Grolsch NV is a medium-size international brewing group, established in 1615. With overall sales in 2005 of €313m, it is less than a twentieth of the size of Heineken. Its key products include Grolsch premium lager and new flavoured beers (Grolsch lemon and Grolsch pink grapefruit). In The Netherlands Grolsch holds the rights for the sale and distribution of the valued US Miller brand. About half its sales are obtained overseas, either through export or licensing of production: the United Kingdom is its second largest market. In 2005, Grolsch centralised its own production on a single new Dutch brewery to increase efficiency and volume, and opened a small additional 'trial' brewery in order to support innovation.

Innovation and branding are core to the company's strategy. The company believes that its strong and distinctive beers can succeed in a market of increased homogenisation. Its brand is reinforced by its striking green bottles and its unique swing-tops.

InBev (Belgium/Brazil)

InBev was created in 2004 from the merger of Belgian InterBrew and Brazilian AmBev. With a turnover of €13.3bn in 2006, it is the largest brewer in the world, holding number one or number two positions in 20 different countries. Its well-known international brands include Beck's and Stella Artois. Through a series of acquisitions, InBev has become the second largest brewer in China.

The company is frank about its strategy: to transform itself from the biggest brewing company in the world to the best. It aims to do this by building strong global brands and increasing efficiency. Efficiency gains will come from more central coordination of purchasing, including media and IT; from the optimisation of its inherited network of breweries; and from the sharing of best practice across sites internationally. Although acquisitions continue, InBev is now emphasising organic growth and improved margins from its existing businesses.

Scottish and Newcastle (UK)

Scottish and Newcastle is a European-focused brewing group based in Edinburgh. In 2005, its turnover was £3.9bn (€5.5bn). Its key brands include John Smiths, Kronenbourg, Kanterbrau, Baltika and (in Europe) Fosters. It is the fourth largest brewer in Europe in volume terms, and market leader in the UK, France and Russia. The company has made many acquisitions in the UK (including Bulmer's cider), France, Greece and Finland. The group's 50 per cent investment in Baltic Beverages has given it exposure to the fast-growing markets of Russia, Ukraine and the Baltic countries. In China, Scottish and Newcastle has a 20 per cent stake in CBC, the country's fifth largest brewery. In India, the company's United Breweries is the country's largest brewer, with the Kingfisher brand. In the USA, Scottish and Newcastle is the second largest importer of foreign beers. The company emphasises the development of innovative and premium beers, and is closing down its more inefficient breweries.

Questions

1 Using the data from the case (and any other sources available), carry out for the European brewing industry (i) a PESTEL analysis and (ii) a five forces analysis. What do you conclude?

2 For the four breweries outlined above (or breweries of your own choice) explain:
   (a) how these trends will impact differently on these different companies; and
   (b) the relative strengths and weaknesses of each company.

Strategic Capability

LEARNING OUTCOMES

After reading this chapter you should be able to:

→ Distinguish elements of strategic capability in organisations: resources, competences, core competences and dynamic capabilities.

→ Recognise the role of continual improvement in cost efficiency as a strategic capability.

→ Analyse how strategic capabilities might provide sustainable competitive advantage on the basis of their value, rarity, inimitability and non-substitutability.

→ Diagnose strategic capability by means of value chain analysis, activity mapping, benchmarking and SWOT analysis.

→ Consider how managers can develop strategic capabilities of organisations.

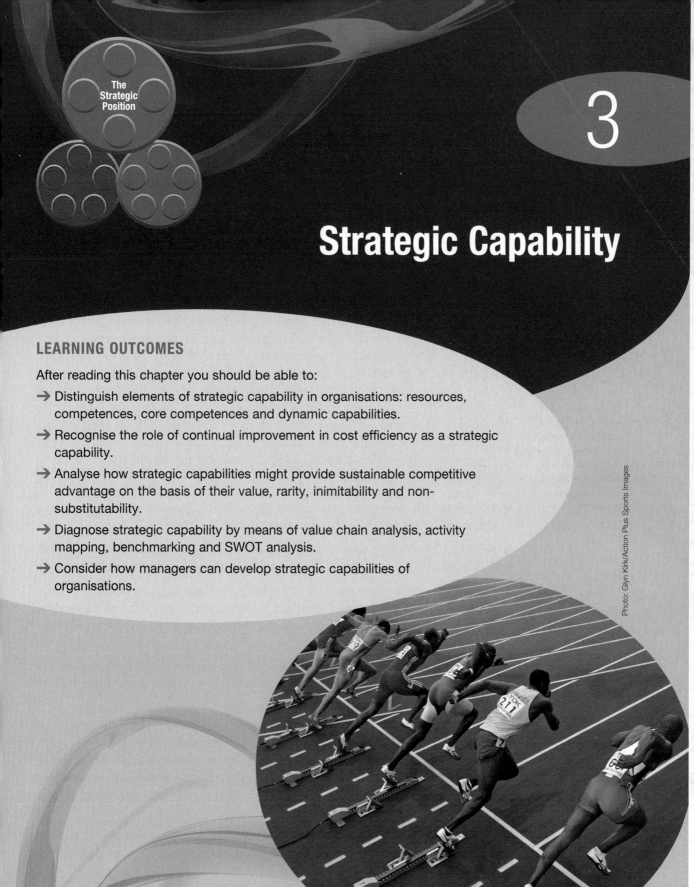

Photo: Glyn Kirk/Action Plus Sports Images

3.1 INTRODUCTION

Chapter 2 outlined how the external environment of an organisation can create both strategic opportunities and threats. However, Tesco, Sainsbury's and Asda all compete in the same environment, yet Tesco is a superior performer. It is not the environment that distinguishes between them but their internal *strategic capabilities*. The importance of strategic capability is the focus of this chapter. There are three key concepts that underpin the discussion. The first is that organisations are not identical, but have different capabilities; they are 'heterogeneous' in this respect. The second is that it can be difficult for one organisation to obtain or copy the capabilities of another. For example, Sainsbury's cannot readily obtain the whole of Tesco's retail sites, its management or its experience. The third arises from these: if an organisation is to achieve competitive advantage, it will do so on the basis of capabilities that its rivals do not have or have difficulty in obtaining. In turn this helps explain how some organisations are able to achieve superior performance compared with others. They have capabilities that permit them to produce at lower cost or generate a superior product or service at standard cost in relation to other organisations with inferior capabilities.[1] These concepts underlie what has become known as the **resource-based view** of strategy[2] (though it might more appropriately be labelled the 'capabilities view'): that the competitive advantage and superior performance of an organisation is explained by the distinctiveness of its capabilities.

The chapter has six sections:

● Section 3.2 discusses the *foundations of strategic capability* and considers the distinction between *resources* and *competences*.

● Section 3.3 is concerned with a vital basis of strategic capability of any organisation, namely the ability to achieve and continually improve *cost efficiency*.

● Section 3.4 considers what sort of capabilities allow organisations to *sustain* competitive advantage over time (in a public sector context the equivalent concern might be how some organisations sustain relative superior performance over time).

● Section 3.5 discusses how the concept of *organisational knowledge* relates to strategic capability and how it might contribute to competitive advantage of organisations.

● Section 3.6 moves on to consider different ways strategic capability might be analysed. These include *value chain* and *value network* analyses, *activity mapping* and *benchmarking*. The section concludes by explaining the use of *SWOT* analysis as a basis for pulling together the insights from the analyses of the environment (explained in Chapter 2) and of strategic capability in this chapter.

● Finally section 3.7 discusses how managers can *develop strategic capability* through internal and external development, the management of people and the building of dynamic capabilities.

The **resource-based view** of strategy: the competitive advantage and superior performance of an organisation is explained by the distinctiveness of its capabilities

3.2 FOUNDATIONS OF STRATEGIC CAPABILITY

Strategic capability is the resources and competences of an organisation needed for it to survive and prosper

Different writers, managers and consultants use different terms and concepts in explaining the importance of strategic capability. Given such differences, it is important to understand how the terms are used here. Overall, **strategic capability** can be defined as the resources and competences of an organisation needed for it to survive and prosper. Exhibit 3.1 shows the elements of strategic capability that are employed in the chapter to explain the concept.

Exhibit 3.1 Strategic capabilities and competitive advantage

	Resources	Competences
Threshold capabilities	**Threshold resources** ● Tangible ● Intangible	**Threshold competences**
Capabilities for competitive advantage	**Unique resources** ● Tangible ● Intangible	**Core competences**

3.2.1 Resources and competences

Tangible resources are the physical assets of an organisation such as plant, labour and finance

Intangible resources are non-physical assets such as information, reputation and knowledge

Perhaps the most basic concept is that of *resources*. **Tangible resources** are the physical assets of an organisation such as plant, people and finance. **Intangible resources**[3] are non-physical assets such as information, reputation and knowledge. Typically, an organisation's resources can be considered under the following four broad categories:

● *Physical resources* – such as the machines, buildings or the production capacity of the organisation. The nature of these resources, such as the age, condition, capacity and location of each resource, will determine the usefulness of such resources.

● *Financial resources* – such as capital, cash, debtors and creditors, and suppliers of money (shareholders, bankers, etc.).

● *Human resources* – including the mix (for example, demographic profile), skills and knowledge of employees and other people in an organisation's networks.

● *Intellectual capital* – as an intangible resource – includes patents, brands, business systems and customer databases. An indication of the value of these is that when businesses are sold, part of the value is 'goodwill'. In a knowledge-based economy intellectual capital is likely to be a major asset of many organisations.

Such resources are certainly important, but what an organisation does – how it employs and deploys these resources – matters at least as much as what resources it has. There would be no point in having state-of-the-art equipment or valuable knowledge or a valuable brand if they were not used effectively. The efficiency and effectiveness of physical or financial resources, or the people in an organisation, depends on not just their existence but how they are managed, the cooperation between people, their adaptability, their innovatory capacity, the relationship with customers and suppliers, and the experience and learning about what works well and what does not. The term **competences** is used to mean the skills and abilities by which resources are deployed effectively through an organisation's activities and processes.

Within these broad definitions, other terms are commonly used. As the explanation proceeds, it might be useful to refer to the two examples provided in Exhibit 3.2, one relating the concepts to a business and the other to sport.

> **Competences** are the skills and abilities by which resources are deployed effectively through an organisation's activities and processes

3.2.2 Threshold capabilities

A distinction needs to be made between capabilities (resources or competences) that are at a threshold level and those that might help the organisation achieve

---

Exhibit 3.2 **Strategic capability: the terminology**

Term	Definition	Example (athletics)
Strategic capability	The ability to perform at the level required to survive and prosper. It is underpinned by the resources and competences of the organisation	Equipment and athletic ability suited to a chosen event
Threshold resources	The resources needed to meet customers' minimum requirements and therefore to continue to exist	A healthy body (for individuals) Medical facilities and practitioners Training venues and equipment Food supplements
Threshold competences	Activities and processes needed to meet customers' minimum requirements and therefore to continue to exist	Individual training regimes Physiotherapy/injury management Diet planning
Unique resources	Resources that underpin competitive advantage and are difficult for competitors to imitate or obtain	Exceptional heart and lungs Height or weight World-class coach
Core competences	Activities that underpin competitive advantage and are difficult for competitors to imitate or obtain	A combination of dedication, tenacity, time to train, demanding levels of competition and a will to win

Threshold capabilities are those capabilities needed for an organisation to meet the necessary requirements to compete in a given market

competitive advantage and superior performance. **Threshold capabilities** are those needed for an organisation to meet the necessary requirements to compete in a given market. These could be *threshold resources* required to meet minimum customer requirements: for example, the increasing demands by modern multiple retailers of their suppliers mean that those suppliers have to possess a quite sophisticated IT infrastructure simply to stand a chance of meeting retailer requirements. Or they could be the *threshold competences* required to deploy resources so as to meet customers' requirements and support particular strategies. Retailers do not simply expect suppliers to have the required IT infrastructure, but to be able to use it effectively so as to guarantee the required level of service.

Identifying and managing threshold capabilities raises at least two significant challenges:

- *Threshold levels of capability will change* as critical success factors change (see section 2.4.4) or through the activities of competitors and new entrants. To continue the example, suppliers to major retailers did not require the same level of IT and logistics support a decade ago. But the retailers' drive to reduce costs, improve efficiency and ensure availability of merchandise to their customers means that their expectations of their suppliers have increased markedly in that time and continue to do so. So there is a need for those suppliers continuously to review and improve their logistics resource and competence base just to stay in business.

- *Trade-offs* may need to be made to achieve the threshold capability required for different sorts of customers. For example, businesses have found it difficult to compete in market segments that require large quantities of standard product as well as market segments that require added value specialist products. Typically, the first requires high-capacity, fast-throughput plant, standardised highly efficient systems and a low-cost labour force; the second a skilled labour force, flexible plant and a more innovative capacity. The danger is that an organisation fails to achieve the threshold capabilities required for either segment.

KEY CONCEPT

Core competences 3.2.3

Unique resources are those resources that critically underpin competitive advantage and that others cannot easily imitate or obtain

Core competences are the skills and abilities by which resources are deployed through an organisation's activities and processes such as to achieve competitive advantage in ways that others cannot imitate or obtain

3.2.3 Unique resources and core competences

While threshold capabilities are important, they do not of themselves create competitive advantage or the basis of superior performance. These are dependent on an organisation having distinctive or unique capabilities that competitors will find difficult to imitate. This could be because the organisation has **unique resources** that critically underpin competitive advantage and that others cannot imitate or obtain – a long-established brand, for example. It is, however, more likely that an organisation achieves competitive advantage because it has distinctive, or core, competences. The concept of core competences was developed, most notably, by Gary Hamel and C.K. Prahalad. While various definitions exist, here **core competences**[4] are taken to mean the skills and abilities by which resources are deployed through an organisation's activities and processes such as to achieve competitive advantage in ways that others cannot imitate or obtain. For example, a supplier that achieves competitive advantage in a retail market

Illustration 3.1

Strategic capabilities

Executives emphasise different strategic capabilities in different organisations.

Freeport-McMoRan Copper and Gold, Inc. is an international mining company in North America. It claims a leading position in the mining industry on the basis of 'large, long lived, geographically diverse assets and significant proven and probable reserves of copper, gold and molybdenum'. More specifically, in terms of its Indonesian operation it points to a 'principal asset' as the 'world class Grasberg mine discovered in 1988' which has 'the world's largest single copper reserve and world's largest single gold reserve'.

Source: Annual Report 2006.

Daniel Bouton, Chairman and CEO of **Société Générale**, in response to the question: *How do you maintain your competitive advantage in equity derivatives?*

The barrier to entry is high, because of two significant costs. The first is IT. The systems you need to perform well cost at least €200 million a year, and it's not something you can buy from Dell or SAP. The second is the sheer number of people you need to work on managing your risk. Before you launch a product, you need to have the front office guys that propose, calculate and write the first model. Then you need the IT guy that creates the IT system in order to be able to calculate risks every 10 seconds. And you need a good validating team in order to verify all the hypotheses. After that, you need high-quality middle and back office people.

Source: Interviewed by Clive Horwood in *Euromoney*, vol. 27, no. 447 (July 2006), pp. 84–89.

Tony Hall, Chief Executive of the **Royal Opera House**:

'world-class' is neither an idle nor boastful claim. In the context of the Royal Opera House the term refers to the quality of our people, the standards of our productions and the diversity of our work and initiatives. Unique? Unashamedly so. We shy away from labels such as 'elite', because of the obvious negative connotations of exclusiveness. But I want people to take away from here the fact that we are elite in the sense that we have the best singers, dancers, directors, designers, orchestra,

chorus, backstage crew and administrative staff. We are also amongst the best in our ability to reach out to as wide and diverse a community as possible.

Source: Annual Review 2005/6, p. 11.

Dave Swift, President of **Whirlpool** North America:

Executing our strategy requires a unique toolkit of competencies that we continue to build for our people globally. The starting point of building new competencies is what we call 'Customer Excellence' – our ability to proactively understand and anticipate the needs of customers. Customer Excellence is a collection of tools that allows our people to analytically assess and prioritize the needs and desires of customers along all aspects of the purchase cycle – from when they first might investigate an appliance on a web site, to the in-store experience on a retailer's floor, to the features and aesthetics of the product, to the installation and service experience, and ultimately to their need to repeat this cycle. With these consumer insights in-hand, we then turn them into customer solutions through our innovation tools. As a result, our innovation capability has produced a robust pipeline of products, achieving a steady-state estimated value of over $3 billion. . . . Our knowledge of customers, coupled with our innovative customer solutions, is driving the attractiveness of our brands and creating greater value for our shareholders.

Source: Whirlpool Corporation 2005 Annual Report.

Questions

1 Categorise the range of capabilities highlighted by the executives in terms of section 3.2 and Exhibit 3.2.

2 With reference to section 3.4, which of the capabilities might be especially important in terms of achieving competitive advantage and why?

3 For an organisation of your choice undertake the same exercise as in questions 1 and 2 above.

might have done so on the basis of a unique resource such as a powerful brand, or by finding ways of providing service or building relationships with that retailer in ways that its competitors find difficult to imitate – a core competence. Section 3.4 of this chapter discusses in more depth the role played by unique resources and core competences in contributing to long-term competitive advantage.

Putting these concepts together, the summary argument is this. To survive and prosper an organisation needs to address the challenges of the environment that it faces, discussed in Chapter 2. In particular it must be capable of performing in terms of the critical success factors that arise from demands and needs of its customers, discussed in section 2.4.4. The strategic capability to do so is dependent on the resources and the competences it has. These must reach a threshold level in order for the organisation to survive. The further challenge is to achieve competitive advantage. This requires it to have strategic capabilities that its competitors find difficult to imitate or obtain. These could be unique resources but are more likely to be the core competences of the organisation. Illustration 3.1 shows how executives of different organisations describe the strategic capabilities of their organisations.

3.3 COST EFFICIENCY

Managers often refer to the management of costs as a key strategic capability. So it is. Moreover, understanding the management of cost efficiency as a strategic capability illustrates some of the points made in section 3.2.

Customers can benefit from cost efficiencies in terms of lower prices or more product features for the same price. The management of the cost base of an organisation could also be a basis for achieving competitive advantage (see sections 6.3.1 and 6.4.1). However, for many organisations the management of costs is becoming a threshold strategic capability for two reasons:

● *Customers do not value product features at any price*. If the price rises too high they will sacrifice value and opt for lower price. So the challenge is to ensure that an appropriate level of value is offered at an acceptable price. This means that everyone is forced to keep costs as low as possible, consistent with the value to be provided. Not to do so invites customers to switch products or invites competition.

● *Competitive rivalry* will continually require the driving down of costs because competitors will be trying to reduce their cost so as to underprice their rivals while offering similar value.

If cost is to be managed effectively, attention has to be paid to key *cost drivers* (see Exhibit 3.3), as follows:

● *Economies of scale* may be especially important in manufacturing organisations, since the high capital costs of plant need to be recovered over a high volume of output. Traditionally manufacturing sectors where this has been especially important have been motor vehicles, chemicals and metals. In other industries, such as drinks and tobacco and food, scale economies are important in distribution or marketing.[5]

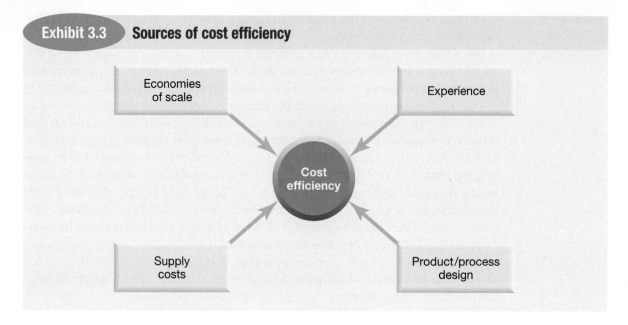

Exhibit 3.3 **Sources of cost efficiency**

- *Supply costs* can be important. Location may influence supply costs, which is why, historically, steel and glass manufacturing were close to raw material or energy sources. In some instances, ownership of raw materials was a unique resource, giving cost advantage. Supply costs are of particular importance to organisations that act as intermediaries, where the value added through their own activities is low and the need to identify and manage input costs is critically important to success. For example, retailers pay a great deal of attention to trying to achieve lower costs of supply than their competitors.

- *Product/process design* also influences cost. Efficiency gains in production processes have been achieved by many organisations through improvements in *capacity-fill*, *labour productivity*, *yield* (from materials) or *working capital* utilisation. Understanding the relative importance of each of these to maintaining a competitive position is important. For example, in terms of managing capacity-fill: an unfilled seat in a plane, train or theatre cannot be 'stocked' for later sale. So marketing special offers (while protecting the core business) and having the IT systems to analyse and optimise revenue are important capabilities. Product design will also influence costs in other parts of the value system – for example, in distribution or after-sales service. In the photocopier market, for example, Canon eroded Xerox's advantage (which was built on service and a support network) by designing a copier that needed far less servicing.

- *Experience*[6] can be a key source of cost efficiency and there is evidence it may provide competitive advantage in particular in terms of the relationship between the cumulative experience gained by an organisation and its unit costs – described as the *experience curve*. See Exhibit 3.4. The experience curve suggests that an organisation undertaking any activity develops competences in this activity over time and therefore does it more efficiently. Since companies with higher market share have more 'cumulative experience' – simply because high share gives them greater volumes of production or service – it follows that it is important to gain and hold market share, as discussed in Chapter 2. It is important to remember that it is the *relative market share* in

| Exhibit 3.4 | The experience curve |

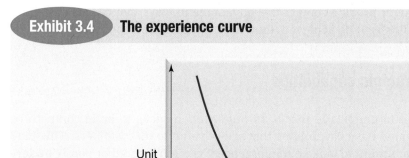

The lessons of sections 3.2 and 3.3 are these: if the capabilities of an organisation do not meet customer needs, at least to a threshold level, the organisation cannot survive; and if managers do not manage costs efficiently and continue to improve on this, it will be vulnerable to those who can. However, if the aim is to achieve *competitive advantage* then the further question is: what strategic

definable market segments that matters. There are important implications of the experience curve concept that could influence an organisation's competitive position.

- *Growth is not optional* in many markets. If an organisation chooses to grow more slowly than the competition, it should expect the competitors to gain cost advantage in the longer term – through experience.

- *Unit costs should decline year on year* as a result of cumulative experience. In high-growth industries this will happen quickly, but even in mature industries this decline in costs should occur. Organisations that fail to achieve this are likely to suffer at the hands of competitors who do. The implication of this is that *continual reduction in costs is a necessity* for organisations in competitive markets. Even if it is not able to provide competitive advantage, it is a threshold competence for survival.

- *First-mover advantage* can be important. The organisation that moves down the experience curve by getting into a market first should be able to reduce its cost base because of the accumulated experience it builds up over its rivals by being first.

3.4 CAPABILITIES FOR ACHIEVING AND SUSTAINING COMPETITIVE ADVANTAGE

The lessons of sections 3.2 and 3.3 are these: if the capabilities of an organisation do not meet customer needs, at least to a threshold level, the organisation cannot survive; and if managers do not manage costs efficiently and continue to improve on this, it will be vulnerable to those who can. However, if the aim is to achieve *competitive advantage* then the further question is: what strategic capabilities might provide competitive advantage in ways that can be sustained over time? If this is to be achieved, then other criteria are important.[7]

3.4.1 Value of strategic capabilities

It is important to emphasise that if an organisation seeks to build competitive advantage it must have capabilities that are of value to its customers. This may seem an obvious point to make but in practice it is often ignored or poorly understood. Managers may argue that some distinctive capability of their organisation is of value simply because it is distinctive. Having capabilities that are different from other organisations is not, of itself, a basis of competitive advantage. So the discussion in section 2.4.4 and the lessons it draws are important here too. Managers should consider carefully which of their organisation's activities are especially important in providing such value. They should also consider which are less valued. Value chain analysis and activity mapping explained in sections 3.6.1 and 3.6.2 can help here.

3.4.2 Rarity of strategic capabilities

Competitive advantage might be achieved if a competitor possesses a unique or rare capability. This could take the form of *unique resources*. For example, some libraries have unique collections of books unavailable elsewhere; a company may have a powerful brand; retail stores may have prime locations. Some organisations have patented products or services that give them advantage – resources that may need to be defended by a willingness to bring litigation against illegal imitators. For service organisations unique resources may be intellectual capital – particularly talented individuals.

Competitive advantage could also be based on rare competences: for example, unique skills developed over time. However, there are three important points to bear in mind about the extent to which rarity of competences might provide sustainable competitive advantage:

- *Ease of transferability*. Rarity may depend on who owns the competence and how easily transferable it is. For example, the competitive advantage of some professional service organisations is built around the competence of specific individuals – such as a doctor in 'leading-edge' medicine, individual fund managers, the manager of a top sports team or the CEO of a business. But since these individuals may leave or join competitors, this resource may be a fragile basis of advantage. More durable advantage *may* be found in competences that exist for recruiting, training, motivating and rewarding such individuals or be embedded in the culture that attracts them to the organisation – so ensuring that they do not defect to 'competitors'.

- *Sustainability*. It may be dangerous to assume that competences that are rare will remain so. *Rarity could be temporary*. If an organisation is successful on the basis of a unique set of competences, then competitors will seek to imitate or obtain those competences. So it may be necessary to consider other bases of sustainability.

- *Core rigidities*. There is another danger of redundancy. Rare capabilities may come to be what Dorothy Leonard-Barton refers to as *'core rigidities'*,[8] difficult to change and therefore damaging to the organisation. Managers may be so wedded to these bases of success that they perceive them as strengths of the organisation and 'invent' customer values around them.

3.4.3 Inimitable strategic capabilities[9]

It should be clear by now that the search for strategic capability that provides sustainable competitive advantage is not straightforward. It involves identifying capabilities that are likely to be durable and which competitors find difficult to imitate or obtain.

At the risk of overgeneralisation, it is unusual for competitive advantage to be explainable by differences in the tangible resources of organisations, since over time these can usually be imitated or traded. Advantage is more likely to be determined by the way in which resources are deployed to create competences in the organisation's activities. For example, as suggested earlier, an IT system itself will not improve an organisation's competitive standing: it is how it is used that matters. Indeed, what will probably make most difference is how the system is used to bring together customer needs with activities and knowledge both inside and outside the organisation. It is therefore to do with linking sets of competences. So, extending the earlier definition, *core competences* are likely to be the skills and abilities to *link* activities or processes through which resources are deployed so as to achieve competitive advantage. In order to achieve this advantage, core competences therefore need to fulfil the following criteria:

- They must relate to an activity or process that underpins the value in the product or service features – as seen through the eyes of the customer (or other powerful stakeholder). This is the value criterion discussed earlier.

- The competences must lead to levels of performance that are significantly better than competitors (or similar organisations in the public sector).

- The competences must be difficult for competitors to imitate – or inimitable.

With regard to this third requirement of inimitability, Exhibit 3.5 summarises how this might be achieved and Illustration 3.2 also gives an example. The three main reasons are:

Complexity[10]

The core competences of an organisation may be difficult to imitate because they are complex. This may be for two main reasons.

- *Internal linkages*. It may be the ability to link activities and processes that, together, deliver customer value. The managers in Plasco (see Illustration 3.2) talked about 'flexibility' and 'innovation', but 'flexibility' or 'innovation' are themselves made up of and dependent on sets of related activities as Illustration 3.2 shows. Section 3.6.2 and Exhibit 3.8 below show how such linked sets of activities might be mapped so that they can be better understood. However, even if a competitor possessed such a map, it is unlikely that it would be able to replicate the sort of complexity it represents.

Illustration 3.2

Strategic capability for Plasco

Strategic capability underpinning competitive success may be based on complex linkages rooted in the history and culture of an organisation.

Plasco, a manufacturer of plastics goods, had won several major retail accounts from competitors. Managers were keen to understand the bases of these successes as a way of understanding strategic capabilities better. To do this they undertook an analysis of customer value (as explained in section 2.4.4). From this they identified that the major retailers with whom it had been successful particularly valued a powerful brand, a good product range, innovation, good service and reliable delivery. In particular, Plasco was outperforming competitors when it came to delivery, service and product range.

They then undertook an activity mapping exercise, as explained in section 3.6.2 (see Exhibit 3.8). Some of what emerged from this the senior management knew about; but they were not aware of some of the other explanations for success that emerged.

When they analysed the bases of reliable delivery, they could not find reasons why they were outperforming competitors. The logistics of the company were no different from other companies. They were essential but not unique – threshold resources and competences.

When they examined the activities that gave rise to the good service they provided, however, they found other explanations. They were readily able to identify that much was down to their having a more flexible approach than their competitors, the main one of which was a major US multinational. But the explanations for this flexibility were less obvious. The flexibility took form, for example, in the ability to amend the requirements of the retailers' orders at short notice; or when the buyers in the retailers had made an error, to 'bale them out' by taking back stock that had been delivered. What was much less obvious were the activities underpinning this flexibility. The mapping surfaced some explanations:

- The junior manager and staff within the firm were 'bending the rules' to take back goods from the major retailers when, strictly speaking, the policies and systems of the business did not allow it.
- Plant utilisation was relatively lower and less automated than competitors, so it was easier to change production runs at short notice. Company policy, on the other hand, was to improve productivity through increased utilisation and to begin to automate the plans. Lower levels of production management were not anxious to do this, knowing that if they did, it would reduce the flexibility and therefore diminish their ability to provide the service customers wanted.

Much of this was down to the knowledge of quite junior managers, sales representatives and staff in the factory as to 'how to work the system' and how to work together to solve the retailers' problems. This was not a matter of company policy or formal training, but custom and practice that had built up over the years. The result was a relationship between sales personnel and retail buyers in which buyers were encouraged to 'ask the impossible' of the company when difficulties arose.

Sound logistics and good-quality products were vital, but the core competences which underpinned their success were the result of linked sets of activities built up over the years which it was difficult, not only for competitors but also for people in the organisation, to identify clearly.

Questions

1 Why might it be difficult for a large, automated US plastics manufacturer to deal with retailers in the same way as Plasco?

2 How should Plasco senior managers respond to the explanations of strategic capability surfaced by the mapping?

3 What could erode the bases of competitive advantage that Plasco has?

Exhibit 3.5 **Criteria for inimitability of strategic capabilities**

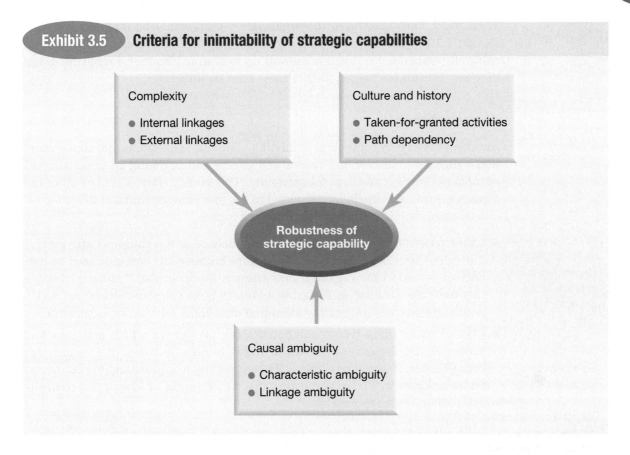

● *External interconnectedness*. Organisations can make it difficult for others to imitate or obtain their bases of competitive advantage by developing activities together with the customer on which the customer is dependent on them. This is sometimes referred to as *co-specialisation*. For example, an industrial lubricants business moved away from just selling its products to customers by coming to agreements with them to manage the applications of lubricants within the customers' sites against agreed targets on cost savings. The more efficient the use of lubricants, the more both parties benefited. Similarly software businesses can achieve advantage by developing computer programs that are distinctively beneficial to specific customer needs.

Culture and history

Core competences may become embedded in an organisation's culture. Indeed, managers within an organisation may not understand them *explicitly* themselves. So coordination between various activities occurs 'naturally' because people know their part in the wider picture or it is simply 'taken for granted' that activities are done in particular ways. For example, in Plasco the experience in rapid changes in production runs and the close links between sales personnel, production and despatch were not planned or formalised: they were the way the firm had come to operate over the years.

Linked to this cultural embeddedness, therefore, is the likelihood that such competences have developed over time and in a particular way. The origins and history by which competences have developed over time are referred to as *path dependency*,[11] are specific to the organisation and cannot be imitated (also see section 5.3.1). Again, however, it should be noted that there is a danger that culturally embedded competences built up over time become so embedded that they are difficult to change: they become core rigidities.

Causal ambiguity[12]

Another reason why competences might be difficult to imitate is that competitors find it difficult to discern the causes and effects underpinning an organisation's advantage. This is called *causal ambiguity*. This could relate to any or all of the aspects of strategic capability discussed in the preceding sections of this chapter. Causal ambiguity may exist in two different forms:[13]

● *Characteristic ambiguity* – where the significance of the characteristic itself is difficult to discern or comprehend, perhaps because it is based on tacit knowledge or rooted in the organisation's culture. For example, it is quite possible that the 'rule bending' in Plasco would have been counter-cultural for its US rival and therefore not readily identified or seen as relevant or significant.

● *Linkage ambiguity* – where competitors cannot discern which activities and processes are dependent on which others to form linkages that create core competences. It would be difficult for competitors to understand the cause and effect linkages in Plasco given that the management of Plasco did not fully comprehend them themselves.

3.4.4 Non-substitutability of strategic capabilities[14]

Providing value to customers and possessing competences that are complex, culturally embedded and causally ambiguous may mean that it is very difficult for organisations to copy them. However, the organisation may still be at risk from substitution. Substitution could take two different forms:

● *Product or service substitution*. As already discussed in Chapter 2 in relation to the five forces model of competition, a product or service as a whole might be a victim of substitution. For example, increasingly e-mail systems have substituted for postal systems. No matter how complex and culturally embedded were the competences of the postal service, it could not avoid this sort of substitution.

● *Competence substitution*. Substitution might, however, not be at the product or service level but at the competence level. For example, task-based industries have often suffered because of an over-reliance on the competences of skilled craftworkers that have been replaced by expert systems and mechanisation.

In summary and from a resource-based view of organisations, managers need to consider whether their organisation has strategic capabilities to achieve and sustain competitive advantage. To do so they need to consider how and to what extent it has capabilities which are (i) valuable to buyers, (ii) rare, (iii) inimitable and (iv) non-substitutable. If such capabilities for competitive advantage do not exist, then managers need to consider if they can be developed. How this might be done is considered in section 3.7 below.

3.4.5 Dynamic capabilities

The discussion so far has tended to assume that strategic capabilities can provide sustainable competitive advantage over time: that they are durable. However, managers often claim that hypercompetitive conditions (see section 2.3.2) are becoming increasingly prevalent. Technology is giving rise to innovation at a faster rate and therefore greater capacity for imitation and substitution of existing products and services. None the less, even in such circumstances, some firms do achieve competitive advantage over others. To explain this, more emphasis has to be placed on the organisation's capability to change, innovate, to be flexible and to learn how to adapt to a rapidly changing environment.

David Teece[15] argued that the strategic capabilities that achieve competitive advantage in such dynamic conditions are **dynamic capabilities**, by which he means an organisation's ability to *renew and recreate its strategic capabilities* to meet the needs of a changing environment.[16] Dynamic capabilities may be relatively formal, such as systems for new product development or procedures for agreement for capital expenditure. They may take the form of major strategic moves, such as acquisitions or alliances by which new skills are learned by the organisation. Or they may be more informal, such as the way in which decisions get taken faster than usual when a fast response is needed. They could also take the form of embedded 'organisational knowledge' (see section 3.5 below) about how to deal with particular circumstances the organisation faces, or how to innovate. Indeed, dynamic capabilities are likely to have both formal and informal, visible and invisible, characteristics associated with them. For example, Kathy Eisenhardt[17] has shown that successful acquisition processes that bring in new knowledge to organisations depend on high-quality pre- and post-acquisition analysis of how the acquisition can be integrated into the new organisation so as to capture synergies and bases of learning from that acquisition. However, hand in hand with these formal procedures will be more informal ways of doing things in the acquisition process built on informal personal relationships and the exchange of knowledge in more informal ways.

In summary, whereas in more stable conditions competitive advantage might be achieved by building capabilities that may be durable over time, in more dynamic conditions competitive advantage requires the building of capacity to change, innovate and learn – to build dynamic capabilities. Illustration 3.3 provides an example.

Dynamic capabilities are an organisation's abilities to renew and recreate its strategic capabilities to meet the needs of a changing environment

3.5 ORGANISATIONAL KNOWLEDGE[18]

As interest in strategic capabilities has grown, writers have come to emphasise the importance of organisational knowledge. **Organisational knowledge** is the collective experience accumulated through systems, routines and activities of sharing across the organisation. As such it is closely related to what has so far been discussed as the competences of an organisation.

There are several reasons why organisational knowledge has been highlighted as important. First, as organisations become more complex and larger, the need to share what people know becomes more of a challenge. Second, information systems have started to provide more sophisticated ways of doing this.[19] And

Organisational knowledge is the collective experience accumulated through systems, routines and activities of sharing across the organisation

Illustration 3.3

Building dynamic capabilities in a new venture

Networks and partnerships can be a source of dynamic capabilities and learning for firms and for managers.

HMD Clinical is an Edinburgh-based clinical technological new venture that seeks to make large-scale clinical trials more efficient for drug development companies. HMD initially provided bespoke services using telephony technology (for example, interactive voice recognition) to monitor clinical trials. However, this was problematic, principally due to human error. HMD therefore sought to develop a product based on another technology – radiofrequency identification. HMD felt this would also offer the prospect of market diversification, especially through international expansion. However, making changes to the company's product market domain called for capabilities to expand or modify HMD's current configuration of resources and capabilities – in other words, for dynamic capabilities.

HMD decided to partner with a large established firm, which HMD saw as a potential source of legitimacy, resources and opportunities: Sun Microsystems, a multinational corporation with a significant presence in Scotland. Co-founder Ian Davison commented, 'There's a certain cache in being associated with a big company.' Sun was interested in HMD's product idea and within months there was progress in establishing the alliance. Davison believes that considerable benefit was derived by HMD: 'We got what we wanted out of the relationship because we managed to build a prototype using the Sun technology.' HMD's experience also illustrates the building of dynamic capabilities at various levels.

Opportunities arose for mutual learning. From HMD's perspective, the venture benefited from exposure to new technological ideas. Of particular advantage was Sun's ability to tap into its widespread resources and capabilities elsewhere in the UK and beyond (for example, Western Europe). Also, Sun's reputation opened doors for HMD. When the prototype was built, HMD made a joint sales call with Sun to a prospective international customer and a demonstration was subsequently held on Sun's Scottish premises. Such activities facilitated experiential learning about processes such as product development and sales.

There were also further benefits for HMD:

- *Product development*. In developing a prototype with Sun, HMD engaged in integrating resources and capabilities to achieve synergies; for example, its own customer-centric technological knowledge in the clinical trials domain was combined with Sun's hardware technology architecture.

- *Alliancing*. Through inputs from a public sector intermediary, HMD gained vital knowledge about formal aspects of alliancing, such as the legalities of sharing intellectual property; equally, HMD came to appreciate the utility of informal social networking in ensuring the smooth progress of joint activity.

- *Strategic decision making*. HMD was able to build new thinking within the firm in terms of, for example, the identification of external knowledge sources as evident from subsequent decisions to expand the alliance to include a third partner.

At the individual level within HMD managers also learned 'new tricks' by engaging in informal routines such as brainstorming sessions and everyday activities such as negotiating. Managers claimed that such learning would help HMD approach its next alliance by replicating certain aspects while modifying others. Davison commented: 'In future we would approach this sort of relationship in a broadly similar manner [but] I think we would attempt to set some clearer company goals and boundaries at the outset.'

Prepared by Shameen Prashantham, Department of Management, University of Glasgow.

Questions

1 At what levels could dynamic capabilities benefit organisations?

2 How do network relationships, such as strategic partnerships, potentially contribute to dynamic capability development?

3 What other joint activity within, and across, organisations could give rise to dynamic capabilities? How?

4 Can dynamic capability development be deliberately planned? How?

third, as explained already in this chapter, it is less likely that organisations will achieve competitive advantage through their physical resources and more likely that it will be achieved through the way they do things and their accumulated experience. So knowledge about how to do things that draws on that experience becomes crucially important.

Two points should be highlighted here:

- *Explicit and tacit organisational knowledge*. Organisational knowledge may take different forms. Nonaka and Takeuchi[20] distinguish between two types of knowledge. *Explicit knowledge* is codified, and 'objective' knowledge is transmitted in formal systematic ways. It may, indeed, take the form of a codified information resource such as a systems manual. In contrast, *tacit knowledge* is personal, context specific and therefore hard to formalise and communicate. As for individuals, organisational competence usually requires both kinds of knowledge. For example, a learner driver uses explicit knowledge, probably taught by an instructor, to develop knowledge on how to drive a car. The tacit knowledge required is, however, achieved through practical experience of driving. Arguably, the more formal and systematic the system of knowledge, the greater is the *danger of imitation*, and therefore the less valuable the knowledge becomes in competitive strategy terms. If knowledge can be codified, then there is more of a chance of it being copied. Non-imitatable competitive advantage is much more likely to exist where knowledge is lodged in the experience of groups of individuals.

- *Communities of practice*. The sharing of knowledge and experience in organisations is an essentially social and cultural process relying on *communities of practice*[21] developing and sharing information because it is mutually beneficial. This may happen through formal systems such as the Internet but it is also highly dependent on social contact and trust. Indeed, exchange of knowledge is more likely to occur in *cultures of trust* without strong hierarchical or functional boundaries. For example, organisations have tried to improve the sharing of knowledge by setting up IT-based systems to do it. However, there has been an increasing realisation that, while some of this knowledge can be codified and built into computer-based systems, it is very difficult to codify knowledge where its value is especially dependent on knowledge sharing.

These observations in turn flag up the links between organisational knowledge and other concepts discussed in this book. Organisational knowledge may be beneficial but needs to develop as the environment changes. As such, organisational knowledge and learning are closely linked concepts. In turn both need to be thought of in terms of the *dynamic capabilities* to adapt to changing conditions referred to in section 3.4.5 above. The links between knowledge, experience and social interaction also need to be considered in relation to cultural aspects of strategy addressed further in Chapter 5.

3.6 DIAGNOSING STRATEGIC CAPABILITY

So far this chapter has been concerned with explaining strategic capability and associated concepts. This section now provides some ways in which strategic capabilities can be diagnosed.

3.6.1 **The value chain and value network**

Value chain and value network

If organisations are to achieve competitive advantage by delivering value to customers, managers need to understand which activities they undertake are especially important in creating that value and which are not. Value chain and value network concepts can be helpful in understanding this.

The value chain

A value chain describes the categories of activities within and around an organisation, which together create a product or service

The **value chain** describes the categories of activities within and around an organisation, which together create a product or service. The concept was developed in relation to competitive strategy by Michael Porter.[22] Exhibit 3.6 is a representation of a value chain. **Primary activities** are *directly* concerned with the creation or delivery of a product or service. For example, for a manufacturing business:

Primary activities are directly concerned with the creation or delivery of a product or service

- *Inbound logistics* are activities concerned with receiving, storing and distributing inputs to the product or service including materials handling, stock control, transport, etc.
- *Operations* transform these inputs into the final product or service: machining, packaging, assembly, testing, etc.
- *Outbound logistics* collect, store and distribute the product to customers, for example warehousing, materials handling, distribution, etc.
- *Marketing and sales* provide the means whereby consumers/users are made aware of the product or service and are able to purchase it. This includes sales administration, advertising and selling.
- *Service* includes those activities that enhance or maintain the value of a product or service, such as installation, repair, training and spares.

Exhibit 3.6 **The value chain within an organisation**

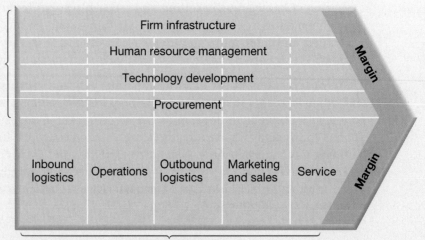

Source: Adapted with the permission of The Free Press, a Division of Simon & Schuster Adult Publishing Group, from *Competitive Advantage: Creating and Sustaining Superior Performance* by Michael E. Porter. Copyright © 1985, 1998 by Michael E. Porter. All rights reserved.

Each of these groups of primary activities is linked to support activities.

Support activities help to improve the effectiveness or efficiency of primary activities:

● *Procurement*. The *processes* that occur in many parts of the organisation for acquiring the various resource inputs to the primary activities.

● *Technology development*. All value activities have a 'technology', even if it is just know-how. Technologies may be concerned directly with a product (for example, R&D, product design) or with processes (for example, process development) or with a particular resource (for example, raw materials improvements).

● *Human resource management*. This transcends all primary activities. It is concerned with those activities involved in recruiting, managing, training, developing and rewarding people within the organisation.

● *Infrastructure*. The formal systems of planning, finance, quality control, information management, and the structures and routines that are part of an organisation's culture (see section 5.4).

The value chain can help with the analysis of the strategic position of an organisation in two different ways.

● As *generic descriptions of activities* that can help managers understand if there is a cluster of activities providing benefit to customers located within particular areas of the value chain. Perhaps a business is especially good at outbound logistics linked to its marketing and sales operation and supported by its technology development. It might be less good in terms of its operations and its inbound logistics. The value chain also prompts managers to think about the role different activities play. For example, in a local family-run sandwich bar, is sandwich making best thought of as 'operations' or as 'marketing and sales', given that its reputation and appeal may rely on the social relations and banter between customers and sandwich makers? Arguably it is 'operations' if done badly but 'marketing and sales' if done well.

● In terms of the *cost and value of activities*.[23] Illustration 3.4 shows this in relation to fish farming. Value chain analysis was used by Ugandan fish farmers as a way of identifying what they should focus on in developing a more profitable business model.

The value network

A single organisation rarely undertakes in-house all of the value activities from design through to delivery of the final product or service to the final consumer. There is usually specialisation of role so any one organisation is part of a wider *value network*. The **value network**[24] is the set of interorganisational links and relationships that are necessary to create a product or service (see Exhibit 3.7). So an organisation needs to be clear about what activities it ought to undertake itself and which it should not and, perhaps, should outsource. However, since much of the cost and value creation will occur in the supply and distribution chains, managers need to understand this whole process and how they can manage these linkages and relationships to improve customer value. It is not sufficient to look within the organisation alone. For example, the quality of a cooker or a

Illustration 3.4

A value chain for Ugandan chilled fish fillet exports

Even small enterprises can be part of an international value chain. Analysing it can provide strategic benefits.

A fish factory in Uganda barely made any profit. Fish were caught from small motorboats owned by poor fishermen from local villages. Just before they set out they would collect ice and plastic fish boxes from the agents who bought the catch on their return. The boxes were imported, along with tackle and boat parts. All supplies had to be paid for in cash in advance by the agents. Sometimes ice and supplies were not available in time. Fish landed with insufficient ice achieved half of the price of iced fish, and sometimes could not be sold to the agents at all. The fish factory had always processed the fillets in the same way – disposing of the waste back into the lake. Once a week, some foreign traders would come and buy the better fillets; they didn't say who they sold them to, and sometimes they didn't buy very much.

By mapping the value chain it was clear that there were opportunities for capturing more value along the chain and reducing losses. Together with outside specialists, the fish factory and the fishing community developed a strategy to improve their capabilities, as indicated in the figure, until they became a flourishing international business, The Lake Victoria Fish Company, with regular air-freight exports around the world. You can see more of their current operations at http://www.ufpea.co.ug/, and find out more about the type of analytical process applied at www.justreturn.ch.

(The approximate costs and prices given represent the situation before improvements were implemented.)

Questions

1 Draw up a value chain for another business in terms of the activities within its component parts.

2 Estimate the relative costs and/or assets associated with these activities.

3 What are the strategic implications of your analysis?

television when it reaches the final purchaser is influenced not only by the activities undertaken within the manufacturing company itself, but also by the quality of components from suppliers and the performance of the distributors.

It is therefore important that managers understand the bases of their organisation's strategic capabilities in relation to the wider value network. Four key issues are:

● *Which activities are centrally important* to an organisation's strategic capability and which less central? A firm in a highly competitive market may have to cut costs in key areas and decide it can only do so by outsourcing to lower-cost producers. Another firm may decide that it is important to retain direct control of centrally important capabilities, especially if they relate to activities and processes that it believes are central to its achieving competitive advantage. For example, diamond cutting businesses have traditionally had to source rough diamonds from the giant De Beers. However, in a revolutionary move

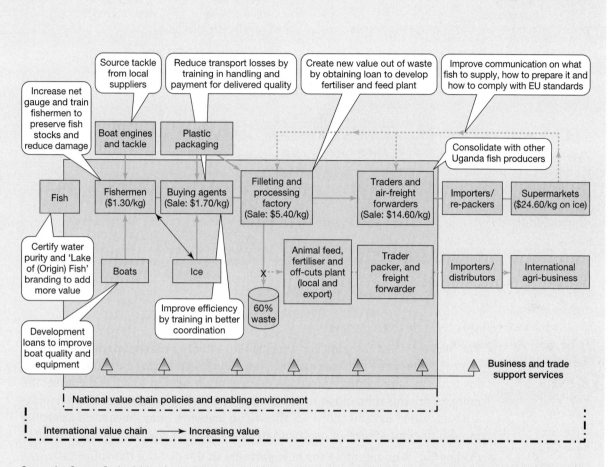

Source: Ian Sayers, Senior Adviser for the Private Sector, Division of Trade Support Services, International Trade Centre, Geneva. E-mail: sayers@intracen.org.

Profit pools refer to the different levels of profit available at different parts of the value network

the Lev Leviev Group decided to invest in its own diamond mining operations, arguing: 'Nothing is stable unless you own your own mine.'[25]

- *Where are the profit pools?*[26] **Profit pools** refer to the different levels of profit available at different parts of the value network. Some parts of a value network may be inherently more profitable than others because of the differences in competitive intensity. For example, in the computer industry microprocessors and software have historically been more profitable than hardware manufacture. The strategic question becomes whether it is possible to focus on the areas of greatest profit potential. Care has to be exercised here. It is one thing to identify such potential; it is another to be successful in it given the capabilities the organisation has. For example, in the 1990s many car manufacturers recognised that greater profit potential lay in services such as car hire and financing rather than manufacturing but they did not have the relevant competences to succeed in such sectors.

Exhibit 3.7   **The value network**

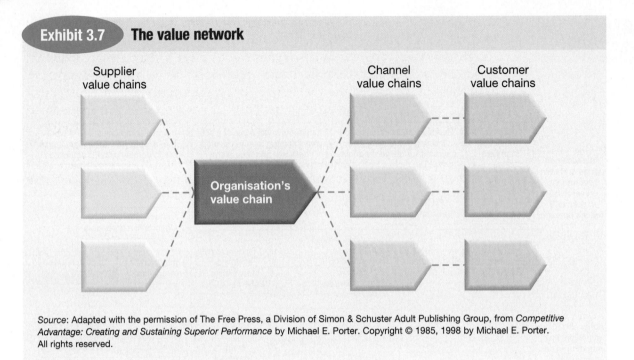

- *The 'make or buy'* decision for a particular activity or component is therefore critical. This is the *outsourcing* decision. There are businesses that now offer the benefits of outsourcing (see the discussion in section 12.4.2). Of course, the more an organisation outsources, the more its ability to influence the performance of other organisations in the value network may become a critically important competence in itself and even a source of competitive advantage.

- *Partnering.* Who might be the best partners in the parts of the value network? And what kind of *relationships* are important to develop with each partner? For example, should they be regarded as suppliers or should they be regarded as alliance partners (see section 10.2.3)? Some businesses have benefited from closer relationships with suppliers such that they increasingly cooperate on such things as market intelligence, product design and R&D.

3.6.2 Activity maps

Managers often find it difficult to identify with any clarity the strategic capability of their organisation. Too often they highlight capabilities not valued by customers but seen as important within the organisation, perhaps because they were valuable in the past. Or they highlight what are, in fact, critical success factors (product features particularly valued by customers) like 'good service' or 'reliable delivery', whereas strategic capability is about the resources, processes and activities that underpin the ability to meet such critical success factors. Or they identify capabilities at too generic a level. This is not surprising given that strategic capability is likely to be rooted in a complex, causally ambiguous set of linked activities (see section 3.4.3). But if they are to be managed proactively, finding a way of identifying and understanding capabilities and the linkages that are likely to characterise competences is important.

One way of undertaking such diagnosis is by means of an activity map that tries to show how the different activities of an organisation are linked together. Illustration 3.2 described the search by Plasco's management for the company's strategic capabilities using activity mapping. There are computer programs in existence that can be used,[27] or such analysis may be done more basically, for example by drawing network diagrams, as shown in Exhibit 3.8.[28] This map was generated by groups of managers from within the organisation, working with a facilitator, mapping the activities of their organisation on a large blank wall initially by using Post-Its.[29]

Exhibit 3.8   An activity system map*

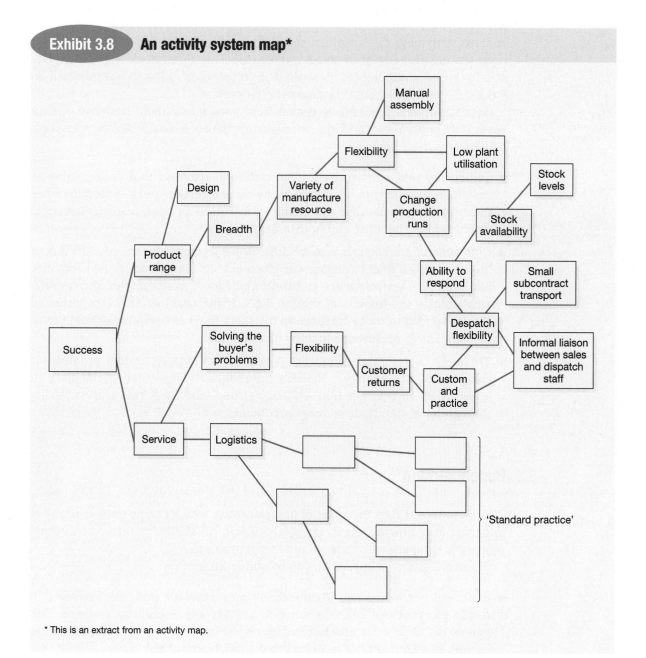

* This is an extract from an activity map.

They began by undertaking a competitor analysis as explained in section 2.4.4. The aim here was to identify (i) the critical success factors in relation to their customers and (ii) on which of these their business outperformed competitors. They identified the critical success factors of brand reputation, product range, innovation, excellence of service and reliability of delivery and that Plasco was seen as particularly successful in relation to competitors in terms of its level of service and its product range. Managers were relatively easily able to identify what Porter refers to as *higher order strategic themes*:[30] that the main benefits offered were to do with flexibility and rapid response. But the reasons why Plasco outperformed competitors did not emerge until these themes themselves were 'unpacked' by identifying the resources and competences that underpinned them. To do this managers kept asking themselves more and more specifically what activities 'delivered' the customer benefits. Exhibit 3.8 is only a selection of these activities. The eventual map consisted of hundreds of Post-Its, each representing an activity in some way contributing to strategic capability. The activity-based competences described in Illustration 3.2 and summarised in Exhibit 3.8 emerged from this diagnostic process.

General lessons that can be drawn from such maps about how competitive advantage is achieved and the relationship between competences and competitive advantage include:

- *Consistency and reinforcement*. The different activities that create value to customers are likely to be pulling in the same direction and supporting rather than opposing each other (for example, in Plasco an open management style facilitated rule bending and in turn flexibility).

- *Difficulties of imitation*. It is more difficult for a competitor to imitate a mix of linked activities than to imitate any given one. In Plasco such linked activities had been built up over years, culturally embedded, were complex and causally ambiguous – the lessons of section 3.4.3. If the multinational competitor of Plasco decided to try to compete on the same basis of flexibility it would have no comparable experience to draw on to do this.

- *Trade-offs*. Even if imitation were possible it could pose another problem for competitors. For example, Plasco's international competitor might place in jeopardy its current position with its existing customers that it is satisfying through more standardised mass production.

3.6.3 Benchmarking[31]

This section considers the value of *benchmarking*, which can be used as a way of understanding how an organisation's strategic capability, in terms of internal processes, compare with those of other organisations.

There are different approaches to benchmarking:

- *Historical benchmarking*. Organisations may consider their performance in relation to previous years in order to identify any significant changes. The danger is that this can lead to complacency since it is the rate of improvement compared with that of competitors that is really important.

- *Industry/sector benchmarking*. Insights about performance standards can be gleaned by looking at the comparative performance of other organisations in the same industry sector or between similar service providers against a set of performance indicators. Some public sector organisations have, in effect, acknowledged the existence of strategic groups by benchmarking against similar organisations rather than against everybody: for example, local government services and police treat 'urban' differently from 'rural' in their benchmarking and league tables. An overriding danger of industry norm comparisons (whether in the private or public sector) is, however, that the whole industry may be performing badly and losing out competitively to other industries that can satisfy customers' needs in different ways. Another danger with benchmarking within an industry is that the boundaries of industries are blurring through competitive activity and industry convergence. For example, supermarkets are (incrementally) entering retail banking and their benchmarking needs to reflect this (as does the benchmarking of the traditional retail banks).

- *Best-in-class benchmarking*. Best-in-class benchmarking compares an organisation's performance against 'best-in-class' performance – wherever that is found – and therefore seeks to overcome the limitations of other approaches. It may also help challenge managers' mindsets that acceptable improvements in performance will result from incremental changes in resources or competences. It can therefore encourage a more fundamental reconsideration of how to improve organisational competences. For example, British Airways improved aircraft maintenance, refuelling and turnround time by studying the processes surrounding Formula One Grand Prix motor racing pit stops.[32] A police force wishing to improve the way in which it responded to emergency telephone calls studied call centre operations in the banking and IT sectors.

The importance of benchmarking is, then, not so much in the detailed 'mechanics' of comparison but in the impact that these comparisons might have on behaviours. It can be usefully regarded as a process for gaining momentum for improvement and change. But it has dangers too:

- *Measurement distortion*. Benchmarking can lead to a situation where *you get what you measure* and this may not be what is intended strategically. It can therefore result in changes in behaviour that are unintended or dysfunctional. For example, the university sector in the UK has been subjected to rankings in league tables on research output, teaching quality and the success of graduating students in terms of employment and starting salaries. This has resulted in academics being 'forced' to orientate their published research to certain types of academic journals that may have little to do directly with the quality of the education in universities.

- *Surface comparisons*. Benchmarking compares inputs (resources), outputs or outcomes; it does not identify the reasons for the good or poor performance of organisations since the process does not compare competences directly. For example, it may demonstrate that one organisation is poorer at customer service than another but not show the underlying reasons. However, if well directed it could encourage managers to seek out these reasons and hence understand how competences could be improved.

Illustration 3.5

SWOT analysis of Pharmcare

A SWOT analysis explores the relationship between the environmental influences and the strategic capabilities of an organisation compared with its competitors.

(a) SWOT analysis for Pharmcare

	Environmental change (opportunities and threats)					
	Health care rationing	Complex and changing buying structures	Increased integration of health care	Informed patients	+	−
Strengths						
Flexible salesforce	+3	+5	+2	+2	12	0
Economies of scale	0	0	+3	+3	+6	0
Strong brand name	+2	+1	0	−1	3	−1
Health care education department	+4	+3	+4	+5	+16	0
Weaknesses						
Limited competences in biotechnology and genetics	0	0	−4	−3	0	−7
Ever lower R&D productivity	−3	−2	−1	−2	0	−8
Weak ICT competences	−2	−2	−5	−5	0	−14
Over-reliance on leading product	−1	−1	−3	−1	0	−6
Environmental impact scores	+9	+9	+9	+10		
	−6	−5	−14	−12		

(b) Competitor SWOT analyses

	Environmental change (opportunities and threats)				
	Health care rationing	Complex and changing buying structures	Increased integration of health care	Informed and passionate patients	Overall impact
Pharmcare *Big global player suffering fall in share price, low research productivity and post mega-merger bureaucracy*	−3 Struggling to prove cost-effectiveness of new drugs to new regulators of health care rationing	+6 Well-known brand, a flexible salesforce combined with a new health care education department creates positive synergy	−3 Weak ICT and lack of integration following mergers means sales, research and admin. are all underperforming	−2 Have yet to get into the groove of patient power fuelled by the Internet	−2 Declining performance over time worsened after merger
Company W *Big pharma with patchy response to change, losing ground in new areas of competition*	−4 Focus is on old-style promotional selling rather than helping doctors control costs through drugs	−4 Traditional salesforce not helped by marketing which can be unaccommodating of national differences	+0 Alliances with equipment manufacturers but little work done across alliance to show dual use of drugs and new surgical techniques	+4 New recruits in the ICT department have worked cross-functionally to involve patients like never before	−4 Needs to modernise across the whole company
Organisation X *Partnership between a charity managed by people with venture capital experience and top hospital geneticists*	+3 Potentially able to deliver rapid advances in genetic-based illnesses	+2 Able possibly to bypass these with innovative cost effective drug(s)	+2 Innovative drugs can help integrate health care through enabling patients to stay at home	+3 Patients will fight for advances in treatment areas where little recent progress has been made	+10 Could be the basis of a new business model for drug discovery – but all to prove as yet
Company Y *Only develops drugs for less common diseases*	+3 Partnering with big pharma allows the development of drugs discovered by big pharma but not economical for them to develop	0 Focus on small market segments so not as vulnerable to overall market structure, but innovative approach might be risky	+2 Innovative use of web to show why products still worthwhile developing even for less common illnesses	+1 Toll-free call centres for sufferers of less common illnesses Company, like patients, is passionate about its mission	+6 Novel approach can be considered either risky or a winner, or both!

Questions

1 What does the SWOT analysis tell us about the competitive position of Pharmcare with the industry as a whole?

2 How readily do you think executives of Pharmacare identify the strengths and weaknesses of competitors?

3 Identify the benefits and dangers (other than those identified in the text) of a SWOT analysis such as that in the illustration.

Prepared by Jill Shepherd, Segal Graduate School of Business, Simon Fraser University, Vancouver, Canada.

3.6.4 SWOT[33]

SWOT summarises the key issues from the business environment and the strategic capability of an organisation that are most likely to impact on strategy development

KEY CONCEPT

SWOT

The key 'strategic messages' from both the business environment (Chapter 2) and this chapter can be summarised in the form of an analysis of strengths, weaknesses, opportunities and threats (SWOT). **SWOT** summarises the key issues from the business environment and the strategic capability of an organisation that are most likely to impact on strategy development. This can also be useful as a basis against which to generate strategic options and assess future courses of action.

The aim is to identify the extent to which strengths and weaknesses are relevant to, or capable of dealing with, the changes taking place in the business environment. However, in the context of this chapter, if the strategic capability of an organisation is to be understood, it must be remembered that it is not absolute but relative to its competitors. So SWOT analysis is really only useful if it is comparative – if it examines strengths, weaknesses, opportunities and threats in relation to competitors. Illustration 3.5 takes the example of a pharmaceuticals firm (Pharmcare).[34] It assumes that key environmental impacts have been identified from analyses explained in Chapter 2 and that major strengths and weaknesses have been identified using the analytic tools explained in this chapter. A scoring mechanism (plus 5 to minus 5) is used as a means of getting managers to assess the interrelationship between the environmental impacts and the strengths and weaknesses of the firm. A positive (+) denotes that the strength of the company would help it take advantage of, or counteract, a problem arising from an environmental change or that a weakness would be offset by that change. A negative (–) score denotes that the strength would be reduced or that a weakness would prevent the organisation from overcoming problems associated with that change.

Pharmcare's share price had been declining because investors were concerned that its strong market position was under threat. This had not been improved by a merger that was proving problematic. The pharmaceutical market was changing with new ways of doing business, driven by new technology, the quest to provide medicines at lower cost and politicians seeking ways to cope with soaring health care costs and an evermore informed patient. But was Pharmcare keeping pace? The strategic review of the firm's position (Illustration 3.5a) confirmed its strengths of a flexible salesforce, well-known brand name and new health care department. However, there were major weakness, namely relative failure on low-cost drugs, competence in information and communication technology (ICT) and a failure to get to grips with increasingly well-informed users. When the impact of environmental forces on competitors was analysed (Illustration 3.5b), it showed that Pharmcare was still outperforming its traditional competitor (Company W), but potentially vulnerable to changing dynamics in the general industry structure courtesy of niche players (X and Y).

A SWOT analysis should help focus discussion on future choices and the extent to which an organisation is capable of supporting these strategies. There are, however, two main dangers:

● A SWOT exercise can generate very *long lists* of apparent strengths, weaknesses, opportunities and threats, whereas what matters is to be clear about what is really important and what is less important.

- There is a danger of *overgeneralisation*. Remember the lessons of sections 3.6.1 and 3.6.2. Identifying a very general explanation of strategic capability does not explain the underlying reasons for that capability. SWOT analysis is not a substitute for more rigorous, insightful analysis, for example by using the techniques and concepts explained in Chapters 2 and 3.

3.7   MANAGING STRATEGIC CAPABILITY

The previous section has been concerned with diagnosing strategic capability. This section considers what managers might do, other than such diagnosis, to manage and improve the strategic capability of their organisation.

3.7.1   Limitations in managing strategic capabilities

One lesson that emerges from an understanding of strategic capabilities is that the most valuable bases of strategic capability may lie in aspects of the organisation that are difficult to discern or be specific about. So, how is it possible to manage that which it is not always easy to be clear about? For example, in the Plasco illustration, some of the capabilities of that organisation were lodged in activities that the top management were not directly managing. It is important to understand what managers might be able to do and what they cannot do in terms of how much they understand and how much they value bases of strategic capability.[35] There may be different circumstances:

- *Competences are valued but not understood*. Managers may know that there are activities in their organisation that have a positive impact and may value them, but may not understand just how such positive impact arises. For example, the delivery of value may be dependent on highly specialised skills as in a cutting-edge hi-tech firm, or on complex linkages far down in the organisation. The lesson here is that managers may have to be careful about disturbing the bases of such capabilities while ensuring that they *monitor the outputs and benefits* created for customers.

- *Competences are not valued*. Managers may know that activities and processes exist in the organisation but not recognise their positive impact or value such activities. There are dangers here that managers take the wrong course of action. For example, they may cut out areas of activity that create actual or potential competitive advantage, perhaps because they are intent on cutting costs. Plasco managers might, for example, have sought to improve production efficiency so that they could have reduced flexibility. It would be wise to understand the value-creating capabilities more clearly using value chain analysis or activity mapping before as Plasco managers did before taking such decisions.

- *Competences are recognised, valued and understood*. This might be the outcome of the sort of analysis done by Plasco. Here managers may be able to nurture and further develop such competences, for example by ensuring that overall company policies support and enhance them. The danger can be that top management may seek to preserve such capabilities by over-formalising or codifying them such that they become 'set in stone'.

3.7.2 Developing strategic capabilities[36]

There are different ways in which managers might develop strategic capabilities:

● *Adding and changing capabilities*. Could capabilities be added, or changed so that they become more reinforcing of outcomes that deliver against critical success factors? For example, in Plasco, could even faster internal ways of responding to customer needs be found?

● *Extending capabilities*. Managers might identify strategic capabilities in one area of the business, perhaps customer service in one geographic business unit of a multinational, that are not present in other business units. They might then seek to extend this throughout all the business units. Whilst this seems straightforward, studies[37] find it is not. The capabilities of one part of an organisation might not be easily transferred to another because of the problems of managing change (see Chapter 14).

● *Stretching capabilities*. Managers may see the opportunity to build new products or services out of existing capabilities. Indeed, building new businesses in this way is the basis of related diversification, as explained in section 7.3.1.[38]

● *Entrepreneurial bricolage*. There is evidence[39] that strategic capabilities may be built by exploiting resources, skills and knowledge that have been ignored or rejected by others; indeed that this is often what entrepreneurs who develop new business models do. For example, the development of Danish wind turbines was based on improvising around available 'modest resources' and the skills of a 'constellation of different players';[40] social networks ignored by others have been used for building technology businesses and information systems designers experiment with different configurations to create new systems drawing from their and others' experience.

● *Ceasing activities*. Could current activities not central to the delivery of value to customers be done away with, outsourced or reduced in cost? This is what new industry entrants, such as Ryanair or easyJet in the airline industry, did to create new business models for low-cost airlines.

● *External capability development*. There may be ways of developing capabilities by looking externally. For example, managers may seek to develop or learn new capabilities by acquisition or by entering into alliances and joint ventures (see section 10.2.3).

3.7.3 Managing people for capability development

One of the lessons of this chapter is that strategic capability often lies in the day-to-day activities that people undertake in organisations, so developing the ability of people to recognise the relevance of what they do in terms of the strategic capability of the organisation is important. More specifically:

- *Targeted training and development* may be possible. Often companies design training and development programmes that are very general. For strategic purposes it may be important to target the development of competences which can provide competitive advantage. For example, an engineering business, whilst acknowledging the abilities its personnel had in the technical aspects of engineering products, recognised that these were attributes that competitors had too, and that there was a need to develop people's abilities to innovate more around value-adding customer service. The business therefore changed its training and development programmes to emphasise these requirements.

- *Staffing policies* might be employed to develop particular competences. For example, an oil company that sought to build its competitive advantage around the building of close customer relationships in markets for industrial oils did so by ensuring that senior field managers with an aptitude for this were promoted and sent to different parts of the world that needed to be developed in such ways.

- *Organisational learning* may be recognised as central, particularly in fast-changing conditions. Here successful firms may be those that have grown the *dynamic capabilities* (see section 3.4.5) to readjust required competences continually. In effect their competence becomes that of learning and development. In this context the characteristics of what has become known as a 'learning organisation' may become especially important (see section 11.5.2). Since this may require the acceptance that different, even conflicting ideas and views are valuable and that experimentation is the norm, managers need to consider how to protect and foster such behaviour. For example, it may be that those within the organisation who show most ability to contribute to such learning are the least powerful, perhaps quite junior in the hierarchy. They may need the protection of more powerful people.

- *Develop people's awareness* that what they do in their jobs can matter at the strategic level. It is a common complaint in organisations that 'no one values what I do'. Helping people see how their work relates to the bigger strategic picture can both enhance the likelihood that they will, indeed, contribute positively to helping achieve competitive success and increase their motivation to do so.

Illustration 3.6 summarises a key debate that writers on the strategic capabilities are pursuing.

SUMMARY

- *Strategic capability* is concerned with the adequacy and suitability of resources and competences required for an organisation to survive and prosper. Strategic capabilities comprise resources and competences, which are the way such resources are used and deployed.

- If organisations are to achieve *competitive advantage*, they require resources and competences which are both valuable to customers and difficult for competitors to imitate (such competences are known as *core competences*).

- The continual improvement of *cost efficiency* is a vital strategic capability if an organisation is to continue to prosper.

- The sustainability of competitive advantage is likely to depend on strategic capabilities being of *value to customers, rare, inimitable* or *non-substitutable*.

- In dynamic conditions, it is unlikely that such strategic capabilities will remain stable. In such circumstances *dynamic capabilities* are important, that is the ability to change strategic capabilities continually.

- Ways of *diagnosing organisational capabilities* include:
  - Analysing an organisation's *value chain and value network* as a basis of understanding how value to a customer is created and can be developed.
  - *Activity mapping* as a means of identifying more detailed activities which underpin strategic capabilities.
  - *Benchmarking* as means of understanding the relative performance of organisations and challenging the assumptions managers have about the performance of their organisation.
  - *SWOT analysis* as a way of drawing together an understanding of strengths, weaknesses, opportunities and threats an organisation faces.

- Managers need to think about how and to what extent they can manage the *development of the strategic capabilities* of their organisation by stretching and adding to such capabilities and by the way they manage people in their organisation.

Illustration 3.6

key debate

The resource-based view of competitive advantage: is it useful to managers?

The view that the management of strategic capability is central for achieving competitive advantage has been questioned.

Since the early 1990s, the resource-based view (RBV) of strategy has become highly influential. Much academic research is carried out on it and managers readily talk about the importance of building on core competences to gain competitive advantage. However, two US academics, Richard Priem and John Butler, have raised questions about the value of RBV.[1]

The critique

In the context of this chapter, two of Priem and Butler's observations are especially significant:

1 *The risk of tautology.* The underlying explanation of RBV is that the resource characteristics (or capabilities) that lead to competitive advantage are those that are valuable and rare. Since competitive advantage is defined in terms of value and rarity, they argue that this verges on tautology. To say that a business performs better than another because it has superior resources or is better at some things than other businesses is not helpful unless it is possible to be specific about what capabilities are important, why and how they can be managed.

2 *The lack of specificity.* However, there is typically little specific in what is written about RBV. And some would say the same is true when managers talk about capabilities or competences. 'Top management skills' or 'innovatory capacity' mean little without being specific about the activities and processes that comprise them. And there is relatively little research that identifies such specifics or how they can be managed. Priem and Butler suggest this is particularly so with regard to the argued importance of tacit knowledge in bestowing competitive advantage: 'This may be descriptively correct, but it is likely to be quite difficult for practitioners to effectively manipulate that which is inherently unknowable.' (The problem raised at the beginning of section 3.6.2.)

The response

Jay Barney,[2] one of the main proponents of RBV, accepts that there is a need to understand more about how resources are used and how people behave in

bestowing competitive advantage. However, he defends the managerial relevance of RBV because he believes it highlights that managers need to identify and develop the most critical capabilities of a firm.

In his earlier writing[3] Barney had argued that an organisation's culture could be a source of sustainable advantage provided it was valuable, rare and difficult to imitate. In such circumstances he suggested managers should 'nurture these cultures'. However, he went on to argue that:

If one firm is able to modify its culture, then it is likely that others can as well. In this case the advantages associated with the culture are imitable and thus only a source of normal economic performance. Only when it is not possible to manage a firm's culture in a planned way does that culture have the potential of generating expected sustained superior financial performance.

In other words, he argues that valuable sources of competitive advantage are the intangible assets and resources or competences embedded in a culture in such a way that not only can competitors not imitate them, but managers cannot manage them.

Priem and Butler would no doubt argue that this makes their point: that RBV is not very helpful in providing practical help to managers.

Notes

1. R. Priem and J.E. Butler, 'Is the resource based view a useful perspective for strategic management research?', *Academy of Management Review*, vol. 26, no. 1 (2001), pp. 22–40.
2. J.B. Barney, 'Is the resource based view a useful perspective for strategic management research? Yes', *Academy of Management Review*, vol. 26, no. 1 (2001), pp. 41–56.
3. J.B. Barney, 'Organizational culture: can it be a source of sustained competitive advantage?', *Academy of Management Review*, vol. 11, no. 3 (1986), pp. 656–665.

Questions

1 How specific would the identification of strategic capabilities need to be to permit them to be managed to achieve competitive advantage?

2 Do you agree that if it were possible to identify and manage such capabilities they would be imitated?

3 Is the RBV useful?

Work assignments

*Denotes more advanced work assignments.   * Refers to a case study in the Text and Cases edition.

3.1   Using Exhibits 3.1 and 3.2 identify the resources and competences of an organisation with which you are familiar. You can answer this in relation to Amazon* or Formula One* if you so wish.

3.2 ✳ Undertake an analysis of the strategic capability of an organisation with which you are familiar in order to identify which capabilities, if any, meet the criteria of (a) value, (b) rarity, (c) robustness and (d) inimitability (see section 3.4). You can answer this in relation to Amazon* or Formula One* if you so wish.

3.3 ✳ For an industry or public service consider how the strategic capabilities that have been the basis of competitive advantage (or best value in the public sector) have changed over time. Why have these changes occurred? How did the relative strengths of different companies or service providers change over this period? Why?

3.4   Map out a value chain/network analysis for an organisation of your choice (referring to Illustration 3.4 could be helpful). You can answer this in relation to a case study in the book such as eBay, Tesco, Tui* or Ryanair* if you wish.

3.5 ✳ For a benchmarking exercise which you have access to, make a critical assessment of the benefits and dangers of the approach that was taken.

Integrative assignment

3.6   Prepare a SWOT analysis for an organisation of your choice and in relation to competitors (see Illustration 3.5). Explain why you have chosen each of the factors you have included in the analysis, in particular their relationship to other analyses you have undertaken in Chapters 2 and 3. What are the conclusions you arrive at from your analysis?

An extensive range of additional materials, including audio summaries, weblinks to organisations featured in the text, definitions of key concepts and self-assessment questions, can be found on the *Exploring Corporate Strategy* Companion Website at **www.pearsoned.co.uk/ecs**

Recommended key readings

- For an understanding of the resource-based view of the firm, an early and much cited paper is by Jay Barney, 'Firm resources and sustained competitive advantage', *Journal of Management*, vol. 17 (1991), pp. 99–120. Also see the introductory paper by D. Hoopes, T. Madsen and G. Walker, 'Why is there a resource based view', in the special issue of the *Strategic Management Journal*, vol. 24, no. 10 (2003), pp. 889–902.

- The concept of dynamic capabilities is reviewed in C.L. Wang and P.K. Ahmed, 'Dynamic capabilities: a review and research agenda', *International Journal of Management Reviews*, vol. 9, no. 1 (2007), pp. 31–52.

- Michael Porter explains how mapping what he calls 'activity systems' can be important in considering competitive strategy in his article 'What is strategy?', *Harvard Business Review*, November–December (1996).

- For a critical discussion of the use and misuse of SWOT analysis see T. Hill and R. Westbrook, 'SWOT analysis: its time for a product recall', *Long Range Planning*, vol. 30, no. 1 (1997), pp. 46–52.

- For an understanding of the challenges of managing capability development see C. Bowman and N. Collier, 'A contingency approach to resource-creation processes', *International Journal of Management Reviews*, vol. 8, no. 4 (2006), pp. 191–211. Also T. Baker and R.E. Nelson, 'Creating something from nothing: resource construction through entrepreneurial bricolage', *Administrative Science Quarterly*, vol. 50, no. 3 (2005), pp. 329–366.

References

1. Extraordinary profits as defined here are also sometimes referred to by economists as rents. For an explanation related to strategy, see R. Perman and J. Scoular, *Business Economics*, Oxford University Press, 1999, pp. 67–73.

2. The concept of resource-based strategies was introduced by B. Wernerfelt, 'A resource-based view of the firm', *Strategic Management Journal*, vol. 5, no. 2 (1984), pp. 171–180. A much cited paper is by J. Barney, 'Firm resources and sustained competitive advantage', *Journal of Management*, vol. 17, no. 1 (1991), pp. 99–120. There are now many books and papers that explain and summarise the approach. See for example the beginning of D.J. Teece, G. Pisano and A. Shuen, 'Dynamic capabilities and strategic management', *Strategic Management Journal*, vol. 18, no. 7 (1997), pp. 509–534; and the introductory paper by D. Hoopes, T. Madsen and G. Walker, 'Why is there a resource based view?', to the special issue of the *Strategic Management Journal*, vol. 24, no. 10 (2003), pp. 889–902.

3. Intangible resources have become increasingly recognised as being of strategic importance. See T. Clarke and S. Clegg, *Changing Paradigms: The transformation of management knowledge for the 21st century*, Harper Collins, 2000, p. 342 (this outlines Arthur Andersen's classification of intangible assets); R. Hall, 'The strategic analysis of intangible resources', *Strategic Management Journal*, vol. 13, no. 2, (1992), pp. 135–144; and also 'A framework linking intangible resources and capabilities to sustainable competitive advantage', *Strategic Management Journal*, vol. 14, no. 8 (1993), pp. 607–618.

4. Gary Hamel and C.K. Prahalad were the academics who promoted the idea of core competences. For example, G. Hamel and C.K. Prahalad, 'The core competence of the corporation', *Harvard Business Review*, vol. 68, no. 3 (1990), pp. 79–91. The idea of driving strategy development from the resources and competences of an organisation is discussed in G. Hamel and C.K. Prahalad, 'Strategic intent', *Harvard Business Review*, vol. 67, no. 3 (1989), pp. 63–76; and G. Hamel and C.K. Prahalad, 'Strategy as stretch and leverage', *Harvard Business Review*, vol. 71, no. 2 (1993), pp. 75–84. Also see G. Hamel and A. Heene (eds), *Competence-based Competition*, Wiley, 1994.

5. Perman and Scoular discuss economies of scale and differences between industry sectors in pages 91–100 of their book (see reference 1).

6. P. Conley, *Experience Curves as a Planning Tool*, available as a pamphlet from the Boston Consulting Group. See also A.C. Hax and N.S. Majluf, in R.G. Dyson (ed.), *Strategic Planning: Models and analytical techniques*, Wiley, 1990.

7. The headings used in this chapter are those used most commonly by writers in academic papers on RBV. These are sometimes referred to as VRIN, which stands for Valuable, Rare, difficult to Imitate and non-Substitutable, and were first identified by J. Barney, 'Firm resources and sustained competitive advantage', *Journal of Management*, vol. 17, no. 1 (1991), pp. 99–120.

8. For a full explanation of 'core rigidities' see D. Leonard-Barton, 'Core capabilities and core rigidities: a paradox in managing new product development', *Strategic Management Journal*, vol. 13 (Summer 1992), pp. 111–125.

9. See reference 7.

10. We use the word 'complexity'. Others use the word 'interconnectedness'. See for example K. Cool, L.A. Costa and I. Dierickx, 'Constructing competitive advantage', in A. Pettigrew, H. Thomas and R. Whittington (eds), *Handbook of Strategy and Management*, pp. 55–71, Sage, 2002.

11. For a fuller discussion of path dependency in the context of strategic capabilities, see the paper by Teece *et al.* (reference 2) and D. Holbrook, W. Cohen, D. Hounshell and S. Klepper, 'The nature, sources and consequences of firm differences in the early history of the semiconductor industry', *Strategic Management Journal*, vol. 21, nos 10–11 (2000), pp. 1017–1042.

12. The seminal paper on causal ambiguity is S. Lippman and R. Rumelt, 'Uncertain imitability: an analysis of interfirm differences in efficiency under competition', *Bell Journal of Economics*, vol. 13 (1982), pp. 418–438.

13. The distinction between and importance of characteristic and linkage ambiguity is explained in detail by A.W. King and C.P. Zeithaml, 'Competencies and firm performance: examining the causal ambiguity paradox', *Strategic Management Journal*, vol. 22, no. 1 (2001), pp. 75–99.

14. The importance of non-substitutability and ways of identifying possible bases of substitution are discussed in M.A. Peteraf and M.E. Bergen, 'Scanning dynamic competitive landscapes: a market and resource based framework', *Strategic Management Journal*, vol. 24, no. 10 (2003), pp. 1027–1042.

15. David Teece has written about dynamic capabilities in the paper referred to in reference 2. Also see C. Helfat, S. Finkelstein, W. Mitchell, M. Peteraf, H. Singh, D. Teece and S. Winter, *Dynamic Capabilities: Understanding strategic change in organizations*, Blackwell Publishing, 2007. Different writers have different views on what dynamic capabilities are but tend to emphasise relatively formal organisational processes such as product development, alliances and particular ways of taking decisions in firms: for example, K.M. Eisenhardt and J.A. Martin,

'Dynamic capabilities: what are they?', *Strategic Management Journal*, vol. 21, nos 10/11 (2000), pp. 1105–1121; M. Zollo and S. Winter, 'Deliberate learning and the evolution of dynamic capabilities', *Organization Science*, vol. 13, no. 3 (2002), pp. 339–351. A different view is that dynamic capabilities are about organisational learning (see the Commentary to Part I) which places more emphasis on the way the organisation is run, on the capacity of its culture to allow for or facilitate learning and adaptation.

16. For a summary paper on dynamic capabilities see C.L. Wang and P.K. Ahmed, 'Dynamic capabilities: a review and research agenda', *International Journal of Management Reviews*, vol. 9, no. 1 (2007), pp. 31–52.

17. See Eisenhardt and Martin, reference 15.

18. The importance of analysing and understanding knowledge is discussed in I. Nonaka and H. Takeuchi, *The Knowledge Creating Company*, Oxford University Press, 1995; and V. von Krogh, K. Ichijo and I. Nonaka, *Enabling Knowledge Creation: How to unlock the mystery of tacit knowledge and release the power of innovation*, Oxford University Press, 2000. There are also collections of articles on organisational knowledge: for example, the special issue of the *Strategic Management Journal*, ed. R. Grant and J.-C. Spender, vol. 17 (1996); and the *Harvard Business Review on Knowledge Management*, HBR Press, 1998.

19. Indeed Peter Drucker (see *Management Challenges for the 21st Century*, Butterworth–Heinemann, 1999) and others have referred to the growth of a 'knowledge-based economy'.

20. See reference 18.

21. E.C. Wenger and W.M. Snyder, 'Communities of practice: the organizational frontier', *Harvard Business Review*, vol. 73, no. 3 (2000), pp. 201–207; and E. Wenger, *Communities of Practice: Learning, Meaning and Identity*, Cambridge University Press, 1999.

22. An extensive discussion of the value chain concept and its application can be found in M.E. Porter, *Competitive Advantage*, Free Press, 1985.

23. For an extended example of value chain analysis see A. Shepherd, 'Understanding and using value chain analysis', in Veronique Ambrosini (ed.), *Exploring Techniques of Analysis and Evaluation in Strategic Management*, Prentice Hall, 1998.

24. P. Timmers, *Electronic Commerce*, Wiley, 2000, pp. 182–193, provides an interesting discussion of how value networks are being created and changed by IT.

25. This quote is attributed to Lev Leviev in the *Financial Times*, 14 December (2006), p. 10.

26. The importance of profit pools is discussed by O. Gadiesh and J.L. Gilbert, 'Profit pools: a fresh look at strategy', *Harvard Business Review*, vol. 76, no. 3 (1998), pp. 139–147.

27. A good example of such computer-based systems for analysing organisational capabilities can be found in a paper by C. Eden and F. Ackermann, 'Mapping distinctive competencies: a systemic approach', *Journal of the Operational Research Society*, vol. 51, no. 1 (2000), pp. 12–20.

28. For a more comprehensive account of the use of such network mapping, see V. Ambrosini, *Tacit and Ambiguous Resources as Sources of Competitive Advantage*, Palgrave Macmillan, 2003. Also see F. Ackermann and C. Eden with I. Brown, *Making Strategy*, Sage, 2005, chapter 6.

29. The paper by P. and G. Johnson, 'Facilitating group cognitive mapping of core competencies' (in *Mapping Strategic Knowledge*, ed. Anne Huff and Mark Jenkins, Sage, 2002), explains some of the problems of undertaking such mapping.

30. Michael Porter explains how mapping what he calls 'activity systems' can be important in considering competitive strategy in his article 'What is strategy?' (*Harvard Business Review*, vol. 74, no. 6 (1996), pp. 61–78).

31. Benchmarking is used extensively in both private and public sectors. S. Codling, *Benchmarking Basics*, Gower, 1998, is a practical guide to benchmarking. Also see J. Holloway, *Identifying Best Practices in Benchmarking*, Chartered Institute of Management Accountants, 1999. And for a review of the use of benchmarking in the public sector see M. Wisniewski, 'Measuring up to the best: a manager's guide to benchmarking', in G. Johnson and K. Scholes (eds), *Exploring Public Sector Strategy*, Financial Times/Prentice Hall, 2001, chapter 5.

32. See A. Murdoch, 'Lateral benchmarking, or what Formula One taught an airline', *Management Today*, November (1997), pp. 64–67. See also the Formula One case study in the case study section of this book (Text and Cases version only).

33. The idea of SWOT as a common-sense checklist has been used for many years: for example, S. Tilles, 'Making strategy explicit', in I. Ansoff (ed.), *Business Strategy*, Penguin, 1968. See also T. Jacobs, J. Shepherd and G. Johnson's chapter on SWOT analysis in V. Ambrosini (ed.), *Exploring Techniques of Strategy Analysis and Evaluation*, Prentice Hall, 1998. For a critical discussion of the (mis)use of SWOT, see T. Hill and R. Westbrook, 'SWOT analysis: it's time for a product recall', *Long Range Planning*, vol. 30, no. 1 (1997), pp. 46–52.

34. For background reading on the pharmaceutical industry see, for example, 'The drug industry – from bench to bedside', *The Economist*, 4 November (2006), and G. Pisano, *Science Business*, Harvard Business School Press, 2006.

35. This section draws on the work of Veronique Ambrosini; see reference 28.

36. For a fuller discussion of how managers may manage strategic capabilities, see C. Bowman and N. Collier, 'A contingency approach to resource-creation processes', *International Journal of Management Reviews*, vol. 8, no. 4 (2006), pp. 191–211.

37. See C.A. Maritan and T.H. Brush, 'Heterogeneity and transferring practices: implementing flow practices in multiple plants', *Strategic Management Journal*, vol. 24, no. 10 (2003), pp. 945–960.

38. In their 1990 paper, Hamel and Prahalad (see reference 4) discuss the stretching of competences as the basis of related diversification.

39. See T. Baker and R.E. Nelson, 'Creating something from nothing: resource construction through entrepreneurial bricolage', *Administrative Science Quarterly*, vol. 50, no. 3 (2005), pp. 329–366.

40. These quotes are from a study by R. Garud and P. Karnoe, 'Bricolage versus breakthrough: distributed and embedded agency in technological entrepreneurship', *Research Policy*, vol. 32, no. 2 (2003), pp. 277–300.

Making eBay work

Jill Shepherd, Segal Graduate School of Business
Simon Fraser University, Canada

In 2006, there were over 200 million eBayers worldwide. For around 750,000 people, eBay (http://www.ebay.com/) was their primary source of income. A survivor of the dot.com bust of the late 1990s, eBay represents a new business model courtesy of the Internet. Whatever statistics you choose – from most expensive item sold to number of auctions in any one day – the numbers amaze. 'This is a whole new way of doing business,' says Meg Whitman, the CEO and President since 1998. 'We're creating something that didn't exist before.'

eBay's business model

Value in eBay is created by providing a virtual worldwide market for buyers and sellers and collecting a tax on transactions as they happen. The business model of eBay relies on its customers being the organisation's product development team, sales- and marketing force, merchandising department and the security department. It is arguably the first web 2.0 company.

According to eBay managers, of key importance is listening to customers: keeping up with what they want to sell, buy and how they want to do it. If customers speak, eBay listens. Technology allows every move of every potential customer to be traced, yielding rich information. Conventional companies might spend big money on getting to know their customers and persuading them to provide feedback; for eBay such feedback is often free and offered without the need for enticement. Even so some of the company's most effective ways of getting user input do not rely on the net and do not come free. eBay organises Voice of the Customer groups which involve flying in a new group of about 10 sellers and buyers from around the country to its offices every few months to discuss the company in depth. Teleconferences are held for new features and policies, however small a change they involve.

Even workshops and classes are held to teach people how to make the most of the site. Participants tend to double their selling activity on eBay after taking a class. Others run their own websites offering advice on how to sell on eBay. Rumours have it that buyers have devised computer programs that place bids in the last moment. Sellers that leave the site unable to compete any more are known to write blogs on what went wrong to help others.

The company is governed from both outside and within. The eBay system has a source of automatic control in the form of buyers and sellers rating each other on each transaction, creating rules and norms. Both buyers and sellers build up reputations which are valuable, in turn encouraging further good behaviour in themselves and others. Sales of illegal products are dealt with by withdrawing what is on sale and invariably banning the seller.

eBay's management

Meg Whitman's style and past have heavily influenced the management of eBay. When she joined the company in 1998, it was more of a collection of geeks, handpicked by the pony-tailed founder Pierre Omidyar, than a blue-chip, something which underpinned Omidyar's recruitment of Meg. Meg, an ex-consultant, filled many of the senior management roles including the head of the US business, head of international operations and vice president of consumer marketing with consultants. The result: eBay has become data and metric driven. 'If you can't measure it, you can't control it', Meg says. Whereas in the early days you could touch and feel the way the organisation worked, its current size means it needs to be measured. Category managers, reminiscent of Meg's days in Procter and Gamble, are expected to spend their days measuring and acting upon data within their fiefdom.

However, unlike their counterparts in Procter and Gamble, category managers in eBay can only indirectly control their products. They have no stock to reorder once levels of toothpaste or washing-up liquid run low on the supermarket shelves. They provide tools to buy and sell more effectively:

What they can do is endlessly try to eke out small wins in their categories – say, a slight jump in scrap-metal listings or new bidders for comic books. To get there, they use marketing and merchandising schemes such as enhancing the presentation of their users' products and giving them tools to buy and sell better.

Over and above this unusual existence, the work environment can be tough and ultra competitive, say ex-eBayers. Changes often come only after PowerPoint slides are exchanged and refined at a low level, eventually presented at a senior level and after the change has been approved in a sign-off procedure which includes every department.

In time eBay has upgraded its ability to ensure the technology does not rule. Until the late 1990s, the site was plagued with outages, including one in 1999 which shut the site down for 22 hours courtesy of software problems and no backup systems. Former Gateway Inc. Chief Information Officer Maynard Webb, who joined as president of eBay's technology unit, quickly took action to upgrade systems. Its use of technology is upgraded constantly. In 2005, Chris Corrado was appointed Senior Vice President and Chief Technology Officer. In eBay's press release COO Maynard Webb said:

Chris is one of the leading technology platform experts in the corporate world, and we are thrilled that he is joining us. It is testament to the tremendous reputation of the eBay technology organization that we were able to bring Chris to the team.

Meg is a leader who buys into the company in more ways than one. Having auctioned some $35,000 (€28,000; £19,500) worth of furnishings in her ski condo in Colorado to understand the selling experience, she became a top seller among the company's employees and ensured that her learning from the experience was listened to by fellow top execs. Meg is also known for listening carefully to her employees and expects her managers to do the same. As the business is as much, if not more, its customers, any false move can cause revolts within the community that is eBay.

Most of all, eBay tries to stay aware and flexible. Nearly all of its fastest-growing new categories emerged from registering seller activity in the area and quietly giving it a nudge at the right moment. For example, after noticing a few car sales, eBay created a separate site called eBay Motors in 1999, with special features such as vehicle inspections and shipping. Some four years later, eBay expects to gross some $1 billion worth of autos and parts, many of which are sold by professional dealers.

The democratic underpinning of eBay, whilst easily embraced by customers, can, however, take some getting used too. New managers take time to understand the ethos. 'Some of the terms you learn in business school – drive, force, commit – don't apply,' says former PepsiCo Inc. exec William C. Cobb, now President eBay North America, with a background in restaurants and PepsiCo, 'We're over here listening, adapting, enabling.'

Competition and cooperation

As the Internet has become a more competitive arena eBay has not stood still. In 2005 it bought Skype, the Internet telephony organisation (http://www.skype.com/), surrounded by much debate in the press as to the logic of the $2.6bn deal. With Skype, eBay argues it can create an unparalleled e-commerce engine, pointing to the 2002 purchase of online payment system PayPal (http://www.paypal.com/) that spurred on the business at that time. All three benefit from so-called network effects – the more members, the more valuable the company – and eBay has to be a world leader in managing network effects.

In 2006 it also announced a deal with Google. eBay is one of Google's biggest advert customers. Google in turn is attracted to eBay's Skype customers for click-to-call adverts. This deal was after eBay signed an advertising deal with Yahoo! which made some think eBay was teaming up with Yahoo! against Google's dominance. But in the interconnected world of the Internet, defining competition and cooperation is a new game. eBay also formed a partnership between Baidu Inc., a Chinese web portal bought by eBay in 2002, and eBay EachNet. Baidu promotes PayPal Beibao as the preferred payment method on Baidu whilst EachNet uses Baidu as its exclusive search provider. The development of a co-branded toolbar is set to cement the partnership. So whilst in the West Yahoo! and eBay are partnering against Google, in the East Yahoo! is a rival.

Despite eBay being the Internet auction phenomenon, it does not do as well in the East as the West. It pulled out of Japan, is suffering in Taiwan and lags behind a rival in China. In Korea, GMarket, partly owned by Yahoo!, is more or less equal in size to eBay's Internet Auction. GMarket offers less emphasis on open auctions than eBay, although eBay now does have eBay Express where new products from multiple sellers can be purchased in one transaction backed as ever by customer support including live chat.

Innovative marketing that makes the experience fun for shoppers and helps sellers improve their performance is perhaps another way GMarket differentiates itself from eBay. GMarket has itself attracted imitators.

Once a web 2.0 company always a web 2.0 company? Although the news did not produce much reaction when announced during an eBay Live! Session, in 2006 eBay created eBay Wiki (http://www.ebaywiki.com/), hosted by Jotspot, allowing people to contribute their knowledge of eBay to others, along with eBay blogs (http://blogs.ebay.com/). But eBay has always been about community so perhaps they will catch on in time.

Questions

1 Analyse eBay's strategic capability using an analytical framework(s) from the chapter.

2 What are the capabilities that have provided eBay with competitive advantage and why?

3 Using the concepts of sustainability and dynamic capabilities, how would you manage this capability (create new resources and competences, invest/divest in others, extend others), given:
   (a) New entrants in the marketplace?
   (b) The changing nature of eBay?

The
Strategic
Position

4

Strategic Purpose

LEARNING OUTCOMES

After reading this chapter you should be able to:

→ Identify the components of the governance chain of an organisation.

→ Understand differences in governance structures across the world and the advantages and disadvantages of these.

→ Identify differences in the corporate social responsibility stances taken by organisations and how ethical issues relate to strategic purpose.

→ Undertake stakeholder analysis as a means of identifying the influence of different stakeholder groups in terms of their power and interest.

→ Consider appropriate ways to express the strategic purpose of an organisation in terms of statements of values, vision, mission or objectives.

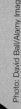

Photo: David Ball/Alamy Images

4.1 INTRODUCTION

The previous two chapters have looked respectively at the influence of the environment and capabilities on an organisation's strategic position. However, a fundamental decision that has to be taken concerns the *purpose* of the strategy that is to be followed. This is the focus of this chapter, together with the influences on such purpose by the expectations of *stakeholders* of an organisation. **Stakeholders** are those individuals or groups who depend on an organisation to fulfil their own goals and on whom, in turn, the organisation depends. An underlying issue raised by this chapter is whether the strategic purpose of the organisation should be determined in response to a particular stakeholder, for example shareholders in the case of a commercial enterprise, or to broader stakeholder interests – at the extreme society and the social good. This theme is considered in relation to a number of key issues.

Stakeholders are those individuals or groups who depend on an organisation to fulfil their own goals and on whom, in turn, the organisation depends

● Section 4.2 considers *corporate governance* and the *regulatory framework* within which organisations operate. Here the concern is with the way in which formally constituted bodies such as investors or boards influence strategic purpose through the formalised processes of supervising executive decisions and actions. In turn this raises issues of *accountability*: who are strategists accountable to? There are significant differences in the approach to corporate governance internationally, broadly relating to either shareholder or wider stakeholder orientations, and these are also discussed.

● Section 4.3 is concerned with issues of *social responsibility and ethics*. Here the question is which purposes an organisation *should* fulfil. How should managers respond to the expectations society has of their organisations, both

Exhibit 4.1   **Influences on strategic purpose**

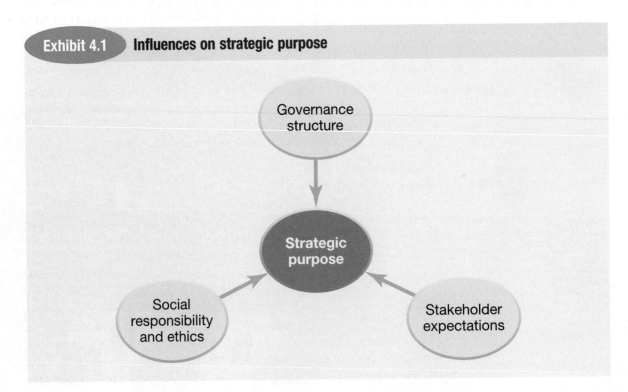

in terms of *corporate social responsibility* and in terms of the *behaviour of individuals* within organisations, including themselves?

● In all this it is, then, important to understand *different stakeholder expectations* and their relative influence on strategic purpose. This requires an understanding of both the *power* and *interest* of different stakeholder groups. This is addressed through *stakeholder analysis*.

● The chapter concludes by considering different ways in which organisations *express strategic purpose*. This may include statements of *values, vision, mission* or *objectives*.

Exhibit 4.1 summarises these different influences on strategic purpose discussed in the chapter.

4.2 CORPORATE GOVERNANCE[1]

Corporate governance is concerned with the structures and systems of control by which managers are held accountable to those who have a legitimate stake in an organisation

Corporate governance is concerned with the structures and systems of control by which managers are held accountable to those who have a legitimate stake in an organisation.[2] It has become an increasingly important issue for organisations for three main reasons.

● *The separation of ownership and management control* of organisations (which is now the norm except with very small businesses) means that most organisations operate within a hierarchy, or chain, of governance. This chain represents those groups that influence an organisation through their involvement in either ownership or management of an organisation.

● *Corporate scandals* since the late 1990s have increased public debate about how different parties in the governance chain should interact and influence each other. Most notable here is the relationship between shareholders and the boards of businesses, but an equivalent issue in the public sector is the relationship between government or public funding bodies and public sector organisations.

● *Increased accountability to wider stakeholder interests* has also come to be increasingly advocated; in particular the argument that corporations need to be more visibly accountable and/or responsive, not only to 'owners' and 'managers' in the governance chain but to wider social interest.

4.2.1 The governance chain

www.pearsoned.co.uk/ecs
KEY CONCEPT
Governance chain

The governance chain illuminates the roles and relationships of different groups involved in the governance of an organisation. In a small family business, the governance chain is quite simple: there are family shareholders; there is a board, with some family members; and there are managers, some of whom may be family too. Here there are just three layers in the chain. However, Exhibit 4.2 shows a governance chain for a typical large, publicly quoted organisation. Here the size of the organisation means there are extra layers of management internally, while being publicly quoted introduces more investor layers as well. Individual investors (the ultimate beneficiaries) often invest in public companies through collective funds, for example unit trusts or pension funds, which then

Exhibit 4.2   **The chain of corporate governance: typical reporting structures**

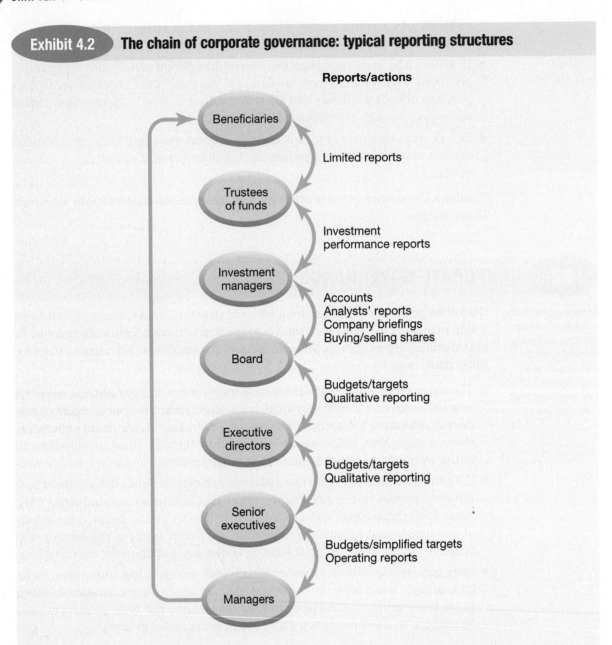

Reports/actions

- Beneficiaries
- Limited reports
- Trustees of funds
- Investment performance reports
- Investment managers
- Accounts
  Analysts' reports
  Company briefings
  Buying/selling shares
- Board
- Budgets/targets
  Qualitative reporting
- Executive directors
- Budgets/targets
  Qualitative reporting
- Senior executives
- Budgets/simplified targets
  Operating reports
- Managers

Source: Adapted from David Pitt-Watson, Hermes.

invest in a range of companies on their behalf. Such funds are of growing importance. In 2006, they owned 50 per cent of the equity of US corporations (19 per cent in 1970) and over 70 per cent in the UK (25 per cent in 1963), with similar growth elsewhere in Europe. Funds are typically controlled by trustees, with day-to-day investment activity undertaken by investment managers. So the ultimate beneficiaries may not even know which companies they have a financial stake in and have little power to influence the companies' boards directly.

The relationships in such governance chains can be understood in terms of the *principal–agent model*[3]. Here 'principals' pay 'agents' to act on their behalf, just as home-owners employ estate agents to sell their homes. In Exhibit 4.2, the beneficiaries are the ultimate principals and fund trustees are their agents in terms of achieving good returns on their investments. Further down the chain, company boards are principals too, with senior executives their agents in managing the company. There are many layers of agents between ultimate principals and the managers at the bottom, with the reporting mechanisms between each layer liable to be imperfect.

Principal–agent theory assumes that agents will not work diligently for principals unless incentives are carefully and appropriately aligned. However, it can be seen from Exhibit 4.2 that in large companies board members and other managers driving strategy are likely to be very remote from the ultimate beneficiaries of the company's performance. In such circumstances, the danger is twofold:

● *Misalignment of incentives and control*. As influence passes down the governance chain, the expectations of one group are not passed on to the next appropriately. For example, ultimate beneficiaries may be mainly concerned with the long-term security of their pension fund, but the investment managers and analysts or the boards with whom they interact may place a greater emphasis on short-term growth.

● *Self-interest*. Any agent in the chain may act out of self-interest. Managers will be striving for promotion and/or increased earnings, investment managers will be seeking to increase their bonuses, and so on.

The result may be that decisions are taken that are not in the best interests of the final beneficiary. This is just what has happened in the case of many of the corporate scandals of recent years, the most notorious of which was probably Enron (see Illustration 4.1).

In this context, the governance chain helps highlight important issues that affect the management of strategy:

● *Responsibility to whom?* A fundamental question in large corporations is whether executives should regard themselves as *solely* responsible to shareholders, or as 'trustees of the assets of the corporation' acting on behalf of a wider range of stakeholders?[4] (See the key debate, Illustration 4.6.) Even in terms of formal governance structures this varies across the world, as section 4.2.3 shows.

● *Who are the shareholders?* If managers do see themselves as primarily responsible to shareholders, what does this mean in terms of the governance chain? As explained above, the final beneficiaries are far removed from the managers, so for many managers responsibility to them is notional. In practical terms, directors of a firm are likely to engage most frequently with institutional representatives of those shareholders – an investment manager or analyst from a pension fund or insurance company perhaps. The principal–agent problem arises here too. The final beneficiaries are also distant for investment managers and analysts, who may also be pursuing their own self-interest. Strategists within a firm therefore face a difficult choice, even if they espouse primary responsibility to shareholders. Do they develop strategies they believe to be in the best interest of a highly fragmented group of unknown shareholders? Or to meet the needs and aspirations of the investment managers? A similar problem exists for public sector managers. They may see themselves as developing strategies in the public good, but they may face direct scrutiny

Illustration 4.1

The Enron corporate scandal

Executive decisions may not always be in the interest of shareholders; sometimes disastrously so.

Enron was one of the world's leading electricity, natural gas, pulp, paper and communications companies, based in Houston, Texas. It employed around 21,000 people with claimed revenues of $101bn (€80bn) in 2000. However at the end of 2001 it was revealed that its reported financial condition was sustained mostly by systematic and creative accounting fraud. When Enron sought Chapter 11 protection in the USA in late 2001, it was the biggest bankruptcy in US history and cost 4,000 employees their jobs. The scandal also caused the dissolution of Arthur Andersen, a Big Five accounting firm.

Many of Enron's recorded assets and profits were inflated, fraudulent and non-existent. Enron had put debts and losses into 'offshore' companies not included in the company's financial statements and used sophisticated financial transactions with related companies known as 'special purposes entities' (SPEs) to take unprofitable transactions off the company's books. Later investigations revealed that some executives at Enron knew about the offshore accounts that were hiding losses for the company. Chief Financial Officer Andrew Fastow led the team which created the off-books companies and manipulated the deals to provide himself, his family and friends with hundreds of millions of dollars in guaranteed revenue, at the expense of the stockholders. As the scandal unfolded, Enron shares dropped from over $90.00 to $0.30.

US Congressional hearings revealed that a group of Enron employees had been expressing concerns as early as 1998. Growing apprehension led to an all-employee meeting in mid-2001, where other related issues were discussed. Following the meeting, Sherron Watkins, Vice President, met with the then CEO, the late Ken Lay, handing him a memo detailing her concerns. She especially highlighted the roles of Vinson & Elkins, LLP, a large and reputable US law firm, and Arthur Andersen, LLP, as complicit with dubious deals. Top management asked Vinson & Elkins to investigate the concerns. However, the law firm reported that apart from some 'bad cosmetics',

and 'aggressive and creative accounting', they found no problem with the SPEs. Arthur Andersen in turn confirmed that it was comfortable with the accounting.

Late in October 2002, the Securities and Exchange Commission opened a formal inquiry into Enron, which also started a devastating trail of events at Arthur Andersen. By the time Andersen received notice from the SEC in mid-November, a large number of Enron-related audit documents had been destroyed. This subsequently led to Andersen's indictment in June 2002. The trial of Arthur Andersen also exposed its accounting fraud at WorldCom, setting off a wave of other accounting scandals.

J.P. Morgan Chase, Citigroup, Merrill Lynch, Credit Suisse First Boston, Canadian Imperial Bank of Commerce (CIBC), Bank America, Barclays Bank, Deutsche Bank; and Lehman Brothers were also named as players in the series of fraudulent transactions that ultimately cost shareholders more than $25bn. Two law firms were identified as involved in the fraud: Vinson & Elkins and Chicago-based Kirkland & Ellis, which Enron used to represent a number of SPEs.

By mid-2006, 16 of Enron's top executives, including Ken Lay, Jeff Skilling (CEO), David Delainey (Head of Enron's Energy Trading Unit), Richard Causey (Chief Accounting Officer), Andrew Fastow (Chief Financial Officer) and Mark Koenig (Head of Investor Relations), pleaded guilty or were convicted and in the process of being sentenced.

Prepared by Rajshree Prakash, University of Lancaster Management School.

Questions

1 What mechanisms in the governance chain should (or could) have prevented what happened at Enron?

2 What changes in corporate governance are required to prevent similar occurrences?

from an agency acting on behalf of the government. Is the strategy to be designed for the general public good, or to meet the scrutiny of the agency? For example, managers and doctors in the UK health service are dedicated to the well-being of their patients. But increasingly how they manage their services is governed by the targets placed upon them by a government department, which presumably also believes it is acting in the public good.

- *The role of institutional investors.* The role of institutional investors with regard to the strategy of firms differs according to governance structures around the world (see section 4.2.3). However, a common issue is the extent to which they do or should actively seek to influence strategy. Historically, in economies like those of the UK or USA investors have exerted their influence on firms simply through the buying and selling of shares rather than through an in-depth engagement with the company on strategic issues. The stock market becomes the judge of their actions through share price movements. There are signs, however, that investors are becoming more actively involved in the strategies of the firms in which they invest.[5] Such involvement varies a good deal[6] but has grown, and there is evidence that institutional investors that seek to work proactively with boards to develop strategy do better for beneficiaries than those who do not.[7]

- *Scrutiny and control.* Given the concerns about governance that have grown in the last decade, there have been increasing attempts to build means of scrutinising and controlling the activities of 'agents' in the chain to safeguard the interests of the final beneficiaries. Exhibit 4.2 indicates the information typically available to each 'player' in the chain to judge the performance of others in that chain. There are increasing statutory requirements as well as voluntary codes placed upon boards to disclose information publicly and regulate their activities. None the less managers are still left with a great deal of discretion as to what information to provide to whom and, indeed, what information to require of those who report to them. For example, what information should be presented to investment analysts who will influence a firm's share price? How specific should a chief executive be in explaining future strategy to shareholders in public statements such as annual reports? There are also issues of internal reporting that have to be resolved. What are the appropriate targets and measures to incentivise and control management within a firm? Should these primarily be concerned with the achievement of shareholder value? Or is a more balanced scorecard approach appropriate to meet the needs of various stakeholders (see section 12.3.5)? Are the typical accountancy methods (such as return on capital employed) the most appropriate measures or should measures be specifically designed to fit the needs of particular strategies or particular stakeholder/shareholder expectations? There are no categoric answers to these questions. How managers answer them will depend on what they decide the strategic purpose of the organisation is, which itself will be influenced by their view on whom they see themselves responsible to.

The governance chain, then, typically operates imperfectly for at least five reasons: (i) a lack of clarity on who the end beneficiaries are; (ii) unequal division of power between the different 'players' in the chain; (iii) with different levels of access to information available to them; (iv) potentially agents in the chain pursuing their own self-interest; and (v) using measures and targets reflecting their own interests rather than those of end beneficiaries. In such circumstances it is not surprising that there are attempts to reform corporate governance and that governance structures are changing around the world.

4.2.2 Corporate governance reforms

Many governments have been proactive in reforming aspects of corporate governance. The most notable has been the Sarbanes–Oxley Act in the USA that was one outcome of the Enron scandal. This tightened accounting standards and increased auditor independence from management.[8] Other governments have sponsored committees to advise on specific issues of corporate governance.[9] Initially these concentrated on internal financial controls and external disclosure of information.[10] Later committees focused on the broadening of internal control requirements beyond simply financial controls and looked at the role and effectiveness of non-executive directors.[11] The public sector picked up a similar agenda; in the UK there was particular interest in *risk management* of public sector organisations' strategies – a traditionally weak area.[12] These reforms have had significant impacts. For example, accountancy firms have been forced to separate their audit function from their advisory services and, indeed, sell off their managing consulting services as a result of the Sarbanes–Oxley Act, so the strategy of accounting firms was directly affected, as was the source of consultancy services for firms.

Surveys have also found that finance directors have switched their attention more to stewardship roles than to strategy roles,[13] and more emphasis has been placed on the role of independent non-executive directors to scrutinise the behaviour of firms. However, some executives have voiced concerns: for example, the managing director of the Bank of Queensland in Australia: 'Over regulation can and will kill the entrepreneurial spirit, it will crush innovation as more and more resources are shifted towards compliance and away from staying ahead of the pack.'[14] There is also a concern that, although changes in the structure of board committees might be needed, the really important issue is the behaviour of boards of directors. The implication for policy makers (in government) is that there is a need to find ways of sponsoring governance changes that will demonstrably encourage or require directors and managers (as 'agents') to behave in ways and pursue strategies that are in the interests of 'principals' in their governance chain as discussed above. Promoting such changes is a major challenge, given the concerns voiced about top executives' focus on building empires, climbing up through the hierarchy and increasing their personal financial rewards without due regard to the consequences on the final beneficiaries.

4.2.3 Different governance structures

The governing body of an organisation is typically a board of directors. The primary statutory responsibility of a board is to ensure that an organisation fulfils the wishes and purposes of the primary stakeholders. However, who these stakeholders are varies. In the private sector in some parts of the world it is shareholders, but in other parts of the world it is a broader or different stakeholder base. In the public sector, the governing body is accountable to the political arm of government – possibly through some intermediate 'agency' such as a funding body. These differences lead to differences in the way firms operate, how the purposes of an organisation are shaped and how strategies are developed as well as the role and composition of boards.[15]

At the most general level there are two governance structures: the shareholder model and the stakeholder model.[16] These are more or less common in different parts of the world.

A shareholder model of governance

Here shareholders have the legitimate primacy in relation to the wealth generated by the corporations, though proponents argue that maximising shareholder value benefits other stakeholders too. There is dispersed shareholding, though a large proportion of shares is held by financial institutions. At least in principle, the trading of shares provides a regulatory mechanism for maximising shareholder value, given that dissatisfied shareholders may sell their shares, the result being a drop in share price and the threat of takeovers for underperforming firms.

The shareholder model is epitomised by the economies of the USA and UK. Firms in the USA usually have a single-tier board structure, with a majority of non-executive directors. This emphasis on outside directors is intended to bring greater independence to the primary role of the board, that of oversight on behalf of shareholders. However, this is not without its problems. Typically the CEO plays a major role in selecting non-executives, which raises questions about their independence. There are also concerns that outside directors may not have sufficient time, or the requisite knowledge of firms' problems.[17]

The UK also has a single-tier board structure and increasingly a separation of the chair and the CEO, with the chair often non-executive. The proportion of the executive directors on the board of large companies is typically between one-third and one-half of the total board membership. The board has an executive role of driving the company forward as well as an oversight role on behalf of shareholders.

There are arguments for and against the shareholder model. The *argued advantages* include:

- *Benefits for investors*. Relative to the stakeholder model the investor gets a higher rate of return. Shareholders can also reduce risk through diversifying their holdings in an equity market where shares can be readily traded.

- *Benefits to the economy*. Since the system facilitates higher risk taking by investors, there is a higher likelihood of the encouragement of economic growth and of entrepreneurship. It is also argued that one reason why the UK gets more than its 'fair share' of inward investment to the EU is because the ownership structures are more open to new investors than elsewhere.

- *Benefits for management*. Arguably the separation of ownership and management makes strategic decisions more objectively related to the potentially different demands and constraints of financial, labour and customer markets. A diversified shareholding also means that no one shareholder is likely to control management decisions, provided the firm performs well.

The *argued disadvantages* include:

- *Disadvantages for investors*. Dispersed shareholdings prevent close monitoring of the management. This may result in the managers sacrificing shareholder value to pursue their own agendas. For example, CEOs may further their own egos at the expense of the shareholders with mergers that add no value.

- *Disadvantages for the economy: the risk of short-termism*. Lack of control of management may lead to them taking decisions to benefit their own careers (for example, to gain promotion). This, combined with the threat of takeovers, may encourage managers to focus on short-term gains at the expense of long-term projects.[18]

- *Corporate reputation and top management greed*. The lack of management control allows for the huge compensations the managers reward themselves in the form of salary, bonuses and stock options. In the USA CEOs have 531 times more compensation than their employees in comparison with Japan where the comparable figure is closer to a multiple of 10.[19]

The stakeholder model of governance

An alternative model of governance pursued in various forms is the stakeholder model. This is founded on the principle that wealth is created, captured and distributed by a variety of stakeholders. This may include shareholders but could include other investors, such as banks, as well as employees or their union representatives. As such, management need to be responsive to multiple stakeholders who, themselves, may be formally represented on boards.

However, stakeholder models are also sometimes known as the *block holder system of governance*.[20] One or two large group of investors come to dominate ownership. For example, in Germany just less than three-quarters of all the German listed companies have a majority owner. In addition, in countries like Germany and Sweden banks play a dominant role and Japanese banks tend to have shareholdings in organisations, as against simply providing loan capital. There is also likely to be a complex web of cross-shareholdings between companies.

Germany and Japan are often cited as examples of the stakeholder model. In Germany there is a two-tier board system. The supervisory board (*Aufsichtsrat*), mandatory for companies having more than 500 employees, and the management board (*Vorstand*). The supervisory board is a forum where the interest of various groups is represented, including shareholders and employees but also typically bankers, lawyers and stock exchange experts. Strategic planning and operational control are vested with the management board, but major decisions like mergers and acquisitions require approval of the supervisory board. In other European countries, notably The Netherlands and France, two-tier boards also exist.

In Japan, profit maximisation or shareholder value is not viewed as the ultimate goal of business enterprises so much as long-term growth and security of the company. There is concentrated ownership of firms, with a small group of shareholders owning a large percentage of the company, and a system of cross-shareholding, where large companies own shares of other companies and banks finance the same subgroup. Japanese firms have a single-tier board system. Directors are appointed from the executive managers of the company, so the board consists almost entirely of insiders.[21] A prerequisite of a good director has traditionally been someone who promotes the interests of employees.

There are *argued advantages* for the stakeholder model of governance:

- *Advantages for stakeholders*. Apart from the argument that the wider interests of stakeholders are taken into account, it is also argued that employee influence in particular is a deterrent to high-risk decisions and investments.

- *Advantages for investors*. Perhaps ironically it is argued that it is block investments that provide economic benefits in several ways. There may be a closer level of monitoring of management, with investors having greater access to information from within the firm. Given that power may reside with relatively few block investors, intervention may also be easier in case of management failure.

- *Long-term horizons*. It is argued that the major investors – banks or other companies, for example – are likely to regard their investments as long term, thus reducing the pressure for short-term results[22] as against longer-term performance.

There are also *argued disadvantages* of the stakeholder model of governance:

- *Disadvantages for management*. Close monitoring could lead to interference, slowing down of decision processes and the loss of management objectivity when critical decisions have to be made.

- *Disadvantages for investors*. Due to lack of pressure from shareholders, long-term investments are made on projects where the returns may be below market expectations.

- *Disadvantage for the economy*. There are fewer alternatives for raising finance, thus limiting the possibilities of growth and entrepreneurial activity.

These argued advantages and disadvantages are summarised in Exhibit 4.3.

It is also worth noting that there are implications with regard to the financing of businesses. In the shareholder model, equity is the dominant form of long-term finance and commercial banks provide debt capital, so relationships with bankers are essentially contractual. There are significant implications. Managers need to limit gearing to a prudent level, so more equity is needed for major strategy developments. It also means that the company itself has a higher degree of influence over strategic decisions since the banks are not seeking a strategic involvement with the company. However, if strategies start to fail, the organisation can become increasingly dependent on the bank as a key stakeholder. This often happens in family-owned small businesses. In the extreme banks may exercise their power through *exit* (that is, withdrawing funds), even if this liquidates the company. In contrast, in some stakeholder systems (notably Japan and to a lesser extent Germany), banks often have significant equity stakes or are part of the same parent company. They are less likely to adopt an arm's-length relationship and more likely to seek active strategic involvement.

Governance structures in transition

There are pressures for change to traditional governance models. Some of these have already been discussed in relation to the governance chain in section 4.2.1.

Exhibit 4.3　Benefits and disadvantages of governance systems

	Shareholder model	Stakeholder model
Benefits	For investors: ● Higher rate of return ● Reduced risk For the economy: ● Encourages entrepreneurship ● Encourages inward investment For management: ● Independence	For investors: ● Closer monitoring of management ● Longer-term decision horizons For stakeholders: ● Deterrent to high-risk decisions
Disadvantages	For investors: ● Difficult to monitor management For the economy: ● The risk of short-termism And top management greed	For management: ● Potential interference ● Slower decision making ● Reduced independence For the economy: ● Reduced financing opportunities for growth

There are, none the less, suggestions that there is a convergence around the world on the shareholder model of governance. This is because of many of the advantages explained above, in particular the view that there is mutual advantage to both shareholders and wider stakeholders. It is also because of the increasing role of institutional investors acting on behalf of a growing mass shareholder class and increasing globalisation and cross-country mergers and acquisitions.[23]

So, for example, in Japan, institutional and foreign investors are gaining influence, and deregulation and liberalisation are increasing the pressure to change governance structures. In Germany, too, there are pressures for change. In mid-2006, for example, Jürgen Thumann of the BDI industry federation argued that if German companies were to remain globally competitive, the employee representation on boards needed to be reviewed: not least because this would help reduce costs and speed decision making.

Similarly elsewhere, governance systems are in transition. In Sweden historically firms were privately owned or in the hands of family-controlled foundations, holding companies and investment companies. By 2005, however, less than 15 per cent of the market capitalisation was held by individual owners as institutional ownership increased.[24] Sweden's entry into the EU has also reduced restrictions on capital inflow and increasingly companies are becoming foreign owned. However, most companies still have a majority owner that gives them a controlling position akin to the stakeholder model.

In India there was a high level of state protectionism till the 1980s, with major industries like airlines and banks nationalised and restrictions on inward foreign investment. However, since 1991 there has been radical change. Import licensing has been abolished and import tariffs reduced. Restrictions on foreign equity have been relaxed in certain industries, some public sector enterprises have been disinvested and firms allowed to register on the international stock exchanges.[25] India is still characterised by family firms, but with increasing separation of ownership and management. The codes of governance being proposed indicate a move towards a shareholder model of governance with a single board and between 30 and 50 per cent non-executive directors.

In China the major stakeholders in firms are the state or quasi-state institutions. China has a two-tier board model. The supervisory board has a minimum of one-third of employees as members, but with limited influence on organisational activities, which is the responsibility of operating boards. Boards are required to have non-executive directors who have recently been required to be independent. The appointment of top management was tightly controlled by government but this has diminished over the years. Senior managers have, however, usually started their careers in government positions.[26]

Public services have a wide variety of arrangements for governing bodies, but there are some commonalities. Governing bodies are often 'representational' of key stakeholders, in practice even if not by regulation. This particularly applies to the place of employees and unions on governing bodies. There has been a move in many countries to increase the proportion of (so-called) independent members on governing bodies. These independent members are the nearest equivalent of the non-executive director in the private sector.

4.2.4 How governing bodies influence strategy

A common issue increasingly debated is, then, the role of boards of directors and of directors themselves. Since boards have the ultimate responsibility for the success or failure of an organisation as well as the benefits received by shareholders or wider stakeholders, they must be concerned with strategy. However, there are two broad choices on how they do this:

● Strategic management can be entirely *delegated to management* – with the board receiving and approving plans/decisions. Here the 'stewardship' role of the board requires processes that ensure that the purpose of the organisation and its strategies are not 'captured' by management at the expense of other stakeholders – particularly the owners. The Enron case is an extreme example of how this can happen.

● The board can *engage with management* in the strategic management process. But this has many practical problems concerning the time and knowledge level of (particularly) non-executive directors to perform their role this way. This problem can be especially pronounced in organisations such as charities or public bodies with governing boards or trustees of people committed to the mission of the organisation, keen to become involved but with limited operational understanding of it.

In the guidelines increasingly issued by governments[27] or advocated by commentators to try to ensure that boards act in the interests of their shareholders and beneficiaries, there are some common themes:

- Boards must be seen to *operate 'independently' of the management* of the company. So the role of non-executive directors is heightened.

- Boards must be *competent to scrutinise the activities of managers*. So the collective experience of the board, its training and the information at its disposal are crucially important.

- Directors must have the *time* to do their job properly. So limitations on the number of directorships that an individual can hold are also an important consideration.

- However, it is the *behaviour of boards* and their members that is likely to be most significant[28] whatever structural arrangements are put in place. For example, respect, trust, 'constructive friction' between board members, fluidity of roles, individual as well as collective responsibility, and the evaluation of individual director and collective board performance.

4.2.5 Ownership choices

Within the broad governance structures that exist, different forms of ownership will have an effect on the purposes of an organisation and the strategies pursued. There may in turn be issues as to whether the form of ownership is appropriate to the strategic purposes of an organisation.

- *Private or public ownership of equity* is an issue for commercial organisations. As they develop and grow, many organisations – for example, family businesses – move from private ownership to a publicly quoted corporation. Such a decision might be made because the owners decide that increased equity is required to finance the growth of the business. The family members who own the business need to recognise that their role will change. They become answerable to a much wider group of shareholders and to institutions acting for those shareholders.

- *Sale of all or part of the company* may be a choice faced by the board of directors of a business which has a responsibility to provide shareholders with a return on their investment. A board may arrive at the view that a different corporate parent would better achieve this primary purpose. Or a business may become the *target for an acquisition* and a board might decide that such an offer is more attractive to shareholders than the returns it can promise in the future.

- *Acquisition of another business* may also be considered. Acquiring other businesses may raise significant issues about the purpose of the corporate entity as Chapter 7 (section 7.4) shows. However, questions have been raised as to whether acquisitions are in the best interests of shareholders. Many fail to deliver the promised benefits to shareholders; at least in the short/medium term, they are likely to lead to loss of shareholder value. The concern centres on the principal–agent issue and the potential *conflict of interest* between a board of directors and the best interests of shareholders. Directors may pursue such acquisitions because they enlarge their empire, improve their financial rewards or because they feel that investment analysts expect acquisitive growth. Mergers and acquisitions are discussed more fully in Chapter 10 (section 10.2.2).

- *Mutual ownership and partnerships* have been the tradition in some sectors. Insurance companies and building societies were traditionally owned by their customers rather than by shareholders. In theory, such an arrangement might seem to bring together the principal beneficiaries of shareholders and customers and facilitate strategy being developed in the interest of both. However, ownership can remain highly fragmented under such a structure, leading to the same principal–agent problems discussed earlier. Indeed, many UK building societies have become banks and changed their form of ownership by de-mutualising, thus changing governance arrangements to be more similar to companies. There are also signs that law firms and accountancy firms, so long wedded to partnership structures, are also moving to more corporate models of ownership.

- *Privatisation* of public sector bodies has occurred in many countries. Historically, most public sector bodies were tightly controlled by central or local government. Governments took decisions to privatise in order to require organisations to face up to market forces, become more aware of customer needs and competitive pressures, and so as to provide access to private sector capital. In turn, managers found more latitude in terms of strategic choice – what they could provide in terms of product or services; the ability to diversify, raise capital for expansion, and so on.

4.3 BUSINESS ETHICS AND SOCIAL RESPONSIBILITY[29]

Underlying the discussion of corporate governance is the issue highlighted in the Introduction. Is the purpose of an organisation and its strategy for the benefit of a primary stakeholder such as the shareholders of a company, or is it there for the benefit of a wider group of stakeholders? In turn this raises the question of societal expectations placed on organisations and how these impact on an organisation's purposes. Governments have increasingly taken the view that these expectations cannot be achieved through regulation alone. This is the province of *business ethics* and it exists at two levels:

- At the *macro* level, there are issues about the role of businesses and other organisations in society. Expectations range from laissez-faire free enterprise at one extreme to shapers of society at the other. The broad ethical stance of an organisation is a matter of *corporate social responsibility*.

- At the *individual* level, business ethics is about the behaviour and actions of people in organisations. This is clearly an important issue for the management of organisations in general, but it is discussed here in terms of the role of managers in the strategic management process.

4.3.1 Corporate social responsibility

The regulatory environment and the corporate governance arrangements for an organisation determine its minimum obligations towards its stakeholders.

Corporate social responsibility is concerned with the ways in which an organisation exceeds its minimum obligations to stakeholders specified through regulation

Corporate social responsibility (CSR) is concerned with the ways in which an organisation exceeds its minimum obligations to stakeholders specified through regulation. However, the legal and regulatory frameworks under which businesses operate pay uneven attention to the rights of different stakeholders. For example, *contractual stakeholders* – such as customers, suppliers or employees – have a legal relationship with an organisation, and *community stakeholders* – such as local communities, consumers (in general) and pressure groups – do not have the protection of the law.[30] CSR policies of companies will be particularly important to these community stakeholders.

Different organisations take very different stances on social responsibility. These different stances will also be reflected in how they manage such responsibilities. Exhibit 4.4 outlines four stereotypes to illustrate these differences. They represent a progressively more inclusive 'list' of stakeholder interests and a greater breadth of criteria against which strategies and performance will be judged. The discussion that follows also explains what such stances typically involve in terms of the ways companies act.[31]

The laissez-faire view (literally 'let do' in French) represents an extreme stance where organisations take the view that the only responsibility of business is the short-term interests of shareholders and to 'make a profit, pay taxes and provide jobs'.[32] It is for government to prescribe, through legislation and regulation, the

Exhibit 4.4 Corporate social responsibility stances

	Laissez-faire	Enlightened self-interest	Forum for stakeholder interaction	Shaper of society
Rationale	Legal compliance: make a profit, pay taxes and provide jobs	Sound business sense	Sustainability or triple bottom line	Social and market change
Leadership	Peripheral	Supportive	Champion	Visionary
Management	Middle management responsibility	Systems to ensure good practice	Board-level issue; organisation-wide monitoring	Individual responsibility throughout the organisation
Mode	Defensive to outside pressures	Reactive to outside pressures	Proactive	Defining
Stakeholder relationships	Unilateral	Interactive	Partnership	Multi-organisation alliances

constraints which society chooses to impose on businesses in their pursuit of economic efficiency. The organisation will meet these minimum obligations but no more. Expecting companies to exercise social duties beyond this can, in extreme cases, undermine the authority of government.

This stance may be taken by executives who are persuaded of it ideologically or by smaller businesses that do not have the resources to do other than minimally comply with regulations. Insofar as social good is pursued, this is justified in terms of improving profitability.[33] This might occur, for example, if social obligations were imposed as a requirement for gaining contracts (for example, if equal opportunities employment practices were required from suppliers to public sector customers) or to defend their reputation. Responsibility for such actions is likely to be with middle managers or functional heads rather than with the chief executive who is unlikely to see this role as part of his or her brief. Relationships with stakeholders are likely to be largely unilateral and one way rather than interactive. The danger here is, of course, that this may not be how society expects organisations to act. Indeed, it seems that society increasingly expects more than this from large organisations and the evidence is that chief executives themselves are aware of this and agree organisations should play a more proactive role.[34]

Enlightened self-interest is tempered with recognition of the *long-term financial benefit to the shareholder* of well-managed relationships with other stakeholders. The justification for social action is that it makes good business sense. An organisation's *reputation*[35] is important to its long-term financial success and there is a business case to be made for a more proactive stance on social issues in order to recruit and retain staff, for example. So corporate philanthropy[36] or welfare provision might be regarded as sensible expenditure like any other form of investment or promotion expenditure. The sponsorship of major sporting or arts events by companies is an example. The avoidance of 'shady' marketing practices is also necessary to prevent the need for yet more legislation in that area. Managers here would take the view that organisations not only have responsibility to their shareholders but also a responsibility for *relationships with* other stakeholders (as against *responsibilities to* other stakeholders) and communication with stakeholder groups is likely to be more interactive than for laissez-faire-type organisations. They may well also set up systems and policies to ensure compliance with best practice (for example, ISO 14000 certification, the protection of human rights in overseas operations, etc.) and begin to monitor their social responsibility performance. Top management may also play more of a part, at least insofar as they support the firm taking a more proactive social role.

A *forum for stakeholder interaction*[37] explicitly incorporates multiple stakeholder interests and expectations rather than just shareholders as influences on organisational purposes and strategies. Here the argument is that the performance of an organisation should be measured in a more pluralistic way than just through the financial bottom line. Companies in this category might retain uneconomic units to preserve jobs, avoid manufacturing or selling 'anti-social' products, and be prepared to bear reductions in profitability for the social good. Some financial service organisations have also chosen to offer socially responsible investment (SRI) 'products' to investors. These only include holdings in organisations that meet high standards of social responsibility in their activities.

However, here there are difficult issues of balance between the interests of different stakeholders. For example, many public sector organisations are, rightly, positioned within this group as they are subject to a wide diversity of expectations, and unitary measures of performance are often inadequate in reflecting this diversity. There are also many family-owned small firms that are in this category through the way that they operate. They will balance their own self-interest with that of their employees and local communities even where this might constrain the strategic choices they make (for example, overseas sourcing vs. local production). Organisations in this category inevitably take longer over the development of new strategies as they are committed to wide consultation with stakeholders and with managing the difficult political trade-offs between conflicting stakeholders' expectations as discussed in section 4.3.

BP claims to have embraced the logic of 'multi-stakeholder capitalism', believing that its long-term survival is not just dependent on its economic performance but on its social and environmental performance. Organisations such as BP may elevate CSR to board-level appointments and set up structures for monitoring social performance across its global operations. Targets, often through balanced scorecards, may be built into operational aspects of business and issues of social responsibility managed proactively and in a coordinated fashion. The expectation is that such a corporate stance will, in turn, be reflected in the ethical behaviour of individuals within the firm. Organisations that take this position do, of course, suffer if they are not seen to be meeting the standards of performance they espouse (see Illustration 4.2). Indeed, BP found this in 2006 when it suffered both in the US courts and worldwide in the press for its shortcomings in health and safety procedures that led to a fatal explosion at its refinery in Texas City.

Shapers of society regard financial considerations as of secondary importance or a constraint. These are activists, seeking to change society and social norms. The firm may have been founded for this purpose, as in the case of the Body Shop. The social role is, then, the *raison d'être* of the business. They may see their strategic purpose as 'changing the rules of the game' through which they may benefit but by which they wish to assure that society benefits. In this role it is unlikely that they will be operating on their own: rather they are likely to be partnering with other organisations, commercial and otherwise, to achieve their purposes.

The extent to which this is a viable ethical stance depends upon issues of regulation, corporate governance and accountability. It is easier for a privately owned organisation to operate in this way, since it is not accountable to external shareholders. Some would argue that the great historical achievements of the public services in transforming the quality of life for millions of people were largely because they were 'mission driven' in this way, supported by a political framework in which they operated. However, in many countries there have been challenges to the legitimacy of this mission-driven stance of public services and demands for citizens (as taxpayers) to expect demonstrable best value from them. Charitable organisations face similar dilemmas. It is fundamental to their existence that they have zeal to improve the interests of particular groups in society, but they also need to remain financially viable, which can lead to them being seen as over-commercial and spending too much on administration or promotional activities.

Illustration 4.2

BP, 'Beyond Petroleum' and the Texas City disaster

Companies have increasingly been explicit about their stance on social responsibility. But in so doing they can increase their vulnerability when things go wrong.

The global energy company BP under the leadership of John Browne has been applauded for developing an explicit code of social responsibility emphasising efficient and sustainable energy, energy diversity, concern for climate change, local development where it operates and high levels of safety. This stance was publicised in an advertising campaign promoting the slogan 'Beyond Petroleum'. Further, as John Browne stated (*Business Strategy Review*, vol. 17, no. 3 (2006), pp. 53–56), 'Our commitment to responsibility has to be expressed not in words, but in the actions of the business, day in and day out, in every piece of activity and every aspect of behaviour.'

It was, therefore, a major disaster, not only to the local community and its families, but also to BP when, in 2005, an explosion at BP's Texas City oil refinery killed 15 workers. In September 2005 BP was given a £12m (€17m) fine by the US Department of Labor for 300 safety violations at the Texas City plant.

The press were unremitting in their criticism. The disaster had happened in the same year as BP profits soared and Browne, himself, was given pay and share remuneration in 2005 estimated at £6.5m. BPs top management were aware of 'significant safety problems' not only at the Texas City refinery but at 34 other locations around the world. They emphasised cost cutting over safety. They didn't listen to people lower down in the organisation; they reported a staff survey that rated 'making money' as the top priority and 'people' as the lowest. Too many jobs have been outsourced to cheaper contractors, and so it went on.

In January 2007 John Browne announced that he would be quitting BP 18 months early to be succeeded by Tony Haywood who had been in charge of BP's exploration and production division.

Passed over was John Manzoni, the board director in charge of refining, with the responsibility of refineries.

In 2005 BP had asked James Baker, former US Secretary of State, to undertake an independent investigation. In January 2007, Baker reported:

BP has not provided effective process safety leadership and has not adequately established process safety as a core value across all its five U.S. refineries. . . . BP tended to have a short-term focus and its decentralized management system and entrepreneurial culture have delegated substantial discretion to U.S. refinery plant managers without clearly defining process safety expectations, responsibilities or accountabilities. . . . The company did not always insure that adequate resources were effectively allocated to support or sustain a high level of process safety performance.

The company relied excessively on monitoring injury rates which 'significantly hindered its perception of process risk'. Incidents and near misses were probably under-reported and, when spotted, root causes often not identified correctly.

BP responded that it planned 'significant external recruitment . . . to increase underlying capability in operations and engineering' and that modern process control systems would be installed at its refineries. But the company's social responsibility stance had taken a battering.

Questions

1 How would you categorize BP's stance on social responsibility in terms of Exhibit 4.4?

2 Can top management effectively manage social responsibility at local level? How?

3 Will the negative publicity around the Texas City disaster affect BP's strategy?

On the face of it, shapers of society represent the other end of the spectrum from laissez-faire firms. However, it is worth noting that some large firms that espouse a laissez-faire approach, arguably such as NewsCorp or Haliburton, are actively engaged in trying to shape society, albeit towards their view of the social role of business.

Increasingly there is a view by managers themselves that the laissez-faire position is not acceptable;[38] that businesses need to take a socially responsible position. This is not solely for ethical reasons but because there is a belief that there are advantages to businesses in so doing and dangers if they do not. Being socially responsible reduces the risk of negative stakeholder (not least customer) reactions and can help retain loyal, motivated employees. Social responsibility is therefore justified in terms of the 'triple bottom line' – social and environmental benefits as well as increased profits. Indeed it is argued that socially responsible strategies should be followed because they can provide a basis of gaining competitive advantage. The need is to seek 'win–win' situations to optimise the economic return on environmental investments:[39] 'The essential test . . . is not whether a cause is worthy but whether it presents an opportunity to create shared value – that is meaningful benefit for society that is also valuable to the business.'[40] Fighting the AIDS pandemic in Africa is not just a matter of 'good works' for a pharmaceutical company or an African mining company, it is central to their own interests. Similarly helping reduce carbon emissions provides a business opportunity for a car manufacturer.[41] The lobby for more eco-friendly packaging in Sweden prompted Ecolean to produce packaging that is not only environmentally friendly but costs 25 per cent less than its competitors.[42]

However, it is less clear whether there really are economic pay-offs. Arguably, if the competitive advantage case is to be taken seriously, then this should be evident in terms of enhanced profits. The evidence is equivocal. There is a claim for the links of an enlightened self-interest approach to superior financial performance.[43] For example, researchers have sought to establish if ethical investment funds outperform other funds because they invest in socially responsible firms? Some claim such funds perform no better or worse than others and argue that the case for CSR cannot be based on profit performance.[44] Others argue that there is evidence for higher performance if the abilities of such investors to spot the best investments is taken into account.[45] In short, the jury is out on this.

Exhibit 4.5 provides some questions against which an organisation's actions on CSR can be assessed. *Social auditing*[46] is a way of ensuring that issues of CSR are systematically reviewed and has been championed by a number of progressive organisations. This takes several forms, ranging from social audits undertaken by independent external bodies, through aspects of the social agenda that are now mandatory in company reporting (for example, some environmental issues) to voluntary social accounting by organisations themselves.

4.3.2 The role of individuals and managers

Ethical issues have to be faced at the individual as well as corporate level and can pose difficult dilemmas for individuals and managers. Some examples are shown in Illustration 4.3. These raise questions about the responsibility of an individual who believes that the strategy of his or her organisation is unethical (for

Exhibit 4.5   **Some questions of corporate social responsibility**

Should organisations be responsible for . . .

INTERNAL ASPECTS

Exployee welfare
. . . providing medical care, assistance with housing finance, extended sick leave, assistance for dependants, etc.?

Working conditions
. . . job security, enhancing working surroundings, social and sporting clubs, above-minimum safety standards, training and development, etc.?

Job design
. . . designing jobs to the increased satisfaction of workers rather than just for economic efficiency? This would include issues of work/life balance?

Intellectual property
. . . respecting the private knowledge of individuals and not claiming corporate ownership?

EXTERNAL ASPECTS

Environmental issues
. . . reducing pollution to below legal standards if competitors are not doing so?
. . . energy conservation?

Products
. . . dangers arising from the careless use of products by consumers?

Markets and marketing
. . . deciding not to sell in some markets?
. . . advertising standards?

Suppliers
. . . 'fair' terms of trade?
. . . blacklisting suppliers?

Employment
. . . positive discrimination in favour of minorities?
. . . maintaining jobs?

Community activity
. . . sponsoring local events and supporting local good works?

Human rights
. . . respecting human rights in relation to: child labour, workers' and union rights, oppressive political regimes? Both directly and in the choice of markets, suppliers and partners?

example, its trading practices) or is not adequately representing the legitimate interests of one or more stakeholder groups. Should that person leave the company on the grounds of a mismatch of values; or is *whistleblowing*[47] appropriate, such as divulging information to outside bodies, for example regulatory bodies or the press?

Given that strategy development can be an intensely political process with implications for the personal careers of those concerned, managers can find difficulties establishing and maintaining a position of integrity. There is also

Illustration 4.3

Ethical dilemmas

Managers face a range of different ethical dilemmas that need to be resolved.

Conflicting objectives

You are a Dutch manager in charge of the mining operations of your multinational company in Namibia. You employ mainly local workers on very low wages. Your operation provides livelihood for 1,000 families and is the mainstay of the local economy. There is no other local work other than subsistence farming. You have discovered many safety problems with the mine but the company engineer has advised that the cost of upgrading facilities would make the mine uneconomic. Closing the mine would cause a major political stir and harm the parent company's reputation. But keeping it open risks the chance of a major disaster.

Performance data

You are the recently appointed head teacher of a school that is now improving following a period of very poor performance under your predecessor. It has been made clear that one important performance indicator is pupil attendance levels – that must be brought up to the national average (95 per cent). You have now collected all the data for your regular statistical return and notice to your disappointment that your attendance record has fallen just below your required target. On discussing this with your deputy she asks if you would like her to 're-examine and correct' the attendance data before submission.

Bribery

You are the newly appointed manager in charge of a new sales office in New York set up following extensive market research by your British company. After a few months you discover that none of the company's products can be sold in New York without code approval from an obscure New York authority that is controlled by Local 4 of the electricians' union. Further investigation reveals that Local 4 had Mafia connections.

Shortly afterwards you are visited by Local 4 representatives who offer you a deal. If the company pays an annual 'consultative fee' of $12,000 (€10,000) (with escalation clauses as sales grew) you will secure approval in six months. The alternative is to attempt to secure approval alone, which informed sources say is unlikely to succeed.

Company policy is opposed to bribery. But the project is a make-or-break one for the company's ventures in the USA and your own career. Given the potential gains $12,000 is a small amount and would probably be approved if presented 'appropriately'.

Rationing

Rationing is one of the most important issues in many public sector organisations. You are a Swedish doctor working on secondment in charge of a local hospital in rural Nigeria. It receives financial support from the Nigerian government and a European medical charity. However, the medical facilities are poor, particularly supplies of medicines and blood. A bus leaving town has collided with a tourist vehicle. Apart from several fatalities there are four seriously injured survivors. Two are local children (one aged 2, the other 10), one is an elderly leader of a local tribe and the fourth is a German tourist. Unless they have urgent blood transfusions they are likely to die. There is only enough blood for two patients.

Questions

You are the 'player' faced with each of these dilemmas:

1 What choices of action do you have?

2 List the pros and cons of each choice to your organisation, the external parties and yourself.

3 Explain what you would do and justify your actions from an ethical point of view.

Exhibit 4.6	Ethical guidelines (based on Texas Instruments' approach to business ethics)

Questions	Appropriate responses
Is action legal?	If no, stop immediately
Does it comply with our values?	If it does not, stop
If you do it, will you feel bad?	Ask your own conscience if you can live with it
How would this look in the newspaper?	Ask, if this goes public tomorrow would you do it today?
If you know it is wrong . . .	Don't do it
If you are not sure . . .	Ask
	And keep asking till you get an answer

Source: Angela Sutherland, Glasgow Caledonian University.

potential conflict between what strategies are in managers' own best interest and what strategies are in the longer-term interests of their organisation and the shareholders. Some organisations, such as Texas Instruments, set down explicit guidelines they expect their employees to follow (see Exhibit 4.6). Perhaps the biggest challenge for managers is to develop a high level of self-awareness of their own behaviour in relation to the issues raised above.[48] This can be difficult because it requires them to stand apart from often deep-rooted and taken-for-granted assumptions that are part of the culture of their organisation – a key theme of the next chapter.

4.4 STAKEHOLDER EXPECTATIONS[49]

KEY CONCEPT

Stakeholders

It should be clear from the preceding sections that the decisions managers have to make about the purpose and strategy of their organisation are influenced by the expectations of stakeholders. This poses a challenge because there are likely to be many stakeholders, especially for a large organisation (see Exhibit 4.7), with different, perhaps conflicting, expectations. This means that managers need to take a view on (i) which stakeholders will have the greatest influence, therefore (ii) which expectations they need to pay most attention to and (iii) to what extent the expectations and influence of different stakeholders vary.

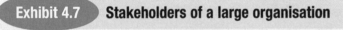

Exhibit 4.7 **Stakeholders of a large organisation**

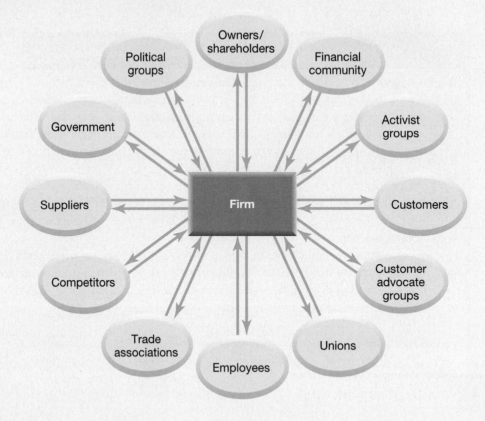

Source: From R.E. Freeman, *Strategic Management: A Stakeholder Approach*, pub. Pitman 1984 Copyright 1984 by R. Edward Freeman.

External stakeholders can be usefully divided into three types in terms of the nature of their relationship with the organisation and, therefore, how they might affect the success or failure of a strategy:[50]

- *Economic stakeholders*, including suppliers, competitors, distributors (whose influence can be identified using the five-forces framework from Chapter 2 (Exhibit 2.2) and shareholders (whose influence can be considered in terms of the governance chain discussed in section 4.2.1).

- *Socio/political stakeholders*, such as policy makers, regulators and government agencies who will influence the 'social legitimacy' of the strategy.

- *Technological stakeholders*, such as key adopters, standards agencies and owners of competitive technologies who will influence the diffusion of new technologies and the adoption of industry standards.

The influence of these different types of stakeholders is likely to vary in different situations. For example, the 'technological group' will be crucial for strategies of new product introduction whilst the 'social/political' group is usually particularly influential in the public sector context.

There are also stakeholder groups internal to an organisation, which may be departments, geographical locations or different levels in the hierarchy. Individuals may belong to more than one stakeholder group, and such groups may 'line up' differently depending on the issue or strategy in hand. Of course, external stakeholders may seek to influence an organisation's strategy through their links with internal stakeholders. For example, customers may exert pressure on sales managers to represent their interests within the company.

Since the expectations of stakeholder groups will differ, it is normal for conflict to exist regarding the importance or desirability of many aspects of strategy. In most situations, a compromise will need to be reached. Exhibit 4.8 shows some of the typical stakeholder expectations that exist and how they might conflict. Global organisations may have added complications as they are operating in multiple arenas. For example, an overseas division is part of the parent company, with all that implies in terms of expectations about behaviour and performance, but is also part of a local community, which has different expectations. These two 'worlds' may not sit comfortably alongside each other.[51]

For these reasons, the stakeholder concept is valuable when trying to understand the political context within which strategic developments take place. Indeed, taking stakeholder expectations and influence into account is an important aspect of strategic choice, as will be seen in Chapter 10.

Exhibit 4.8 Some common conflicts of expectations

- In order to grow, short-term profitability, cash flow and pay levels may need to be sacrificed.

- 'Short-termism' may suit managerial career aspirations but preclude investment in long-term projects.

- When family businesses grow, the owners may lose control if they need to appoint professional managers.

- New developments may require additional funding through share issue or loans. In either case, financial independence may be sacrificed.

- Public ownership of shares will require more openness and accountability from the management.

- Cost efficiency through capital investment can mean job losses.

- Extending into mass markets may require a decline in quality standards.

- In public services, a common conflict is between mass provision and specialist services (e.g. preventative dentistry or heart transplants).

- In large multinational organisations, conflict can result because of a division's responsibilities to the company and also to its host country.

4.4.1 Stakeholder mapping[52]

Stakeholder mapping identifies stakeholder expectations and power and helps in understanding political priorities

There are different ways in which stakeholder mapping can be used to gain an understanding of stakeholder influence.[53] The approach to **stakeholder mapping** here identifies stakeholder expectations and power and helps in understanding political priorities. It underlines the importance of two issues:

● How *interested* each stakeholder group is in impressing its expectations on the organisation's purposes and choice of strategies.

● Whether stakeholders have the *power* to do so (see section 4.4.3).

Power/interest matrix

The power/interest matrix can be seen in Exhibit 4.9. It describes the context within which a strategy might be pursued by classifying stakeholders in relation to the power they hold and the extent to which they are likely to show interest in supporting or opposing a particular strategy. The matrix helps in thinking through stakeholder influences on the development of strategy. However, it must be emphasised that how managers handle relationships will depend on the governance structures under which they operate (see section 4.2) and the stance taken on corporate responsibility (section 4.3.1). For example, in some countries unions may be very weak but in others they may be represented on supervisory boards; banks may take an 'arm's-length' relationship with regard to strategy in some countries, but be part of the governance structures in others. A laissez-faire type of business may take the view that it will only pay attention to stakeholders with the most powerful economic influence (for example, investors), whereas shapers of society might go out of their way to engage with

Exhibit 4.9   Stakeholder mapping: the power/interest matrix

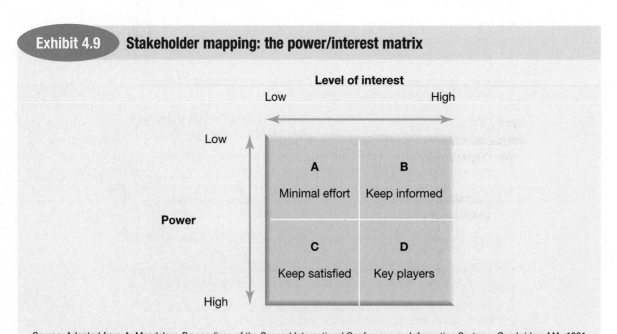

Source: Adapted from A. Mendelow, *Proceedings of the Second International Conference on Information Systems*, Cambridge, MA, 1991.

and influence the expectations and involvement of stakeholders who would not typically see themselves as influential.

In order to show the way in which the matrix may be used, the discussion here takes the perspective of a business where managers see themselves as formulating strategy by trying to ensure the compliance of stakeholders to their own assessment of strategic imperatives. In this context the matrix indicates the type of relationship that such an organisation might typically establish with stakeholder groups in the different quadrants. Clearly, the acceptability of strategies to *key players* (segment D) is of major importance. It could be that these are major investors, but it could also be particular individuals or agencies with a lot of power – for example, a major shareholder in a family firm or a government funding agency in a public sector organisation. Often the most difficult issues relate to stakeholders in segment C. Although these might, in general, be relatively passive, a disastrous situation can arise when their level of interest is underrated and they suddenly *reposition* to segment D and frustrate the adoption of a new strategy. Institutional shareholders such as pension funds or insurance firms can fall into this category. They may show little interest unless share prices start to dip, but may then demand to be heard by senior management.

Similarly, organisations might address the expectations of stakeholders in segment B, for example community groups, through information provision. It may be important not to alienate such stakeholders because they can be crucially important 'allies' in influencing the attitudes of more powerful stakeholders: for example, through *lobbying*.

Stakeholder mapping might help in understanding better some of the following issues:

- In *determining purpose and strategy*, which stakeholder expectations need to be most considered?

- Whether the *actual levels of interest and power* of stakeholders properly reflect the corporate governance framework within which the organisation is operating, as in the examples above (institutional investors, community groups).

- Who the key *blockers* and *facilitators* of a strategy are likely to be and how this could be responded to – for example, in terms of education or persuasion.

- Whether *repositioning* of certain stakeholders is desirable and/or feasible. This could be to lessen the influence of a key player or, in certain instances, to ensure that there are more key players who will champion the strategy (this is often critical in the public sector context).

- *Maintaining* the level of interest or power of some key stakeholders may be essential. For example, public 'endorsement' by powerful suppliers or customers may be critical to the success of a strategy. Equally, it may be necessary to discourage some stakeholders from repositioning themselves. This is what is meant by *keep satisfied* in relation to stakeholders in segment C, and to a lesser extent *keep informed* for those in segment B. The use of *side payments* to stakeholders as a means of securing the acceptance of new strategies can be a key maintenance activity. For example, a 'deal' may be done with another department to support them on one of *their* strategies if they agree not to oppose *this* strategy.

Illustration 4.4a

Stakeholder mapping at Tallman GmbH

Stakeholder mapping can be a useful tool for determining the political priorities for specific strategic developments or changes.

Tallman GmbH was a German bank providing both retail and corporate banking services throughout Germany, Benelux and France. There were concerns about its loss in market share in the corporate sector which was serviced from two centres – Frankfurt (for Germany and Benelux) and Toulouse (for France). It was considering closing the Toulouse operation and servicing all corporate clients from Frankfurt. This would result in significant job losses in Toulouse, some of which would be replaced in Frankfurt alongside vastly improved IT systems.

Two power/interest maps were drawn up by the company officials to establish likely stakeholder reactions to the proposed closure of the Toulouse operation. Map A represents the likely situation and

map B the preferred situation – where support for the proposal would be sufficient to proceed.

Referring to map A, it can be seen that, with the exception of customer X and IT supplier A, the stakeholders in box B are currently opposed to the closure of the Toulouse operation. If Tallman was to have any chance of convincing these stakeholders to change their stance to a more supportive one, the company must address their questions and, where possible, alleviate their fears. If such fears were overcome, these people might become important allies in influencing the more powerful stakeholders in boxes C and D. The supportive attitude of customer X could be usefully harnessed in this quest. Customer X was a multinational with

Map A: The likely situation

	Shareholder M (–) Toulouse office (–) Customer X (+) French minister (–) Marketing (–)
A	**B** IT supplier A (+)
Customer Z German minister	Customer Y (+) Frankfurt office (+) Corporate finance (+)
C	**D**

Map B: The preferred situation

French minister	Shareholder M (–) Toulouse office (–) Marketing (–) IT supplier A (+)
A	**B**
Customer Z German minister	Customer X (+) Customer Y (+) Frankfurt office (+) Corporate finance (+)
C	**D**

These questions can raise difficult ethical issues for managers in deciding the role they should play in the political activity surrounding stakeholder management. This takes the debate back to the considerations of governance and ethics discussed earlier in the chapter. For example, are managers really the honest brokers who weigh the conflicting expectations of stakeholder groups? Or should they be answerable to one stakeholder – such as shareholders – and hence is their role to ensure the acceptability of their strategies to other operations throughout Europe. It had shown dissatisfaction with the inconsistent treatment that it received from Frankfurt and Toulouse.

The relationships Tallman had with the stakeholders in box C were the most difficult to manage since, whilst they were considered to be relatively passive, largely due to their indifference to the proposed strategy, a disastrous situation could arise if their level of interest was underrated. For example, if the German minister were replaced, her successor might be opposed to the strategy and actively seek to stop the changes. In this case they would shift to box D.

The acceptability of the proposed strategy to the current players in box D was a key consideration. Of particular concern was customer Y (a major French manufacturer who operated only in France – accounting for 20 per cent of Toulouse corporate banking income). Customer Y was opposed to the closure of the Toulouse operation and could have the power to prevent it from happening, for example by the withdrawal of its business. The company clearly needed to have open discussions with this stakeholder.

By comparing the position of stakeholders in map A and map B, and identifying any changes and mismatches, Tallman could establish a number of tactics to change the stance of certain stakeholders to a more positive one and to increase the power of certain stakeholders. For example, customer X could be encouraged to champion the proposed strategy and assist Tallman by providing media access, or even convincing customer Y that the change could be beneficial.

Tallman could also seek to dissuade or prevent powerful stakeholders from changing their stance to a negative one: for example, unless direct action were taken, lobbying from her French counterpart may well raise the German minister's level of interest. This has implications for how the company handles the situation in France. Time could be spent talking the strategy through with the French minister and also customer Y to try to shift them away from opposition at least to neutrality, if not support.

Question

To ensure that you are clear about how to undertake stakeholder mapping, produce your own complete analysis for Tallman GmbH against a different strategy, that is *to service all corporate clients from Toulouse*. Ensure that you go through the following steps:

1 Plot the most likely situation (map A) – remembering to be careful to *reassess* interest and power for each stakeholder in relation to this *new* strategy.

2 Map the preferred situation (map B).

3 Identify the mismatches – and hence the political priorities. Remember to include the need to *maintain* a stakeholder in its 'opening' position (if relevant).

4 Finish off by listing the actions you would propose to take and give a final view of the degree of political risk in pursuing this new strategy.

stakeholders? Or are they, as many authors suggest, the real power themselves, constructing strategies to suit their own purposes and managing stakeholder expectations to ensure acceptance of these strategies?

Illustration 4.4a shows some of the practical issues of using stakeholder mapping to understand the political context surrounding a new strategy and to establish political priorities. The example relates to a German bank with head-quarters in Frankfurt (Germany) and providing corporate banking services from head office and a regional office in Toulouse (France). It is considering the closure of its Toulouse office and providing all corporate banking services from Frankfurt.

The example illustrates two further issues.

- Stakeholder groups are *not usually 'homogeneous'* but contain a variety of sub-groups with different expectations and power. In the illustration, *customers* are shown divided into those who are largely supportive of the strategy (customer X), those who are actively hostile (customer Y) and those who are indifferent (customer Z). So when using stakeholder mapping, there is clearly a balance to be struck between describing stakeholders too generically – hence hiding important issues of diversity – and too much subdivision, making the situation confusing and difficult to interpret.

- The *role and the individual* currently undertaking that role need to be distinguished. It is useful to know if a new individual in that role would shift the positioning. Serious misjudgements can be made if care is not paid to this point. In the example, it has been concluded that the German minister (segment C) is largely indifferent to the new development – it is low in her priorities. However, a change of minister might change this situation. Although it will be impossible for the bank to remove such uncertainties entirely, there are implications for the political priorities. For example, those permanent officials who are advising the minister need to be kept satisfied, since they will outlive individual ministers and provide a continuity which can diminish uncertainty. It is also possible, of course, that the German minister's level of interest will be raised by lobbying from her French counterpart. This would have implications for how the company handles the situation in France.

4.4.2 Power[54]

The previous section was concerned with understanding stakeholder expectations and highlighted the importance of power. It has been seen that, in most organisations, power will be unequally shared between the various stakeholders. For the purposes of this discussion, **power** is the ability of individuals or groups to persuade, induce or coerce others into following certain courses of action. This is the mechanism by which one set of expectations will influence strategic development or seek compromise with others.

Power is the ability of individuals or groups to persuade, induce or coerce others into following certain courses of action

There are many different sources of power. On the one hand, there is power that people or groups derive from their position within the organisation, the resources or know-how they control, and through the formal corporate governance arrangements. Stakeholders may also have power by other means, as summarised in Exhibit 4.10. This exhibit can be used to understand how powerful each stakeholder is in influencing a particular strategy (as part of stakeholder mapping).

The relative importance of these sources will vary over time. Indeed, major changes in the business environment can significantly shift the power balance between organisations and their stakeholders. For example, consumers' knowledge of different companies' offerings through Internet browsing has increased

Exhibit 4.10	Sources and indicators of power

Sources of power	
Within organisations	**For external stakeholders**
• Hierarchy (formal power), e.g. autocratic decision making	• Control of strategic resources, e.g. materials, labour, money
• Influence (informal power), e.g. charismatic leadership	• Involvement in strategy implementation, e.g. distribution outlets, agents
• Control of strategic resources, e.g. strategic products	• Possession of knowledge or skills, e.g. subcontractors, partners
• Possession of knowledge and skills, e.g. computer specialists	• Through internal links, e.g. informal influence
• Control of the human environment, e.g. negotiating skills	
• Involvement in strategy implementation, e.g. by exercising discretion	

Indicators of power	
Within organisations	**For external stakeholders**
• Status	• Status
• Claim on resources	• Resource dependence
• Representation	• Negotiating arrangements
• Symbols	• Symbols

their power considerably as they compare different offerings and reduce their traditional loyalty to a particular supplier. Deregulation and 'citizen empowerment' have required public service organisations to adopt more customer-focused strategies.

Since there are a variety of different sources of power, it is useful to look for *indicators of power*, which are the visible signs that stakeholders have been able to exploit sources of power. Indicators of power include: the *status* of the individual or group (such as job grade or reputation); the *claim on resources* (such as budget size); *representation* in powerful positions; and *symbols* of power (such as office size or use of titles and names). It should be remembered, however, that the distribution of power will vary *in relation to the strategy under consideration*. For example, a corporate finance function will be more powerful in relation to developments requiring new capital or revenue commitments than in relation to ones which are largely self-financing or within the financial authority of separate divisions or subsidiaries.

Illustration 4.4b

Assessment of power at Tallman GmbH

Assessing the power of stakeholders is an important part of stakeholder mapping.

The corporate finance department is seen as powerful by all measures, and the marketing department universally weak. Equally, the Frankfurt operation is particularly powerful compared with Toulouse. This analysis provides important data in the process of stakeholder mapping, since the strategic importance of power is also related to whether individuals or groups are likely to exercise their power. This assessment thus helped in deciding where to locate the stakeholders on the power/interest maps.

Combining the results of this analysis with the stakeholder mapping exercise, it can be seen that Toulouse's only real hope is to encourage supplier A to reposition by convincing it of the increased IT opportunities which a two-centre operation would provide. Perhaps shareholder M could be helpful in this process through lobbying the supplier.

Internal stakeholders

Indicators of power	Corporate finance	Marketing	Frankfurt	Toulouse
Status				
Position in hierarchy (closeness to board)	H	L	H	M
Salary of top manager	H	L	H	L
Average grade of staff	H	M	H	L
Claim on resources				
Number of staff	M	H	M	M
Size of similar company	H	L	H	L
Budget as per cent of total	H	M	H	L
Representation				
Number of directors	H	None	M	None
Most influential directors	H	None	M	None
Symbols				
Quality of accommodation	H	L	M	M
Support services	H	L	H	L

H = high   M = medium   L = low

External stakeholders

Indicators of power	IT supplier A	Customer Y	Shareholder M
Status	M	H	L
Resource dependence	M	H	H
Negotiating arrangements	M	H	L
Symbols	M	H	L

H = high   M = medium   L = low

A similar understanding of the power held by external stakeholders can be useful. The indicators of power here are slightly different:

● The *status* of an external stakeholder can often be inferred by the speed with which the company responds.

● *Resource dependence* in terms of the relative size of shareholdings or loans, or the proportion of a company's business tied up with any one customer, or a similar dependence on suppliers. A key indicator could be the ease with which a supplier, financier or customer could switch or *be switched* at short notice.

● *Symbols* are also valuable clues about power. For example, whether the management team wine and dine a customer or supplier, or the level of person in the company who deals with a particular supplier.

Again, no single indicator will give a full understanding of the extent of the power held by external stakeholders. Illustration 4.4b shows these indicators of power for the bank from the previous illustration. It can be seen that Toulouse's only real hope of survival is to encourage supplier A to 'reposition' by convincing it of the increased IT opportunities that a two-centre operation would provide. Perhaps shareholder M could be helpful in this process through lobbying the supplier.

4.5 ORGANISATIONAL PURPOSES: VALUES, MISSION, VISION AND OBJECTIVES

The previous sections have looked at factors that influence the overall purpose of an organisation. However, it is managers who will need to form a view on this purpose and find a way of expressing it. It may be that an explicit statement of such a purpose is a formal requirement of corporate governance or expected of the organisation by one or more stakeholders. Or it may be that managers themselves decide such a statement is useful. This section will look at the different ways in which such purpose may be expressed explicitly through statements of *corporate values*, *vision*, *mission* and *objectives*.

4.5.1 Corporate values

Core values are the underlying principles that guide an organisation's strategy

Increasingly organisations have been keen to develop and communicate a set of corporate values that define the way that the organisation operates.[55] Of particular importance are an organisation's **core values** – these are the underlying 'principles' that guide an organisation's strategy. For example, emergency services such as ambulance and the fire brigades have an overriding commitment to saving life that employees are committed to the extent that they will break strike action or risk their own lives to attend emergencies when life is threatened. Jim Collins and Jerry Porras have argued that the long-run success of many US corporates – such as Disney, General Electric or 3M – can be attributed (at least in part) to strong core values.[56] There are again, however, potential downsides to public statements of corporate values if an organisation demonstrably fails to live them out in practice (see Illustration 4.2). It is also important to distinguish between the *core values* expressing the way the organisation *is*, as distinct from those to which the organisation wishes to *aspire*. Unless this distinction is clear there is room for considerable misunderstanding and cynicism about statements of corporate values. In either case such statements may be concerned with aspects of corporate social responsibility as discussed in section 4.3.

4.5.2 Mission and vision statements

Whereas corporate values may be a backcloth and set boundaries within which strategies are developed, a **mission statement** and a **vision statement** are typically more explicitly concerned with the purpose of an organisation in terms of its strategic direction. In practice the distinction between mission and vision statements can be hazy but they are intended to be different as follows:

A **mission statement** aims to provide employees and stakeholders with clarity about the overall purpose and *raison d'être* of the organisation.

A **vision statement** is concerned with what the organisation aspires to be

Mission and vision

- *A mission statement* aims to provide employees and stakeholders with clarity about the overall purpose and *raison d'être* of the organisation. It is therefore to do with building understanding and confidence about how the strategy of the organisation relates to that purpose.

- *A vision statement* is concerned with what the organisation aspires to be. Its purpose is to set out a view of the future so as to enthuse, gain commitment and stretch performance.

Although both mission and vision statements became widely adopted by the early 2000s, many critics regard them as bland and wide ranging.[57] However, arguably if there is substantial disagreement within the organisation or with stakeholders as to its mission (or vision), it may well give rise to real problems in resolving the strategic direction of the organisation. So, given the political nature of strategic management, they can be a useful means of focusing debate on the fundamentals of the organisation. Illustration 4.5 shows examples of mission, vision and value statements.

4.5.3 Objectives

Objectives are statements of specific outcomes that are to be achieved

Objectives are statements of specific outcomes that are to be achieved. Objectives – both at the corporate and at the business unit level – are often expressed in financial terms. They could be the expression of desired sales or profit levels, rates of growth, dividend levels or share valuations.[58] However, organisations may also have market-based objectives, many of which are quantified as targets – such as market share, customer service, repeat business and so on.

There are three related issues that managers need to consider with regard to setting objectives.

- *Objectives and measurement*. Objectives are typically quantified. Indeed, some argue[59] that objectives are not helpful unless their achievement can be measured. However, this does raise the question as to how many objectives

Illustration 4.5

Mission, vision and values statements

Can well-crafted statements of mission, vision or values be an important means of motivating an organisation's stakeholders?

Tata Steel

Mission 2007

Consistent with the vision and values of the founder Jamsetji Tata, Tata Steel strives to strengthen India's industrial base through the effective utilisation of staff and materials. The means envisaged to achieve this are high technology and productivity, consistent with modern management practices.

Tata Steel recognises that while honesty and integrity are the essential ingredients of a strong and stable enterprise, profitability provides the main spark for economic activity.

Overall, the company seeks to scale the heights of excellence in all that it does in an atmosphere free from fear, and thereby reaffirms its faith in democratic values.

Vision 2007

To seize the opportunities of tomorrow and create a future that will make us an EVA positive company.

To continue to improve the quality of life of our employees and the communities we serve.

To revitalise the core business for a sustainable future.

To venture into new businesses that will own a share of our future.

To uphold the spirit and values of Tatas towards nation building.

The Metropolitan Police

Mission and values

Our mission: Working together for a safer London.

Our values: Working together with all our citizens, all our partners, all our colleagues:

We will have pride in delivering quality policing. There is no greater priority.

We will build trust by listening and responding.

We will respect and support each other and work as a team.

We will learn from experience and find ways to be even better.

We are one team – we all have a duty to play our part in making London safer.

Villeroy & Boch

Company vision

To be the leading European lifestyle brand with high competence and trend-setting style for high-end design and living.

Five values – one philosophy

I. *Customers*. Our success is measured by the enthusiasm our customers show for our products and services. A constant challenge is to satisfy the high expectations architects, retailers, the trade and end consumers have of the 'Villeroy & Boch' brand. We convince them with competence and experience.

II. *Employees*. In the long run a strong market position can only be achieved by having innovative and committed employees. Our priority task is to motivate them and cultivate their team spirit, encouraging them to achieve personal and joint goals.

III: *Innovation*. If we lay claim to a leading position on the international markets it is not enough to follow trends. Those who want to secure their competitive edge worldwide must recognise and shape trends early on.

IV: *Earning power*. An important concern for us is to maintain the independence of the company and achieve long-term success. The fundamentals for this are a balanced portfolio, earnings-oriented growth, high and constant rates of return and appropriate dividends.

V: *Responsibility*. Not many companies have made regional economic history as well as European cultural and social history. Villeroy & Boch is one of them, and thus bears many responsibilities. We feel obligated not only to our employees, shareholders and customers, but also to the environment and society.

Questions

1 Which of these statements do you think are likely to motivate which stakeholders? Why?

2 Could any of them have been improved? How?

3 Identify other statements of mission, vision, purpose or values that you think are especially well crafted and explain why.

expressed in such ways are useful. Certainly there are times when specific quantified objectives are required, for example when urgent action is needed and it becomes essential for management to focus attention on a limited number of priority requirements – as in a *turnaround* situation (see section 14.5.1). If the choice is between going out of business and surviving, there is no room for latitude through vaguely stated requirements. However, it may be that in other circumstances – for example, in trying to raise the aspirations of people in the organisation – more attention needs to be paid to qualitative statements of purpose such as mission or vision statements.

- *Objectives and control.* A recurring problem with objectives is that managers and employees 'lower down' in the hierarchy are unclear as to how their day-to-day work contributes to the achievement of higher level of objectives. This could, in principle, be addressed by a 'cascade' of objectives – defining a set of detailed objectives at each level in the hierarchy. Many organisations attempt to do this to some extent. Here consideration needs to be given to a trade-off: how to achieve required levels of clarity on strategy without being over-restrictive in terms of the latitude people have. There is evidence, for

---

Exhibit 4.11 **Simple rules**

Turbulent markets require strategic flexibility to seize opportunities – but flexibility can be disciplined. Different types of simple rules help.

Type	Purpose	Example
How-to rules	Spell out key features of how a process is executed – 'What makes our process unique?'	Dell focus on focused customer segments. So a Dell business must be split in two when its revenue hits $1 billion.
Boundary rules	Focus managers on which opportunities can be pursued and which should not	In Miramax movie-picking process, every movie must: i) revolve around a central human condition, such as love; ii) have a main character appealing but deeply flawed; iii) have a clear story line.
Priority rules	Help managers rank the accepted opportunities	Intel's rule for allocating manufacturing capacity: allocation is based on a product's gross margin. (See Chapter 11 case example.)
Timing rules	Synchronise managers with the pace of emerging opportunities and other parts of the company	Nortel's product development time must be less than 18 months, which forces it to move quickly into new opportunities.
Exit rules	Help managers decide when to pull out of yesterday's opportunities	In Oticon, the Danish hearing aid company, if a key team member – manager or not – chooses to leave a project for another within the company, the project is killed.

Source: Reprinted by permission of *Harvard Business Review*. Exhibit adapted from 'Strategy as simple rules' by K.M. Eisenhardt and D.N. Sull, January 2001. Copyright © 2001 by the Havard Business School Publishing Corporation; all rights reserved.

example, that innovation is stymied by over-restrictive target setting and measurement.[60]

- *Simple rules.* Especially in organisations in which innovation and flexibility are important, there is evidence that managers need to be very clear about the very few overarching objectives that have to be met, sometimes known as 'simple rules', but then allow flexibility and latitude in how they are achieved. Research by Kathy Eisenhardt and her colleagues has begun to establish the nature of these simple rules.[61] Exhibit 4.11 summarises the types of rules they identify as important in organisations facing fast-changing environments; and gives some examples of how they take form and their effects. The suggestion is that the number of rules does not need to be many to result in consistent patterns of behaviour. In this respect the proposal builds on the arguments advanced by complexity theorists and explained in the Commentary on the lenses (see pages 36–41).

An underlying theme in this chapter has been that strategists have to consider the overall strategic purpose of their organisations. However, a central question that arises is what stakeholder expectations they should respond to in so doing. The key debate in Illustration 4.6 provides three views on this in the context of publicly quoted large commercial organisations.

SUMMARY

- The purpose of an organisation will be influenced by the expectations of its stakeholders.

- The influence of some key stakeholders will be represented formally within the governance structure of an organisation. This can be represented in terms of a governance chain, showing the links between ultimate beneficiaries and the managers of an organisation.

- There are two generic governance structures systems: the shareholder model and the stakeholder model. There are variations of these internationally, but some signs that there is convergence towards a shareholder model.

- There are also ethical dimensions to the purpose of an organisation. At an organisational level, this takes the form of its stance on corporate social responsibility. However, individual managers may also be faced with ethical dilemmas relating to the purpose of their organisation or the actions it takes.

- Different stakeholders exercise different influence on organisational purpose and strategy, dependent on the extent of their power and interest. Managers can assess the influence of different stakeholder groups through stakeholder analysis.

- An important managerial task is to decide how the organisation should express its strategic purpose through statements of values, vision, mission or objectives.

Illustration 4.6

key debate

Three views on the purpose of a business?

Since there is no one categoric view of the overarching purpose of a business, stakeholders, including managers, have to decide.

Milton Friedman and profit maximisation

Milton Friedman, the renowned economist, wrote:[1]

In a free enterprise, private property system, a corporate executive is an employee of the owners of the business. He has direct responsibility to his employers. That responsibility is to conduct the business in accordance with their desires, which generally will be to make as much money as possible while conforming to the basic rules of society. . . . What does it mean to say that the corporate executive has a 'social responsibility'? . . . If the statement is not pure rhetoric, it must mean that he is to act in some way that is not in the interests of his employers. . . . Insofar as his actions in accord with his 'social responsibility' reduce returns to stockholders, he is spending their money. Insofar as his actions raise the price to customers, he is spending the customers' money. Insofar as his actions lower the wages of some employees he is spending their money.

Milton Friedman's maxim was that 'the business of business is business', that the 'only social responsibility of business is to increase its profit'. Market mechanisms are then adequate in themselves. If customers are not satisfied, they take their business elsewhere. If employees are not satisfied they work elsewhere. It is the job of government to ensure that there is a free market to allow those conditions to take effect.

Charles Handy's stakeholder view

Citing the corporate scandals of the last decade, Charles Handy[2] argues that the driving for shareholder value linked to stock options for executives, especially in the USA, has resulted in the system 'creating value where none existed'. He accepts

that there is, first, a clear and important need to meet the expectations of a company's theoretical owners: the shareholders. It would, however, be more accurate to call them investors, perhaps even gamblers. They have none of the pride or responsibility of ownership and are . . . only there for the money. . . . But to turn shareholders' needs into a purpose is to be guilty of a logical confusion. To mistake a necessary condition for a sufficient one. We need to eat to live; food is a necessary condition of life. But if we lived mainly to eat, making food a sufficient or sole purpose of life, we would become gross. The purpose of a business, in other words, is not to make a profit. It is to make a profit so that the business that can do something more or better. That 'something' becomes the real justification for the business.

The new capitalists' argument: 'Society and share owners are becoming one and the same'[3]

In their book *The New Capitalists*, the authors also recognise that 'a corporation is the property of its stock owners and should serve their interests'. However, it is the 'millions of pension holders and other savers . . . [who] . . . own the world's giant corporations'. These 'new capitalists are likely to be highly diversified in their investments'. Investment funds, such as pension funds, are their representatives and 'hold a tiny share in hundreds, perhaps even thousands, of companies around the world'. They then argue:

Imagine that all your savings were invested in one company. The success of that company alone would be your only interest. You would want it to survive, prosper and grow, even if that did damage to the economic system as a whole. But your perspective would change if you had investments in lots of companies. [Then] it is to your disadvantage that any business should seek to behave socially irresponsibly towards other businesses, the customers, employees or society generally. By so doing they will damage the interests of other firms in which you have an interest. The new capitalist has an interest in all the firms in which he or she is investing behaving responsibly: 'in creating rules that lead to the success of the economic system as a whole, even if, in particular circumstances, those rules may tie the hands of an individual company'. . . . managers of a business should quite properly 'concentrate single mindedly on the success of their own organisations . . . however they will not be serving their share owners interest if they undertake activities that may be good for them individually, but damaging to the larger economic system.

Notes

1. M. Friedman 'The social responsibility of business is to increase its profits', *New York Times. Magazine*, 13 September (1970).
2. C. Handy, 'What's a business for?', *Harvard Business Review*, December (2002), pp. 49–55.
3. S. Davies, J. Lukommik and D. Pitt-Watson, *The New Capitalists*, Harvard Business School Press, 2006.

Questions

1 Which view do you hold:
   (a) As a manager? (b) As a shareholder?

2 What are the implications of the different views for managers' development of organisational strategy?

Work assignments

*Denotes more advanced work assignments.   * Refers to a case study in the Text and Cases edition.*

4.1 ✳ For an organisation of your choice, map out a governance chain that identifies the key players through to the beneficiaries of the organisation's good (or poor) performance. To what extent do you think managers are:

(a) knowledgeable about the expectations of beneficiaries;
(b) actively pursuing their interests;
(c) keeping them informed?

How would you change any of these aspects of the organisation's operations? Why?

4.2 ✳ It is argued that many economies are shifting from a stakeholder to a shareholder model of governance. What are your own views of the strengths and weaknesses of these systems? Consider this in relation to an economy that is in transition in terms of governance.

4.3 For an organisation of your choice, use Exhibit 4.4 to establish the *overall stance* of the organisation on corporate social responsibility.

4.4 ✳ Identify the key corporate social responsibility issues which are of major concern in an industry or public service of your choice (refer to Exhibit 4.5). Compare the approach of two or more organisations in that industry, and explain how this relates to their competitive standing.

4.5 Using Illustration 4.4 as a worked example, identify and map out the stakeholders for Manchester United*, Direct and Care* or an organisation of your choice in relation to:

(a) current strategies;
(b) different future strategies of your choice.

What are the implications of your analysis for the management?

4.6 Write mission and vision statements for an organisation of your choice and suggest what strategic objectives managers might set. Explain why you think these are appropriate.

Integrative assignment

4.7 Using specific examples explain how changes in corporate governance and in expectations about corporate social responsibility are requiring organisations to develop new competences (Chapter 3) and also creating dilemmas in the pursuit of shareholder value and managing people in organisations (see Chapter 13).

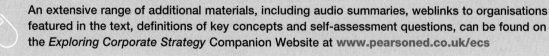

An extensive range of additional materials, including audio summaries, weblinks to organisations featured in the text, definitions of key concepts and self-assessment questions, can be found on the *Exploring Corporate Strategy* Companion Website at **www.pearsoned.co.uk/ecs**

Recommended key readings

- For books providing a fuller explanation of corporate governance: R. Monks and N. Minow (eds), *Corporate Governance*, 3rd edition, Blackwell, 2003; and J. Solomon, *Corporate Governance and Accountability*, 2nd edition, Wiley, 2007. For a provocative critique and proposals for the future of corporate governance linked to issues of social responsibility see S. Davies, J. Lukomnik and D. Pitt-Watson, *The New Capitalists*, Harvard Business School Press, 2006.

- For a review of different stances on corporate social responsibility see P. Mirvis and B. Googins, 'Stages of corporate citizenship', *California Management Review*, vol. 48, no. 2 (2006), pp. 104–126. Also D.A. Whetten, G. Rands and P. Godfrey, 'What are the responsibilities of business to society?', in A. Petigrew, H. Thomas and R. Whittington (eds), *Handbook of Strategy and Management*, Sage, 2002.

- For more about the stakeholder concept and analysis see K. Scholes' chapter in V. Ambrosini with G. Johnson and K. Scholes (eds), *Exploring Techniques of Analysis and Evaluation in Strategic Management*, Prentice Hall, 1998. For a case example of stakeholder analysis see J. Bryson, G. Cunningham and K. Lokkesmoe, 'What to do when stakeholders matter: the case of problem formulation for the African American men project of Hennepin County, Minnesota', *Public Administration Review*, vol. 62, no. 5 (2002), pp. 568–584.

- The case for the importance of clarity of strategic values and vision is especially strongly made by J. Collins and J. Porras, *Built to Last: Successful habits of visionary companies*, Harper Business, 2002 (in particular see chapter 11).

References

1. Useful general references on corporate governance are: R. Monks and N. Minow (eds), *Corporate Governance*, 3rd edition, Blackwell, 2003; and J. Solomon, *Corporate Governance and Accountability*, 2nd edition, Wiley, 2007. Those interested in an annual research update can find this in 'Corporate governance digest', *Business Horizons* (usually the May issue).

2. This definition is based on, but adapted from, that in S. Jacoby, 'Corporate governance and society', *Challenge*, vol. 48, no. 4 (2005), pp. 69–87.

3. The principal–agent model is part of agency theory which developed within organisational economics but is now widely used in the management field as described here. Two useful references are: K. Eisenhardt, 'Agency theory: an assessment and review', *Academy of Management Review*, vol. 14, no. 1 (1989), pp. 57–74; J.-J. Laffont and D. Martimort, *The Theory of Incentives: The Principal–Agent Model*, Princeton University Press, 2002.

4. The issue of to whom corporate managers should be accountable is discussed by J. Kay, 'The stakeholder corporation', in G. Kelly, D. Kelly and A. Gamble, *Stakeholder Capitalism*, Macmillan, 1997.

5. For a strong advocacy of this position see S. Davies, J. Lukomnik and D. Pitt-Watson, *The New Capitalists*, Harvard Business School Press, 2006.

6. For a typology and examples of ways in which investors engage with firms, see N. Amos and W. Oulton, 'Approaching and engaging with CR', *Corporate Responsibility Management*, vol. 2, no. 3 (2006), pp 34–37.

7. See M. Becht, J. Franks, C. Mayer and S. Rossi, *Returns to Shareholder Activism: Evidence from a clinical study of the Hermes UK Focus Fund*, European Corporate Governance Institute: http://www.ecgi.org/activism/index.php.

8. Sarbanes–Oxley Act of 2002, PL 107-204, 116 Stat 745 (30 July 2002).

9. The contribution of each of these reports is neatly summarised by G. Vinten, 'Corporate governance: the need to know', *Industrial and Commercial Training*, vol. 32, no. 5 (2000), pp. 173–178.

10. The Treadway (1987) and COSO (1992) Reports in the USA and the Cadbury Reports (1992 and 1996) in the UK.

11. For example, in the UK the Hampel (1998), Turnbull (1999) and Higgs (2003) Reports.

12. The importance of risk management in the public sector was addressed in 'Supporting innovation: managing risk in government departments', *Report by the Comptroller and Auditor General*, The Stationery Office, July 2000.

13. Role of CFOs in J. Weber, M. Arndt, E. Thornton, A. Barrett and D. Frost, 'CFOs in the hot seat', *Business Week*, 17 March (2003), pp. 65–68.

14. S. Wiesenthal, 'CFOs caught up in red tape', *Australian Financial Review*, 2003, p. 16.

15. These differences between countries are discussed in the general books (reference 1) and also in T. Clarke and S. Clegg, *Changing Paradigms: The transformation of management knowledge in the 21st century*, HarperCollins, 2000, chapter 5.

16. Within this broad classification there are other models. The market-oriented system, long-term investor system (A. Murphy and K. Topyan, 'Corporate governance: a critical survey of key concepts, issues, and recent reforms in the US', *Employee Responsibility and Rights Journal*, vol. 17, no. 2 (2005), pp. 75–89) is similar to the shareholder model as it advocates views like dispersed shareholdings and takeovers as a mechanism for corporate control. The long-term investor model and the Rhine model (M. Albert, *Capitalism against Capitalism*, Whurr Publishers, 1992) resemble the stakeholder model with a philosophy of a consensual approach towards group success with characteristics like stakeholder representation

on the boards and labour unions sharing power with the management.

17. From a Korn/Ferry International Survey cited by K. Keasey, S. Thompson and M. Wright, *Corporate Governance: Accountability, Enterprise and International Comparisons*, Wiley, 2005.

18. See Keasey *et al.* (reference 17) and also J.A. McCahery, P. Moerland, T. Raijmakers and L. Renneboog, *Corporate Governance Regimes: Convergence and diversity*, Oxford University Press, 2002.

19. See S. Jacoby (2005) (see reference 2).

20. J. Zwiebel, 'Block investment and partial corporate control', *Review of Economic Studies*, vol. 62, no. 211 (1995), p. 161.

21. See C.A. Mallin, *Corporate Governance*, Oxford University Press, 2004; and S.F. Copp, 'The institutional architecture of UK corporate governance reform: an evaluation', *Journal of Banking Regulation*, vol. 7, nos 1/2 (2006), pp. 41–63.

22. Short-termism as an issue in the Anglo-American tradition is contrasted with the 'Rhine model' more typical of Germany, Switzerland, Benelux and Northern European countries by M. Albert, 'The Rhine model of capitalism: an investigation', in W. Nicoll, D. Norburn and R. Schoenberg (eds), *Perspectives on European Business*, Whurr Publishers, 1995.

23. For further discussion on convergence, see H. Hansmann, and R. Kraakman, 'Toward a single model of corporate law?', in J.A. McCahery, P. Moerland, T. Raijmakers and L. Renneboog (eds), *Corporate Governance Regimes: Convergence and diversity*, Oxford University Press, 2002.

24. See R. Skog, 'A remarkable decade: the awakening of Swedish institutional investors', *European Business Law Review*, vol. 16, no. 5 (2005), pp. 1017–1031.

25. See V. Gupta and K. Gollakota, 'History, ownership forms and corporate governance in India', *Journal of Management History*, vol. 12, no. 2 (2006), pp. 185–197.

26. For further explanations of developments in China, see G.S. Liu and P. Sun, 'The class of shareholdings and its impacts on corporate performance: a case of state shareholdings in Chinese public corporations', *Corporate Governance*, vol. 13, no. 1 (2005), pp. 46–59; and G. Chen, M. Firth, D. Gao and O.M. Rui, 'Ownership structure, corporate governance, and fraud: evidence from China', *Journal of Corporate Finance*, vol. 12, no. 3 (2006), pp. 424–448.

27. In the USA: the Sarbanes–Oxley Act (2002). In the UK: D. Higgs, 'Review of the role and effectiveness of non-executive directors', UK Department of Trade and Industry, 2003.

28. See D. Norburn, B. Boyd, M. Fox and M. Muth, 'International corporate governance reform', *European Business Journal*, vol. 12, no. 3 (2000), pp. 116–133; J. Sonnenfeld, 'What makes great boards great', *Harvard Business Review*, vol. 80, no. 9 (2002), pp. 106–113.

29. There is a prolific flow of literature on business ethics. Readers can gain some useful insights into the field by reading P. Werhane and R.E. Freeman, 'Business ethics: the state of the art', *International Journal of Management Research*, vol. 1, no. 1 (1999), pp. 1–16. This is a useful summary of the recent publications on business ethics. Practising managers might wish to consult B. Kelley, *Ethics at Work*, Gower, 1999, which covers many of the

issues in this section and includes the Institute of Management guidelines on ethical management. Also see M.T. Brown, *Corporate Integrity: Rethinking organizational ethics and leadership*, Cambridge University Press, 2005.

30. J. Charkham, 'Corporate governance lessons from abroad', *European Business Journal*, vol. 4, no. 2 (1992), pp. 8–16.

31. Based on research undertaken at the Center for Corporate Citizenship at the Boston College, reported in P. Mirvis and B. Googins, 'Stages of corporate citizenship', *California Management Review*, vol. 48, no. 2 (2006), pp. 104–126.

32. Often quoted as a summary of Milton Friedman's argument is M. Friedman: 'The social responsibility of business is to increase its profits', *New York Times Magazine*, 13 September (1970).

33. See A. McWilliams and D. Seigel, 'Corporate social responsibility: a theory of the firm perspective', *Academy of Management Review*, vol. 26 (2001), pp. 117–127.

34. See *The State of Corporate Citizenship in the US: A view from inside, 2003–2004*, Center for Corporate Citizenship, Boston College; also reported in Mirvis and Googins, reference 31.

35. See S. Macleod, 'Why worry about CSR?', *Strategic Communication Management*, Aug/Sept (2001), pp. 8–9.

36. See M. Porter and M. Kramer, 'The competitive advantage of corporate philanthropy', *Harvard Business Review*, vol. 80, no. 12 (2002), pp. 56–68.

37. H. Hummels, 'Organizing ethics: a stakeholder debate', *Journal of Business Ethics*, vol. 17, no. 13 (1998), pp. 1403–1419.

38. D. Vogel, 'Is there a market for virtue? The business case for corporate social responsibility', *California Management Review*, vol. 47, no. 4 (2005), pp. 19–45.

39. S.A. Waddock and C. Bodwell, 'Managing responsibility: what can be learned from the quality movement', *California Management Review*, vol. 47, no. 1 (2004), pp. 25–37; and R. Orsato, 'Competitive environmental strategies: when does it pay to be green?', *California Management Review*, vol. 48, no. 2 (2006), pp. 127–143.

40. This quote is from Porter and Kramer, reference 36, p. 80.

41. These examples are given by Porter and Kramer, reference 36.

42. From Orsato, reference 39.

43. K. Schnietz and M. Epstein, 'Does a reputation for corporate social responsibility pay off?', *Social Issues in Management Conference Papers*, Academy of Management Proceedings, 2002. This paper shows that the Fortune 500 firms that were also in the Domini Social Index outperformed the others in terms of stock return.

44. See D. Vogel, reference 38.

45. M.L. Barnett and R.M. Salomon ('Beyond dichotomy: the curvilinear relationship between social responsibility and financial performance', *Strategic Management Journal*, vol. 27, no. 11 (2006), pp. 1101–1122) argue that research such as that by Vogel does not take sufficient account of the screening programmes of the investors. The more such screening takes place and depending on the type of screening, so performance may increase.

46. For a discussion of the range of performance measures being used in relation to CSR and their effectiveness, see A. Chatterji and D. Levine, 'Breaking down the wall of codes: evaluating non-financial performance measures',

California Management Review, vol. 48, no. 2 (2006), pp. 29–51.

47. See: T.D. Miethe, *Tough Choices in Exposing Fraud, Waste and Abuse on the Job*, Westview Press, 1999; G. Vinten, *Whistleblowing: Subversion or corporate citizenship?*, Paul Chapman, 1994; R. Larmer, 'Whistleblowing and employee loyalty', *Journal of Business Ethics*, vol. 11, no. 2 (1992), pp. 125–128.

48. M.R. Banaji, M.H. Bazerman and D. Chugh, 'How (UN)ethical are you?', *Harvard Business Review*, vol. 81, no. 12 (2003), pp. 56–64.

49. The early writings about stakeholders are still worthy of note. For example, the seminal work by R.M. Cyert and J.G. March, *A Behavioural Theory of the Firm*, Prentice Hall, 1964; I.I. Mitroff, *Stakeholder of the Organisational Mind*, Jossey Bass, 1983; R.E. Freeman, *Strategic Management: A stakeholder approach*, Pitman, 1984. Also see J. Bryson, 'What to do when stakeholders matter: stakeholder identification and analysis techniques', *Public Management Review*, vol. 6, no. 1 (2004), pp. 21–53.

50. Details of how these three groups interact with organisations can be found in J. Cummings and J. Doh, 'Identifying who matters: mapping key players in multiple environments', *California Management Review*, vol. 42, no. 2 (2000), pp. 83–104.

51. T. Kostova and S. Zaheer, 'Organisational legitimacy under conditions of complexity: the case of the multinational enterprise', *Academy of Management Review*, vol. 24, no. 1 (1999), pp. 64–81.

52. This approach to stakeholder mapping has been adapted from A. Mendelow, *Proceedings of the 2nd International Conference on Information Systems*, Cambridge, MA, 1991. See also K. Scholes' chapter, 'Stakeholder analysis', in V. Ambrosini with G. Johnson and K. Scholes (eds), *Exploring Techniques of Analysis and Evaluation in Strategic Management*, Prentice Hall, 1998. For a public sector explanation, see K. Scholes, 'Stakeholder mapping: a practical tool for public sector managers', in G. Johnson and K. Scholes (eds), *Exploring Public Sector Strategy*, Financial Times/Prentice Hall, 2001, chapter 9; and

J. Bryson, G. Cunningham and K. Lokkesmoe, 'What to do when stakeholders matter: the case of problem formulation for the African American men project of Hennepin County, Minnesota', *Public Administration Review*, vol. 62, no. 5 (2002), pp. 568–584.

53. For example, see J. Bryson *et al.* reference 52. Also see Kalle Pajunen, 'Stakeholder influences in organizational survival', *Journal of Management Studies*, vol. 43, no. 6 (2006), pp. 1261–1288.

54. D. Buchanan and R. Badham, *Power, Politics and Organisational Change: Winning the turf game*, Sage, 1999, provide a useful analysis of the relationship between power and strategy. See also S. Clegg, D. Courpasson and N. Phillips, *Power and Organizations*, Sage, 2006.

55. P. Lencioni, 'Make your values mean something', *Harvard Business Review*, vol. 80, no. 7 (2002), pp. 113–117.

56. See J. Collins and J. Porras, *Built to Last: Successful habits of visionary companies*, Harper Business, 2002.

57. For example, see B. Bartkus, M. Glassman and B. McAfee, 'Mission statements: are they smoke and mirrors?', *Business Horizons*, vol. 43, no. 6 (2000), pp. 23–28; and B. Bartkus, M. Glassman and B. McAfee, 'Mission statement quality and financial performance', *European Management Journal*, vol. 24, no. 1 (2006), pp. 86–94.

58. Communicating effectively with the investing community is essential, as discussed by A. Hutton, 'Four rules', *Harvard Business Review*, vol. 79, no. 5 (2001), pp. 125–132.

59. For example, I. Ansoff, *Corporate Strategy*, Penguin, 1968, p. 44, argued that objectives should be precise and measurable.

60. See A. Neely, 'Measuring performance in innovative firms', in R. Delbridge, L. Grattan and G. Johnson (eds), *The Exceptional Manager*, Oxford University Press, 2006, chapter 6.

61. This discussion is based on research by K.M. Eisenhardt and D.N. Sull, reported in 'Strategy as simple rules', *Harvard Business Review*, vol. 79, no. 1 (2001), pp. 107–116.

CASE EXAMPLE

(PRODUCT) RED and Gap

(RED) was created by Bono and Bobby Shriver, Chairman of DATA, to raise awareness and money for The Global Fund by teaming up with the world's most iconic brands to produce (PRODUCT) RED-branded products. A percentage of each (PRODUCT) RED product sold is given to The Global Fund. The money helps women and children with HIV/AIDS in Africa.[1]

The (RED) initiative was set up in early 2006, with Rwanda selected as the initial country to benefit from sales of the (RED) products. The first products launched in the UK were the (PRODUCT) RED American Express card and a (PRODUCT) RED vintage T-shirt from Gap launched in March 2006. Other companies joining the scheme included Motorola, Converse, Apple (introducing a (PRODUCT) RED iPod) and Emporio Armani. There was also a special (PRODUCT) RED edition of the *Independent*, guest edited by Bono.

THE (RED)™ MANIFESTO

ALL THINGS BEING EQUAL, THEY ARE NOT.

AS FIRST WORLD CONSUMERS, WE HAVE TREMENDOUS POWER. WHAT WE COLLECTIVELY CHOOSE TO BUY, OR NOT TO BUY, CAN CHANGE THE COURSE OF LIFE AND HISTORY ON THIS PLANET.

(RED) IS THAT SIMPLE AN IDEA. AND THAT POWERFUL. NOW, YOU HAVE A CHOICE. THERE ARE (RED) CREDIT CARDS, (RED) PHONES, (RED) SHOES, (RED) FASHION BRANDS. AND NO, THIS DOES NOT MEAN THEY ARE ALL RED IN COLOR, ALTHOUGH SOME ARE.

IF YOU BUY A (RED) PRODUCT OR SIGN UP FOR A (RED) SERVICE, AT NO COST TO YOU, A (RED) COMPANY WILL GIVE SOME OF ITS PROFITS TO BUY AND DISTRIBUTE ANTI-RETROVIRAL MEDICINE TO OUR BROTHERS AND SISTERS DYING OF AIDS IN AFRICA.

WE BELIEVE THAT WHEN CONSUMERS ARE OFFERED THIS CHOICE, AND THE PRODUCTS MEET THEIR NEEDS, THEY WILL CHOOSE (RED). AND WHEN THEY CHOOSE (RED) OVER NON-(RED), THEN MORE BRANDS WILL CHOOSE TO BECOME (RED) BECAUSE IT WILL MAKE GOOD BUSINESS SENSE TO DO SO. AND MORE LIVES WILL BE SAVED.

(RED) IS NOT A CHARITY. IT IS SIMPLY A BUSINESS MODEL. YOU BUY (RED) STUFF. WE GET THE MONEY, BUY THE PILLS AND DISTRIBUTE THEM. THEY TAKE THE PILLS, STAY ALIVE, AND CONTINUE TO TAKE CARE OF THEIR FAMILIES AND CONTRIBUTE SOCIALLY AND ECONOMICALLY IN THEIR COMMUNITIES.

IF THEY DON'T GET THE PILLS, THEY DIE. WE DON'T WANT THEM TO DIE. WE WANT TO GIVE THEM THE PILLS. AND WE CAN. AND YOU CAN. AND IT'S EASY.

ALL YOU HAVE TO DO IS UPGRADE YOUR CHOICE.

Source: http://www.joinred.com/manifesto.asp.

Support for the (RED) campaign has come from Bill Gates, interviewed in *Advertising Age*: 'Red is about saving lives . . . if there's not enough money to buy drugs, people die, and so we can say, "Hey, let's just let that happen," or we can take all the avenues available to us.' He acknowledged that this included governments being more generous, but also believed that consumers wanted 'to associate themselves with saving lives' and that what Gap or Armani were doing through (PRODUCT) RED provided this opportunity.

Other commentators were not so positive. Another article in *Advertising Age*[2] claimed that the campaign had raised only $18m (€15m; £10m) in a year despite a marketing outlay by companies involved in the scheme (including Gap) of $100m. Gap was the biggest spender here with an advertising budget of $7.8m. A spokeswoman for (RED) claimed that the

Ad Age figure of 100 million was merely a 'phantom number pulled out of thin air'.

An article in the *Independent* went on to do its own mathematics, concluding that the figure raised was $25 million in six months and that, on an advertising investment of $40 million, this was a 'staggeringly good rate of return'.

They went on to argue:[3]

what the RED initiative has set out to do – and with some success if $25 million in six months is half the profits RED products would have made – is create a stream of revenue for the fight against AIDS in Africa which will far exceed one-off payments from corporate philanthropy budgets. It looks set to create a major source of cash for the global fund, and one which is sustainable. It is an entirely new model for fund raising.

But wouldn't it be better if people simply gave the money that they spend on the products directly to charity? 'If only that were the choice. But most people wouldn't give the cost of a new ipod to the global fund.' They continued:

The money RED has raised means that some 160,000 Africans will be put on life saving anti-retrovirals in the coming months, orphans are being fed and kept in school in Swaziland and a national HIV treatment and prevention programme has begun in Rwanda.

(RED) Gap

On their website Gap's Senior Vice President for Social Responsibility, Dan Henkle, explained Gap's commitment in relation to its work in Lesotho. Lesotho has a population of 1.8 million, with almost one-third HIV positive. Gap has invested significantly in the manufacture of T-shirts in that country, as well as in community initiatives, for example in HIV testing and treatment to garment workers. It has also promoted forums to encourage the growth of the garment industry in that country.

The British pressure group, Labour Behind the Label, which campaigns to improve the working conditions of garment workers around the world, expressed its support for efforts being made by Gap to move towards more responsible sourcing of products. By deciding to manufacture the (PRODUCT) RED T-shirts in Lesotho, Gap had helped to safeguard workers' likelihoods there at a time when other companies were increasingly sourcing garments from China and India:

While GAP, like all clothing companies, is a long way from resolving all workers' rights issues in its supply chain, it has come further than many. Whilst we would like to see initiatives like RED being more comprehensive in their attitude towards combining charity and political change, so far indications suggest that the way the RED T-shirt has been put together could be a positive step for the African garment industry as well as for the fight against AIDS.[4]

Others were less supportive. A parodying website, mirroring the Gap advertising, was set up by protesters in San Francisco. It urged people to support causes directly, rather than via shopping. Its message: 'Shopping is not a solution. Buy (Less). Give More. Join us in rejecting the ti(red) notion that shopping is a reasonable response to human suffering.'

And in October 2006 there was a lengthy critique in *The Times*:[5]

GAP, America's still-trendy mass-market clothing retailer, is winning plaudits over here for its new campaign . . .

designed to generate awareness and money to alleviate suffering in Africa. . . . It is pledging to give half of the profits from its iconic red T-shirts and leather jackets to Aids/HIV relief. The campaign was launched here last week, with the always crucial imprimatur of Hollywood. It features stars such as Steven Spielberg and Penelope Cruz in red T-shirts with one-word messages that say, with a modesty that doesn't fit quite as well as the clothes, INSPI(RED) and ADMI(RED). The message is that, by buying these products, ordinary mortals such as you and I (well, all right, you) can look like Hollywood stars and save lives in Africa too. You can almost taste the pity and charity oozing from Ms Cruz's pouted lips, the love pouring from Mr Spielberg's dewy eyes.

Sorry to play the curmudgeon here. But this latest concession to the galloping forces of corporate social responsibility, far from helping the benighted of the world, is actually going to make things worse. I am sick and TI(RED) of companies trying to demonstrate to me how seriously they take their supposed duty to bring joy to and remove pain from the world. They can take their charge card (S, CREWnecks and mobile phones and ask THEMSELVES) whether this is really the sort of thing they should be doing with their shareholders' money.

Now I don't here intend to demean the charitable spirit or the work of good people such as Bono or Bob Geldof, nor the perfectly decent motivation of millions in the wealthy world who genuinely want to help to improve the wretched lives of those less fortunate than themselves. Don't get me

Photo: Associated Press/PA Photos

Bono and Oprah promoting Gap

wrong; charity remains one of the finest of virtues and should, in almost all instances, be encouraged.

Nor am I going to point out the nauseating conspicuousness of the consumption represented by the RED campaign ('Look,' it says, 'I not only look good. I AM good!'). Nor am I even going to dwell on the fact, though I could, that for all the aid Africa has received over the past 50 years, the continent remains poorer than ever, and certainly poorer than parts of the world that have received little in the way of charity in that time.

My problem here is with what this does for the very idea of capitalism, for companies pursuing their real and entirely wholesome responsibility of making money. Free market capitalism, untrammelled by marketing people in alliance with special interest groups on a mission to save the world, has done more to alleviate poverty than any well-intentioned anti-poverty campaign in the history of the globe.

By concentrating on selling quality, low-priced goods, some of them made with labour that would otherwise lie idle (and dying) in the developing world, Gap saves lives. By helping to keep prices down and generating profits, Gap ploughs money back into the pockets of people in the US, the UK and elsewhere. Which creates the demand for imports of products from the developing world. Which keeps the poor of those countries from suffering even more than they do now.

In a complex world, we all operate in a division of labour. Companies make profits. It is what they are designed to do. It is what they do best. When they depart from that mission, they lead their employees and their shareholders down a long, slow route to perdition.

You think that is over the top? What is most troubling about campaigns such as Product Red is that they represent an accommodation with groups who think the business of capitalism is fundamentally evil. By appeasing people who regard globalisation as a process of exploitation, companies such as Gap are making the world much worse for all of us. They are implicitly acknowledging that their main business – selling things that people want for a profit – is inherently immoral and needs to be expiated by an occasional show of real goodness.

Rather than resisting it, they are nurturing and feeding an anti-business sentiment that will impoverish us all. What's more, this encroachment by companies is fundamentally undemocratic. Companies should not collude with interest groups and non-governmental organisations to decide on public priorities. That is for free people, through their elected governments, to do.

None of this is to say companies – or the people who run them – should not behave morally. They should observe not only the law, but the highest ethical standards, which means honesty, straight dealing and openness. It might even at times be in their corporate interests (ie, longer-term profitability) to contribute to political or charitable causes – in those cases shareholders can and should vote on the appropriation of funds for such purposes.

But shareholders – all of us – should be concerned when managements decide, for whatever reason, to make common cause with those who oppose the very principals on which their business is conducted. That represents a case of misguided corporate BULLS(HIT) TING the wrong target.

Notes

1. *Source*: (PRODUCT) RED website http://joinred.blogspot.com/.
2. M. Frazier, 'Costly Red Campaign reaps meager $18m', *Advertising Age*, vol. 78, no. 10 (5 March 2007).
3. P. Vallely, 'The Big Question: Does the RED campaign help big Western brands more than Africa', *Independent*, p. 50, 9 March (2007). Copyright The Independent, 9.3.07.
4. *Source*: http://www.labourbehindthelabel.org/content/view/67/51/.
5. Gerard Baker, 'Mind the Gap – with this attack on globalisation', *The Times*, 24 October (2006). © Gerard Baker. N.I. Syndication Limited, 24.10.06.

Questions

1 Drawing on the three perspectives in the key debate (Illustration 4.6) or the four stances in Exhibit 4.4, what is the rationale of:
   (a) The founders of (PRODUCT) RED?
   (b) Dan Henkle and Gap?
   (c) The author of the article in *The Times*?

2 What views might shareholders of Gap have of Product Gap?

3 In your view is (PRODUCT) RED an appropriate corporate activity?

4 If you were a shareholder of a company and wished to persuade top management to join the (PRODUCT) RED initiative, how might you do this? (Use stakeholder analysis as a means of considering this.)

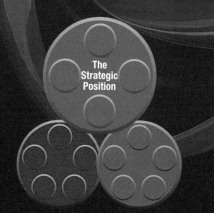

The Strategic Position

5

Culture and Strategy

LEARNING OUTCOMES

After reading this chapter you should be able to:

→ Identify organisations that have experienced strategic drift and the symptoms of strategic drift.

→ Analyse how history influences the strategic position of organisations.

→ Analyse the influence of an organisation's culture on its strategy using the cultural web.

→ Recognise the importance of strategists questioning the taken-for-granted aspects of a culture.

5.1   INTRODUCTION

Chapters 2, 3 and 4 have considered the important influences of the environment, organisational capabilities and stakeholder expectations on the development of strategy. Vital as these are to understand, there is a danger that managers only take into account relatively recent phenomena without understanding how those phenomena have come about or how the past influences current and future strategy. Many organisations have long histories. The large Japanese Mitsui Group was founded in the seventeenth century; Daimler-Chrysler was founded in the nineteenth century and there has been evident continuity in its values and design principles; managers in the UK retailer Sainsbury's still refer to the founding principles of the Sainsbury family in the nineteenth century; many public sector organisations – government departments, the police, universities, for example – are strongly influenced by their historical legacies that have become embedded in their cultures.

Historical and cultural perspectives can help an understanding of both opportunities and constraints that organisations face, many of which are also discussed in other chapters of this book. The business environment (Chapter 2) cannot be understood without considering how it has developed over time. The capabilities of an organisation (Chapter 3), especially those that provide organisations with competitive advantage, may have historical roots and have built up over time in

Exhibit 5.1   **Chapter structure**

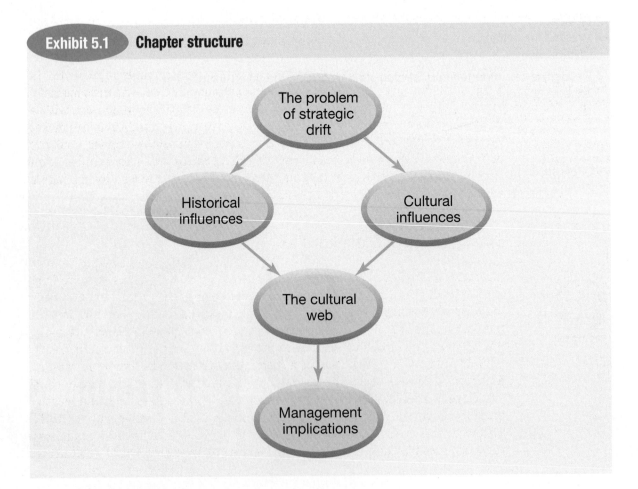

ways unique to that organisation. In so doing such capabilities may become part of the culture of an organisation – the taken-for-granted way of doing things – therefore difficult for other organisations to copy. However, they may also be difficult to change. So understanding the historical and cultural bases of such capabilities also informs the challenges of strategic change (Chapter 14). The powers and influence of different stakeholders are also likely to have historical origins that are important to understand. The theme of this chapter is, then, that the strategic position of an organisation has historical and cultural roots and that understanding those roots helps managers develop the future strategy of their organisations.

The chapter begins by explaining the phenomenon of strategic drift that highlights the importance of history and culture in relation to strategy development and identifies important challenges managers face in managing that development. The chapter then considers the two important and linked perspectives of history and culture. Section 5.3 examines the influence of the history of an organisation on its current and future strategy and goes on to consider how that history can be analysed. Section 5.4 then explains what is meant by culture and how cultural influences at the national, institutional and organisational levels influence current and future strategy. It then suggests how a culture can be analysed and its influence on strategy understood. Exhibit 5.1 summarises the chapter structure.

5.2   STRATEGIC DRIFT

Strategic drift is the tendency for strategies to develop incrementally on the basis of historical and cultural influences but fail to keep pace with a changing environment

Historical studies of organisations have shown a pattern that is represented in Exhibit 5.2. **Strategic drift**[1] is the tendency for strategies to develop incrementally on the basis of historical and cultural influences, but fail to keep pace with a changing environment. An example of strategic drift is given in Illustration 5.1. The reasons and consequences of strategic drift are important to understand, not only because it is common, but because it helps explain why organisations often 'run out of steam'. It also highlights some significant challenges for managers which, in turn, point to some important lessons.

5.2.1   Strategies change incrementally

www.pearsoned.co.uk/ecs
KEY CONCEPT

Strategic drift

Strategies of organisations tend to change gradually. This is discussed more fully in Chapter 11. Here it is sufficient to summarise by explaining that there is a tendency for strategies to develop on the basis of what the organisation has done in the past – especially if that has been successful.[2] For example, Sainsbury's was one of the most successful retailers in the world for decades till the early 1990s, with its formula of selling food of a higher quality than competitors at reasonable prices. Always under the patriarchal guidance of a Sainsbury family chief executive, it gradually extended its product lines, enlarged its stores and its geographical coverage, but it did not deviate from its tried and tested ways of doing business. This is shown in phase 1 of the exhibit. In most successful businesses there are usually long periods of relative *continuity* during which established

Exhibit 5.2   Strategic Drift

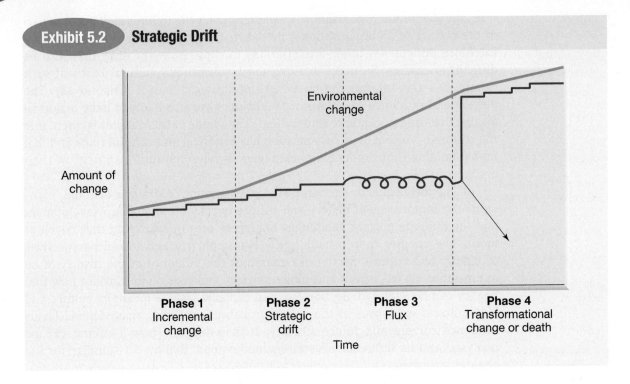

strategy remains largely unchanged or changes very *incrementally*. There are three main reasons for this:

- *Alignment with environmental change*. It could well be that the environment, particularly the market, is changing gradually and the organisation is keeping in line with those changes by such incremental change. It would make no sense for the strategy to change dramatically when the market is not doing so.

- *The success of the past*. There may be a natural unwillingness by managers to change a strategy significantly if it has been successful in the past, especially if it is built on capabilities that have been shown to be the basis of competitive advantage (see Chapters 3 and 6) or of innovation (see section 5.3.1 and Chapter 7).

- *Experimentation around a theme*. Indeed managers may have learned how to build variations around their successful formula, in effect experimenting without moving too far from their capability base. (This is akin to what some writers have referred to as 'logical incrementalism'; see section 11.3.1).

This poses challenges for managers, however. For how long and to what extent can they rely on incremental change building on the past being sufficient? When should they make more fundamental strategic changes? How are they to detect when this is necessary?

5.2.2 The tendency towards strategic drift

Whilst an organisation's strategy may continue to change incrementally, it may not change in line with the environment. This does not necessarily mean that there has to be dramatic environmental changes; phase 2 of Exhibit 5.2 shows environmental change accelerating, but it is not sudden. For Sainsbury's there

Illustration 5.1

Motorola: an analogue history facing a digital revolution

The bases of a firm's success may in turn be a cause of strategic drift.

In 1994 Motorola had 60 per cent of the US mobile telephone market. Founded in 1928, it was known for its technological innovation. It introduced the two-way walkie-talkie radio device commonly used in the Second World War, it marketed the first television to sell for under $200 in 1948. By the 1950s it had developed capabilities in printed circuit, ceramic substrate technology and electronic system design. By the 1970s it was a leading producer of microprocessors and was regarded as a world leader in technology.

However, even in the early days it was evident that the emphasis was on technology, rather than the market. Critics suggested that the firm put technology before consumers.

Mobile phones had been developed by Bell Labs in the 1970s. By the mid-1980s Motorola was the leading producer of cell phones using analogue technology, but none the less a logical progression from its military walkie-talkie systems using the post-war technology it had developed. However, these devices were bulky and expensive, targeted at business managers who were on the move and could not use landlines. The phones were not widely known or available.

By the mid-1990s Motorola was highly successful. From 1992 to 1995 sales revenue grew at an average of 27 per cent a year to reach $27bn (€22bn) and net income 58 per cent a year to reach $1.8bn.

However, by the mid-1990s digital technology for mobile phones was being developed through what was known as the Personal Communication System (PCS). This technology overcame some of the shortcomings of analogue technology. It reduced interference, allowed security codes to be encrypted and could deal with more subscribers than analogue. It was a technology that supported mass market development. The demand for digital phones grew rapidly, not amongst business people alone, but amongst a wider consumer market.

These consumers were much less concerned about functionality and much more concerned about ease of use and aesthetic appeal.

According to a Motorola chief executive of the time, Robert Galvin, the company 'was at the forefront of the development of digital technology'. However, it chose to stay with analogue technology for many years, licensing its digital to Nokia and Ericsson through which it earned increasing royalties. Indeed Motorola launched a new analogue phone, Star-TAC, and embarked on an aggressive marketing campaign to promote it.

Not only was it clear from the growing royalties that digital phones were taking off, wireless carrier customers were lobbying Motorola to develop digital phones: 'They told us we didn't know what we were talking about. . . . These were not friendly conversations. But Motorola didn't do it. Instead we launched with Ericsson, then Nokia.'

By 1998 Motorola's market share had dropped to 34 per cent and it was forced to lay off 20,000 people.

Source: Adapted from S. Finkelstein, 'Why smart executives fail: four case histories of how people learn the wrong lessons from history', *Business History*, vol. 48, no. 2 (2006), pp. 153–170.

Questions

1 Identify on a timeline between 1928 and 1998 the major events identified here. What does this analysis tell you about the reasons for the resistance of Motorola to new technology?

2 Given that Motorola had the technology and knew that the digital market was developing, give reasons as to why it persisted with analogue technology. (See Chapter 11 and the Commentaries as well as this chapter to help with this question.)

was the growing share of its rival, Tesco, accompanied by the growth of larger-size stores, with wider ranges of goods (for example, non-food) and changes in distribution logistics of competitors. These changes, however, had been taking place for many years. The problem that gives rise to strategic drift is that, as with many organisations, Sainsbury's strategy was not keeping pace with these changes. There are at least five reasons for this:

- *The problem of hindsight*. Chapter 2 has provided ways to analyse the environment and such analyses may yield insights. But how are managers to be sure of the direction and significance of such changes? Or changes may be seen as temporary. Managers may be understandably wary of changing what they are likely to see as a winning strategy on the basis of what might only be a fad in the market, or a temporary downturn in demand. It may be easy to see major changes with hindsight, but it may not be so easy to see their significance as they are happening.

- *Building on the familiar*. Managers may see changes in the environment about which they are uncertain or which they do not entirely understand. In these circumstances they may try to minimise the extent to which they are faced with such uncertainty by looking for answers that are familiar, which they understand and which have served them well in the past. This will lead to a bias towards continued incremental strategic change. For example, Sainsbury's managers clung to the belief that they had loyal customers who valued the superior quality of Sainsbury's goods. Tesco had been a cheaper retailer with what they saw as inferior goods. Surely the superior quality of Sainsbury's would continue to be recognised.

- *Core rigidities*. As Chapter 3 explains, success in the past may well have been based on capabilities that are unique to an organisation and difficult for others to copy. However, the capabilities that have been bases of advantage can become difficult to change, in effect *core rigidities*.[3] There are two reasons. First, over time, the ways of doing things that have delivered past success may become taken for granted. This may well have been an advantage in the past because it was difficult for competitors to imitate them. However, taken-for-granted core competences rarely get questioned and therefore tend to persist beyond their usefulness. Second, ways of doing things develop over time and become more and more embedded in organisational routines that reinforce and rely on each other and are difficult to unravel; this is discussed further in section 5.3.1.

- *Relationships become shackles*.[4] Success has probably been built on the basis of excellent relationships with customers, suppliers and employees. Maintaining these may very likely be seen as fundamental to the long-term health of the organisation. Yet these relationships may make it difficult to make fundamental changes to strategy that could entail changing routes to market or the customer base, developing products requiring different suppliers or changing the skill base of the organisation with the risk of disrupting relationships with the workforce.

- *Lagged performance effects*. The effects of such drift may not be easy to see in terms of the performance of the organisation. Financial performance may continue to hold up in the early stages of strategic drift. Customers may be loyal and the organisation, by becoming more efficient, cutting costs or simply trying harder, may continue to hold up its performance. So there may not be internal signals of the need for change or pressures from managers, or indeed external observers to make major changes.

However, over time, if strategic drift continues, there will be symptoms that become evident: a downturn in financial performance; a loss in market share to competitors perhaps; a decline in the share price. Indeed such a downturn may happen quite rapidly once external observers, not least competitors and financial analysts, have identified that such drift has occurred. Even the most successful companies may drift in this way. Indeed, there is a tendency – which Danny Miller has called the Icarus Paradox[5] – for businesses to become victims of the very success of their past. They become captured by the formula that has delivered that success.

5.2.3 A period of flux

The next phase (phase 3) may be a period of *flux* triggered by the downturn in performance. Strategies may change but in no very clear direction. There may also be management changes, often at the very top as the organisation comes under pressure to make changes from its stakeholders, not least shareholders in the case of a public company. There may be internal rivalry as to which strategy to follow, quite likely based on differences of opinion as to whether future strategy should be based on historic capabilities or whether those capabilities are becoming redundant. Indeed, there have been highly publicised boardroom rows when this has happened. All this may result in a further deterioration of confidence in the organisation: perhaps a further drop in performance or share price, a difficulty in recruiting high-quality management, or a further loss of customers' loyalty.

5.2.4 Transformational change or death

As things get worse it is likely that the outcome (phase 4) will be one of three possibilities: (i) the organisation may die (in the case of a commercial organisation it may go into receivership, for example); (ii) it may get taken over by another organisation; or (iii) it may go through a period of *transformational change*. Such change could take form in multiple changes related to the organisation's strategy: for example, a change in products, markets or market focus, changes of capabilities on which the strategy is based, changes in the top management of the organisation and perhaps the way the organisation is structured.

Transformational change does not take place frequently in organisations and is usually the result of a major downturn in performance. Often it is transformational changes that are heralded as the success stories of top executives; this is where they most visibly make a difference. The problem is that, from the point of view of market position, shareholder wealth and jobs, it may be rather too late. Competitive position may have been lost, shareholder value has probably already been destroyed and, very likely, many jobs will have been lost too. The time when 'making a difference' really matters most is in phase 2 in Exhibit 5.2, when the organisation is beginning to drift. However, a study of 215 major UK firms identified just 8 that had effected major transformational change without performance decline.[6] The problem is that, very likely, such drift is not easy to see before performance suffers. So in understanding the strategic position of an organisation so as to avoid the damaging effects of strategic drift, it is vital to take seriously the extent to which historical tendencies in strategy development tend to persist in the cultural fabric of organisations. The rest of this chapter focuses on this. The challenge is, then, how to manage change in such circumstances and this challenge is taken up in Chapter 11 on managing strategic change.

5.3 WHY IS HISTORY IMPORTANT?

If the tendency for strategic drift is to be understood, the history of organisations needs to be taken seriously by strategists. There are also other reasons why understanding history can help in understanding the strategic position of an organisation and in the management of strategy:

● *Managers' organisational experience*. Managers may have spent many years in an organisation or in an industry. The experience on which they base their decisions may be heavily influenced by that history (see the discussion on the 'experience lens' in the Commentary). It is helpful if managers can 'stand apart' from that history so as to understand the influence it has on themselves and their colleagues.

● *Avoiding recency bias*. Managers can give too much weight to recent events or performance, forgetting past patterns, resulting in either undue optimism or undue pessimism. Understanding the current situation in terms of the past can provide useful lessons. For example, have there been historical trends that may repeat themselves? How have competitors responded to strategic moves in the past? A historical perspective may also help managers see what gave rise to events that were seen as surprises in the past and learn from how their organisation dealt with them.

● *Misattribution of success?* Is it clear where current bases of success originate, how they developed and how this might inform future strategy development? The danger is that there may be a misattribution of causes of success, which may lie elsewhere than thought or even be the result of luck. Such misattribution could in turn lead to the reinforcement of wrong behaviours. For example, the future strategy of an engineering firm stressed the importance of proactively managing innovation of new products and services. This was because managers saw that its current growth was coming from just such an innovation, whilst the rest of its offering was showing no growth. However, a study of the origins of innovatory products in the firm showed that the limited extent to which they occurred was largely due to what appeared to be happenchance, or as a result of technologies inherited from acquisitions happening to be relevant to the business's core activities. Historically there was no evidence of innovation being internally planned or proactively managed. This historical perspective raised important questions about what the firm saw as its capabilities for managing future innovation.

● *'What if' questions.* History can also encourage managers to ask the 'what if' question. It can encourage them to imagine what might have happened had there been other influences in the environment, different responses from customers or competitors, or different initiatives or leadership within their organisation. It makes the present more evidently a product of circumstances and thus less fixed. So potentially it opens up the possibilities for changes in the future.

● *Detecting and avoiding strategic drift.* If managers sensitise themselves to the influence of the history of their organisation they stand a better chance of seeing current strategy as part of what Henry Mintzberg describes strategy as: 'a pattern in a stream of decisions'.[7] As such, managers are more likely to be able to question the extent to which the strategy they are seeking to develop is usefully informed by that history as distinct from being driven or captured by it. The discussion on the influence of organisational culture in section 5.4 is especially relevant here.

5.3.1 Path dependency

Path dependency is where early events and decisions establish policy paths that have lasting effects on subsequent events and decisions

A useful way of thinking of the role and influence of history is through the concept of *path dependency* and the associated notion of historical *lock-in*. **Path dependency** is where early events and decisions establish 'policy paths' that have lasting effects on subsequent events and decisions.[8] It has already been discussed in Chapter 3 in relation to the potential bases of competitive advantage and path-dependent capabilities (see section 3.4.3). Its origins, its impact and how it can be understood are therefore important.

Examples often relate to technology. There are many instances where the technology we employ is better explained by path dependency than by the optimisation of such technology. A famous one is the layout used for typewriter keyboards in many countries: QWERTY. This was originated in the nineteenth century for two main reasons. First, it is a layout that reduced the problem of the keys on mechanical typewriters getting tangled when typing fast. The second was to help salespeople at that time demonstrate the machine at maximum speed by putting all the letters of the word 'typewriter' on the top line. There are more optimal layouts, but QWERTY has remained with us in most countries for over 150 years despite the elimination of mechanical keys and the eventual development of personal computers.[9] There are countless other examples ranging from technologies in nuclear power stations through to VCR systems. Early decisions and commitments become 'locked in' over time, through widespread repeated usage by networks of suppliers and users who, in turn, build their own support systems around such technology.

Path dependency is not just about technology. It also relates to any form of behaviour that has its origins in the past and becomes entrenched. In an organisational and strategic context this is likely to take form over time in the development of behavioural routines supported by hardware and technology that make up systems of selling, marketing, recruiting, accounting, and so on.[10] Such routines also often become more widely 'institutionalised' than the organisation. Take the example of accounting systems. The lock-in of these has occurred at multiple levels involving networks comprising what people do, those with whom

| Exhibit 5.3 | **Path dependency and lock-in** |

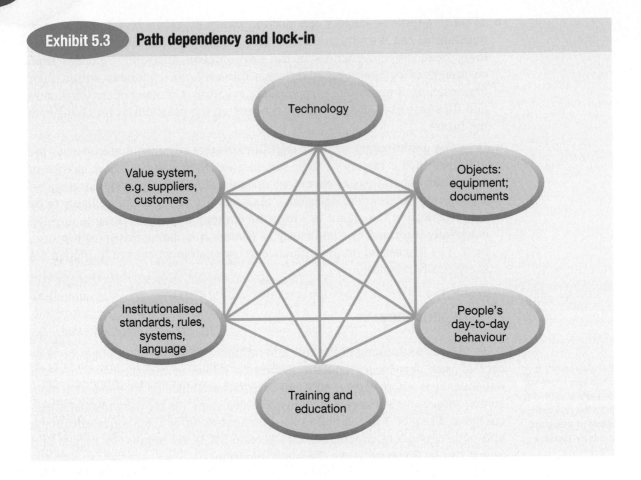

they interact within and outside their organisation, the standards and systems in which they are trained, and the objects and technologies they generate or use. All these have developed over time and mutually reinforce each other as Exhibit 5.3 illustrates. Rather like QWERTY, the 'rightness' or at least inevitability of such systems tends to be taken for granted. They also strongly influence decision making, not least in relation to strategic analysis and strategic choice. Historic accounting systems also persist despite increasing numbers of experts, both in the accountancy profession and elsewhere,[11] who point to fundamental weaknesses in such systems, not least the failure of accounting systems to provide measures for many of the factors that account for the market value of firms.

Path dependency is, then, a way of thinking about how historical events and decisions, within and around an organisation, have an effect on that organisation for good or ill. These include:

● *Building strategy around the path-dependent capabilities* that may have developed within an organisation. This is at the root of much of the arguments put forward for the building of competitive advantage discussed in Chapter 3 and further developed in Chapter 6. Indeed there is evidence that this is so. Path dependency has been shown to explain organisational strategies.[12] Firms tend to enter markets, focus on market segments and diversify in line with the previous path-dependent capabilities they have developed. In so doing they tend to focus on types of customers that they have serviced or capabilities on which their success has been based. This may be a basis for success but can also be dangerous as the Motorola example in Illustration 5.1 shows.

● The concept of *path creation* is, however, also relevant here. This suggests that some managers may actively seek to amend and deviate from path-dependent ways of doing things to the benefit of their organisations. They may be sensitive enough to history to recognise what they can and cannot change. Going too far may be risky (see the discussion on 'legitimacy' in section 5.4.2), but setting in motion changes that are accepted as appropriate and beneficial by others in the network may be a way of achieving advantage. Arguably this is what new players in the insurance market such as Tesco have done. They have not tried to change basic principles of insurance provision; they have significantly changed the way in which insurance is sold and distributed.

● *Innovation based on historic capabilities.* In the BMW museum in Munich there is a quote: 'Anyone who wants to design for the future has to leaf through the past.'[13] The museum may be about the history of BMW, but it is also about how the lessons of the past can give rise to new ideas and innovation. Indeed the Innovation and Technology Division of BMW is sited next to the museum and the archives of BMW. Innovation may build on historic capabilities in at least two ways. First, as technologies change, firms with experience and skills built over time that are most appropriate to those changes tend to innovate more than those that do not.[14] Or it could be that there are new combinations of knowledge as capabilities built up in adjacent technologies are adapted in innovative ways to new technological opportunities. For example, the development of lighting systems was derived from the way gas was distributed.[15] Similarly successful firms that created the TV industry were previously radio manufacturers and it was they that exhibited greater innovation as the industry developed than the non-radio producers.[16]

In relation to both path creation and innovation managers need to see the past in relation to the future and in so doing challenge the one with the other: ask what is relevant from the past that can help with the future and what does the future demand but also not require from the past? In doing this they also need to ask themselves the extent to which the environment is changing in such a way that their path-dependent capabilities will be relevant. In other words, if strategy is to evolve on the back of such capabilities, it can only do so if simultaneously the changes in markets, technologies and other aspects of the environment discussed in Chapter 2 are potentially converging with those capabilities. They need to develop a sensitivity, not only to the historic capabilities that matter, but also to the relationship of these to an evolving environment.

● *Management style* may also have its roots in history. This may be not only in terms of the values of the founder, which indeed may have a strong influence, but also in the interplay between past ways of doing things and the lessons learned from the organisation's evolving environment.[17] To take Tesco as an example again, it is now one of the most successful international retailers. In its early days it was a family firm run by Jack Cohen renowned for his blunt and authoritative style. This gave rise to internal conflicts within the firm and between suppliers and Tesco. Things are different in Tesco now, but the historic conflict has evolved into productive challenge and rivalry between managers and different parts of the firm that, arguably, have substantially contributed to its innovation and success.[18]

However, again there is another side to these potential benefits. The evolution of management style may not be in line with the needs of a changing environment, but over-influenced and bound by the legacy of the past. Similarly capabilities that are path dependent and rooted in history may become highly entrenched. Path dependency has sometimes been described as like the 'furrows in a road' that become deeper and deeper as more and more traffic goes along. Once that happens the traffic has no option but to go along those furrows. Hence capabilities, once the bases of competitive advantage and success, become core rigidities leading to the phenomenon of strategic drift explained in section 5.2.

5.3.2 Historical analysis

How then might managers undertake a historical strategic analysis of their organisation? There are a number of ways this may be done:[19]

- *Chronological analysis*. At the most basic level this involves setting down a chronology of key events showing changes in the organisation's environment – especially its markets – how the organisation's strategy itself has changed and with what consequences – not least financial. Some firms have done this much more extensively by commissioning extensive corporate histories. These may sometimes be little more than public relations exercises, but the better ones are serious exercises in documenting the history.[20] At the very least this historical understanding can help sensitise managers to the sort of questions raised above.

- *Cyclical influences*. Is there evidence of cyclical influences? Certainly these have been shown to exist in terms of economic cycles, but also in terms of cycles of industry activity, such as periods of high acquisition activity or indeed divestment activity. Understanding when these cycles might occur and how industry and market forces might change during such cycles can inform decisions on whether to build strategy in line with those cycles or in a counter-cyclical fashion.

- *Anchor points*. History may be regarded as continuous but historical events can also be significant for an organisation at particular points in time, sometimes known as 'anchor points'. These could be particularly significant events, either in terms of industry change or organisational strategic decisions. Or they might be policies laid down by a founder or by powerful senior executives; or major successes or failures or defining periods of time that have informed received wisdom or which managers have come to see as especially important. Such anchor points may be traced to many years ago in the organisation's history, yet may have profound effects on current organisational strategy, strategic thinking or exercise significant constraints on future strategy. This could, of course, be for the good: they may provide a very clear overall direction strategically that contributes to the sort of vision discussed in the previous chapter. They could, on the other hand, be a major barrier to challenging existing strategies or changing strategic direction. A famous example is Henry Ford's maxim 'You can have any colour provided it's black', which set a trajectory for mass production and low variety in the car industry for decades. Currently government (and political opposition) health policy in the UK is constrained by the historical mantra that health provision should be 'free at point of delivery' when it clearly is not. Apple's 1984 advertising campaign marked its clear positioning against IBM: the peak time TV ad featured a young female athlete hurling a sledgehammer at a sinister TV image of *Big Brother*, clearly referring to the then dominant IBM .

● *Historical narratives*. How do people in the organisation talk about and explain the history of their organisation? In trying to understand the foundations of the strategy of an organisation a new chief executive or an external consultant will typically spend a good deal of time talking with people to try to gain insights from their personal accounts of history.[21] What do they have to say about the way they see their organisation and its past, not least in terms of anchor points and origins of success? In turn, what are the implications for future strategy development? Does what they say suggest an organisation with the historic capabilities of relevance to particular markets and customers, one capable of innovation and change or one so rooted in past ways of doing things that there are risks of strategic drift?

History, then, is important in terms of how it influences current strategy for better or worse. As suggested here, there are ways in which history can be analysed. It is not always easy, however, to trace the links to the organisation as it currently exists. It is here that understanding the organisation's culture becomes important. The current culture of an organisation is, to a great extent, the legacy of its history; history becomes 'encapsulated in culture'.[22] So understanding an organisation's culture is one way of understanding the historical influences that, as we have seen, can be very powerful. The next section goes on to explain what culture is and how it can be analysed.

5.4 WHAT IS CULTURE AND WHY IS IT IMPORTANT?

Organisational culture is the 'basic *assumptions and beliefs* that are shared by members of an organisation, that operate unconsciously and define in a basic taken-for-granted fashion an organisation's view of itself and its environment'

There are many definitions of culture. Earlier in the book (see page xx) it was defined as 'socially established structures of meaning'.[23] Edgar Schein defines **organisational culture** more specifically as the 'basic *assumptions and beliefs* that are shared by members of an organisation, that operate unconsciously and define in a basic taken-for-granted fashion an organisation's view of itself and its environment'.[24] Related to this are taken-for-granted ways of doing things, the routines, that accumulate over time. In other words, culture is about that which is taken for granted but none the less contributes to how groups of people respond and behave in relation to issues they face. It therefore has important influences on the development and change of organisational strategy.

In fact cultural influences exist at multiple levels as Exhibit 5.4 shows. The sections that follow will identify the important factors and issues in terms of different cultural frames of reference and then show how organisational culture can be analysed and characterised as a means of understanding the influences of culture on both current and future organisational purposes and strategies.

KEY CONCEPT

Organisational culture

Exhibit 5.4	**Cultural frames of reference**

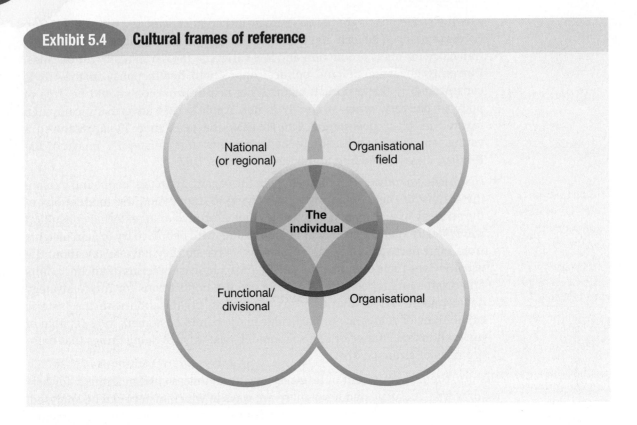

5.4.1 National and regional cultures

Many writers, perhaps the most well known of which is Geert Hofstede,[25] have shown how attitudes to work, authority, equality and other important factors differ from one country to another. Such differences have been shaped by powerful cultural forces concerned with history, religion and even climate over many centuries. Organisations that operate internationally need to understand and cope with such differences that can manifest themselves in terms of different standards, values and expectations in the various countries in which they operate.[26] For example, Euro Disney's attempt to replicate the success of the Disney theme parks in the USA was termed 'cultural imperialism' in the French media and has experienced difficulties. There was a decline in visitors of 0.3 per cent a year between 1999 and 2005. Illustration 5.2 also shows how cultural differences can pose challenges for managers seeking to develop markets in China.

Although they are not shown separately in Exhibit 5.4 (for reasons of simplification), it may also be important to understand *subnational* (usually regional) cultures. For example, attitudes to some aspects of employment and supplier relationships may differ at a regional level even in a relatively small and cohesive country like the UK, and quite markedly elsewhere in Europe (for example, between northern and southern Italy). There may also be differences between urban and rural locations.

Illustration 5.2

When in China . . .

As Western firms move into China, understanding Chinese ways of doing business becomes crucial.

David Hands has operated in Beijing for real estate firm Jones Lang Lasalle (JLL), where he had to develop the business in China. *Management Today* reported an interview with him:

There are a huge number of opportunities in China but it's crucial to sort the wheat from the chaff and you need to work on efficiency to do that. For example, we had problems with time management in the early stages. Imagine trying to set up a meeting where everybody is turning up at different times, and where nobody has thought to specify an agenda for the meeting. Or there will be three multi-hour meetings for a client who barely gives us any business. It was tough to make people understand the importance of breaking down costs versus benefits.

It took time to get the Chinese to value the advice that JLL could provide because, whilst they are accustomed to paying for goods, paying for services came as a culture shock:

You have to learn to go step by step and give a little. You can't turn up at someone's office and say: 'Pay me a large amount of money in advance'. And you have to really show them where you can add value to their operations.

There are also problems of understanding hierarchy:

You may think you are dealing with the top guy and he is asking you for a discount. You give him one. But then you meet up with another five managers in gradually ascending order and they all ask for discounts. So beware!

The symbols of hierarchy are not the same either. Unlike in some Western countries where status symbols such as car and clothing brands may signify status, in China senior management are likely to dress 'more drably':

Cheap clothing is important in a culture plagued by corruption: dressing down diverts attention from any ill-gotten gains, but the head honcho still wants to assert his authority and one way he does that is by having an entourage of flunkies. . . . I learnt early on that if I didn't reciprocate by going to meetings with one or more assistants, people would just take me less seriously.

To the Westerner there may also seem to be a lack of courtesy: 'They basically think they own you, in the same way as they own a car or luxury watch after they have paid for them.'

Staff relationships to the boss are also more important than staff relationships to the company: 'That's why you'll find staff cleaning their boss' cars on the weekend. We have to teach staff that this will not earn them promotion . . .'.

Another interviewee had experience of Chinese bureaucracy:

When you are negotiating with the government you need to find somebody who feels you can help him personally benefit from the deal. Once your interests are aligned, he can then guide you through the maze. . . . It's not a matter of getting somebody's name card and going out for a drink. In China you have to earn that person's gratitude and trust and you do that by doing them favours. The bigger the favour, the more they will help you professionally as well as privately.

Source: D. Slater, 'When in China . . .', *Management Today*, May (2006). Reproduced from *Management Today* magazine with the permission of the copyright owner, Haymarket Publications Limited.

Questions

1 On the evidence of these interviews identify how the cultural norms and taken-for-granted assumptions of Chinese managers differ from those of Western managers.

2 If you are seeking to operate in a country with a very different culture, other than talking with people experienced in that market, how else would you set about trying to understand the culture and its underlying assumptions?

5.4.2 The organisational field[27]

An organisational field is a community of organisations that interact more frequently with one another than with those outside the field and that have developed a shared meaning system

A recipe is a set of assumptions, norms and routines held in common within an organisational field about organisational purposes and a 'shared wisdom' on how to manage organisations

The culture of an organisation is also shaped by 'work-based' groupings such as an industry (or sector), a profession or what is sometimes known as an **organisational field**, which is a community of organisations that interact more frequently with one another than with those outside the field and that have developed a shared meaning system.[28] Such organisations may share a common technology, set of regulations or education and training. In turn this can mean that they tend to cohere around a **recipe**:[29] a set of assumptions, norms and routines held in common within an organisational field about organisational purposes and a 'shared wisdom' on how to manage organisations. For example, there are many organisations in the organisational field of 'justice', such as lawyers, police, courts, prisons and probation services. The roles of each are different and their detailed prescriptions as to how justice should be achieved differ. However, they are all committed to the principle that justice is a good thing which is worth striving for, they interact frequently on this issue, have developed shared ways of understanding and debating issues that arise and operate common routines or readily accommodate the routines of others in the field. Similar coherence around a recipe is common in other organisational fields, for example professional services such as accountancy (see Illustration 5.3) and many industries.

This links to the concept of path dependency discussed above. The different parties in an organisational field form a self-reinforcing network built on such assumptions and behaviours that, very likely, will lead to behavioural lock-in. Indeed professions, or trade associations, often attempt to formalise an organisational field where the membership is exclusive and the behaviour of members is regulated. Such cultural influences can be advantageous – say to customers – in maintaining standards and consistency between individual providers. Managers can, however, become 'institutionalised' such that they do not see the opportunities or indeed threats from outside their organisational field and their recipes are also likely to be very difficult to change.

Just as previous chapters have shown the importance of environmental forces (Chapter 2), strategic capabilities (Chapter 3) and stakeholder expectations (Chapter 4), within an organisational field *legitimacy* is an important influence.

Legitimacy is concerned with meeting the expectations within an organisational field in terms of assumptions, behaviours and strategies

Legitimacy is concerned with meeting the expectations within an organisational field in terms of assumptions, behaviours and strategies. Strategies can be shaped by the need for legitimacy in several ways. For example, through *regulation* (for example, standards and codes of behaviour specified, perhaps by a professional body), *normative expectations* (what is socially expected), or simply that which is taken for granted as being appropriate (for example, the *recipe*). Over time, there tends to develop a consensus within an organisational field about strategies that will be successful or acceptable – so strategies themselves become legitimised. By conforming to such norms, organisations may secure approval, support and public endorsement, thus increasing their legitimacy. Stepping outside that strategy may be risky because important stakeholders (such as customers or bankers) may not see such a move as legitimate. Therefore, organisations tend to mimic each other's strategies. There may be differences in strategies between organisations but within bounds of legitimacy.[30] This is shown in the discussion of strategy in Illustration 5.3. Of course, some fringe players may actually represent successful future strategies (for example,

Illustration 5.3

Strategy debate in an accounting firm

The perceived legitimacy of a strategy may have different roots.

Edward Gray, the managing partner of QDG, one of the larger accountancy firms in the world, is discussing its global development with two of his senior partners. Global development had been the main issue at the firm's international committee in the USA the previous week. Like most accountancy firms, QDG is organised along national lines. Its origins were in auditing but it now offers tax and financial advice, corporate recovery and information systems services. International cooperation is based on personal contacts of partners across the world. However, large clients are beginning to demand a 'seamless global service'. At the meeting is Alan Clark, with 20 years' experience as a partner and a high reputation in the accountancy profession, and Michael Jones: new to QDG and unlike the others not an accountant, he heads up the information systems arm of QDG, having been recruited from a consultancy firm.

Gray:

Unless we move towards a more global form of business, QDG could lose its position as one of the leading accountancy firms in the world. Our competitors are moving this way, so we have to. The issue is how?

Clark was sympathetic but cautionary. He pointed out that clients were entering growing economies such as China:

Governments there will insist on international standards of practice, but they have difficulties. For example, in China there is often no real concept of profit, let alone how to measure it. If there is to be a market economy, the need for the services we provide is high. There are however major problems, not least, the enormous number of people required. It is not possible to churn out experienced accountants overnight. Our professional standards would be compromised. The firm cannot be driven by market opportunity at the expense of standards. There is another issue. Our business is based on personal relationships and trust; this must not be compromised in the name of 'global integration'.

Jones suggested that the problem was more challenging:

All our competitors are going global. They will be pitching for the same clients, offering the same services and the same standard of service. Where is the difference? To achieve any competitive advantage we need to do things differently and think beyond the obvious. For example why not a two-tier partnership, where smaller countries are non-equity partners? That would allow us to make decisions more quickly, allow us to enforce standards and give formal authority to senior partners looking after our major international clients.

Clark had expected this:

This is not an opportunity to make money; it's about the development of proper systems for the economies of previously closed countries. We need to co-operate with other firms to make sure that there are compatible standards. This cannot be helped by changing a partnership structure that has served well for a hundred years.

Gray:

The view of at last week's meeting was certainly that there is a need for a more internationally co-ordinated firm, with a more effective client management system, less reliance on who knows whom and more on drawing on the best of our people when we need them.

Clark:

I could equally argue that we have an unparalleled network of personal relationships throughout the world which we have been building for decades. That what we have to do is strengthen this using modern technology and modern communications.

Gray reconciled himself to a lengthy discussion.

Source: Adapted from the case study in G. Johnson and R. Greenwood, 'Institutional theory and strategic management', in Mark Jenkins and V. Ambrosini (eds), *Strategic Management: A Multiple-Perspective Approach*, Palgrave, 2007.

Questions

1 What are the underlying assumptions of the arguments being advanced by the three partners?

2 What may be the origins of these assumptions?

3 How do the different views correspond to the discussions of strategic capabilities (Chapter 3) and competitive strategy (Chapter 6)?

Internet providers of downloadable music), but *initially* this may not be seen – customers may remain loyal to established investors, bankers may be reluctant to fund such ventures and existing players in the market may dismiss what they see as aberrations.

Because the recipe varies from one field to another, the transition of managers between sectors can also prove difficult. For example, private sector managers have been encouraged to join public services in an attempt to inject new ways of doing things into the public sector. Many have expressed difficulties in gaining acceptance of their ways of working and in adjusting their management style to the different traditions and expectations of their new organisation, for example in issues like consensus building as part of the decision-making process. Or, to take the example in Illustration 5.3, Michael Jones's different career background means he has some quite different views on strategy from his accountant colleagues.

5.4.3 Organisational culture

The culture of an organisation is often conceived as consisting of four layers[31] (see Exhibit 5.5):

● *Values* may be easy to identify in an organisation, and are often written down as statements about an organisation's mission, objectives or strategies (see section 4.5). However, they can be vague, such as 'service to the community' or 'honouring equal employment opportunities'.

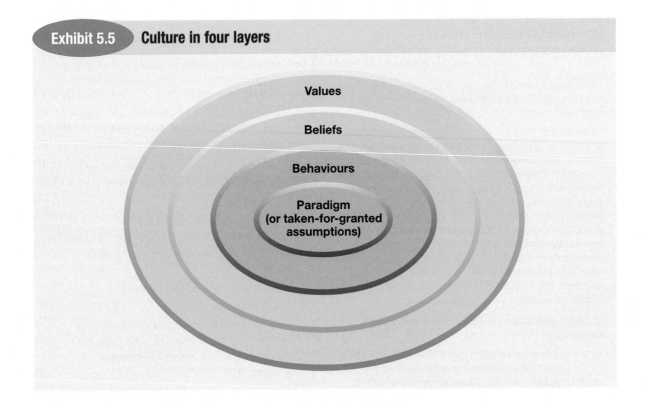

Exhibit 5.5   Culture in four layers

Values

Beliefs

Behaviours

Paradigm
(or taken-for-granted
assumptions)

- *Beliefs* are more specific, but again they can typically be discerned in how people talk about issues the organisation faces; for example, a belief that the company should not trade with particular countries, or that professional staff should not have their professional actions appraised by managers.

With regard to both values and beliefs it is important to remember that in relation to culture, the concern is with the collective rather than individuals' values and beliefs. Indeed it may be that individuals in organisations have values and beliefs that at times run counter to their organisation's, which can give rise to the sort of ethical tensions and problems discussed in section 4.3.2.

- *Behaviours* are the day-to-day way in which an organisation operates and can be seen by people both inside and outside the organisation. This includes the work routines, how the organisation is structured and controlled and 'softer' issues around symbolic behaviours.

- *Taken-for-granted assumptions* are the core of an organisation's culture. They are the aspects of organisational life which people find difficult to identify and explain. Here they are referred to as the organisational paradigm. The **paradigm** is the set of assumptions held in common and taken for granted in an organisation. For an organisation to operate effectively there is bound to be such a generally accepted set of assumptions. As mentioned above, these assumptions represent *collective experience* without which people would have to 'reinvent their world' for different circumstances that they face. The paradigm can underpin successful strategies by providing a basis of common understanding in an organisation, but can also be a major problem, for example when major strategic change is needed (see Chapter 14), or when organisations try to merge and find they are incompatible. The importance of the paradigm is discussed further in section 5.4.6.

A paradigm is the set of assumptions held relatively in common and taken for granted in an organisation

5.4.4 Organisational subcultures

In seeking to understand the relationship between culture and an organisation's strategies, it may be possible to identify some aspects of culture that pervade the whole organisation. However, there may also be important *subcultures* within organisations. These may relate directly to the structure of the organisation: for example, the differences between geographical divisions in a multinational company, or between functional groups such as finance, marketing and operations. Differences between divisions may be particularly evident in organisations that have grown through acquisition. Also different divisions may be pursuing different types of strategy and these different market positionings require or foster different cultures. Indeed, aligning strategic positioning and organisational culture is a critical feature of successful organisations. Differences between business functions also can relate to the different nature of work in different functions. For example, in a company like Shell or BP differences are likely between those functions engaged in 'upstream' exploration, where time horizons may be in decades, and those concerned with 'downstream' retailing, with much shorter market-driven time horizons. Arguably, this is one reason why both Shell and BP pay so much attention to trying to forge a corporate culture that crosses such functions.

5.4.5 Culture's influence on strategy

The taken-for-granted nature of culture is what makes it centrally important in relation to strategy and the management of strategy. There are two primary reasons for this:

- *Managing culture*. Because it is difficult to observe, identify and control that which is taken for granted, it is difficult to manage (see the key debate in Illustration 5.5 at the end of the chapter). This is why having a way to analyse culture so as to make it more evident is important – the subject of the next section.

- *Culture as a driver of strategy*. Organisations can be 'captured' by their culture and find it very difficult to change their strategy outside the bounds of that culture. Managers, faced with a changing business environment, are more likely to attempt to deal with the situation by searching for what they can understand and cope with in terms of the existing culture. The result is likely to be incremental strategic change with the risk of eventual strategic drift explained in section 5.2. Culture is, in effect, an unintended driver of strategy.

The effect of culture on strategy is shown in Exhibit 5.6.[32] Faced with a stimulus for action, such as declining performance, managers first try to improve the implementation of existing strategy. This might be through trying to lower cost,

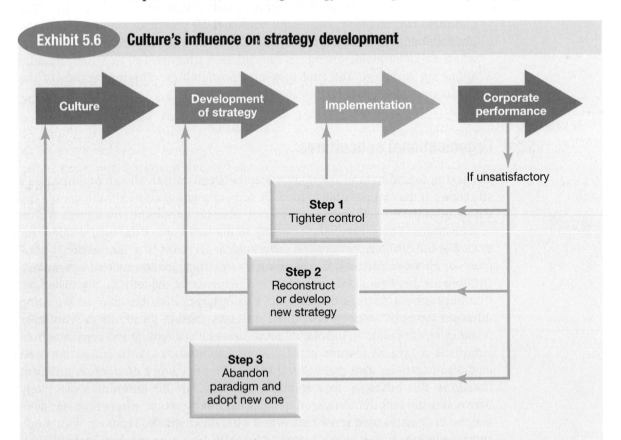

Exhibit 5.6 Culture's influence on strategy development

Source: Adapted from P. Grinyer and J.-C. Spender, *Turnaround: Managerial Recipes for Strategic Success*, Associated Business Press, 1979, p. 203.

improve efficiency, tighten controls or improve accepted ways of doing things. If this is not effective, a change of strategy may occur, but a change in line with the existing culture. For example, managers may seek to extend the market for their business, but assume that it will be similar to their existing market, and therefore set about managing the new venture in much the same way as they have been used to. Alternatively, even where managers know intellectually that they need to change, indeed know technologically how to do so, they find themselves constrained by path-dependent organisational routines and assumptions or political processes, as seems likely in Illustration 5.1. This often happens, for example, when there are attempts to change highly bureaucratic organisations to be customer oriented. Even if people who accept intellectually the need to change a culture's emphasis on the importance of conforming to established rules, routines and reporting relationships, they do not readily do so. The notion that reasoned argument necessarily changes deeply embedded assumptions rooted in collective experience built up over long periods of time is flawed. Readers need only think of their own experience in trying to persuade others to rethink their religious beliefs, or indeed allegiances to sports teams, to realise this. What occurs is the predominant application of the familiar and the attempt to avoid or reduce uncertainty or ambiguity. This is likely to continue until there is, perhaps, dramatic evidence of the redundancy of the culture, quite likely as the result of the organisation entering phases 3 or 4 of strategic drift (see Exhibit 5.2).

5.4.6 Analysing culture: the cultural web

The **cultural web** shows the behavioural, physical and symbolic manifestations of a culture that inform and are informed by the taken-for-granted assumptions, or paradigm

KEY CONCEPT

Cultural web

In order to understand both the existing culture and its effects it is important to be able to analyse culture. The **cultural web**[33] is a means of doing this. The cultural web shows the behavioural, physical and symbolic manifestations of a culture that inform and are informed by the taken-for-granted assumptions, or paradigm, of an organisation (see Exhibit 5.7). It is in effect the inner two ovals in Exhibit 5.5. The cultural web can be used to understand culture in any of the frames of reference discussed above but is most often used at the organisational and/or functional levels in Exhibit 5.4.[34] The elements of the cultural web are as follows:

● The *paradigm* is at the core of Exhibit 5.5. In effect, the taken-for-granted assumptions and beliefs of the paradigm are the *collective experience* applied to a situation to make sense of it and inform a likely course of action. The assumptions of the paradigm may be very basic. For example, it may seem self-evident that a newspaper business's core assumptions are about the centrality of news coverage and reporting. However, from a strategic point of view, increasingly newspapers' revenues are reliant on advertising income and the strategy may need to be directed to this. The paradigm of a charity may be about doing good works for the needy: but this cannot be achieved if it is not run effectively for the purpose of raising money. So understanding what the paradigm is and how it informs debate on strategy matters. The problem is that, since it is unlikely to be talked about, trying to identify it can be difficult, especially if you are part of that organisation. Outside observers may find it relatively easy to identify simply by listening to what people say

| Exhibit 5.7 | **The cultural web of an organisation** |

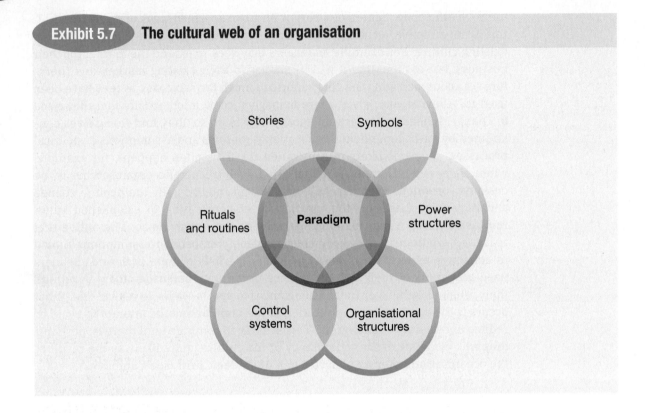

and watching what they do and emphasise, but this may not be so easy for insiders who are part of the culture. One way of 'insiders' getting to see the assumptions they take for granted is to focus initially on other aspects of the cultural web because these are to do with more visible manifestations of culture. Moreover, these other aspects are likely to act to reinforce the assumptions within that paradigm.

Routines are 'the way we do things around here on a day-to-day basis'.

- **Routines** are 'the way we do things around here' on a day-to-day basis. These may have a long history and may well be common across organisations (see section 5.3). At their best, these lubricate the working of the organisation, and may provide a distinctive organisational competence. However, they can also represent a taken-for-grantedness about how things should happen which, again, can be difficult to change.

Rituals are activities or events that emphasise, highlight or reinforce what is especially important in the culture.

- The **rituals** of organisational life are activities or events that emphasise, highlight or reinforce what is especially important in the culture. Examples include training programmes, interview panels, promotion and assessment procedures, sales conferences, and so on. An extreme example, of course, is the ritualistic training of army recruits to prepare them for the discipline required in conflict. However, rituals can also be informal activities such as drinks in the pub after work or gossiping around photocopying machines. A checklist of rituals is provided in Chapter 14 (see Exhibit 14.6).

- The *stories*[35] told by members of an organisation to each other, to outsiders, to new recruits, and so on, may act to embed the present in its organisational history and also flag up important events and personalities. They typically have to do with successes, disasters, heroes, villains and mavericks (who deviate from the norm). They can be a way of letting people know what is important in an organisation.

Symbols are objects, events, acts or people that convey, maintain or create meaning over and above their functional purpose

- **Symbols**[36] are objects, events, acts or people that convey, maintain or create meaning over and above their functional purpose. For example, offices and office layout, cars and titles have a functional purpose but are also typically signals about status and hierarchy. Particular people may come to represent specially important aspects of an organisation or historic turning points. The form of language used in an organisation can also be particularly revealing, especially with regard to customers or clients. For example, the head of a consumer protection agency in Australia described his clients as 'complainers'. In a major teaching hospital in the UK, consultants described patients as 'clinical material'. Whilst such examples might be amusing, they reveal an underlying assumption about customers (or patients) that might play a significant role in influencing the strategy of an organisation. Although symbols are shown separately in the cultural web, it should be remembered that many elements of the web are symbolic. So, routines, control and reward systems and structures are not only functional but also symbolic.

- *Power structures*. The most powerful groupings within an organisation are likely to be closely associated with the core assumptions and beliefs. For example, in firms that experience strategic drift, it is not unusual to find powerful executives who have long association with long-established ways of doing things. In analysing power the guidance given in Chapter 4 (section 4.4.2) is useful.

- *Organisational structure* is likely to reflect power and show important roles and relationships. Formal hierarchical, mechanistic structures may emphasise that strategy is the province of top managers and everyone else is 'working to orders'. Highly devolved structures (as discussed in Chapter 12) may signify that collaboration is less important than competition and so on.

- *Control systems*, measurements and reward systems emphasise what is important to monitor in the organisation. For example, public service organisations have often been accused of being concerned more with stewardship of funds than with quality of service. This is reflected in their procedures, which are more about accounting for spending rather than with quality of service. Individually based bonus schemes related to volume are likely to signal a culture of individuality, internal competition and an emphasis on sales volume rather than teamwork and an emphasis on quality.

Illustration 5.4 shows a cultural web drawn up by managers and staff in the Forestry Commission of the UK as part of a strategy development programme, together with a commentary on the significance of its elements. The key point to emerge was that at a time when this public body was charged with changing strategy towards opening up forests to the public, the staff saw themselves as technical experts and the public as a nuisance. Similar problems can often emerge through such an analysis. A cultural web analysis for an accountancy firm espousing closeness to clients as central to its strategy revealed a culture of 'partner care and centrality', rather than clients. Perhaps most significant, politicians and managers of the British Labour Party undertook a cultural web

Illustration 5.4

The cultural web of the UK Forestry Commission

The cultural web can be used to identify the behaviours and taken-for-granted assumptions of an organisation.

This is an adapted version of a cultural web produced by managers and staff of the UK Forestry Commission. The Forestry Commission (FC) was a public sector organisation charged with managing the forests of the UK.

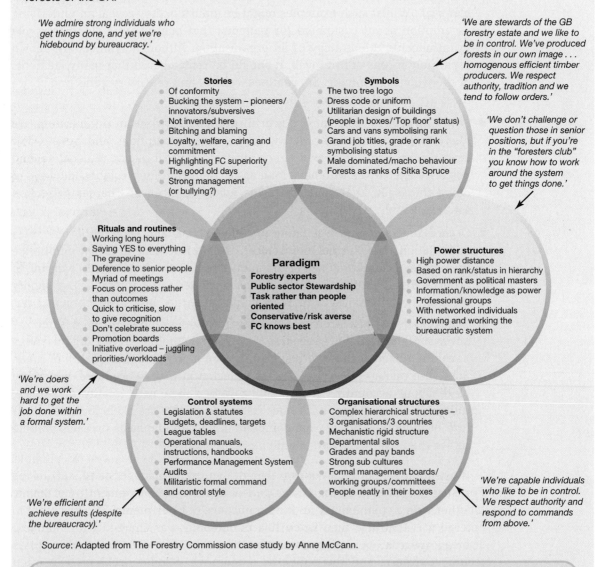

'We admire strong individuals who get things done, and yet we're hidebound by bureaucracy.'

'We are stewards of the GB forestry estate and we like to be in control. We've produced forests in our own image . . . homogenous efficient timber producers. We respect authority, tradition and we tend to follow orders.'

'We don't challenge or question those in senior positions, but if you're in the "foresters club" you know how to work around the system to get things done.'

Stories
- Of conformity
- Bucking the system – pioneers/innovators/subversives
- Not invented here
- Bitching and blaming
- Loyalty, welfare, caring and commitment
- Highlighting FC superiority
- The good old days
- Strong management (or bullying?)

Symbols
- The two tree logo
- Dress code or uniform
- Utilitarian design of buildings (people in boxes/'Top floor' status)
- Cars and vans symbolising rank
- Grand job titles, grade or rank symbolising status
- Male dominated/macho behaviour
- Forests as ranks of Sitka Spruce

Rituals and routines
- Working long hours
- Saying YES to everything
- The grapevine
- Deference to senior people
- Myriad of meetings
- Focus on process rather than outcomes
- Quick to criticise, slow to give recognition
- Don't celebrate success
- Promotion boards
- Initiative overload – juggling priorities/workloads

Paradigm
- **Forestry experts**
- **Public sector Stewardship**
- **Task rather than people oriented**
- **Conservative/risk averse**
- **FC knows best**

Power structures
- High power distance
- Based on rank/status in hierarchy
- Government as political masters
- Information/knowledge as power
- Professional groups
- With networked individuals
- Knowing and working the bureaucratic system

'We're doers and we work hard to get the job done within a formal system.'

Control systems
- Legislation & statutes
- Budgets, deadlines, targets
- League tables
- Operational manuals, instructions, handbooks
- Performance Management System
- Audits
- Militaristic formal command and control style

Organisational structures
- Complex hierarchical structures – 3 organisations/3 countries
- Mechanistic rigid structure
- Departmental silos
- Grades and pay bands
- Strong sub cultures
- Formal management boards/working groups/committees
- People neatly in their boxes

'We're efficient and achieve results (despite the bureaucracy).'

'We're capable individuals who like to be in control. We respect authority and respond to commands from above.'

Source: Adapted from The Forestry Commission case study by Anne McCann.

Questions

1 How would you characterise the dominant culture here?

2 What are the strategic implications?

analysis in the mid-1990s prior to their election victory of 1997. It revealed a party culturally 'built to oppose', as it had done with every government in power through its history – including Labour governments! Not surprisingly, Tony Blair, who became Prime Minister, saw culture change of the party as a major necessity.

5.4.7 Undertaking cultural analysis

If an analysis of the culture of an organisation is to be undertaken, there are some important issues to bear in mind:

● *The questions to ask*. Exhibit 5.8 outlines some of the questions that might help build up an understanding of culture using the cultural web.

● *Statements of cultural values*. As organisations increasingly make visible often carefully considered public statements of their values, beliefs and purposes – for example, in annual reports, mission or values statements and business plans – there is a danger that these are seen as useful and accurate descriptions of the organisational culture. But this is likely to be at best only partially true, and at worst misleading. This is not to suggest that there is any organised deception. It is simply that the statements of values and beliefs are often statements of the aspirations of a particular stakeholder (such as the CEO) rather than accurate descriptions of the actual culture. For example, an outside observer of a police force might conclude from its public statements of purpose and priorities that it had a balanced approach to the various aspects of police work – catching criminals, crime prevention, community relations. However, a deeper probing might quickly reveal that (in cultural terms) there is the 'real' police work (catching criminals) and the 'lesser work' (crime prevention, community relations).

● *Pulling it together*. The detailed 'map' produced by the cultural web is a rich source of information about an organisation's culture, but it is useful to be able to characterise the culture that the information conveys. Sometimes this is possible by means of graphic descriptors. For example, the managers who undertook a cultural analysis in the UK National Health Service (NHS) summed up their culture as 'The National Sickness Service'. Although this approach is rather crude and unscientific, it can be powerful in terms of organisational members seeing the organisation as it really is – which may not be immediately apparent from all of the detailed points in the cultural web. It can also help people to understand that culture drives strategies; for example, a 'national sickness service' would clearly prioritise strategies that are about spectacular developments in curing sick people above strategies of health promotion and prevention. So those favouring health promotion strategies need to understand that they are facing the need to change a culture and that in doing so they may not be able to assume that rational processes like planning and resource allocation will be enough (see Chapter 14).

The cultural analysis suggested in this chapter is also valuable in ways that relate to other parts of this book and the management of strategy:

● *Strategic capabilities*. As Chapter 3 makes clear, historically embedded capabilities are, very likely, part of the culture of the organisation. The cultural

| Exhibit 5.8 | **The cultural web: some useful questions** |

Stories
- What core beliefs do stories reflect?
- How pervasive are these beliefs (through levels)?
- Do stories relate to:
  - strengths or weaknesses?
  - successes or failures?
  - conformity or mavericks?
- Who are the heroes and villains?
- What norms do the mavericks deviate from?

Symbols
- Are there particular symbols which denote the organisation?
- What status symbols are there?
- What does the language and jargon signify?
- What aspects of strategy are highlighted in publicity?

Routines and rituals
- Which routines are emphasised?
- Which are embedded in history?
- What behaviour do routines encourage?
- What are the key rituals?
- What core beliefs do they reflect?
- What do training programmes emphasise?
- How easy are rituals/routines to change?

Power structures
- How is power distributed in the organisation?
- What are the core assumptions and beliefs of the leadership?
- How strongly held are these beliefs (idealists or pragmatists)?
- Where are the main power blockages to change?

Stories   Symbols

Routines and rituals   **Paradigm**   Power structures

Control systems   Organisational structures

Control systems
- What is most closely monitored/controlled?
- Is emphasis on reward or punishment?
- Are controls related to history or current strategies?
- Are there many/few controls?

Organisational structures
- How mechanistic/organic are the structures?
- How flat/hierarchical are the structures?
- How formal/informal are the structures?
- Do structures encourage collaboration or competition?
- What types of power structure do they support?

Overall
- What do the answers to these questions suggest are the (four) fundemental assumptions that are the paradigm?
- How would you characterise the dominant culture?
- How easy is this to change?

analysis of the organisation therefore provides a complementary basis of analysis to an examination of strategic capabilities (see Chapter 3). In effect, such an analysis of capabilities should end up digging into the culture of the organisation, especially in terms of its routines, control systems and the everyday way in which the organisation runs, very likely on a 'taken-for-granted' basis.

- *Strategy development*. An understanding of organisational culture sensitises managers to the way in which historical and cultural influences will likely affect future strategy for good or ill. It therefore relates to the discussion on strategy development in Chapter 11.

- *Managing strategic change*. An analysis of the culture also provides a basis for the management of strategic change, since it provides a picture of the existing culture that can be set against a desired strategy so as to give insights as to what may constrain the development of that strategy or what needs to be changed in order to achieve it. This is discussed more extensively in Chapter 14.

- *Culture and experience*. There have been repeated references in this section to the role culture plays as a vehicle by which meaning is created in organisations. This was discussed more fully in the Commentary on the experience lens and provides a useful way in which many aspects of strategy can be considered (see the commentaries throughout the book).

5.5 MANAGING IN AN HISTORIC AND CULTURAL CONTEXT

History and culture are, then, important influences on the strategy of organisations. This leaves the challenging question of what managers can do about managing history and managing culture. Arguably there is little to be done about managing history; it has happened. There are, however, many examples in history of governments that have set about rewriting history and some would argue that corporations attempt to do much the same in their public relations. There is, however, a good deal written about the need to create or 'manage culture' (and it is a theme taken up in the context of managing strategic change in Chapter 14). This raises the question – or the challenge for managers – of just how realistic it is to be able to manage that which is taken for granted and historically based. This is the subject of the key debate in Illustration 5.5.

What is evident is that, if managers are to become path creators in strategy development, they need to be able to challenge, question and potentially change path dependent capabilities rooted in history and culture. To do this managers have, at the very least, to learn to be questioning of the very history that they have, perhaps, been part of or that has led to their existing positions. It should, therefore, be evident that one of the major requirements of a manager of strategy is to be able to encourage the questioning of that which is taken for granted. This may be possible through the sort of analytical tools covered in this chapter and in this book. However, it is also likely to require a management style – indeed a culture – that allows and encourages such questioning. If, on the other hand, the culture is such as to discourage such questioning, it is very unlikely that the lessons of history will be learned and much more likely that the dictates of history will be followed.

Illustration 5.5   key debate

Path dependency

Is history a powerful constraint on managers or an excuse for managerial inertia?

Brian Arthur, the Stanford economist, argued that when technologies compete for adoption, 'insignificant events may by chance give one of them an initial advantage in adoptions'. Such a technology may be technically inferior to alternatives but

may then improve more than the others, so it may appeal to a wider proportion of potential adopters. It may therefore become further adopted and further improved. Thus it may happen that a technology that by chance gains an early lead in adoption may eventually 'corner the market' of potential adopters.

This has become known as 'path dependency', defined by Paul David as where 'important influences upon the eventual outcome can be exerted by temporally remote events, including happenings dominated by chance'. The result can be the unplanned 'lock-in' of that technology and the 'lock-out' of others.

Examples given of this include the QWERTY typewriter keyboard (see section 5.3.1), petrol cars over steam cars and the VHS video system over Betamax. All came to dominate, though the alternative systems were initially considered technically superior. The concept of path dependency has also come to be applied to strategy. Just as it may to be too expensive or too complex for managers to see it as worthwhile to change course to a potentially superior technology, so it may be for a strategy.

Others have argued that the notion of path dependency is exaggerated. Stephen Margolis and S.J. Liebowitz raise questions about the extent to which 'inferior technologies', persisting through path dependence, were really that inferior. For example, in typing contests typists using the QWERTY system were victorious over those who did not. And there were features of the VHS system preferred over Betamax when they were in competition.

In relation to public policy Adrian Kay also has reservations about the concept of path dependence. He likens it more to policies becoming institutionalised, taken for granted or just more complex: all creating problems for managing change, but none the less amenable to it. For example, there

are many reasons why it is difficult to change the UK state pensions provision, not least the large sunk costs in the scheme and the shear complexity surrounding it. However, his studies show both policy stability and policy change and 'the notion of path dependency is only useful for accounting for the former'. Management can create the latter.

Luis Araujo and Debbie Harrison also argue that managers are not captured by history to the extent that path dependency suggests. Managers are able to make choices and overcome potential forces for inertia by having 'one foot in the past, the present and the future.' They are capable of reflecting on the benefits and disbenefits of history and doing something about it.

Sources:

L. Araujo and D. Harrison, 'Path dependence, agency and technological evolution', *Technology Analysis and Strategic Management*, vol. 14, no. 1 (2007), pp. 5–19.

W.B. Arthur, 'Competing technologies, increasing returns and lock in by historical events', *Economic Journal*, vol. 99 (1989), pp. 116–131.

P.A. David, 'Clio and the economics of QWERTY', *American Economic Review*, vol. 75 (1985), pp. 332–337.

A. Kay, 'A critique of the use of path dependency in policy studies', *Public Administration*, vol. 83, no. 3 (2005), pp. 553–571.

S.E. Margolis and S.J. Liebowitz, *Path Dependence: the New Palgrave of Economics and the Law*, 1998.

Questions

1 Summarise the arguments above in terms of the extent to which the authors believe that managers are locked into path-dependent histories.

2 Drawing on your own experience, and the arguments in this chapter and in the Commentaries, summarise the path dependency, institutional and cultural forces on managers.

3 What are your views about the extent to which such forces are a powerful constraining influences or an excuse for fatalism and management inertia?

SUMMARY

www.pearsoned.co.uk/ecs
AUDIO
SUMMARY

- The history and culture of an organisation may contribute to its strategic capabilities, but may also give rise to strategic drift as its strategy develops incrementally on the basis of such influences and fails to keep pace with a changing environment.

- Historical, path-dependent processes play a significant part in the success or failure of an organisation and need to be understood by managers. There are historical analyses that can be conducted to help uncover these influences.

- Cultural and institutional influences both inform and constrain the strategic development of organisations.

- Organisational culture is the basic assumptions and beliefs that are shared by members of an organisation, operate unconsciously and define in a basic taken-for-granted fashion an organisation's view of itself and its environment.

- An understanding of the culture of an organisation and its relationship to organisational strategy can be gained by using the cultural web.

Work assignments

∗ *Denotes more advanced work assignments.* * *Refers to a case study in the Text and Cases edition.*

5.1 Identify four organisations that, in your view, are in the different phases of strategic drift (see Exhibit 5.2). Justify your selection.

5.2 ∗ In the context of section 5.3, undertake an historical analysis of the strategy development of an organisation and consider the question: 'Does history matter in managing strategy?'

5.3 Map out an organisational field (see section 5.4.2) within which an organisation of your choice operates. (As a basis for this you could for example use accountancy, a public sector organisation such as Direct and Care* or Formula One*.)

5.4 Identify (a) an organisation where its publicly stated values correspond with your experience of it and (b) one where they do not. Explain why (a) and (b) might be so.

5.5 Use the questions in Exhibit 5.8 to plot out a cultural web for Marks & Spencer A or an organisation of your choice.

5.6 ∗ By using a number of the examples from above, critically appraise the assertion that 'culture can only really be usefully analysed by the symptoms displayed in the way the organisation operates'. (You may wish to refer to Schein's book in the recommended key readings to assist you with this task.)

Integrative assignment

5.7 ∗ What is the relationship between strategic capabilities, competitive advantage, organisation culture, strategy development and the challenge of managing strategic change? (Refer to Chapters 3, 5, 6, 11 and 14.) Consider this in relation to a major change in strategy such as the development or adoption of a different basis of competitive strategy (see section 6.3) or the change to an e-business model.

An extensive range of additional materials, including audio summaries, weblinks to organisations featured in the text, definitions of key concepts and self-assessment questions, can be found on the *Exploring Corporate Strategy* Companion Website at **www.pearsoned.co.uk/ecs**

Recommended key readings

- For a more thorough explanation of the phenomenon of strategic drift see Gerry Johnson, 'Rethinking incrementalism', *Strategic Management Journal*, vol. 9 (1988), pp. 75–91; and 'Managing strategic change – strategy, culture and action', *Long Range Planning*, vol. 25, no. 1 (1992), pp. 28–36. (These papers also explain the cultural web.) Also see Donald S. Sull, 'Why good companies go bad', *Harvard Business Review*, July/August (1999), pp. 42–52.

- For an historical perspective on strategy see I. Greener, 'Theorizing path dependency: how does history come to matter in organizations?', *Management Decision*, vol. 40, no. 6 (2002), pp. 614–619; and

D.J. Jeremy, 'Business history and strategy', in A. Pettigrew, H. Thomas and A. Pettigrew (eds), *Handbook of Strategy and Management*, Sage, 2002, pp. 436–460.

- For a summary and illustrated explanation of institutional theory see Gerry Johnson and Royston Greenwood, 'Institutional theory and strategy', in Mark Jenkins and V. Ambrosini (eds), *Strategic Management: A Multiple-Perspective Approach*, Palgrave, 2007.

- For a comprehensive and critical explanation of organisational culture see Mats Alvesson, *Understanding Organizational Culture*, Sage, 2002.

References

1. For an explanation of strategic drift see G. Johnson, 'Rethinking incrementalism', *Strategic Management Journal*, vol. 9 (1988), pp. 75–91; and 'Managing strategic change – strategy, culture and action', *Long Range Planning*, vol. 25, no. 1 (1992), pp. 28–36. Also see E. Romanelli and M.L. Tushman, 'Organizational transformation as punctuated equilibrium: an empirical test', *Academy of Management Journal*, vol. 7, no. 5 (1994), pp. 1141–1166. They explain the tendency of strategies to develop very incrementally with periodic transformational change.

2. See D. Miller and P. Friesen, 'Momentum and revolution in organisational adaptation', *Academy of Management Journal*, vol. 23, no. 4 (1980), pp. 591–614.

3. See D. Leonard–Barton, 'Core capabilities and core rigidities: a paradox in managing new product development', *Strategic Management Journal*, vol. 13 (1992), pp. 111–125.

4. This is a term used by Donald S. Sull in accounting for the decline of high performing firms (see 'Why good companies go bad', *Harvard Business Review*, July/August (1999), pp. 42–52).

5. In the *Icarus Paradox* (D. Miller, Harper Collins, 1990) Danny Miller makes a convincing case that organisations' success leads to a number of potentially pathological tendencies, not least of which are the tendencies to inflate the durability of bases of success and to build future strategies relatively uncritically.

6. This research, known as the Successful Strategic Transformers (SST) Project, was in progress at the time of writing, a part of the UK Advanced Institute of Management Research initiative. The research was being undertaken

by Timothy Devinney, Gerry Johnson, George Yip and Manuel Hensmans.

7. The phrase 'Strategy as a pattern in a stream of decisions' is taken from H. Mintzberg, 'Patterns in strategy formation', *Management Science*, May (1978), pp. 934–948.

8. W.B. Arthur, 'Competing technologies, increasing returns and lock in by historical events', *Economic Journal*, vol. 99 (1989), 116–131.

9. P.A. David, 'Clio and the economics of QWERTY', *Economic History*, vol. 75, no. 2 (1985), pp. 332–337.

10. See I. Greener, 'Theorizing path dependency: how does history come to matter in organizations?', *Management Decision*, vol. 40, no. 6 (2002), pp. 614–619.

11. The world's biggest accounting firms have called for radical reform: 'Big four in call for real time accounts', *Financial Times*, 8 November (2006), p. 1.

12. From D. Holbrook, W. Cohen, D. Hounshell and S. Klepper, 'The nature, sources and consequences of firm differences in the early history of the semiconductor industry', *Strategic Management Journal*, vol. 21, nos 10–11 (2000), pp. 1017–1042.

13. This quote by André Malraux and the story of the BMW museum was provided by Mary Rose

14. See Holbrook *et al.*, reference 12.

15. Private correspondence with Mary Rose, the business historian, who suggests that: 'it links to Schumpeter and his notion of boundary crossing which may be between sectors, between technologies or informing the development and application of old technology with new knowledge'.

16. S. Klepper and K.L. Simons, 'Dominance by birthright: entry of prior radio producers and competitive ramifications in the US television receiver industry', *Strategic Management Journal*, vol. 21, nos 10–11 (2000), pp. 987–1016.

17. See J.R. Kimberley and H. Bouchikhi, 'The dynamics of organizational development and change: how the past shapes the present and constrains the future', *Organization Science*, vol. 6, no. 1 (1995), pp. 9–18.

18. This example is also taken from the SST research project referred to in reference 6.

19. Also see D.J. Jeremy, 'Business history and strategy', in A. Pettigrew, H. Thomas and R. Whittington (eds), *Handbook of Strategy and Management*, Sage, 2002, pp. 436–460.

20. For good examples of corporate histories see G. Jones, *Renewing Unilever: Transformation and Tradition*, Oxford University Press, 2005; R. Fitzgerald, *Rowntrees and the Marketing Revolution, 1862–1969*, Cambridge University Press, 1995; T.R. Gourvish, *British Railways 1948–73*, Cambridge University Press, 1986.

21. Walsh and Ungson make the point that 'Organisational memory' is stored in a number of ways but these include shared interpretations and individual recollections. See J.P. Walsh and G.R. Ungson, 'Organizational memory', *Academy of Management Review*, vol. 16, no. 1 (1991), pp. 57–91.

22. This quote is from S. Finkelstein, 'Why smart executives fail: four case histories of how people learn the wrong lessons from history', *Business History*, vol. 48, no. 2 (2006), pp. 153–170.

23. See C. Geertz, *The Interpretation of Culture*, Basic Books, 1973, p. 12; and M. Alvesson, *Understanding Organizational Culture*, Sage, 2002, p. 3.

24. This definition of culture is taken from E. Schein, *Organisational Culture and Leadership*, 2nd edition, Jossey-Bass, 1997, p. 6.

25. See G. Hofstede, *Culture's Consequences*, 2nd edition, Sage, 2001. For a critique of Hofstede's work see B. McSweeney, 'Hofstede's model of national cultural differences and their consequences: a triumph of faith – a failure of analysis', *Human Relations*, vol. 55, no. 1 (2002), pp. 89–118.

26. On cross-cultural management also see R. Lewis, *When Cultures Collide: Managing successfully across cultures*, 2nd edition, Brealey, 2000, a practical guide for managers. It offers an insight into different national cultures, business conventions and leadership styles. Also S. Schneider and J.-L. Barsoux, *Managing Across Cultures*, 2nd edition, Financial Times/Prentice Hall, 2003. T. Jackson, 'Management ethics and corporate policy: a cross-cultural comparison', *Journal of Management Studies*, vol. 37, no. 3 (2000), pp. 349–370, looks at how national culture influences management ethics and provides a useful link to section 4.4 of this book.

27. A useful review of research on this topic is T. Dacin, J. Goodstein and R. Scott, 'Institutional theory and institutional change: introduction to the special research forum', *Academy of Management Journal*, vol. 45, no. 1 (2002), pp. 45–57. For a more general review see G. Johnson and R. Greenwood, 'Institutional theory and strategy', in Mark Jenkins and V. Ambrosini (eds), *Strategic Management: A Multiple-Perspective Approach*, Palgrave, 2007.

28. This definition is taken from W. Scott, *Institutions and Organizations*, Sage, 1995.

29. The term 'recipe' was introduced to refer to *industries* by J. Spender, *Industry Recipes: The nature and sources of management judgement*, Blackwell, 1989. We have broadened its use by applying it to *organisational fields*. The fundamental idea that behaviours are driven by a collective set of norms and values remains unchanged.

30. D. Deephouse, 'To be different or to be the same? It's a question (and theory) of strategic balance', *Strategic Management Journal*, vol. 20, no. 2 (1999), pp. 147–166.

31. E. Schein, *Organisation Culture and Leadership*, 2nd edition, Jossey-Bass, 1997, and A. Brown, *Organisational Culture*, FT/Prentice Hall, 1998, are useful in understanding the relationship between organisational culture and strategy. For a useful critique of the concept of organisational culture see M. Alvesson, *Understanding Organizational Culture*, Sage, 2002.

32. Exhibit 5.4 is adapted from the original in P. Grinyer and J.C. Spender, *Turnaround: Managerial Recipes for Strategic Success*, Associated British Press, (1979) p. 203.

33. A fuller explanation of the cultural web can be found in G. Johnson, *Strategic Change and the Management Process*, Blackwell, 1987, and 'Managing strategic change: strategy, culture and action', *Long Range Planning*, vol. 25, no. 1 (1992), pp. 28–36. Also forthcoming at the time of writing is G. Johnson and A. McCann, *Changing Strategy: Changing Culture*, FT Publications.

34. A practical explanation of cultural web mapping can be found in G. Johnson, 'Mapping and re-mapping organisational culture', in V. Ambrosini with G. Johnson and K. Scholes (eds), *Exploring Techniques of Analysis and Evaluation in Strategic Management*, Prentice Hall, 1998.

35. See A.L. Wilkins, 'Organisational stories as symbols which control the organisation', in L.R. Pondy, P.J. Frost, G. Morgan and T.C. Dandridge (eds), *Organisational Symbolism*, JAI Press, 1983.

36. The significance of organisational symbolism is explained in G. Johnson, 'Managing strategic change: the role of symbolic action', *British Journal of Management*, vol. 1, no. 4 (1990), pp. 183–200.

Marks & Spencer (A)

Nardine Collier

The M&S formula for success

Michael Marks began his penny bazaars in the late 1880s. He soon decided he needed a partner to help run the growing firm and Tom Spencer, a cashier of Marks' supplier, was recommended. From this partnership Marks & Spencer (M&S) steadily grew. Simon Marks took over the running of M&S from his father, turning the penny bazaars into stores, establishing a simple pricing policy and introducing the 'St Michael' logo as a sign of quality. There was a feeling of camaraderie and a close-knit family atmosphere within the stores, with staff employed whom the managers believed would 'fit in' and become part of that family. The staff were also treated better and paid more than in other companies. The family nature of this firm dominated top management too: until the late 1970s the board was made up of family members only.

Marks was renowned for his personal, top-down, autocratic management style and his attention to detail. This also manifested itself in the way he dealt with suppliers. He always used the same UK-based suppliers and meticulously ensured that goods were exactly to specification, a relationship designed to build reliance of the suppliers and ensure high and consistent quality.

Until the late 1990s M&S was hugely successful in terms of profit and market share, running its operations according to a set of fundamental principles; namely to:

- offer customers high-quality, well-designed and attractive merchandise at reasonable prices under the brand name St Michael;

Photo: Charles Hewitt/Picture Post/Getty Images

- encourage suppliers to use the most modern and efficient production techniques;
- work with suppliers to ensure the highest standards of quality control;
- provide friendly, helpful service and greater shopping comfort and convenience to customers;
- improve the efficiency of the business, by simplifying operating procedures;
- foster good human relations with customers, suppliers and staff and in the communities in which M&S trade.

Its specialist buyers operated from a central buying office from which goods were allocated to the stores. The store managers followed central direction on merchandising, layout, store design and training. Every M&S store was identical in the procedures it followed, leading to a consistency of image and a guarantee of M&S standards. However, it also meant store managers were severely restricted in how they could respond to the local needs of customers.

During M&S's growth there were few changes to its methods of operation or strategies. Its reputation for good-quality clothing was built on basics, the essentials which every customer needed and would outlast the current fashion and trends seen in other high street retailers. As it did not have fitting rooms till the 1990s, all assistants carried tape measures and M&S would give a 'no quibble' refund to any customer who was unhappy with the product he or she had purchased. As its products remained in the stores all year round for most of its history it never held sales.

The success of M&S continued into the 1990s. Richard Greenbury, the CEO from 1991, explained this success:

we followed absolutely and totally the principles of the business with which I was embued. . . . I ran the business with the aid of my colleagues based upon the very long standing, and proven ways of running it. (Radio 4, August 2000)

Successive chief executives were renowned for their attention to detail in terms of supplier control, merchandise and store layout; and it seemed to work. M&S's success under Marks was often attributed to his understanding of customer preferences and trends. However, because of this, it could also mean that buyers tended to select merchandise which they knew chief executives would approve of. For example, since it was known Greenbury did not want M&S to be at the cutting edge of fashion, buyers concentrated on the types of product they knew he would like – 'classic, wearable fashions'.

There were other problems of centralised authority. On one occasion Greenbury had decided that to control costs there would be less full-time sales assistants. Although this led to an inability in stores to meet the service levels required by M&S, when Greenbury visited, all available employees were brought in so that it appeared the stores were giving levels of service that, at other times, they were not. It also meant there was little disagreement with directives from the top, so policies and decisions remained unchallenged even when executives or store managers were concerned about negative effects. Customer satisfaction surveys that showed decreasing satisfaction throughout the late 1990s

were kept from Greenbury by senior executives who felt he might be annoyed by the results.

A hitch in the formula

M&S's problems began to hit the headlines in October 1998 when it halted its expansion programme in Europe and America and in November announced a 23 per cent decline in first-half profits, causing its shares to fall drastically. Greenbury blamed a turbulent competitive environment, saying that M&S had lost sales and market share to its competitors from both the top and bottom ends of the retail market. Competitors at the top end of the market, such as the Gap, Oasis and Next, offered similarly priced goods, but more design focused with up-to-date fashions. At the bottom end, Matalan and supermarkets ranges such as the 'George' range at Asda offered basic clothing at significantly lower prices. Moreover, Tesco and Sainsbury's were now offering added value foods which had been pioneered by M&S.

Commentators suggested that M&S no longer understood or reacted to its customers' needs. It misread its target market, and could not understand that customers who purchased food or underwear might not want products from its home furnishings range. It had continued too long with its traditional formula and ignored changes in the marketplace. Greenbury was too focused on the day-to-day operations of the firm rather than long-term strategy. M&S was tied to a generalised view of the market, instead of trying to understand and tailor offerings to the various market segments. It had no loyalty card at a time when almost every other retailer did. Although a large proportion of M&S customers were women and much of the merchandise was womenswear, top management were dominated by men. Almost all managers and executives were promoted internally, starting at the bottom of the organisation and becoming immersed in its routines and traditions. It had an inward-looking culture strongly reinforced by Greenbury and his autocratic approach.

In November 1998, Greenbury announced that he would be stepping down. There followed a series of heavily publicised arguments between Keith Oates, Greenbury's deputy, and Peter Salsbury, another director, whom the media suggested was Greenbury's favoured successor. It was Salsbury who was eventually appointed as CEO. Oates elected to take early retirement. Analysts commented that, as Salsbury had only worked in womenswear, one of the worst-performing units in M&S, it might have been wiser to bring in an outsider.

During this period of boardroom scuffles, M&S's problems were compounded by its £192m (€270m) purchase of 19 Littlewoods department stores. These required refurbishment at a cost of £100m at the same time as existing M&S stores were being refurbished. The disruption had a far worse effect on customers than M&S had expected, leading Greenbury to describe the clothing section as a 'bloodbath'. In January 1999 M&S announced its second profits warning. It had been a bad Christmas trading period made worse by M&S overestimating sales and buying £250m worth of stock that then had to be heavily discounted.

New tactics . . . but more problems

In an attempt to regain confidence, Salsbury implemented a restructuring strategy, splitting the company into three: UK retail business, overseas business and financial services. He also established a company-wide marketing department to break down the power of the traditional buying fiefdoms established around product lines. The marketing department would adopt a customer-focused approach, rather than allowing buyers to dictate what the stores should stock. There were new clothing and food ranges, reinforced by a large-scale promotional campaign, to attempt to restore its image as an innovative retailer offering unique, quality products. Explaining that he wanted to move away from a bureaucratic culture by creating a decision-making environment that was unencumbered by hierarchy, Salsbury stripped away of layers of hierarchy and established a property division so that rents were charged to stores to make store managers more accountable for branch performance.

In June Greenbury retired a year early, a decision which came just before the board entered a three-day meeting to discuss 'a few hundred pages of its new strategy'. Salsbury commented:

What we are doing has moved away from his [Greenbury's] methodology and thought processes . . . decisions were reached without him being able to have an input. (*Financial Times*, 23 June 1999)

In September M&S stated that it was in the process of overseas sourcing while severing links with some UK suppliers, streamlining international operations, diversifying into home and Internet shopping, and creating a department dedicated to identifying new business opportunities. However, customers continued to voice their concerns regarding the clothing range:

There are so many items here to find and they don't tend to segregate it out, so there's something I might like next to something my granny might like. (*Financial Times*, 28 September 1999)

By November M&S had more bad news for its shareholders when it revealed its shares had fallen to the lowest price since 1991. There followed reports of Tesco, American pension fund companies and Philip Green, the retail entrepreneur, being interested in acquiring M&S. To counteract these rumours M&S implemented another management restructuring to become more customer focused, establishing seven business units: lingerie, womenswear, menswear, childrenswear, food, home, and beauty. Executives were appointed at just below board level to head the units, reporting directly to Salsbury who believed the flatter structure allowed M&S to be more responsive to market changes and customer needs.

A new horizon

In January 2000 Luc Vandevelde was appointed chairman. Belgian-born Vandevelde had left his managing director role at Promodés, the French food retailer, where he had achieved a sixfold increase in stock value. This was the first time anyone from outside M&S had been appointed to the position of chairman.

In the next two years there followed more changes. He unveiled an exclusive clothes collection from haute couture designers. Purchasing of the clothing range was shifted to almost 100 per cent Asian sources. M&S stopped using its famous green carrier bags, and relegated the St Michael logo to inside clothing. Stores were grouped on the basis of demographic characteristics and lifestyle patterns, instead of operating with the old system which allocated merchandise dependent on floor space. Still the fortunes of the company declined. In May 2000 M&S announced a fall in profit of £71.2m.

There was another restructuring into five operating divisions: UK retail; international retail; financial services; property; and ventures. Within the UK retail division seven customer business units were established, and to ensure customer focus each unit would have dedicated buying and selling teams. There was further store modernisation; more customer advisers on the shop floor; and the opening of three prototype stores where all new initiatives and concepts would be tested. M&S disclosed plans to offer clothes at a discounted price in factory outlet malls. Early in 2001 it announced its plans to withdraw from its stores in Europe and Brooks Brothers in America and franchise those in Hong Kong. In the midst of this, in September 2000, Salsbury retired.

Discussing the still disappointing end-of-year results, Vandevelde scaled back on the promises he had made on his arrival for recovery within two years. However, he was confident that he had the right recipe for recovery, it was just a matter of time.

There followed the decision to move out of its headquarters in Baker Street, London, and into a new building in Paddington. For those who had worked in M&S's headquarters, the grey and imposing building symbolised much that had gone wrong with the retailer. Its endless corridors were described as Kremlin-like, and the small individual offices reflected the status of the occupant by the thickness of the carpet. Former managers described the building as 'oppressive', with facilities that were not conducive to modern working practices, few casual meeting rooms, and a highly structured hierarchy for the 4,000 employees who worked there. Commentators were delighted with the move; they felt it showed M&S was at last tackling the problems at its core, not just altering merchandise and store layout.

It was not till the end of November 2001 that there were signs of an upturn in trading performance. This followed the arrival of Yasmin Yousef, a new creative designer, and the much heralded collaboration with George Davies, founder of Next and the creator of the 'George' clothing range at Asda. Davies introduced the Per Uno women's range targeted at 25–35 fashion-conscious customers to compete with brands like Mango and Kookai. Davies had secured a deal whereby he owned Per Una, and retained the profits from supplying M&S. To operate so autonomously he had invested £21m of his own money. He was therefore designing, manufacturing and distributing the clothes independently of M&S.

In 2001 Vandevelde also head-hunted Roger Holmes to be Head of UK Retailing. Holmes started his career as a consultant for McKinsey, moving to become Financial Director of DIY chain B&Q, Managing Director of retailers Woolworths, and finally Chief of Electricals for the Kingfisher group. Was a new era for M&S beginning?

Sources:

BBC2, 'Sparks at Marks', *The Money Programme*, 1 November (2000).

BBC2, 'Marks and Spencer', *Trouble at the Top*, 6 December (2001).

G. Beaver, 'Competitive advantage and corporate governance: shop soiled and needing attention, the case of Marks and Spencer plc', *Strategic Change*, vol. 8 (1999), pp. 325–334.

J. Bevan, *The rise and fall of Marks and Spencer*, Profile Books, (2001).

Channel 4, 'Inside Marks and Spencer', 25 February (2001).

Radio 4, Interview with Sir Richard Greenbury, 22 August (2000).

G. Rees, *St Michael: A history of Marks and Spencer*, Weidenfeld and Nicolson, (1969).

K. Tse, *Marks and Spencer: Anatomy of Britain's most efficiently managed company*, Pergamon, (1985).

Questions

1 Analyse the organisational culture of M&S in the 1990s.

2 Why was M&S so successful for so long?

3 Why did it suffer the downturn in the 1990s?

4 Why did the changes made from 1998 to 2001 fail to overcome the problems?

Part I of the book has discussed some of the main influences that managers in organisations have to take into account in developing the strategies of their organisations. The underlying theme here is that reconciling these different forces is problematic. Not only are there many of them, but also their effects are difficult to predict and they are likely to change, creating potentially high levels of uncertainty. The forces may also be in conflict with one another, or pulling in different directions. Understanding the strategic position of an organisation is therefore challenging for managers.

In this commentary the four strategy lenses introduced in the initial Commentary are now used to reconsider *how managers can and do make sense of the strategic position they face* and some of the key issues discussed in the chapters in Part I. Note that:

● There is no suggestion here that one of these lenses is better than another, but they do provide different insights into the problems faced and the ways managers cope with the challenge.

● If you have *not* read the Commentary following Chapter 1 that explains the four lenses, you should now do so.

Design lens

The concepts and analytic tools of strategy can be used to understand the complex and uncertain world managers face in developing strategy. So it makes sense to:

● Undertake rigorous analysis of environmental forces, strategic capabilities, stakeholder power and cultural influences.
● Build scenarios to sensitise possible futures.
● Integrate the insights from such analyses into a clear view of the strategic position.
● Involve managers in such analysis through systematic strategic planning.

A clear understanding of the strategic position by managers is then helpful in their managing the development of a future strategy because it provides a basis upon which they can consider how different strategic options might address the issues identified.

Experience lens

Managers' individual or collective experience based on prior events is drawn upon by them to make sense of the strategic position of the organisation. This can be useful because it provides short-cuts in sense making. It is, however, also dangerous because such experience becomes fixed, determines how stimuli are made sense of and biases responses to such stimuli. An uncertain future is therefore likely to be understood in terms of past experience that acts as an 'uncertainty reduction mechanism'.

The strategic capabilities (especially core competences) that have driven past success are likely to have become embedded in its history and organisational culture. Over time this may well give rise to strategic drift.

Questioning and challenging that which is taken for granted is vital. It is at least as important to surface the assumptions that managers have as to undertake careful strategic analysis, because it is likely to be such assumptions that are driving strategic decisions. A major role of the frameworks of analysis described in Part I is to do just this.

Commentary on Part I

The Strategic Position

Ideas lens

It is not possible to reduce uncertainty sufficiently to arrive at a clear strategic position upon which strategies can be rationally evaluated. Knowledge and understanding of the bases of the strategic position of the organisation can never be sufficiently complete. Indeed, rigorous analysis may foster conformity and a 'right way' of seeing things.

However, the ambiguity and uncertainty of the future may be beneficial in that it can give rise to a variety of different perspectives that can stimulate new ideas from within and around the organisation. These new ideas are just as likely to bubble up from below as be originated at the top of an organisation. So, if innovation is important, managers need to learn how to foster and harness such variety.

Managers may not be able to determine an objectively based 'right' view of the strategic position of their organisation, but they may be able to establish a sufficiently clear overarching vision or a set of 'simple rules' that allows for the necessary variety to encourage the emergence of new ideas.

With regard to strategic drift, there are different views here:

- That sufficient variety could give rise to new ideas and experimentation that help avoid drift.
- That drift is an inevitability but that the resulting instability will itself help generate new ideas and be an opportunity for renewal.

Discourse lens

The strategic position of an organisation is not so much a matter of objective 'fact' as that which is represented and privileged in the discourse of major stakeholders and powerful people, for example a CEO, investors, government. What such stakeholders say shows how influential people are making sense of their strategic position and the key issues that are driving the strategy of organisations. This has a very real influence on organisations' strategies.

Discourse is also linked to identity. So:

- Each stakeholder has their own identity and associated with this is their own way of talking about their relationship to the strategy of an organisation. This is a route to understanding stakeholder interest and influence.
- The concepts and tools associated with strategy can be employed by managers so that they can look as though they have insights that give them a special place with regard to the destiny of the organisation. In this sense strategy discourse is linked to power.
- People get locked into their ways of talking about their strategic perspective. It can be difficult to change this. In this sense dominant discourse can contribute to strategic drift.

STRATEGIC CHOICES

This part explains strategic choices in terms of:

→ How an organisation positions itself in relation to competitors in terms of its overall competitive strategy.

→ The scope and diversity of an organisation's products and therefore the nature of its corporate portfolio and how that portfolio is managed.

→ The geographic scope of the organisation and the bases of its international strategy.

→ The extent to which and how it seeks to foster innovation and entrepreneurial endeavour.

→ Ways in which it might pursue strategic options in terms of organic development, acquisitions or joint ventures.

→ The criteria and tools by which these choices might be evaluated.

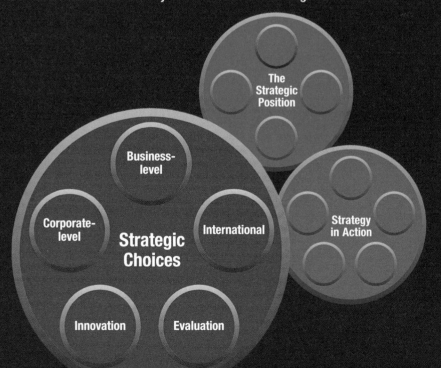

The Strategic Position

Business-level

Corporate-level

Strategic Choices

International

Innovation

Evaluation

Strategy in Action

Introduction to Part II

Strategic choices are concerned with decisions about an organisation's future and the way in which it needs to respond to the many pressures and influences discussed in Part I of the book. In turn, the consideration of future strategies must be mindful of the realities of translating strategy into action which, in turn, can be significant constraints on strategic choice.

There are three overarching choices to be made as shown in Exhibit II.i. These are:

- The choices as to *how an organisation positions itself in relation to competitors*. This is a matter of deciding the overall basis of how to compete in a market. For example, if the aim is to pursue a strategy that provides lasting superior financial performance, is this to be achieved by competitive advantage on the basis of price or differentiation? Or is competitive advantage possible through being more flexible and fleeter of foot than competitors? Or is a more cooperative approach to competitors appropriate? These questions are addressed in Chapter 6.

- The choices of *products and markets for an organisation*. Should the organisation be very focused on just a few products and markets? Or should it be much broader in scope, perhaps very diversified in terms of both products (or services) and markets? This raises questions of corporate strategy addressed

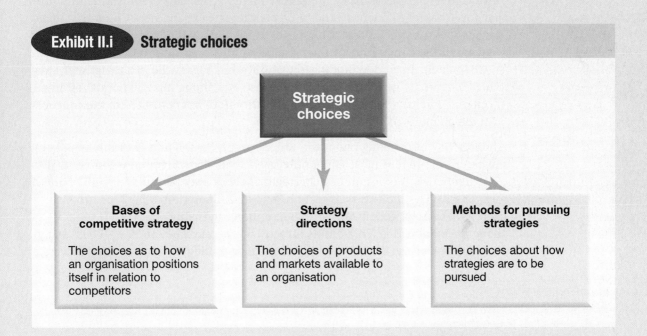

Exhibit II.i   Strategic choices

in Chapter 7, international strategy in Chapter 8 and the extent of innovative and entrepreneurial endeavour in the organisation, which is discussed in Chapter 9.

● The choices about *how strategies are to be pursued*. For any of these choices, should they be pursued by organic development, acquisitions or through joint ventures with other organisations? This is the theme of the first part of Chapter 10.

This part of the book also asks:

● *How are these choices to be evaluated?* What are the criteria that might be used and the tools that are useful for this? This is the theme of the second part of Chapter 10.

The discussion in these chapters provides explanations and rationales for a wide range of strategic options. However, a word of warning: there is a potentially misleading distinction between undertaking the sort of strategy analysis that was explained in Part I of the book and considering the choices discussed in Part II. In two respects, they are not separate and disconnected:

1 *Key strategic issues*. The choices described here have to be considered in the context of the understanding of an organisation's strategic position. Here it is important that there is clarity on the *key strategic issues*. This means that strategists should be able to identify the really important issues that a strategy has to address from the very many other issues that, no doubt, will have arisen in their analysis. Too often the outcome of such analysis is a very long list of observations without any clarity of what such key issues are. There is no 'strategy tool' for this. This is a matter of informed judgement and, because managers usually work in groups, of debate. The analytic tools provided can help inform, but are not a substitute for judgement.

2 *Strategic analysis generates strategic options*. Part I of the book has provided ways in which strategists can identify forces at work in the business environment (Chapter 2), identify and build on strategic capabilities (Chapter 3), meet stakeholder expectations (Chapter 4) and build on the benefits, as well as be aware of the constraints of their organisation's historical and cultural context (Chapter 5). In understanding these different forces the strategist will have also begun to generate ideas and raise questions that generate strategic options. Identifying strategic options is therefore not restricted to the concepts in the chapters of Part II.

Another way of thinking about the link between Parts I and II of the book is by means of one of the most commonly used tools of strategy development. It is quite likely that the output of a strategic analysis may be pulled together in the form of a SWOT analysis (see section 3.6.4 and Illustration 3.5). This can also be used as a way of generating strategic options by using the TOWS matrix* as shown in Exhibit II.ii. This builds directly on the information in a SWOT analysis. Each box of the TOWS matrix can be used to identify options that address a

---

* See H . Weihrich 'The TOWS matrix – a tool for situational analysis', *Long Range Planning*, April (1982), pp. 54–66.

Exhibit II.ii	The TOWS matrix

Internal factors

External factors		Strengths (S)	Weaknesses (W)
	Opportunities (O)	**SO Strategic options** Generate options here that use strengths to take advantage of opportunities	**WO Strategic options** Generate options here that take advantage of opportunities by overcoming weaknesses
	Threats (T)	**ST Strategic options** Generate options here that use strengths to avoid threats	**WT Strategic options** Generate options here that minimise weaknesses and avoid threats

different combination of the internal factors (strengths and weaknesses) and the external factors (opportunities and threats). For example, the top left-hand box prompts a consideration of options that use the strengths of the organisation to take advantage of opportunities in the business environment. An example might be the extension of sales into an adjacent geographical market where demand is expected to grow quickly. The bottom right-hand box prompts options that minimise weaknesses and also avoid threats; for example, the avoidance of major competitors by focusing activities on specialist niches that the organisation is capable of servicing successfully.

6

Business-Level Strategy

LEARNING OUTCOMES

After reading this chapter you should be able to:

→ Identify strategic business units (SBUs) in organisations.

→ Explain bases of achieving competitive advantage in terms of 'routes' on the strategy clock.

→ Assess the extent to which these are likely to provide sustainable competitive advantage.

→ Identify strategies suited to hypercompetitive conditions.

→ Explain the relationship between competition and collaboration.

→ Employ principles of game theory in relation to competitive strategy.

Photo: BAA Aviation Photo Library

6.1 INTRODUCTION

This chapter is about a fundamental strategic choice: what competitive strategy to adopt in order to gain competitive advantage in a market at the business unit level. For example, faced with increasing competition from low-price airlines, should British Airways seek to compete on price or maintain and improve its strategy of differentiation? Exhibit 6.1 shows the main themes that provide the structure for the rest of the chapter:

● First, *strategic business units (SBUs)* are explained. Most organisations have a number of SBUs, because they compete in different markets or market segments. These SBUs may or may not be organisationally separate but it may be necessary to consider if different competitive strategies are required for them. So it helps to identify the SBUs of an organisation.

● Next, *bases of competitive strategy* available to SBUs are considered. These include price-based strategies, differentiation strategies, hybrid and focus strategies.

● The later sections consider *ways of achieving competitive advantage*. This starts in section 6.4 by explaining bases for the *sustainability of competitive strategy* over time.

● However, in a fast-changing and uncertain world the sustainability of competitive advantage can be problematic, so other ways of competing successfully are discussed. The idea of *hypercompetition* (introduced in section 2.3.2) is revisited in section 6.5 to consider lessons for strategic choices.

● The potential benefits of *cooperative* strategies with competitors are then discussed in section 6.6.

● Finally *game theory* is introduced as a way of achieving advantage through an understanding of the interdependence of competitors' actions (section 6.7).

Exhibit 6.1   Business-level strategies

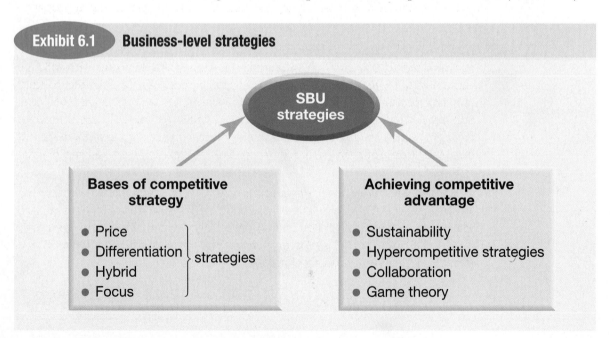

6.2 IDENTIFYING STRATEGIC BUSINESS UNITS

A strategic business unit (SBU) is a part of an organisation for which there is a distinct external market for goods or services that is different from another SBU

KEY CONCEPT
SBU

A **strategic business unit (SBU)** is a part of an organisation for which there is a distinct external market for goods or services that is different from another SBU. The identification of an organisation's SBUs helps the development of business-level strategies since these may need to vary from one SBU to another. In the sections that follow in the rest of this chapter the concepts discussed therefore relate to the SBUs that have been identified. The identification of SBUs does, however, raise three other issues considered briefly here but also elsewhere in the book:

- *A confusion of SBUs.* Since bases of competitive strategy may need to differ by markets (or market segment) the SBUs considered need to reflect this. However, potentially, managers may subdivide markets into many segments based on different criteria (see Exhibit 2.7). The result could be unmanageable in terms of identifying compatible bases of competitive strategy. So sensible judgements need to be made about which SBUs are most useful for strategy-making purposes.

- *Corporate complexity.* Similarly, too many SBUs can create excessive complexity in developing corporate-level strategy (see Chapter 7).

- *Organisational structure.* An SBU is an organisational unit for strategy-making purposes. An organisation may not actually be structured on the basis of SBUs, so consideration needs to be given to the relationship of SBUs and organisational design (see Chapter 13).[1] In the public sector the frequent 'repackaging' of activities within ministries in central government shows how difficult these judgements can be. For example, in the UK over the last few decades 'Education' has been partnered with 'Science', then 'Employment' and then with 'Skills'

There are external and internal criteria that can help in identifying appropriate SBUs:

- *Market-based criteria.* Different parts of an organisation might be regarded as the same SBU if they are targeting the same *customer types*, through the same sorts of *channels* and facing similar *competitors*. For example, a 'unit' tailoring products or services to specific local needs is a different SBU from one that offers standardised products or services globally. So are units that offer the same products to a customer group through significantly different channels (for example, retailing to consumers versus direct selling via the Internet).

- *Capabilities-based criteria.* Parts of an organisation should only be regarded as the same SBU if they have similar strategic capabilities. So for a food manufacturer branded goods should probably be considered a different SBU from retail 'own-brand' goods even though they are selling to the same end customers through the same channels.

6.3   BASES OF COMPETITIVE ADVANTAGE: THE 'STRATEGY CLOCK'

Competitive strategy is concerned with the basis on which a business unit might achieve competitive advantage in its market

Strategy clock

This section reviews different ways of thinking about **competitive strategy**, the bases on which a business unit might achieve competitive advantage in its market. For public service organisations, the equivalent concern is the bases on which the organisation chooses to achieve superior quality of services in competition with others for funding; that is, how it provides 'best value'.

Michael Porter[2] proposed three different 'generic' strategies by which an organisation could achieve competitive advantage: 'overall cost leadership', 'differentiation' and 'focus'. There is much debate as to exactly what each of these categories means. In particular many confuse Porter's 'cost leadership' with 'low price'. To remove such confusions this book employs 'market-facing' generic strategies similar to those used by Cliff Bowman and Richard D'Aveni.[3] These are based on the principle that competitive advantage is achieved by providing customers with what they want, or need, better or more effectively than competitors. Building on this proposition, the strategy clock (Exhibit 6.2) enshrines Porter's categories of differentiation and focus alongside price – as discussed in the sections below.

In a competitive situation, customers make choices on the basis of their perception of value for money, the combination of price and perceived product/ service benefits. The 'strategy clock' represents different positions in a market where customers (or potential customers) have different 'requirements' in terms of value for money. These positions also represent a set of generic strategies for achieving competitive advantage. Illustration 6.1 shows examples of different competitive strategies followed by firms in terms of these different positions on the strategy clock. The discussion of each of these strategies that follows also acknowledges the importance of an organisation's costs – particularly relative to competitors. But it will be seen that cost is a strategic consideration for all strategies on the clock – not just those where the lead edge is low price.

Since these strategies are 'market facing' it is important to understand the critical success factors for each position on the clock. Customers at positions 1 and 2 are primarily concerned with price, but only if the product/service benefits meet their threshold requirements as discussed in Chapter 2 (section 2.4.3). This usually means that customers emphasise functionality over service or aspects such as design or packaging. In contrast, customers at position 5 require a customised product or service for which they are prepared to pay a price premium. The volume of demand in a market is unlikely to be evenly spread across the positions on the clock. In commodity-like markets demand is substantially weighted towards positions 1 and 2. Many public services are of this type too. Other markets have significant demand in positions 4 and 5. Historically professional services were of this type. However, markets change over time. Commodity-like markets develop value-added niches which grow as disposable incomes rise. For example, this has occurred in the drinks market with premium and speciality beers. And customised markets may become more commodity-like particularly where IT can demystify and routinise the professional content of the product – as in financial services.

So the strategy clock can help managers understand the changing requirements of their markets and the choices they can make about positioning and competitive advantage. Each position on the clock will now be discussed.

Exhibit 6.2   **The strategy clock: competitive strategy options**

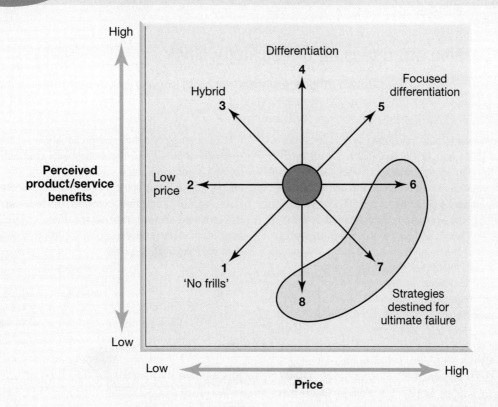

		Needs/risks
1	'No frills'	Likely to be segment specific
2	Low price	Risk of price war and low margins; need to be cost leader
3	Hybrid	Low cost base and reinvestment in low price and differentiation
4	Differentiation	
	(a) Without price premium	Perceived added value by user, yielding market share benefits
	(b) With price premium	Perceive added value sufficient to bear price premium
5	Focused differentiation	Perceived added value to a particular segment, warranting price premium
6	Increased price/standard value	Higher margins if competitors do not follow; risk of losing market share
7	Increased price/low value	Only feasible in monopoly situation
8	Low value/standard price	Loss of market share

Note: The strategy clock is adapted from the work of Cliff Bowman (see D. Faulkner and C. Bowman, *The Essence of Competitive Strategy*, Prentice Hall, 1995). However, Bowman uses the dimension 'Perceived Use Value'.

Illustration 6.1

Competitive strategies on the strategy clock

The competitive strategies of UK grocery retailers have shifted in the last three decades.

The supermarket retail revolution in the UK began in the late 1960s and 1970s as, initially, Sainsbury's began to open up supermarkets. Since the dominant form of retailing at that time was the corner grocery shop, Sainsbury's supermarkets were, in effect, a hybrid strategy: very clearly differentiated in terms of the physical layout and size of the stores as well as the quality of the merchandise, but also lower priced than many of the corner shop competitors.

As more and more retailers opened up supermarkets a pattern emerged. Sainsbury's was the dominant differentiated supermarket retailer. Tesco grew as a 'pile it high, sell it cheap' no frills operator. Competing in between as lower priced, but also lower quality than Sainsbury's, were a number of other supermarket retailers.

The mid-1990s saw a major change. Under the leadership of Ian Maclaurin, Tesco made a dramatic shift in strategy. It significantly increased the size and number of its stores, dropped the 'pile it high, sell cheap' stance and began offering a much wider range of merchandise. Still not perceived as equal to Sainsbury's on quality, it none the less grew its market share at the expense of the other retailers and began to challenge Sainsbury's dominance. However the big breakthrough came for Tesco when it also shifted to higher-quality merchandise but still at perceived lower prices than Sainsbury's. In effect it was now adopting a hybrid strategy. In so doing it gained massive market share. By early 2007 this stood at over 30 per cent of the retail grocery market in the UK. In turn Sainsbury's had seen its share eroded to just 16 per cent, as it sought to find a way to resurrect its differentiated image of quality in the face of this competition.

In the meantime, other competitive strategy positions had consolidated. The low-price strategy was being followed by Asda (Wal-Mart) which also had a 16 per cent share of the market and Morrison's (with 11 per cent). In the no-frills segment was Netto, Lidl and Aldi, all retail formats that arrived in the 1990s from European neighbours and with a combined share of around 6 per cent.

The strategy of differentiation no longer really existed in a pure form. The closest was Waitrose (almost 4 per cent) emphasising a higher-quality image, but targeting a more select, upper-middle-class, market in selected locations. The focused differentiated stance remained the domain of the specialists: delicatessens and, of course in a London context, Harrods Food Hall.

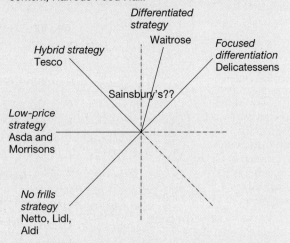

Questions

1 Who is 'stuck in the middle' here? Why?

2 Is a differentiated strategy or a low-price strategy defensible if there is a successful hybrid strategy, similar to that being followed by Tesco?

3 What might prevent other competitors following the Tesco strategy and competing successfully with them? (That is, does Tesco have strategic capabilities that provide sustainable competitive advantage?)

4 For another market of your choice, map out the strategic positions of the competitors in that market in terms of the strategy clock.

(Tesco is the case example in Chapter 10.)

6.3.1 Price-based strategies (routes 1 and 2)

A 'no frills' strategy combines a low price, low perceived product/service benefits and a focus on a price-sensitive market segment

Route 1 is the **'no frills' strategy**, which combines a low price with low perceived product/service benefits and a focus on a price-sensitive market segment. These segments might exist because of the following:

- The existence of *commodity markets*. These are markets where customers do not value or discern differences in the offering of different suppliers, so price becomes the key competitive issue. Basic foodstuffs – particularly in developing economies – are an example.

- There may be *price-sensitive customers*, who cannot afford, or choose not, to buy better-quality goods. This market segment may be unattractive to major providers but offers an opportunity to others (Aldi, Lidl and Netto in Illustration 6.1, for example). In the public services funders with tight budgets may decide to support only basic-level provision (for example, in subsidised spectacles or dentistry).

- Buyers have *high power and/or low switching costs* so there is little choice – for example, in situations of tendering for government contracts.

- The strategy offers an opportunity to *avoid major competitors*. Where major providers compete on other bases, a low-price segment may be an opportunity for smaller players or a new entrant to carve out a niche or to use route 1 as a bridgehead to build volume before moving on to other strategies.

A low-price strategy seeks to achieve a lower price than competitors whilst trying to maintain similar perceived product or service benefits to those offered by competitors

Route 2, the **low-price strategy**, seeks to achieve a lower price than competitors whilst maintaining similar perceived product or service benefits to those offered by competitors. Increasingly this has been the competitive strategy chosen by Asda (owned by Wal-Mart) and Morrisons in the UK supermarket sector (see Illustration 6.1). In the public sector, since the 'price' of a service to the provider of funds (usually government) is the unit costs of the organisation receiving the budget, the equivalent is year-on-year efficiency gains achieved without loss of perceived benefits.

Competitive advantage through a low-price strategy might be achieved by focusing on a market segment that is unattractive to competitors and so avoiding competitive pressures eroding price. However, a more common and more challenging situation is where there is competition on the basis of price, for example in the public sector and in commodity-like markets. There are two pitfalls when competing on price:

- *Margin reductions for all*. Although tactical advantage might be gained by reducing price this is likely to be followed by competitors, squeezing profit margins for everyone.

- An *inability to reinvest*. Low margins reduce the resources available to develop products or services and result in a loss of perceived benefit of the product.

So, in the long run, both a 'no frills' strategy and a low-price strategy cannot be pursued without a *low-cost base*. However, low cost in itself is not a basis for advantage. Managers often pursue low cost that does not give them competitive advantage. The challenge is how costs can be reduced in ways which others cannot match such that a low-price strategy might give sustainable advantage. This is difficult but possible ways are discussed in section 6.4.1. Illustration 6.2 also shows how easyJet has sought to reduce costs to pursue its 'no frills' strategy.

Illustration 6.2

easyJet's 'no frills' strategy

Multiple bases for keeping costs down can provide a basis for a successful 'no frills' strategy.

Launched in 1995, easyJet was seen as the brash young upstart of the European airline industry and widely tipped to fail. But by the mid-2000s this Luton-based airline had done more than survive. From a starting point of six hired aircraft working one route, by 2006 it had 122 aircraft flying 262 routes to 74 airports and carrying over 33 million passengers per annum and impressive financial results: £129m profit on £1,619m revenue (≈ €187m on ≈ €2,348m).

The principles of its strategy and its business model were laid down in annual reports year by year. For example, in 2006:

- The internet is used to reduce distribution costs . . . now over 95% of all seats are sold online, making Easy Jet one of Europe's biggest internet retailers;
- Maximizing the utilization of substantial assets. We fly our aircraft intensively, with swift turnaround times each time we land. This gives us a very low unit cost;
- Ticket-less travel. Passengers receive booking details via an email rather than paper. This helps to significantly reduce the cost of issuing, distributing, processing and reconciling millions of transactions each year;
- No 'free lunch'. We eliminate unnecessary services, which are complex to manage such as free catering, pre-assigned seats, interline connections and cargo services. This allows us to keep our total costs of production low;
- Efficient use of airports. Easy Jet flies to main destination airports throughout Europe, but gains efficiencies compared to traditional carriers with rapid turnaround times, and progressive landing charge agreements with airports. [It might have added here that since it does not operate a hub system, passengers have to check in and offload their luggage at each stage. This means that aircraft are not held up whilst luggage is transferred between flights.]

It might also have added that other factors contributed to low costs:

- A focus on the Airbus A319 aircraft, and the retirement of 'old generation' Boeing 737 aircraft, meant 'a young fleet of modern aircraft secured at very competitive rates' benefiting maintenance costs. And, since an increasing proportion of these were owned by easyJet, financing costs were being reduced.
- A persistent focus on reducing ground handling costs.
- In the face of rising fuel costs, hedging on future buying of fuel.

In addition to all the factors above the 2006 annual report stated that easyJet's customer proposition is defined by

low cost with care and convenience. . . . We fly to main European destinations from convenient local airports and provide friendly onboard service. People are a key point of difference at Easy Jet and are integral to our success. This allows us to attract the widest range of customers to use our services – both business and leisure.

Source: easyJet annual report 2006.

Questions

1 Read sections 6.3.1 and 6.4.1 and identify the bases of easyJet's 'no frills' strategy.

2 How easy would it be for larger airlines such as BA to imitate the strategy?

3 On what bases could other low-price airlines compete with easyJet?

6.3.2 (Broad) Differentiation strategies (route 4)

A differentiation strategy seeks to provide products or services that offer benefits that are different from those of competitors and that are widely valued by buyers

The next option is a broad **differentiation strategy** providing products or services that offer benefits different from those of competitors and that are widely valued by buyers.[4] The aim is to achieve competitive advantage by offering better products or services at the same price or enhancing margins by pricing slightly higher. In public services, the equivalent is the achievement of a 'centre of excellence' status, attracting higher funding from government (for example, universities try to show that they are better at research or teaching than other universities).

The success of a differentiation approach is likely to be dependent on two key factors:

● *Identifying and understanding the strategic customer*. The concept of the strategic customer is helpful because it focuses consideration on who the strategy is targeting. However, this is not always straightforward, as discussed in section 2.4.3. For example, for a newspaper business, is the customer the reader of the newspaper, the advertiser, or both? They are likely to have different needs and be looking for different benefits. For a branded food manufacturer is it the end consumer or the retailer? It may be important that public sector organisations offer perceived benefits, but to whom? Is it the service user or the provider of funds? However, *what is valued* by the strategic customer can also be dangerously taken for granted by managers, a reminder of the importance of identifying critical success factors (section 2.4.2).

● *Identifying key competitors*. Who is the organisation competing against? For example, in the brewing industry there are now just a few major global competitors, but there are also many local or regional brewers. Players in each strategic group (see section 2.4.1) need to decide who they regard as competitors and, given that, which bases of differentiation might be considered. Heineken appears to have decided that it is the other global competitors – Carlsberg and Anheuser-Busch, for example. SABMiller built its global reach on the basis of acquiring and developing national brands and competing on the basis of local tastes and traditions, but has more recently also acquired Miller to compete globally.

The competitor analysis explained in section 2.4.4 (and Exhibit 2.8) can help in both of these regards:

● The *difficulty of imitation*. The success of a strategy of differentiation must depend on how easily it can be imitated by competitors. This highlights the importance of non-imitable strategic capabilities discussed in section 3.4.3.

● The extent of *vulnerability to price-based competition*. In some markets customers are more price sensitive than others. So it may be that bases of differentiation are just not sufficient in the face of lower prices. Managers often complain, for example, that customers do not seem to value the superior levels of service they offer. Or, to take the example of UK grocery retailing (see Illustration 6.1), Sainsbury's could once claim to be the broad differentiator on the basis of quality but customers now perceive that Tesco is comparable and seen to offer lower prices.

6.3.3 The hybrid strategy (route 3)

A **hybrid strategy** seeks simultaneously to achieve differentiation and low price relative to competitors. The success of this strategy depends on the ability to deliver enhanced benefits to customers together with low prices whilst achieving sufficient margins for reinvestment to maintain and develop bases of differentiation. It is, in effect, the strategy Tesco is seeking to follow. It might be argued that, if differentiation can be achieved, there should be no need to have a lower price, since it should be possible to obtain prices at least equal to the competition, if not higher. Indeed, there is a good deal of debate as to whether a hybrid strategy can be a successful competitive strategy rather than a suboptimal compromise between low price and differentiation.[5] If it is the latter, very likely it will be ineffective. However, the hybrid strategy could be advantageous when:

A hybrid strategy seeks simultaneously to achieve differentiation and a price lower than that of competitors

- Much *greater volumes* can be achieved than competitors so that margins may still be better because of a low-cost base, much as Tesco is achieving given its market share in the UK.

- *Cost reductions are available outside its differentiated activities*. For example, IKEA concentrates on building differentiation on the basis of its marketing, product range, logistics and store operations, but low customer expectations on service levels allow cost reduction because customers are prepared to transport and build its products.

- Used as an *entry strategy* in a market with established competitors. For example, in developing a global strategy a business may target a poorly run operation in a competitor's portfolio of businesses in a geographical area of the world[6] and enter that market with a superior product at a lower price to establish a foothold from which it can move further.

6.3.4 Focused differentiation (route 5)

A **focused differentiation** strategy provides high perceived product/service benefits, typically justifying a substantial price premium, usually to a selected market segment (or niche). These could be premium products and heavily branded, for example. Manufacturers of premium beers, single malt whiskies and wines from particular chateaux all seek to convince customers who value or see themselves as discerning of quality that their product is sufficiently differentiated from competitors' products to justify significantly higher prices. In the public services, centres of excellence (such as a specialist museum) achieve levels of funding significantly higher than more generalist providers. However, focused differentiation raises some important issues:

A focused differentiation strategy seeks to provide high perceived product/service benefits justifying a substantial price premium, usually to a selected market segment (niche)

- A *choice* may have to be made between a focus strategy (position 5) and broad differentiation (position 4). A firm following a strategy of international growth may have to choose between building competitive advantage on the basis of a common global product and brand (route 4) or tailoring its offering to specific markets (route 5) – an issue taken up again in Chapter 8 (section 8.4).

- *Tensions between a focus strategy and other strategies*. For example, broad-based car manufacturers, such as Ford, acquired premier marques, such as

Jaguar and Aston Martin, but learned that trying to manage these in the same way as mass market cars was not possible. By 2007 Ford had divested Aston Martin and was seeking to divest others. Such tensions limit the degree of diversity of strategic positioning that an organisation can sustain, an important issue for corporate-level strategy discussed in Chapter 7.

● *Possible conflict with stakeholder expectations*. For example, a public library service might be more cost efficient if it concentrated its development efforts on IT-based online information services. However, this would very likely conflict with its purpose of social inclusion since it would exclude people who were not IT literate.

● *Dynamics of growth for new ventures*. New ventures often start in very focused ways – offering innovative products or services to meet particular needs. It may, however, be difficult to find ways to grow such new ventures. Moving from route 5 to route 4 means a lowering of price and therefore cost, whilst maintaining differentiation features.

● *Market changes may erode differences between segments*, leaving the organisation open to much wider competition. Customers may become unwilling to pay a price premium as the features of 'regular' offerings improve. Or the market may be further segmented by even more differentiated offerings from competitors. For example, 'up-market' restaurants have been hit by rising standards elsewhere and by the advent of 'niche' restaurants that specialise in particular types of food.

6.3.5 Failure strategies (routes 6, 7 and 8)

A **failure strategy** is one that does not provide perceived value for money in terms of product features, price or both

A **failure strategy** is one which does not provide perceived value for money in terms of product features, price or both. So the strategies suggested by routes 6, 7 and 8 are probably destined for failure. Route 6 suggests increasing price without increasing product/service benefits to the customer, the strategy that monopoly organisations are accused of following. Unless the organisation is protected by legislation, or high economic barriers to entry, competitors are likely to erode market share. Route 7 is an even more disastrous extension of route 6, involving the reduction in product/service benefits whilst increasing relative price. Route 8, reduction in benefits whilst maintaining price, is also dangerous, though firms have tried to follow it. There is a high risk that competitors will increase their share substantially. There is also another basis of failure, which is for a business to be unclear as to its fundamental generic strategy such that it ends up being 'stuck in the middle' – a recipe for failure.

6.4 SUSTAINING COMPETITIVE ADVANTAGE

Organisations that try to achieve competitive advantage hope to preserve it over time and much of what is written about competitive strategy takes the need for sustainability as a central expectation. This section builds on the discussion in Chapter 3 (section 3.3.2) relating to strategic capability to consider how sustainability might be possible. However, increasingly, questions have been raised as to whether sustainability of competitive advantage is possible, so section 6.5 looks at competitive strategy in circumstances where sustainability is not possible or very difficult.

6.4.1 Sustaining price-based advantage

An organisation pursuing competitive advantage through low prices might be able to sustain this in a number of ways (see Exhibit 6.3):

- *Operating with lower margins* may be possible for a firm either because it has much greater sales volume than competitors or because it can cross-subsidise a business unit from elsewhere in its portfolio (see Chapter 7).

- *A unique cost structure.* Some firms may have unique access to low-cost distribution channels, be able to obtain raw materials at lower prices than competitors or be located in an area where labour cost is low.

- *Organisationally specific capabilities* may exist for a firm such that it is able to drive down cost throughout its value chain. Indeed Michael Porter defines cost leadership as '*the* low-cost producer in its industry . . . [who] must find and exploit all sources of cost advantage'[7] (see section 3.3 and Exhibit 3.3).

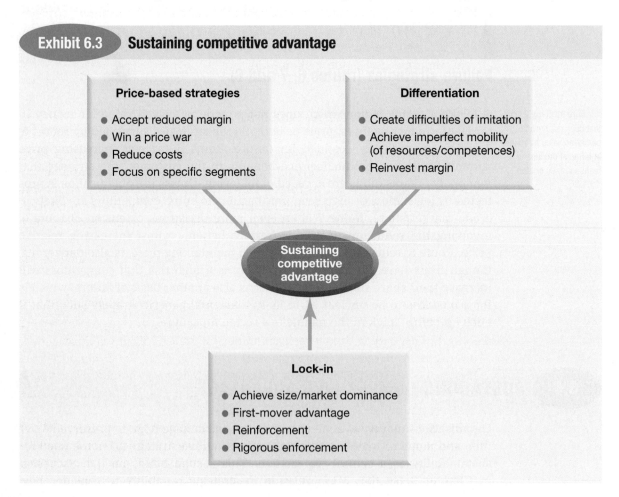

Exhibit 6.3 **Sustaining competitive advantage**

Price-based strategies
- Accept reduced margin
- Win a price war
- Reduce costs
- Focus on specific segments

Differentiation
- Create difficulties of imitation
- Achieve imperfect mobility (of resources/competences)
- Reinvest margin

Sustaining competitive advantage

Lock-in
- Achieve size/market dominance
- First-mover advantage
- Reinforcement
- Rigorous enforcement

Of course, if either of these last two approaches is to be followed it matters that the operational areas of low cost do truly deliver cost advantages to support real price advantages over competition. It is also important that competitors find these advantages difficult to imitate, as discussed in Chapter 3. This requires a mindset where innovation in cost reduction is regarded as essential to survival. An example of this is Ryanair in the low-price (no frills) airline sector which, in 2006, declared its ambition to be able to eventually offer passengers flights for free.

● *Focusing on market segments* where low price is particularly valued by customers but other features are not. An example is the success of dedicated producers of own-brand grocery products for supermarkets. They can hold prices low because they avoid the high overhead and marketing costs of major branded manufacturers. However, they can only do so provided they focus on that product and market segment.

There are, however, dangers with trying to pursue low-price strategies:

● *Competitors may be able to do the same*. There is no point in trying to achieve advantage through low price on the basis of cost reduction if competitors can do it too.

● Customers start to *associate low price with low product/service benefits* and an intended route 2 strategy slips to route 1 by default.

● Cost reductions may result in an *inability to pursue a differentiation strategy*. For example, outsourcing IT systems for reasons of cost efficiency may mean that no one takes a strategic view of how competitive advantage might be achieved through IT (see section 12.3).

6.4.2 Sustaining differentiation-based advantage

There is little point in striving to be different if competitors can imitate readily; there is a need for sustainability of the basis of advantage. For example, many firms that try to gain advantage through launching new products or services find them copied rapidly by competitors. Illustration 6.3 shows how wine producers in France and Australia have been seeking bases of differentiation over each other over the years.

Ways of attempting to sustain advantage through differentiation include the following (see Exhibit 6.3):

● *Create difficulties of imitation*. Section 3.3 discussed the factors that can make strategies difficult to imitate.

● *Imperfect mobility* such that the capabilities that sustain differentiation cannot be *traded*. For example, a pharmaceutical firm may gain great benefits from having top research scientists, or a football club from its star players, but they may be poached by competitors: they are tradable. On the other hand, some bases of advantage are very difficult to trade. For example:
  – *Intangible assets* such as brand, image or reputation that are intangible or competences rooted in an organisation's culture are difficult for a competitor to imitate or obtain. Indeed even if the competitor acquires the company to gain these, they may not readily transfer given new ownership.

Illustration 6.3

The strategy battle in the wine industry: Australia vs. France

The benefits of successful differentiation may be difficult to sustain.

For centuries French wines were regarded as superior. Building on the Appellation d'Origine Contrôlée (AOC) system, with its separate label requirements and controls for nearly 450 wine-growing regions, the emphasis was on the distinct regionality of the wines and the chateau-based branding. In the AOC system the individual wine-grower is a custodian of the *terroir* and its traditions. The quality of the wines and the distinct local differences are down to the differences in soil and climate as well as the skills of the growers, often on the basis of decades of local experience.

However, by 2001 the traditional dominance of French wines in the UK seemed to have ended, with sales of Australian wine outstripping them for the first time. This went hand in hand with huge growth in wine consumption as it became more widely available in supermarkets, where Australian wine was especially succesful. The success of Australian wines with retailers was for several reasons. The quality was consistent, compared with French wines that could differ by year and location. Whilst the French had always highlighted the importance of the local area of origin of the wine, in effect Australia 'branded' the country as a wine region and then concentrated on the variety of grape – a Shiraz or a Chardonnay, for example. This avoided the confusing details of the location of vineyards and the names of chateaux that many customers found difficult about French wines. The New World approach to the production of wine in terms of style, quality and taste was also based around consumer demand, not local production conditions. Grapes were sourced from wherever necessary to create a reliable product. French wines could be unpredictable – charming to the connoisseur, but infuriating to the dinner-party host, who expects to get what he or she paid for.

Between 1994 and 2003 France lost 84,000 growers. There was so much concern that in 2001, the French government appointed a committee to study the problem. The committee's proposals were that France should both improve the quality of its appellation wine and also create an entirely new range of quality, generic wines, so-called 'vins de cepage' (wines based on a grape variety). A company called

OVS planned to market the Chamarré brand – French for 'bursting with colours', to sell between £5 and £7 (€7.25 and €10.15), the price range where New World wines have made the biggest inroads. OVS President Pascal Renaudat, who has had 20 years in the wine business, explained:

We have to simplify our product and reject an arrogant approach that was perhaps natural to us. It is important to produce wine that corresponds to what people want to drink and at a good price. . . . This is not wine for connoisseurs. It is for pleasure.

'It's time to get rid of the stuffy pretentiousness that surrounds French wine,' said Renaud Rosari, Chamarré's master wine-maker. 'Chamarré is about bringing our wines to life for the consumers – the brand is lively, uncomplicated and approachable and means consistently high quality wines, with the fresh easy drinking style customers are looking for.'

There was qualified optimism: Jamie Goode of wineanorak.com saw it as a brave commercial decision. However: 'The trouble is that everybody is doing it. . . . Access to market is key. You need to get into the supermarkets, but you need to have a strong brand with which to negotiate or else they will savage you on price.'

Sources: Adapted from *Financial Times*, 11 February and 3/4 March (2001); *Independent*, 4 August (2003); *Sunday Times*, 5 February (2006); Guardian Unlimited, 7 February (2006).

Questions

1 Explain the high and distinct reputation of French wines of the past in terms of the bases of sustainable differentiation explained in sections 6.4.2 and 3.4.

2 What were the reasons for the success of Australian wines? Are these as sustainable?

3 What competitive strategy is Chamarré adopting to respond to the challenge of Australian (and other 'New World') wines?

- There may be *switching costs*. The actual or perceived cost for a buyer of changing the source of supply of a product or service may be high. Or the buyer might be dependent on the supplier for particular components, services or skills. Or the benefits of switching may simply not be worth the cost or risk.

- *Co-specialisation*, if one organisation's resources or competences are intimately linked with the buyers' operations. For example, a whole element of the value chain for one organisation, perhaps distribution or manufacturing, may be undertaken by another.

● A *lower-cost position* than competitors can allow an organisation to sustain better margins that can be reinvested to achieve and maintain differentiation. For example, Kellogg's or Mars may well be the lowest cost in their markets, but they reinvest their profits into branding and product and service differentiation, not low prices.

6.4.3 Strategic lock-in

Another approach to sustainability, whether for price-based or differentiation strategies, is the creation of **strategic lock-in**.[8] This is where an organisation achieves a proprietary position in its industry; it becomes an industry standard. For example, Microsoft became an industry standard. Many argue that technically the Apple Macintosh had a better operating system, but Microsoft Windows became the industry standard by working to ensure that the 'architecture' of the industry was built around it. Other businesses had to conform or relate to that standard in order to prosper.

The achievement of lock-in is likely to be dependent on (see Exhibit 6.3):

● *Size or market dominance*. It is unlikely that others will seek to conform to such standards unless they perceive the organisation that promotes it as dominant in its market.

● *First-mover dominance*. Such standards are likely to be set *early in life cycles of markets*. In the volatility of growth markets it is more likely that the single-minded pursuit of lock-in by the *first-movers* will be successful than when the market is mature. For example, Sky, with the financial support of News Corporation, was able to undercut competitors and invest heavily in technology and fast market share growth, sustaining substantial losses over many years, in order to achieve dominance.

● *Self-reinforcing commitment*. When one or more firms support the standard, more come on board, then others are obliged to, and so on.

● *Insistence on the preservation* of the lock-in position. Insistence on conformity to the standard is strict so rivals will be seen off fiercely. This can of course lead to problems, as Microsoft found in the US courts when it was deemed to be operating against the interests of the market.

Strategic lock-in is where an organisation achieves a proprietary position in its industry; it becomes an industry standard

6.4.4 **Responding to competitive threat**[9]

The preservation of competitive advantage in the face of competitors who attack by targeting customers on the basis of a different competitive strategy can be a serious threat. One of the most common is low-price competitors entering markets dominated by firms that have built a strong position through differentiation. For example, low-price airlines have taken substantial share from most of the leading airlines throughout the world. An equivalent situation in the public sector arises given the insistence by funding providers on year-on-year 'efficiency gains'. It is an opportunity for new entrants to undercut existing service providers, or indeed it may be that those providers find themselves being forced to undercut themselves.

Exhibit 6.4 suggests the series of questions that might be asked and the appropriate responses; there are also some general guidelines. First, *if a strategy of differentiation is retained* as the basis of retaliation (or in the public sector if the decision is to maintain a 'centre of excellence' status):

- *Build multiple bases of differentiation*. There is more likelihood of highlighting relative benefits if they are multiple; for example, Bang and Olufson's design of hi-fi systems linked to product innovation and its relationships with retailers to ensure they present its products distinctly in stores.

- *Ensure a meaningful basis of differentiation*. Customers need to be able to discern a meaningful benefit. For example, Gillette has found it difficult to persuade customers of the benefit of long-life Duracell batteries not only because low-price competitors offer multi-packs of cheap batteries to compete, but also because the demand for batteries has diminished.

- *Minimise price differences* for superior products or services. This is one reason why a hybrid strategy can be so effective of course.

- *Focus on less price-sensitive market segments*. For example, British Airways has switched its strategic focus to long-haul flights with a particular emphasis on business travellers.

Second, if differentiators decide to *set up a low-price business*:

- *Establish a separate brand* for the low-price business to avoid customer confusion.

- *Run the business separately* and *ensure it is well resourced*. The danger is that the low-price alternative is regarded as 'second class' or is over-constrained by the procedures and culture of the traditional business.

- *Ensure benefits to the differentiated offering* from the low-price alternative. For example, some banks offer lower charges through Internet banking subsidiaries. These lower-priced alternatives reach customers that the traditional banks might not reach and raise funds they would otherwise not have.

- *Allow the businesses to compete*. Launching the low-price business purely defensively is unlikely to be effective. It has to be allowed to compete as a viable separate SBU; as such, quite likely there will be substitution of one offering with another. Managers need to build this into their strategic plans and financial projections.

Exhibit 6.4   A framework for responding to low-cost rivals

When a low-cost player enters your indurtry:

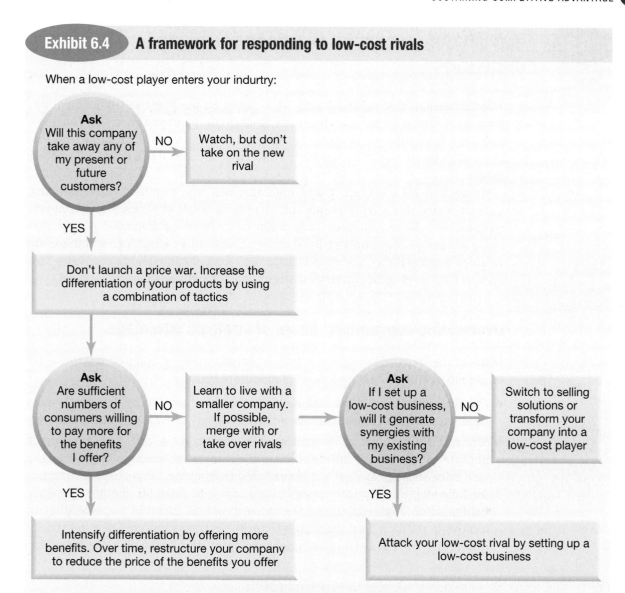

A third possibility is that differentiated businesses may *change their own business model*. For example:

- *Become solutions providers*. Low-price entrants are likely to focus on basic products or services so it may be possible to reconstruct the business model to focus on higher-value services. Many engineering firms have realised, for example, the higher-value potential of design and consultancy services rather than labour-based engineering operations that are easily undercut in price.

- *Become a low-price provider*. The most radical response would be to abandon the reliance on differentiation and learn to compete head-on with the low-price competitor.[10] Perhaps not surprisingly, there is not much evidence of the success of such a response, not least because it would mean competing on the basis of competences better understood by the incumbent.

6.5 COMPETITIVE STRATEGY IN HYPERCOMPETITIVE CONDITIONS

The discussion in sections 6.3 and 6.4 is based on the premise that competitive strategy is driven by the search for sustainable competitive advantage. However, there are arguments to suggest that this is not necessarily achievable and that there are other bases of competitive strategies. Sections 6.5, 6.6 and 6.7 address these.

As section 2.3.2 argued, many organisations face turbulent, fast-changing, uncertain business environments and increasing levels of competition, or *hyper-competition*.[11] Here imitation, innovation or changes of customer preferences mean advantage may be short-lived at best. Competitive advantage will therefore relate to organisations' ability to change fast, to be flexible and to innovate. This section considers competitive strategies in such conditions (see Exhibit 6.5).

6.5.1 Overcoming competitors' bases of strategic advantage

Some of the ways one competitor may undermine others' competitive strategies or defend against the incursions of competitors include:

- *Imitation*. One competitor may seek to achieve advantage by developing new products or entering new markets. Such moves may be relatively easily imitated.

- *Strategic (re)positioning*. As indicated in section 6.4.4, one firm may attack another by adopting a different basis of competitive strategy; for example, a low-price strategy against a differentiated competitor. Or perhaps a competitor following a low-price strategy may attempt to stave off another by establishing some degree of differentiation without an increase in price (that is, a move to position 3 on the strategy clock). As this is imitated new sources of differentiation will need to be sought. So innovation and agility are essential.

Exhibit 6.5   **Competitive strategies in hypercompetitive conditions**

Overcoming bases of competitive advantage by:

- Imitation
- Strategic (re)positioning
- Blocking first-mover advantage
- Overcoming barriers to entry

← Competitive strategies in hypercompetitive conditions →

Characteristics of successful hypercompetitive strategies:

- Cannibalise bases of success
- Smaller moves may be more effective than bigger ones
- Disruption of the status quo
- Be unpredictable
- Mislead the competition

- *Blocking first-mover advantages.* One competitor may try to achieve advantage as a *first-mover*. The key lesson here is not to allow that competitor to establish a dominant position before a response is made. Further, instead of launching an imitation product, the response might be a product with enhanced features, seeking to leapfrog or outflank the first-mover.

- *Overcoming barriers to entry.* Attempts to build barriers to entry may take different forms, but may be overcome. For example:
  - *Undermining competitors' strongholds.* Competitors may try to dominate a geographic area or market segment. However, these can be undermined. For example, in globalising markets the benefits of economies of scale built up in one area can be undermined by a competitor using the economies of scale from its own home territory to enter a market. Or in education, established institutions have become vulnerable to IT/Internet-based training offered by competitors who have written off the costs of materials development through sales in their home markets. Or where an organisation has built strongholds by tying up distribution channels, entrants may be able to use different distribution channels (for example, online retailing).
  - *Countering deep pockets.* Some competitors may have substantial surplus resources (sometimes called 'deep pockets') by which they try to withstand an intensive competitive war (see section 6.4.1). Such advantages may be overcome, for example by competitors *merging or building alliances* so they can compete from a stronger base.

6.5.2 Characteristics of successful hypercompetitive strategies

The radical argument put forward by Richard D'Aveni[12] is not only that managers need to rethink their approach to business-level strategy because it may no longer be possible to plan for sustainable positions of competitive advantage, but also that planning for long-term sustainability may actually destroy competitive advantage by slowing down response. Managers have to learn to be better at doing things faster than competitors. He provides some guidelines:

- *Cannibalise bases of success.* Sustaining old advantages distracts from developing new advantages. An organisation has to be willing to cannibalise the basis of its own success.

- *Attacking competitors' weaknesses can be unwise* as they learn about how their strengths and weaknesses are perceived and build their strategies accordingly.

- A series of *smaller moves may be more effective than bigger ones* because the longer-term direction is not as easily discernible by competitors and smaller moves create more flexibility and give a series *of temporary advantages*.

- *Disruption of the status quo* is strategic behaviour, not mischief. The ability constantly to 'break the mould' could be a core competence.

- *Be unpredictable.* If competitors can see a pattern they can predict the next competitive moves and quickly learn how to imitate or outflank an organisation. So surprise, unpredictability, even apparent irrationality can be important. Managers must learn ways of appearing to be unpredictable to the external world whilst, internally, thinking strategies through.

- *Mislead the competition.* Drawing on the lessons of game theory (see section 6.7), the strategist may signal moves competitors expect but which are not the moves that actually occur. Or the strategist might disguise its own success in a market.[13]

6.6   COMPETITION AND COLLABORATION[14]

So far the emphasis has been on competition and competitive advantage. However, advantage may not always be achieved by competing. Collaboration between organisations may be a way of achieving advantage or avoiding competition. Collaboration between potential competitors or between buyers and sellers is likely to be advantageous when the combined costs of purchase and buying transactions (such as negotiating and contracting) are lower through collaboration than the cost of operating alone. Collaboration also helps build switching costs. This can be shown by returning to the five forces framework from section 2.3.1 (also see Exhibit 6.6):

- *Collaboration to increase selling power.* In the aerospace industry component manufacturers might seek to build close links with customers. Achieving accredited supplier status can be tough, but may significantly increase seller power once achieved. It may also help in research and development activities, in reducing stock and in joint planning to design new products.

- *Collaboration to increase buying power.* Historically, the power and profitability of pharmaceutical companies were aided by the fragmented nature of their buyers – individual doctors and hospitals. But many governments have promoted, or required, collaboration between buyers of pharmaceuticals and centralised government drug-specifying agencies, the result of which has been more coordinated buying power.

- *Collaboration to build barriers to entry or avoid substitution.* Faced with threatened entry or substitute products, firms in an industry may collaborate to invest in research and development or marketing. Trade associations may promote an industry's generic features such as safety standards or technical specifications to speed up innovation and pre-empt the possibility of substitution.

- *Collaboration to gain entry and competitive power.* Organisations seeking to develop beyond their traditional boundaries (for example, geographical expansion) may collaborate with others to gain entry into new arenas. Gaining local market knowledge may also require collaboration with local operators. Indeed, in some parts of the world, governments require entrants to collaborate in such ways. Collaboration may also help in developing required infrastructure such as distribution channels, information systems or research and development activities. It may also be needed because buyers may prefer to do business with local rather than expatriate managers. Especially in hi-tech and hypercompetitive situations there is increasing disintegration (or 'unbundling') of value chains because there is innovatory competition at each stage of that chain. In such circumstances there also is likely to be increasing need for cooperative strategies between such competitors to offer coherent solutions for customers.[15]

Exhibit 6.6   **Competition and collaboration**

- *Collaboration to share work with customers.* An important trend in public services is *co-production* with clients,[16] for example self-assessment of income tax. The motives include cost efficiency, quality/reliability improvement or increased 'ownership/responsibility' from the clients. Websites also facilitate customers' self-service (the virtual shopping basket is an example) or allow them to design or customise a product or service to their own specification (for example, when ordering a new computer).

- In the public sector *gaining more leverage from public investment* may require collaboration to raise the overall standards of the sector or to address social issues that cross several professional fields (such as drugs or community safety). One difference from the private sector is that sharing of knowledge and dissemination of best practice is regarded as a duty or a requirement.

However, collaborating with competitors is not as easy as it sounds. Illustration 6.4 is an example of public/private sector collaboration in one sector.

6.7   GAME THEORY[17]

Game theory is concerned with the interrelationships between the competitive moves of a set of competitors

Game theory is concerned with the interrelationships between the competitive moves of a set of competitors. It is helpful in understanding the competitive dynamics of markets and in considering appropriate strategies in this light. There are two key assumptions in relation to understanding competitive dynamics in terms of game theory:

- *Rationality.* Competitors will behave rationally in trying to win to their own benefit.

www.pearsoned.co.uk/ecs
KEY CONCEPT
Game theory

Illustration 6.4

Business–university collaboration in the creative and cultural industries

Public/private sector collaboration may bring benefits to both parties.

In 2003 the UK government set up a committee (The Lambert Committee) to report on business–university collaboration in the UK and to propose how it might be improved. The first stage was to seek ideas from a wide range of stakeholders. The following is an extract from the Arts and Humanities Research Council (AHRC), which supported work that was fundamental to a range of creative and cultural industries:

We are in the early stages of exploring a range of partnerships and possible strategic interventions (see below). In collaboration with the Department for Culture, Media and Sports (DCMS) and others, a Creative Industries/Higher Education Forum has been established. This group will seek to bring together the supply and demand side of this relationship to foster stronger links and new activities.

Creative and cultural industries: a role for creative clusters

Many universities have developed links with businesses in the creative and cultural industries. . . . However, many of the companies in the creative industries are small (SMEs). . . . An organic development in recent years has been the creation of a number of 'creative clusters' bringing together local or regional HEIs with business for the generation of new ideas, products and processes. Examples exist from around the country, including Scotland, Sheffield, London, Bristol, Nottingham. Such creative clusters supported by business enterprise and support services could provide the basis for supporting small-scale individual entrepreneurship.

Working with Regional Development Agencies (RDAs)

Both the Research Councils and RDAs are channels to their respective communities, and work has already commenced on identifying ways in which jointly they can be both a catalyst for new ideas and a facilitator of knowledge transfer. Such activities might cover individual projects, jointly-sponsored schemes, and facilitation of sector clusters, such as creative clusters.

Embedding practitioners and professionals in HEIs

Many traditional models of the relationship between HEIs and business describe a linear process in which

knowledge is passed to industry. However, it can be argued that, increasingly, knowledge transfer is not a process, but an interaction based on access to people, information, data and infrastructure. In the creative and performing arts the concept of portfolio careers is not uncommon. Individuals can hold part-time research or teaching positions alongside other forms of employment or self-employment, including artistic performance. In addition, it is not uncommon for businesses and other non-private sector organisations to provide visiting professorships or lectureships.

Widening the definition of knowledge transfer in a knowledge economy

Increasingly a large number of people are trading their knowledge, expertise and experience through non-conventional employment means. However, in looking for evidence of knowledge transfer from academia to business the focus tends to be on the numbers of patents, spin-outs and companies created. These are undoubtedly important indicators to industrial performance, but a wider evidence base looking at employment patterns and self-employment would give a wider perspective.

Charting this new landscape

It is the role of bodies such as the AHRC to provide an environment that enables the ideas and creativity of the academic community to be unlocked and developed. Working with analogous bodies in other sectors, such as the RDAs, the aspiration is to find ways to improve the links out from academia to the wider society and economy.

Source: AHRC Response from the AHRC to the Lambert Review of Business–University Collaboration, http://www.ahrc.ac.uk.

Questions

1 Look at section 6.6 and then identify the potential benefits from business–university collaboration to a number of the important stakeholders.

2 What are the risks of collaboration to each of these stakeholders (as against 'going it alone')?

- *Interdependence*. Competitors are in an interdependent relationship with each other. So one competitor's move is likely to galvanise response from another and the outcome of choices made by one competitor is dependent on the choices made by another. Moreover, to a greater or lesser extent competitors are aware of such interdependencies and the moves that competitors could take.

Arising from these assumptions, there are then two principles guiding the development of successful competitive strategies:

- *'Get in the mind' of the competitors*. Strategists need to put themselves in the position of competitors, take a rational view about what competitors are likely to do and choose their own strategy in this light. They need to get to know their game to plan their own.

- *'Think forwards and reason backwards'*. Decide strategy on the basis of understanding the outcomes of possible strategic moves of competitors. Game theory therefore emphasises the importance of the dynamics of market competition.

6.7.1 The 'prisoner's dilemma': the problem of cooperation

The term *coopetition* has been coined[18] to denote that, to varying degrees, all competitors cooperate (see section 6.6). The decision on whether or not to cooperate is the theme of one of the most famous examples of game theory: the prisoners' dilemma. This is most commonly illustrated in terms of the dilemma two prisoners face. They are being held in separate cells. They have to decide on the relative benefits of supporting each by refusing to divulge information to their interrogators or seeking an advantage by 'ratting' on the other. Here the same situation is illustrated in terms of a competitive business situation represented in Exhibit 6.7. Suppose two firms have to decide whether to compete head-on or work together to develop a new market opportunity. They may know that the cost of cooperating on the venture would be much lower and the returns higher and realised sooner than competing. The notional pay-off of cooperation is represented in the bottom right-hand quadrant of Exhibit 6.7. However, there are reasons they may not do this. For example, each knows that if they invest in

Exhibit 6.7   **A prisoner's dilemma**

		Competitor A	
		Don't cooperate	Cooperate
Competitor B	Don't cooperate	B = 5 A = 5	B = 12 A = 2
	Cooperate	B = 2 A = 12	B = 9 A = 9

trying to achieve a dominant position in the new market and the other does not, they would achieve even higher returns (represented in the top right and bottom left quadrants) so may be tempted to do this, or may fear that their rival will be tempted to do so if they do not. They each may also fear that, if they collaborate, after the early joint investment, the other may begin to dominate the market and benefit at the disproportionality. Or they may simply not trust each other. It is therefore quite likely that both parties will decide to go it alone to ensure that the other competitor does not get an advantage. This may mean that the returns from the investment needed to develop the market would be much lower for both than if they decided to cooperate – as shown in the top left quadrant.

A dominant strategy is one that outperforms other strategies whatever rivals choose

This is an example of what game theorists refer to as a **dominant strategy**: one that outperforms other strategies whatever rivals choose. In the prisoner's

Illustration 6.5

Innova and Dolla play a sequential game

The principles of game theory can provide insights into competitive strategy.

Innova and Dolla, competitors in the market for computer games, face a decision on investment in research and development. Innova has highly innovative designers but is short of the finance required to invest heavily in rapid development of products. Dolla is strong financially but relatively weak in terms of its research and design.

In terms of the crucial choice of investing in research and design or not, they both know that investing heavily would shorten the development time but would incur considerable costs. Indeed high levels of investment by both is the worst outcome: for Innova because its financial position is weak and it could be a risky route to follow; for Dolla because, if it can raise the finance, Innova has better chances of winning given its design capabilities.

Innova has a dominant strategy; to keep its investment low. If Dolla were to invest low, Innova would get a better pay-off because of its innovative capabilities. Indeed Dolla probably expects that Innova will keep levels of investment down. It also knows that if it goes for a low level of investment, it

has no advantage over Innova's superior innovative capabilities. For Dolla a low level of investment is a *dominated strategy* so the likelihood is that it will go for high levels of investment.

However, this can be reconsidered sequentially (see Figure 1). If Innova decides to invest low, it knows that Dolla is likely to respond high and gain the advantage (pay-off C). However, if Innova moves first and invests high, it places Dolla in a difficult position. If Dolla also invests high, it ends up with a low pay-off as does Innova (pay-off A). In these circumstances – provided that Dolla's strategist is a game theorist – Dolla might well reject that strategy and choose to invest low (with pay-off B).

Working through these different game logics, Innova should realise that if it waits for Dolla to make a move, it is bound to lose, but if it moves first and invests high, it stands a chance of winning. Of course there are risks here for Innova, not least financial. Also that Dolla may not believe that Innova will really invest high, so Innova has to be credible in its move. If it appears to waver, or not make a dilemma example it would be better for there to be cooperation between the competitors. However, the fact is that if either of the competitors breaks rank the other one will suffer badly. So the dominant strategy is to go it alone. A general principle is that if there is a dominant strategy it makes sense to use it. It may well be that the end result is a lesser pay-off than could optimally be achieved, but it is better than losing out to the competitor.

In practice this 'lose–lose' outcome is not likely if there is a limited number of competitors interacting over time, because they learn to understand and accommodate each other. But something similar often occurs when there are many competitors jostling for position in a fragmented market. For example, whilst it might be logical for all competitors to hold prices at a relatively high level in such circumstances, no one expects anyone else to do so, and price wars result.

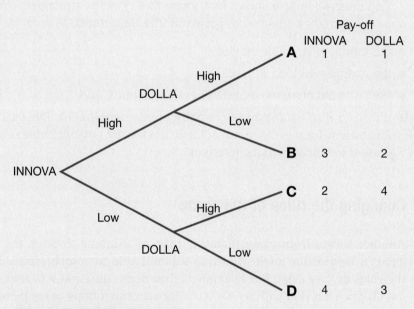

Figure 1 A sequential move game

Source: From *Thinking Strategically: The Competitive Edge in Business, Politics and Everyday Life* by Avinash K. Dixit and Barry J. Nalebuff. Copyright © 1991 by Avinash K. Dixit and Barry J. Natebuff. Used by permission of W.W. Norton & Company, Inc.

substantial enough investment, Dolla may invest high too and both lose out (pay-off A). Of course, if there is some way of Innova appearing to be credible in a decision to invest high whilst actually investing low, thus persuading Dolla to invest low too, then Innova achieves its *dominant strategy* (pay-off D).

Questions

1 Suggest other situations where game theory approaches might be useful and explain why.

2 What might prevent strategic decisions being made in this way?

6.7.2 Sequential games

The prisoner's dilemma is a simultaneous game, where competitors make decisions or strategic moves at the same time. This is not usually the case. A series of strategic decisions will typically be sequential, one party making a move, followed by the other. Here the guiding principle of 'think forwards and reason backwards' becomes especially important. The strategist needs to consider (i) what that competitor desires as the outcome, (ii) the sequence of moves that competitor might make based on that desired outcome and therefore (iii) the most advantageous strategy for itself. In doing this, it needs to be borne in mind that competitors will have different strategic capabilities and, linked to this, their own dominant strategies – for example, easyJet or Ryanair clearly have a dominant strategy of low price in the airline industry.

Illustration 6.5 shows how game theory reasoning might play out given these more complex conditions. If the situation is considered in terms of a sequential game, as in section 6.7.1, the best Innova can do is to follow its dominant strategy of investing low, which results in the least worst pay-off. Given that Innova will not be happy with this outcome, the illustration shows how considering the problem as a sequential game might help Innova gain advantage over its rival.

The illustration also shows how game theory helps strategists consider some important strategic lessons, in particular the importance of:

● the timing of strategic moves;

● the careful weighing of risk;

● the potential benefits of bluff and counter-bluff; and

● linked to this, establishing credibility and commitment. For example, in the illustration Innova could not achieve its desired outcome unless it had a reputation for sticking to its decisions.

6.7.3 Changing the rules of the game

Another lesson from game theory is that, by thinking through the logic of the game, a competitor might find that it is not able to compete effectively within the rules as they exist. For example, a firm might find that it is always battling it out on price but that with its cost structure it cannot hope to compete effectively. Or, as with the examples given here, that competition is always played out on the basis of a particular capability, such as heavy investment in research and development; this is a battle it cannot win. In such circumstances it may make sense to try to change the rules of the game. For example, in a market dominated by price-based strategies, a competitor might try to shift the rules of the game towards:

● *Clearer differentiation* based on what customers really value (see section 6.3.2).

● *More transparent pricing*, for example by trying to get published price lists established as the norm. On the face of it, this may not seem to avoid price competition, but the evidence is that greater transparency in this respect removes a significant basis for trying to achieve tactical advantage and therefore encourage more cooperative behaviour amongst competitors.

● *More incentives for customer loyalty*. The growth of loyalty cards in retailing is a good example. The principles of differentiation suggest that this is a weak strategy because competitors will imitate it. However, the pressure on competition through price can be reduced for all competitors.

Game theory does of course rely heavily on the principle of rationality, and it may well be that competitors do not always behave rationally. However, it does provide a way of thinking through the logic of interactive competitive markets and, in particular, when it makes sense to compete, on what bases, and when it makes sense to cooperate. At the very least it is important for managers to consider how competitors will respond to their preferred strategy.

An underlying theme in this chapter is the search for competitive advantage and the need for distinctiveness and strategies of differentiation to achieve this. The key debate in Illustration 6.6 reconsiders this theme and questions the extent to which differentiation does provide competitive advantage.

SUMMARY

www.pearsoned.co.uk/ecs
AUDIO SUMMARY

● Competitive strategy is concerned with seeking competitive advantage in markets at the business level or, in the public services, providing best value services.

● Competitive strategy needs to be considered and defined in terms of strategic business units (SBUs).

● Different bases of competitive strategy include:
  – A *'no frills'* strategy, combining low price and low perceived added value.
  – A *low-price* strategy providing lower price than competitors at similar added value of product or service to competitors.
  – A *differentiation* strategy, which seeks to provide products or services which are unique or different from competitors.
  – A *hybrid* strategy, which seeks simultaneously to achieve differentiation and prices lower than competitors.
  – A *focused differentiation* strategy, which seeks to provide high perceived value justifying a substantial price premium.

● Managers need to consider the bases upon which price-based or differentiation strategies can be sustained based on strategic capabilities, developing durable relationships with customers or the ability to achieve a 'lock-in' position so becoming the 'industry standard' recognised by suppliers and buyers.

● In hypercompetitive conditions sustainable competitive advantage is difficult to achieve. Speed, flexibility, innovation and the willingness to change successful strategies are then important bases of competitive success.

● Strategies of collaboration may offer alternatives to competitive strategies or may run in parallel.

● Game theory provides a basis for thinking through competitors' strategic moves in such a way as to pre-empt or counter them.

Illustration 6.6

key debate

To be different or the same?

Can differentiation strategies rebound, making an organisation seem dangerously eccentric rather than delivering competitive advantage?

This chapter has introduced the potential value of differentiation strategies, in which the organisation emphasises its uniqueness. This is consistent also with the argument of the resource-based view (Chapter 3) in favour of the distinctiveness and inimitability of an organisation's resources. But how far should an organisation push its uniqueness, especially if there is a danger of it beginning to be seen as simply eccentric?

McKinsey & Co. consultant Philipp Natterman makes a strong case for differentiation.[1] He tracks the relationship between profitability and differentiation (in terms of pricing and product features) over long periods in both the personal computer and mobile phone industries. He finds that as differentiation falls over time, so too do industry profit margins. Natterman blames management techniques such as benchmarking (Chapter 3), which tend to encourage convergence on industry 'best practices'. The trouble with best practices is that they easily become standard practices. There is no competitive advantage in following the herd.

However, 'institutional theorists' such as Paul DiMaggio and Walter Powell point to some advantages in herd-like behaviour.[2] They think of industries as 'organisational fields' in which all sorts of actors must interact – customers, suppliers, employees and regulators. The ability of these actors to interact effectively depends upon being legitimate in the eyes of other actors in the field. Over time, industries develop institutionalised norms of legitimate behaviour, which it makes sense for everybody to follow. It is easier for customers and suppliers to do business with organisations that are more or less the same as the others in the industry. It is reassuring to potential employees and industry regulators if organisations do not seem highly eccentric. Especially when there is high uncertainty about what drives performance – for example, in knowledge-based industries – it can be a lot better to be legitimate than different. To the extent that customers, suppliers, employees and regulators value conformity, then it is valuable in itself. Being a 'misfit' can be costly.

This institutionalist appreciation of conformity makes sense of a lot of strategic behaviour. For example, merger waves in some industries seem to be driven by bandwagons, in which organisations become panicked into making acquisitions simply for fear of being left behind. Likewise, many management initiatives, such as business process re-engineering, e-business or outsourcing, are the product of fads and fashions as much as hard objective analysis. The insight from institutionalist theory, however, is that following the fashion is not necessarily a bad thing.

Thus institutional theory and the resource-based view appear to have opposing perspectives on the value of differentiation. David Deephouse has investigated this apparent trade-off between differentiation and conformity in the American banking industry and found a curvilinear relationship between differentiation and financial performance.[3] Strong conformity led to inferior performance; moderate differentiation was associated with improved performance; extreme differentiation appeared to damage performance.

Deephouse concludes in favour of 'balance' between differentiation and conformity. He also suggests that the value of differentiation depends on the extent to which key actors in the industry – customers, suppliers, employees, and so on – have converged on institutionalised norms of appropriate strategy. It seems that strategies can be too differentiated, but that how much 'too differentiated' is depends on the kind of industry that one is in.

Sources:
1. P.M. Natterman, 'Best practice does not equal best strategy', *McKinsey Quarterly*, no. 2 (2000), pp. 22–31.
2. P. DiMaggio and W. Powell, 'The iron cage revisited: institutional isomorphism and collective rationality in organizational fields', *American Sociological Review*, vol. 48 (1983), pp. 147–160.
3. D. Deephouse, 'To be different or to be the same? It's a question (and theory) of strategic balance', *Strategic Management Journal*, vol. 20 (1999), pp. 147–166.

Questions

1 To what extent do (a) universities and (b) car manufacturers compete by being different or the same?

2 Considering the nature of their industries, and key players within them, why might these organisations adopt these approaches to conformity or differentiation?

Work assignments

✱ *Denotes more advanced work assignments.*   * *Refers to a case study in the Text and Case edition.*

6.1   Using Exhibit 6.2, the strategy clock, identify examples of organisations following strategic routes 1 to 5. If you find it difficult to be clear about which route is being followed, note down the reasons for this, and consider if the organisations have a clear competitive strategy.

6.2   You have been appointed personal assistant to the chief executive of a major manufacturing firm, who has asked you to explain what is meant by 'differentiation' and why it is important. Write a brief report addressing these questions.

6.3 ✱ How appropriate are bases of competitive advantage explained in section 6.3 for considering the strategies of public sector organisations? Illustrate your argument by reference to a public sector organisation of your choice.

6.4   Applying the lessons from section 6.4, consider how sustainable are the strategies of any of:

(a) Tesco

(b) Ryanair*

(c) an organisation of your choice.

6.5 ✱ Choose an industry or sector which is becoming more and more competitive (for example, financial services or fashion retailing). How might the principles of hypercompetitive strategies apply to that industry?

6.6   Drawing on sections 6.6 (on collaborative strategies) write a report for the chief executive of a business in a competitive market (for example, pharmaceuticals* or Formula One*) explaining when and in what ways cooperation rather than direct competition might make sense.

Integrative assignment

6.7 ✱ Refer to section 6.4.3 and Exhibit 6.3. If the achievement of 'lock-in' were to be the basis of an international strategy (Chapter 8) explain how this might influence the choices around both the direction and methods of strategy development (Chapter 10).

An extensive range of additional materials, including audio summaries, weblinks to organisations featured in the text, definitions of key concepts and self-assessment questions, can be found on the *Exploring Corporate Strategy* Companion Website at **www.pearsoned.co.uk/ecs**

Recommended key readings

- The foundations of the discussions of generic competitive strategies are to be found in the writings of Michael Porter, which include *Competitive Strategy* (1980) and *Competitive Advantage* (1985), both published by Free Press. Both are recommended for readers who wish to understand the background to discussions in sections 6.3 and 6.4 on competitive strategy and competitive advantage.

- Hypercompetition, and the strategies associated with its conditions, are explained in Richard D'Aveni, *Hypercompetitive Rivalries: Competing in highly dynamic environments*, Free Press, 1995. There is a lively debate about whether sustainable competitive advantage is possible. Two papers offering different evidence on this are: R.W. Wiggins and T.W. Ruefli, 'Schumpeter's ghost: is hypercompetition making the best of times shorter?', *Strategic Management Journal*, vol. 26 (2005), pp. 887–911, which argues there is no evidence for sustainable competitive advantage; and G. Mcnamara, P.M. Vaaler and C. Devers, 'Same as it ever was: the search for evidence of increasing hypercompetition', *Strategic Management Journal*, vol. 24 (2003), pp. 261–278, which argues that it is.

- There is much written on game theory but a good deal of it can be rather inaccessible to the lay reader. An exception is the book by A.K. Dixit and B.J. Nalebuff, *Thinking Strategically*, W.W. Norton, 1991. R. McCain, *Game Theory: A Non-Technical Introduction to the Analysis of Strategy*, South Western, 2003, considers business strategy in game theory terms.

References

1. For a detailed discussion as to how organisational structures might 'address' an organisation's mix of SBUs see M. Goold and A. Campbell, *Designing Effective Organisations: How to create structured networks*, Jossey Bass, 2002. Also K. Eisenhardt and S. Brown, 'Patching', *Harvard Business Review*, vol. 77, no. 3 (1999), p. 72.

2. M. Porter, *Competitive Advantage*, Free Press, 1985.

3. See D. Faulkner and C. Bowman, *The Essence of Competitive Strategy*, Prentice Hall, 1995. A similar framework is also used by Richard D'Aveni, *Hypercompetitive Rivalries: Competing in highly dynamic environments*, Free Press, 1995.

4. B. Sharp and J. Dawes, 'What is differentiation and how does it work?', *Journal of Marketing Management*, vol. 17, nos 7/8 (2001), pp. 739–759, reviews the relationship between differentiation and profitability.

5. See, for example, D. Miller, 'The generic strategy trap', *Journal of Business Strategy*, vol. 13, no. 1 (1992), pp. 37–42; C.W.L. Hill, 'Differentiation versus low cost or differentiation and low cost: a contingency framework', *Academy of Management Review*, vol. 13, no. 3 (1998), pp. 401–412; and S. Thornhill and R. White, 'Strategic purity: a multi-industry evaluation of pure vs hybrid business strategies', *Strategic Management Journal*, vol. 28, no. 5 (2007), pp. 553–561.

6. See G. Hamel and C.K. Prahalad, 'Do you really have a global strategy?', *Harvard Business Review*, vol. 63, no. 4 (1985), pp. 139–148.

7. These quotes concerning Porter's three competitive strategies are taken from his book *Competitive Advantage*, Free Press, 1985, pp. 12–15.

8. The Delta Model is explained and illustrated more fully in A.C. Hax and D.L. Wilde II, 'The Delta Model', *Sloan Management Review*, vol. 40, no. 2 (1999), pp. 11–28.

9. This section is based on research by N. Kumar, 'Strategies to fight low cost rivals', *Harvard Business Review*, vol. 84, no. 12 (2006), pp. 104–113.

10. For a discussion of how to compete in such circumstances, see A. Rao, M. Bergen and S. Davis, 'How to fight a price war', *Harvard Business Review*, vol. 78, no. 2 (2000), pp. 107–115.

11. The extent to which hypercompetitive conditions exist is a matter of debate. There is evidence in support: see R.W. Wiggins and T.W. Ruefli, 'Schumpeter's ghost: is hypercompetition making the best of times shorter?', *Strategic Management Journal*, vol. 26 (2005), pp. 887–911. But there is also evidence against: see G. Mcnamara, P.M. Vaaler and C. Devers, 'Same as it was: the search for evidence of increasing hypercompetition', *Strategic Management Journal*, vol. 24 (2003), pp. 261–278.

12. See D'Aveni, reference 3.

13. For other examples of misleading signals see G. Stalk Jr, 'Curveball: strategies to fool the competition', *Harvard Business Review*, September (2006), pp. 115–122.

14. Useful books on collaborative strategies are Y. Doz and G. Hamel, *Alliance Advantage: The art of creating value through partnering*, Harvard Business School Press, 1998; *Creating Collaborative Advantage*, ed. Chris Huxham, Sage, 1996; and D. Faulkner, *Strategic Alliances: Co-operating to compete*, McGraw-Hill, 1995.

15. This case for cooperation in hi-tech industries is argued and illustrated by V. Kapur, J. Peters and S. Berman: 'High tech 2005: the horizontal, hypercompetitive future', *Strategy and Leadership*, vol. 31, no. 2 (2003), pp. 34–47.

16. See J. Brudney and R. England, 'Towards a definition of the co-production concept', *Public Administration Review*, vol. 43, no. 10 (1983), pp. 59–65; and J. Alford, 'A public management road less travelled: clients as co-producers of public services', *Australian Journal of Public Administration*, vol. 57, no. 4 (1998), pp. 128–137.

17. For readings on game theory see A.K. Dixit and B.J. Nalebuff, *Thinking Strategically*, W.W. Norton, 1991; A. Brandenburger and B. Nalebuff, *Co-opetition*, Profile Books, 1997; R. McCain, *Game Theory: A Non-Technical Introduction to the Analysis of Strategy*, South Western, 2003; and, for a summary, S. Regan, 'Game theory perspective', In M. Jenkins and V. Ambrosini (eds), *Advanced Strategic Management: A Multi-Perspective Approach*, 2nd edition, Palgrave Macmillan, 2007, pp. 83–101.

18. A. Brandenburger and B.J. Nalebuff, *Co-opetition*, Profile Books, 1997.

CASE EXAMPLE

Madonna: still the reigning queen of pop?

Phyl Johnson, Strathclyde University Business School

The music industry has always been the backdrop for one-hit wonders and brief careers. Pop stars who have remained at the top for decades are very few. Madonna is one such phenomenon; the question is, after over 25 years at the top, how much longer can it last?

Described by *Billboard Magazine* as the smartest business woman in show business, Madonna, Louise Ciccone, began her music career in 1983 with the hit single 'Holiday' and in 2005–2006 once again enjoyed chart success for her album 'Confessions on a Dance Floor'. In the meantime she had consistent chart success with her singles and albums, multiple sell-out world tours, major roles in six films, picked up 18 music awards, been the style icon behind a range of products from Pepsi and Max Factor to the Gap and H&M, and became a worldwide best-selling children's author.

The foundation of Madonna's business success was her ability to sustain her reign as the 'queen of pop' since 1983. Along with many others, Phil Quattro, the President of Warner Brothers, has argued that 'she always manages to land on the cusp of what we call contemporary music, every established artist faces the dilemma of maintaining their importance and relevance, Madonna never fails to be relevant.' Madonna's chameleon-like ability to change persona, change her music genre with it and yet still achieve major record sales has been the hallmark of her success.

Madonna's early poppy style was targeted at young 'wannabe' girls. The image that she portrayed through hits such as 'Holiday' and 'Lucky Star' in 1983 was picked up by Macy's, the US-based department store. It produced a range of *Madonna lookalike* clothes that mothers were happy to purchase for their daughters. One year later in 1984, Madonna then underwent her first image change and, in doing so, offered the first hint of the smart cookie behind the media image. In the video for her hit

Photo: DPA/PA Photos

'Material Girl', she deliberately mirrored the glamour-based, sexual pussycat image of Marilyn Monroe whilst simultaneously mocking both the growing materialism of the late 1980s and the men fawning after her. Media analysts Sam and Diana Kirschner commented that with this kind of packaging, Madonna allowed the record companies to keep hold of a saleable 'Marilyn image' for a new cohort of fans, but also allowed her original fan base of now growing up wannabe girls to take the more critical message from the music. The theme of courting controversy but staying marketable enough has been recurrent throughout her career, if not slightly toned down in later years.

Madonna's subsequent image changes were more dramatic. First she took on the Catholic Church in her 1989 video 'Like a Prayer' where, as a red-dressed 'sinner', she kissed a black saint easily interpreted as a Jesus figure. Her image had become increasingly sexual whilst also holding on to a critical social theme: for example, her pointed illustration of white-only imagery in the Catholic Church. At this point in her career, Madonna took full control of her image in the $60m (€48m; £33m) deal with Time-Warner that created her record company Maverick. In 1991, she published a coffee-table soft-porn book entitled *Sex* that exclusively featured pictures of herself in erotic poses. Her image and music also reflected this erotic theme. In her 'Girlie' tour, her singles 'Erotica' and 'Justify my Love' and her fly-on-the-wall movie 'In bed with Madonna' she played out scenes of sadomasochistic and lesbian fantasies. Although allegedly a period of her career she would rather forget, Madonna more than survived it. In fact, she gained a whole new demography of fans who not only respected her artistic courage, but also did not miss the fact that Madonna was consistent in her message: her sexuality was her own and not in need of a male gaze. She used the media's love affair with her, and the *cause célèbre* status gained from having MTV ban the video for 'Justify my Love', to promote the message that women's sexuality and freedom is just as important and acceptable as men's.

Changing gear in 1996, Madonna finally took centre stage in the lead role in the film *Evita* that she had chased for over five years. She beat other heavyweight contenders for the role including Meryl Streep and Elaine Page, both with more acceptable pasts than Madonna. Yet she achieved the image transition from erotica to saint-like persona of Eva Peron and won critical acclaim to boot. Another vote of confidence from the 'establishment' came from Max Factor, who in 1999 signed her up to front its relaunch campaign that was crafted around a glamour theme. Procter and Gamble (owners of the Max Factor make-up range) argued that they saw Madonna as 'the closest thing the 90s has to an old-style Hollywood star . . . she is a real woman'.

With many pre-release leaks, Madonna's keenly awaited album 'Ray of Light' was released in 1998. Radio stations worldwide were desperate to get hold of the album being billed as her most successful musical voyage to date. In a smart move, Madonna had teamed up with techno pioneer William Orbit to write and produce the album. It was a huge success, taking Madonna into the super-trendy techno sphere, not the natural environment for a pop star from the early 1980s. Madonna took up an 'earth mother/ spiritual' image and spawned a trend for all things Eastern in fashion and music. This phase may have produced more than just an image as it is the time in Madonna's life which locates the beginning of her continued faith in the Kabbalah tradition of Eastern spiritual worship.

By 2001, her next persona was unveiled with the release of her album 'Music'. Here her style had moved on again to 'acid rock'. With her marriage to British movie director Guy Ritchie, the ultimate 'American Pie' had become a fully fledged Brit babe earning the endearing nick name of 'Madge' in the British press.

By 2003 some commentators were suggesting that an interesting turn of events hinted that perhaps 'the cutting-edge' Madonna, 'the fearless', was starting to think about *being part of* rather than *beating* the establishment when she launched her new Che-Guevara-inspired image. Instead of maximising the potential of this image in terms of its political and social symbolism during the Second Gulf War, in April 2003 she withdrew her militaristic image and video for the album 'American Life'. That action timed with the publication of her children's book *The English Roses*, based on the themes of compassion and friendship, which sparked questions in the press around the theme 'has Madonna gone soft?'

By late 2003 she had wiped the military image from the West's collective memory with a glitzy high-profile ad campaign for the Gap, the clothing retailer in which she danced around accompanied by rapper Missy Elliot to a retrospective remix of her 1980s' track 'Get into the Groove'. Here Madonna was keeping the 'thirty-somethings', who remembered the track from first time around, happy. They could purchase jeans for themselves and their newly teenage daughters whilst also purchasing the re-released CD (on sale in store) for them to share and a copy of *The English Roses* (also promoted in the Gap stores) for perhaps the youngest member of the family.

Late 2005 saw the release of the 'Confessions on a Dance Floor' album that was marketed as her

Releases	Year	Image	Target audience
Lucky Star	1982	Trashy pop	Young wannabe girls, dovetailing from fading disco to emerging 'club scene'
Like a Virgin *Like a Prayer*	1984	Originally a Marilyn glamour image, then became a saint and sinner	More grown-up rebellious fan base, more critical female audience and male worshippers
Vogue *Erotica* *Bedtime Stories*	1990 1992 1994	Erotic porn star, sadomasochistic, sexual control, more Minelli in *Cabaret* than Monroe	Peculiar mix of target audiences: gay club scene, 1990s' women taking control of their own lives, also pure male titillation
Something to Remember Evita	1995	Softer image, ballads preparing for glamour image of *Evita* film role	Broadest audience target, picking up potential film audiences as well as regular fan base. Most conventional image. Max Factor later used this mixture of Marilyn and Eva Peron to market its glamour image
Ray of Light	1998	Earth mother, Eastern mysticism, dance music fusion	Clubbing generation of the 1990s, new cohort of fans plus original fan base of now 30-somethings desperately staying trendy
Music	2000	Acid rock, tongue in cheek Miss USA/cow girl, cool Britannia	Managing to hit the changing club scene and 30-something Brits
American Life	2003	Militaristic image Che Guevara Anti-consumerism of American dream	Unclear audience reliant on existing base
Confessions on a Dance Floor	2005	Retro-1980s' disco imagery, high-motion dance–pop sound	Strong gay–icon audience, pop–disco audience, dance-based audience

comeback album after her lowest-selling 'American Life'. It and the linked tour achieved one of the highest-selling peaks of her career. The album broke a world record for solo-female artists when it debuted at number one in 41 countries. By February 2007 it had sold 8 million copies. Here Madonna focused on the high-selling principal of *remix*, choosing samples of the gay–iconic disco favourites of Abba and Giorgio Moroder to be at the heart of her symbolic reinvention of herself from artist to DJ. By cross-marketing the album image with Dolce & Gabbana in its men's fashion shows, Madonna cashed in on her regaining the dance–pop crown. Will this, her latest album, stand the musical test of time? Who knows? But for now it seems to have more than met the moment.

Sources: 'Bennett takes the reins at Maverick', *Billboard Magazine*, 7 August (1999); 'Warner Bros expects Madonna to light up international markets', *Billboard Magazine*, 21 February (1998);

'Maverick builds on early success', *Billboard Magazine*, 12 November (1994); A., Jardine 'Max Factor strikes gold with Madonna', *Marketing*, vol. 29, (1999), pp. 14–15; S. Kirschner and D. Kirschner, 'MTV, adolescence and Madonna: a discourse analysis', in *Perspectives on Psychology & the Media*, American Psychological Association, Washington, DC, 1997; 'Warner to buy out maverick co-founder', *Los Angeles Times*, 2 March (1999); 'Why Madonna is back in Vogue', *New Statesman*, 18 September (2000); 'Madonna & Microsoft', *Financial Times*, 28 November (2000).

Questions

1 Describe and explain the strategy being followed by Madonna in terms of the explanation of competitive strategy given in Chapter 6.

2 Why has she experienced sustained success over the past two decades?

3 What might threaten the sustainability of her success?

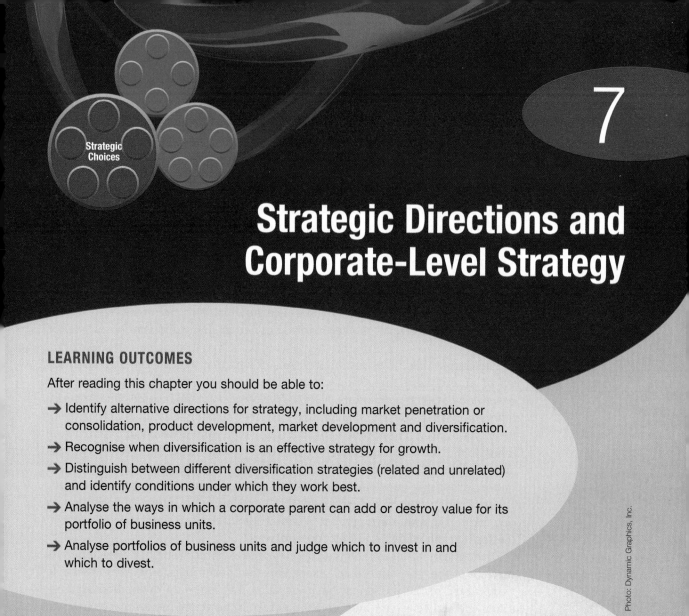

Strategic Choices

7

Strategic Directions and Corporate-Level Strategy

LEARNING OUTCOMES

After reading this chapter you should be able to:

→ Identify alternative directions for strategy, including market penetration or consolidation, product development, market development and diversification.

→ Recognise when diversification is an effective strategy for growth.

→ Distinguish between different diversification strategies (related and unrelated) and identify conditions under which they work best.

→ Analyse the ways in which a corporate parent can add or destroy value for its portfolio of business units.

→ Analyse portfolios of business units and judge which to invest in and which to divest.

7.1 INTRODUCTION

Chapter 6 was concerned with choices at the level of single business or organisational units, for instance through pricing strategies or differentiation. This chapter is about choices of *products and markets* for an organisation to enter or exit (see Exhibit II.i in the Part Introduction). Should the organisation be very focused on just a few products and markets? Or should it be much broader in scope, perhaps very diversified in terms of both products (or services) and markets? Many organisations do choose to enter many new product and market areas. For example, the Virgin Group started out in the music business, but is now highly diverse, operating in the holiday, cinema, retail, air travel and rail markets. Sony began by making small radios, but now produces games, music and movies, as well as a host of electronic products. As organisations add new units, their strategies are no longer concerned just with the business-level but with the corporate-level choices involved in having many different businesses or markets.

The chapter begins by introducing Ansoff's matrix, which generates an initial set of alternative strategic directions. The four basic directions are *increased penetration* of existing markets; *market development*, which includes building new markets, perhaps overseas or in new customer segments; *product development*, referring to product improvement and innovation; and *diversification*, involving a significant broadening of an organisation's scope in terms of both markets and products. This chapter takes a particularly hard look at the diversification option, proposing good reasons for doing so and warning of less good reasons. Diversification does not always pay. Chapter 8 takes up internationalisation as one form of market development; Chapter 9 addresses product development in the form of innovation and entrepreneurship.

Diversification raises the other themes of the chapter. The first theme here is the role of the 'corporate-level' executives that perform a **corporate parent** role with regard to the individual business units that make up diversified organisations' portfolios. Given their detachment from the actual marketplace, how can corporate-level activities, decisions and resources add value to the actual businesses? As will be seen in this chapter's key debate (Illustration 7.6), there is considerable scepticism about the role of corporate-level strategy. The second theme is how to achieve a good mix of businesses within the corporate portfolio. Which businesses should corporate parents cultivate and which should they divest? Here various portfolio matrices help structure corporate-level choices.

The chapter is not just about large commercial businesses. Even small businesses may consist of a number of business units. For example, a local builder may be undertaking contract work for local government, work for industrial buyers and for local homeowners. Not only are these different market segments, but the mode of operation and capabilities required for competitive success are also likely to be different. Moreover, the owner of that business has to take decisions about the extent of investment and activity in each segment. Public sector organisations such as local government or health services also provide different services, which correspond to business units in commercial organisations. Corporate-level strategy is highly relevant to the appropriate drawing of organisational boundaries in the public sector, and privatisation and outsourcing

The **corporate parent** refers to the levels of management above that of the business units, and therefore without direct interaction with buyers and competitors

| Exhibit 7.1 | Strategic directions and corporate-level strategy |

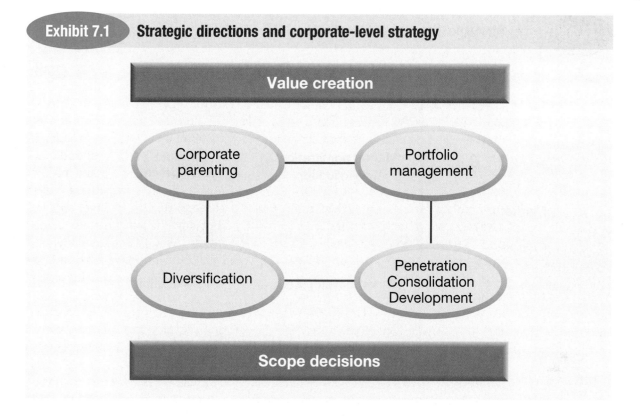

decisions can be considered as responses to the failure of public sector organisations to add sufficient value by their parenting.

Exhibit 7.1 summarises the key themes of this chapter. After reviewing Ansoff's strategic directions, the chapter focuses specifically on diversification. Diversification in turn raises the two related topics of the role of the corporate parent and the use of business portfolio matrices.

7.2   STRATEGIC DIRECTIONS

Strategic
directions

The Ansoff product/market growth matrix[1] provides a simple way of generating four basic alternative directions for strategic development: see Exhibit 7.2. An organisation typically starts in box A, the top left-hand one, with its existing products and existing markets. According to the matrix, the organisation basically has a choice between *penetrating* still further within its existing sphere (staying in box A); moving rightwards by *developing new products* for its existing markets (box B); moving downwards by bringing its *existing products into new markets* (box C); or taking the most radical step of full *diversification*, with altogether new markets and new products (box D).

The Ansoff matrix explicitly considers growth options. Growth is rarely a good end in itself. Public sector organisations are often accused of growing out-of-control bureaucracies; similarly, some private sector managers are accused of empire building at the expense of shareholders. This chapter therefore adds

Exhibit 7.2	Strategic directions (Ansoff matrix)

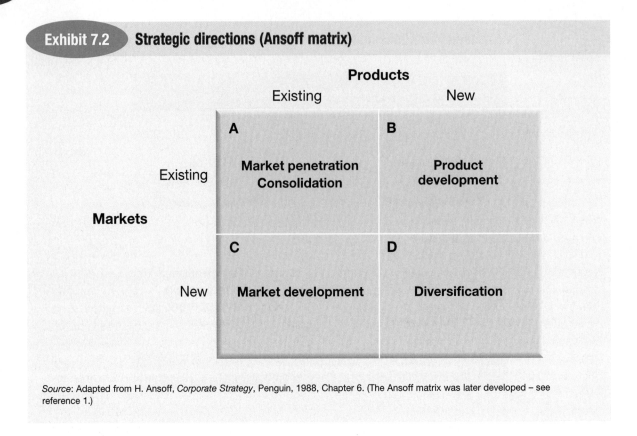

Source: Adapted from H. Ansoff, *Corporate Strategy*, Penguin, 1988, Chapter 6. (The Ansoff matrix was later developed – see reference 1.)

consolidation as a fifth option. Consolidation involves protecting existing products and existing markets and therefore belongs in box A. The rest of this section considers the five strategic directions in more detail. See Illustration 7.1 for an application of the Ansoff matrix to Springer publishers.

7.2.1 Market penetration

Market penetration is where an organisation gains market share

Further **market penetration**, by which the organisation takes increased share of its existing markets with its existing product range, is on the face of it the most obvious strategic direction. It builds on existing strategic capabilities and does not require the organisation to venture into uncharted territory. The organisation's scope is exactly the same. Moreover, greater market share implies increased power vis-à-vis buyers and suppliers (in terms of the five forces), greater economies of scale and experience curve benefits.

However, organisations seeking greater market penetration may face two constraints:

● *Retaliation from competitors*. In terms of the five forces (section 2.2), increasing market penetration is likely to exacerbate industry rivalry as other competitors in the market defend their share. Increased rivalry might involve price wars or expensive marketing battles, which may cost more than any market share gains are actually worth. The dangers of provoking fierce retaliation are greater in low-growth markets, as any gains in volume will be much more

Illustration 7.1

Strategic directions for Axel Springer

This German publishing company has many opportunities, and the money to pursue them.

In 2007, Mathias Döpfner, Chairman and Chief Executive of Axel Springer publishers, had about €2bn (£1.5bn) to invest in new opportunities. The previous year, the competition authorities had prohibited his full takeover of Germany's largest television broadcaster, ProSiebenSat.1. Now Döpfner was looking for alternative directions.

Founded in 1946 by Axel Springer himself, the company was in 2007 already Germany's largest publisher of newspapers and magazines, with more than 10,000 employees and over 150 titles. Famous print titles included *Die Welt*, the *Berliner Morgenpost*, *Bild* and *Hörzu*. Outside Germany, Axel Springer was strongest in Eastern Europe. The company also had a scattering of mostly small investments in German radio and television companies, most notably a continuing 12 per cent stake in ProSieben Sat.1. Axel Springer described its strategic objectives as market leadership in the German-language core business, internationalisaton and digitalisation of the core business.

Further digitalisation of the core newspaper and magazine business was clearly important and would require substantial funding. There were also opportunities for the launch of new print magazine titles in the German market. But Döpfner was considering acquisition opportunities: 'it goes without saying,' he told the *Financial Times*, 'that

whenever a large international media company comes on to the market (i.e. is up for sale), we will examine it very closely – whether in print, TV or the online sector'.

Döpfner mentioned several specific kinds of acquisition opportunity. For example, he was still interested in buying a large European television broadcaster, even if it would probably have to be outside Germany. He was also attracted by the possibility of buying undervalued assets in the old media (namely, print), and turning them around in the style of a private equity investor: 'I would love to buy businesses in need of restructuring, where we can add value by introducing our management and sector expertise'. However, Döpfner reassured his shareholders by affirming that he felt no need 'to do a big thing in order to do a big thing'. He was also considering what to do with the 12 per cent minority stake in ProSiebenSat.1.

Main source: *Financial Times Deutschland*, 2 April (2007).

Questions

1 Referring to Exhibit 7.1, classify the various strategic directions considered by Mattias Döpfner for Axel Springer.

2 Using the Ansoff matrix, what other options could Döpfner pursue?

---

at the expense of other players. Where retaliation is a danger, organisations seeking market penetration need strategic capabilities that give a clear competitive advantage. In low-growth or declining markets, it can be more effective simply to acquire competitors. Some companies have grown quickly in this way. For example, in the steel industry the Indian company LNM (Mittal) moved rapidly in the 2000s to become the largest steel producer in the world by acquiring struggling steel companies around the world. Acquisitions can actually reduce rivalry, by taking out independent players and consolidating them under one umbrella: see also the consolidation strategy in section 7.2.2.

● *Legal constraints*. Greater market penetration can raise concerns from official competition regulators concerning excessive market power. Most countries have regulators with the powers to restrain powerful companies or prevent mergers and acquisitions that would create such excessive power. In the United Kingdom, the Competition Commission can investigate any merger or acquisition that would account for more than 25 per cent of the national market, and either halt the deal or propose measures that would reduce market power. The European Commission has an overview of the whole European market and can similarly intervene. For example, when Gaz de France and Suez, two utility companies with dominant positions in France and Belgium, decided to merge in 2006, the European Commission insisted that the two companies reduce their power by divesting some of their subsidiaries and opening up their networks to competition.[2]

7.2.2 Consolidation

Consolidation is where organisations focus defensively on their current markets with current products

Consolidation is where organisations focus defensively on their current markets with current products. Formally, this strategy occupies the same box in the Ansoff matrix as market penetration, but is not orientated to growth. Consolidation can take two forms:

● *Defending market share*. When facing aggressive competitors bent on increasing their market share, organisations have to work hard and often creatively to protect what they already have. Although market share should rarely be an end in itself, it is important to ensure that it is sufficient to sustain the business in the long term. For example, turnover has to be high enough to spread essential fixed costs such as R&D. In defending market share, differentiation strategies in order to build customer loyalty and switching costs are often effective.

● *Downsizing or divestment*. Especially when the size of the market as a whole is declining, reducing the size of the business through closing capacity is often unavoidable. An alternative is divesting (selling) some activities to other businesses. Sometimes downsizing can be dictated by the needs of shareholders, for instance an entrepreneur wishing to simplify his or her business on approaching retirement. Divesting or closing peripheral businesses can also make it easier to sell the core business to a potential purchaser.

The term 'consolidation' is sometimes also used to describe strategies of *buying up rivals* in a fragmented industry, particularly one in decline. By acquiring weaker competitors, and closing capacity, the consolidating company can gain market power and increase overall efficiency. As this form of consolidation increases market share, it could be seen as a kind of market penetration, but here the motivation is essentially defensive.

Although both consolidation and market penetration strategies are by no means static ones, their limitations often propel managers to consider alternative strategic directions.

7.2.3 **Product development**

Product development is where organisations deliver modified or new products to existing markets

Product development is where organisations deliver modified or new products (or services) to existing markets. This is a limited extension of organisational scope. In practice, even market penetration will probably require some product development, but here product development implies greater degrees of innovation. For Sony, such product development would include moving the Walkman portable music system from audio tapes, through CDs to MP3-based systems. Effectively the same markets are involved, but the technologies are radically different. In the case of the Walkman, Sony probably had little choice but to make these significant product developments. However, product development can be an expensive and high-risk activity for at least two reasons:

- *New strategic capabilities.* Product development typically involves mastering new technologies that may be unfamiliar to the organisation. For example, many banks entered online banking at the beginning of this century, but suffered many setbacks with technologies so radically different to their traditional high street branch means of delivering banking services. Success frequently depended on a willingness to acquire new technological and marketing capabilities, often with the help of specialised IT and e-commerce consultancy firms.[3] Thus product development typically involves heavy investments and high risk of project failures.

- *Project management risk.* Even within fairly familiar domains, product development projects are typically subject to the risk of delays and increased costs due to project complexity and changing project specifications over time. A famous recent case was the €11bn (£7.6bn) Airbus A380 double-decker airline project, which suffered two years of delays in the mid-2000s because of wiring problems. Airbus had managed several new aircraft developments before, but the high degrees of customisation required by each airline customer, and incompatibilities in computer-aided design software, led to greater complexity than the company's project management staff could handle.

Strategies for product development are considered further in Chapter 9.

7.2.4 **Market development**

Market development is where existing products are offered in new markets

If product development is risky and expensive, an alternative strategy is market development. **Market development** involves offering existing products to new markets. Again, the extension of scope is limited. Typically, of course, this may entail some product development as well, if only in terms of packaging or service. Market development might take three forms:

- *New segments.* For example, in the public services, a college might offer its educational services to older students than its traditional intake, perhaps via evening courses.

- *New users.* Here an example would be aluminium, whose original users in packaging and cutlery manufacture are now supplemented by users in aerospace and automobiles.

● *New geographies*. The prime example of this is internationalisation, but the spread of a small retailer into new towns would also be a case.

In all cases, it is essential that market development strategies are based on products or services that meet the *critical success factors* of the new market (see section 2.4.4).

Strategies based on simply offloading traditional products or services in new markets are likely to fail. Moreover, market development faces similar problems as product development. In terms of strategic capabilities, market developers often lack the right marketing skills and brands to make progress in a market with unfamiliar customers. On the management side, the challenge is coordinating between different segments, users and geographies, which might all have different needs. International market development strategy is considered in Chapter 8.

7.2.5 Diversification

Diversification is defined as a strategy that takes an organisation away from both its existing markets and its existing products

Diversification is strictly a strategy that takes the organisation away from both its existing markets and its existing products (box D in Exhibit 7.1). In this sense, it radically increases the organisation's scope. In fact, much diversification is not as extreme as implied by the closed boxes of the Ansoff growth matrix. Box D tends to imply unrelated or conglomerate diversification (see section 7.3.2), but a good deal of diversification in practice involves building on relationships with existing markets or products. Frequently too, market penetration and product development entail some diversifying adjustment of products or markets. Diversification is a matter of degree.

None the less, the Ansoff matrix does make clear that the further the organisation moves from its starting point of existing products and existing markets, the more the organisation has to learn to do. Diversification is just one direction for developing the organisation, and needs to be considered alongside its alternatives. The drivers of diversification, its various forms and the ways it is managed are the main topics of this chapter.

7.3 REASONS FOR DIVERSIFICATION

In terms of the Ansoff matrix, diversification is the most radical strategic direction.[4] Diversification might be chosen for a variety of reasons, some more value creating than others. Three potentially value-creating reasons for diversification are as follows.

● *Efficiency gains* can be made by applying the organisation's existing resources or capabilities to new markets and products or services. These are often described as *economies of scope*, by contrast to economies of scale.[5] If an organisation has underutilised resources or competences that it cannot effectively close or sell to other potential users, it can make sense to use these resources or competences by diversification into a new activity. In other words, there are economies to be gained by extending the scope of the organisation's activities. For example, many universities have large resources in terms of halls of residence, which they must have for their students but which are underutilised out of term-time. These halls of residence are more efficiently used if the universities expand the scope of their activities into conferencing and tourism during vacation periods. Economies of scope may apply to both *tangible* resources, such as halls of residence, and *intangible* resources and competences, such as brands or staff skills. Sometimes these scope advantages are referred to as the benefits of **synergy**,[6] by which is meant that activities or assets are more effective together than apart (the famous 2 + 2 = 5 equation). Thus a film company and a music publisher would be synergistic if they were worth more together than separately. Illustration 7.2 shows how a French company, Zodiac, has diversified following this approach.

> **Synergy** refers to the benefits that are gained where activities or assets complement each other so that their combined effect is greater than the sum of the parts

- *Stretching corporate parenting capabilities* into new markets and products or services can be another source of gain. In a sense, this extends the point above about applying existing competences in new areas. However, this point highlights corporate parenting skills that can otherwise easily be neglected. At the corporate parent level, managers may develop a competence at managing a range of different products and services which can be applied even to businesses which do not share resources at the operational unit level. C.K. Prahalad and R. Bettis have described this set of corporate parenting skills as the 'dominant general management logic', or 'dominant logic' for short.[7] Thus the French conglomerate LVMH includes a wide range of businesses – from champagne, through fashion and perfumes, to financial media – that share very few operational resources or competences. LVMH creates value for these specialised companies by adding parenting skills – for instance, the support of classic brands and the nurturing of highly creative people – that are relevant to all these individual businesses (see section 7.4.1).

- *Increasing market power* can result from having a diverse range of businesses. With many businesses, an organisation can afford to cross-subsidise one business from the surpluses earned by another, in a way that competitors may not be able to. This can give an organisation a competitive advantage for the subsidised business, and the long-run effect may be to drive out other competitors, leaving the organisation with a monopoly from which good profits can then be earned. This was the fear behind the European Commission's refusal to allow General Electric's $43bn (£24bn; €37bn) bid for electronic controls company Honeywell in 2001. General Electric might have bundled its jet engines with Honeywell's aviation electronics in a cheaper package than rival jet engine manufacturers could possibly match. As aircraft manufacturers and airlines increasingly chose the cheaper overall package, rivals could have been driven out of business. General Electric would then have the market power to put up its prices without threat from competition.

There are several other reasons that are often given for diversification, but which are less obviously value creating and sometimes serve managerial interests more than shareholders' interests:

- *Responding to market decline* is one common but doubtful reason for diversification. It is arguable that Microsoft's diversification into electronic games such as the Xbox – whose launch cost $500m (£280m; €415m) in marketing

Illustration 7.2

Zodiac: inflatable diversifications

An organisation may seek the benefits of synergies by building a portfolio of businesses through related diversification.

The Zodiac company was founded near Paris, France, in 1896 by Maurice Mallet just after his first hot-air balloon ascent. For 40 years, Zodiac manufactured only dirigible airships. In 1937, the German Zeppelin *Hindenburg* crashed near New York, which abruptly stopped the development of the market for airships. Because of the extinction of its traditional activity, Zodiac decided to leverage its technical expertise and moved from dirigibles to inflatable boats. This diversification proved to be very successful: in 2004, with over 1 million units sold in 50 years, the Zodiac rubber dinghy (priced at approximately €10,000 (£7,000)) was extremely popular worldwide.

However, because of increasing competition, especially from Italian manufacturers, Zodiac diversified its business interests. In 1978, it took over Aerazur, a company specialising in parachutes, but also in life vests and inflatable life rafts. These products had strong market and technical synergies with rubber boats and their main customers were aircraft manufacturers. Zodiac confirmed this move to a new market in 1987 by the takeover of Air Cruisers, a manufacturer of inflatable escape slides for aircraft. As a consequence, Zodiac became a key supplier to Boeing, McDonnell Douglas and Airbus. Zodiac strengthened this position through the takeover of the two leading manufacturers of aircraft seats: Sicma Aero Seats from France and Weber Aircraft from the USA. In 1997, Zodiac also took over, for €150m, MAG Aerospace, the world leader for aircraft vacuum waste systems. Finally, in 1999, Zodiac took over Intertechnique, a leading player in active components for aircraft (fuel circulation, hydraulics, oxygen and life support, electrical power, flight-deck controls and displays, systems monitoring, etc.). By combining these competences with its traditional expertise in inflatable products, Zodiac launched a new business unit: airbags for the automobile industry.

In parallel to these diversifications, Zodiac strengthened its position in inflatable boats by the takeover of several competitors: Bombard-L'Angevinière in 1980, Sevylor in 1981, Hurricane and Metzeler in 1987.

Finally, Zodiac developed a swimming-pool business. The first product line, back in 1981, was based on inflatable structure technology, and Zodiac later moved – again through takeovers – to rigid above-ground pools, modular in-ground pools, pool cleaners and water purification systems, inflatable beach gear and air mattresses.

In 2003, total sales of the Zodiac group reached €1.48bn with a net profit of €115m. Zodiac was a very international company, with a strong presence in the USA. It was listed on the Paris Stock Exchange and rumours of takeovers from powerful US groups were frequent. However, the family of the founder, institutional investors, the management and the employees together held 55 per cent of the stocks.

Far above the marine and the leisure businesses, aircraft products accounted for almost 75 per cent of the total turnover of the group. Zodiac held a 40 per cent market share of the world market for some airline equipment: for instance, the electrical power systems of the new Airbus A380 were Zodiac products. In 2004, Zodiac even reached Mars: NASA Mars probes *Spirit* and *Opportunity* were equipped with Zodiac equipment, developed by its US subsidiary Pioneer Aerospace.

Prepared by Frédéric Fréry, ESCP-EAP European School of Management.

Questions

1 What were the bases of the synergies underlying each of Zodiac's diversifications?

2 What are the advantages and potential dangers of such a basis of diversification?

alone – is a response to slowing growth in its core software businesses. Shareholders might have preferred the Xbox money to have been handed back to shareholders, leaving Sony and Nintendo to make games, while Microsoft gracefully declined. Microsoft itself defends its various diversifications as a necessary response to convergence in electronic and computer media.

● *Spreading risk* across a range of businesses is another common justification for diversification. However, conventional finance theory is very sceptical about risk spreading by business diversification. It argues that investors can diversify more effectively themselves by investing in a diverse portfolio of quite different companies. Whilst managers might like the security of a diverse range of businesses, investors do not need each of the companies they invest in to be diversified as well – they would prefer managers to concentrate on managing their core business as well as they can. On the other hand, for private businesses, where the owners have a large proportion of their assets tied up in the business, it can make sense to diversify risk across a number of distinct activities, so that if one part is in trouble, the whole business is not pulled down.

● *The expectations of powerful stakeholders*, including top managers, can sometimes drive inappropriate diversification. Under pressure from Wall Street analysts to deliver continued revenue growth, in the late 1990s the US energy company Enron diversified beyond its original interest in energy trading into trading commodities such as petrochemicals, aluminium and even bandwidth.[8] By satisfying the analysts in the short term, this strategy boosted the share price and allowed top management to stay in place. However, it soon transpired that very little of this diversification had been profitable, and in 2001 Enron collapsed in the largest bankruptcy in history.

In order to decide whether or not such reasons make sense and help organisational performance, it is important to be clear about different forms of diversification, in particular the degree of relatedness (or unrelatedness) of business units in a portfolio. The next sections consider related and unrelated diversification.

7.3.1 Related diversification

Related diversification is corporate development beyond current products and markets, but within the capabilities or value network of the organisation

Vertical integration is backward or forward integration into adjacent activities in the value network

Backward integration is development into activities concerned with the inputs into the company's current business

Related diversification can be defined as corporate development beyond current products and markets, but within the capabilities or the value network of the organisation (see sections 3.4 and 3.8.1). For example, Procter and Gamble and Unilever are diversified corporations, but virtually all of their interests are in fast-moving consumer goods distributed through retailers. Their various businesses benefit therefore from shared capabilities in R&D, consumer marketing, building relationships with powerful retailers and global brand development.

The value network provides one way of thinking about different forms of related diversification as shown in Exhibit 7.3:

● **Vertical integration** describes either backward or forward integration into adjacent activities in the value network. **Backward integration** refers to development into activities concerned with the inputs into the company's current business (that is, they are further back in the value network). For example, the acquisition by a car manufacturer of a component supplier would be related

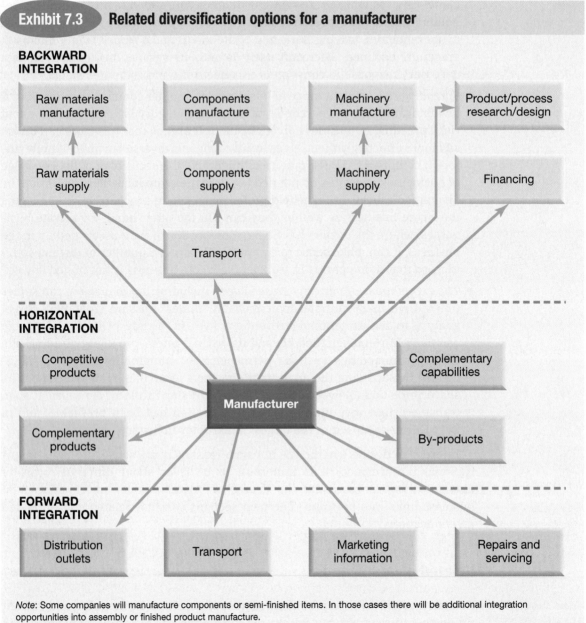

Exhibit 7.3   Related diversification options for a manufacturer

BACKWARD INTEGRATION

| Raw materials manufacture | Components manufacture | Machinery manufacture | Product/process research/design |

| Raw materials supply | Components supply | Machinery supply | Financing |

Transport

HORIZONTAL INTEGRATION

Competitive products

Complementary capabilities

Manufacturer

Complementary products

By-products

FORWARD INTEGRATION

| Distribution outlets | Transport | Marketing information | Repairs and servicing |

Note: Some companies will manufacture components or semi-finished items. In those cases there will be additional integration opportunities into assembly or finished product manufacture.

Forward integration is development into activities which are concerned with a company's outputs

Horizontal integration is development into activities which are complementary to present activities

diversification through backward integration. **Forward integration** refers to development into activities which are concerned with a company's outputs (that is, are further forward in the value system): for a car manufacturer, this might be distribution, repairs and servicing.

● **Horizontal integration** is development into activities which are complementary or adjacent to present activities. For example, the Internet search company Google has spread horizontally into news, images and maps, amongst other services (another example is Zodiac – see Illustration 7.2).

It is important to recognise that capabilities and value links are distinct. A link through the value network does not necessarily imply the existence of capabilities. For example, in the late 1990s some car manufacturers began to integrate forward into repairs and servicing following a value network logic. The car manufacturers thought they could create value by using forward links to ensure a better overall customer experience with their cars. However, the manufacturers rapidly realised that these new businesses involved quite different capabilities: not manufacturing in large factories, but service in many scattered small units. In the end, the absence of relevant capabilities outweighed the potential from the value network links, and the car manufacturers generally withdrew from these forward integration initiatives. Synergies are often harder to identify and more costly to extract in practice than managers like to admit.[9]

It is also important to recognise that relationships have potential disadvantages. Related diversification can be problematic for at least two reasons:

- *corporate-level time and cost* as top managers try to ensure that the benefits of relatedness are achieved through sharing or transfer across business units;
- *business unit complexity*, as business unit managers attend to the needs of other business units, perhaps sharing resources or adjusting marketing strategies, rather than focusing exclusively on the needs of their own unit.

In summary, a simple statement such as 'relatedness matters' has to be questioned.[10] Whilst there is evidence that it may have positive effects on performance (see section 7.3.3), each individual diversification decision needs careful thought about just what relatedness means and what gives rise to performance benefits.

7.3.2 Unrelated diversification

Unrelated diversification is the development of products or services beyond the current capabilities and value network

If related diversification involves development within current capabilities or the current value network, **unrelated diversification** is the development of products or services beyond the current capabilities or value network. Unrelated diversification is often described as a *conglomerate* strategy. Because there are no obvious economies of scope between the different businesses, but there is an obvious cost of the headquarters, unrelated diversified companies' share prices often suffer from what is called the 'conglomerate discount' – in other words, a lower valuation than the individual constituent businesses would have if they stood alone. In 2003, the French conglomerate Vivendi-Universal, with interests spreading from utilities to mobile telephony and media, was trading at an estimated discount of 15–20 per cent. Naturally, shareholders were pressurising management to break the conglomerate up into its more highly valued parts.

However, the case against conglomerates can be exaggerated and there are certainly potential advantages to unrelated diversification in some conditions:

- *Exploiting dominant logics*, rather than concrete operational relationships, can be a source of conglomerate value creation. As at Berkshire Hathaway, a skilled investor such as Warren Buffett, the so-called Oracle of Omaha and one of the richest men in the world, may be able to add value to diverse businesses within his dominant logic.[11] Berkshire Hathaway includes businesses in different areas of manufacturing, insurance, distribution and retailing, but Buffet focuses on mature businesses that he can understand and whose managers he can trust. During the e-business boom of the late 1990s, Buffet deliberately avoided buying high-technology businesses because he knew they were outside his dominant logic. (See Illustration 7.3.)

Illustration 7.3

Berkshire Hathaway Inc.

A portfolio manager may seek to manage a highly diverse set of business units on behalf of its shareholders.

Berkshire Hathaway's Chairman is Warren Buffett, one of the world's richest men, and Charles Munger is Vice Chairman. The businesses in the portfolio are highly diverse. There are insurance businesses, including GEICO, the sixth largest automobile insurer in the USA, manufacturers of carpets, building products, clothing and footwear. There are service businesses (the training of aircraft and ship operators), retailers of home furnishings and fine jewellery, a daily and Sunday newspaper and the largest direct seller of housewear products in the USA.

The annual report of Berkshire Hathaway (2002) provides an insight into its rationale and management. Warren Buffett explains how he and his vice chairman run the business.

Charlie Munger and I think of our shareholders as owner-partners and of ourselves as managing partners. (Because of the size of our shareholdings we are also, for better or worse, controlling partners.) We do not view the company itself as the ultimate owner of our business assets but instead view the company as a conduit through which our shareholders own the assets. . . . Our long term economic goal . . . is to maximise Berkshire's average annual rate of gain in intrinsic business value on a per-share basis. We do not measure the economic significance or performance of Berkshire by its size; we measure by per-share progress.

Our preference would be to reach our goal by directly owning a diversified group of businesses that generate cash and consistently earn above average returns on capital. Our second choice is to own parts of similar businesses, attained primarily through purchases of marketable common stocks by our insurance subsidiaries. . . . Charlie and I are interested only in acquisitions that we believe will raise the per-share intrinsic value of Berkshire's stock.

Regardless of price we have no interest at all in selling any good businesses that Berkshire owns. We are also very reluctant to sell sub-par businesses as long as we expect them to generate at least some cash and as long as we feel good about their managers and labour relations. . . . Gin rummy managerial behaviour (discard your least promising business at each turn) is not our style. We would rather have our overall results penalised a bit than engaged in that kind of behaviour.

Buffett then explains how they manage their subsidiary businesses:

. . . we delegate almost to the point of abdication: though Berkshire has about 45,000 employees, only 12 of these are at headquarters. . . . Charlie and I mainly attend to capital allocation and the care and feeding of our key managers. Most of these managers are happiest when they are left alone to run their businesses and that is customarily just how we leave them. That puts them in charge of all operating decisions and of despatching the excess cash they generate to headquarters. By sending it to us, they don't get diverted by the various enticements that would come their way were they responsible for deploying the cash their businesses throw off. Further more, Charlie and I are exposed to a much wider range of possibilities for investing these funds than any of our managers could find in his/her own industry.

Questions

1 In what ways does Berkshire Hathaway conform (and not conform) to the archetypal portfolio manager described in section 7.4.2?

2 Using the checklist explained in section 7.4, suggest how and in what ways Berkshire Hathaway may or may not add value to its shareholders.

- *Countries with underdeveloped markets* can be fertile ground for conglomerates. Where external capital and labour markets do not yet work well, conglomerates offer a substitute mechanism for allocating and developing capital or managerial talent within their own organisational boundaries. For example, Korean conglomerates (the chaebol) were successful in the rapid growth phase of the Korean economy partly because they were able to mobilise investment and develop managers in a way that standalone companies in South Korea traditionally were unable to. Also, the strong cultural cohesion amongst managers in these chaebol reduced the coordination and monitoring costs that would be necessary in a Western conglomerate, where managers would be trusted less.[12] The same may be true today in other fast-growing economies that still have underdeveloped capital and labour markets.

It is important also to recognise that the distinction between related and unrelated diversification is often a matter of degree. As in the case of Berkshire Hathaway, although there are very few operational relationships between the constituent businesses, there is a relationship in terms of similar parenting requirements (see section 7.4.4). As in the case of the car manufacturers diversifying forwards into apparently related businesses such as repairs and servicing, operational relationships can turn out to be much less valuable than they appear at first. The blurred boundary between related and unrelated diversification is important for considering the performance consequences of diversification.

7.3.3 Diversification and performance

Because most large corporations today are diversified, but also because diversification can sometimes be in management's self-interest, many scholars and policy makers have been concerned to establish whether diversified companies really perform better than undiversified companies. After all, it would be deeply troubling if large corporations were diversifying simply to spread risk for managers, to save managerial jobs in declining businesses or to preserve the image of growth, as in the case of Enron.

Research studies of diversification have generally found some performance benefits, with *related diversifiers* outperforming both firms that remain *specialised* and those which have *unrelated* diversified strategies.[13] In other words, the diversification–performance relationship tends to follow an inverted (or upside down) U-shape, as in Exhibit 7.4. The implication is that some diversification is good – but not too much.

However, these performance studies produce statistical averages. Some related diversification strategies fail – as in the case of the vertically integrating car manufacturers – while some conglomerates succeed – as in the case of Berkshire Hathaway. The case against unrelated diversification is not solid, and effective dominant logics or particular national contexts can play in its favour. The conclusion from the performance studies is that, although on average related diversification pays better than unrelated, any diversification strategy needs rigorous questioning on its particular merits.

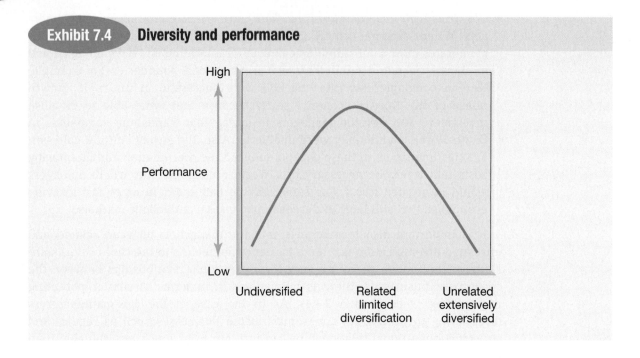

Exhibit 7.4 **Diversity and performance**

7.4 VALUE CREATION AND THE CORPORATE PARENT

Given the doubtful benefits of conglomerate diversification strategies, it is clear that some corporate parents do not add value. During 2006, two large US conglomerates, Tyco and Cendant, decided to break themselves up voluntarily, recognising that their subsidiary business units would be more valuable apart than together under their parenting. In the public sector too, units such as schools or hospitals are increasingly being given freedom from parenting authorities, because independence is seen as more effective. Some theorists even challenge the notion of corporate-level strategy altogether, the subject of the key debate in Illustration 7.6. This section examines how corporate parents can both add and destroy value, and considers three different parenting approaches that can be effective.

7.4.1 Value-adding and value-destroying activities of corporate parents[14]

Any corporate parent needs to demonstrate that it creates more value than it costs. This applies to both commercial and public sector organisations. For public sector organisations, privatisation or outsourcing is likely to be the consequence of failure to demonstrate value. Companies whose shares are traded freely on the stock markets face a further challenge. They must demonstrate that they create more value than any other rival corporate parent could create. Failure to do so is likely to lead to a hostile takeover or break-up (see Illustration 7.4 for a possible break-up of Cadbury Schweppes). Rival companies that think they can create

Illustration 7.4

A sweet deal for Nelson Peltz?

Financiers can make money out of over-diversified corporations, and managers have to respond.

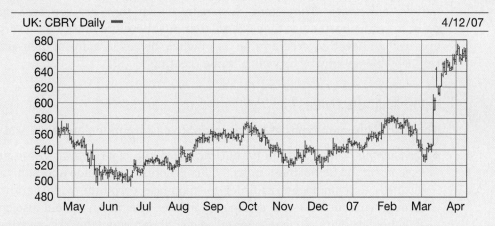

UK: CBRY Daily —   4/12/07

Figure 1 Cadbury Schweppes share price, 2006–2007

Source: www.bigcharts.com. Marketwatch.Online by BigCharts.com. Copyright 2007 by Dow Jones & Company, Inc. Reproduced with permission of Dow Jones & Company, Inc. in format Textbook via Copyright Clearance Center.

In March 2007, American financier Nelson Peltz used his hedge fund Trian Fund Management LP to take a 3 per cent stake in Cadbury Schweppes PLC. Peltz was known as an activist shareholder, keen to extract maximum shareholder value through pressuring management or breaking up underperforming groups. Over the next few days, the Cadbury Schweppes share price rose by 15 per cent (see Figure 1).

Since 1969, Cadbury Schweppes had combined the chocolate and confectionary businesses of the original Cadbury company (founded 1824) with the carbonated drinks business of Schweppes (founded 1790). Cadbury's major confectionary brands included Dairy Milk, Creme Eggs and Dentyne gum. The company was the largest confectionery producer in the world, with 10 per cent market share, just ahead of Mars and Nestlé. The Schweppes business owned 7 Up and Dr Pepper, as well as the original Schweppes drinks. However, in its main market of the USA, it was still a distant number three to Coca-Cola and PepsiCo, who together accounted for 75 per cent of the carbonated drinks market. Cadbury Schweppes management were investing substantially in the drinks business, having bought up major bottling facilities during 2006. Todd Stitzer, the Cadbury Schweppes Chief Executive, had played a leading role in acquiring Dr Pepper and 7 Up back in 1995.

Two days after the announcement of Peltz's stake, Cadbury Schweppes stated it was actively considering the demerger of its drinks business. Options that were being examined for the drinks business included: making it a stand-alone company; selling the business outright to another company or private equity house; and floating a minority stake in the business and, over time, selling the remaining shares.

Soon after, rumours began to emerge of a possible merger between Cadbury Schweppes and Hershey, the American confectioner with over 5 per cent of the world confectionery market. Such a deal would give the merged company a commanding lead over competitors and substantial leverage over powerful retailers. Cadbury was weak in the US confectionary market, while Hershey was weak in Europe.

Sources: *Wall Street Journal* and *Financial Times*, various dates.

Questions

1 Why has the Cadbury Schweppes share price behaved in the way it has?

2 Why do you think Cadbury Schweppes had not acted earlier on the demerger option?

more value out of the business units can bid for the company's shares, on the expectation of either running the businesses better or selling them off to other potential parents. If the rival's bid is more attractive and credible than what the current parent can promise, shareholders will back it at the expense of incumbent management.

In this sense, competition takes place between different corporate parents for the right to own and control businesses. In the competitive market for the control of businesses, corporate parents must show that they have 'parenting advantage', on the same principle that business units must demonstrate competitive advantage. They must demonstrate that they are the best possible parents for the businesses they control. Parents therefore must have a very clear approach to how they create value. In practice, however, many of their activities can be value destroying as well as value creating.

Value-adding activities[15]

There are four main types of activity by which a corporate parent can add value.

- *Envisioning*. The corporate parent can provide a clear overall vision or *strategic intent* for its business units.[16] This vision should guide and motivate the business unit managers in order to maximise corporate-wide performance through commitment to a common purpose. The vision should also provide stakeholders with a *clear external image* about what the organisation as a whole is about: this can reassure shareholders about the rationale for having a diversified strategy in the first place. Finally, a clear vision provides a *discipline* on the corporate parent to stop it wandering into inappropriate activities or taking on unnecessary costs.

- *Coaching and facilitating*. The corporate parent can help business unit managers *develop strategic capabilities*, by coaching them to improve their skills and confidence. It can also facilitate cooperation and sharing across the business units, so improving the *synergies* from being within the same corporate organisation. Corporate-wide management courses are one effective means of achieving these objectives, as bringing managers across the business to learn management skills also provides an opportunity for them to build relationships between each other and see opportunities for cooperation.

- *Providing central services and resources*. The centre is obviously a provider of capital for *investment*. The centre can also provide central services such as treasury, tax and human resource advice, which if centralised can have *sufficient scale* to be efficient and to build up *relevant expertise*. Centralised services often have greater *leverage*: for example, combining the purchases of separate business units increases their bargaining power for shared inputs such as energy. This leverage can be helpful in *brokering* with external bodies, such as government regulators, or other companies in negotiating alliances. Finally, the centre can have an important role in managing expertise within the corporate whole, for instance by *transferring managers* across the business units or by creating shared *knowledge management* systems.

- *Intervening*. Finally, the corporate parent can also intervene within its business units in order to ensure appropriate performance. The corporate parent should be able closely to *monitor* business unit performance and *improve performance* either by replacing weak managers or by assisting them in turning around their businesses. The parent can also *challenge and develop* the strategic ambitions of business units, so that satisfactorily performing businesses are encouraged to perform even better.

Value-destroying activities

However, there are also three broad ways in which the corporate parent can inadvertently destroy value:

● *Adding management costs*. Most simply, the staff and facilities of the corporate centre are expensive. The corporate centre typically has the best-paid managers and the most luxurious offices. It is the actual businesses that have to generate the revenues that pay for them. If their costs are greater than the value they create, then the corporate centre's managers are net value destroying.

● *Adding bureaucratic complexity*. As well as these direct financial costs, there is the 'bureaucratic fog' created by an additional layer of management and the need to coordinate with sister businesses. These typically slow down managers' responses to issues and lead to compromises between the interests of individual businesses.

● *Obscuring financial performance*. One danger in a large diversified company is that the underperformance of weak businesses can be obscured. Weak businesses might be cross-subsidised by the stronger ones. Internally, the possibility of hiding weak performance diminishes the incentives for business unit managers to strive as hard as they can for their businesses: they have a parental safety net. Externally, shareholders and financial analysts cannot easily judge the performance of individual units within the corporate whole. Diversified companies' share prices are often marked down, because shareholders prefer the 'pure plays' of stand-alone units, where weak performance cannot be hidden.

These dangers suggest clear paths for corporate parents that wish to avoid value destruction. They should keep a close eye on centre costs, both financial and bureaucratic, ensuring that they are no more than required by their corporate strategy. They should also do all they can to promote financial transparency, so that business units remain under pressure to perform and shareholders are confident that there are no hidden disasters.

Overall, there are many ways in which corporate parents can add value. It is, of course, difficult to pursue them all and some are hard to mix with others. For example, a corporate parent that does a great deal of top-down intervening is less likely to be seen by its managers as a helpful coach and facilitator. Business unit managers will concentrate on maximising their own individual performance rather than looking out for ways to cooperate with other business unit managers for the greater good of the whole. For this reason, corporate parenting roles tend to fall into three main types, each coherent within itself but distinct from the others.[17] These three types of corporate parenting role are summarised in Exhibit 7.5.

Exhibit 7.5 **Portfolio managers, synergy managers and parental developers**

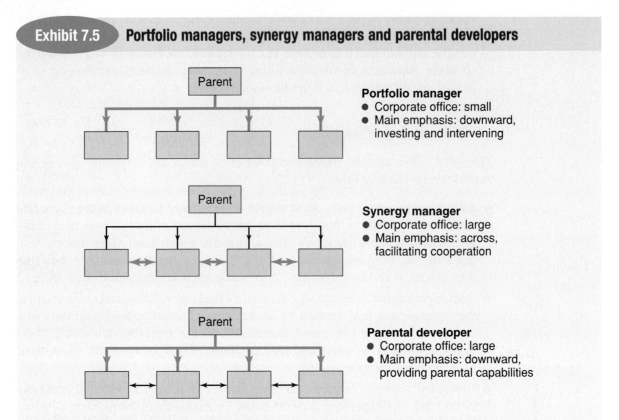

Portfolio manager
● Corporate office: small
● Main emphasis: downward, investing and intervening

Synergy manager
● Corporate office: large
● Main emphasis: across, facilitating cooperation

Parental developer
● Corporate office: large
● Main emphasis: downward, providing parental capabilities

Source: Adapted from M. Goold, A. Campbell and M. Alexander, *Corporate Level Strategy*, Wiley, 1994.

7.4.2 The portfolio manager

A portfolio manager is a corporate parent acting as an agent on behalf of financial markets and shareholders

The **portfolio manager** operates as an active investor in a way that shareholders in the stock market are either too dispersed or too inexpert to be able to do. In effect, the portfolio manager is acting as an agent on behalf of financial markets and shareholders with a view to extracting more value from the various businesses than they could achieve themselves. Its role is to identify and acquire undervalued assets or businesses and improve them. The portfolio manager might do this, for example, by acquiring another corporation, divesting low-performing businesses within it and intervening to improve the performance of those with potential. Such corporations may not be much concerned about the relatedness (see sections 7.2.1 and 7.2.2) of the business units in their portfolio, typically adopting a conglomerate strategy. Their role is not to get closely involved in the routine management of the businesses, only to act over short periods of time to improve performance. In terms of the value-creating activities identified earlier, the portfolio manager concentrates on intervening and the provision (or withdrawal) of investment.

Portfolio managers seek to keep the cost of the centre low, for example by having a small corporate staff with few central services, leaving the business units alone so that their chief executives have a high degree of autonomy. They set clear financial targets for those chief executives, offering high rewards if they achieve them and likely loss of position if they do not. Such corporate parents can, of course, manage quite a large number of such businesses because they are not directly managing the everyday strategies of those businesses. Rather they are acting from above, setting financial targets, making central evaluations about the well-being and future prospects of such businesses, and investing, intervening or divesting accordingly.

Some argue that the days of the portfolio manager are gone. Improving financial markets mean that the scope for finding and investing cheaply in underperforming companies is much reduced. However, some portfolio managers remain and are successful. Private equity firms such as Apax Partners or Blackstone are a new way of operating a portfolio management style, typically investing in, improving and then divesting companies in loosely knit portfolios. For example, in 2006, Apax had investments in 360 separate businesses at different stages of development, ranging from Philips' former semiconductor division to Tommy Hilfiger clothing. Illustration 7.3 includes a description of the portfolio parenting approach of Warren Buffett at Berkshire Hathaway.

7.4.3 The synergy manager

The **synergy manager** is a corporate parent seeking to enhance value across business units by managing synergies across business units

Obtaining synergy is often seen as the prime *raison d'être* of the corporate parent.[18] Synergies are likely to be particularly rich in the case of related diversification. In terms of value-creating activities, the focus of a **synergy manager** is threefold: envisioning to build a common purpose; facilitating cooperation across businesses; and providing central services and resources. For example, at Apple, Steve Jobs' vision of his personal computers being the digital hub of the new digital lifestyle guides managers across the iMac computer business, iTunes and iPod to ensure seamless connections between the fast-developing offerings. The result is enhanced value through better customer experience. American giant GE facilitates cooperation by investing heavily in its management training activities, making it easier for managers to pass value-creating knowledge between businesses. A metals company diversified into both steel and aluminium might centralise its energy procurement, gaining synergy benefits through increased bargaining power over suppliers.

However, the problems in achieving such synergistic benefits are similar to those in achieving the benefits of relatedness (see section 7.3.1). Three problems are worth highlighting here:

● *Excessive costs*. The benefits in sharing and cooperation need to outweigh the costs of undertaking such integration, both direct financial costs and opportunity costs. Managing synergistic relationships tends to involve expensive investments in management time.

● *Overcoming self-interest*. Managers in the business units have to want to cooperate. Especially where managers are rewarded largely according to the performance of their own particular business unit, they are likely to be unwilling to sacrifice their time and resources for the common good.

● *Illusory synergies*. It is easy to overestimate the value of skills or resources to other businesses. This is particularly common when the corporate centre needs to justify a new venture or the acquisition of a new company. Claimed synergies often prove illusory when managers actually have to put them into practice.

The failure of many companies to extract expected synergies from their businesses has led to growing scepticism about the notion of synergy. Synergistic benefits are not as easy to achieve as would appear. It has proven very hard for Daimler Chrysler to find the promised synergies between its luxury Mercedes car business and mass market manufacturer Chrysler. However, synergy continues to be a common theme in corporate-level strategy, as Illustration 7.2 on Zodiac exemplifies.

7.4.4 The parental developer[19]

The **parental developer** is a corporate parent seeking to employ its own competences as a parent to add value to its businesses and build parenting skills that are appropriate for its portfolio of business units

The **parental developer** seeks to employ its own capabilities as a parent to add value to its businesses. This is not so much about how the parent can develop benefits *across* business units or transfer capabilities between business units, as in the case of managing synergy. Rather parental developers focus on the resources or capabilities they have as parents which they can transfer *downwards* to enhance the potential of business units. For example, a parent could have a valuable brand (as in the case of Virgin), or specialist skills in financial management or product development. If such parenting capabilities exist, corporate managers then need to identify a *parenting opportunity*: a business which is not fulfilling its potential but which could be improved by applying the parenting capability, such as branding or product development. Such parenting opportunities are therefore more common in the case of related rather than unrelated diversified strategies and are likely to involve exchanges of managers and other resources across the businesses. Key value-creating activities for the parent will be the provision of central services and resources.

The capabilities that parents have will vary. Royal Dutch Shell would argue that it is not just its huge financial muscle that matters but also that it is adept at negotiating with governments, as well as developing high-calibre internationally mobile executives who can work almost anywhere in the world within a Shell corporate framework. These capabilities are especially valuable in allowing it to develop businesses globally. 3M is single-mindedly concerned with inculcating a focus on innovation in its businesses. It tries to ensure a corporate culture based on this, set clear innovation targets for its businesses and elevate the standing of technical personnel concerned with innovation. Unilever has increasingly sought to focus on developing its core expertise in global branding and marketing in the fast-moving consumer goods market, with state-of-the-art R&D facilities to back it up. It would argue that this is where it can add greatest value to its businesses, and this belief has guided its investments and divestments over the years.

Managing an organisation on this basis does, however, pose at least four challenges:

● *Identifying parental capabilities*. A big challenge for the corporate parent is being sure about just how it can add value to business units. If the value-adding capabilities of the parent are wrongly identified then its contribution will be only counter-productive. There needs to be some hard evidence of such value-adding capabilities.

● *Parental focus*. If the corporate parent identifies that it has value-adding capabilities in particular and limited ways, the implication is that it should not be providing services in other ways, or if it does they should be provided at minimal cost. Corporate executives should focus their energy and time on activities where they really do add value. Some central services could be outsourced to specialist companies who can do it better.

- *The 'crown jewel' problem.* Some diversified companies have business units in their portfolios which are performing well but to which the parent adds little value. These can become 'crown jewels', to which corporate parents become excessively attached. The logic of the parental development approach is if the centre cannot add value, it is just a cost and therefore destroying value. Parental developers should divest businesses they do not add value to, even profitable ones. Funds raised by selling a profitable business can be reinvested in businesses where the parent can add value.

- *Sufficient 'feel'.* If the logic of the parental developer is to be followed then the executives of the corporate parent must also have 'sufficient feel' or understanding of the businesses within the portfolio to know where they can

Exhibit 7.6 **Value-adding potential of corporate rationales**

Value-adding activities (see section 7.4.1)	Portfolio manager	Synergy manager	Parental developer
Envisioning			
Developing strategic intent/mission		●	●
Clear external image		●	●
Setting disciplinary expectations	●		
Coaching and training			
Developing strategic capabilities		●	
Achieving synergies		●	
Central services and resources			
Investment	●	●	●
Scale advantages		●	
Transferring capabilities and knowledge		●	
Specialist expertise			●
Leverage and brokering		●	
Intervening			
Monitoring performance	●		
Improving business and performance			●
Challenging/developing strategy		●	●

add value and where they cannot: this is an issue taken up in section 7.5.3 in relation to the logic of portfolios.

The three roles of the parent can be considered in terms of the possible value-adding roles of corporate parents suggested in section 7.4.1. Exhibit 7.6 identifies how the main value-adding roles of corporate parents might differ in line with the discussion in sections 7.4.2–7.4.4.

7.5 PORTFOLIO MATRICES

The discussion in section 7.4 was about the rationales that corporate parents might adopt for the management of a multi-business organisation. This section introduces models by which managers can manage the various parts of their portfolio differently, or add and subtract business units within the portfolio. Each model gives more or less attention to the following three criteria:

● the *balance* of the portfolio, for example in relation to its markets and the needs of the corporation;

● the *attractiveness* of the business units in terms of how strong they are individually and how profitable their markets or industries are likely to be; and

● the *fit* that the business units have with each other in terms of potential synergies or the extent to which the corporate parent will be good at looking after them.

7.5.1 The growth/share (or BCG) matrix[20]

KEY CONCEPT
www.pearsoned.co.uk/ecs

BCG and portfolio matrices

One of the most common and long-standing ways of conceiving of the balance of a portfolio of businesses is the Boston Consulting Group (BCG) matrix (see Exhibit 7.7). Here market share and market growth are critical variables for determining attractiveness and balance. High market share and high growth are, of course, attractive. However, the BCG matrix also warns that high growth demands heavy investment, for instance to expand capacity or develop brands. There needs to be a balance within the portfolio, so that there are some low-growth businesses that are making sufficient surplus to fund the investment needs of higher growth businesses.

The growth/share axes of the BCG matrix define four sorts of business:

A **star** is a business unit which has a high market share in a growing market

● A **star** is a business unit which has a high market share in a growing market. The business unit may be spending heavily to keep up with growth, but high market share should yield sufficient profits to make it more or less self-sufficient in terms of investment needs.

A **question mark** (or problem child) is a business unit in a growing market, but without a high market share

● A **question mark** (or problem child) is a business unit in a growing market, but not yet with high market share. Developing question marks into stars, with high market share, takes heavy investment. Many question marks fail to develop, so the BCG advises corporate parents to nurture several at a time. It is important to make sure that some question marks develop into stars, as existing stars eventually become cash cows and cash cows may decline into dogs.

Exhibit 7.7   The growth share (or BCG) matrix

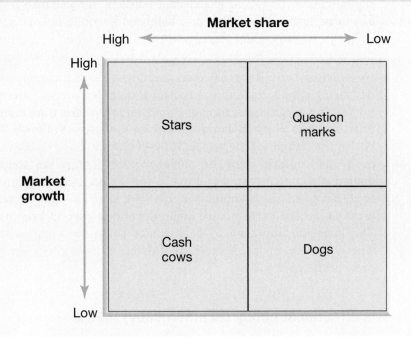

A **cash cow** is a business unit with a high market share in a mature market

- A **cash cow** is a business unit with a high market share in a mature market. However, because growth is low, investment needs are less, while high market share means that the business unit should be profitable. The cash cow should then be a cash provider, helping to fund investments in question marks.

Dogs are business units with a low share in static or declining markets

- **Dogs** are business units with a low share in static or declining markets and are thus the worst of all combinations. They may be a cash drain and use up a disproportionate amount of company time and resources. The BCG usually recommends divestment or closure.

The BCG matrix has several advantages. It provides a good way of visualising the different needs and potential of all the diverse businesses within the corporate portfolio. It warns corporate parents of the financial demands of what might otherwise look like a desirable portfolio of high-growth businesses. It also reminds corporate parents that stars are likely eventually to wane. Finally, it provides a useful discipline to business unit managers, underlining the fact that the corporate parent ultimately owns the surplus resources they generate and can allocate them according to what is best for the corporate whole. Cash cows should not hoard their profits. Incidentally, surplus resources may not only be investment funds: the corporate parent can also reallocate business unit managers who are not fully utilised by low-growth cash cows or dogs.

However, there are at least three potential problems with the BCG matrix:

- *Definitional vagueness*. It can be hard to decide what high and low growth or share mean in particular situations. Managers are often keen to define themselves as 'high share' by defining their market in a particularly narrow way (for example, ignoring relevant international markets).

● *Capital market assumptions*. The notion that a corporate parent needs a balanced portfolio to finance investment from internal sources (cash cows) assumes that capital cannot be raised in external markets, for instance by issuing shares or raising loans. The notion of a balanced portfolio may be more relevant in countries where capital markets are underdeveloped or in private companies that wish to minimise dependence on external shareholders or banks.

● *Unkind to animals*. Both cash cows and dogs receive ungenerous treatment, the first being simply milked, the second terminated or cast out of the corporate home. This treatment can cause *motivation problems*, as managers in these units see little point in working hard for the sake of other businesses. There is also the danger of the *self-fulfilling prophecy*. Cash cows will become dogs even more quickly than the model expects if they are simply milked and denied adequate investment. Finally, the notion that a dog can be simply sold or closed down also assumes that there are *no ties to other business units* in the portfolio, whose performance might depend in part on keeping the dog alive. This portfolio approach to dogs works better for conglomerate strategies, where divestments or closures are unlikely to have knock-on effects on other parts of the portfolio.

7.5.2   The directional policy (GE–McKinsey) matrix

The **directional policy matrix** positions SBUs according to (i) how attractive the relevant market is in which they are operating, and (ii) the competitive strength of the SBU in that market

Another way to consider a portfolio of businesses is by means of the *directional policy matrix*[21] which categorises business units into those with good prospects and those with less good prospects. The matrix was originally developed by McKinsey & Co. consultants in order to help the American conglomerate General Electric manage its portfolio of business units. Specifically, the **directional policy matrix** positions business units according to (i) how attractive the relevant market is in which they are operating, and (ii) the competitive strength of the SBU in that market. Attractiveness can be identified by PESTEL or five forces analyses; business unit strength can be defined by competitor analysis (for instance, the strategy canvas): see Chapter 2. Some analysts also choose to show graphically how large the market is for a given business unit's activity, and even the market share of that business unit, as shown in Exhibit 7.8. For example, managers in a firm with the portfolio shown in Exhibit 7.8 will be concerned that they have relatively low shares in the largest and most attractive market, whereas their greatest strength is in a market with only medium attractiveness and smaller markets with little long-term attractiveness.

The matrix also provides a way of considering appropriate corporate-level strategies given the positioning of the business units, as shown in Exhibit 7.9. It suggests that the businesses with the highest growth potential and the greatest strength are those in which to invest for growth. Those that are the weakest and in the least attractive markets should be divested or 'harvested' (that is, used to yield as much cash as possible before divesting).

The directional policy matrix is more complex than the BCG matrix. However, it can have two advantages. First, unlike the simpler four-box BCG matrix, the nine cells of the directional policy matrix acknowledge the possibility of a difficult middle ground. Here managers have to be carefully selective. In this sense, the directional policy matrix is less mechanistic than the BCG matrix,

Exhibit 7.8   Directional policy (GE–McKinsey) matrix

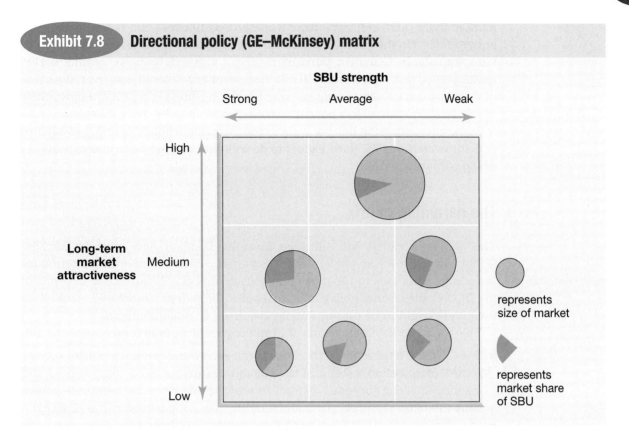

encouraging open debate on less clear-cut cases. Second, the two axes of the directional policy matrix are not based on single measures (that is, market share and market growth). Business strength can derive from many other factors than

Exhibit 7.9   Strategy guidelines based on the directional policy matrix

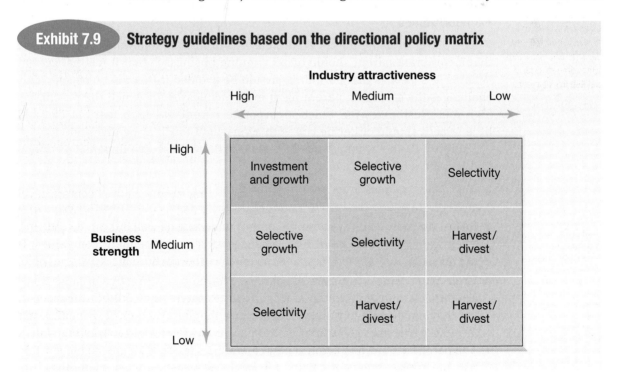

market share, and industry attractiveness does not just boil down to industry growth rates. On the other hand, the directional policy matrix shares some problems with the BCG matrix, particularly about vague definitions, capital market assumptions, motivation and self-fulfilling prophecy. Overall, however, the value of the matrix is to help managers invest in the businesses which are most likely to pay off.

So far the discussion has been about the logic of portfolios in terms of balance and attractiveness. The third logic is to do with 'fit' with the particular capabilities of the corporate parent.

7.5.3 The parenting matrix

The *parenting matrix* (or Ashridge Portfolio Display) developed by Michael Goold and Andrew Campbell introduces parental fit as an important criterion for including businesses in the portfolio.[22] Businesses may be attractive in terms of the BCG or directional policy matrices, but if the parent cannot add value, then the parent ought to be cautious about acquiring or retaining them.

There are two key dimensions of fit in the parenting matrix (see Exhibit 7.10):

- *'Feel'*. This is a measure of the fit between each business unit's *critical success factors* (see section 2.4.4) and the capabilities (in terms of competences and resources) of the corporate parent. In other words, does the corporate parent have the necessary 'feel', or understanding, for the businesses it will parent?
- *'Benefit'*. This measures the fit between the *parenting opportunities*, or needs, of business units and the capabilities of the parent. Parenting opportunities are about the upside, areas in which good parenting can benefit the business (for instance, by bringing marketing expertise). For the benefit to be realised, of course, the parent must have the right capabilities to match the parenting opportunities.

The power of using these two dimensions of fit is as follows. It is easy to see that a corporate parent should avoid running businesses that it has no *feel* for. What is less clear is that parenting should be avoided if there is no *benefit*. This challenges the corporate parenting of even businesses for which the parent has high feel. Businesses for which a corporate parent has high feel but can add little benefit should either be run with a very light touch or be divested.

Exhibit 7.10 shows four kinds of business along these two dimensions of feel and benefit:

- *Heartland* business units are ones which the parent understands well and can continue to add value to. They should be at the core of future strategy.
- *Ballast* business units are ones the parent understands well but can do little for. They would probably be at least as successful as independent companies. If not divested, they should be spared as much corporate bureaucracy as possible.
- *Value trap* business units are dangerous. They appear attractive because there are opportunities to add value (for instance, marketing could be improved), but they are deceptively attractive, because the parent's lack of feel will result in more harm than good (that is, the parent lacks the right marketing skills). The parent will need to acquire new capabilities if it is to be able to move value trap businesses into the heartland. It might be easier to divest to another corporate parent who could add value, and will pay well for the chance.

Illustration 7.5

Splitting the Home Office

After 225 years of combining justice and national security responsibilities, the British 'Home Office' was declared no longer 'fit for purpose'.

Since the eighteenth century, the British Home Office (roughly equivalent to many countries' Interior Ministry) had been an unusual combination of both justice and national security functions. By 2007, it had 70,000 civil servants responsible for running the justice system (courts and so on), the police, the prisons, the probation service, counter-terrorism, intelligence, drug control, passports, identity cards, border controls, the asylum system, anti-social behaviour policy and equality and diversity policy (concerned with race, gender, the disabled, etc.).

But the Home Office was seen as a failed organisation. During 2006, the Home Office had been involved in many apparent fiascos. It was revealed that records had not been kept on British citizens committing crimes abroad, that there was no tally on escaped convicts, that foreign criminals were not being deported, that there was a backlog for the consideration of asylum seekers running to many thousands, that convicted criminals were being kept long term in police cells because of a lack of suitable prison accommodation, and so on. A former Home Office adviser commented:

This department has become too big to manage. Its left hand does not know what its right is doing. The government can no longer avoid confronting the hard question of whether it is safe to leave it intact. It has turned into a dinosaur with a brain too small to co-ordinate its gigantic body.

Charles Clarke, Home Secretary (Home Office Minister), was forced to resign. His successor,

John Reid, declared the Home Office as 'unfit for purpose'. The Home Office was split. A new Ministry for Justice took charge of running the criminal justice system, with responsibilities for criminal law, sentencing and the prison and probation services. The Home Office meanwhile took on additional tasks in counter-terrorism, while retaining its other existing responsibilities such as the police, crime reduction, immigration and asylum, and identity and passports. The change was widely summarised as 'separating catching criminals from sentencing them'.

Ousted minister Charles Clarke commented on the changes to his old department: 'I think the problem with the department is a lack of coordination between its various elements. Dividing the Home Office will make those problems far worse.'

Sources: *Guardian*, 5 February (2007); *The Economist*, 31 March (2007).

Questions

1 How could the old Home Office 'add value' to its constituent parts? How might it 'destroy value'?

2 What corporate parenting style is appropriate for the new Home Office (portfolio management, synergy management or parental developer)?

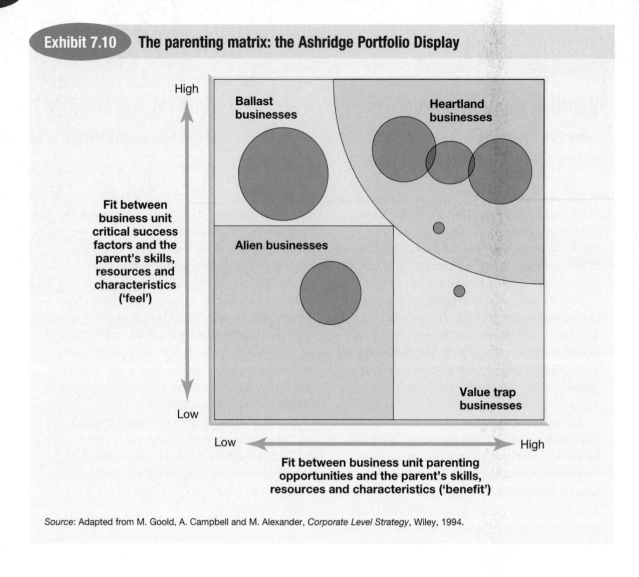

Exhibit 7.10 The parenting matrix: the Ashridge Portfolio Display

Source: Adapted from M. Goold, A. Campbell and M. Alexander, *Corporate Level Strategy*, Wiley, 1994.

● *Alien* business units are clear misfits. They offer little opportunity to add value and the parent does not understand them anyway. Exit is definitely the best strategy.

This approach to considering corporate portfolios places the emphasis firmly on how the parent benefits the business units. It requires careful analysis of both parenting capabilities and business unit parenting needs. The parenting matrix can therefore assist hard decisions where either high feel or high parenting opportunities tempt the corporate parent to acquire or retain businesses. Parents should concentrate on actual or potential heartland businesses, where there is both high feel and high benefit.

The concept of fit has equal relevance in the public sector (see Illustration 7.5). The implication is that public sector managers should control directly only those services and activities for which they have special managerial expertise. Other services should be outsourced or set up as independent agencies. Whilst outsourcing, privatising and setting up independent agencies are often driven as much by political dogma as by corporate-level strategy analysis (see Illustration 7.6), the trend in many countries recently has been in this direction.

Illustration 7.6

Why have corporate-level strategies anyway?

Do we really need diversified corporations?

The notion of corporate strategy assumes that corporations should own and control businesses in a range of markets or products. But 'transaction cost' economist Oliver Williamson believes that diversified corporations should only exist in the presence of 'market failures'.[1] If markets worked well, there would be no need for business units to be coordinated through managerial structures. Business units could be independent, coordinating where necessary by simple transactions in the marketplace. The 'invisible hand' of the market could replace the 'visible hand' of managers at corporate headquarters. There would be no 'corporate strategy'.

Market failures favouring the diversified corporation occur for two reasons:

- '*Bounded rationality*'. People cannot know everything that is going on in the market, so perfectly rational market transactions are impossible. Information, for instance on quality and costs, can sometimes be better inside the corporate fold.

- '*Opportunism*'. Independent businesses trading between each other may behave opportunistically, for example by cheating on delivery or quality promises. Cheating can sometimes be policed and punished more easily within a corporate hierarchy.

According to Williamson, activities should only be brought into the corporation when the 'transaction costs' of coping with bounded rationality (gaining information) and opportunism (guarding against cheats) are lower inside the corporate hierarchy than they would be if simply relying on transactions in the marketplace.

This comparison of the transaction costs of markets and hierarchies has powerful implications for trends in product diversification:

- Improving capital markets may reduce the relative information advantages of conglomerates in managing a set of unrelated businesses. As markets get better at capturing information there will be less need for conglomerates, something that may account for the recent decline in conglomerates in many economies.

- Improving protection of intellectual property rights may increase the incentives for corporations to license out their technologies to companies, rather than trying to do everything themselves. If the prospect of collecting royalties improves, there is less advantage for corporations keeping everything in-house.

Thus fewer market failures also mean narrower product scope.

Williamson's 'transaction cost' view puts a heavy burden on corporations to justify themselves. Two defences are possible. First, knowledge is hard to trade in the market. Buyers can only know the value of new knowledge once they have already bought it. Because they can trust each other, colleagues in sister business units within the same corporation are better at transferring knowledge than independent companies are in the open market.[2] Second, corporations are not just about minimising the costs of information and cheating, but also about maximising the value of the combined resources. Bringing creative people together in a collective enterprise enhances knowledge exchange, innovation and motivation. Corporations are value creators as well as cost minimisers.[3]

Sources:
1. O.E. Williamson, 'Strategy research: governance and competence perspectives', *Strategic Management Journal*, vol. 12 (1998), pp. 75–94.
2. B. Kogut and U. Zander, 'What firms do? Coordination, identity and learning', *Organization Science*, vol. 7, no. 5 (1996), pp. 502–519.
3. S. Ghoshal, C. Bartlett and P. Moran, 'A new manifesto for management', *Sloan Management Review*, Spring (1999), pp. 9–20.

Question

Consider a diversified corporation such as Cadbury Schweppes or Unilever: what kinds of hard-to-trade knowledge might it be able to transfer between product and country subsidiaries and is such knowledge likely to be of increasing or decreasing importance?

SUMMARY

- Many corporations comprise several, sometimes many, business units. Decisions above the level of business units are the concern of what in this chapter is called the corporate parent.

- Corporate strategy is concerned with decisions of the corporate parent about (i) the product and market scope, and (ii) how it seeks to add value to that created by its business units.

- Product diversity is often considered in terms of related and unrelated diversification.

- Performance tends to suffer if organisations become very diverse, or unrelated, in their business units.

- Corporate parents may seek to add value by adopting different parenting roles: the portfolio manager, the synergy manager or the parental developer.

- Corporate parents can destroy value as well as create it, and should be ready to divest units for which they cannot create value.

- There are several portfolio models to help corporate parents manage their businesses, of which the most common are: the BCG matrix, the directional matrix and the parenting matrix.

Work assignments

✱ *Denotes more advanced work assignments.   * Refers to a case study in the Text and Cases edition.*

7.1   Using the Ansoff matrix (Exhibit 7.2), identify and explain possible strategic directions for any one of these case organisations: CRH*, Numico*, News Corporation*.

7.2   Go to the website of any large multi-business organisation (for example, Google, Tata Group, Siemens) and assess the degree to which its corporate-level strategy is characterised by (a) related or unrelated diversification and (b) a coherent 'dominant logic' (see section 7.3.1).

7.3   For any large multi-business corporation (as in 7.2), explain how the corporate parent should best create value for its component businesses (as portfolio manager, synergy manager or parental developer: see section 7.4). Would all the businesses fit equally well?

7.4 ✱ For any large multi-business corporation (as in 7.2), plot the business units on a portfolio matrix (for example, the BCG matrix: section 7.5). Justify any assumptions about the relative positions of businesses on the relevant axes of the matrix. What managerial conclusions do you draw from this analysis?

7.5   For any large multi-business organisation (see 7.2), map the business units on the Ashridge parenting matrix (Exhibit 7.10).

Integrative assignment

7.6   Take a case of a recent merger or acquisition (see Chapter 10), and assess the extent to which it involved related or unrelated diversification (if either) and how far it was consistent with the company's existing dominant logic. Using share price information (see www.bigcharts.com or similar), assess shareholders' reaction to the merger or acquisition. How do you explain this reaction?

An extensive range of additional materials, including audio summaries, weblinks to organisations featured in the text, definitions of key concepts and self-assessment questions, can be found on the *Exploring Corporate Strategy* Companion Website at **www.pearsoned.co.uk/ecs**

Recommended key readings

● An accessible discussion of strategic directions is provided by A. Campbell and R. Park, *The Growth Gamble: When leaders should bet on big new businesses*, Nicholas Brealey, 2005.

● M. Goold and K. Luchs, 'Why diversify: four decades of management thinking', in D. Faulkner and A. Campbell (eds), *The Oxford Handbook of Strategy*, vol. 2, Oxford University Press, pp. 18–42,

provides an authoritative overview of the diversification option over time.

● A summary of different portfolio analyses is provided in D. Faulkner, 'Portfolio matrices', in V. Ambrosini (ed.), *Exploring Techniques of Analysis and Evaluation in Strategic Management*, Prentice Hall, 1998.

References

1. This figure is an extension of the product/market matrix: see I. Ansoff, *Corporate Strategy*, Penguin, 1988, chapter 6. The Ansoff matrix was later developed into the one show below.

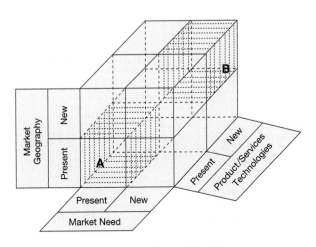

Source: H. Ansoff, *The New Corporate Strategy*, Wiley, 1988.

2. For the European Commission competition authority, see http://ec.europa.eu/comm/competition; for the UK Competition Commission, see http://www.competition-commission.org.uk/.

3. See, for example, J. Huang, M. Enesi and R. Galliers, 'Opportunities to learn from failure with electronic commerce: a case study of electronic banking', *Journal of Information Technology*, vol. 18, no. 1 (2003), pp. 17–27.

4. For discussions of the challenge of sustained growth and diversification, see A. Campbell and R. Parks, *The Growth*

Gamble, Nicholas Brearly, 2005, and D. Laurie, Y. Doz and C. Sheer, 'Creating new growth platforms', *Harvard Business Review*, vol. 84, no. 5 (2006), pp. 80–90.

5. On economies of scope, see D.J. Teece, 'Towards an economic theory of the multi-product firm', *Journal of Economic Behavior and Organization*, vol. 3 (1982), pp. 39–63.

6. M. Goold and A. Campbell, 'Desperately seeking synergy', *Harvard Business Review*, vol. 76, no. 2 (1998), pp. 131–145.

7. See C.K. Prahalad and R. Bettis, 'The dominant logic: a new link between diversity and performance', *Strategic Management Journal*, vol. 6, no. 1 (1986), pp. 485–501; and R. Bettis and C.K. Prahalad, 'The dominant logic: retrospective and extension', *Strategic Management Journal*, vol. 16, no. 1 (1995), pp. 5–15.

8. For a theoretical discussion and empirical study of management interests and diversification, see M. Goranova, T. Alessandri, P. Brandes and R. Dharwadkar, 'Managerial ownership and corporate diversification: a longitudinal view', *Strategic Management Journal*, vol. 28, no. 3 (2007), pp. 211–226.

9. A. Pehrson, 'Business relatedness and performance: a study of managerial perceptions', *Strategic Management Journal*, vol. 27, no. 3 (2006), pp. 265–282.

10. A. Campbell and K. Luchs, *Strategic Synergy*, Butterworth–Heinemann, 1992.

11. See Prahalad and Bettis, reference 7.

12. See C. Markides, 'Corporate strategy: the role of the centre', in A. Pettigrew, H. Thomas and R. Whittington (eds), *Handbook of Strategy and Management*, Sage, 2002. For a discussion of recent chaebol changes, see J. Chang and H.-H. Shin, 'Governance system effectiveness following the crisis: the case of Korean business group headquarters', *Corporate Governance: an International Review*, vol. 14, no. 2 (2006), pp. 85–97.

13. L.E. Palich, L.B. Cardinal and C. Miller, 'Curvilinearity in the diversification-performance linkage: an examination of over three decades of research', *Strategic Management Journal*, vol. 21 (2000), pp. 155–174. The inverted-U relationship is the research consensus, but studies often disagree, particularly finding variations over time and across countries. For recent context sensitive studies, see M. Mayer and R. Whittington, 'Diversification in context: a cross national and cross temporal extension', *Strategic Management Journal*, vol. 24 (2003), pp. 773–781; and A. Chakrabarti, K. Singh and I. Mahmood, 'Diversification and performance: evidence from East Asian firms', *Strategic Management Journal*, vol. 28 (2007), pp. 101–120.

14. For a good discussion of corporate parenting roles, see Markides in reference 11. A recent empirical study of corporate headquarters is D. Collis, D. Young and M. Goold, 'The size, structure and performance of corporate headquarters', *Strategic Management Journal*, vol. 28, no. 4 (2007), pp. 383–406.

15. M. Goold, A. Campbell and M. Alexander, *Corporate Level Strategy*, Wiley, 1994, is concerned with both the value-adding and value-destroying capacity of corporate parents.

16. For a discussion of the role of a clarity of mission, see A. Campbell, M. Devine and D. Young, *A Sense of Mission*, Hutchinson Business, 1990. However, G. Hamel and C.K. Prahalad argue in chapter 6 of their book, *Competing for the Future*, Harvard Business School Press, 1994, that mission statements have insufficient impact for the competence of a clarity of 'strategic intent'. This is more likely to be a brief but clear statement which focuses more on clarity of strategic direction (they use the word 'destiny') than on how that strategic direction will be achieved. See also Hamel and Prahalad on strategic intent in the *Harvard Business Review*, vol. 67, no. 3 (1989), pp. 63–76.

17. The first two rationales discussed here are based on a paper by M. Porter, 'From competitive advantage to corporate strategy', *Harvard Business Review*, vol. 65, no. 3 (1987), pp. 43–59.

18. See A. Campbell and K. Luchs, *Strategic Synergy*, Butterworth–Heinemann, 1992.

19. The logic of parental development is explained extensively in Goold *et al.*, reference 15.

20. For a more extensive discussion of the use of the growth/share matrix see A.C. Hax and N.S Majluf, 'The use of the growth-share matrix in strategic planning', *Interfaces*, vol. 13, no. 1 (1992), pp. 40–46; and D. Faulkner, 'Portfolio matrices', in V. Ambrosini (ed.), *Exploring Techniques of Analysis and Evaluation in Strategic Management*, Prentice Hall, 1998; for source explanations of the BCG matrix see B.D. Henderson, *Henderson on Corporate Strategy*, Abt Books, 1979.

21. A. Hax and N. Majluf, 'The use of the industry attractiveness-business strength matrix in strategic planning', in R. Dyson (ed.), *Strategic Planning: Models and analytical techniques*, Wiley, 1990.

22. The discussion in this section draws on M. Goold, A. Campbell and M. Alexander, *Corporate Level Strategy*, Wiley, 1994, which provides an excellent basis for understanding issues of parenting.

The Virgin Group

Aidan McQuade

Introduction

The Virgin Group is one of the UK's largest private companies. The group included, in 2006, 63 businesses as diverse as airlines, health clubs, music stores and trains. The group included Virgin Galactic, which promised to take paying passengers into sub-orbital space.

The personal image and personality of the founder, Richard Branson, were highly bound up with those of the company. Branson's taste for publicity has led him to stunts as diverse as appearing as a cockney street trader in the US comedy *Friends*, to attempting a non-stop balloon flight around the world. This has certainly contributed to the definition and recognisability of the brand. Research has showed that the Virgin name was associated with words such as 'fun', 'innovative', 'daring' and 'successful'.

In 2006 Branson announced plans to invest $3bn (€2.4bn; £1.7bn) in renewable energy. Virgin, through its partnership with a cable company NTL, also undertook an expansion into media challenging publicly the way NewsCorp operated in the UK and the effects on British democracy. The nature and scale of both these initiatives suggests that Branson's taste for his brand of business remains undimmed.

Origins and activities

Virgin was founded in 1970 as a mail order record business and developed as a private company in music publishing and retailing. In 1986 the company was floated on the stock exchange with a turnover of £250m (€362.5m). However, Branson became tired of the public listing obligations: he resented making presentations in the City to people whom, he believed, did not understand the business. The pressure to create short-term profit, especially as the share price began to fall, was the final straw: Branson decided to take the business back into private ownership and the

Photo: Steve Bell/Rex Features

shares were bought back at the original offer price.

The name Virgin was chosen to represent the idea of the company being a virgin in every business it entered. Branson has said that: 'The brand is the single most important asset that we have; our ultimate objective is to establish it as a major global name.' This does not mean that Virgin underestimates the importance of understanding the *businesses* that it is branding. Referring to his intent to set up a 'green' energy company producing ethanol and cellulosic ethanol fuels in competition with the oil industry, he said, 'We're a slightly unusual company in that we go into industries we know nothing about and immerse ourselves.'

Virgin's expansion had often been through joint ventures whereby Virgin provided the brand and its partner provided the majority of capital. For example, the Virgin Group's move into clothing and cosmetics required an initial outlay of only £1,000, whilst its partner, Victory Corporation, invested £20m. With Virgin Mobile, Virgin built a business by forming partnerships with existing wireless operators to sell services under the Virgin brand name. The carriers' competences lay in network management. Virgin set out to differentiate itself by offering innovative

This case was updated and revised by Aidan McQuade, University of Strathclyde Graduate School of Business, based upon work by Urmilla Lawson.

services. Although it did not operate its own network, Virgin won an award for the best wireless operator in the UK.

Virgin Fuels appears to be somewhat different in that Virgin is putting up the capital and using the Virgin brand to attract attention to the issues and possibilities that the technology offers.

In 2005 Virgin announced the establishment of a 'quadruple play' media company providing television, broadband, fixed-line and mobile communications through the merger of Branson's UK mobile interests with the UK's two cable companies. This Virgin company would have 9 million direct customers, 1.5 million more than BSkyB, and so have the financial capacity to compete with BSkyB for premium content such as sports and movies.[1] Virgin tried to expand this business further by making an offer for ITV. This was rejected as undervaluing the company and then undermined further with the purchase of an 18 per cent share of ITV by BSkyB. This prompted Branson to call on regulators to force BSkyB to reduce or dispose of its stake citing concerns that BSkyB would have material influence over the free-to-air broadcaster.[2]

Virgin has been described as a 'keiretsu' organisation – a structure of loosely linked, autonomous units run by self-managed teams that use a common brand name. Branson argued that, as he expanded, he would rather sacrifice short-term profits for long-term growth of the various businesses.

Some commentators have argued that Virgin had become an endorsement brand that could not always offer real expertise to the businesses with which it was associated. However, Will Whitehorn, Director of Corporate Affairs for Virgin, stated, 'At Virgin we know what the brand means and when we put our brand name on something we are making a promise.'

Branson saw Virgin adding value in three main ways, aside from the brand. These were their public relations and marketing skills; its experience with greenfield start-ups; and Virgin's understanding of the opportunities presented by 'institutionalised' markets. Virgin saw an 'institutionalised' market as one dominated by few competitors, not giving good value to customers because they had become either inefficient or preoccupied with each other. Virgin believed it did well when it identified such complacency and offered more for less. The entry into fuel and media industries certainly conforms to the model of trying to shake up 'institutionalised' markets.

Corporate rationale

In 2006 Virgin still lacked the trappings of a typical multinational. Branson described the Virgin Group as 'a branded venture capital house'.[3] There was no 'group' as such; financial results were not consolidated either for external examination or, so Virgin claimed, for internal use. Its website described Virgin as a family rather than a hierarchy. Its financial operations were managed from Geneva.

In 2006 Branson explained the basis upon which he considered opportunities: they have to be global in scope, enhance the brand, be worth doing and have an expectation of a reasonable return on investment.[4] Each business was 'ring-fenced', so that lenders to one company had no rights over the assets of another. The ring-fencing seems also to relate not just to provision of financial protection, but also to a business ethics aspect. In an interview in 2006 Branson cricitised supermarkets for selling cheap CDs. His criticism centred on the supermarkets' use of loss leading on CDs damaging music retailers rather than fundamentally challenging the way music retailers do business. Branson has made it a central feature of Virgin that it shakes up institutionalised markets by being innovative. Loss leading is not an innovative approach.

Virgin has evolved from being almost wholly comprised of private companies to a group where some of the companies are publicly listed.

Virgin and Branson

Historically, the Virgin Group had been controlled mainly by Branson and his trusted lieutenants, many of whom had stayed with him for more than 20 years. The increasing conformity between personal interest and business initiatives could be discerned in the establishment of Virgin Fuels. In discussing his efforts to establish a 'green' fuel company in competition with the oil industry Branson made the geopolitical observation that non-oil-based fuels could 'avoid another Middle East war one day'; Branson's opposition to the Second Gulf War is well publicised.[5] In some instances the relationship between personal conviction and business interests is less clear cut. Branson's comments on the threat to British democracy posed by NewsCorp's ownership of such a large percentage of the British media could be depicted as either genuine concern from a public figure or sour grapes from a business rival just been beaten out of purchasing ITV.

More recently Branson has been reported as talking about withdrawing from the business 'which more or less ran itself now',[6] and hoping that his son Sam might become more of a Virgin figurehead.[7] However, while he was publicly contemplating this withdrawal from business, Branson was also launching his initiatives in media and fuel. Perhaps Branson's idea of early retirement is somewhat more active than most.

Corporate performance

By 2006 Virgin had, with mixed results, taken on one established industry after another in an effort to shake up 'fat and complacent business sectors'. It had further set its sights on the British media sector and the global oil industry.

Airlines clearly were an enthusiasm of Branson's. According to Branson, Virgin Atlantic, which was 49 per cent owned by Singapore Airways, was a company that he would not sell outright: 'There are some businesses you preserve, which wouldn't ever be sold, and that's one.' Despite some analysts' worries that airline success could not be sustained given the 'cyclical' nature of the business, Branson maintained a strong interest in the industry, and included airline businesses such as Virgin Express (European), Virgin Blue (Australia) and Virgin Nigeria in the group. Branson's engagement with the search for 'greener' fuels and reducing global warming had not led him to ground his fleets. but rather to prompt a debate on measures to reduce carbon emissions from aeroplanes.

At the beginning of the twenty-first century the most public problem faced by Branson was Virgin Trains, whose Cross Country and West Coast lines were ranked 23rd and 24th out of 25 train-operating franchises according to the Strategic Rail Authority's Review in 2000. By 2002 Virgin Trains was reporting profits and paid its first premium to the British government.

The future

The beginning of the twenty-first century also saw further expansion by Virgin, from airlines, spa finance and mobile telecoms in Africa, into telecoms in Europe, and into the USA. The public flotation of individual businesses rather than the group as a whole has become an intrinsic part of the 'juggling' of finances that underpins Virgin's expansion.

Some commentators have identified a risk with Virgin's approach: 'The greatest threat [is] that . . . Virgin brand . . . may become associated with failure.'[8] This point was emphasised by a commentator[9] who noted that 'a customer who has a bad enough experience with any one of the product lines may shun all the others'. However, Virgin argues that its brand research indicates that people who have had a bad experience will blame that particular Virgin company or product but will be willing to use other Virgin products or services, due to the very diversity of the brand. Such brand confidence helps explain why Virgin should even contemplate such risky and protracted turnaround challenges as its rail company.

Sarah Sands recounts that Branson's mother 'once proudly boasted that her son would become Prime Minster'. Sands futher commented that she thought his mother underestimated his ambition.[10] With Virgin's entry into fuel and media and Branson's declarations that he is taking on the oil corporations and NewsCorp, Sands may ultimately prove to have been precient in her comment.

Notes

1. *Sunday Telegraph*, 4 December (2005).
2. *Independent*, 22 November (2006).
3. Hawkins (2001a, b).
4. PR Newswire Europe, 16 October (2006).
5. *Fortune*, 6 February (2006).
6. *Independent on Sunday*, 26 November (2006).
7. Ibid.
8. *The Times* 1998, quoted in Vignali (2001).
9. Wells (2000).
10. *Independent on Sunday*, 26 November (2006).

Sources: *The Economist*, 'Cross his heart', 5 October (2002); 'Virgin on the ridiculous', 29 May (2003); 'Virgin Rail: tilting too far', 12 July (2001). P. McCosker, 'Stretching the brand: a review of the Virgin Group', *European Case Clearing House*, 2000. *The Times*, 'Virgin push to open up US aviation market', 5 June (2002); 'Branson plans $1bn US expansion', 30 April (2002). *Observer*, 'Branson eyes 31bn float for Virgin Mobile', 18 January (2004). *Strategic Direction*, 'Virgin Flies High with Brand Extensions', vol. 18, no. 10, (October 2002). R. Hawkins, 'Executive of Virgin Group outlines corporate strategy' *Knight Ridder/Tribune Business News*, July 29 (2001a). R. Hawkins, 'Branson in new dash for cash', *Sunday Business*, 29 July (2001b); *South China Morning Post*, 'Virgin shapes kangaroo strategy aid liberalisation talks between Hong Kong and Australia will determine carrier's game-plan', 28 June (2002). C. Vignali, 'Virgin Cola', *British Food Journal*, vol. 103, no. 2 (2001), pp. 131–139. M. Wells, 'Red Baron', *Forbes Magazine*, vol. 166, no. 1, 7 March (2000).

Questions

1　What is the corporate rationale of Virgin as a group of companies?

2　Are there any relationships of a strategic nature between businesses within the Virgin portfolio?

3　How does the Virgin Group, as a corporate parent, add value to its businesses?

4　What were the main issues facing the Virgin Group at the end of the case and how should they be tackled?

8

Strategic
Choices

International Strategy

LEARNING OUTCOMES

After reading this chapter you should be able to:

→ Assess the internationalisation potential of different markets, sensitive to variations over time.

→ Identify sources of competitive advantage in international strategy, both through global sourcing and exploitation of local factors embodied in Porter's Diamond.

→ Distinguish between four main types of international strategy.

→ Rank markets for entry or expansion, taking into account attractiveness, cultural and other forms of distance and competitor retaliation threats.

→ Assess the relative merits of different market entry modes, including joint ventures, licensing and foreign direct investment.

8.1   INTRODUCTION

The last chapter introduced market development as a strategy, in relation to the Ansoff matrix. This chapter focuses on a specific but important kind of market development, operating in different geographical markets. This kind of internationalisation raises choices about which countries to compete in, how far to modify the organisation's range of products or services and how to manage across borders. These kinds of questions are relevant to a wide range of organisations nowadays. There are of course the large traditional multinationals such as Nestlé, Toyota and McDonald's, but increasingly new small firms are also 'born global', building international relationships right from the start. Public sector organisations too are having to make choices about collaboration, outsourcing and even competition with overseas organisations. European Union legislation requires public service organisations to accept tenders from non-national providers.

Exhibit 8.1 places international strategy as the core theme of the chapter. International strategy, however, depends ultimately on both the external environment (as in Chapter 2) and organisational capabilities (as in Chapter 3). On the environmental side, Exhibit 8.1 highlights internationalisation drivers; on the capabilities side, it emphasises international and national sources of advantage. The choice of international strategy in turn tends to shape the selection of country markets and the modes of market entry.

This chapter examines key issues in international strategy as follows. The next section introduces the *drivers of internationalisation*. The chapter then considers international and national sources of competitive advantage, particularly those located in *global sourcing* and those in the nationally specific factors embodied

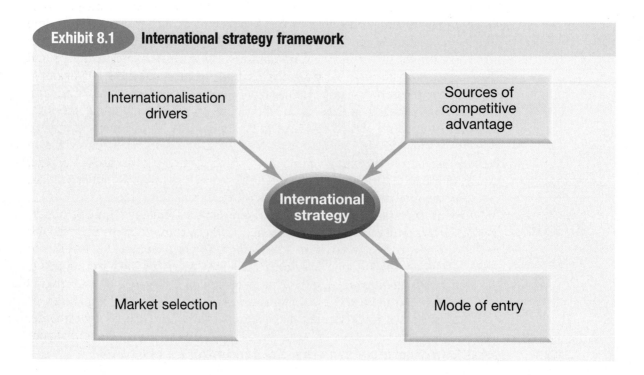

Exhibit 8.1   International strategy framework

Internationalisation drivers

Sources of competitive advantage

International strategy

Market selection

Mode of entry

in Michael Porter's *Diamond framework*. In the light of these drivers and sources of competitive advantage, the chapter describes different *types of international strategy*. As different geographical markets tend to demand significant product or service modifications, some international strategies take the organisation from simple market development to increasingly diversified strategies.[1] From here, the chapter moves on to analyse market selection and market entry. Here, the chapter stresses the interdependence of market attractiveness with *various kinds of distance* and the threat of *competitor retaliation*. The relative advantages of different *entry modes* are then considered, including joint ventures, foreign direct investment and licensing. *Entry sequences* are discussed, including those for new firms and emerging market multinationals. The final two sections examine parallel issues to those addressed with regard to diversification in Chapter 7: internationalisation and *performance* and *portfolio* management.

8.2   INTERNATIONALISATION DRIVERS

Yip's interna-
tionalisation
drivers

There are many general pressures increasing internationalisation. Barriers to international trade, investment and migration are all now much lower than they were a couple of decades ago. International regulation and governance have improved, so that investing and trading overseas is less risky. Improvements in communications – from cheaper air travel to the Internet – make movement and the spread of ideas much easier around the world. Not least, the success of new economic powerhouses such as the so-called BRICs – Brazil, Russia, India and China – is generating new opportunities and challenges for business internationally.[2]

However, not all these internationalisation trends are one way. Nor do they hold for all industries. For example, migration is now becoming more difficult between some countries. The Internet and cheap air travel are making it easier for expatriate communities to stick with home cultures, rather than merging into a single global 'melting pot' of tastes and ideas. Many so-called multinationals are concentrated in quite particular markets, for example North America and Western Europe, or have a very limited set of international links, for example supply or outsourcing arrangements with just one or two countries overseas. Markets vary widely in the extent to which consumer needs are standardising – compare computer operating systems to tastes in chocolate. In short, managers need to beware 'global baloney', by which economic integration into a single homogenised and competitive world is wildly exaggerated (see the key debate, Illustration 8.6). As in the Chinese retail market (Illustration 8.1), international drivers are usually a lot more complicated than that.

Given internationalisation's complexity, international strategy should be underpinned by a careful diagnosis of the strength and direction of trends in particular markets. George Yip's 'drivers of globalisation' framework provides a basis for such a diagnosis (see Exhibit 8.2).[3] Note though that, while this framework refers to the need for a *global strategy*, with all parts of the business carefully coordinated around the world, most of these drivers also apply to broader *international strategies*, allowing for more limited overseas operations and looser coordination between them (see section 8.4). Accordingly, Yip's drivers can be thought of simply as 'internationalisation drivers'. The four drivers are as follows:

Illustration 8.1

Chinese retail: global or local?

Internationalisation is not a simple process, as supermarket chains Carrefour and Wal-Mart have found in China.

At the start of the twenty-first century, China is a magnet for ambitious Western supermarket chains. Growing at 13 per cent a year, the Chinese market is predicted by Euromonitor to reach $747bn. (£418bn; €380bn) by 2010. Some 520 million people are expected to join the Chinese upper middle class by 2025. With the local industry fragmented and focused on particular regions, large Western companies might have an advantage.

In 1995, after six years' experience in neighbouring Taiwan, French supermarket chain Carrefour was the first to enter the Chinese market in a substantial fashion. By 2006, Carrefour was the sixth largest retailer in China, though the market being what it is, this meant only 0.6 per cent overall market share. The world's largest retailer, the American Wal-Mart, was close behind, especially with its acquisition in 2006 of a Taiwanese chain with outlets on the mainland. These two rivals are pursuing very different strategies. Wal-Mart is pursuing its standard centralised purchasing and distribution strategy, supplying as much as it can from its new, state-of-the-art distribution centre in Shenzen. Carrefour is following a decentralised strategy: except in Shanghai, where it has several stores, Carrefour allows its local store managers, scattered across the many different regions of China, to make their own purchasing and supply decisions.

The growth of companies such as Carrefour and Wal-Mart, as well as local chains, demonstrates that already there is a substantial market for the Western supermarket experience. Carrefour, for example, was a pioneer of 'private label' goods in China, while Wal-Mart brings logistical expertise. Growing wealth and exposure to foreign ideas will no doubt increase Chinese receptiveness. None the less, progress has been slow. Wal-Mart has yet to make a profit in China; Carrefour finally is, but its 2–3 per cent margins are significantly below the nearly 5 per cent margins it enjoys in France.

One early discovery for Wal-Mart was that Chinese consumers prefer frequent shopping trips, buying small quantities each time. While Wal-Mart assumed that Chinese consumers would drive to out-of-town stores and fill their cars with large frozen multi-packs on a once-a-week shop, much like Americans, in fact Chinese customers would break open the multi-packs to take just the smaller quantities they required. Now Wal-Mart supplies more of its frozen foods loose, offering customers a scoop so they can take exactly the amount they want. In 2006, moreover, Wal-Mart allowed trade unions into its stores, in marked contrast to its policy in the rest of the world.

Another discovery for Western retailers is the amount of regional variation in this vast and multi-ethnic country. In the north of China, soya sauces are important; in central China, chilli pepper sauces are required; in the South, it is oyster sauces that matter. For fruit, northerners must have dates; southerners want lychees. In the north, the cold means more demand for red meat and, because customers are wearing layers of clothing, wider store aisles. Northerners do not have much access to hot water, so they wash their hair less frequently, meaning that small sachets of shampoo sell better than large bottles.

Sources: Financial Times, Wall Street Journal and Euromonitor (various dates).

Questions

1 What are the pros and cons of the different China strategies pursued by Carrefour and Wal-Mart?

2 What might be the dangers for a large Western retailer in staying out of the Chinese market?

Exhibit 8.2	Drivers of internationalisation

Market drivers

- Similar customer needs
- Global customers
- Transferable marketing

Government drivers

- Trade policies
- Technical standards
- Host government policies

International strategies

Cost drivers

- Scale economies
- Country-specific differences
- Favourable logistics

Competitive drivers

- Interdependence between countries
- Competitors' global strategies

Source: Adapted from G. Yip, *Total Global Strategy II*, FT/Prentice Hall, 2003, Chapter 2.

- *Market drivers*. A critical facilitator of internationalisation is some standardisation of markets. There are three components underlying this driver. First, the presence of *similar customer needs and tastes*: the fact that in most societies consumers have similar needs for easy credit has promoted the worldwide spread of a handful of credit card companies such as Visa. Second, the presence of *global customers*: for example, car component companies have become more international as their customers, such as Toyota or Ford, have internationalised, and required standardised components for all their factories around the world. Finally, *transferable marketing* promotes market globalisation: brands such as Coca-Cola are still successfully marketed in very similar ways across the world.

- *Cost drivers*. Costs can be reduced by operating internationally. Again, there are three main elements to cost drivers. First, increasing volume beyond what a national market might support can give *scale economies*, both on the production side and in purchasing of supplies. Companies from smaller countries such as The Netherlands and Switzerland tend therefore to become proportionately much more international than companies from the USA, which have a vast market at home. Scale economies are particularly important in industries with high product development costs, as in the aircraft industry, where initial costs need to be spread over the large volumes of international markets. Second, internationalisation is promoted where it is possible to take advantage of *country-specific differences*. Thus it makes sense to locate the manufacture of clothing in China or Africa, where labour is still considerably cheaper, but to keep design activities in cities such as New York, Paris, Milan or London, where fashion expertise is concentrated. The third element is *favourable logistics*, or the costs of moving products or services across borders relative to their final value. From this point of view, microchips are easy to source internationally, while bulky materials such as assembled furniture are harder.

● *Government drivers*. These can both facilitate and inhibit internationalisation. The relevant elements of policy are numerous, including tariff barriers, technical standards, subsidies to local firms, ownership restrictions, local content requirements, controls over technology transfer, intellectual property (patenting) regimes and currency and capital flow controls. No government allows complete economic openness and openness typically varies widely from industry to industry, with agriculture and high-tech industries related to defence likely to be particularly sensitive. Nevertheless, the World Trade Organization continues to push for greater openness and the European Union and the North American Free Trade Agreement have made significant improvements in their specific regions.[4]

● *Competitive drivers*. These relate specifically to globalisation as an integrated worldwide strategy rather than simpler international strategies. Such drivers have two elements. First, *interdependence* between country operations increases the pressure for global coordination. For example, a business with a plant in Mexico serving both the American and the Japanese markets has to coordinate carefully between the three locations: surging sales in one country, or a collapse in another, will have significant knock-on effects on the other countries. The second element relates directly to competitor strategy. The presence of *globalised competitors* increases the pressure to adopt a global strategy in response because competitors may use one country's profits to cross-subsidise their operations in another. A company with a loosely coordinated international strategy is vulnerable to globalised competitors, because it is unable to support country subsidiaries under attack from targeted, subsidised competition. The danger is of piecemeal withdrawal from countries under attack, and the gradual undermining of any overall economies of scale that the international player may have started with.[5]

The key insight from Yip's drivers framework is that the internationalisation potential of industries is variable. There are many different factors that can support or inhibit it, and an important step in determining an internationalisation strategy is a realistic assessment of the true scope for internationalisation in the particular industry. Illustration 8.2 explains some of the reasons for Deutsche Post's increasing international diversity since the late 1990s.

Deutsche Post's increasing international diversity

Globalising markets and political and regulatory change are amongst the reasons for an organisation's increasing international diversity.

The internationalisation of Deutsche Post is closely linked to the opportunities and pressures resulting from the deregulation of national and international markets and the associated globalisation of the transport and logistics industries. The foundation was laid by the 'big bang' reform of the German postal system in 1990. The 'Law concerning the Structure of Posts and Telecommunication' retained Deutsche Post as a state-owned company but aimed to prepare the company for gradual privatisation (the firm went public in 2000 with an initial sale of 29 per cent of share capital). In the following years the company went through a period of consolidation and restructuring which saw the integration of the former East German Post. By 1997, a year which saw a liberalisation of the German postal market, the company had put into place the groundwork for a period of rapid international expansion.

The subsequent globalisation of Deutsche Post's activities was largely driven by the demands of a growing number of business customers for a single provider of integrated national and international shipping and logistics services. Over the next five years Deutsche Post responded by acquiring key players in the international transport and logistics market, notably Danzas and DHL, with the aim of 'becoming the leading global provider of express and logistics services'. This international expansion enabled Deutsche Post – renamed Deutsche Post World Net (DPWN) in order to highlight its global ambitions – to gain, for example, a major contract with fellow German company BMW for the transport, storage and delivery of cars to its Asian dealerships. As part of its so-called 'START' programme, DPWN initiated, in 2003, a programme aimed at harmonising its products and sales structures, creating integrated networks and implementing group-wide process management in order to

realise the benefits of the economies of scale resulting from its global operations. At the same time DPWN implemented its 'One brand – One face to the customer' motto by making the DHL brand its global 'public face' with the expectation that this 'familiar and trusted brand name will aid us as we continue to develop globalised services'.

Deregulation and wider political changes, reflected in the elimination of trade restrictions, continued to drive international expansion. China's entry into the World Trade Organization enhanced the potential for growth in its international postal market. Accordingly, DPWN strengthened its commitment to this increasingly important market and was rewarded with a 35 per cent growth rate over the period from 2002 to 2004 and, through a joint venture with Sinotrans, gained a 40 per cent market share of Chinese cross-border express services. DPWN aimed to exploit regulatory changes closer to home as well. With its subsidiary Deutsche Post Global Mail (UK) gaining a long-term licence for unlimited bulk mail delivery from the British regulator 'Postcomm', DPWN saw further opportunity for growth in the UK and continued to expand its presence in the British postal market through the acquisition of postal operator Speedmail.

Sources: www.dpwn.de/enrde/press/news; DPWN Annual Report 2002.

Prepared by Michael Mayer, Bath University.

Questions

1 What were the internationalisation drivers associated with DPWN's strategy?

2 Evaluate the pros and cons of both a multidomestic strategy and a global strategy for DPWN.

8.3 NATIONAL AND INTERNATIONAL SOURCES OF ADVANTAGE

As is clear from the earlier discussion of cost drivers in international strategy, the location of activities is a crucial source of potential advantage and one of the distinguishing features of international strategy relative to other diversification strategies. As Bruce Kogut has explained, an organisation can improve the configuration of its *value chain and network*[6] by taking advantage of country-specific differences (see section 3.6.1). There are two principal opportunities available: the exploitation of particular *national advantages*, often in the company's home country, and sourcing advantages overseas via an *international value network*.

8.3.1 Porter's Diamond[7]

Porter's
diamond

As for any strategy, internationalisation needs to be based on possession of some sustainable competitive advantage (see Chapter 3). This competitive advantage has usually to be substantial. After all, a competitor entering a market from overseas typically starts with considerable *dis*advantages relative to existing home competitors, which will usually have superior market knowledge, established relationships with local customers, strong supply chains and the like. A foreign entrant must have significant competitive advantages to overcome such disadvantages. The example of the American giant retailer Wal-Mart provides an illustration: Wal-Mart has been successful in many Asian markets with relatively underdeveloped retail markets, but was forced to withdraw from Germany's maturer market after nearly a decade of failure in 2006. In Germany, unlike in most Asian markets, Wal-Mart had no significant competitive advantage over domestic retailers.

Chapter 3 addresses competitive advantage in general, but the international context raises specifically national sources of advantage that can be substantial and hard to imitate. Countries, and regions within them, often become associated with specific types of enduring competitive advantage: for example, the Swiss in private banking, the north Italians in leather and fur fashion goods, and the Taiwanese in computer laptops. Michael **Porter's Diamond** helps explain why some nations tend to produce firms with sustained competitive advantages in some industries more than others (see Exhibit 8.3). The degree of national advantage varies from industry to industry.

Porter's Diamond
suggests that there are
inherent reasons why
some nations are more
competitive than others,
and why some industries
within nations are more
competitive than others

Porter's Diamond suggests there are four interacting determinants of national, or home base, advantage in particular industries (these four determinants together make up a diamond-shaped figure). The home base determinants are:

● *Factor conditions*. These refer to the 'factors of production' that go into making a product or service (that is, raw materials, land and labour). Factor condition advantages at a national level can translate into general competitive advantages for national firms in international markets. For example, the linguistic ability of the Swiss has provided a significant advantage to their banking industry. Cheap energy has traditionally provided an advantage for the North American aluminium industry.

| Exhibit 8.3 | Porter's Diamond – the determinants of national advantages |

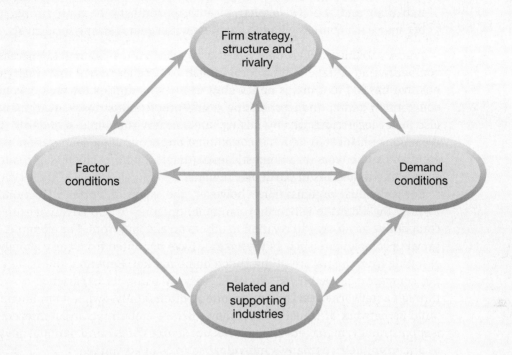

- *Home demand conditions*. The nature of the domestic customers can become a source of competitive advantage. Dealing with sophisticated and demanding customers at home helps train a company to be effective overseas. For example, Japanese customers' high expectations of electrical and electronic equipment provided an impetus for those industries in Japan leading to global dominance of those sectors. Sophisticated local customers in France and Italy have helped keep their local fashion industries at the leading edge for many decades.

- *Related and supporting industries*. Local 'clusters' of related and mutually supporting industries can be an important source of competitive advantage. These are often regionally based, making personal interaction easier. In northern Italy, for example, the leather footwear industry, the leather working machinery industry, and the design services which underpin them, group together in the same regional cluster to each other's mutual benefit. Silicon Valley forms a cluster of hardware, software, research and venture capital organisations which together create a virtuous circle of high-technology enterprise.

- *Firm strategy, industry structure and rivalry*. The characteristic strategies, industry structures and rivalries in different countries can also be bases of advantage. German companies' strategy of investing in technical excellence gives them a characteristic advantage in engineering industries and creates large pools of expertise. A competitive local industry structure is also helpful: if too dominant in their home territory, local organisations can become complacent and lose advantage overseas. Some domestic rivalry can actually be an advantage, therefore. For example, the long-run success of the Japanese car companies is partly based on government policy sustaining several national players (unlike in the United Kingdom, where they were all merged into one) and the Swiss pharmaceuticals industry became strong in part because each company had to compete with several strong local rivals.

Porter's Diamond has been used by governments aiming to increase the competitive advantage of their local industries. The argument that rivalry can be positive has led to a major policy shift in many countries towards encouraging competition rather than protecting home-based industries. Governments can also foster local industries by raising safety or environmental standards (that is, creating sophisticated demand conditions) or encouraging cooperation between suppliers and buyers on a domestic level (that is, building clusters of related and supporting industries in particular regions).

For individual organisations, however, the value of Porter's Diamond is to identify the extent to which they can build on home-based advantages to create competitive advantage in relation to others on a global front. For example, Dutch brewing companies – such as Heineken – have benefited from early globalisation resulting from the nature of the Dutch home market. Benetton, the Italian clothing company, has achieved global success by using its experience of working through a network of largely independent, often family-owned manufacturers to build its network of franchised retailers. Before embarking on an internationalisation strategy, managers should seek out sources of general national advantage to underpin their company's individual sources of advantage.

8.3.2 The international value network

However, the sources of advantage need not be purely domestic. For international companies, advantage can be drawn from the international configuration of their *value network*. Here the different skills, resources and costs of countries around the world can be systematically exploited in order to locate each element of the value chain in that country or region where it can be conducted most effectively and efficiently. This may be achieved both through foreign direct investments and joint ventures but also through **global sourcing**, that is by purchasing services and components from the most appropriate suppliers around the world, regardless of their location. For example, in the UK, the National Health Service has been sourcing medical personnel from overseas to offset a shortfall in domestic skills and capacity.

Different locational advantages can be identified:

Global sourcing:
purchasing services and
components from the
most appropriate
suppliers around the
world regardless of
their location

- *Cost advantages* include labour costs, transportation and communications costs and taxation and investment incentives. Labour costs are important. American and European firms, for example, are increasingly moving software programming tasks to India where a computer programmer costs an American firm about one-quarter of what it would pay for a worker with comparable skills in the USA. As wages in India have risen, Indian IT firms have already begun moving work to even more low-cost locations such as China with some predicting that subsidiaries of Indian firms will come to control as much as 40 per cent of China's IT service exports.

Illustration 8.3

Boeing's global R&D network

Organisations may seek to exploit locational advantages worldwide.

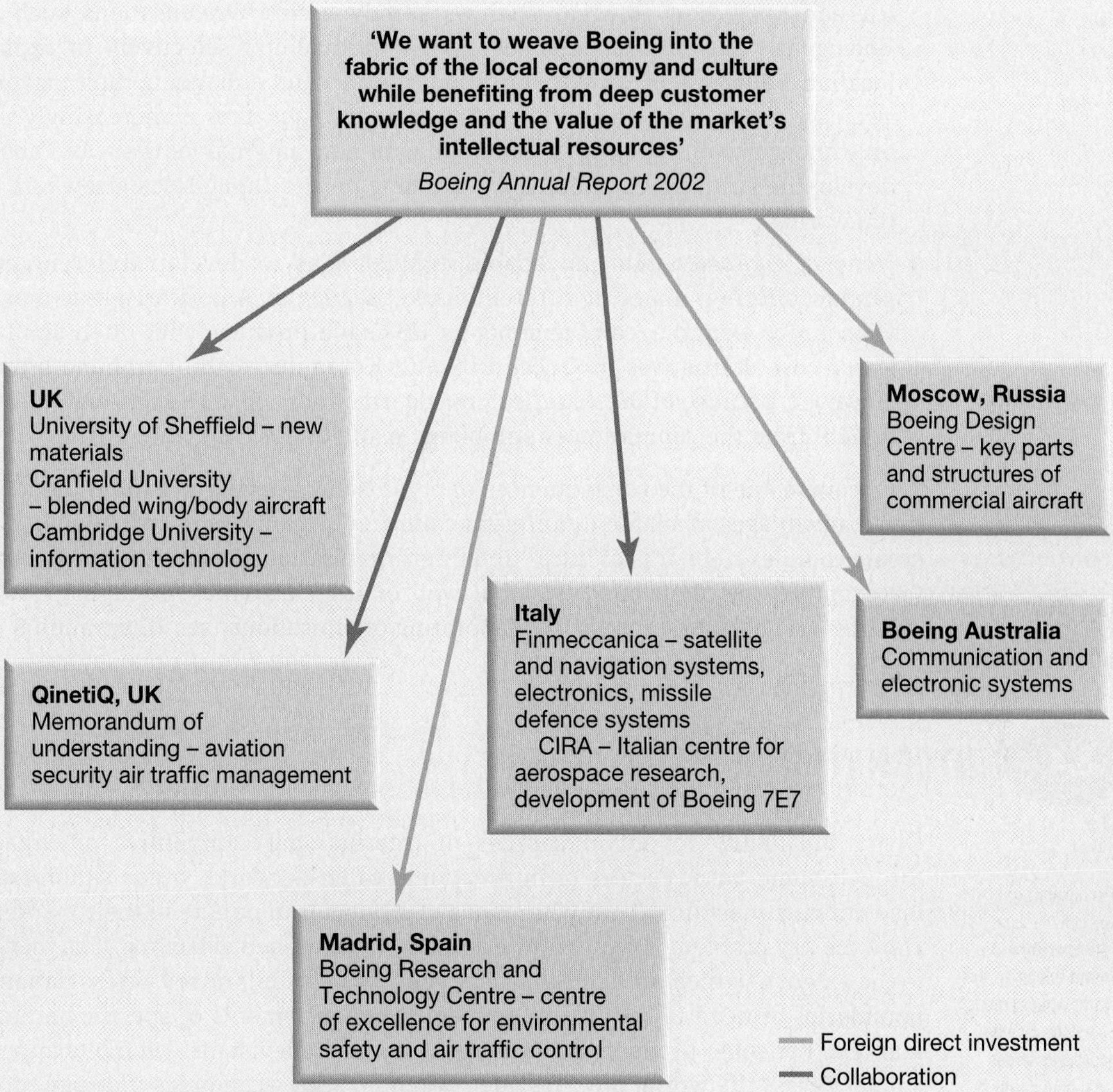

> **'We want to weave Boeing into the fabric of the local economy and culture while benefiting from deep customer knowledge and the value of the market's intellectual resources'**
> *Boeing Annual Report 2002*

UK
University of Sheffield – new materials
Cranfield University
– blended wing/body aircraft
Cambridge University –
information technology

Moscow, Russia
Boeing Design Centre – key parts and structures of commercial aircraft

QinetiQ, UK
Memorandum of understanding – aviation security air traffic management

Italy
Finmeccanica – satellite and navigation systems, electronics, missile defence systems
   CIRA – Italian centre for aerospace research, development of Boeing 7E7

Boeing Australia
Communication and electronic systems

Madrid, Spain
Boeing Research and Technology Centre – centre of excellence for environmental safety and air traffic control

— Foreign direct investment
— Collaboration

Sources: Boeing.com, Boeing Annual Report 2002, Aviation International News Online.
Prepared by Michael Mayer, Bath University.

Questions

1 What reasons might be driving the internationalisation of Boeing's R&D activities?

2 What challenges might Boeing face as it internationalises its R&D activities?

- *Unique capabilities* may allow an organisation to enhance its competitive advantage. A reason for Accenture to locate a rapidly expanding software development office in the Chinese city of Dalian was that communication with potential Japanese and Korean multinational firms operating in the region was easier than if an equivalent location in India or the Philippines had been chosen. Organisations may also seek to exploit advantages related to specific technological and scientific capabilities. Boeing, for example, located its largest engineering centre outside of the USA in Moscow to help it access Russian know-how in areas such as aerodynamics. Organisations such as Boeing are thus increasingly leveraging their ability selectively to exploit locational advantages with a view to building on and enhancing their existing strategic capabilities. Put differently, internationalisation is increasingly not only about exploiting existing capabilities in new national markets, but about developing strategic capabilities by drawing on the capabilities elsewhere in the world.

- *National characteristics* can enable organisations to develop differentiated product offerings aimed at different market segments. American guitar-maker Gibson, for example, complements its US-made products with often similar, lower-cost alternatives produced in South Korea under the Epiphone brand. However, because of the American music tradition, Gibson's high-end guitars benefit from the reputation of still being 'made in the USA'.

Of course one of the consequences of organisations trying to exploit the locational advantages available in different countries' organisations can be that they create complex networks of intra- and interorganisational relationships. Boeing, for example, has developed a global web of R&D activities through its subsidiaries and partnerships with collaborating organisations (see Illustration 8.3).

8.4 INTERNATIONAL STRATEGIES

The **global–local dilemma** relates to the extent to which products and services may be standardised across national boundaries or need to be adapted to meet the requirements of specific national markets

Given the ability to obtain sources of international competitive advantage through home-based factors or international value networks, organisations still face difficult questions about what kinds of strategies to pursue in their markets. Here the key problem is typically the so-called **global–local dilemma**. This relates to the extent to which products and services may be standardised across national boundaries or need to be adapted to meet the requirements of specific national markets. For some products and services – such as televisions – markets appear similar across the world, offering huge potential scale economies if design, production and delivery can be centralised. For other products and services – such as television programming – tastes still seem highly nationally specific, drawing companies to decentralise operations and control as near as possible to the local market. This global–local dilemma can evoke a number of responses from companies pursuing international strategies, ranging from decentralisation to centralisation, with positions in between.

This section introduces four different kinds of international strategy, based on choices about the international *configuration* of the various activities an organisation has to carry out and the degree to which these activities are then *coordinated*

Exhibit 8.4	**Four international strategies**

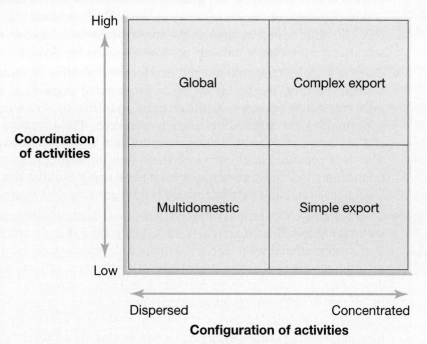

Four
international
strategies

internationally (see Exhibit 8.4). More precisely, configuration refers to the geographical dispersion or concentration of activities such as manufacturing and R&D, while coordination refers to the extent to which operations in different countries are managed in a decentralised way or a centrally coordinated way. The four basic international strategies are:[8]

- *Simple export*. This strategy involves a concentration of activities (particularly manufacturing) in one country, typically the country of the organisation's origin. At the same time, marketing of the exported product is very loosely coordinated overseas, perhaps handled by independent sales agents in different markets. Pricing, packaging, distribution and even branding policies may be determined locally. This strategy is typically chosen by organisations with a strong locational advantage – as determined by the Porter Diamond, for example – but where either the organisation has insufficient managerial capabilities to coordinate marketing internationally or where coordinated marketing would add little value, for example in agricultural or raw material commodities.

- *Multidomestic*. This strategy is similarly loosely coordinated internationally, but involves a dispersion overseas of various activities, including manufacturing and sometimes product development. Instead of export, therefore, goods and services are produced locally in each national market. Each market is treated independently, with the needs of each local domestic market given priority – hence 'multidomestic'. Local adaptations can make the overall corporate portfolio increasingly diversified. This strategy is appropriate where there are few economies of scale and strong benefits to adapting to local needs. This multidomestic strategy is particularly attractive in professional services, where local relationships are critical, but it carries risks towards brand and reputation if national practices become too diverse.

● *Complex export.* This strategy still involves the location of most activities in a single country, but builds on more coordinated marketing. Economies of scale can still be reaped in manufacturing and R&D, but branding and pricing opportunities are more systematically managed. The coordination demands are, of course, considerably more complex than in the simple export strategy. This is a common stage for companies from emerging economies, as they retain some locational advantages from their home country, but seek to build a stronger brand and network overseas with growing organisational maturity.

● *Global strategy.* This strategy describes the most mature international strategy, with highly coordinated activities dispersed geographically around the world. Using international value networks to the full, geographical location is chosen according to the specific locational advantage for each activity, so that product development, manufacturing, marketing and headquarters functions might all be located in different countries. For example, Detroit-based General Motors designed its Pontiac Le Mans at the firm's German subsidiary Opel, with its high engineering skills; developed its advertising via a British agency with the creativity strengths of London; produced many of the more complex components in Japan, exploiting its sophisticated manufacturing and technological capabilities; and assembled the car in South Korea, a location where a lower-cost, yet skilled, labour force was available. All this, of course, required high investments and skill in coordination (see also the discussion of the transnational structure in Chapter 12).

In practice, these four international strategies are not absolutely distinct. Managerial coordination and geographical concentration are matters of degree rather than sharp distinctions. Companies may often oscillate within and between the four strategies. Their choices, moreover, will be influenced by changes in the internationalisation drivers introduced earlier. Where, for example, tastes are highly standardised, companies will tend to favour complex export or global strategies. Where economies of scale are few, the logic is more in favour of multidomestic strategies.

8.5 MARKET SELECTION AND ENTRY

Having decided on an international strategy built on significant sources of competitive advantage and supported by strong internationalisation drivers, managers need next to decide which countries to enter. Not all countries are equally attractive. To an extent, however, countries can initially be compared using the standard environmental analysis techniques, for example along the dimensions identified in the PESTEL framework (see section 2.2.1) or according to the industry five forces (section 2.3). However, there are specific determinants of market attractiveness that need to be considered in internationalisation strategy, and they can be analysed under two main headings: the intrinsic characteristics of the market and the nature of the competition. A key point here is how initial estimates of country attractiveness can be modified by various measures of *distance* and the likelihood of competitor *retaliation*. The section concludes by considering different *entry modes* into national markets.

8.5.1 Market characteristics

At least four elements of the PESTEL framework are particularly important in comparing countries for entry:

- *Political*. Political environments vary widely between countries and can alter rapidly. Russia since the fall of communism has seen frequent swings for and against private foreign enterprise. Governments can of course create significant opportunities for organisations. For example, the official regional development agency Scottish Enterprise provided a subsidy in order to attract the 2003 MTV music awards to the Scottish capital Edinburgh, while political and regulatory changes can create opportunities for international expansion as with Deutsche Post (see Illustration 8.2). It is important, however, to determine the level of *political risk* before entering a country.

- *Economic*. Key comparators in deciding entry are levels of gross domestic product and disposable income which help in estimating the potential size of the market. Fast-growth economies obviously provide opportunities, and in developing economies such as China growth is translating into an even faster creation of a high-consumption middle class. However, companies must also be aware of the stability of a country's currency which may affect its income stream. There can be considerable *currency risk*.

- *Social*. Social factors will clearly be important, for example the availability of a well-trained workforce or the size of demographic market segments – old or young – relevant to the strategy. Cultural variations need to be considered, for instance in defining tastes in the marketplace.

- *Legal*. Countries vary widely in their legal regime, determining the extent to which businesses can enforce contracts, protect intellectual property or avoid corruption. Similarly, policing will be important for the security of employees, a factor that in the past has deterred business in some South American countries.

It is quite common to rank country markets against each other on criteria such as these and then to choose the countries for entry that offer the highest relative scores. However, Pankaj Ghemawat has pointed out that what matters is not just the attractiveness of different countries relative to each other, but also the compatibility of the possible countries with the internationalising firm itself.[9] The argument is that, for firms coming from any particular country, some countries are more 'distant' – or incompatible – than others. In other words, companies with different nationalities would not fit equally well in all the top-ranked countries. A South American market might rank the same as an East African market in terms of attractiveness, but a Spanish company would probably be more at home in the first than the second. As well as a relative ranking of countries, therefore, each company has to add its assessment of countries according to their 'closeness'.

In arguing that 'distance still matters', Ghemawat offers a 'CAGE framework', with each letter of the acronym highlighting different dimensions of distance:

- *Cultural distance*. The distance dimension here relates to differences in language, ethnicity, religion and social norms. Cultural distance is not just a matter of similarity in consumer tastes, but extends to important compatibilities in terms of managerial behaviours. Here, for example, American firms might be closer to Canada than to Mexico, which Spanish firms might find relatively compatible.

- *Administrative and political distance*. Here distance is in terms of incompatible administrative, political or legal traditions. Colonial ties can diminish difference, so that the shared heritage of France and its former West African colonies creates certain understandings that go beyond linguistic advantages. Institutional weaknesses – for example, slow or corrupt administration – can open up distance between countries. So too can political differences: Chinese companies are increasingly able to operate in parts of the world that American companies are finding harder, for example parts of the Middle East and Africa.

- *Geographical distance*. This is not just a matter of the kilometres separating one country from another, but involves other geographical characteristics of the country such as size, sea access and the quality of communications infrastructure. For example, Wal-Mart's difficulties in Europe relate to the fact that its logistics systems were developed in the geographically enormous space of North America, and proved much less suitable for the smaller and more dense countries of Europe. Transport infrastructure can shrink or exaggerate physical distance. France is much closer to large parts of Continental Europe than to the UK, because of the barrier presented by the English Channel and the UK's relatively poor road and rail infrastructure.

- *Economic*. The final element of the CAGE framework refers particularly to wealth distances. Here, instead of simply assuming that a wealthy market is a good one to enter, and a poor market a bad one, the framework points to the differing capabilities of companies from different countries. Multinationals from rich countries are typically weak at serving consumers in poorer markets (see Illustration 8.4 for how Unilever approaches this problem). In developing countries, rich-country multinationals often end up focusing on economic elites. In reverse, it often takes a long time for companies from developing countries to learn all the requirements that the middle classes from wealthy countries routinely expect.[10]

8.5.2 Competitive characteristics

Assessing the relative attractiveness of markets by PESTEL and CAGE analyses is only the first step. The second element relates to competition. Here, of course, Porter's five forces framework can help (see section 2.3). For example, country markets with many existing competitors, powerful buyers (perhaps large retail chains such as in much of North America and Northern Europe) and low barriers to further new entrants from overseas would typically be unattractive.

Illustration 8.4

Strategic innovation at Hindustan Lever Ltd

Large multinational corporations may still need to tailor their products and services to local market needs.

Unilever is one of the world's biggest consumer products companies. It seeks to establish its brands on a global basis and support them with state-of-the-art research and development. However, it is acutely aware that markets differ and that, if it is to be global, it has to be prepared to adapt to local market conditions. It also recognises that if it is to have global reach, it has to be able to market its goods in poorer areas as well as richer areas. Indeed it estimates that by 2010 half of its sales will come from the developing world – an increase of over 30 per cent from the equivalent figure in 2000.

In the rural areas of India Hindustan Lever is setting about marketing Unilever's branded goods in ways suited to local conditions.

Much of the effort goes into marketing branded goods in local 'haats' or market places, where Unilever representatives sell the products from the back of trucks using loudspeakers to explain the brand proposition. Local executives argue that, poor as people are, they 'aren't naturally inclined to settle for throwaway versions of the real deal – if the companies that make the real deal bother to explain the difference'.

To help develop the skills to do this Lever management trainees in India begin their careers by spending weeks living in rural villages where they eat, sleep and talk with the locals: 'Once you have spent time with consumers, you realise that they want the same things you want. They want a good quality of life.'

The same executives have innovated further in the way goods are marketed. They have developed direct sales models where women, belonging to self-help groups that run micro credit operations, sell Lever products so as to make their collectives' savings grow. Where television viewing is uncommon, Hindustan Lever marketing executives have also mounted thousands of live shows at cattle and trade markets, employing rural folklore. The aim here is not just to push the Lever brands, it is to explain the importance of more frequent washing and better hygiene. Indeed sales personnel attend religious festivals and use ultraviolet light wands on people's hands to show the dangers of germs and dirt.

But it is not just the way the goods are marketed that is tailored to rural India. Product development is also different. For example, Indian women are very proud of the care of their hair and regard hair grooming as a luxury. However, they tend to use the same soap for body washing as for washing their hair. So Lever has dedicated research and development efforts into finding a low-cost soap that can be used for the body and for the hair and which is targeted to smaller towns and rural areas.

As Keki Dadiseth, a director of Hindustan Lever, puts it: 'Everyone wants brands. And there are a lot more poor people in the world than rich people. To be a global business . . . you have to participate in all segments.'

Source: Rekha Balu, 'Strategic innovation: Hindustan Lever Ltd', *FastCompany.com* (www.fastcompany.com/magazine), issue 47, June (2001).

Questions

1 What are the challenges a multinational such as Unilever faces in developing global brands whilst encouraging local responsiveness?

2 What other examples of local tailoring of global brands can you think of?

3 Multinationals have been criticised for marketing more expensive branded goods in poorer areas of developing countries. What are your views of the ethical dimensions to Hindustan Lever's activities?

Exhibit 8.5	International competitor retaliation

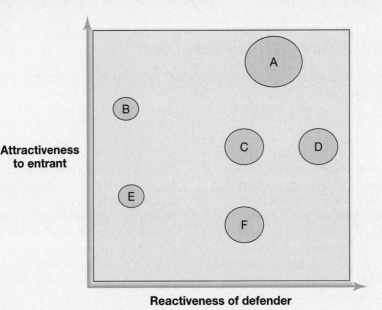

Note: Size of bubble indicates defender's relative clout.

Source: Reprinted by permission of *Harvard Business Review*. Exhibit adapted from 'Global gamesmanship' by I. MacMillan, S. van Putten and R. McGrath, May 2003. Copyright © 2003 by the Harvard Business School Publishing Corporation; all rights reserved.

However, an additional consideration is the likelihood of retaliation from other competitors.

In the five forces framework, retaliation potential relates to rivalry, but managers can extend this by using insights directly from 'game theory' (see section 6.7). Here the likelihood and ferocity of potential competitor reactions are added to the simple calculation of relative country market attractiveness. As in Exhibit 8.5, country markets are aligned against two axes.[11] The first is *market attractiveness* to the new entrant, based on PESTEL, CAGE and five forces analyses, for example. In the exhibit, countries A and B are the most attractive to the entrant. The second is the *defender's reactiveness*, likely to be influenced by the market's attractiveness to the defender but also by the extent to which the defender is working with a globally integrated, rather than multidomestic, strategy. A defender will be more reactive if the markets are important to it and it has the managerial capabilities to coordinate its response. Here, the defender is highly reactive in countries A and D. The third element is the *clout* (that is, power) that the defender is able to muster in order to fight back. Clout is typically a function of share in the particular market, but might be influenced by connections to other powerful local players, such as retailers or government. In Exhibit 8.5, clout is represented by the size of the bubbles, with the defender having most clout in countries A, C, D and F.

Choice of country to enter can be significantly modified by adding reactiveness and clout to calculations of attractiveness. Relying only on attractiveness, the top-ranked country to enter in Exhibit 8.5 is country A. Unfortunately, it is also one in which the defender is highly reactive, and the one in which it has most clout. Country B becomes a better international move than A. In turn, country C is a better prospect than country D, because, even though they are equally attractive, the defender is less reactive. One surprising result of taking defender reactiveness and clout into account is the re-evaluation of country E: although ranked fifth on simple attractiveness, it might rank second overall if competitor retaliation is allowed for.

This sort of analysis is particularly fruitful for considering the international moves of two interdependent competitors, such as Unilever and Procter and Gamble or British Airways and Singapore Airlines. In these cases the analysis is relevant to any aggressive strategic move, for instance the expansion of existing operations in a country as well as initial entry. Especially in the case of globally integrated competitors, moreover, the overall clout of the defender must be taken into account. The defender may choose to retaliate in other markets than the targeted one, counter-attacking wherever it has the clout to do damage to the aggressor. Naturally, too, this kind of analysis can be applied to interactions between diversified competitors as well as international ones: each bubble could represent different products or services.

8.5.3 Entry modes

Once a particular national market has been selected for entry, an organisation needs to choose how to enter that market. Entry modes differ in the degree of resource commitment to a particular market and the extent to which an organisation is operationally involved in a particular location. The key entry mode types are: exporting; contractual arrangement through licensing and franchising; joint ventures and alliances; and foreign direct investment, which in turn may involve the acquisition of established companies or 'greenfield' investments, the development of facilities 'from scratch'. These alternative methods of strategy development are explained further in section 10.3, but the specific advantages and disadvantages for international market entry are summarised in Exhibit 8.6.

Entry modes are often selected according to stages of organisational development. Internationalisation brings organisations into new and often unknown territory, requiring managers to learn new ways of doing business.[12] Internationalisation is therefore traditionally seen as a sequential process whereby companies gradually increase their commitment to newly entered markets, accumulating knowledge and increasing their capabilities along the way. This

Staged international expansion: firms initially use entry modes that allow them to maximise knowledge acquisition whilst minimising the exposure of their assets

strategy of **staged international expansion** means that firms begin by using entry modes such as licensing and exporting that allow them to acquire local knowledge whilst minimising the exposure of their assets. Once firms have sufficient knowledge and confidence, they can then sequentially increase their exposure, perhaps first by a joint venture and finally by direct foreign investment. An example is the entry of automobile manufacturer BMW into the American market. After a lengthy period of exporting from Germany to the USA, BMW set up a manufacturing plant in Spartanburg, South Carolina, in order to strengthen its competitive position in the strategically important American market.

In contrast to the gradual internationalisation followed originally by many large and established firms, some small firms are now internationalising rapidly at early stages in their development using multiple modes of entry to several countries. These are the so-called 'born global' firms.[13] GNI, the mini-multinational

Exhibit 8.6 **Market entry modes: advantages and disadvantages**

Exporting

Advantages

- No operational facilities needed in the host country
- Economies of scale can be exploited
- By using Internet, small/inexperienced firms can gain access to international markets

Disadvantages

- Does not allow the firm to benefit from the locational advantages of the host nation
- Limits opportunities to gain knowledge of local markets and competitors
- May create dependence on export intermediaries
- Exposure to trade barriers such as import duties
- Incurs transportation costs
- May limit the ability to respond quickly to customer demands

Joint ventures and alliances

Advantages

- Investment risk shared with partner
- Combining of complementary resources and know-how
- May be a governmental condition for market entry

Disadvantages

- Difficulty of identifying appropriate partner and agreeing appropriate contractual terms
- Managing the relationship with the foreign partner
- Loss of competitive advantage through imitation
- Limits ability to integrate and coordinate activities across national boundaries

Licensing

Advantages

- Contractually agreed income through sale of production and marketing rights
- Limits economic and financial exposure

Disadvantages

- Difficulty of identifying appropriate partner and agreeing contractual terms
- Loss of competitive advantage through imitation
- Limits benefits from the locational advantages of host nation

Foreign direct investment

Advantages

- Full control of resources and capabilities
- Facilitates integration and coordination of activities across national boundaries
- Acquisitions allow rapid market entry
- Greenfield investments allow development of state-of-the-art facilities and can attract financial support from the host government

Disadvantages

- Substantial investment in and commitment to host country leading to economic and financial exposure
- Acquisition may lead to problems of integration and coordination
- Greenfield entry time consuming and less predictable in terms of cost

in Illustration 8.5, illustrates this born global process. In achieving this rapid internationalisation, born global firms need to manage simultaneously the process of internationalisation and develop their wider strategy and infrastructure, whilst often lacking the usually expected experiential knowledge to do so.

Emerging country multinationals too are often moving quickly through entry modes. Prominent examples are the Chinese white goods multinational Haier, the Indian pharmaceuticals company Ranbaxy Laboratories and Mexico's Cemex cement company. These companies' international strategies are not simply

Illustration 8.5

The mini-multinational

GNI, a biotechnology start-up, has fewer than 100 employees, but operates in five countries in four continents.

Christopher Savoie is an American entrepreneur who originally studied medicine in Japan, becoming fluent in Japanese and adopting Japanese citizenship. In 2001, he founded GNI, a biotechnology company that by 2006 had raised 3bn yen (€20m) in investment funds, including a stake from famed global investment bank Goldman Sachs. The company already has operations in Tokyo and Fukuoka, Japan; in Shanghai, China; in Cambridge and London, UK; and in San Jose in California. There is also collaboration with a laboratory in Auckland, New Zealand. Savoie comments: 'We take the best in each country and put them together.'

GNI's strategy is to focus on Asian ailments that have been neglected by big Western pharmaceutical companies, for example stomach cancer and hepatitis. According to Savoie: 'Asia has been getting the short end of the stick. As a small company, we had to choose a niche, and we thought that half of humanity was an acceptable place to start.'

GNI's scientists work on umbilical cords, providing genetic tissue that has been virtually unaffected by the environment. However, Japanese parents traditionally keep their children's umbilical cords. GNI therefore works with the Rosie Maternity Hospital in Cambridge to source its basic genetic materials. On the other hand, GNI in Japan has ready access to supercomputers, and Japanese scientists have worked out the

algorithms required to analyse the genetic codes. Japan also has been the main source of investment funds, where regulations on start-ups are relaxed. China comes in as an effective place to test treatments on patients. Regulatory advantages mean that trials can be carried out more quickly in China, moreover for one-tenth of the cost in Japan. In 2005, GNI merged with Shanghai Genomics, a start-up run by two US-educated entrepreneurs. Meanwhile, in San Jose, there is a business development office seeking out relationships with the big American pharmaceutical giants.

Savoie describes the business model as essentially simple:

We have a Chinese cost structure, Japanese supercomputers and, in Cambridge, access to ethical materials (umbilical cords) and top clinical scientists. This is a network we can use to take high-level science and turn it into molecules to compete with the big boys.

Sources: D. Pilling, 'March of the mini-multinational', *Financial Times*, 4 May (2006); www.gene-networks.com.

Questions

1 Analyse GNI's value network in terms of cost advantages, unique capabilities and national characteristics.

2 What managerial challenges will GNI face as it grows?

export and cost based.[14] Typically they develop *unique capabilities* in their home market, in areas neglected by established multinationals. They then move on to establish outposts in more developed markets. For example, because of the needs of the Chinese market, Haier became skilled at very efficient production of simple white goods, providing a cost advantage that is transferable outside a Chinese manufacturing base. In 1999, Haier set up a manufacturing operation in South Carolina in the USA, competing head-on with Western giant multinationals such as General Electric and Whirlpool on their home territory.

8.6   INTERNATIONALISATION AND PERFORMANCE

Just as for product and service diversity discussed in section 7.2.3 the relationship between internationalisation and performance has been extensively researched.[15] Some of the main findings from such research are these:

- *An inverted-U curve*. While the potential performance benefits of internationalisation are substantial, in that it allows firms to realise economies of scale and scope and benefit from the locational advantages available in countries around the globe, the combination of diverse locations and diverse business units also gives rise to high levels of organisational complexity. After a point, the costs of organisational complexity may exceed the benefits of internationalisation. Accordingly, theory and the balance of evidence suggest an inverted-U-shaped relationship between internationalisation and performance (similar to the findings on product/service diversification shown in Exhibit 7.4 and reported in section 7.2.3), with moderate levels of internationalisation leading to the best results. However, Yip's recent research on large British companies suggests that managers may be getting better at internationalisation, with substantially internationalized firms actually seeing performance improving at the point where international sales are above about 40 per cent of total sales.[16] Experience and commitment to internationalisation may be able deliver strong performance for highly internationalised firms.

- *Service sector disadvantages*. A number of studies have suggested that, in contrast to firms in the manufacturing sector, internationalisation may not lead to improved performance for service sector firms. There are three possible reasons for such an effect. First, the operations of foreign service firms in some sectors (such as accountants or banks) remain tightly regulated and restricted in many countries; second, due to the intangible nature of services, they are often more sensitive to cultural differences and require greater adaptation than manufactured products which may lead to higher initial learning costs; third, services typically require a significant local presence and reduce the scope for the exploitation of economies of scale in production compared with manufacturing firms.[17]

- *Internationalisation and product diversity*. An important question to consider is the interaction between internationalisation and product/service diversification. Compared with single-business firms it has been suggested that product-diversified firms are likely to do better from international expansion because they have already developed the necessary skills and structures for managing internal diversity. At the other end of the spectrum there is general consensus that firms that are highly diversified in terms of both product and international markets are likely to face excessive costs of coordination and control leading to poor performance. As many firms have not yet reached levels of internationalisation where negative effects outweigh possible gains, and because of current scepticism with regard to the benefits of high levels of product diversification, many companies currently opt for reducing their product diversity while building their international scope. Unilever, for example, has been combining a strategy of growing internationalisation with de-diversification.

8.7 ROLES IN AN INTERNATIONAL PORTFOLIO

Just as for product diversification, international strategies imply different relationships between subsidiary operations and the corporate centre. The complexity of the strategies followed by organisations such as General Motors or Unilever can result in highly differentiated networks of subsidiaries with a range of distinct strategic roles. Subsidiaries may play different roles according to the level of local resources and capabilities available to them and the strategic importance of their local environment (see Exhibit 8.7):[18]

Exhibit 8.7 **Subsidiary roles in multinational firms**

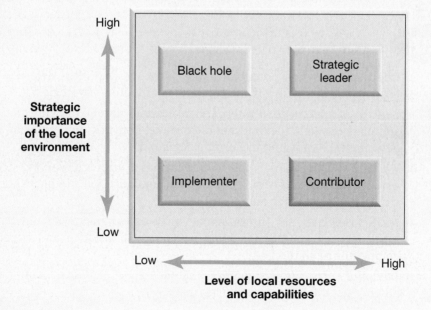

Source: Reprinted by permission of Harvard Business School Press. From *Managing Across Borders: The Transnational Solution* by C.A. Bartlett and S. Ghoshal. Boston, MA 1989, pp. 105–11. Copyright © 1989 by the Harvard Business School Publishing Corporation; all rights reserved.

Strategic leaders (in the context of international strategy) are subsidiaries that not only hold valuable resources and capabilities but are also located in countries that are crucial for competitive success

Contributors are subsidiaries with valuable internal resources but located in countries of lesser strategic significance, which none the less play key roles in a multinational organisation's competitive success

Implementers simply execute strategies developed elsewhere and may generate surplus financial resources to help fund initiatives elsewhere

Black holes are subsidiaries located in countries that are crucial for competitive success but with low-level resources or capabilities

- **Strategic leaders** are subsidiaries that not only hold valuable resources and capabilities but are also located in countries that are crucial for competitive success because of, for example, the size of the local market or the accessibility of key technologies. Japanese and European subsidiaries in the USA often play this role.

- **Contributors**, subsidiaries with valuable internal resources but located in countries of lesser strategic significance, can nevertheless play key roles in a multinational organisation's competitive success. The Australian subsidiary of the Swedish telecommunications firm Ericsson played such a role in developing specialized systems for the firm's mobile phone business.

- **Implementers**, though not contributing substantially to the enhancement of a firm's competitive advantage, are important in the sense that they help generate vital financial resources. In this sense, they are similar to the 'cash cows' of the BCG matrix. The danger is that they turn into the equivalent of 'dogs'.

- **Black holes** are subsidiaries located in countries that are crucial for competitive success but with low-level resources or capabilities. This is a position many subsidiaries of American and European firms found themselves in over long periods in Japan. They have some of the characteristics of 'question marks' in the BCG matrix, requiring heavy investment (like an astrophysicist's black hole, sucking matter in). Possibilities for overcoming this unattractive position include the development of alliances and the selective and targeted development of key resources and capabilities.[19]

Again this does, of course, in turn relate to how these subsidiaries are controlled and managed and this is discussed in Chapter 12. See also the key debate in Illustration 8.6.

SUMMARY

- Internationalisation potential in any particular market is determined by four drivers: market, cost, government and competitors' strategies.

- Sources of advantage in international strategy can be drawn from both global sourcing through the international value network and national sources of advantage, as captured in Porter's Diamond.

- There are four main types of international strategy, varying according to extent of coordination and geographical configuration: simple export, complex export, multidomestic and global.

- Market selection for international entry or expansion should be based on attractiveness, multidimensional measures of distance and expectations of competitor retaliation.

- Modes of entry into new markets include export, licensing, joint ventures and alliances and foreign direct investment.

- Internationalisation has an uncertain relationship to financial performance, with an inverted-U curve warning against over-internationalisation.

- Subsidiaries in an international firm can be managed by portfolio methods just as businesses in a diversified firm.

Illustration 8.6

Global, local or regional?

Debate rages over whether companies are really becoming more global, or whether local or indeed regional pressures remain strong.

Ted Levitt, Harvard Business School professor and former non-executive director of the international advertising firm Saatchi & Saatchi, has provocatively made the case for deep commitment to global strategies in all kinds of markets. He argues that modern communications technologies are creating homogeneous market needs, while manufacturing technologies are increasing the benefits of scale. Given the cost advantages of scale, and the diminishing importance of consumer differences, companies that commit to truly global strategies will be able to use low prices to sweep out all competitors still focused on local needs. He argues: 'The global company will seek to standardize its offering everywhere. . . . Companies that do not adopt to the new global realities will become victims of those that do.' He cites Coca-Cola, Rolex, Sony and McDonald's as exemplars of the trend. Companies should not hanker over detailed differences left over from the past, but recognise the big picture of coming globalisation.

Levitt's sweeping argument brought a spirited response from American academics Gerry Wind and Susan Douglas, warning of 'the Myth of Globalisation'. They challenge both the trend to homogenisation and the growing role of scale economies. Even apparently global companies adapt to country needs: for example, Coca-Cola sells local products in Japan alongside its classic Coke, and its Dasani bottled water is a success in the USA, but a failure in Europe. As to scale, new flexible automation technologies may even be reducing economic order sizes, allowing short production runs adapted to local needs. Besides, as the world gets richer, consumers will be less price sensitive and more ready to spend on indulging their local tastes. Wind and Douglas warn that blind confidence in the inevitability of globalisation will surely lead to business disappointment.

Between the two poles of global and local there is a third position: regional. Pankaj Ghemawat points out that most international trade is intra-regional. European countries trade predominantly with each other. The trend towards intra-regional trade is actually growing, from about 40 per cent of all trade 40 years ago to 55 per cent at the beginning of the twenty-first century. This is reflected in the nature of multinational companies as well. Alan Rugman calculates that in the early years of the twenty-first century over 300 out of the world's largest corporations still have more than half their sales in their home region. An apparently global company like McDonald's is effectively bi-regional, with 80 per cent of its sales concentrated in North America and Europe. Established multinationals such as General Electric and Procter and Gamble have 60 per cent and 55 per cent of their sales respectively back home in North America.

Ted Levitt might be impatient with these empirical details. The essential issue for him is: where are things going in the future? Certainly there are still local differences in taste, but are these declining overall? Maybe there is a growth of intra-regional trade, but is this just the result of transitional events such as the creation of the North American Free Trade Agreement or the sucking-in of imports by China? We should not be distracted by temporary blips on the grand highway to global integration.

Sources: T. Levitt, 'The globalization of markets', *Harvard Business Review*, May–June (1983), pp. 92–102; S. Douglas and G. Wind, 'The myth of globalization', *California Journal of World Business*, vol. 22, no. 4 (1987), pp. 19–30; P. Ghemawat, 'Regional strategies for global leadership', *Harvard Business Review*, December (2005), pp. 98–108; A. Rugman, *The regional multinationals*, Cambridge University Press, 2005.

Questions

1 Make a list of products and services which are getting more 'global' over time; then make a list of products and services which are getting less 'global'.

2 How many countries in the world have you visited in your lifetime? How many countries had your parents visited by the same age?

Work assignments

✱ Denotes more advanced work assignments.   * Refers to a case study in the Text and Case edition.

8.1   Using Exhibit 8.2 (Yip's globalisation drivers), compare two markets you are familiar with and analyse how strong each of the drivers is for increased international strategy.

8.2 ✱ Taking an industry you are familiar with that is strong in your home country (for example, fashion in France, cars in Germany), use the four determinants of Porter's Diamond (Exhibit 8.3) to explain that industry's national advantage.

8.3   Using the four international strategies of Exhibit 8.4, classify the international strategy of AIB*, SABMiller* or any other multinational corporation with which you are familiar.

8.4 ✱ Using the CAGE framework (section 8.5.1), assess the relative distance of possible overseas markets for a small entrepreneurial company such as MacPac* or Brown Bag Films* to expand into. What entry modes (export, alliances, licensing or direct investment) would you recommend for the most attractive markets?

8.5 ✱ Take any part of the public or not-for-profit sector (for example, education, health) and explain how far internationalisation has affected its management and consider how far it may do in the future.

Integrative assignment

8.6   As in 8.3, use the four international strategies of Exhibit 8.4 to classify the international strategy of AIB*, SABMiller* or any other multinational corporation with which you are familiar. Drawing on section 12.2, how does this corporation's organisational structure fit (or not fit) this strategy?

An extensive range of additional materials, including audio summaries, weblinks to organisations featured in the text, definitions of key concepts and self-assessment questions, can be found on the *Exploring Corporate Strategy* Companion Website at **www.pearsoned.co.uk/ecs**

Recommended key readings

- An eye-opening introduction to the detailed workings – and inefficiencies – of today's global economy is P. Rivoli, *The Travels of a T-Shirt in the Global Economy: an Economist Examines the Markets, Power and Politics of World Trade*, Wiley, 2006. A more optimistic view is in T. Friedman, *The World is Flat: the Globalized World in the Twenty First Century*, Penguin, 2006.

- An invigorating perspective on international strategy is provided by G. Yip, *Total Global Strategy II*, Prentice Hall, 2003. A comprehensive general

textbook is A. Rugman and S. Collinson, *International Business*, 4th edition, FT/Prentice Hall, 2006.

- A useful collection of academic articles on international business is in A. Rugman and T. Brewer (eds), *The Oxford Handbook of International Business*, Oxford University Press, 2003.

- For information on the financial considerations with respect to international developments see G. Arnold *Corporate Financial Management*, 3rd edition, FT/Prentice Hall, 2005, Chapter 7.

References

1. Indeed, many authors refer to internationalisation simply as 'international diversification': see N. Capar and M. Kotabe, 'The relationship between international diversification and performance in service firms', *Journal of International Business Studies*, vol. 34 (2003), pp. 345–355.

2. T. Friedman, *The World is Flat: the Globalized World in the Twenty First Century*, Penguin, 2006; and P. Rivoli, *The Travels of a T-Shirt in the Global Economy: an Economist Examines the Markets, Power and Politics of World Trade*, Wiley, 2006.

3. G. Yip, *Total Global Strategy II*, Prentice Hall, 2003.

4. Useful industry-specific data on trends in openness to trade and investment can be found at the World Trade Organization's site, www.wto.org.

5. G. Hamel and C.K. Prahalad, 'Do you really have a global strategy?', *Harvard Business Review*, vol. 63, no. 4 (1985), pp. 139–148.

6. B. Kogut, 'Designing global strategies: comparative and competitive value added changes', *Sloan Management Review*, vol. 27 (1985), pp. 15–28.

7. M. Porter, *The Competitive Advantage of Nations*, Macmillan, 1990.

8. This typology builds on the basic framework of M. Porter, 'Changing patterns of international competition', *California Management Review*, vol. 28, no. 2 (1987), pp. 9–39, but adapts its terms for the four strategies into more readily understandable terms: note particularly that here 'global' strategy is transposed to refer to the top left box, and the top right box is described as 'complex export'.

9. P. Ghemawat, 'Distance still matters', *Harvard Business Review*, September (2001), pp. 137–147.

10. For a good analysis of developing country companies and their opportunities, see T. Khanna and K. Palepu, 'Emerging giants: building world-class companies in developing countries', *Harvard Business Review*, October (2006), pp. 60–69.

11. This framework is introduced in I. Macmillan, A. van Putten and R. McGrath, 'Global gamesmanship', *Harvard Business Review*, vol. 81, no. 5 (2003), pp. 62–71.

12. For detailed discussions about the role of learning and experience in market entry see M.F. Guillén, 'Experience, imitation, and the sequence of foreign entry: wholly owned and joint-venture manufacturing by South Korean firms and business groups in China, 1987–1995', *Journal of International Business Studies*, vol. 83 (2003), pp. 185–198; and M.K. Erramilli, 'The experience factor in foreign market entry modes by service firms', *Journal of International Business Studies*, vol. 22, no. 3 (1991), pp. 479–501.

13. G. Knights and T. Cavusil, 'A taxonomy of born-global firms', *Management International Review*, vol. 45, no. 3 (2005), pp. 15–35.

14. For analyses of emerging country multinationals, see T. Khanna and K. Palepu, 'Emerging giants: building world-class companies in developing countries', *Harvard Business Review*, October (2006), pp. 60–69; and J. Sinha, 'Global champions from emerging markets', *McKinsey Quarterly*, no. 2 (2005), pp. 26–35.

15. A useful review of the international dimension is M. Hitt and R.E. Hoskisson, 'International diversification: effects on innovation and firm performance in product-diversified firms', *Academy of Management Journal*, vol. 40, no. 4 (1997), pp. 767–798.

16. For detailed results on British companies, see G. Yip, A. Rugman and A. Kudina, 'International success of British companies', *Long Range Planning*, vol. 39, no. 1 (2006), pp. 241–264.

17. See N. Capar and M. Kotabe, 'The relationship between international diversification and performance in service firms', *Journal of International Business Studies*, vol. 34 (2003), pp. 345–355; and F.J. Contractor, S.K. Kundu and C. Hsu, 'A three-stage theory of international expansion: the link between multinationality and performance in the service sector', *Journal of International Business Studies*, vol. 34 (2003), pp. 5–18.

18. C.A. Bartlett and S. Ghosal, *Managing Across Borders: The Transnational Solution*, The Harvard Business School Press, 1989, pp. 105–111; A.M. Rugman and A. Verbeke, 'Extending the theory of the multinational enterprise: internalization and strategic management perspectives', *Journal of International Business Studies*, vol. 34 (2003), pp. 125–137.

19. For a more far-reaching exploration of the role of subsidiaries in multinational corporations see J. Birkinshaw, *Entrepreneurship and the Global Firm*, Sage, 2000.

Lenovo computers: East meets West

Introduction

In May 2005, the world's thirteenth largest personal computer company, Lenovo, took over the world's third largest personal computer business, IBM's PC division. Lenovo, at that time based wholly in China, was paying $1.75bn (€1.4bn, £1bn) to control a business that operated all over the world and had effectively invented the personal computer industry back in 1981. Michael Dell, the creator of the world's largest PC company, commented simply: 'it won't work'.

Lenovo had been founded back in 1984 by Liu Chuanzhi, a 40-year-old researcher working for the Computer Institute of the Chinese Academy of Sciences. His early career had included disassembling captured American radar systems during the Vietnam War and planting rice during the Chinese Cultural Revolution. Liu Chuanzhi had started with $25,000 capital from the Computer Institute and promised his boss that he would build a business with revenues of $250,000. Working in the Computer Institute's old guardhouse, and borrowing its office facilities, one of Liu's first initiatives was reselling colour televisions. But real success started to come in 1987, when Lenovo was one of the first to package Chinese-character software with imported PCs.

Lenovo began to take off, with Liu using the support of his father, well placed in the Chinese government, to help import PCs cheaply through Hong Kong. During 1988, Lenovo placed its first job advertisement, and recruited 58 young people to join the company. Whilst the founding generation of Lenovo staff were in their forties, the new recruits were all in their twenties, as the Cultural Revolution had prevented any university graduates for a period of 10 years in China. Amongst the new recruits was Yang Yuanqing, who would be running Lenovo's PC business before he was 30, and later become Chairman of the new Lenovo–IBM venture at the age of 41. It was this new team which helped launch the

Lenovo's Chairman, Yang Yuanqing

production of the first Lenovo PC in 1990, and drove the company to a 30 per cent market share within China by 2005. The company had partially floated on the Hong Kong Stock Exchange in 1994.

The deal

Work on the IBM PC deal had begun in 2004, with Lenovo assisted by management consultancy McKinsey & Co. and investment banker Goldman Sachs. IBM wanted to dispose of its PC business, which had only 4 per cent market share in the USA and suffered low margins in a competitive market dominated by Dell and Hewlett Packard. Higher margin services and mainframe computers would be IBM's future. As well as Lenovo, IBM had private equity firm Texas Pacific Group in the bidding. Lenovo offered the best price, but Texas Pacific was persuaded enough to take a stake in the new group, while IBM took 13 per cent ownership. The government-owned Chinese Academy of Sciences still owned 27 per cent of the stock, the largest single shareholder.

The new Chairman, Yang Yuanqing, had a clear vision of what the company was to achieve, while recognising some of the challenges:

In five years, I want this (Lenovo) to be a very famous PC brand, with maybe double the growth of the industry. I want to have a very healthy profit margin, and maybe some other businesses beyond PCs, worldwide. We are at the beginnings of this new company, so we can define some fundamentals about the culture. The three words I use to describe this are trust, respect, compromise.

He continued:

As a global company maybe we have to sacrifice some speed, especially during our first phase. We need more communication. We need to take time to understand each other. But speed was in the genes of the old Lenovo. I hope it will be in the genes of the new Lenovo.

IBM was not leaving its old business to sink or swim entirely on its own. Lenovo had the right to use the IBM brand for PCs for five years, including the valuable ThinkPad name. IBM's salesforce would be offered incentives to sell Lenovo PCs, just as they had with IBM's own-brand machines. IBM Global Services was contracted to provide maintenance and support. IBM would have two non-voting observers on the Lenovo board. Moreover, Stephen Ward, the 51-year-old former head of IBM's PC division, was to become Lenovo's Chief Executive Officer.

Managing the new giant

Having an IBM CEO was not entirely a surprise. After all, the $13bn business was nearly 80 per cent ex-IBM and customers and employees had to be reassured of continuity. But there were some significant challenges for the new company to manage none the less.

Things had not started well. When the Chinese team first flew to New York to meet the IBM team, they had not been met at the airport as they had expected and was normal polite practice in China. Yang and Ward had disagreed about the location of the new headquarters, Yang wishing it to be shared between Beijing and near New York. Ward had prevailed, and Yang moved his family to the USA. The new organisation structure kept the old IBM business and the original Lenovo business as separate divisions. But still the new company needed considerable liaison with China, a 13-hour flight away, across 12 time zones. Teleconferencing between the East Coast and China became a way of life, with the Americans calling typically at either 6.00 in the morning or 11.00 at night to catch their Chinese colleagues. Calls were always in English, with many Chinese less than fluent and body language impossible to observe.

The Chinese nature of the company was an issue for some constituencies. IBM had had a lot of government business, and populist members of the US Congress whipped up a scare campaign about Chinese computers entering sensitive domains. In Germany, labour laws allowed a voluntary transition of IBM employees to Lenovo, and many German workers chose not to transfer, leaving the company short staffed. There was some discomfort amongst former IBM employees in Japan about Chinese ownership. Between the two dominant cultures, American and Chinese, there were considerable differences. Qiao Jian, Vice President for Human Resources, commented:

Americans like to talk; Chinese people like to listen. At first we wondered why they kept talking when they had nothing to say. But we have learnt to be more direct when we have a problem, and the Americans are learning to listen.

Cultural differences were not just national. Lenovo was a new and relatively simple company – basically one country, one product. Multinational giant IBM Corporation, founded in 1924, was far more complex. The Lenovo management team, mostly in their thirties, were much younger than IBM's, and the average age of the company as a whole was just 28. IBM was famous for its management processes and routines. Qiao Jian commented: 'IBM people set a time for a conference call and stick to it every week. But why have the call if there is nothing to report?' On the other hand, IBM people had a tendency for being late for meetings, something that was strictly discouraged within Lenovo.

Some results

At first, the response to the new Lenovo was positive. IBM customers stayed loyal and the stock price began to climb (see Figure 1). Remaining IBM executives recognised that at least they were part of a business committed to PCs, rather than the Cinderella in a much larger IBM empire. The fact that a Lenovo PC manufactured in China had a labour cost of just $3.00 offered a lot of opportunity.

However, market leader Dell responded to the new company with heavy price cuts, offering $100 savings

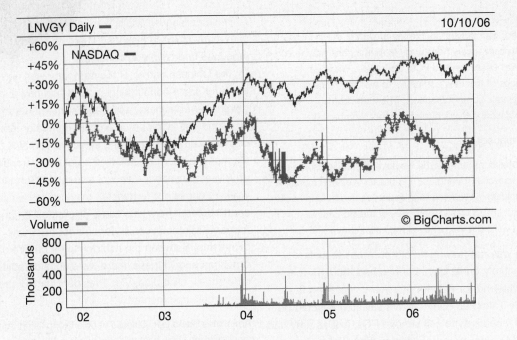

Figure 1 Lenovo Group's stock price, 2001–2006, compared with NASDAQ index

Source: www.bigcharts.com (11 October 2006). Marketwatch.Online by BigCharts.com. Copyright 2006 by Dow Jones & Company, Inc. Reproduced with permission of Dow Jones & Company, Inc. in the format Textbook via Copyright Clearance Center.

on the average machine. With market share in the crucial American market beginning to slip, ex-IBM CEO Stephen Ward was replaced in December 2005 by William Amelio. This was a coup for Lenovo, as Amelio had been running Dell's Asia–Pacific region. As well as knowing Lenovo's competitor from the inside, Amelio, based for several years in Singapore, had a good understanding of Asian business:

In the five years I have been in Asia, one thing I have learned . . . is to have a lot more patience. I have to be someone who has a high sense of urgency and drive, but I have also learned how to temper that in the various cultures that I have dealt with in order to be more effective.

Amelio started by addressing costs, removing 1,000 positions, or 10 per cent, from Lenovo's non-China workforce. He integrated the IBM business and the old Lenovo business into a single structure. The company launched a new range of Lenovo-branded PCs for small and medium-sized American business, a market traditionally ignored by IBM. To improve its reach in this segment, Lenovo expanded sales to big American retailers such as Office Depot. US market share began to recover, pushing beyond 4 per cent again. Lenovo began to consider entry into the Indian market.

Amelio's actions seemed to pay off. After a precipitous slide during the first half of 2006, the stock price turned up. But there was no disguising that the stock price in the autumn of 2006 was still below where it was five years earlier, and that it continued to trail the hi-tech American NASDAQ index.

Sources: L. Zhijun, *The Lenovo Affair*, Wiley, Singapore, 2006; *Business Week*, 7 August (2006), 20 April (2006), 22 December (2005) and 9 May (2005); *Financial Times*, 8 November (2005), 9 November (2005) and 10 November (2005).

Questions

1 What national sources of competitive advantage might Lenovo draw from its Chinese base? What disadvantages derive from its Chinese base?

2 In the light of the CAGE framework and the MacMillan *et al.* Competitor Retaliation framework (Exhibit 8.5), comment on Lenovo's entry into the American market.

3 Now that Lenovo is international, what type of generic international strategy should it pursue – simple export, multidomestic, complex export or global?

Innovation and Entrepreneurship

LEARNING OUTCOMES

After reading this chapter you should be able to:

→ Identify and respond to key innovation dilemmas, such as the relative emphases to place on technologies or markets, product or process innovations, and the broad business model.

→ Anticipate and to some extent influence the diffusion (or spread) of innovations.

→ Decide when being a first-mover or a follower is most appropriate in innovation, and how an incumbent organisation should respond to innovative challengers.

→ Anticipate key issues facing entrepreneurs as they go through the stages of growth, from start-up to exit.

→ Evaluate opportunities and choices facing social entrepreneurs as they create new ventures to address social problems.

Photo: Tracey Fahy/Alamy Images

9.1 INTRODUCTION

Innovation and entrepreneurship are fundamental drivers in today's economy. Steve Jobs is a technological innovator, whose creativity in computers, electronics and film led to Apple Computers and built Pixar into one of the world's leading animation companies. Sir Stelios Haji-Ioannou is a business model innovator, whose introduction of online ticketing and simplified airline routing has been at the heart of the easyJet airline. Nobel Prize winner Muhammad Yunus is a social entrepreneur and innovator, pioneer of microcredit – small loans to entrepreneurs too poor to be considered by ordinary banks – and founder of the Grameen Bank in Bangladesh.

This chapter centres on innovation, both as driven by independent entrepreneurs and as generated by people inside established organisations. Innovation is a key aspect of business-level strategy as introduced in Chapter 6, with implications for quality, price and sustainability. It is also one of the directions of growth highlighted in Chapter 7. Entrepreneurship is at the origins of all businesses. Innovation and entrepreneurship are linked by a common concern for the creation of new phenomena, whether new organisations or new products, services or processes. For private sector organisations operating in increasingly competitive markets, innovation is often a condition of simple survival. For public sector organisations too, ceaseless cost pressures and increasing public demands are compelling constant innovation and even new kinds of entrepreneurship.

Two themes run through this chapter. The first is timing. Critical timing decisions include when to be *first-mover* or *fast second* in innovation; when, and if, an innovation will reach its *tipping point*, the point where demand takes off; and, for an entrepreneurial new venture, when to bring in external managers or finally to exit. The other theme is relationships. Creating innovations or new organisations is very rarely done alone. Successful innovation and entrepreneurship are typically done through relationships. These relationships come in many forms: sometimes relationships between organisations and their customers; sometimes relationships between big business and small start-ups; sometimes between business and 'social entrepreneurs'. Exhibit 9.1 summarises the links between timing, relationships and both innovation and entrepreneurship.

Within this broad framework, this chapter will examine first innovation, then entrepreneurship:

- Section 9.2 starts with three *fundamental dilemmas* with regard to which managers must decide their focus: technology push as against market pull; product innovation rather than process innovation; and finally technological as opposed to broader business model innovation. None of these are absolute 'either–or' dilemmas, but managers must choose where to concentrate their limited resources.

- Section 9.3 considers issues surrounding the *diffusion*, or spread, of innovations in the marketplace. Diffusion can be accelerated or inhibited by managerial choices on both the supply side, for example product design, and the demand side, for example marketing. Diffusion processes often follow *S-curve patterns*, raising further typical issues for decision, particularly with regard to tipping points and tripping points.

| Exhibit 9.1 | **The innovation–entrepreneurship framework** |

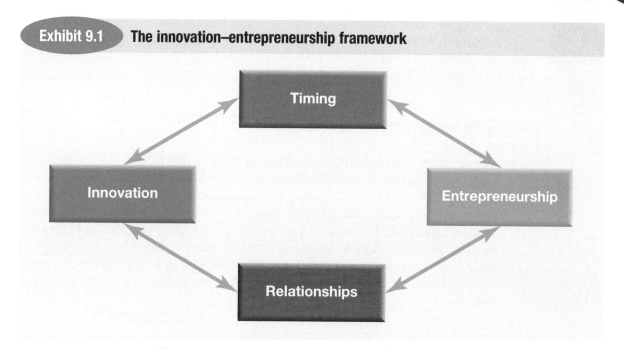

- Section 9.4 completes the discussion of innovation by considering choices with regard to timing. This includes *first-mover* advantages and disadvantages, the opportunities of being *fast second* into a market, and the issue of how established incumbents should respond to innovative challengers.

- Section 9.5 addresses *entrepreneurship*. The section discusses typical choices facing entrepreneurs as their ventures progress through the uncertain *stages of growth*, from start-up to exit. It also examines the kinds of *relationships* that entrepreneurs may have to form, particularly with larger firms practising 'open innovation'.

- Section 9.6 finally introduces *social entrepreneurship*, by which individuals and small groups can launch innovative and flexible new initiatives that larger public agencies are often unable to pursue. Again, social entrepreneurs face choices with regard to relationships, particularly with big business.

The key debate of the chapter (Illustration 9.6) brings entrepreneurship and innovation together again by considering the issue of whether small or large firms are better at innovation.

Innovation involves the conversion of new knowledge into a new product, process or service and the putting of this new product, process or service into use, either via the marketplace or by other processes of delivery

9.2   INNOVATION DILEMMAS

www.pearsoned.co.uk/ecs

KEY CONCEPT

Innovation dilemmas

Innovation raises fundamental strategic dilemmas for strategists. Innovation is more complex than just invention. Invention involves the conversion of new knowledge into a new product, process or service. **Innovation** adds the critical extra step of putting this new product, process or service into use, in the private sector typically via the marketplace and in the public sector through service delivery.[1] The strategic dilemmas stem from this more complex and extended process. Strategists have to make choices with regard to three fundamental issues:

how far to follow technological opportunity as against market demand; how much to invest in product innovation rather than process innovation; and finally whether to focus on technological innovation rather than extending innovation to their whole business model.[2]

9.2.1 Technology push or market pull

People often see innovation as driven by technology. In this *technology push*[2] view, technologists or scientists carry out research in their laboratories in order to create new knowledge. This new knowledge forms the basis for new products, processes or services that are then 'handed over' to the rest of the organisation to make, market and distribute. Technological advances push what goes into the marketplace. According to this perspective, managers should listen primarily to their scientists and technologists, let them follow their hunches and support them with ample resources. Generous R&D budgets are crucial to making innovation happen.

An alternative approach to innovation is *market pull*. Market pull reflects a view of innovation that goes beyond invention and sees the importance of actual use. The role of market pull has been promoted since Eric von Hippel's discovery that in many sectors users, not producers, are common sources of important innovations.[3] In designing their innovation strategies, therefore, organisations should listen in the first place to users rather than their own scientists and technologists. Von Hippel refines this focus on users to point out that in many markets it is not ordinary users that are the source of innovation, but *lead-users*. In medical surgery, top surgeons often adapt existing surgical instruments in order to carry out new types of operation. In extreme sports such as snowboarding or windsurfing, it is leading sportspeople who make the improvements necessary to greater performance. In this view, then, it is the pull of users in the market that is responsible for innovation. Managers need to build close relationships with lead-users such as the best surgeons or sporting champions. Marketing and sales functions identify the lead-users of a field and then scientists and technologists translate their inventive ideas into commercial products, processes or services that the wider market can use.

There are merits to both the technology push and market pull views. Relying heavily on existing users can make companies too conservative, and vulnerable to disruptive technologies that uncover needs unforeseen by existing markets (see section 9.4.3). On the other hand, history is littered with examples of companies that have blindly pursued technological excellence without regard to real market needs. Technology push and market pull are best seen as extreme views, therefore, helping to focus attention on a fundamental choice: relatively how much to rely on science and technology as sources of innovation, rather than what people are actually doing in the market. In practice, most organisations find a compromise between the two views, with the balance varying between industries and often over time. As at the skateboarding company Sole Technology, users may be key at start-up, but internally led innovation can become more important with growth (see Illustration 9.1). The key issue for managers is to be aware of the dilemma and to review their organisation's balance between the two extremes consciously rather than relying on habit or prejudice.

Illustration 9.1

Shoes for skateboarders

Innovation at Sole Technologies is driven by both users and technology.

After taking a degree in industrial software, Pierre André Senizergues started his career as a professional skateboarder in France. In less than 20 years, he created an action shoe and apparel business with $200m (£112m; €160m) sales, and seven brands, including Etnies with its famous upside-down 'E' and the big snowboarding boot brand ThirtyTwo. He also created the first skateboard shoe research laboratory in the world.

Things had not started out so promisingly for Senizergues. In 1988 he signed to ride for the skateboard brand of a new French venture. The very next year he was forced to retire from professional skateboarding with back problems. Although he spoke poor English and had little business experience, he persuaded his employer to grant him the licence to sell its Etnies shoes in the USA. The first five years were very hard, but Senizergues introduced his own designs and from the mid-1990s Etnies began to take off. In 1996, Senizergues bought the Etnies brand from the French venture and incorporated it and other brands – including éS, Emerica and ThirtyTwo – under the Sole Technology umbrella. Growth over the next 10 years ran at double digits per annum.

From the first, Senizergues had been able to use his expertise as a professional skateboarder in his designs. He told the *Financial Times*: 'In this market, you have to be authentic, you have to come from skateboarding.' For example, in the 1990s he had noticed that skateboarders were buying unsuitable low-top shoes for their looks, rather than high-top shoes with the proper performance characteristics. Senizergues responded by designing low-top shoes that had the necessary durability. His company has stayed close to its sports, sponsoring more than 100 athletes around the world. It listens closely to customers. The company's website has a design-your-own shoe facility and it often releases potential specifications for its new products through blogs, in order to solicit feedback and ideas. The average age of Sole Technology's 400 employees is 28, with many still involved in action sports.

However, Senizergues has also built the world's first skateboarding research facility, the Sole Technology Institute. With 10,000 square feet (930m^2), it reproduces typical skateboarding obstacles such as rails, stairs and ledges. Senizergues believes that it is time for skateboarding to do its own biomechanical research, instead of borrowing technologies developed in other sports. One of the outputs of the Sole Technology Institute has been the G202 gel-and-air bag technology. As the trend for girls' shoes moved towards slim silhouettes during 2006, this gel-and-air technology has allowed Sole Technology to keep right abreast of fashion.

Sources: *Financial Times*, 23 August (2006); *Footwear News*, 20 February (2006); www.soletechnology.com.

Questions

1 For what reasons is it important to be 'authentic' in the skateboarding shoe market?

2 If a big company like Nike or Adidas was looking to grow in this market, what would you advise it to do?

9.2.2 Product or process innovation

Just as managers must find a balance between technological push and market pull, so must they determine the relative emphasis to place on product or process innovation. *Product innovation* relates to the final product (or service) to be sold, especially with regard to its features; *process innovation* relates to the way in which this product is produced and distributed, especially with regard to improvements in cost or reliability. Some firms specialise more in product innovation, others more in process innovation. For example, in computers, Apple has generally pioneered in terms of product features (for instance, the iMac), while Dell has innovated in terms of efficient processes, for instance direct sales, modularity and build to order.

Industries often follow technological trajectories according to which the relative importance of product innovation and process innovation change over time. Periods of product innovation based on new features are often followed by periods of process innovation based on efficiency in production and delivery. William Abernathy, for example, has shown how the early history of the automobile was dominated by competition in product design, as pioneers competed as to whether cars should be fuelled by steam, electricity or petrol, place their engines at the front or at the rear, and have three wheels or four.[3] Once Henry Ford introduced the Model T, the industry settled on a *dominant design*: cars would generally be petrol driven, with their engines at the front and four wheels. As soon as this dominant design was established, the rate of product innovation fell as competition shifted to producing this basic type of car as efficiently as possible. Establishing the dominant design thus promoted a surge of process innovation. Here Ford pioneered again, with the epochal process innovation of the automated assembly line allowing mass production.

This sequence of product innovation leading to the establishment of a dominant design, after which competition shifts to process innovation, is a common one across many industries.[4] Exhibit 9.2 provides a general model of the relationship between product and process innovation. The model has several strategic implications:

- *New developing industries* typically favour product innovation, as competition is still around defining the basic features of the product or service.

- *Maturing industries* typically favour process innovation, as competition shifts towards efficient production of a dominant design of product or service.

- *Small new entrants* typically have the greatest opportunity in the early stages of an industry, competing with new features. Before the Model T, there were more than 100 competitors in the American automobile industry.

- *Large incumbent firms* typically have the advantage later as the dominant design is established and scale economies and the ability to roll out process innovations matter most. By the 1930s, there were just four large American automobile manufacturers, Ford, General Motors, Chrysler and American Motors, all producing very similar kinds of cars.

This sequence of product to process innovation is not always a neat one. In practice, product and process innovation are often pursued in tandem.[5] For example, each new generation of microprocessor also requires simultaneous process

Exhibit 9.2   **Product and process innovation**

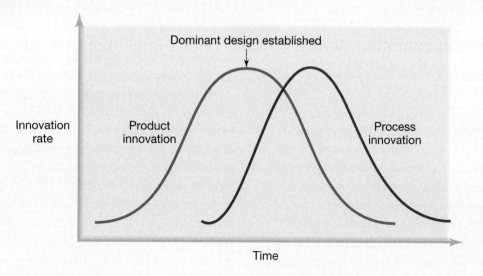

Source: Adapted from W.J. Abernathy and J.M. Utterback, 'A dynamic model of process and product innovation', *Omega*, vol. 3, no. 6 (1975), pp. 639–656.

innovation in order to manufacture the new microprocessor with increasing precision. However, the model does help managers confront the issue of where to focus, whether more on product features or more on process efficiency. It also points to whether competitive advantage is likely to be with small new entrants or large incumbent firms.

9.2.3 Technological or business model innovation

A key question for innovators is the importance of new knowledge in the form of scientific or technological advances. Many successful innovations do not rely simply upon new science or technology, but the reorganisation of all the elements of business into new combinations. Here innovators are creating whole new *business models*, bringing customers, producers and suppliers together in new ways, with or without new technologies. To return to easyJet, the entrepreneurial airline's business model cut out travel agents by using direct sales through the Internet, bringing customers and the airline together in a new way, while also using cheap secondary airports. Simplification of service and choice of airports were much more important than technological innovation. The Internet technology itself was not easyJet's creation and it had the same aircraft as most of its competitors.

A **business model** describes the structure of product, service and information flows and the role of participating parties

Gary Hamel defines a business model as essentially a 'way of doing business'.[6] More formally, a **business model** describes the structure of product, service and information flows and the role of participating parties. The crucial elements of a business model can be seen in terms of two halves of the value chain framework, introduced in section 3.6.1:[7]

Illustration 9.2

A Russian computer games entrepreneur's new business model

An upstart from the East takes on the best from the West.

In April 2006, 10 years after founding Nival Interactive, Sergey Orlovskiy announced a radical change of business model. From being a Russian-based developer of PC games, the company was shifting its headquarters to Los Angeles, taking on new management and targeting both PC and console markets. The games line-up already included 'Blitzkrieg', 'Heroes of Might and Magic', 'Night Watch' and 'Hammer and Sickle'. Orlovskiy explained: 'Normally our revenue increases from 20 to 50 per cent a year. Now we are going to increase it by 100 per cent, because we're changing the business model.'

Orlovskiy, then a 23-year-old IT student, originally founded the company as a PC games specialist. The first product sold 100,000 copies worldwide, a strong start for a PC game. Nival continued to design new PC games, with 'Blitzkrieg', a Second World War strategy game, launched in 2003, selling 1.5 million copies, three times the norm for a reasonably successful PC game. That same year, Nival partnered with French games publisher Ubisoft on the fifth edition of 'Heroes of Might and Magic', a top-selling fantasy strategy game. Nival had a significant cost advantage: Russian programmers cost four or five times less than American programmers.

But the PC games market is limited. PC games sales were less than $1bn (£560m; €800m) in 2005, while console games such as for the Xbox and PlayStation were five times that. In 2005, American venture capital fund Ener1 Group acquired 70 per cent of Nival for an undisclosed amount estimated to be around $10m. Ener1 proposed the change of model: a shift of leadership to the USA, an injection of capital and an expansion into console games, alongside the continued exploitation of programming cost advantages.

Sergey Orlovskiy became President of Nival, while the company took on new talent at the top. The new CEO was Kevin Bachus, one of the original four creators of the Xbox. Other new American managers had held senior positions at companies such as Atari, Electronic Arts, Sega and Sony. This management team were ready to launch the new business model. Described as 'reverse outsourcing', the model was not about a Western company outsourcing production to cheap locations in developing countries, but a low-cost company acquiring the very best American creativity and management. With its new talents and new capital, Nival expected its low-cost development teams – not just in Russia, but potentially in China or anywhere else around the world – to offer an unbeatable combination of economy and innovation.

Sources: Business Week, 3 March (2006) and www.nival.com. See also case example in Chapter 13.

Questions

1 In what respects would you describe Nival's recent transformation as a change in business model rather than a change in strategy?

2 What advantages and what problems might Orlovskiy personally find in this new set-up?

- *The product*. A business model may involve a particular way of defining what the product or service is and how it is produced. In terms of the value chain, this concerns technology development, procurement, inbound logistics, operations and procurement. Thus the business model for Linux open-source operating systems is based on a network of thousands of volunteer programmers, both freelancers and dedicated employees at companies such as IBM and Hewlett Packard. This is very different to Microsoft, for instance, whose business model is based on performing technology development in-house with its own employees.

- *The selling*. A business model may involve a particular way of selling or diffusing a product or service. In terms of the value chain, this concerns outbound logistics, marketing and sales and service. Thus Linux software is free to users, not sold as Microsoft software is. IBM and Hewlett Packard preload the free operating systems on their machines, benefiting through not having to pay a license fee to Microsoft. Linux distributors such as Red Hat earn their money by packaging Linux with user manuals, regular updates and service, and then charging customers annual subscription fees for support.

The business model concept overlaps strongly with the concept of business-level strategy.[8] However, the two concepts have useful differences in emphasis:

- *Radical versus incremental*. Business model change involves radical strategic transformation. On the other hand, many strategic initiatives are essentially incremental, making small adjustments within an existing business model: for example, investment in extra capacity or entry into new geographical markets. The business model concept can help managers confront the limitations of incremental adjustments and address the need sometimes for radical transformation.

- *Standard versus competitive*. In many industries, especially mature ones, business models are effectively standardised, with little difference in basic structure. Business-level strategy is more focused on how to obtain and sustain differentiation and advantage vis-à-vis competitors in the same industry. Business-level strategy thus keeps managers focused on how to position themselves against their competition.

Finally, the business model concept is valuable in helping managers to consider new scientific and technological knowledge as just one part of the whole package that contributes to innovation. Innovation can be drawn from all parts of the value chain, not just technology development (see Illustration 9.2).

9.3 INNOVATION DIFFUSION

Diffusion is the process by which innovations spread amongst users, varying in pace and extent

So far, this chapter has been concerned with sources and types of innovation, for example technology push or market pull. This section moves on to the **diffusion** of innovations after they have been introduced.[9] Since innovation is typically expensive, its commercial attractiveness can hinge on the pace – extent and speed – at which the market adopts new products and services. This pace of diffusion is something managers can influence from both the supply and demand sides, and which they can also model using the S-curve.

9.3.1 The pace of diffusion

The pace of diffusion can vary widely according to the nature of the products concerned. It took 20 years for personal computers to reach 60 per cent of American households. It took 10 years for the Internet to achieve equivalent usage. The pace of diffusion is influenced by a combination of supply-side and demand-side factors, over which managers have considerable control. On the *supply side*, pace is determined by product features such as the following:

- *Degree of improvement* in performance above current products (from a customer's perspective) that provides incentive to change. For example, 3G mobile phones did not provide sufficient performance improvement to prompt rapid switch in many markets.

- *Compatibility* with other factors, for example digital TV becomes more attractive as the broadcasting networks change more of their programmes to that format.

- *Complexity*, either in the product itself or in the marketing methods being used to commercialise the product: unduly complex pricing structures, as with many financial service products such as pensions, discourage consumer adoption.

- *Experimentation* – the ability to test products before commitment to a final decision – either directly or through the availability of information about the experience of other customers. This is why new product marketing often features satisfied customers and/or endorsements from suitable role models such as sports or pop celebrities.

- *Relationship management*, in other words how easy it is to get information, place orders and receive support. This relates to the choice of business model as described in section 9.2.3 above.

On the *demand side*, key factors driving the pace of diffusion are as follows:

- *Market awareness*. Many potentially successful products have failed through lack of consumer awareness – particularly when the promotional effort of the manufacturer has been confined to 'push' promotion to its intermediaries (for example, distributors).

- *Observability* (to potential adopters) of the benefits of the product or service in use. This is an important determinant in spreading adoption – for example, through creating a 'band wagon' effect. For some products this can be difficult if the benefits are intangible or do not accrue immediately (for example, financial investments). Intermediaries (such as distributors) also need to observe that there is benefit to them too. This could be observed if they see *their* competitors gaining commercial advantage from the new product.

- *Customer innovativeness*. The distribution of potential customers from early adopter groups (keen to adopt first) through to laggards (typically indifferent to innovations). Innovations are often targeted initially at early adopter groups – typically the young and the wealthy – in order to build the critical mass that will encourage more laggardly groups – the poorer and older – to join the bandwagon. Innovations targeted at laggardly groups will take off more slowly.

The various factors listed above provide a checklist against which innovation strategies can be assessed. For example, a manager writing a 'business case' to secure funds for improving particular product features would need to address many of the issues listed above. The business case should start by showing why the improved features might be *valued by customers* sufficiently to switch purchase or upgrade. It should also address issues of *compatibility* with other equipment that the consumer or distributor uses in conjunction with the product. In other words, at a minimum it is essential that the product or service matches the threshold requirements of both consumers and intermediaries. This may entail considerable effort to allay some of their concerns about switching to the new product. Adoption would be more likely if the product matches the *critical success factors (CSFs)* of consumers and intermediaries (see section 2.4.3). The marketing plan should address how these attributes would be *communicated* and who would be the initial *target audiences*. It should address how initial adoptions would then be *rolled out* into wider uptake in the market.[10]

9.3.2 The diffusion S-curve

The pace of diffusion is typically not steady. Successful innovations often diffuse according to an *S-curve* pattern.[11] The shape of the S-curve reflects a process of slow adoption in the early stages, followed by a rapid acceleration in diffusion, and ending with a plateau representing the limit to demand (Exhibit 9.3). The height of the S-curve shows the extent of diffusion; the shape of the S-curve shows the speed.

Exhibit 9.3   The diffusion S-curve

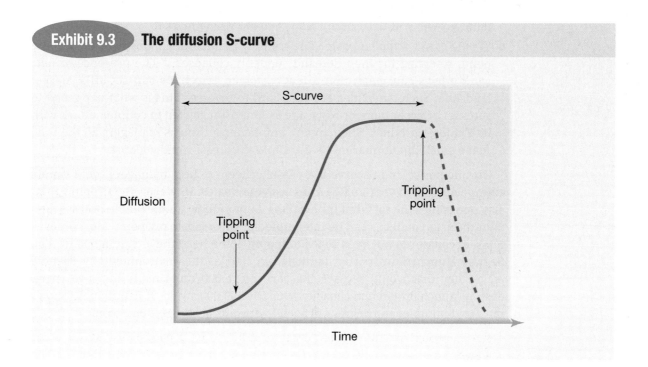

Diffusion rarely follows exactly this pattern, but none the less the S-curve can help managers anticipate upcoming issues. In particular, the S-curve points to four likely decision points:

● *Timing of the 'tipping point'.* Demand for a new product and service may initially be slow but then reach a **tipping point** when it explodes onto a rapid upwards path of growth.[12] Tipping points are particularly explosive where there are strong *network effects*: in other words, where the value of a product or service is increased the more people in a network use them. Text messaging exploded in this way, because once some members of a social circle began to text each other, it became very worthwhile for all the other members to learn to do the same. Being aware of a possible tipping point ahead can help managers plan investment in capacity and distribution. Companies can easily underestimate demand. In the mid-1980s, American companies predicted that by 2000 there would be 900,000 mobile phones worldwide. That year came, and 900,000 phones were sold every 19 hours. The Finnish company Nokia was able to seize worldwide leadership.[13] Failing to anticipate a tipping point leads to missed sales and easy opportunities for competitors.

● *Timing of the plateau.* The S-curve also alerts managers to a likely eventual slow-down in demand growth. Again, it is tempting to extrapolate existing growth rates forwards, especially when they are highly satisfactory. But heavy investment immediately before growth turns down is likely to leave firms with overcapacity and carrying extra costs in a period of industry shake-out.

● *Extent of diffusion.* The S-curve does not necessarily lead to 100 per cent diffusion amongst potential users. Most innovations fail to displace previous-generation products and services altogether. For example, in music, traditional turntables and LP discs are still preferred over CD and MP3 players by many disc jockeys and music connoisseurs. A critical issue for managers then is to estimate the final ceiling on diffusion, being careful not to assume that tipping point growth will necessarily take over the whole market.

● *Timing of the 'tripping point'.* The tripping point is the opposite of the tipping point, referring to when demand suddenly collapses.[14] The presence of network effects can mean that a few customer defections can set off a market landslide. Such landslides are very hard to reverse. This is what happened to Internet browser pioneer Netscape as Microsoft started to counter-attack with its Explorer product. The tripping point concept warns managers all the time that a small dip in quarterly sales could presage a rapid collapse.

To summarise, the S-curve is a useful concept to help managers avoid simply extrapolating next year's sales from last year's sales. However, the tripping point also underlines the fact that innovations do not follow an inevitable process, and their diffusion patterns can be interrupted or reversed at any point. Most innovations, of course, do not even reach a tipping point, let alone a tripping point. The Segway Human Transporter, launched in 2001 as the environmentally-friendly technology that would replace the car, sold 6,000 units in its first two years, despite launch production capacity of nearly 500,000 a year. Illustration 9.3 shows the rapid but uneven progress of social networking site MySpace.com.

*A **tipping point** is where demand for a product or service suddenly takes off, with explosive growth*

Illustration 9.3

The MySpace snowball

How long can the explosive growth of the social networking site MySpace continue?

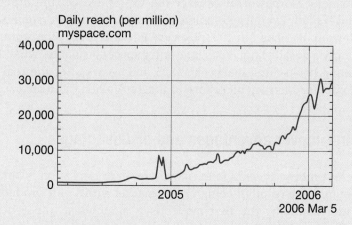

Figure 1 The traffic data is based on the set of Alexa toolbar uses, which may not be a representative sample of the global Internet population

Source: Alexa.com. © 2006 Alexa.

MySpace began in 2003 as a networking site for independent musicians in Los Angeles. By 2006 it was the most popular website in the USA, and had easily overtaken rival social networking sites such as Friendster and Facebook to claim nearly 80 per cent of online networking site visits. The site became highly attractive to advertisers such as Coca-Cola and Procter and Gamble, seeking access to the youth market. The Alexa market research company monitored MySpace's explosive growth in daily 'reach' from less than 1,000 in every million Internet users in 2004 to around 30,000 in early 2006: see Figure 1. Rupert Murdoch, owner of the multinational media conglomerate News Corporation, was so impressed that he bought the two-year-old company in 2005 for $580m (£324m; €259m).

Acquisition by News Corporation gave MySpace the capital to fund rapid innovation. During 2006, the company had 20 new products in development, including VoIP telephony, plus 11 new international sites. But there were many threats to continued growth. The sheer volume and chaos of user-controlled postings was creating capacity and reliability problems. There was mounting controversy about online predators and malicious gossip. New competitors were entering the market, such as YouTube with its popular video service. Ownership by the News Corporation was beginning to impose constraints in terms of content and style. Finally, there was the fear that as MySpace matured, it would no longer be so cool.

Sources: *Business Week*, 13 June (2005); www.wikipedia.org.

Questions

1 How should potential advertisers on MySpace have interpreted the upwards blip in its daily reach in late 2004 and the downwards blip in early 2006?

2 How would you forecast future demand for MySpace?

9.4   INNOVATORS AND FOLLOWERS

A key choice for managers is whether to lead or to follow in innovation. The S-curve concept seems to promote leadership in innovation. First-movers get the easy sales of early fast growth and can establish a dominant position. There are plenty of examples of first-movers who have built enduring positions on the basis of innovation leadership: Coca-Cola in drinks and Hoover in vacuum cleaners are powerful century-old examples. On the other hand, many first-movers fail. Even Apple failed with its pioneering Personal Digital Assistant, the Newton, launched in 1993. Hewlett Packard and Palm captured the PDA market nearly a decade later. This late-entry success is not unusual. Amazon entered the online bookselling market in 1995, four years after the real online pioneer, the Computer Literacy bookstore of Silicon Valley, California.

9.4.1   First-mover advantages and disadvantages

A first-mover advantage exists where an organisation is better off than its competitors as a result of being first to market with a new product, process or service

KEY CONCEPT

First mover advantages

A **first-mover advantage** exists where an organisation is better off than its competitors as a result of being first to market with a new product, process or service. Fundamentally, the first-mover is a monopolist, theoretically able to charge customers high prices without fear of immediate undercutting by competitors. In practice, however, innovators often prefer to sacrifice profit margins for sales growth and, besides, monopoly is usually temporary. There are five potentially more robust first-mover advantages:[15]

● *Experience curve benefits* accrue to first-movers, as their rapid accumulation of experience with the innovation gives them greater expertise than late entrants still relatively unfamiliar with the new product, process or service (see Exhibit 3.4).

● *Scale benefits* are typically enjoyed by first-movers, as they establish earlier than competitors the volumes necessary for mass production and bulk purchasing, for example.

● *Pre-emption of scarce resources* is an opportunity for first-movers, as late-movers will not have the same access to key raw materials, skilled labour or components, and will have to pay dearly for them.

● *Reputation* can be enhanced by being first, especially since consumers have little 'mind-space' to recognise new brands once a dominant brand has been established in the market.

● *Buyer switching costs* can be exploited by first-movers, by locking in their customers with privileged or sticky relationships that later challengers can only break with difficulty. Switching costs can be increased by establishing and exploiting a *technological standard* (see Chapter 6).

Experience curve benefits, economies of scale and the pre-emption of scarce resources all confer cost advantages on first-movers. It is possible for them to retaliate against challengers with a price war. Superior reputation and customer lock-in provide a marketing advantage, allowing first-movers to charge high prices, which can then be reinvested in order to consolidate their position against late-entry competitors.

But the experience of Apple with its Newton shows that first-mover advantages are not necessarily overwhelming. Late-movers have two principal potential advantages:[16]

● *Free-riding*. Late-movers can imitate technological and other innovation at less expense than originally incurred by the pioneers. Research suggests that the costs of imitation are typically only 65 per cent of the cost of innovation.

● *Learning*. Late-movers can observe what worked well and what did not work well for innovators. They may not make so many mistakes and be able to get it right first time.

9.4.2 First or second?

Given the potential advantages of late-movers, managers face a hard choice between striving to be first or coming in later. They should assess the likely value of first-mover and late-mover advantages in their particular case. In addition, there are three contextual factors managers should consider that might swing the balance between moving first or not:

● *Capacity for profit capture*. David Teece emphasises the importance of innovators being able to capture for themselves the profits of their innovations.[17] This depends on the ease with which followers can imitate. The likelihood of imitation depends on two primary factors. First, imitation is likely if the innovation is in itself *easy to replicate*: for example, if there is little tacit knowledge involved or if it is embedded in a product that is sold in the external marketplace (unlike many process technologies) and is therefore easy to 'reverse-engineer'. Second, imitation is facilitated if *intellectual property rights* are weak, for example where patents are hard to define or impractical to defend.[18] It is unwise for companies to invest in being first-movers if imitators are likely to be able quickly to seize their share of innovation profits.

● *Complementary assets*. Possession of the assets or resources necessary to scale up the production and marketing of the innovation is often critical.[19] Many small European biotech start-up companies face this constraint in the pharmaceuticals industry, where marketing and distribution in the USA, the world's largest market, are essential complementary assets, but are controlled by the big established pharmaceutical companies. Small European start-ups can find themselves obliged either to sell out to a larger company with the complementary marketing and distribution assets, or to license their innovation to it on disadvantageous terms. For organisations wishing to remain independent and to exploit their innovations themselves, there is little point in investing heavily to be first-mover in the absence of the necessary complementary assets.

● *Fast-moving arenas*. Where markets or technologies are moving very fast, and especially where both are highly dynamic, first-movers are unlikely to establish a durable advantage. The American electronics company Magnavox was the first to launch an electronic video game console in 1972, the Odyssey. But both the market and the technologies were evolving quickly. Magnavox only survived into the second generation of video game consoles, finally exiting in 1984. The seventh generation is now firmly dominated by Microsoft (entered in 2001), Sony (entered in 1994) and Nintendo (entered in 1983). In slower-moving markets and technologies, such as Coca-Cola's drinks arena, durable first-mover advantages are more probable. Managers need, therefore, to assess future market and technological dynamism in calculating the likely value of first-mover advantage.

For large established companies, Costas Markides and Paul Geroski argue, the most appropriate response to innovation, especially radical innovation, is often not to be a first-mover, but to be a 'fast second'.[20] Established companies typically do not have the cultures and systems to create new markets from scratch. What they do have are the financial, manufacturing, marketing and distribution assets that allow them to dominate a market once it has begun to emerge. The goal of a 'fast-second' organisation is to consolidate the early experiments of first-movers into a durable business model (see section 9.2.3). Fast-second companies may not be literally the second company into the market, but they dominate the second generation of competitors. For example, the established mainframe computer company IBM followed smaller innovative companies like Osborne and Apple into personal computers. The established Apple in turn followed pioneers such as Napster into online music. But, as the next section shows, even being 'fast second' can be challenging for incumbents.

9.4.3 The incumbents' response

For established companies in a market, innovation is often not so much an opportunity as a threat. Kodak's dominance of the photographic film market was made nearly worthless by the sudden rise of digital photography. As Clay Christensen has shown, the problem is that relationships between incumbent organisations and their customers can become too close.[21] Customers typically prefer incremental improvements to existing technologies, and are unable to imagine completely new technologies. Even lead-users typically adapt what they already have. Incumbents become used to making incremental innovations that meet, and even modestly surpass, existing customers' expectations. As in Exhibit 9.4, incumbents can usually improve their existing technology along a steady upwards trajectory, here Technology 1. Innovations on this trajectory are termed 'sustaining innovations', because they keep the existing basic technology up to date.

A disruptive innovation creates substantial growth by offering a new performance trajectory that, even if initially inferior to the performance of existing technologies, has the potential to become markedly superior

The challenge for incumbents, however, is switching from the existing trajectory of sustaining innovations for Technology 1 to the trajectory offered by the **disruptive innovation** represented by Technology 2. With a disruptive innovation, the new technology, even if initially inferior to the performance of existing technologies, has the potential quickly to become markedly superior. This superior performance can produce spectacular growth, either by creating new sets of customers or by undercutting the cost base of rival existing business models. Disruptive innovations are hard for incumbents to respond to because their initial poor performance is likely to upset existing customer relationships and because they typically involve changing their whole business model (see also Illustration 9.4). For example, in the music industry, the major record companies were long content to keep on selling traditional CDs through retailers, marketing them through promotions and radio-plugging. They responded to MP3 online music simply by prosecuting operators such as Napster for breach of copyright and highlighting the relatively poor sound quality of peer-to-peer file sharing.

| Exhibit 9.4 | Disruptive Innovation |

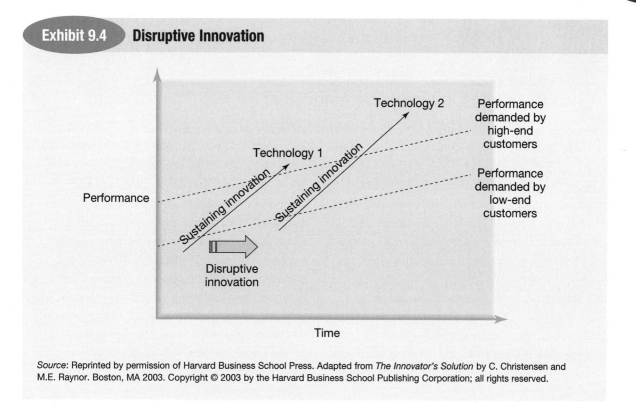

However, the British band Arctic Monkeys, and their small independent record company Domino, radically disrupted the majors' marketing model by giving away MP3 tracks free over the Internet in order to create an independent fan base. In 2006, the Arctic Monkeys' debut CD ended up selling nearly 400,000 copies in its first week, a record for the top 20 British album chart.

Incumbents can follow two policies to help keep them responsive to potentially disruptive innovations:

● *Develop a portfolio of real options.* Companies that are most challenged by disruptive innovations tend to be those built upon a single business model and with one main product or service. Rita McGrath and Ian MacMillan recommend that companies build portfolios of *real options* in order to maintain organisational dynamism.[22] Real options are limited investments that keep opportunities open for the future (for a more technical discussion, see Chapter 10). Establishing an R&D team in a speculative new technology or acquiring a small start-up in a nascent market would both be examples of real options, each giving the potential to scale up fast should the opportunity turn out to be substantial. McGrath and MacMillan's portfolio identifies three different kinds of options (Exhibit 9.5). Options where the market is broadly known, but the technologies are still uncertain, are *positioning options*: a company might want several of these, to ensure some position in an important market, by one technology or another. On the other hand, a company might have a strong technology, but be very uncertain about appropriate markets, in which case it would want to bet on several *scouting options* to explore which markets are actually best. Finally, a company would want some *stepping stone* options, very unlikely in themselves to work, but possibly leading to something more promising in the future. Even if they do not turn a profit,

Illustration 9.4

Lush Cosmetics, a disruptive innovator?

Continuous innovation is at the heart of this entrepreneurial venture

Lush Cosmetics is a fast-growing British bath products company, making distinctive (and even plain odd) shampoos, soaps, moisturisers and the like. The motto of its founder and CEO Mark Constantine is 'Innovate like mad, then start over again.'

Constantine's first career break was as a cosmetician at the Body Shop. By the late 1980s, products conceived by him accounted for 80 per cent of Body Shop sales. But the Body Shop was becoming conservative and rejected his concept of the 'bath bomb', a fizzing aromatic ball that dissolves in water. Constantine and a small team of fellow-believers left. After failure with a catalogues business, Cosmetics to Go, Constantine and his team set up Lush with one store in the small south coast town of Poole in 1994. In just over 10 years, Constantine built a €100m (£69m) business, with 320 stores in 35 countries. Bath bombs made up 40 per cent of the business, with up to 60,000 sold a day. The Body Shop meanwhile lost momentum and was sold to the French multinational L'Oréal in 2006.

Not willing to repeat the Body Shop's mistake, Constantine is committed to constant renewal of his range. The rule is that one-third of Lush products should be discontinued each year. An annual 'mafia meeting' of senior managers ruthlessly enforces the rule, despite frequent protests from loyal customers (on one occasion, customers threatened to parade naked through London's Trafalgar Square to keep a product). But the consequence of the rule is a commitment to introduce at least 100 new products a year to replace the old ones. Innovation is built into the Lush system.

One driver of innovation is the customers themselves. The name Lush came from a customer as a result of a company competition to find a name. Since then, customers have been constantly involved in product development. The eccentric and ethical style of the company generates fierce loyalty, so that customers describe themselves as 'Lushies' and participate in lively discussions in the chatroom on the company's website. Lushies propose new products, vote on alternatives and send in evocative names such as 'whoosh', 'aurora' and 'smitten' to inspire the company's cosmeticians to create new products. Lushies also post photographs of themselves, their pets and even their collections of Lush products, described as 'Lush porn'.

The company also works hard at generating new ideas itself. Constantine continues personally to work at new products, but he also hires new product designers with a brief to push the boundaries. Thus Japanese designer Noriko Miura has experimented with flavours for toothpaste such as green apple, salt and charcoal. Lush is determined not to meet the same fate as its failed progenitor, the Body Shop.

Sources: Fast Company, July (2005); www.lush.co.uk.

Questions

1 What are the advantages and disadvantages of a fixed rule such as discontinuing one-third of a product range annually?

2 What are the limits and dangers of customer-driven innovation as at Lush?

Exhibit 9.5 | **Portfolio of innovation options**

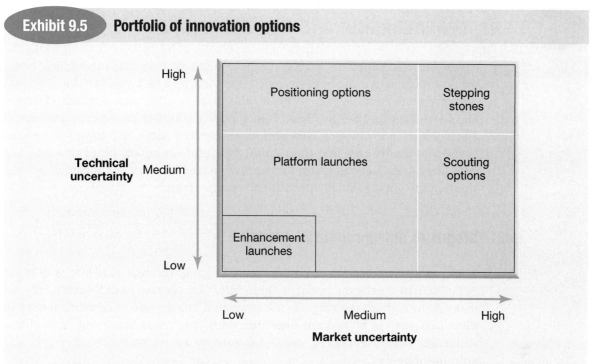

stepping stones should provide valuable learning opportunities. An important principle for options is: 'Fail fast, fail cheap, try again.'

- *Develop independent business units.* New ventures, especially when under-taken from a real options perspective, may need protection from the usual systems and disciplines of a core business. It would make no sense to hold the managers of a real option strictly accountable for sales growth and profit margin: their primary objective is preparation and learning. For this reason, large incumbent organisations often set up innovative businesses as inde-pendent business units, sometimes called *new venture divisions*, typically with managers hired specially from outside.[23] For example, in 2003 Delta Airlines, the American international airline dating from the 1920s, responded to the threat of low-cost airlines in its domestic markets by establishing Song Airlines as a stand-alone competitor. Song adopted the low-cost airline busi-ness model but also innovated with free personal entertainment systems at every seat, including audio MP3 selections, trivia games that could be played against other passengers and satellite television. In-flight safety instructions would be sung in different musical styles, by request. The risks of such independent business units are twofold.[24] First, the new units may be denied resources that the core business could easily supply, such as branding or management information systems. Second, innovation becomes isolated from the core business: for the core organisation, innovation is something that somebody else does. Delta responded to the second risk by reabsorbing Song into its main operations, at the same time incorporating several of Song's innovations such as satellite television.

9.5   ENTREPRENEURSHIP AND RELATIONSHIPS

Given the difficulties of large incumbent firms in fostering innovation, many would conclude that the best approach is to start up a new venture. Independent entrepreneurs such as James Dyson, the pioneer of bagless vacuum cleaners, and Larry Page and Sergey Brin of Google are exemplars of this entrepreneurial approach to innovation.[25] This section introduces some key issues for entrepreneurial innovators, and then points to a more complex set of relationships with large firms, raising further choices for entrepreneurs. It concludes by considering the opportunities of social entrepreneurship.

9.5.1   Stages of entrepreneurial growth

Entrepreneurial ventures are often seen as going through four stages of a life cycle: start-up; growth; maturity; and exit.[26] Of course, most ventures do not make it through all the stages – the estimated failure rate of new businesses in their first year is more than one-fifth, with two-thirds going out of business within six years.[27] However, each of these four stages raises key questions for entrepreneurs:

- *Start-up*. There are many challenges at this stage, but one key question with implications for both survival and growth is sources of capital. Loans from family and friends are common sources of funds, but these are typically limited and, given the new business failure rate, likely to lead to embarrassment. Bank loans and credit cards can provide funding too, but often they are too rigid in their requirement for interest and repayment to fit the irregular revenue streams of a start-up. *Venture capitalists* are specialised investors in new ventures. They usually insist on a seat on the venture's board of directors and may install their preferred managers. Venture capitalist backing has been shown to increase significantly the chances of a venture's success, but venture capitalists typically accept only about 1 in 400 propositions put to them.[28]

- *Growth*. A key challenge for growth ventures is management. Entrepreneurs have to be ready to move from doing to managing. Typically this transition occurs as the venture grows beyond about 20 employees. Many entrepreneurs make poor managers: if they had wanted to be managers, they would probably be working in a large corporation in the first place. The choice entrepreneurs have to make is whether to rely on their own managerial skills or to bring in professional managers. In 2001, the youthful founders of Google, Larry Page and Sergey Brin, responded to pressure from their venture capitalists by recruiting 46-year-old Eric Schmidt, former Chief Executive of the large software company Novell, to run their company.

- *Maturity*. The challenge for entrepreneurs at this stage is retaining their enthusiasm and commitment and generating new growth. This is a period when entrepreneurship changes to *intrapreneurship*, the generation of new ventures from inside the organisation. An important option is usually *diversification* into new business areas, a topic dealt with in Chapter 7. The move of the Russian computer games company Nival into console games is a typical example. When generating new ventures at this stage, it is critical to

| Exhibit 9.6 | Stages of entrepreneurial growth and typical challenges |

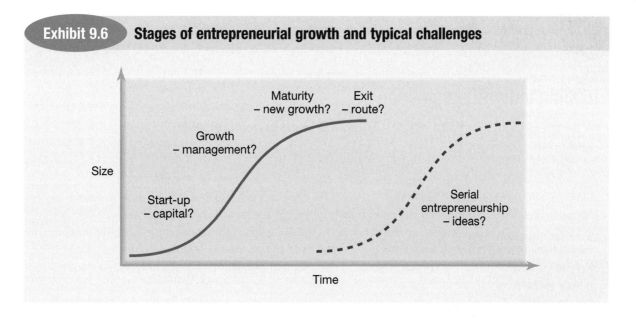

recall the odds on success. Research suggests that many small high-tech firms fail to manage the transition to a second generation of technology, and that it is often better at this point simply to look for exit.[29]

- *Exit*. This refers to departure from the venture, either by the founding entrepreneurs or by the original investors, or both. At the point of exit, entrepreneurs and venture capitalists will seek to release capital as a reward for their input and risk taking. Entrepreneurs may consider three prime routes to exit. A simple *trade sale* of the venture to another company is a common route. Thus MySpace was bought by NewsCorp just two years after foundation: see Illustration 9.3. Some entrepreneurs may sell to their own managers, in the form of a *management buy-out* (MBO). Another exit route for highly successful enterprises is an *Initial Public Offering* (IPO), the sale of shares to the public, for instance on the American NASDAQ exchange. IPOs usually involve just a portion of the total shares available, and may thus allow entrepreneurs to continue in the business and provide funds for further growth. Google raised $1.67bn (£0.93bn; €1.36bn) with its 2004 IPO, selling only 7 per cent of its shares. It is often said that good entrepreneurs plan for their exit right from start-up, and certainly venture capitalists will insist on this.

Entrepreneurs who have successfully exited a first venture often become *serial entrepreneurs*. Serial entrepreneurs are people who set up a succession of enterprises, investing the capital raised on exit from earlier ventures into new growing ventures. For serial entrepreneurs, the challenge often is no longer so much funding but good ideas.

9.5.2 Entrepreneurial relationships

For many, entrepreneurship is about independence, working for oneself. This pride in independence is reinforced by a common stereotype of entrepreneurs as heroic individuals, starting their businesses at night in a university laboratory (see Illustration 9.5), or in the spare room at home or in a local lock-up garage.

Illustration 9.5

Fatima's dignified gowns

A business administration degree is just the starting point for this entrepreneurial venture.

Fatima Ba-Alawi graduated in business administration from the University of Portsmouth in 2005. Less than one year later, seven National Health Service hospitals were trialling her innovative hospital gowns, with interest from private sector hospital operator Bupa too. Her new company, DCS Designs (Dignity, Comfort and Safety), had got off to a flying start.

Ba-Alawi had arrived in the United Kingdom in 1998, as a refugee from Somalia speaking no English. After studying for English GCSEs and A-levels, she says: 'I applied to the University of Portsmouth to read business administration because the idea of going into business always appealed to me'. She was keen to have her own business after finding it 'deeply unpleasant working for somebody else at a fast food outlet as a teenager'.

It was while working in a local hospital as a care assistant that her business idea came to her. Conventional hospital gowns were undignified for wearers and awkward for carers. Ba-Alawi designed a new type of gown which provided extra coverage for the back, gave better access points for medical drips and used easy press-stud buttoning. Her design was more dignified, more comfortable and more safe.

While still studying, Ba-Alawi approached the University of Portsmouth's Centre for Enterprise for support. She won £500 (€725) in the University's Enterprise Challenge competition, which she used to fund an initial prototype and carry out some market research. The University's enterprise mentoring service provided her with one-to-one coaching, which helped her develop her business plan. This business plan won a further University

prize, worth £2,000, which she used to fund a patent application and register her company, DCS Designs Ltd. She next put in a bid to the University's Student SEED Fund, gaining more support plus an office in the University's Centre for Enterprise and access to virtual office facilities. The SEED Fund allowed Ba-Alawi to manufacture sample gowns and distribute them to hospitals, at the same time as launching the DCS Designs website, which had a facility for user feedback. The local Enterprise Hub also provided access to a local patent attorney to help protect her intellectual property. Ba-Alawi commented on the University's role:

Having had the support of the University has made all the difference. It's much better to have a real business presence than to try to run this from my room at home! The University has not just given me the start up funds, but it has also given me the confidence and support I needed to take my idea off the ground and make it happen.

Sources: Financial Times, 12 April (2006); Evening Standard, 13 September (2005); www.port.ac.uk.

Questions

1 What challenges would you anticipate for Ba-Alawi's DCS Designs company if it takes off? How should she deal with them?

2 Does your experience of work and organisations give you any ideas for new ventures?

3 What does your university or college do to support student entrepreneurship?

William Hewlett and David Packard, founders of the famous computing and printer company, and Steve Jobs of Apple, are oft-quoted examples of the garage stereotype. But digging beneath the stereotype soon reveals a more complex story, in which relationships with large companies can be important right from the start. Typically entrepreneurs have worked for large companies beforehand, and continue to use relationships afterwards.[30,31] While Hewlett came fairly directly out of Stanford University's laboratories, Packard worked at General Electric and Litton Industries. The Hewlett Packard company used Litton Industries' foundries early on, and later used relationships at General Electric to recruit experienced managers. Steve Jobs worked for William Hewlett for a summer job aged 12, and later was the 40th employee at video games company Atari.

Entrepreneurship often involves close relationships with other companies, especially big companies. Entrepreneurs need to decide how to exploit their relationships, in particular with those powerful organisations that are driving innovation in their markets. Fortunately, the entrepreneurial need for relationships fits with the growing needs of large organisations themselves. These powerful organisations are increasingly shifting to what Henry Chesbrough calls a new 'open' model of innovation. In this *open innovation* model, even big organisations cease to rely on their own internal resources but draw increasingly on independent new ventures and external partners such as universities, suppliers and customers. Two concepts are currently particularly influential here:

● *Corporate venturing*. Many large corporations, such as Intel, Nokia and Shell, have developed corporate venture units that invest externally in new ventures as safeguards against disruptive innovations and potential drivers of future growth.[32] Large corporations gain by increasing the range of ideas they are exposed to, by protecting early stage ventures from internal bureaucracy and by spreading their risk. Entrepreneurs gain by accessing not just capital but also knowledge of large-company thinking in their domain and contacts with other members of the large company's network. It is crucial that both entrepreneurs and corporate venture capitalists continuously monitor the set of expectations behind the investment: is the investment more profit driven in terms of expecting good financial returns or is it more strategic, in the sense of being about technological or market development? Shifting expectations on the part of the corporate venture capitalist can lead to the disruption of longer-term plans by the entrepreneurial new venture. In recent years, companies such as Siemens and Nokia have sold or diluted their stakes in some of their corporate venture units, and companies such as Ericsson and Diageo have had to close them down entirely.

● *Ecosystems*. High-technology companies such as Cisco, IBM and Intel often foster 'ecosystems' of smaller companies: IBM had 1,398 alliances in the late 1990s, most with small firms. These ecosystems are communities of connected suppliers, agents, distributors, franchisees, technology entrepreneurs and makers of complementary products.[33] Apple for example has created an ecosystem around its iPod, in which more than a hundred companies manufacture accessories and peripherals such as cases, speakers and docking units. Large firms get the benefits of increased customer satisfaction through the provision of complementary products. Ecosystem members get the benefit of a large and often lucrative market: iPod accessories get plenty of retail shelf space and superior margins. However, large firms must manage their ecosystems actively for their advantage. These firms take up *platform leadership*, in which they consciously nurture independent companies through successive waves of innovation around their basic technological 'platform'.[34] Platform examples include the Palm Pilot PDA, which needs a continuously evolving range of software and connecting devices to maximise its value, and DoCoMo's i-mode 'always-on' Internet phones, whose launch required a host of web content providers to rewrite their websites in a compatible programming language. For entrepreneurial members of a business ecosystem, each new generation of a technology platform imposes a crucial choice about whether and how much to bet on a platform whose leadership they typically cannot influence.

9.5.3 Social entrepreneurship

Entrepreneurship is not just a matter for the private sector. The public sector has seen increasing calls for a more entrepreneurial approach to service creation and delivery.[35] Recently too the notion of social entrepreneurship has become common. **Social entrepreneurship** involves individuals and groups who create independent organisations to mobilise ideas and resources to address social problems, typically earning revenues but on a not-for-profit basis.[36] Independence and revenues generated in the market give social entrepreneurs the flexibility and dynamism to pursue social problems that pure public sector organisations are often too bureaucratic, or too politically constrained, to tackle. Social entrepreneurs have pursued a wide range of initiatives, including small loans ('microcredit') to peasants by the Grameen Bank in Bangladesh, employment creation by the Mondragon cooperative in the Basque region of Spain, and fair trade by Traidcraft in the United Kingdom. This wide range of initiatives raises at least three key choices for social entrepreneurs:

Social entrepreneurship involves individuals and groups who create independent organisations to mobilise ideas and resources to address social problems, typically earning revenues but on a not-for-profit basis

- *Social mission*. For social entrepreneurs, the social mission is primary. The social mission can embrace two elements: end objectives and operational processes. For example, the Grameen Bank has the end objective of reducing rural poverty, especially for women. The process is empowering poor people's own business initiatives by providing microcredit at a scale and to people that conventional banks would ignore.

- *Organisational form*. Many social enterprises take on cooperative forms, involving their employees and other stakeholders on a democratic basis and thus building commitment and channels for ideas. This form of organisation raises the issue of which stakeholders to include, and which to exclude. Cooperatives can also be slow to take hard decisions. Social enterprises therefore sometimes take more hierarchical charity or company forms of organisation. Cafédirect, the fair-trade beverages company, even became a publicly listed company, paying its first dividend to shareholders in 2006.

- *Business model*. Social enterprises typically rely to a large extent on revenues earned in the marketplace, not just government subsidy or charitable donations. Housing associations collect rents, microcredit organisations charge interest and fair-trade organisations sell produce. Social entrepreneurs are no different to other entrepreneurs, therefore, in having to design an efficient and effective business model. This business model might involve innovative

Illustration 9.6

key debate

Are large firms better innovators than small firms?

Just how much more innovative are small firms really?

The famous Austrian economist Joseph Schumpeter proposed that large firms are proportionately more innovative than small firms. This proposition is a controversial one. If true, it would discourage laboratory scientists and engineers from leaving their large-firm employers to set up their own ventures. It would encourage large firms like Google and Cisco to keep on buying up small innovative firms and absorbing them into their own corporate strategies. It would make government policy makers more tolerant of huge, domineering firms like Microsoft which claim that their large scale is important to continued innovation in computer software.

Schumpeter's proposition for the advantages of large firms in innovation has several points in its favour:

● Large firms have greater and more diverse resources, helping them to bring together all the various necessary elements for innovation.

● Large firms may have a greater propensity for innovation risk, knowing that they can absorb the costs of innovation failure.

● Large firms have better incentives to innovate, because they are more likely to be able to capitalise on innovation, having all the required complementary assets (distribution channels and so on) to roll it out fast and under their control.

On the other hand, there are good reasons why small firms might be more innovative:

● Small firms are typically more cohesive, so that knowledge is more easily shared.

● Small firms are typically more flexible and less bureaucratic, so that they can innovate faster and more boldly.

● Small firms are more motivated to innovate simply to survive, while large firms can simply defend and exploit their dominance of existing markets.

There has been plenty of research on whether small or large firms are proportionately more innovative. Some researchers have focused on the input side, for example measuring whether large firms are more research intensive in terms of R&D expenditure as a percentage of sales. Other researchers have focused on the output side, for example counting whether large firms have proportionately greater numbers of patents for innovations. There is no final consensus on the overall patterns of innovation. However, recent research findings suggest that in general:

● Large firms are relatively less research intensive in high-technology industries, for example electronics and software.

● Large firms are relatively more innovative in service industries than in manufacturing industries.

It seems that the research so far cannot provide any definite rules about whether large or small firms are better innovators in general. However, research scientists, acquisitive large firms and government policy makers need to consider carefully the specifics of particular industries.

Sources:
C. Camisón-Zornosa, R. Lapiedra-Alcani, M. Segarra-Ciprés and M. Boronat-Navarro, 'A meta-analysis of innovation and organizational size', *Organization Studies*, vol. 25, no. 3 (2004), pp. 331–361.

C.-Y. Lee and T. Sung, 'Schumpeter's legacy: a new perspective on the relationship between firm size and R&D', *Research Policy*, vol. 34 (2005), pp. 914–931.

Question

What kinds of managerial action might you consider if you were trying to increase the innovativeness of a large firm in a high-technology manufacturing industry?

changes in the value chain. Thus fair-trade organisations have often become much more closely involved with their suppliers than commercial organisations, for example advising farmers on agriculture and providing education and infrastructure support to their communities.

Social entrepreneurs, just like other entrepreneurs, often have to forge relationships with large commercial companies (see also Illustration 9.6). For example, a new social enterprise called Ten Senses established Bulgaria's first fair-trade shop with assistance from the multinational bank Citigroup and the oil company Royal Dutch Shell. Rosabeth Moss Kanter points out that the benefits to business of involvement with social enterprise can go beyond a feelgood factor and attractive publicity.[37] She shows that involvement in social enterprise can help develop new technologies and services, access new pools of potential employees, and create relationships with government and other agencies that can eventually turn into new markets. Kanter concludes that large corporations should develop clear strategies with regard to social entrepreneurship, not treat it as ad hoc charity.

SUMMARY

- Strategists face three fundamental dilemmas in innovation, concerning: the relative emphasis to put on technology push or market pull; whether to focus on product or process innovation; and finally how far to concentrate on technological innovation as opposed to broader business model innovation.

- Innovations often diffuse into the marketplace according to an S-curve model in which slow start-up is followed by accelerating growth (the tipping point) and finally a flattening of demand. Managers can influence this process by a combination of supply-side and demand-side initiatives. They should not assume that innovations will necessarily follow a smooth S-curve and should watch out for 'tripping points'.

- Managers have a choice between being first into the marketplace and entering later. There are advantages and disadvantages to both. Being first into the market without the required complementary assets and capacity to capture profits can simply be a waste of effort. 'Fast-second' strategies are often more attractive.

- Established incumbents' businesses can easily become too locked into existing customer relationships and should beware disruptive innovations that uncover entirely new market needs. Incumbents can help protect themselves from conservatism by developing portfolios of real options and by organising independent new venture units.

- Entrepreneurs face characteristic dilemmas as their businesses go through the entrepreneurial life cycle of start-up, growth, maturity and exit. Entrepreneurs also have to choose how they relate to large firms, particularly as they may become involved in their ecosystems or strategies for open innovation. There is no conclusive evidence that entrepreneurial small firms are more innovative than large firms. There is not conclusive evidence that entrepreneurial small firms are more innovative than large firms (see Key Debate, Illustration 9.6).

- Social entrepreneurship offers a flexible way of addressing social problems, raising dilemmas over appropriate missions, organisational forms and business models. Social entrepreneurs and large businesses also frequently have to choose how to relate to each other through mutually beneficial partnerships.

Work assignments·

✱ *Denotes more advanced work assignments.*   * *Refers to a case study in the Text and Cases edition.*

9.1 ✱ For a new product or service that you have recently experienced and enjoyed, investigate the strategy of the company responsible. With reference to the dilemmas of section 9.2, explain whether the innovation was more technology push or market pull, product or process driven, or technological or more broadly business model based.

9.2 Go to a web traffic site (such as alexa.com) and compare over time trends in terms of 'page views' or 'reach' for older sites (such as Amazon.com) and newer sites (such as youtube.com, or any that has more recently emerged). With reference to section 9.3, how do you explain these trends and how would you project them forward?

9.3 ✱ With regard to a new product or service that you have recently experienced and enjoyed (as in 9.1), investigate the strategic responses of 'incumbents' to this innovation. To what extent is the innovation disruptive for them (see section 9.4.3)?

9.4 With reference to the entrepreneurial life cycle, identify the position of either MacPac*, Ekomate*, Brown Bag Film* or ACME*. What managerial issues might this case company anticipate in the coming years?

9.5 Use the Internet to identify a social entrepreneurial venture that interests you (via www.skollfoundation.org, for example), and, with regard to section 9.5.3, identify its social mission, its organisational form and its business model.

Integrative assignment

9.6 Consider a for-profit or social entrepreneurial idea that you or your friends or colleagues might have. Drawing on section 15.4.4, outline the elements of a strategic plan for this possible venture. What more information do you need to get?

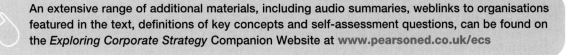

An extensive range of additional materials, including audio summaries, weblinks to organisations featured in the text, definitions of key concepts and self-assessment questions, can be found on the *Exploring Corporate Strategy* Companion Website at www.pearsoned.co.uk/ecs

Recommended key readings

- P. Trott, *Innovation Management and New Product Development*, 3rd edition, FT/Prentice Hall, 2005, provides a comprehensive overview of innovation strategy issues. A lively and accessible survey of many innovation issues, together with a wealth of examples, is C. Markides and P. Geroski, *Fast second: how smart companies bypass radical innovation to enter and dominate new markets*, Josey-Bass, 2005.

- A good collection of accessible articles on specialised innovation topics by leading academics is J. Fagerberg, D. Mowery and R. Nelson (eds), *The Oxford Handbook of Innovation*, Oxford University Press, 2005. An equivalent collection on

entrepreneurship is M. Casson, B. Yeung, A. Basu and N. Wadeson (eds), *The Oxford Handbook of Entrepreneurship*, Oxford University Press, 2006.

- P.A. Wickham, *Strategic Entrepreneurship*, 3rd edition, 2004, is becoming the standard European text with regard to entrepreneurial strategy.

- Social entrepreneurship is discussed usefully in A. Nichols (ed.), *Social Entrepreneurship: New paradigms of sustainable social change*, Oxford University Press, 2006.

- For an overview of the associated financial considerations for new business start ups/proposals see G. Arnold, *Corporate Financial Management*, 3rd edition, FT/Prentice Hall, 2005, Chapter 2.

References

1. This definition adapts, in order to include the public sector, the definition in P. Trott, *Innovation Management and New Product Development*, 3rd edition, FT/Prentice Hall, 2005.

2. A good discussion of the academic models that underpin these dilemmas is in R. Rothwell, 'Successful industrial innovation: critical factors for the 1990s', *R&D Management*, vol. 22, no. 3 (1992), pp. 221–239.

3. W.J. Abernathy and J.M. Utterback, 'A dynamic model of process and product innovation', *Omega*, vol. 3, no. 6 (1975), pp. 142–160.

4. P. Anderson and M.L. Tushman, 'Technological discontinuities and dominant designs: a cyclical model of technological change', *Administrative Science Quarterly*, vol. 35 (1990), pp. 604–633.

5. J. Tang, 'Competition and innovation behaviour', *Research Policy*, vol. 35 (2006), pp. 68–82.

6. G. Hamel, *Leading the Revolution*, Harvard Business School Press, 2000.

7. J. Magretta, 'Why business models matter', *Harvard Business Review*, vol. 80, no. 5 (2002), pp. 86–92

8. Good discussions of business models and their relationship to business-level strategy can be found in G. Yip, 'Using strategy to change your business model', *Business Strategy Review*, vol. 15, no. 2 (2004), pp. 17–24; and G.M. Mansfield and L. Fourie, 'Strategy and business models – strange bedfellows? A case for convergence and its evolution into strategic architecture', *South African Business Management Journal*, vol. 15, no. 1 (2004), pp. 35–44.

9. Innovation diffusion is discussed in the classic E. Rogers, *Diffusion of Innovations*, Free Press, 1995; C. Kim and R. Maubourgne, 'Knowing a winning idea when you see one', *Harvard Business Review*, vol. 78, no. 5 (2000), pp. 129–138; and J. Cummings and J. Doh, 'Identifying who matters: mapping key players in multiple environments', *California Management Review*, vol. 42, no. 2 (2000), pp. 83–104 (see especially pp. 91–97).

10. J. Cummings and J. Doh, 'Identifying who matters: mapping key players in multiple environments', *California Management Review*, vol. 42, no, 2 (2000), pp. 83–104.

11. J. Nichols and S. Roslow, 'The S-curve: an aid to strategic marketing', *Journal of Consumer Marketing*, vol. 3, no. 2 (1986), pp 53–64; and F. Suarez and G. Lanzolla, 'The half-truth of first-mover advantage', *Harvard Business Review*, vol. 83 no. 4 (2005), pp. 121–127. This S-curve refers to innovation diffusion. However, the S-curve effect sometimes also refers to the diminishing performance increases available from a maturing technology: A. Sood and G. Tellis, 'Technological evolution and radical innovation', *Journal of Marketing*, vol. 69, no. 3 (2005), pp. 152–168.

12. M. Gladwell, *The Tipping Point*, Abacus, 2000. Tipping points are also important in public policy and can help anticipate emerging problems, for example crime waves and epidemics.

13. www.bbcnews.com, 12 January (2007).

14. S. Brown, 'The tripping point', *Marketing Research*, vol. 17, no. 1 (2005), pp. 8–13.

15. C. Markides and P. Geroski, *Fast second: how smart companies bypass radical innovation to enter and dominate new markets*, Josey-Bass, 2005; R. Kerin, P. Varadarajan and R. Peterson, 'First-mover advantage: a synthesis, conceptual framework and research propositions', *Journal of Marketing*, vol. 56, no. 4 (1992), pp. 33–52; and P.F. Suarez and G. Lanzolla, 'The half-truth of first-mover advantage', *Harvard Business Review*, vol. 83, no. 4 (2005), pp. 121–127

16. F. Suarez and G. Lanzolla, 'The half-truth of first-mover advantage', *Harvard Business Review*, vol. 83, no. 4 (2005), pp. 121–127. See also S. Min, U. Manohar and W. Robinson, 'Market pioneer and early follower survival risks: a contingency analysis of really new versus incrementally new product-markets', *Journal of Marketing*, vol. 70, no. 1 (2006), pp. 15–33.

17. David Teece, the academic authority in this area, refers to the capacity to capture profits the 'appropriability regime': see D. Teece, *Managing Intellectual Capital*, Oxford University Press, 2000.

18. An excellent survey of intellectual property rights is in *The Economist Magazine*, Survey: Patents and Technology, October 25 (2005).

19. D. Teece, *Managing Intellectual Capital*, Oxford University Press, 2000.

20. C. Markides and P. Geroski, *Fast second: how smart companies bypass radical innovation to enter and dominate new markets*, Jossey-Bass, 2005.

21. See J. Bower and C. Christensen, 'Disruptive technologies: catching the wave', *Harvard Business Review*, vol. 73, no. 1 (1995), pp. 43–53; and C. Christensen and M.E. Raynor, *The Innovator's Solution*, Harvard Business School Press, 2003.

22. R.G. McGrath and I. MacMillan, *The Entrepreneurial Mindset*, Harvard Business School Press, 2000.

23. C. Christensen and M.E. Raynor, *The Innovator's Solution*, Harvard Business School Press, 2003.

24. V. Govindarajan and C. Trimble, 'Organizational DNA for strategic innovation', *California Management Review*, vol. 43, no. 3 (2005), pp. 47–75.

25. Excellent textbooks on strategic entrepreneurship include J.A. Timmons, *New Venture Creation: Entrepreneurship in the 21st Century*, 6th edition, Irwin, 2004; and P.A. Wickham, *Strategic Entrepreneurship*, 3rd edition, FT/Prentice Hall, 2004.

26. Life-cycle models of entrepreneurship are discussed in S. Hanks, C. Watson, E. Jansen and G. Chandler, 'Tightening the life-cycle construct: a taxonomic study of growth stage configurations in high-technology organizations', *Entrepreneurship Theory and Practice*, Winter (1993), pp. 5–28; and D. Flynn and A. Forman, 'Life cycles of new venture organizations: different factors affecting performance', *Journal of Developmental Entrepreneurship*, vol. 6, no. 1 (2001), pp. 41–58.

27. D. Flynn and A. Forman, 'Life cycles of new venture organizations: different factors affecting performance', *Journal of Developmental Entrepreneurship*, vol. 6, no. 1 (2001), pp. 41–58.

28. D. Flynn and A. Forman, 'Life cycles of new venture organizations: different factors affecting performance', *Journal of Developmental Entrepreneurship*, vol. 6, no. 1 (2001), pp. 41–58.

29. R. Kaplinksy, 'Firm size and technical change', *Journal of Industrial Economics*, vol. 32, no. 1 (1983), pp. 39–59. For a detailed account of Cisco's policy of taking over high-technology firms, see D. Mayer and M. Kenney, 'Economic action does not take place in a vacuum: understanding Cisco's acquisition and development strategy', *Industry and Innovation*, vol. 11, no. 4 (2004), pp. 293–325.

30. P. Audia and C. Rider, 'A garage and an idea: what more does an entrepreneur need?', *California Management Review*, vol. 40, no. 1 (2005), pp. 6–28.

31. H. Chesbrough, *Open Innovation: the New Imperatives for Creating and Profiting from Technology*, Harvard Business School Press, 2003. The Research Director of Intel describes his company's 'open' approach in D. Tennenhouse, 'Intel's open-collaborative model of industry-university research', *Research and Technology Management*, July–August (2004), pp. 19–26.

32. H. Chesbrough, 'Making sense of corporate venture capital', *Harvard Business Review*, vol. 80, no. 3 (2002), pp. 4–11; A. Campbell, J. Birkinshaw, A. Morrison and R. van Basten Batenburg, 'The Future of corporate venturing', *MIT Sloan Management Review*, vol. 45, no. 1 (2003), pp. 33–41.

33. IBM's director of research describes ecosystems in P.M. Horn, 'The changing nature of innovation', *Research and Technology Management*, November–December (2005), pp. 28–33; see also B. Iyer, C.-H. Lee and N. Venkatraman, 'Managing in a "Small World Ecosystem"', *California Management Review*, vol. 48, no. 3 (2006), pp. 28–47.

34. A. Gawer and M. Cusumano, *Platform Leadership: how Intel, Microsoft and Cisco drive industry innovation*, Harvard Business School Press, 2002.

35. P. DuGay, 'Against enterprise', *Organization*, vol. 11, no. 1 (2004), pp. 37–48.

36. S. Alvord, L. Brown and C. Letts, 'Social entrepreneurship and societal transformation: an exploratory study', *Journal of Applied Behavioral Science*, vol. 43, no. 3 (2004), pp. 260–282; A. Nichols (ed.) *Social Entrepreneurship: New paradigms of sustainable social change*, Oxford University Press, 2006; J. Austin, H. Stevenson and J. Wei-Skillern, 'Social and commercial entrepreneurship: same, different, or both?', *Entrepreneurship Theory and Practice*, vol. 30, no. 1 (2006), pp. 1–22.

37. R. Moss Kanter, 'From spare change to real change', *Harvard Business Review*, May–June (1999), pp. 122–133.

Skype: innovators and entrepreneurs

Introduction

Niklas Zennström and Janus Friis are a golden pair in the Internet business. For a period during the early 2000s, their Kazaa peer-to-peer file sharing business was the world's largest music sharing site. After selling that business to Sharman Networks, they moved quickly to establish Skype in 2003, which quickly became the dominant player in the world's VoIP (Voice over Internet Protocol) telephone market. Skype's free Internet-based VoIP service was an attractive alternative to the expensive traditional landline and mobile telephone services, gaining 60 million users by 2005. That same year, they sold Skype to eBay for $2.6bn (£1.5bn; €2.1bn) – an impressive figure for a business whose total revenues were just $60m and had still not turned a profit.

Key issues for Zennström and Friis in 2006 were the long-term sustainability of their business model and their future under the ownership of eBay.

Two entrepreneurs

Zennström is the older of the two, aged 40 at the sale to eBay. He took a first degree in business and then an MSc in engineering and computer science from Uppsala University in Sweden. He then entered the telecommunications industry, spending nine years in Tele2, a fast-expanding European telecoms group. He met Friis in 1997, hiring him to manage a help-desk. Friis, a Dane, is 11 years younger and failed even to graduate from high school. But from the late 1990s the two worked closely together on a series of new ventures: as well as Kazaa and Skype, these included Altnet, claimed to be the world's first secure peer-to-peer wholesale network, Joltid, a company in traffic optimisation technologies, and the portal everyday.com.

Zennström has a modest personal style. In his London office, he shares a long desk with half a

Co-founders of Skype – Niklas Zennström (left) and Janus Friis (right)

dozen colleagues and he flies economy class, despite his height of 6ft 4in (1.93m). But he is absolutely committed to the idea of disruptive innovation. He told the *Financial Times*: 'It's everyone's obligation to fight against monopolies and also companies that provide bad services.' Of the traditional landline and mobile telephone companies, he declares: 'They deserve to be challenged. They provide bad and expensive service.'

About his partner Friis, he observes: 'I think he benefited from not having formal schooling. His thought process is much freer. He doesn't think conventionally.' However, he rejects the notion that Friis is the vision guy and he is simply the execution guy. 'We are very complementary with each other. It is a very creative process and it's easier to be creative with two people. You need to try things out and challenge each other.'

The Skype business model

Skype's software allows people to use the Internet to make free calls to other Skype users all over the world. Given the cost of traditional international calls, this was an exciting idea. Initial funding, however, was not easy to find as the music industry was still pursuing a lawsuit against the two founders regarding the illegal filesharing their earlier Kazaa venture appeared to facilitate. For fear of legal action, Zennström and Friis dared not even enter the USA. Most traditional venture capitalists gave the new venture a wide berth. Moreover, it was not easy to see how to make money out of free calls.

The business model is more complicated than that, of course. Most users have free calls, certainly. However, Skype has very low costs, as customers download the software off the Internet and it is the customers' computers and Internet connections that make the network. It costs nothing to keep connections open continuously. Marketing is cheap, because customers naturally invite others to join. Skype has no telephone help-desk, citing the overwhelming number of customers and the effectiveness of its standard Internet queries services. Skype makes its money from its ancillary services, such as SkypeOut, which allows customers to call traditional landline or mobile numbers for a fee, often very small. Zennström explains the model: 'We want to make as little money as possible per user. We don't have any cost per user, but we want a lot of them.'

This overturns the traditional landline and mobile phone business model. Traditional telephone companies of both types face high costs of both marketing and capacity building. Customers are typically charged according to distance and by the minute. The traditional principle is to maximise revenues per customer, completely the opposite to Skype. Zennström summarised to *Business Week*:

When you're a phone company, you have marketing and customer-acquisition costs. When you have a customer, you have an operational cost of running the network. Then you have a cost for billing systems. That's an operator business model.

The business model of Skype is completely different. Skype has a software business model. We don't have any distribution or marketing costs for each user – our software is spread virally. And when we have a new user, we have zero cost for serving that user because they're using P2P (peer-to-peer) software and their own bandwidth. So we have zero costs of getting new users and zero costs of running traffic. Our costs are only business development and software development.

Comparing the positions of the two types of companies, he added: 'Something that is a great business model for us is probably a terrible model for them.'

As shown in Figure 1, Skype's service was immensely attractive. With a tipping point in 2004, user numbers surged ahead. Of course, this success

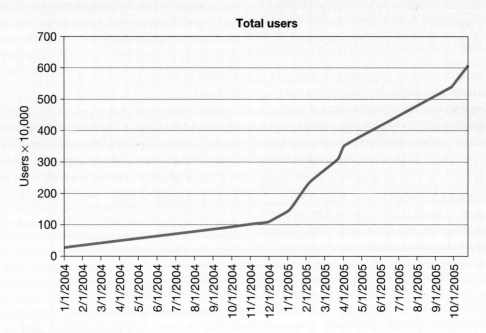

Figure 1 Skype's users

Source: www.wikipedia.com. This material is licensed under the GNU Free Documentation Licence. It uses material from the Wikipedia article 'Skype'.

raised an awkward paradox. If Skype became near universal, who would be left for people to call using the paid service of SkypeOut to access traditional phones?

eBay's move

Skype was always likely to be for sale. Zennström and Friis had sold Kazaa quickly and their initial funders would want a profitable early exit too. It was not surprising that rumours started during 2005 of possible acquisition from technology giants such as Google, Microsoft and Yahoo!. In the end, however, it was online auctioneer eBay who did the deal, slightly surprisingly as it was not seen as a communications company.

There are similarities in the underlying business models of the two companies. Both benefit from 'network effects', where value rises disproportionately fast with increasing members of the network. One more precise rationale from eBay's point of view was that Skype connections could be placed directly on the eBay site, allowing customers potentially to phone sellers with a single click of the button. Also, sellers could place voice links directly on their eBay sites, so that customers could click directly to a message, paying eBay a fee every time they did. On the other hand, Skype would strengthen its links with eBay's subsidiary PayPal, which Skype already used for managing payments for its SkypeOut service.

For Zennström, however, one major attraction of eBay was that it looked likely to leave Skype more alone. Companies like Yahoo! and Microsoft tend to integrate their acquisitions closely into their existing operations, extinguishing autonomy. Zennström and Friis might be working with eBay for some time. The deal included an 'earn-out' arrangement which would push Skype's final sale price to over $4bn if they managed to meet revenue and profit targets over the coming years. Anyway, the two had an exciting vision for the future: to become the world's biggest and best platform for all communication – text, voice or video – from any Internet-connected device, whether a computer or a mobile phone.

eBay's role

eBay had a lot to offer an ambitious company like Skype. Founded only in 1995, it had reached revenues of $4.55bn and 11,600 employees in the space of 10 years. Zennström commented of Meg Whitman, eBay's Chief Executive since 1998: 'I think I can learn a lot of things from Meg. We want to see things through, but we also have some other ideas.' Skype would still have its own strategy, budgets, culture and brands. Zennström insisted to the *Financial Times*:

One of the important things for us, but also one of the great things with eBay, is that we wanted to make sure that we could merge with a bigger company, but that Skype stays as one company. Meg said: 'Take advantage of the resources we have, but we are not going to tell you what to do because you're the best in the world to run your own business'.

The managerial demands of rapid growth were considerable. Staff quadrupled to 300 between 2005 and 2006, and included 30 nationalities scattered all over the world. eBay introduced five of its own senior managers to help, including a new president responsible for day-to-day operations, a chief financial officer and a new human resource director. But Skype was keen to preserve its own culture. According to Zennström, still the CEO, Skype's passionate, pioneering culture had to be both protected and nurtured: 'It's how you operate, how you behave. It starts when we are hiring people. They need to be really thrilled about Skype as a movement, rather than a place to work.' For the new Human Resources Director, Annemie van Rensburg, her job was about 'the fun stuff, such as keeping the Skype culture intact and bringing Skype people together globally'.

Sources: 'Phone Service the "Zero Cost" Way', *Business Week online*, 7 January (2004); www.wikipedia.org; *The Economist*, 15 September (2005); *Financial Times*, 17 and 19 April (2006).

Strategy Methods and Evaluation

LEARNING OUTCOMES

After reading this chapter you should be able to:

→ Identify the *methods* by which strategies can be pursued: *organic development*, *mergers and acquisitions* and *strategic alliances*.

→ Employ three *success criteria* for evaluating strategic options: *suitability*, *acceptability* and *feasibility*.

→ Use a range of different *techniques for evaluating strategic options*.

Photo: John Crum/Alamy Images

10.1 INTRODUCTION

This chapter rounds off Part II of the book, the whole of which has been concerned with strategic choices available to organisations, as outlined in Exhibit II.i. Chapter 6 offered a range of choices about how to position the organisation in relation to competitors. Within this generalised choice about the basis of competitive strategy, there are more specific choices to be made about the strategic direction of the organisation; in particular, which markets and which products are most appropriate. These choices were set out in Chapter 7 and developed further in Chapters 8 and 9 in the context of international strategy and strategy innovation. However, there is a third level of choice concerned with the *methods by which competitive strategy and strategic direction can be pursued*. This is the theme of section 10.2, the first half of this chapter.

Bearing in mind that the use of the concepts and tools introduced in Part I of the book will also have generated ideas about strategies that might be followed, the strategist may well need to consider many possible options. The second half of this chapter therefore discusses the *success criteria* by which they can be assessed and, building on these criteria, explains some of the *techniques for evaluating strategic options*.

Exhibit 10.1 summarises the overall structure of the chapter.

Exhibit 10.1 **Strategy methods and evaluation: chapter structure**

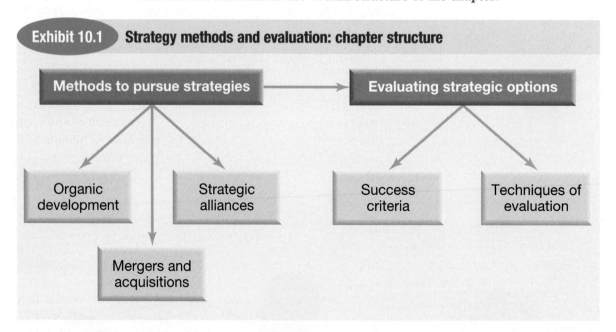

10.2 METHODS OF PURSUING STRATEGIES

A strategic method is the *means* by which a strategy can be pursued

Any of the strategy directions discussed in Chapters 6 to 9 may be undertaken in a different way or by a different **strategic method**: the *means* by which a strategy can be pursued. These methods can be divided into three types: organic development, acquisition (or disposal) and alliances.

10.2.1 Organic development[1]

Organic development is where strategies are developed by building on and developing an organisation's own capabilities

Organic development (or internal development) is where strategies are developed by building on and developing an organisation's own capabilities. For many organisations organic development has been the primary method of strategy development, and there are some compelling reasons why this should be so:

- *Highly technical products* in terms of design or method of manufacture lend themselves to organic development since the process of development may be the best way of acquiring the necessary capabilities to compete successfully. These competences may of course in turn spawn new products and create new market opportunities.

- *Knowledge and capability development* may be enhanced by organic development. For example, a business may feel that the direct involvement gained from having its own salesforce rather than using sales agents gains greater market knowledge and therefore competitive advantage over other rivals more distant from their customers.

- *Spreading investment over time*. The final cost of developing new activities internally may be greater than that of acquiring other companies. However, spreading these costs over time may be a more favourable option than major expenditure at a point in time required for an acquisition. This is a strong motive for organic development in small companies or many public services that may not have the resources for major one-off investments.

- *Minimising disruption*. The slower rate of change of organic development may also minimise the disruption to other activities and avoid the political and cultural problems of acquisition integration that can occur (see section 10.2.2).

- *The nature of markets* may dictate organic development. In many instances organisations breaking new ground may not be in a position to develop by acquisition or joint development, since they are the only ones in the field. Or there may be few opportunities for acquisitions, as, for example, for foreign companies attempting to enter Japan.

10.2.2 Mergers and acquisitions[2]

An acquisition is where an organisation takes ownership of another organisation

A merger is a mutually agreed decision for joint ownership between organisations

An **acquisition** is where an organisation takes ownership of another organisation, whereas a **merger** implies a mutually agreed decision for joint ownership between organisations. In practice, few acquisitions are hostile and few mergers are the joining of equals. So both acquisitions and mergers typically involve the managers of one organisation exerting strategic influence over the other. Worldwide merger and acquisition activity takes place on a major scale but tends to go in waves.[3] Globally the number of completed acquisitions tripled between 1991 and 2001. There was then a decline after 2000 but they still stood at $1.2 trillion (≈ €1 trillion; £690bn) in 2002. Since then it has risen again and stood at almost $3.8 trillion in 2006[4] (see Exhibit 10.2). Global activity in mergers is dominated by North America and Western Europe whereas it is much less common in other economies, for example Japan. This reflects the influence of the differences in governance systems that exist (see section 4.2).

www.pearsoned.co.uk/ecs
KEY CONCEPT

Mergers and acquisitions

Exhibit 10.2 **Worldwide mergers and acquisition by value ($bn)**

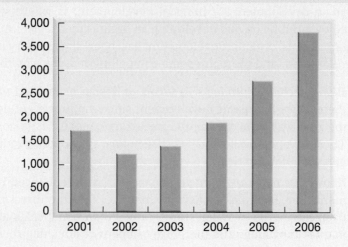

Source: 'All aboard the M&A express', *Sunday Times Business Focus*, 31 December (2006), p. 5. © NI Syndication Limited, 3.12.06.

Motives for acquisitions and mergers

There are different motives for developing through acquisition or merger. A major reason can be the need to keep up with a changing *environment*:

- *Speed of entry*. Products or markets may be changing so rapidly that acquisition becomes the only way of successfully entering the market, since the process of internal development is too slow.

- The *competitive situation* may influence a company to prefer acquisition. In static markets and where market shares of companies are steady it can be difficult for a new company to enter the market, since its presence may create excess capacity. If entry is by acquisition the risk of competitive reaction may be reduced.

- *Consolidation opportunities*. Where there are low levels of industry concentration, there may be an opportunity for improving the balance between supply and demand by acquiring companies and shutting down excess capacity. In many countries, *deregulation* of public utilities has also created a level of fragmentation that was regarded as suboptimal. This was then an opportunity for acquisitive organisations to rationalise provision and/or seek to gain other benefits, for example through the creation of 'multi-utility' companies offering electricity, gas, telecommunications and other services to customers.

- *Financial markets* may provide conditions that motivate acquisitions. If the share value or price/earnings (P/E) ratio of a company is high, it may see the opportunity to acquire a firm with a low share value or P/E ratio. Indeed, this is a major stimulus for the more opportunistic acquisitive companies. An extreme example is asset stripping, where the main motive is short-term gain by buying up undervalued assets and disposing of them piecemeal.

There may also be *capability considerations*:

● *Exploitation of strategic capabilities* can motivate acquisitions, for example through buying companies overseas in order to leverage marketing or R&D skills internationally.

● *Cost efficiency* is a commonly stated reason for acquisitions typically by merging units so as to rationalise resources (for example, head office services or production facilities) or gain scale advantages.

● *Obtaining new capabilities* may also be achieved through acquisitions, or at least be a motive for acquisition. For example, a company may be acquired for its R&D expertise, or its knowledge of particular business processes or markets.

Acquisition can also be driven by the *stakeholder expectations*:

● *Institutional shareholder expectations* may be for continuing growth and acquisitions may be a quick way to deliver this growth. There are considerable dangers, however, that acquisitive growth may result in value destruction rather than creation – for some of the reasons discussed in Chapter 7. For example, the 'parent' may not have sufficient feel for the acquired businesses and thus destroy value.

● *Managerial ambition* may motivate acquisitions because they speed the growth of the company. In turn, this might enhance managers' self-importance, provide better career paths and greater monetary rewards.

● *Speculative motives* of some stakeholders may stimulate acquisitions that bring a short-term boost to share value. Other stakeholders are usually wary of such speculation since their short-term gain can destroy longer-term prospects.

The key debate at the end of the chapter (Illustration 10.7) highlights the debate about the extent to which acquisitions are beneficial to different organisational stakeholders.

Acquisitions and financial performance

Acquisitions are not an easy or guaranteed route to improving financial performance.[5] As many as 70 per cent of acquisitions end up with lower returns to shareholders of both organisations. The most common mistake is in paying too much for a company – possibly through lack of experience in acquisitions, or poor financial advice (for example, from the investment bank involved). In addition the managers of the acquiring company may be over-optimistic about the benefits of the acquisition. An acquisition will probably include poor resources and competences as well as those which were the reason for the purchase. Or it may be that the capabilities of the merging organisations are not compatible. So much was the case, for example, in the 2004 acquisition in the UK of the Safeway supermarket chain by its competitor Morrisons. Amongst the problems was that Morrisons spent a year trying to integrate the IT systems of the two companies before abandoning the attempt. Indeed for this reason acquirers may attempt to buy products or processes rather than whole companies if possible. At the very best it may take the acquiring company considerable time to gain financial benefit from acquisitions.

Making acquisitions work[6]

The implementation agenda following an acquisition or merger will vary depending on its purpose.[7] None the less there are four frequently occurring issues that account for success or failure of an acquisition/merger:

● *Adding value*. The acquirer may find difficulty in adding value to the acquired business (the parenting issue as discussed in section 7.4).

● *Gaining the commitment of middle managers* responsible for the operations and customer relations in the acquired business is important in order to avoid internal uncertainties and maintain customer confidence. Linked to this, deciding which executives to retain in the acquired business needs to be done quickly.

● *Expected synergies may not be realised*, either because they do not exist to the extent expected or because it proves difficult to integrate the activities of the acquired business. For example, where the motive was the transfer of competences or knowledge it may be difficult to identify what these are (see sections 3.4.3 and 3.6.2).

● *Problems of cultural fit*. This can arise because the acquiring business finds that 'everyday' but embedded aspects of culture (for example, organisation routines) differ in ways that prove difficult to overcome but are not readily identifiable before the acquisition. This can be particularly problematic with cross-country acquisitions.[8]

10.2.3 Strategic alliances[9]

A strategic alliance is where two or more organisations share resources and activities to pursue a strategy

KEY
CONCEPT
www.pearsoned.co.uk/ecs

Strategic
alliances

A **strategic alliance** is where two or more organisations share resources and activities to pursue a strategy.[10] They vary from simple two-partner alliances co-producing a product to one with multiple partners providing complex products and solutions. By the turn of the century the top 500 global companies had an average of 60 alliances each.[11] This kind of joint development of new strategies has become increasingly popular. This is because organisations cannot always cope with increasingly complex environments or strategies (such as globalisation)[12] from internal resources and competences alone. They may need to obtain materials, skills, innovation, finance or access to markets but recognise that these may be as readily available through cooperation as through ownership. The choice of acquisition or alliance is therefore one that many organisations face, as Illustration 10.1 shows. However, about half of all alliances fail.[13]

Motives for alliances[14]

A frequent reason for alliances is to obtain resources that an organisation needs but does not itself possess. For example, banks need to gain access to the payment systems that allow credit cards to be used in retail outlets (for example, Visa or MasterCard) and to the automated teller machines (ATMs) to allow cash withdrawals. These resources do not, however, confer competitive advantage on members of the alliance; nor are they intended to so: they are threshold requirements for modern banking. Such arrangements are *infrastructure alliances* that

Illustration 10.1

How law firms are going global

Organisations may have to decide between the benefits and risks of acquisition or alliances.

Both major UK and US law firms are extending their operations globally. However, this has taken different forms. 'Leading U.S. law firms harvest the world's largest legal market at home and plough cautiously elsewhere, while many of the biggest British based firms have placed a huge bet on building extensive international networks and a global presence.' As yet, it is unclear which choices will work best in terms of the preferences of their multinational clients: whether they will 'prefer to be served by one stop shop multinational law firms, or by cherry picking different legal practices in different countries'.

Most of the largest law firms by revenue are from the USA. But the biggest are the 'magic circle' London-based law firms. In the 1990s these firms, with their relatively limited home market,

decided to move beyond their informal relationships with firms in other countries and either put in place formal partnerships or full mergers or open their own offices. . . . Three quarters of the top 25 British based firms have at least one wholly owned office in China, up from one third in 2004.

By 2007 the results were impressive: 'The biggest four magic circle firms out performed even the trend of globally rising profitability last year.'

There were problems, however. One was the differences between the legal systems in different countries. In the face of this 'English lawyers and the law society, their professional body, are keen to promote English law as a jurisdiction of choice for international business' and 'Britain's government and legal profession have begun an openly aggressive effort to persuade other countries to remove restrictions on how it's lawyers can operate'.

US firms have tended to focus at home where they have the benefit of most of the world's largest multinationals – even if they are concerned that more and more of them are choosing to register outside the USA as a result of the Sarbanes–Oxley rules on financial disclosure.

Their approach is that they can 'keep their profitability high by working their home market, running offices in a few key foreign centres and building links with local firms in countries where they have no presence'. This cuts running costs and insulates US firms from the risk of overcommitment to potentially risky markets. Indeed this is an approach that London-based law firm Slaughter and May has also adopted successfully 'shunning international expansion in favour of establishing a network of "best friends" firms in economically significant countries'.

Supporters of this approach also point to survey evidence that has found that the international capability of law firms does not feature in the top 10 requirements by their clients. They also argue that markets outside Europe are much less profitable.

In addition to all this, there is evidence of different overall approaches to mergers and acquisitions between US and UK firms: 'Big British firms are on the prowl almost permanently – if mostly fruitlessly – for merger partners (in the U.S.) that will give them the bigger toehold they want.' Contrast that with the partner at one of the biggest US law firms who says of mergers: 'That's not our way. We have never merged, we have never acquired and we are never going to.'

Source: 'Reach versus risk', *Financial Times*, 14 December (2006), p. 15.

Questions

1 Explain the different rationales for acquisition or alliance building for law firms in terms of the reasons given in sections 10.2.2 and 10.2.3 of the chapter.

2 What are the risks of each approach?

involve the sharing or pooling of resources and mechanism of cooperation, but which are not seeking to gain competitive advantage.[15] Here, however, we are concerned with *strategic alliances* that do seek to gain such advantage.

Motives for such alliances are of three main types:

- The need for *critical mass*, which alliances can achieve by forming partnerships with either competitors or providers of complementary products. This can lead to cost reduction and improved customer offering.

- *Co-specialisation* – allowing each partner to concentrate on activities that best match its capabilities: for example, to enter new geographical markets where an organisation needs local knowledge and expertise in distribution, marketing and customer support. Similarly alliances with organisations in other parts of the value chain (for example, suppliers or distributors) are common.

- *Learning* from partners and developing competences that may be more widely exploited elsewhere. For example, first steps into e-business may be achieved with a partner that has expertise in website development. However, the longer-term intention might be to bring those activities in-house. Organisations may also enter alliances as a means of *experimentation* since it allows them to break out of a sole reliance on the exploitation of their own resources and capabilities. Indeed they may use alliances as a basis for developing strategic options different from those being developed in house organically[16] (see the discussion on real options in section 10.3.2).

Types of alliance

There are different types of strategic alliance. Some may be formalised inter-organisational relationships. At the other extreme, there are loose arrangements of cooperation and informal networking between organisations, with no shareholding or ownership involved:

- *Joint ventures* are relatively formalised alliances and may take different forms themselves. Here organisations remain independent but set up a newly created organisation jointly owned by the parents. Joint ventures are a favoured means of collaborative ventures in China, for example. Local firms provide labour and entry to markets; Western companies provide technology, management expertise and finance.

- *Consortia* may involve two or more organisations in a joint venture arrangement typically more focused on a particular venture or project. Examples include large civil engineering projects, or major aerospace undertakings, such as the European Airbus. They might also exist between public sector organisations where services (such as public transport) cross administrative boundaries.

- *Networks* are less formal arrangements where organisations gain mutual advantage by working in collaboration without relying on cross-ownership arrangements and formal contracts. Carlos Jarillo suggests that characteristic of such network arrangements are a reliance on coordination through mutual adaptation of working relationships, mutual trust (see below) and, typically, a 'hub organisation' that may have promoted the network and maintains a proactive attitude to it.[17] Such networked arrangements may exist between competitors in highly competitive industries where some form of sharing is none the less beneficial. For example, in the Formula One industry,[18] where state-of-the-art know-how tends to flow between firms.

Other alliance arrangements exist usually of a contractual nature and unlikely to involve ownership:

- *Franchising* involves the franchise holder undertaking specific activities such as manufacturing, distribution or selling, whilst the franchiser is responsible for the brand name, marketing and probably training. Perhaps the best-known examples are Coca-Cola and McDonald's.

- *Licensing* is common in science-based industries where, for example, the right to manufacture a patented product is granted for a fee.

- With *subcontracting*, a company chooses to subcontract particular services or part of a process: for example, increasingly in public services responsibility for waste removal, cleaning and IT services may be subcontracted (or 'out-sourced') to private companies.

Exhibit 10.3 shows three important factors that can influence types of alliance:

- *Speed of market change* will require strategic moves to be made quickly. So less formal and flexible network arrangements may be more appropriate than a joint venture, which could take too long to establish.

- *The management of resources and capabilities*. If a strategy requires separate, dedicated, resources then a joint venture will be appropriate. In contrast, if the strategic purpose and operations of the alliance can be supported by the current resources of the partners this favours a looser contractual relationship or network.

Exhibit 10.3 **Types of strategic alliance**

INFLUENCING FACTORS	FORM OF RELATIONSHIP		
	Loose (Market) ● Networks ● Opportunistic alliances	**Contractual** ● Licensing ● Franchising ● Subcontracting	**Ownership** ● Consortia ● Joint ventures
The Market ● Speed of market change	Fast change	⟶	Slow change
Resources ● Asset management	Managed separately by each partner	⟶	Managed together
● Partner's assets	Draws on 'parent's' assets	⟶	Dedicated assets for alliance
● Risk of losing assets to partner	High risk	⟶	Low risk
Expectations ● Spreading financial risk	Maintains risk	⟶	Dilutes risk
● Political climate	Unfavourable climate	⟶	Favourable climate

● The *expectations and motives* of alliance partners will play a part. For example, if alliance partners see the alliance as a means of spreading their financial risk, this will favour more formal arrangements such as joint ventures.

Ingredients of successful alliances[19]

Although organisations may establish an alliance for one or more of the reasons outlined above, the benefits of alliances tend to evolve. It may, for example, be established to address a particularly complex technological opportunity, but yield new and unexpected opportunities. The success of alliances is therefore dependent on how they are managed and the way in which the partners foster the evolving nature of the partnership. Given this, success factors fall under three broad headings:

● *Strategic purpose*. A clear strategic purpose is likely to be helpful at the outset of an alliance. However, alliance members will, quite likely, have differing if compatible reasons for being part of the alliance. As an alliance develops it is likely that their expectations and perceived benefits will evolve – not least because they are often built to cope with dynamic or complex environments. If the expectations of alliance members start to diverge the alliance may eventually disintegrate. If the evolving expectations remain compatible or converge then it is likely the alliance will continue. It is also possible that convergence could give rise to more formalised ownership arrangements such as a merger of the alliance partners.[20]

● *Alliance expectations and benefits*. Similarly, given that the expectations of alliance partners may vary, managing those expectations as the alliance evolves is vital. At the most basic level, expectations cannot be met without a willingness to exchange information, including performance information that would not normally be shared between organisations. However, beyond this, given that many alliances are about learning and experimentation, the acceptance of these as benefits of themselves by alliance members may be important. If one of the partners does not buy into such benefits and attempts to impose a 'static' strategy on the alliance this may well lead to problems.[21] There are also indications that alliances that develop knowledge-based products and services (as distinct from physical product) tend to bind alliance partners more closely together since they are likely to be mutually dependent on shared tacit knowledge in the development of such products and services.[22]

● *Managing alliance relationships*. Senior management support for an alliance is important since alliances require a wider range of relationships to be built and sustained. This can create cultural and political hurdles that senior managers must help to overcome. In turn strong interpersonal relationships to achieve *compatibility at the operational level* is also needed. In cross-country partnerships this includes the need to transcend national cultural differences. Consistently, however, research shows that *trust* is the most important ingredient of success and a major reason for failure if it is absent.[23] But trust has two separate elements. Trust can be *competence based* in the sense that each partner is confident that the other has the resources and competences to fulfil its part in the alliance. Trust is also *character based* and concerns whether partners trust each other's motives and are compatible in terms of attitudes to integrity, openness, discretion and consistency of behaviour. Overall the message is that it is the quality of the relationships in an alliance that are of prime importance; indeed to a greater extent than the physical resources in an alliance.[24]

A consistent message that recurs, then, is that whilst it may be very helpful to ensure that an alliance has clear *goals, governance and organisational arrangements* concerning activities that cross or connect the partners, it is also important to keep the alliance *flexible*, such that it can *evolve and change*.

10.3 STRATEGY EVALUATION

Part II of the book has now introduced an array of strategic choices as summarised in Exhibit 10.4. This section of the chapter turns to how these might be evaluated by asking why some strategies might succeed better than others. It does this in terms of three key success criteria which can be used to assess the viability of strategic options:

● *Suitability* is concerned with whether a strategy addresses the key issues relating to the *strategic position* of the organisation (as discussed in Part I).

Exhibit 10.4 Strategic options

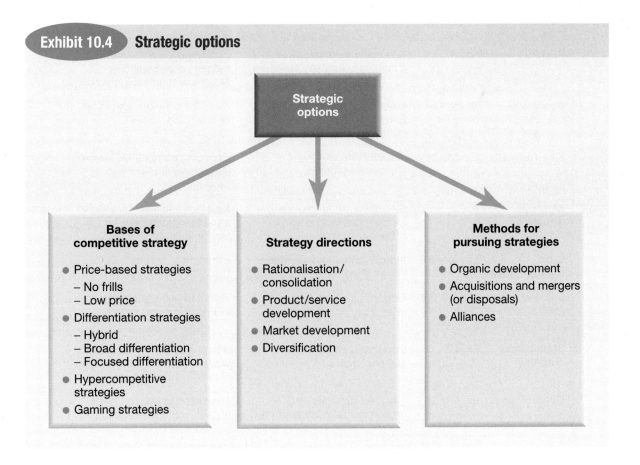

Strategic options

Bases of competitive strategy
- Price-based strategies
  - No frills
  - Low price
- Differentiation strategies
  - Hybrid
  - Broad differentiation
  - Focused differentiation
- Hypercompetitive strategies
- Gaming strategies

Strategy directions
- Rationalisation/ consolidation
- Product/service development
- Market development
- Diversification

Methods for pursuing strategies
- Organic development
- Acquisitions and mergers (or disposals)
- Alliances

● *Acceptability* is concerned with the expected *performance outcomes* (such as the *return* or *risk*) of a strategy and the extent to which these meet the *expectations* of stakeholders.

● *Feasibility* is concerned with whether a strategy could work in practice; therefore, whether it has the capabilities to deliver a strategy.

10.3.1 Suitability

Suitability is concerned with whether a strategy addresses the key issues relating to the strategic position of the organisation

Suitability is concerned with whether a strategy addresses the key issues that have been identified in understanding the strategic position of the organisation. It is therefore concerned with the overall *rationale* of a strategy. In particular this requires an assessment of the extent to which any strategic option would fit with key drivers and expected changes in the *environment*, exploit *strategic capabilities* and be appropriate in the context of *stakeholder expectations and influence* and *cultural influences*. So the concepts and frameworks already discussed in Chapters 2 to 4 can be especially helpful in understanding suitability. Some examples are shown in Exhibit 10.5. However, there is an important point to bear in mind. It is very likely that a great many issues will have been raised if the

Exhibit 10.5 **Suitability of strategic options in relation to strategic position**

Concept	Exhibit Illustrations	Helps with understanding	Suitable strategies must address (examples)
PESTEL	III. 2.1	Key environmental drivers Changes in industry structure	Industry cycles Industry convergence Major environmental changes
Scenarios	III. 2.2	Extent of uncertainty/risk Extent to which strategic options are mutually exclusive	Need for contingency plans or 'low-cost probes'
Five-forces	Ex. 2.2 III. 2.3	Industry attractiveness Competitive forces	Reducing competitive intensity Development of barriers to new entrants
Strategic groups	III. 2.5	Attractiveness of groups Mobility barriers Strategic spaces	Need to reposition to a more attractive group or to an available strategic space
Core competences	Exs 3.1, 3.6 3.8	Industry threshold standards Bases of competitive advantage	Eliminating weaknesses Exploiting strengths
Value chain	Exs 3.6, 3.7	Opportunities for vertical integration or outsourcing	Extent of vertical integration or possible outsourcing
Stakeholder mapping	Ex. 4.5 III. 4.4a, b	Power and interest of stakeholders	Which strategic options are likely to address the interests of which stakeholders
Cultural web	Ex. 5.7 III. 5.4	The links between organisational culture and the current strategy	The strategic options most aligned with the prevailing culture

concepts and tools discussed in Part I have been employed. It is therefore important that the really important issues are identified from amongst all these. Indeed a major skill of a strategist is to be able to discern these *key strategic issues*. Evaluating the suitability of a strategy is extremely difficult unless these have been identified.

The discussions about strategic directions in the preceding chapters in Part II and on strategy methods in section 10.2 above were concerned not only with understanding what directions and methods were 'available' to organisations, but also with providing reasons why each might be considered. So the examples in those sections also illustrate why strategies might be regarded as *suitable*. Exhibit 10.6 summarises these points from earlier sections and provides

Exhibit 10.6 Some examples of suitability

Strategic option	Why this option might be suitable in terms of:		
	Environment	Capability	Stakeholder and/or cultural influences
Directions			
Consolidation	Withdraw from declining markets Maintain market share	Build on strengths through continued investment and innovation	Stick to what the organisation and its stakeholders know best
Market penetration	Gain market share for advantage	Exploit superior resources and competences	
Product development	Exploit knowledge of customer needs	Exploit R&D	Minimise the risk of alienating stakeholders with interests in preserving the status quo or making counter cultural decisions
Market development	Current markets saturated New opportunities for: geographical spread, entering new segments or new uses	Exploit current products and capabilities	
Diversification	Current markets saturated or declining	Exploit core competences in new arenas	Meet the needs of stakeholders with expectations for more rapid growth But potential for culture clash
Methods			
Organic development	Partners or acquisitions not available or not suitable	Building on own capabilities Learning and competence development	Cultural/political ease
Merger/acquisition	Speed Supply/demand P/E ratios	Acquire competences Scale economies	Returns: growth or share value But potential for culture clash
Joint development	Speed Industry norm Required for market entry	Complementary competences Learning from partners	Dilutes risk Fashionable

examples of reasons why strategy directions or methods might be regarded as suitable.

Evaluation tools for assessing suitability

There are a number of tools that can be used to assess the suitability of strategic options. These include:

- *The TOWS matrix*.[25] This was introduced in the Introduction to Part II of the book (see Exhibit II.ii) as a method of identifying strategic options on the basis of a SWOT analysis. However, it can also be used to provide an assessment of suitability by 'justifying' options in terms of the extent to which they address the strengths, weaknesses, threats and opportunities relating to the strategic position of the organisation.

- The *relative suitability* of options that matters. There may be options 'available' to an organisation that are more or less suitable than others. There are useful frameworks that can assist in understanding better the relative suitability of different strategic options:

- *Ranking strategic options*. Options are assessed against key factors relating to the strategic position of the organisation and a score (or ranking) established for each option. See Illustration 10.2 for a detailed example

- *Decision trees* can also be used to assess strategic options against a list of key factors. Here options are 'eliminated' and preferred options emerge by progressively introducing requirements which must be met (such as growth, investment or diversity). See Illustration 10.3.

- *Scenarios*. Here strategic options are considered against a range of possible future situations. This is especially useful where a high degree of uncertainty exists (as discussed in section 2.2.2 – see Illustration 2.2). Suitable options are ones that are sensible in terms of the various scenarios so several need to be 'kept open', or perhaps in the form of contingency plans. Or it could be that an option being considered is found to be suitable in different scenarios.

10.3.2 Acceptability

Acceptability is concerned with the expected performance outcomes of a strategy and the extent to which these meet the expectations of stakeholders

Acceptability is concerned with the expected performance outcomes of a strategy. These can be of three types: *return*, *risk* and *stakeholder reactions*. Exhibit 10.7 summarises some frameworks that can be useful in understanding the acceptability of strategies, together with some of their limitations. It is probably sensible to use more than one approach in assessing the acceptability of a strategy.

Return

Returns are the benefits which stakeholders are expected to receive from a strategy

Returns are the benefits which stakeholders are expected to receive from a strategy. Measures of return are a common way of assessing proposed new ventures or major projects by managers within businesses. So an assessment of financial and non-financial returns likely to accrue from specific strategic options could be a key criterion of acceptability of a strategy – at least to some stakeholders.

Illustration 10.2

Ranking options: Churchill Pottery

Ranking can usefully build on a SWOT analysis by comparing strategic options against the key strategic factors from the SWOT analysis.

In the 1990s Churchill Pottery, based in Stoke-on-Trent, UK, was one of the subjects of a BBC series entitled *Troubleshooter*, where the management teams of a number of companies were invited to discuss their organisation's strategic development with Sir John Harvey-Jones (ex-Chairman of ICI). Like many traditional manufacturing companies at the time, Churchill found itself under increasing pressure from cheaper imports in its traditional markets, and was considering whether to move 'up market' by launching a new range aimed at the design-conscious end of the market. The ranking exercise below was done by a group of participants on a management programme having seen the Churchill Pottery video.

The results of the ranking are interesting. First, they highlight the need to do *something*. Second, the radical departures in strategy – such as moves into retailing or diversification – are regarded as unsuitable. They do not address the problems of the core business, do not fit the capabilities of Churchill and would not fit culturally. This leaves related developments as the front runners – as might be expected in a traditional manufacturing firm like Churchill. The choice boils down to significant investments in cost reduction to support an essentially 'commodity' approach to the market (options 2 and 5) or an 'added value' attack on the growing 'up-market' segments. The company chose the latter and with some success – presumably helped by its wide television exposure through the *Troubleshooter* series.

Source: Based on the BBC *Troubleshooter* series.

Questions

1 Has option 4 been ranked above the others because:
   (a) It has the most ticks?
   (b) It has the least crosses?
   (c) A combination of these?
   (d) Other reasons?
   Justify your answer.

2 List the main strengths and limitations of ranking analysis.

Ranking exercise

	Key strategic factors						
Strategic options	Family ownership	Investment funds	Low-price imports	Lack of marketing/ design skills	Automation low	Consumer taste (design)	Ranking
1. Do nothing	✓	?	✗	?	✗	✗	C
2. Consolidate in current segments (investment/automation)	✓	✗	✓	?	✓	?	B
3. Expand overseas sales (Europe)	✗	✗	✗	✗	✗	?	C
4. Launch 'up-market' range	✓	✓	✓	✗	?	✓	A
5. Expand 'own-label' production (to hotel/ catering industry)	✓	✓	✓	?	✗	?	B
6. Open retail outlets	✗	✗	?	✗	?	?	C
7. Diversify	✗	✗	?	?	?	✓	C

✓ = favourable; ✗ = unfavourable; ? = uncertain or irrelevant.
A = most suitable; B = possible; C = unsuitable.

Illustration 10.3

A strategic decision tree for a law firm

Decision trees evaluate future options by progressively eliminating others as additional criteria are introduced to the evaluation.

A law firm had most of its work related to house conveyancing where profits had been significantly squeezed. Therefore, it wanted to consider a range of new strategies for the future. Using a strategic decision tree it was able to eliminate certain options by identifying a few key criteria which future developments would incorporate, such as growth, investment (in premises, IT systems or acquisitions), and diversification (for example, into matrimonial law which, in turn, often brings house conveyancing work as families 'reshape').

Analysis of the decision tree reveals that if the partners of the firm wish growth to be an important aspect of future strategies, options 1–4 are ranked more highly than options 5–8. At the second step, the need for low-investment strategies would rank options 3 and 4 above 1 and 2, and so on.

The partners were aware that this technique has limitations in that the choice at each branch of the

tree can tend to be simplistic. Answering 'yes' or 'no' to diversification does not allow for the wide variety of alternatives which might exist between these two extremes, for example *adapting the 'style' of the conveyancing service* (this could be an important variant of options 6 or 8). Nevertheless, as a starting point for evaluation, the decision tree provides a useful framework.

> **Questions**
>
> 1 Try reversing the sequence of the three parameters (to diversification, investment and growth) and redraw the decision tree. Do the same eight options still emerge?
>
> 2 Add a fourth parameter to the decision tree. This new parameter is development by *internal methods* or by *acquisition*. List your 16 options in the right-hand column.

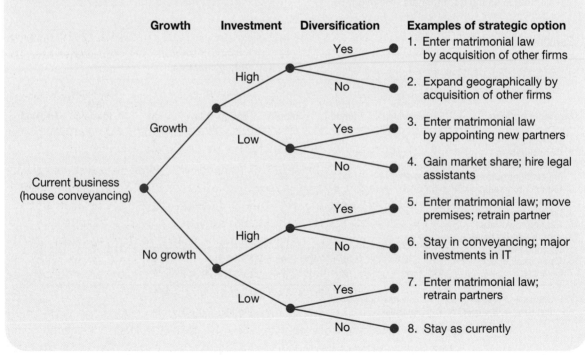

Growth	Investment	Diversification	Examples of strategic option

- **Growth** — High — Yes → 1. Enter matrimonial law by acquisition of other firms
- High — No → 2. Expand geographically by acquisition of other firms
- Low — Yes → 3. Enter matrimonial law by appointing new partners
- Low — No → 4. Gain market share; hire legal assistants
- **No growth** — High — Yes → 5. Enter matrimonial law; move premises; retrain partner
- High — No → 6. Stay in conveyancing; major investments in IT
- Low — Yes → 7. Enter matrimonial law; retrain partners
- Low — No → 8. Stay as currently

Current business (house conveyancing)

Exhibit 10.7	Some criteria for assessing the acceptability of strategic options

Criteria	Used to understand	Examples	Limitations
Return			
Profitability	Financial return on investments in major projects	Return on capital Payback period Discounted cash flow (DCF)	Apply to discrete projects Only tangible costs/benefits
Cost–benefit	Wider costs/benefits (including intangibles)	Major infrastructure projects	Difficulties of quantification
Real options	Sequence of decisions	Real options analysis	Quantification
Shareholder value analysis (SVA)	Impact of new strategies on shareholder value	Mergers/acquisitions Assessment of new ventures	Technical detail often difficult
Risk			
Financial ratio projections	Robustness of strategy	Break-even analysis Impact on gearing and liquidity	
Sensitivity analysis	Test assumptions/robustness	'What if?' analysis	Tests factors separately
Stakeholder reactions	Political dimension of strategy	Stakeholder mapping	Largely qualitative

There are different approaches to understanding return. This section looks briefly at three of these. It is important to remember that there are no absolute standards as to what constitutes good or poor return. It will differ between industries, countries and between different stakeholders. Views also differ as to which measures give the best assessment of return, as will be seen below.

Financial analysis[26]

Traditional financial analyses are used extensively in assessing the acceptability of different strategic options. Three commonly used approaches are (see Exhibit 10.8):

● Forecasting the *return on capital employed (ROCE)* for a specific time period after a new strategy is in place. For example, an ROCE of 15 per cent by year 3. This is shown in Exhibit 10.8(a). The ROCE is a measure of the earning power of the resources used in implementing a particular strategic option.

● Estimating the *payback period*. This is the length of time it takes before the cumulative cash flows for a strategic option become positive. In the example in Exhibit 10.8(b) the payback period is $3\frac{1}{2}$ years. Payback is used as a financial criterion when a significant capital injection is needed to support a new venture. The judgement that has to be made is whether the payback period is too long and the organisation is prepared to wait. Payback periods vary from industry to industry. Public infrastructure projects such as road building may be assessed over payback periods exceeding 50 years.

● Calculating *discounted cash flows (DCFs)*. This is a widely used investment appraisal technique. It is an extension of payback analysis. Once the cash inflows and outflows have been assessed for each of the years of a strategic

Exhibit 10.8 **Assessing profitability**

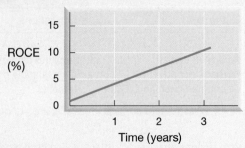

(a) Return on capital employed

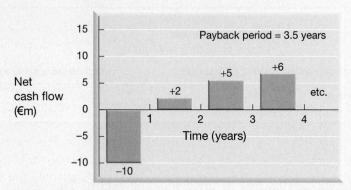

(b) Payback period

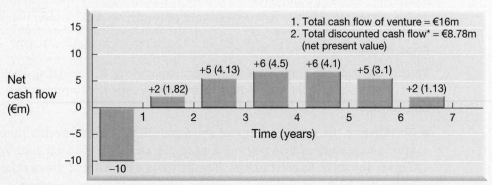

* Using a discounting rate of 10%.
Figures in brackets are discounted by 10% annually.

(c) Discounted cash flow (DCF)

option (see Exhibit 10.8(c)) they are discounted. This reflects the fact that cash generated early is more valuable than cash generated later. In the example, the cost of capital or discounting rate of 10 per cent (after tax) reflects the rate of return required by those providing finance for the venture – shareholders and/or lenders. The 10 per cent cost of capital *includes* an allowance for inflation of about 3–4 per cent. It is referred to as the 'money cost of capital'.

By contrast, the 'real' cost of capital is 6–7 per cent *after* allowing for or *excluding* inflation.

The projected after-tax cash flow of £2m at the start of year 2 is equivalent to receiving £1.82m now (£2m multiplied by 0.91 or 1/1.10); £1.82m is called the *present value* of receiving £2m at the end of year 1/start of year 2 at a cost of capital of 10 per cent. Similarly, the after-tax cash flow of £5m at the end of year 2/start of year 3 has a present value of £4.13m (£5m multiplied by 1/1.10 squared). The *net present value (NPV)* of the venture, as a whole, is calculated by adding up all the annual present values over the venture's anticipated life. In the example, this is 7 years. The NPV works out at £8.78m. Allowing for the time value of money, the £8.78m is the extra cash flow that a strategic option will generate during its entire lifetime. It is important to remember that DCF analysis is only as good as the assumptions on which it is based. For example, if sales volume increases of 3 per cent a year turn out to be unrealistic then the NPV calculation will be too optimistic. The *internal rate of return (IRR)* is that rate of return producing a zero NPV. For example, in Exhibit 10.8(c) a cost of capital or discounting rate of about 32 per cent would produce a zero NPV.

There are also other considerations to be borne in mind when carrying out a financial analysis. In particular, do not be misguided by the apparent thoroughness of the various approaches. Most were developed for the purposes of investment appraisal. Therefore, they focus on discrete projects where the additional cash inflows and outflows can be predicted relatively easily. For example, a retailer opening a new store. Such assumptions are not necessarily valid in many strategic contexts. The precise way in which a strategy develops (and the associated cash flow consequences) tend to become clearer as the implementation proceeds rather than at the outset. Nor are strategic developments and the relevant cash flows easy to isolate from ongoing business activities.

Additionally, financial appraisals tend to focus on the direct *tangible* costs and benefits rather than the strategy more broadly. For example, a new product may look unprofitable as a single project. But it may make strategic sense by enhancing the market acceptability of other products in a company's portfolio. In an attempt to overcome some of these shortcomings, other approaches have been developed in an assessment of return.

Cost–benefit[27]

In many situations, profit is too narrow an interpretation of return, particularly where intangible benefits are an important consideration. This is usually so for major public infrastructure projects, for example, such as the siting of an airport or a sewer construction project, as shown in Illustration 10.4, or in organisations with long-term programmes of innovation (for example, pharmaceuticals or aerospace). The *cost–benefit* concept suggests that a money value can be put on all the costs and benefits of a strategy, including tangible and intangible returns to people and organisations other than the one 'sponsoring' the project or strategy.

Although in practice monetary valuation is often difficult, it can be done and, despite the difficulties, cost–benefit analysis is useful provided its limitations are understood. Its major benefit is in forcing managers to be explicit about the various factors that influence strategic choice. So, even if people disagree on

Illustration 10.4

Sewerage construction project

Investment in items of infrastructure – such as sewers – often requires a careful consideration of the wider costs and benefits of the project.

The UK's privatised water companies were monopolies supplying water and disposing of sewage. One of their priorities was investment in new sewerage systems to meet the increasing standards required by law. They frequently used cost–benefit analysis to assess projects. The figures below are from an actual analysis.

Cost/Benefit	£m	£m
Benefits		
Multiplier/linkage benefits		0.9
Flood prevention		2.5
Reduced traffic disruption		7.2
Amenity benefits		4.6
Investment benefit		23.6
Encouragement of visitors		4.0
Total benefits		42.8
Costs		
Construction cost	18.2	
Less: Unskilled labour cost	(4.7)	
Opportunity cost of construction	(13.5)	
Present value of net benefits (NPV)	29.3	
Real internal rate of return (IRR)	15%	

Note: Figures discounted at a *real* discount rate of 5% over 40 years.

Benefits

Benefits result mainly from reduced use of rivers as overflow sewers. There are also economic benefits resulting from construction. The following benefits are quantified in the table:

- The multiplier benefit to the local economy of increased spending by those employed on the project.

- The linkage benefit to the local economy of purchases from local firms, including the multiplier effect of such spending.

- Reduced risk of flooding from overflows or old sewers collapsing – flood probabilities can be quantified using historical records, and the cost of flood damage by detailed assessment of the property vulnerable to damage.

- Reduced traffic disruption from flooding and road closures for repairs to old sewers – statistics on the costs of delays to users, traffic flows on roads affected and past closure frequency can be used to quantify savings.

- Increased amenity value of rivers (for example, for boating and fishing) can be measured by surveys asking visitors what the value is to them or by looking at the effect on demand of charges imposed elsewhere.

- Increased rental values and take-up of space can be measured by consultation with developers and observed effects elsewhere.

- Increased visitor numbers to riverside facilities resulting from reduced pollution.

Construction cost

This is net of the cost of unskilled labour. Use of unskilled labour is not a burden on the economy, and its cost must be deducted to arrive at opportunity cost.

Net benefits

Once the difficult task of quantifying costs and benefits is complete, standard discounting techniques can be used to calculate net present value and internal rate of return, and analysis can then proceed as for conventional projects.

Source: G. Owen, formerly of Sheffield Business School.

Questions

1 What do you feel about the appropriateness of the listed benefits?

2 How easy or difficult is it to assign money values to these benefits?

the value that should be assigned to particular costs or benefits, at least they can argue their case on common ground and compare the merits of the various arguments.

Real options[28]

The previous approaches assume a reasonable degree of clarity about the outcomes of a strategic option. There are, however, situations where precise costs and benefits of strategies only become clear as implementation proceeds. In these circumstances the traditional DCF approach discussed above will tend to undervalue a 'project' because it does not take into account the value of options that could be opened up by the particular project. Luehrman[29] argues that this extra value arises because

> executing a strategy almost always involves making a sequence of decisions. Some actions are taken immediately, while others are deliberately deferred. . . . The strategy sets the framework within which future decisions will be made, but . . . leaves space for learning from ongoing developments and for discretion to act based on what is learnt.

So the flexibility can be used to expand, extend, contract, defer or close down a project. So a strategy should be seen as a *series* of 'real' options (that is, choices of direction at particular points in time as the strategy takes shape). There are three main benefits of this approach:

- *Bringing strategic and financial evaluation closer together*. Arguably it provides a clearer understanding of both strategic and financial return and risk of a strategy by examining each step (option) separately. For example, the value that will accrue from investing in a technology that creates a 'platform' from which several products or process improvements may spring is not clear at the outset. However, as the project develops learning occurs as to which directions the development should progress or even if it should be terminated early.

- *Valuing emerging options*. In taking such an approach, it then allows a value to be placed on options that might be opened up by an initial strategic decision.

- *Coping with uncertainty*. Advocates of a real options approach argue it overcomes, or provides an alternative to, profitability analyses that require managers to make assumptions about future conditions that may well not be realistic. As such it can be linked into ways of analysing uncertain futures such as scenario analysis (see section 2.2.2). For example, applying a real options approach, as in Exhibit 10.9, shows that high levels of volatility should have two effects. First, to defer decisions as far as possible because (second) the passage of time will clarify expected returns – even to the extent that apparently unfavourable strategies might prove viable at a later date (the category 'maybe invest later' in the exhibit).

Shareholder value analysis[30]

There has been a growing interest in shareholder value analysis (SVA) and 'managing for value' (MFV) (see section 13.4.1). In the main this is because of the growing concern about the need for company directors to pay more attention to providing value for shareholders (see sections 4.2.1 and 4.2.2). A major limitation of traditional accounting measures such as operating profit (profit

Exhibit 10.9 **Real options framework**

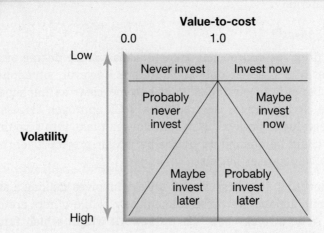

before interest and taxation) is that they ignore the cost of capital. Misleading signals are given, therefore, about whether value is created or destroyed. In turn, this can give misleading views about the acceptability of specific strategic options. In this context there have been increasing questions raised about the extent to which the waves of mergers and acquisitions generate shareholder value (see section 10.2.2).

There are two measures of shareholder value. One is external to the company. The other is internal:

● The external measure is referred to as *total shareholder return (TSR)*. In any financial year, it is equal to the increase in the price of a share plus the dividends received per share actually received in that year. This is then divided by the share price at the start of the financial year. A simple example is given as Exhibit 10.10(a).

● The internal measure is called *economic profit* or *economic value added (EVA)*. If the operating profit (after tax) is greater than the cost of the capital required to produce that profit then EVA is positive. An example is given as Exhibit 10.10(b). Evidence suggests that a positive EVA will lead to positive share price performance. For this reason, EVA is a good internal proxy for shareholder return.

Used effectively, both EVA and the subsequent improvement in TSR performance align the interests of owners and managers. Although shareholder value analysis has helped address the shortcomings of traditional financial analyses, it cannot remove all the inherent uncertainties surrounding strategic choices. It has also been criticised for overemphasising short-term returns.[31] Nevertheless, the idea of valuing a strategy may serve to give greater realism and clarity to otherwise vague claims for strategic benefits. Perhaps the major lesson, however, is that firms that most successfully employ SVA do so within an over-

---

Exhibit 10.10   **Measures of shareholder value**

(a) Total shareholder return (TSR)	(b) Economic profit or economic value added (EVA)
Given • Opening share price, £1 • Closing share price, £1.20 • Dividend per share received during financial year, 5p **Then** • Increase in share price (20p) plus dividend received (5p) = 25p **TSR is** • 25p divided by opening share price of £1 expressed as a percentage = 25%	**Given** • Operating profit after tax, £10m • Capital employed, £100m • Cost of capital, 8% **Then** • The capital or financing charge required to produce the operating profit after tax is the capital employed of £100m × the cost of capital of 8% = (£8m) **EVA is** • Operating profit (after tax) of £10m less the cost of the capital, £8m = £2m

all approach to managing for value throughout the firm rather than merely as a technique for purposes of analysis.[32] SVA is discussed further in section 13.4.1.

Risk

Risk concerns the probability and consequences of the failure of a strategy

Another aspect of acceptability is the *risk* that an organisation faces in pursuing a strategy. **Risk** concerns the probability and consequences of the failure of a strategy. This risk can be high for organisations with major long-term programmes of innovation, where high levels of uncertainty exist about key issues in the environment or where there are high levels of public concern about new developments – such as genetically modified Crops.[33] Formal risk assessments are often incorporated into business plans as well as the investment appraisals of major projects. Importantly, risks other than ones with immediate financial impact are included such as 'risk to corporate or brand image' or 'risk of missing an opportunity'. Developing a good understanding of an organisation's strategic position (Part I of this book) is at the core of good risk assessment. However, some of the concepts below can also be used to establish the detail within a risk assessment.

Financial ratios[34]

The projection of how key financial ratios might change if a strategy were adopted can provide useful insights into risk. At the broadest level, an assessment of how the *capital structure* of the company would change is a good general measure of risk. For example, strategies that would require an increase in long-term debt will increase the gearing (or 'leverage') of the company and, hence, its financial risk.

A consideration of the likely impact on an organisation's *liquidity* (cash position) is also important in assessing risk. For example, a small retailer eager to grow quickly may be tempted to fund the required shop-fitting costs by delaying payments to suppliers and increasing bank overdraft. The extent to which this increased risk of reduced liquidity threatens survival depends on the likelihood of either creditors or the bank demanding payments from the company – an issue that clearly requires judgement.

Sensitivity analysis[35]

Sometimes referred to as *'what if'* analysis, sensitivity analysis allows each of the important assumptions underlying a particular strategy to be questioned and challenged. In particular, it tests how sensitive the predicted performance or

Illustration 10.5

Sensitivity analysis

Sensitivity analysis is a useful technique for assessing the extent to which the success of a preferred strategy is dependent on the key assumptions which underlie that strategy.

In 2007 the Dunsmore Chemical Company was a single-product company trading in a mature and relatively stable market. It was intended to use this established situation as a 'cash cow' to generate funds for a new venture with a related product. Estimates had shown that the company would need to generate some £4m (≈ €6m) cash (at 2007 values) between 2008 and 2013 for this new venture to be possible.

Although the expected performance of the company was for a cash flow of £9.5m over that period (the *base case*), management were concerned to assess the likely impact of three key factors:

- Possible increases in *production costs* (labour, overheads and materials), which might be as much as 3 per cent p.a. in real terms.
- *Capacity-fill*, which might be reduced by as much as 25 per cent due to ageing plant and uncertain labour relations.
- *Price levels*, which might be affected by the threatened entry of a new major competitor. This

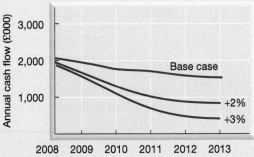

(a) **Sensitivity of cash flow to changes in real production costs**

could squeeze prices by as much as 3 per cent p.a. in real terms.

It was decided to use sensitivity analysis to assess the possible impact of each of these factors on the company's ability to generate £4m. The results are shown in the graphs.

From this analysis, management concluded that their target of £4m would be achieved with *capacity utilisation* as low as 60 per cent, which was certainly outcome (for example, profit) is to each of these assumptions. For example, the key assumptions underlying a strategy might be that market demand will grow by 5 per cent per annum, or that the company will stay strike-free, or that certain expensive machines will operate at 90 per cent loading. Sensitivity analysis asks what would be the effect on performance (in this case, profitability) of variations on these assumptions. For example, if market demand grew at only 1 per cent, or by as much as 10 per cent, would either of these extremes alter the decision to pursue that strategy? This can help develop a clearer picture of the risks of making particular strategic decisions and the degree of confidence managers might have in a given decision. Illustration 10.5 shows how sensitivity analysis can be used.

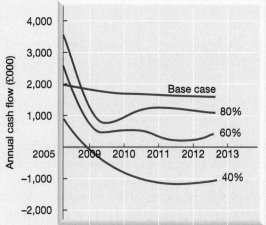

(b) Sensitivity of cash flow to changes in plant utilisation

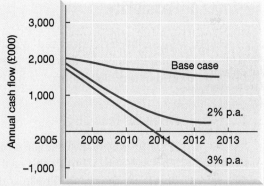

(c) Sensitivity of cash flow to reductions in real price

going to be achieved. Increased *production costs* of 3 per cent p.a. would still allow the company to achieve the £4m target over the period. In contrast, *price* squeezes of 3 per cent p.a. would result in a shortfall of £2m.

Management concluded from this analysis that the key factor which should affect their thinking on this matter was the likely impact of new competition and the extent to which they could protect price levels if such competition emerged. They therefore developed an aggressive marketing strategy to deter potential entrants.

Source: The calculations for the sensitivity test utilise computer programs employed in the Doman case study by Peter Jones (Sheffield Business School).

Question

What should the company do if its marketing campaigns fail to stop real price erosion:

(a) Push to achieve more sales volume/capacity fill?

(b) Reduce unit costs of production?

(c) Something else?

Stakeholder reactions

The discussion of *stakeholder mapping* in Chapter 4 (section 4.4.1) showed how it can be used to understand the political context and consider the political agenda in an organisation. However, stakeholder mapping can also be useful in understanding the likely reactions of stakeholders to new strategies, the ability to manage these reactions, and hence the acceptability of a strategy.

There are many situations where stakeholder reactions could be crucial. For example:

● *Financial restructuring*. A new strategy might require the financial restructuring of a business, for example an issue of new shares, which could be unacceptable to powerful groups of shareholders, since it dilutes their voting power.

● *An acquisition or merger* could be unacceptable to unions, government or some customers.

● *A new business model* might cut out channels (such as retailers), hence running the risk of a backlash, which could jeopardise the success of the strategy.

● *Outsourcing* is likely to result in job losses and could be opposed by unions.

10.3.3 Feasibility

Feasibility is concerned
with whether an
organisation has the
capabilities to deliver
a strategy

Feasibility is concerned with whether an organisation has the resources and competences to deliver a strategy. A number of approaches can be used to understand feasibility.

Financial feasibility

A useful way of assessing financial feasibility is *cash flow analysis and forecasting*.[36] This seeks to identify the cash required for a strategy and the likely sources for obtaining that cash. These sources are sometimes referred to as *funding sources*. They are shown in Illustration 10.6. Cash flow forecasting is, of course, subject to the difficulties and errors of any method of forecasting. However, it should highlight whether a proposed strategy is likely to be feasible in terms of both cash generation and the availability and timing of new funding requirements. This issue of funding strategic developments is an important interface between business and financial strategies and is discussed more fully in section 13.4.2.

Financial feasibility can also be assessed through break-even analysis.[37] This is a simple and widely used approach for judging the feasibility of meeting financial targets such as the ROCE and operating profit. In addition, it provides an assessment of the risks of various strategies particularly where different strategic options require markedly different cost structures.

Resource deployment

Although financial feasibility is important, a wider understanding of feasibility can be achieved by identifying the resources and competences needed for a specific strategy. Indeed the effectiveness of a strategy is likely to be dependent on whether such capabilities are available or can be developed or obtained. For example, geographical expansion in a market might be critically dependent on

Illustration 10.6

Cash flow analysis: a worked example

A cash flow analysis can be used to assess whether a proposed strategy is likely to be feasible in financial terms. It does so, first, by forecasting the cash that would be needed for the strategy and, second, identifying the likely sources of funding that cash requirement.

Kentex plc (a UK electrical goods retailer) was considering pursuing a strategy of expansion. In the immediate future, this would involve opening new stores in the Irish Republic. To evaluate the financial feasibility of this proposal and to establish the cash requirements and funding sources, the company decided to undertake a cash flow analysis.

Stage 1: Estimation of cash inflows

The opening of the new stores was estimated to increase revenues or sales from the current £30m (≈ €45m) to £31.65m over the following three years. In turn, this was expected to generate operating cash flows of £15m during the same time period.

Stage 2: Estimation of cash outflows

There would be a number of costs associated with the new stores. First, Kentex decided to purchase rather than lease property so capital investment would be required to purchase and then fit out the stores. The forecast was £13.25m. Also there would be additional working capital costs to cover extra stock etc. Forecasts for these were based on a simple pro rata estimate. On the previous sales level of £30m, a working capital level of £10m was required, so pro rata, additional sales of £1.65m would require an additional £0.55m in working capital. Tax liability and expected dividend payments were estimated at £1.2m and £0.5m respectively.

Stage 3: Estimation and funding of the cash shortfall

The calculations show a cash shortfall of £0.5m. The issue facing Kentex was how to finance this deficit. It could raise cash through the issue of new share capital but the company decided to seek a short-term loan of £0.65m. In turn, this would incur interest payments of £0.15m over the three-year period assuming simple interest at 7.5 per cent annually. Therefore, the net amount of cash raised would be £0.5m.

The overall cash flow analysis is summarised below:

Cash inflows	Cash outflows
Operating cash flows, £15m	Capital expenditure, £13.25m
	Further working capital, £0.55m
	Tax, £1.2m
	Subtotal of cash outflows, £15m
	Dividends, £0.5m
	Total cash outflows, £15.5m

Note: The shortfall between the cash inflows and the cash outflows is £500,000.

Questions

1 Which parts of this assessment are likely to have the greatest probability of error?

2 What are the implications of your answer to question 1 on how the analysis should be presented to the decision makers?

3 How might this uncertainty influence the management of the implementation phase if approval is given?

marketing and distribution expertise, together with the availability of cash to fund increased stocks. Or a strategy of developing new products to sell to current customers may depend on engineering skills, the capability of machinery and the company's reputation for quality in new products.

A resource deployment assessment can be used to judge (i) the extent to which an organisation's current capabilities need to change to reach or maintain the *threshold* requirements for a strategy; and (ii) if and how unique resources and/or core competences can be developed to sustain competitive advantage. The issue is whether these changes are *feasible* in terms of scale, quality of resource or time-scale of change.

10.3.4 Evaluation criteria: three qualifications

There are three qualifications that need to be made to this discussion of evaluation criteria:

- *Conflicting conclusions and management judgement.* Conflicting conclusions can arise from the application of the criteria of suitability, acceptability and feasibility. A proposed strategy might look eminently suitable but not be acceptable to major stakeholders, for example. It is therefore important to remember that the criteria discussed here are useful in helping think through strategic options but are not a replacement for management judgement. Managers faced with a strategy they see as suitable, but which key stakeholders object to, have to rely on their own judgement on the best course of action, but this should be better informed through the analysis and evaluation they have undertaken.

- There needs to be *consistency between the different elements of a strategy.* It should be clear from the chapters in Part II that there are several elements of a strategy, so an important question is whether the component parts work together as a 'package'. So *competitive strategy* (such as low price or differentiation), strategy *direction* (such as product development or diversification) and strategic *method* (internal, acquisition or alliances) need to be consistent. They need to be considered as a whole and make sense as a whole. There are dangers that they do not. For example, suppose an organisation wishes to develop a strategy built on its inherent competences developed over many years as a basis of differentiation that competitors will find difficult to imitate. It may believe it can do this by using those competences to develop new products or services within a market it knows well. If so there may be dangers in looking to develop those new products through acquiring other businesses which might have very different competences and capabilities that are incompatible with the strengths of the business.

- *The implementation and development of strategies* may throw up issues that might make organisations reconsider whether particular strategic options are, in fact, feasible or uncover factors that change views on the suitability or acceptability of a strategy. This may lead to a reshaping, or even abandonment, of strategic options. It therefore needs to be recognised that, in practice, strategy evaluation may take place through implementation, or at least partial implementation. This is another reason why experimentation and low-cost probes may make sense. The next section of the book (Chapters 11 to 15) will look at the practical issues of translating strategy into action. More generally, care should also be taken in assuming that the careful and systematic evaluation of strategy is necessarily the norm in organisations. Chapters 11 and 15 explain more how strategies actually develop in organisations and what managers actually do in managing strategic issues.

SUMMARY

- There are three broad *methods* of strategy development:
  - *Organic development* has the major benefit of building on the strategic capabilities of an organisation. However, it can result in overstretched resources and is likely to require the development of those capabilities.
  - *Mergers and acquisitions* may have advantages of speed and the ability to acquire competences not already held 'in-house'. However, the track record of acquisitions is not good. (See the key debate in Illustration 10.7).
  - Successful *alliances* appear to be those where partners have a positive attitude to the evolving nature of the alliance and where there is trust between partners.

- The success or failure of strategies will be related to three main *success criteria*:
  - *Suitability* is concerned with whether a strategy addresses the strategic position of the organisation as discussed in Part II of this book. It is about the *rationale* of a strategy.
  - The *acceptability* of a strategy relates to three issues: the expected *return* from a strategy, the level of *risk* and the likely *reaction of stakeholders*.
  - *Feasibility* is concerned with whether an organisation has or can obtain the capabilities to deliver a strategy.

- Since a strategy comprises the broad *competitive strategy*, the *strategy direction* and the *method* of pursuing them, these three elements need to be consistent with each other.

Illustration 10.7   **key debate**

Merger madness?

Mergers and acquisitions involve huge sums of money, but how wisely is it being spent?

This chapter has introduced the importance of mergers and acquisitions as a method of development, but also pointed to some challenges. There have been some spectacular failures. When in 2001 media company Time Warner merged with Internet company AOL, Time Warner shares were worth a total of $90bn (£50bn; €78bn). Just under three years later, Time Warner investors' holdings in the merged company were worth only $36bn, a loss of over $50bn (in the same period, media companies' valuations had fallen on average 16 per cent).

Harvard Business School professor Michael Porter has been a prominent sceptic of mergers and acquisitions, noting that half of all acquired companies are sold off again within a few years.[1] The figure shows the aggregate dollar return (that is, the change in stock price associated with the acquisition announcement) of acquiring companies in the USA between 1996 and 2001.[2] In 2000, acquiring firms' shareholders lost, in all, more than $150bn. The authors of this study calculate that in the whole period of 1991 to 2001, acquiring firms' shareholders lost more than $7 for every $100 spent on acquisitions.

One interpretation of these large losses is that mergers and acquisitions represent a reckless waste of money by managers who are careless of investors' interests. Indeed there is evidence that CEOs suffer the consequences, over half being replaced within a relatively short time period.[3] It might be appropriate therefore to make mergers and acquisitions more difficult by legislating to help target companies resist or refuse hostile bids. If the law restricted hostile bids, wasteful acquisitions could be cut.

There are drawbacks to restricting mergers and acquisitions, however.[4] Even if acquiring companies often fail to make money for their shareholders, they can improve the profitability of the system as a whole in at least two ways:

● The threat of being taken over if they do not satisfy their shareholders helps keep managers focused on performance. The financial press report just such threats regularly.

● Mergers and acquisitions can be an effective way of restructuring stagnant firms and industries. The absence of hostile takeovers in Japan is often blamed for the slow restructuring of Japanese industry since the early 1990s.

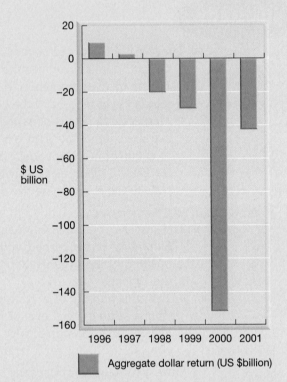

$ US billion

Aggregate dollar return (US $billion)

Sources:
1. M. Porter, 'From competitive advantage to corporate strategy', *Harvard Business Review*, May–June (1987), pp. 43–60.
2. S.B. Moeller, F.P. Schlingemann and R.M. Stulz, 'Wealth destruction on a massive scale? A study of acquiring firm returns in the recent merger wave', *Journal of Finance*, vol. 60, no. 2 (2005), pp. 757–782.
3. K.M. Lehn and M. Zhao, 'CEO turnover after acquisitions: are bad bidders fired?', *Journal of Finance*, vol. LXI, no. 4 (2006), pp. 1759–1810.
4. 'Hostile bids are back again: who should rejoice?', *The Economist*, 21 February (2004).

Questions

1 For a recent large merger or acquisition, track the share prices of the companies involved (using www.bigcharts.com, for instance), for several weeks both before and after the announcement. What do the share price movements suggest about the merits of the deal?

2 Identify a hostile takeover threat from press reports. What action did the company's managemnt do to resist the takeover?

Work assignments

Denotes more advanced work assignments. * *Refers to a case study in the Text and Cases edition.*

10.1 Write a short (one-paragraph) statement to a chief executive who has asked you to advise whether or not the company should develop through mergers/acquisitions. Write a similar statement to the chief executive of a hospital who is considering possible mergers with other hospitals.

10.2 * 'Strategic alliances will not survive in the long term if they are simply seen as ways of "blocking gaps" in an organisation's resource base or competences.' Discuss this in relation to alliances which have recently featured in the business or public sector press.

10.3 Undertake a ranking analysis of the choices available to Numico*, Wimm Bill Dann* or an organisation of your choice similar to that shown in Illustration 10.2.

10.4 * Bearing in mind your answers to the questions in Illustration 10.4:

(a) What is your feeling about the overall 'validity' of cost–benefit analysis?
(b) How could it be improved?

10.5 Using the criteria of suitability, acceptability and feasibility, undertake an evaluation of the strategic options that might exist for Tesco, Wimm Bill Dann* or an organisation of your choice.

10.6 * Using examples from your answer to previous assignments, make a critical appraisal of the statement that 'Strategic choice is, in the end, a highly subjective matter. It is dangerous to believe that, in reality, analytical techniques will ever change this situation.' Refer to the Commentary at the end of Part II of the book.

Integrative assignment

10.7 * Explain how the success criteria (see section 10.3) might differ between public and private sector organisations. Show how this relates to both the nature of the business environment (Chapter 2) and the expectations of stakeholders (Chapter 4).

 An extensive range of additional materials, including audio summaries, weblinks to organisations featured in the text, definitions of key concepts and self-assessment questions, can be found on the *Exploring Corporate Strategy* Companion Website at **www.pearsoned.co.uk/ecs**

Recommended key readings

- A comprehensive book on mergers and acquisitions is P. Gaughan, *Mergers, Acquisitions and Corporate Restructurings*, 4th edition, Wiley, 2007.
- A useful book on strategic alliances is J. Child, *Cooperative strategy*, Oxford University Press, 2005.
- A companion book which explores techniques of strategy evaluation more fully is V. Ambrosini with

G. Johnson and K. Scholes (eds), *Exploring Techniques of Analysis and Evaluation in Strategic Management*, Prentice Hall, 1998.
- Readers can gain useful insights into P/E ratios, financial motives and financial performance of acquisitions and associated financial material on acceptability and feasibility in G. Arnold, *Corporate Financial Management*, 3rd edition, FT/Prentice Hall, 2005.

References

1. See J.F. Mognetti, *Organic Growth: Cost-Effective Business Expansion from Within*, Wiley, 2002.
2. There are many publications on mergers and acquisitions: see P. Gaughan, *Mergers, Acquisitions and Corporate Restructurings*, 4th edition, Wiley, 2007. A practical guide for managers is T. Galpin and M. Herndon, *The Complete Guide to Mergers and Acquisitions*, Jossey-Bass, 2000; also D.M. DePamphilis, *Mergers, acquisitions, and other restructuring activities: An integrated approach to process, tools, cases, and solutions*, Elsevier, 2005. For a briefer discussion see R. Schoenberg, 'Mergers and acquisitions: motives, value creation and implementation', *The Oxford Handbook of Corporate Strategy*, Oxford University Press, 2003, chapter 21.
3. G. Muller-Stewens, 'Catching the right wave', *European Business Forum*, issue 4, Winter (2000), pp. 6–7, illustrates the major waves of mergers over the last 100 years.
4. Data from 'All aboard the M&A express', *Sunday Times Business Focus*, 31 December (2006), p. 5.
5. For example, see M. Zey and T. Swenson, 'The transformation and survival of Fortune 500 industrial corporations through mergers and acquisitions, 1981–1995', *Sociological Quarterly*, vol. 42, no. 3 (2001), pp. 461–486; and A. Gregory, 'An examination of the long term performance of UK acquiring firms', *Journal of Business Finance and Accounting*, vol. 24 (1997), pp. 971–1002.
6. There is a great deal published on the reasons for the success and failure of acquisitions. For example, a good discussion of the practicalities can be found in D. Carey, 'Making mergers succeed', *Harvard Business Review*, vol. 78, no. 3 (2000), pp. 145–154. Also see B. Savill and P. Wright, 'Success factors in acquisitions', *European Business Forum*, issue 4, Winter (2000), pp. 29–33; R. Larsson and S. Finkelstein, 'Integrating strategic, organisational and human resource perspectives on mergers and acquisitions: a case study survey of synergy realisation', *Organisation Science*, vol. 10, no. 1 (1999), pp. 1–26; J. Birkinshaw, H. Bresman and L. Hakanson, 'Managing the post-acquisition integration process: how the human integration and task integration processes interact to foster value creation', *Journal of Management Studies*, vol. 37, no. 3 (2000), pp. 395–425; R. Schoenberg, 'The influence of cultural compatibility within cross-border acquisitions: a review', *Advances in Mergers and*

Acquisitions, vol. 1 (2000), pp. 43–59; D. Fubini, C. Price and M. Zollo: *Mergers: Leadership, Performance and Corporate Health*, Palgrave, 2007; P. Haspeslagh, 'Maintaining momentum in mergers', *European Business Forum*, issue 4, Winter (2000), pp. 53–56; D.N. Angwin *Implementing successful post-acquisition integration*, FT/Prentice Hall, 2000.
7. J. Bower, 'Not all M&As are alike', *Harvard Business Review*, vol. 79, no. 3 (2001), pp. 93–101.
8. See J. Child, D. Faulkner and R. Pitkethly, *The Management of International Acquisitions*, Oxford University Press, 2003.
9. Useful publications on strategic alliances are Y. Doz and G. Hamel, *Alliance Advantage: The art of creating value through partnering*, Harvard Business School Press, 1998; J. Child, *Cooperative strategy*, Oxford University Press, 2005; and R. ul-Haq, *Alliances and Co-Evolution: Insights from the Banking Sector*, Palgrave, 2005. For a detailed theoretical insight see Y. Doz, D. Faulkner and M. de Rond, *Co-operative Strategies: Economic, Business and Organisational Issues*, Oxford University Press, 2001. A practical guide for managers is E. Rigsbee, *Developing Strategic Alliances*, Crisp, 2000.
10. More specifically ul-Haq (reference 9) defines 'The "strategic alliance" is typically one which displays high levels of resource commitment, is of long or open ended duration and whose purposes represent a core activity of a strategic nature for one or more of the partners' (p. 6).
11. D. Ernst and T. Halevy, 'Give alliances their due', *McKinsey Quarterly*, no. 3 (2002), pp. 4–5.
12. For a consideration of the special issues of global strategic alliances see G. Yip, *Total Global Strategy II*, 2nd edition, FT/Prentice Hall, 2003, pp. 82–85.
13. But see J. Dyer, P. Kale and H. Singh, 'How to make strategic alliances work', *Sloan Management Review*, vol. 42, no. 4 (2001), pp. 37–43.
14. See Doz and Hamel, reference 9, chapters 1 and 2; Ernst and Halevy, reference 11; ul-Haq, reference 9; M. Koza and A. Lewin, 'The co-evolution of strategic alliances', *Organisation Science*, vol. 9, no. 3 (1998), pp. 255–264.
15. This definition is based on ul-Haq's explanation of infrastructure alliances (see reference 9, pp. 6–9).
16. For a fuller discussion of the role of alliances and joint ventures in exploration versus exploitation see

W. Kummerle, 'Home base and knowledge management in international ventures', *Journal of Business Venturing*, vol. 17, no. 2 (2002), pp. 99–122.

17. These characteristics are based on J. Carlos Jarillo, 'On strategic networks', *Strategic Management Journal*, vol. 9, no. 1 (1988), pp. 31–41.

18. See M. Jenkins, K. Pasternak and R. West, *Performance at the Limit: Business Lessons from Formula 1 Motor Racing*, Cambridge University Press, 2005.

19. See Doz and Hamel, reference 9; T. Pietras and C. Stormer, 'Making strategic alliances work', *Business and Economic Review*, vol. 47, no. 4 (2001), pp. 9–12; N. Kaplan and J. Hurd, 'Realising the promise of partnerships', *Journal of Business Strategy*, vol. 23, no. 3 (2002), pp. 38–42; A. Parkhe, 'Interfirm diversity in global alliances', *Business Horizons*, vol. 44, no. 6 (2001), pp. 2–4; ul-Haq, reference 9; I. Hipkin and P. Naude, 'Developing effective alliance partnerships', *Long Range Planning*, vol. 39 (2006), pp. 51–69; A. Inkpen, 'Learning and knowledge acquisition through international strategic alliances', *Academy of Management Executive*, vol. 2, no. 4 (1998), pp. 69–80; and 'Learning through joint ventures: a framework of knowledge acquisition, *Journal of Management Studies*, vol. 37, no. 7 (2000), pp. 1019–1045.

20. ul-Haq (reference 9) identifies different patterns of co-evolution he refers to as parallel, divergent and convergent.

21. See Hipkin and Naude, reference 19.

22. Inkpen in the *Academy of Management Executive*, reference 19.

23. See L. Abrams, R. Cross, E. Lesser and D. Levin, 'Nurturing interpersonal trust in knowledge sharing networks', *Academy of Management Executive*, vol. 17, no. 4 (2003), pp. 64–77. Also C. Huxham and S. Vangen, *Managing to Collaborate: The Theory and Practice of Collaborative Advantage*, Routledge, 2005; or their article, S. Vangen, and C. Huxham, 'Nurturing collaborative relations: building trust in interorganizational relationships', *Journal of Applied Behavioural Science*, vol. 39, no. 1 (2003), pp. 5–31.

24. This point is made by D. Lavie, 'The competitive advantage of interconnected firms: an extension of the resource based view', *Academy of Management Review*, vol. 21, no. 3 (2006), pp. 638–658.

25. H. Weihrich, 'The TOWS matrix – a tool for situational analysis', *Long Range Planning*, April (1982), pp. 54–66.

26. Most standard finance and accounting texts explain in more detail the financial analyses summarised here. For example, see G. Arnold, *Corporate Financial Management*, 3rd edition, FT/Prentice Hall, 2005, chapter 4.

27. A 'classic' explanation of cost–benefit analysis is J.L. King, 'Cost-benefit analysis for decision-making', *Journal of Systems Management*, vol. 31, no. 5 (1980), pp. 24–39. A detailed example in the water industry can be found in N. Poew, 'Water companies' service performance and environmental trade-off', *Journal of Environmental Planning and Management*, vol. 45, no. 3 (2002), pp. 363–379.

28. Real options evaluation can get lost in the mathematics so readers wishing to gain more detail of how real options analysis works can consult one of the following: T. Copeland, 'The real options approach to capital allocation', *Strategic Finance*, vol. 83, no. 4 (2001), pp. 33–37; T. Copeland, T. Koller and J. Murrin, *Valuation: Measuring and managing the value of companies*, 3rd edition, Wiley, 2000; T. Copeland and V. Antikarov, *Real Options: A practitioner's guide*, Texere Publishing, 2001; L. Trigeorgis, *Managerial Flexibility and Strategy in Resource Allocation*, MIT Press, 2002; P. Boer, *The Real Options Solution: Finding total value in a high risk world*, Wiley, 2002. Also see M.M. Kayali. 'Real options as a tool for making strategic investment decisions' *Journal of the American Academy of Business*, vol. 8, no. 1 (2006), pp. 282–287.

29. T. Luehrman, 'Strategy as a portfolio of real options', *Harvard Business Review*, vol. 76, no. 5 (1998), pp. 89–99.

30. The main proponent of shareholder value analysis is A. Rappaport, *Creating Shareholder Value: The new standard for business performance*, 2nd edition, Free Press, 1998. See also R. Mill's chapter, 'Understanding and using shareholder value analysis', in V. Ambrosini with G. Johnson and K. Scholes (eds), *Exploring Techniques of Analysis and Evaluation in Strategic Management*, Prentice Hall, 1998.

31. A. Kennedy, *The End of Shareholder Value*, Perseus Publishing, 2000.

32. This point is made clear in a research study reported by P. Haspeslagh, T. Noda and F. Boulos, 'Its not just about the numbers', *Harvard Business Review*, July–August (2001), pp. 65–73.

33. L. Levidow and S. Carr, 'UK: precautionary commercialisation', *Journal of Risk Research*, vol. 3, no. 3 (2000), pp. 261–270.

34. See C. Walsh, *Master the Management Metrics That Drive and Control Your Business*, 4th rev. edition, FT/Prentice Hall, 2005.

35. A brief description of sensitivity analysis can be found in Arnold, reference 26, p. 218. For those readers interested in the details of sensitivity analysis see A. Satelli, K. Chan and M. Scott (eds), *Sensitivity Analysis*, Wiley, 2000. For a more detailed exploration of different approaches see A.G. Hadigheh and T. Terlaky. 'Sensitivity analysis in linear optimization: invariant support set intervals' *European Journal of Operational Research*, vol. 169, no. 3 (2006), pp. 1158–1176.

36. See Arnold, reference 26, chapter 3, p. 108.

37. Break-even analysis is covered in most standard accountancy texts. See, for example, Arnold, reference 26, p. 223.

Tesco conquers the world?

In 2006 Tesco, the UK's most successful grocery retailer (with about 30 per cent market share), again reported a record-breaking year. Over the previous four years it had almost doubled group sales (excluding VAT) and profits to £39bn (≈ €57bn) and £2.28bn respectively. The 'group statistics' painted a picture of what this growth meant on the ground: the number of stores had tripled to 2,672 and employee numbers had grown by about 60 per cent to 273,000. Significantly, sales to the rest of Europe had grown from 9 to 13 per cent of group sales and Asian sales were 11 per cent of group sales (up from 6 per cent in 2002). The company had also extended its product range significantly since 2002 – moving into non-food sectors and retailing services.

Not surprisingly the 2006 annual report was very 'upbeat' and the Chairman, David Reid, summarised the company achievements and prospects for the future:

UK Our sales performance in the UK core business has been strong, as we have invested in all parts of the customer offer.

International has delivered good growth in like-for-like sales, profits and returns. Our largest ever new store development programme delivered 5.4 million sq ft [500,000 m²] of sales area, with a further 6.6 million sq ft planned in the current year.

Non-food has again made strong progress, with UK sales up by over 13%, against the background of cautious consumer spending. Our established areas such as health and beauty (up 10%) have done well and newer departments such as consumer electronics (34% growth) and clothing (16% growth) have performed particularly strongly.

Retailing services have also had a good year with tesco.com delivering record results, Tesco Personal Finance (TPF) performing well in a challenging personal finance sector and good growth in telecoms.

The report went on to explain in more detail exactly how each of the main parts of the business were changing and developing:

Photo: Richard Jones/Rex Features

Core UK business

'giving customers what they want 24/7'

Ranges

Because everyone is welcome at Tesco, we appreciate that our customers have different tastes and requirements. We work hard to give our customers a broad assortment of leading brands, a really good range of Tesco products – from *Finest* to *Value* lines – and lots of new ideas for feeding the family.

Instead of offering a standard product range everywhere, we have put a lot of effort into tailoring our offer for local customers. For example, our new *Extra* store in Slough, Berkshire features over 900 speciality Asian products, from new vegetarian and Halal ready meals to extensive ranges of bulk-pack rice, and even Bollywood DVDs.

Formats

Our store formats are a way of meeting the different needs of our customers wherever they live and however they want to shop – in large stores, in small stores or on-line. Tesco *Express* brings great food and low prices into the heart of neighbourhoods. . . . *Metro* offers the convenience of Tesco in town and city centres where people live and work. At Tesco *Superstores*, customers can find everything they need for their weekly shopping and at our *Extra* stores customers can not only find our full range of food and convenience lines, but also a comprehensive range of non-foods. *Homeplus* non-food only store was trialed in 2005.

NON-FOOD

'offering great quality, range, price and service'

More and more people are choosing to buy not just their household essentials but also bigger ticket items at Tesco, from clothing to TVs and fridges and from sports equipment to toys. They appreciate the convenience of being able to do all their shopping under one roof in our Extra stores.

We will be sourcing products that are common in all countries (UK, Ireland and Central Europe) together as a group. Each country will retain the responsibility of identifying the local needs of their customers and sourcing those products from the appropriate suppliers within their respected country.

RETAILING SERVICES

'making on-line shopping simple'

Tesco.com is the most successful on-line grocery shopping service in the world. What is remarkable about our on-line business is the diversity of customers using it, from busy urban families to people in rural communities. It has also allowed many house-bound people to shop properly for the first time.

DVDs to your door 60,000 customers have now signed up to our DVDs to rent service, giving them access to the 30,000 titles that are available through our on-line DVD service.

Energy We have enabled tens of thousands of customers to save money on their gas and electricity bills (by comparing prices of different suppliers). This service is fully comprehensive, fully independent and fully impartial.

Getting healthy on-line E–diets help customers to tailor their eating plans to what's right for them, taking into account lifestyles, food preferences and health recommendations.

'financial services that are simple'

Tesco Personal Finance now offers 21 financial products and services from loans and savings accounts to credit cards and insurance. We are Britain's third largest on-line car insurer with over 1.4 million active car insurance policies.

We are continually trying to improve our offer for customers and now offer the opportunity to purchase travel money in-store, by providing kiosks in seven stores. We have also made the purchase of premium bonds much more convenient for customers [through] the partnership with National Savings & Investments (NS&I).

Tesco Mobile is a virtual network formed as a joint venture with [the mobile network operator] O2.

International

With the exception of Ireland (91 stores) the company's international expansion had been in Eastern Europe (272 stores) and Asia (450 stores). The company planned to enter the US market in 2007 with a completely new local format for the American consumer modelled on *Express*. What was most interesting was the way that each development reflected local market conditions rather than working to a standard entry model. Some of the details from the 2006 annual report are shown in the box.

Where next from here?

Despite this rosy picture not everyone was convinced that Tesco was yet a major world player. The obvious comparison was with the world's biggest retailer, the US company Wal-Mart, whose turnover of US$312 (≈ €250bn) was more than four times that of Tesco. Although Wal-Mart's US sales were flattening out it had a presence in some 70 countries with 2,285 stores outside the USA – this was almost three times Tesco's international 'footprint'. Importantly Wal-Mart won the race to enter India in the autumn of 2006 leaving Tesco with difficulties in finding a suitable local partner – crucial in that market.

Market research with UK consumers also highlighted issues for the company to think about. In particular, although Tesco had attracted a broad range of customers across demographics and age groups, there was evidence that the market was fragmenting. Tesco customers' loyalty seemed to be declining and in an analysis of people's favourite brands by age,[1] Tesco and other high street retailers did well among the over 55s, but did not feature at all in the top 10 brands of 16 to 24 year olds.

But the Tesco Chief Executive, Sir Terry Leahy, was clear about the Tesco 'formula' for success:

Tesco is about making the shopping experience better for customers and we've built our success and our growth by listening to them.

Note

1. Milward Brown research reported by Carlos Grande, *Financial Times*, 19 December (2006).

Source: Tesco Annual Report 2006 at www.tesco.com/InvestorRelations.

Tesco's international stores in 2006

China (39 stores)
We have begun to accelerate our expansion programme beyond the Yangtse delta and have teams working to develop our network in Beijing, Shenzhen and Guangzhou. We have also invested in capability, bringing Tesco systems and know-how into the business, focusing particularly on improving store design, the supply chain and store replenishment.

Japan (111 stores)
In Japan, we operate discount convenience supermarkets, typically 3,000 sq ft in size. We opened our first trial *Express* store in April 2006.

Malaysia (13 stores)
We are trialling our *Express* format in Malaysia with three stores, situated mainly in the area around Kuala Lumpur. We also opened our first *Value* store, a 3,000 sq m store in Banting. By offering a tailored hypermarket range in a smaller store which is cheaper to build, we have been able to bring a modern retail offer to a community which would not have been able to sustain a larger hypermarket.

South Korea (62 stores)
We opened eight new hypermarkets in South Korea this year, including three compact hypers. We have further adapted our *Express* model in South Korea, enabling us to focus on the key products which customers want to be able to buy, close to where they live and work.

Taiwan (6 stores)
[We have agreed an] asset swap deal with Carrefour . . . [which] will enable us to exit from Taiwan with minimal financial impact, allowing us to focus on investment in Central Europe and our other Asian businesses.

Thailand (219 stores)
[Through] the launch of our *Talad* format we have tailored our offer to customers who are used to shopping in local markets. We now have ten of these stores, which carry between 4,500 and 7,500 product lines in around 10,000 sq ft of selling space.

Czech Republic (35 stores)
We have accelerated our new store development programme, adding 20% to our sales area during the year, with eight new compact hypermarkets. (Also) we opened the Group's first 1,000 sq m, or '1K' store . . . [which] enables us to bring the Tesco offer to smaller towns, carrying a locally-tailored range of around 2,700 products.

Hungary (87 stores)
Customers are facing a more challenging economic and retail environment in Hungary, which has held back our growth but we have still made solid progress. Our customers have benefited from lower prices in store and from the roll-out of petrol stations, making it significantly cheaper to fill-up.

Poland (105 stores)
Customers love the convenience of our small format stores which bring many of the advantages of our larger hypermarkets closer to where they live and work.

Republic of Ireland (91 stores)
We continue to invest in bringing prices down for our Irish customers. . . . We are also focusing on extending our product ranges. With *Finest* growing in popularity, we have increased the number of lines in areas such as cheese, ready meals and wine.

Slovakia (37 stores)
In line with our other Central European businesses, Tesco Slovakia has introduced a price promise on 50 everyday items, guaranteeing that we won't be beaten by any local competitor. Our new store programme is now supported by the growth of our compact hypermarket format.

Turkey (8 stores)
In Turkey, Kipa delivered a very strong performance. . . . We successfully launched the *Kipa Value* brand in Turkey, with over 400 products so far and we plan to extend this in the coming year.

Questions

1 Using Exhibit 7.2 in Chapter 7 identify the development directions that Tesco had followed from its origins as a UK-based grocery retailer.

2 Identify the development directions 'available' to the company in the future and assess the relative suitability of each of these options by ranking them (using Illustration 10.2 as an example).

3 For each of the top four development directions in your ranking compare the relative merits of each development method (internal, acquisition or strategic alliance).

4 Complete your evaluation of the options that now appear most suitable by applying the criteria of acceptability and feasibility (see sections 10.3.2 and 10.3.3 respectively).

In Part II of the book the central issue posed is how strategic choices are to be made. The chapters have offered a range of such strategic choices, evidence as to why some seem more effective than others and criteria by which managers may make judgements about them. But this raises two linked questions on which the four lenses provide differing insights:

1 How do managers actually make such choices?

2 How should managers conceive of strategic choice?

Note that:

- There is no suggestion here that one of these lenses is better than another, but they do provide different insights into the problems faced and the ways managers cope with the challenge.

- If you have *not* read the Commentary following Chapter 1 that explains the four lenses, you should now do so.

Design lens

Strategic choice can be made logically and objectively on the basis of linear, analytic, evaluative procedures driven by top managers or other managers working with them. This involves:

- Establishing clear objectives developed to reflect stakeholder expectations and used as a basis for evaluating options.

- Making argued cases for explicit options on the basis of a clear understanding of the strategic position of the organisation arrived at analytically.

- Evaluating options by systematically examining their relative merits in terms of (i) their suitability in addressing the strategic issues the organisation faces; (ii) the feasibility of implementing the strategic option and (iii) the acceptability of the strategic option to key stakeholders.

Demonstrating this approach to strategic choice is likely to be important in gaining the support for a strategy from some key stakeholders (for example, financial institutions).

Experience lens

There are different but complementary explanations here:

- Strategy develops incrementally based on past strategy, past experience and the culture of the organisation within a political context. So choices made are heavily influenced by that past experience.

- Indeed management experience and 'strong cultures' may militate against innovation or constrain innovation to that which is generated in terms of or acceptable to prevailing experience/culture.

- An extension of this is the 'garbage can' view: managers have ready-made solutions on the basis of their experience and search for opportunities and circumstances to put them into effect.

- Strategies emerge on the basis of experimentation and learning by doing (a logical incremental view).

- Political processes of bargaining and negotiation play an important role in strategic choice.

- The strategies of successful organisations are mimicked by others.

In any of the above, analytic tools may be used as a way of checking *why* a strategy might be worth following or developing. Or they might be used to post-rationalise strategic choice.

Commentary on Part II

Strategic choices

Ideas lens

The emphasis here is on the emergence of 'strategic ideas' as the source of strategic options from within the organisation rather than planned strategy from the top. This is characterised by:

- New ideas arising in conditions of instability or 'adaptive tension' rather than through formal plans.
- Experimentation and trial and error behaviour.
- The importance of imperfect copying: even if successful strategies are imitated, they will not be imitated perfectly; differences emerge.
- Internal and external networking giving rise to new ideas.

Managers cannot determine what these new ideas will be but can create a context where they will emerge and discern patterns of ideas as this happens.

Managers are one, but not the only, mechanism by which such selection takes place.

New ideas also get selected for by:

- attracting 'positive feedback' from inside and outside the organisation (for example, from managers in the organisation or customers in the market);
- winning out in competition with other new ideas;
- becoming embedded in organisational routines.

Discourse lens

What appears to be choice is very constrained by the discourse of which managers are part. For example:

- Managers are likely to be comparing their organisation to competitors delimited by who is talked about as being competitors rather than by objective analysis.
- Similarly, strategic options that prevail are likely to be those that fit within a 'dominant narrative' that prevails inside an organisation or in its organisational field/industry.
- There are also 'strategy fads' – commonly followed strategies popular at particular times.

In whatever way a strategy is selected, it is likely to be explained such as to:

- Achieve legitimacy of the strategy in the eyes of stakeholders; for example, 'achieving competitive advantage' is the sort of term likely to be used by managers to justify a strategy, whether or not there is substance to the claim.
- Signal its inevitable success.
- Or post-rationalise its failure.

Understanding *how* a strategy is talked about therefore needs to be seen as an important influence on what strategies are likely to be favoured in an organisation and which are not.

Part III

STRATEGY IN ACTION

This part explains:

→ How strategies develop in organisations; in particular, the organisational processes that may give rise to intended strategies or to emergent strategies.

→ The way in which organisational structures, organisational processes and the management of relationships is important in organising for strategic success.

→ The relationship between an organisation's overall strategy and the resource areas of people, information, finance and technology.

→ How strategic change might be managed and the importance of understanding organisational context and in managing change.

→ Who strategists are and what they do in practice.

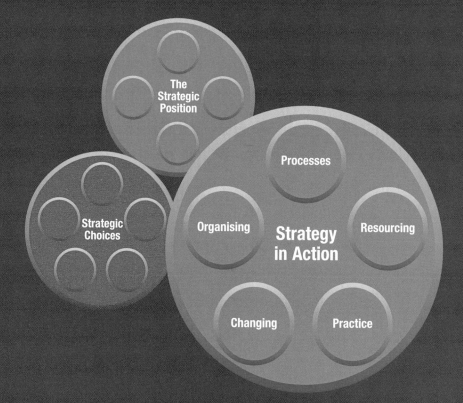

Introduction to Part III

This part of the book is concerned with strategy in action. A continuing question throughout the book has been the extent to which strategy can be seen as pre-planned intent. If this is so, strategy in action is to do with strategy implementation, with 'making strategy happen'. An alternative view is that strategy is more emergent, for example on the basis of people's experience or as a result of responses to competitive action. Here there is less of a separation of intent and action; it is more about 'strategy happening'. In fact elements of both explanations are likely to be evident in organisations and this part of the book reflects that.

The next chapter quite specifically addresses the distinction between intended and emergent explanations of strategy development by reviewing the different organisational processes that can explain how strategies come about. The two chapters that follow consider the relationship between a strategy and how an organisation functions: first in terms of how people work with each other within formal structures but also more informal relationships; second in relation to key resource areas of an organisation. The development of a new strategy may also require significant change for the organisation. Strategic change and how this might be managed is the theme of the penultimate chapter. This part of the book then concludes by discussing what strategists themselves actually do. In so doing it asks the question of the extent to which and how much of what is discussed in this book is put into practice.

More specifically the issues raised in the chapters are as follows:

- Chapter 11 explains how strategies develop in organisations. How intended strategy may be the outcome of the *vision, leadership or 'command'* of individuals, formal *planning systems* or the deliberate *imposition* of strategy from outside an organisation. Also how strategies might emerge out of more routine and day-by-day activities in organisations and through *cultural processes* and *political processes*. The chapter also discusses the implications of these various processes for strategists.

- Chapter 12 is about *organising* for success. It looks at three separate strands of organising: organisational structures, organisational processes and the management of relationships. The chapter highlights the importance for successful organising of making these various elements work together in order to create mutually reinforcing configurations that are well matched to an organisation's strategies.

- Chapter 13 looks at the relationship between an organisation's overall strategy and the strategies in four key resource areas: people, information, finance and technology. The two questions that are pursued through the chapter are these.

First, whether the separate resource areas of an organisation are capable of enabling strategies to be executed successfully. The second question is whether the strategies of an organisation are being shaped to capitalise on the expertise in a particular resource area.

- Chapter 14 examines more specifically how *strategic change* might be managed. This is done in several ways. First, by acknowledging that the challenge of managing change is not the same in all organisations; that the change context matters. Second, by looking at different approaches to managing change, including the roles that managers and others play and the styles of managing change they adopt. Next, by considering a range of levers that might be employed to help manage change in organisations, including changes to organisational routines, the management of political and symbolic processes and other specific tactics for managing change. Finally the chapter considers how these various levers might be employed in different change contexts.

- Chapter 15 examines three issues in the practice of strategy: first, who to include in strategy-making activities, often not just top management but middle managers, consultants and planners as well; second, the kinds of activities that strategists do, from selling strategic issues to communicating chosen strategies; third, the kinds of methodologies that strategists use, including away-days, projects, hypothesis testing and business plans.

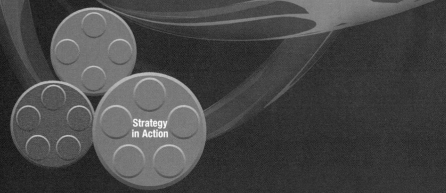

11

Strategy in Action

Strategy Development Processes

LEARNING OUTCOMES

After reading this chapter you should be able to:

→ Explain what is meant by *intended* and *emergent* strategy development.

→ Identify intended processes of strategy development in organisations including the role of vision and command, strategic planning systems and externally imposed strategy.

→ Identify emergent processes of strategy development such as logical incrementalism, resource allocation processes, cultural processes and organisational politics.

→ Consider how different processes of strategy development may be found in *multiple forms* and in *different contexts*.

→ Explain some of the issues managers face in strategy development including the challenge of managing *intended and realised strategy*, the development of the *learning organisation* and strategy development in *uncertain and complex conditions*.

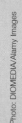

Photo: DIOMEDIA/Alamy Images

11.1 INTRODUCTION

KEY CONCEPT

Intended and emergent strategy

Parts I and II of the book have so far addressed how strategists might understand the strategic position of their organisation and what strategic choices are available. This chapter raises the question as to *how strategies develop*; or more specifically, what overall processes give rise to organisational strategies. (Chapter 15 then examines in more detail which people get involved in these processes, what they actually do in developing strategies, and the methodologies they use.)

There are two broad explanations of strategy development, though they are not mutually exclusive. The first is associated with the idea of *intended strategy*: that strategies come about as a result of careful deliberation typically associated with top management decisions. This is also linked to the idea that strategies are developed using the sorts of concepts and tools so far discussed in the book. This is sometimes known as the *rational/analytic view* of strategy development, or, as in the commentary sections of this book, *a design view* of strategy development. The second view is that of *emergent strategy*: that strategies do not develop on the basis of some grand plan but tend to emerge in organisations over time. The discussion in the commentaries of the experience, ideas and discourse lenses relates to this explanation. This chapter is organised around these two views:

Exhibit 11.1 **Strategy development processes**

Processes of intended strategy development
- Strategic vision, leadership and command
- Strategic planning
- Externally imposed strategies

Processes of emergent strategy development
- Logical incrementalism
- Resource allocation routines
- Cultural processes
- Political processes

Challenges and implications
- Intended and realised strategy
- The learning organisation
- Uncertain and complex conditions

strategy as intended and strategy as emergent. Exhibit 11.1 explains the structure of the chapter:

- The first section (11.2) of the chapter discusses intended strategy. First there is an explanation of how strategies may be the outcome of the *vision, leadership or 'command'* of individuals. This is followed by a discussion of what formal *planning systems* in organisations might look like and the role they play. The section concludes with a discussion of how strategies might be deliberately *imposed* on organisations from the outside.

- The second section of the chapter (11.3) then switches to explanations of how strategies might emerge in organisations. The common feature of the different explanations here is that they do not see strategy making as a distinct and separate organisational activity, but rather see strategies developing out of more day-to-day and routine aspects of organisations. The section begins by considering what has become known as *logical incrementalism*. It then explains how strategies could be the outcome of *resource allocation processes* in organisations. The influence of *cultural processes* in organisations and their *political processes* are then discussed.

- Section 11.4 shows that these different explanations of strategy development should not be seen as independent or mutually exclusive. Indeed that they may all be seen within organisations to different degrees or at different times and in different contexts. However there is evidence that there are *patterns of strategy development* and these are explained in this section.

- The final section of the chapter (11.5) raises some *implications for managing strategy development* including:
  - The distinction between *intended strategy and realised strategy* and the implications for managing strategy development.
  - The challenge of developing what has become known as the *learning organisation*.
  - How different approaches to strategy development may be more or less well suited to *stable, dynamic or complex* environments.

11.2 INTENDED STRATEGY DEVELOPMENT

Intended strategy is an expression of a desired strategy as deliberately formulated or planned by managers

Intended strategy is an expression of a desired strategy as deliberately formulated or planned by managers. Its development may also be associated with the use of the sort of tools, techniques and frameworks for strategic analysis and evaluation explained in this book. These may be used in strategic planning systems, in the thinking of individual strategic leaders or groups of managers about the strategy of their organisation (see Chapter 15).

11.2.1 Strategy development through strategic leadership: the role of vision and command

Strategy development may be strongly associated with a strategic leader, an individual (or perhaps a small group of individuals) upon whom strategy is seen to be dependent. They are individuals whose personality, position or reputation may result in others willingly deferring to them and seeing strategy development as their province. They are therefore personally identified with and central to the strategy of their organisation. That individual may be central because he or she is the owner or founder of the organisation. This is often the case in small businesses and family businesses, some of which may be very large and successful. It may also be that an individual still remains central after a business is publicly quoted: such is the case with Charles Dunstone at Carphone Warehouse, or Rupert Murdoch at NewsCorp. Or it could be that an individual chief executive has turned round a business in times of difficulty and, as such, personifies the success of the organisation's strategy, as is the case with Michael O'Leary at Ryanair. Or perhaps an individual's network of contacts in an industry or organisational field are perceived as especially significant.[1]

In any of these circumstances, strategy may be – or may be seen to be – the deliberate intention of that leader. How such an intention comes about can, however, be explained in different ways:

- *Strategy leadership as design*. It could be that the strategic leader has thought through the strategy analytically. This might be by using the sort of techniques associated with strategic analysis and evaluation, or it might simply be that the individual has consciously, systematically and on the basis of his or her own logic worked through issues the organisation faces and come to his or her own conclusions.

- *Strategy leadership as vision*. It could be that a strategic leader determines or is associated with an overall vision, mission or strategic intent (see section 4.5.2) that motivates others, helps create the shared beliefs within which people can work together effectively and shapes more detailed strategy developed by others in an organisation. Some writers see this as *the* role of the strategic leader.[2]

- *Strategy leadership as command*. The strategy of an organisation might also be dictated by an individual. This is, perhaps, most evident in owner-managed small firms, where that individual is in direct control of all aspects of the business. Danny Miller and Isabel Le-Breton suggest there are advantages and disadvantages here. On the plus side it can mean speed of strategy adaptation and 'sharp, innovative, unorthodox strategies that are difficult for other companies to imitate'. The downside can, however, be 'hubris, excessive risk taking, quirky, irrelevant strategies'.[3]

11.2.2 Strategic planning systems

Strategic planning may take the form of systematised, step-by-step, chronological procedures to develop or coordinate an organisation's strategy

Often, strategy development is equated with formalised **strategic planning** systems.[4] These may take the form of systematised, step-by-step, chronological procedures involving different parts of the organisation. For example, in a study of strategic planning systems of major oil companies, Rob Grant[5] noted the following stages in the cycle for a large corporation:

- *Initial guidelines*. The cycle's starting point is usually a set of guidelines or assumptions about the external environment (for example, price levels and supply and demand conditions) and the overall priorities, guidelines and expectations of the corporate centre.

- *Business-level planning.* Business units or divisions then draw up strategic plans to present to the corporate centre. Corporate centre executives then discuss those plans with the business managers usually in face-to-face meetings. On the basis of these discussions the businesses revise their plans for further discussion.

- *Corporate-level planning.* The corporate plan results from the aggregation of the business plans. This coordination may be undertaken by a corporate planning department that, in effect, has a coordination role. The corporate board then has to approve the corporate plan.

- *Financial and strategic targets* are then likely to be extracted to provide a basis for performance monitoring of businesses and key strategic priorities on the basis of the plan.

Illustration 11.1 is a schematic representation of two different strategic planning systems Robert Grant found in his study of oil companies. Some companies were much more formal and regularised than others (for example, the French Elf Aquitaine and Italian ENI), with greater reliance on written reports and formal presentations, more fixed planning cycles, less flexibility and more specific objectives and targets relating to the formal plans. Where there was more informality/flexibility (for example, BP, Texaco and Exxon), companies placed greater emphasis on more general financial targets. Central corporate planning departments also played different roles. In some organisations they acted primarily as coordinators of business plans. In others they were more like internal consultants.

It is important to note that major strategic decisions may not, themselves, be made within or as a direct result of such planning processes. For example, the decisions about competitive strategy in a business-level strategic plan will quite likely be taken in management meetings in that business. There the processes associated with strategy development may correspond to any of those explained in this chapter and elsewhere in the book (see Chapter 15 and the commentaries). However, such decisions may *then* be built into the formal plan.

None the less a strategic planning system may have many uses. First, it may indeed play a role in how the future organisational *strategy is determined*. For example, it might:

- *Help structure analysis and thinking* about complex strategic problems.

- *Encourage questioning and challenge* of received wisdom taken for granted in an organisation.

- *Encourage a longer-term view* of strategy than might otherwise occur. Planning horizons vary, of course. In a fast-moving consumer goods company, 3–5-year plans may be appropriate. In companies which have to take very long-term views on capital investment, such as those in the oil industry, planning horizons can be as long as 15 years (in Exxon) or 20 years (in Shell).[6]

- *Enhance coordination of business-level strategies* within an overall corporate strategy.

It could be that in any of this planning systems could employ the tools and techniques of strategic analysis and decision making discussed in Parts I and II of this book.

Illustration 11.1

Strategic planning in Shell and ENI

The role of strategic planning systems may differ between firms.

Shell

Shell's strategic planning is based on (i) 20-year plans every 4–5 years on the basis of its scenario planning process and (ii) annual business plans with 5–10-year time horizons. The purpose is to enhance business unit strategies and coordinate strategy across the multinational operation.

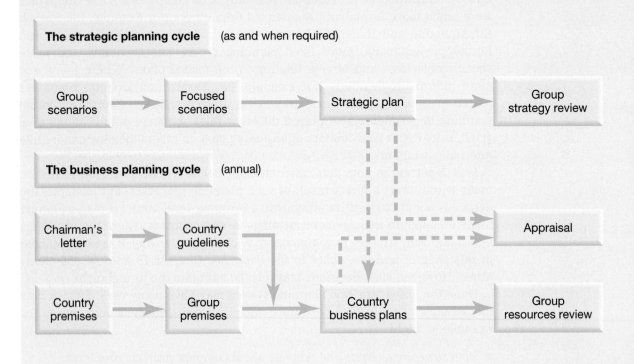

A planning system may also facilitate *converting an intended strategy into organisational action* by:

- *Communicating* intended strategy from the centre to operating units.
- *Providing agreed objectives or strategic milestones* against which performance and progress can be reviewed.
- *Coordinating resources* required to put strategy into effect.

A planning system may also have a *psychological role* by:

- *Involving people* in strategy development, therefore perhaps helping to create *ownership* of the strategy.

ENI

ENI has an annual planning cycle with a four-year time horizon embracing each business unit, sector and the whole group. The first year of the plan forms the basis of the annual budget and performance objectives. The emphasis is on central corporate control of business units and pressure on them to achieve greater efficiencies.

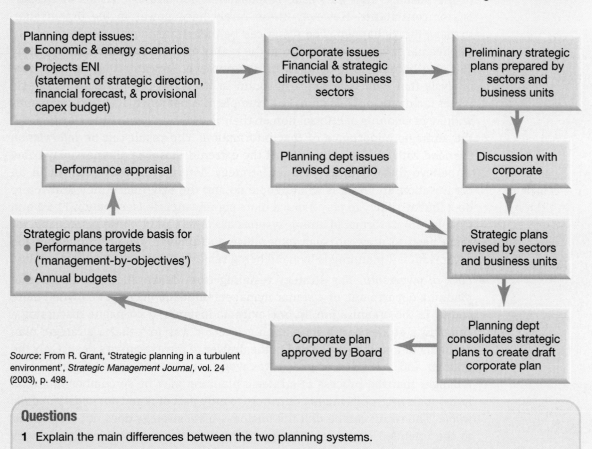

Source: From R. Grant, 'Strategic planning in a turbulent environment', *Strategic Management Journal*, vol. 24 (2003), p. 498.

Questions

1 Explain the main differences between the two planning systems.

2 What other processes of strategy development are likely to be found in a major oil company?

- Providing a *sense of security* and logic for the organisation, not least senior management who believe they *should* be proactively determining the future strategy and exercising control over the destiny of the organisation.

Henry Mintzberg has, however, challenged the extent to which planning provides such benefits.[7] Arguably there are four main dangers in the way in which formal systems of strategic planning have been employed:

- *Confusing strategy with the plan.* Managers may see themselves as managing strategy when what they are doing is going through the processes of planning. Strategy is, of course, not the same as 'the plan': strategy is the long-term direction that the organisation is following, not just a written document.

Linked to this may be a confusion between *budgetary processes* and strategic planning processes; the two may come to be seen as the same. The result is that planning gets reduced to the production of financial forecasts rather than the thinking through of the sort of issues discussed in this book. Of course it may be important to build the output of strategic planning into the budgetary process, but they are not the same.

- *Detachment from reality*. The managers responsible for the implementation of strategies, usually line managers, may be so busy with the day-to-day operations of the business that they cede responsibility for strategic issues to special-ists or consultants. However, these rarely have power in the organisation to make things happen. The result can be that strategic planning becomes an intellectual exercise removed from the reality of operation. Strategic planning can also become over-detailed in its approach, concentrating on extensive analysis that, whilst technically sound in itself, misses the major strategic issues facing the organisation. For example, it is not unusual to find companies with huge amounts of information on their markets, but with little clarity about the strategic importance of that information. The result can be *information overload* with no clear outcome. At the extreme, strategic planners may come to believe that centrally planned strategy determines what goes on in an organisation. In fact it is what people do and the experience they draw on to do it that are likely to play a much more significant role (see section 11.5.1 and Chapter 15). If formal planning systems are to be useful, those responsible for them need to draw on such experience and involve people throughout the organisation if planning is to avoid being removed from organisational reality.

- *Lack of ownership*. The strategy resulting from deliberations of a corporate planning department, or a senior management team, may not be owned more widely in the organisation. In one extreme instance, a colleague discussing a company's strategy with its planning director was told that a strategic plan existed, but found it was locked in the drawer of the executive's desk. Only the planner and a few senior executives were permitted to see it! There is also a danger that the process of strategic planning may be so cumbersome that individuals or groups might contribute to only part of it and *not understand the whole*. The result can be that the business-level strategy does not correspond to the intended corporate strategy. This is particularly problematic in very large firms.

- *Dampening of innovation*. Highly formalised and rigid systems of planning, especially if linked to very tight and detailed mechanisms of control, can result in an inflexible, hierarchical organisation with a resultant stifling of ideas and dampening of innovative capacity.

The evidence of the extent to which the pursuit of such a systemised approach results in organisations performing better than others is equivocal[8] – not least because it is difficult to isolate formal planning as the dominant or determining effect on performance. However, there is some evidence that it may be especially beneficial in dynamic environments, where decentralised authority for strategic decisions is required (see Chapter 12) but where there is a need for coordination of strategies arising from such decentralisation.[9]

Certainly there has been a decline in the use of formal corporate planning departments[10] and a shift to line managers taking responsibility for strategy development and planning (see Chapter 15). Strategic planning is becoming more project based and flexible.[11] In this respect, strategic planning ceases to be a vehicle for the top-down development of intended strategy and more of a vehicle for the coordination of strategy emerging from below (see section 11.4.1 on resource allocation).

11.2.3 Externally imposed strategy

There may be situations in which managers face what they see as the imposition of strategy by powerful external stakeholders. Strategies being imposed in such ways may have been determined using the tools of analysis and evaluation associated with a rational/analytic approach, or perhaps through systematic strategic planning; or they may have developed in a more emergent fashion (see section 11.3). However, to the managers of the organisation having it imposed on them, it is certainly experienced as an 'intended strategy'.

For example, the government may dictate a particular strategic direction as in the public sector, or where it exercises extensive regulation over an industry. Or it may choose to deregulate or privatise a sector or organisation currently in the public sector. Indeed, in the UK public sector a more direct interventionist approach began to be used in the early 2000s. So-called 'special measures' were employed for schools or hospitals deemed to be underperforming badly, with specialist managers being sent in to turn round the ailing organisations and impose a new strategic direction. Businesses in the private sector may also be subject to such imposed strategic direction, or significant constraints on their choices. A multinational corporation seeking to develop businesses in some parts of the world may be subject to governmental requirements to do this in certain ways, perhaps through joint ventures or local alliances. An operating business within a multidivisional organisation may also regard the overall corporate strategic direction of its parent as akin to imposed strategy.

11.3 EMERGENT STRATEGY DEVELOPMENT

Although strategy development is typically associated with intentionality, this may not be so. Research on historical patterns of strategy development in organisations shows a pattern of what has become known as incremental strategy development. Strategies do not typically change in major shifts of direction. They typically change by building on and amending what has gone before. Prior decisions tend to affect future directions giving rise to the sort of pattern described in Exhibit 11.2. An apparently coherent strategy of an organisation may develop on the basis of a series of strategic moves each of which makes sense in terms of previous moves. Perhaps a product launch, or a significant investment decision, establishes a strategic direction which, itself, guides decisions on the next strategic move – an acquisition perhaps. This in turn helps consolidate the strategic direction, and over time the overall strategic approach of the organisation becomes more established. As time goes on, each move is informed by this developing pattern of strategy and, in turn, reinforces it.

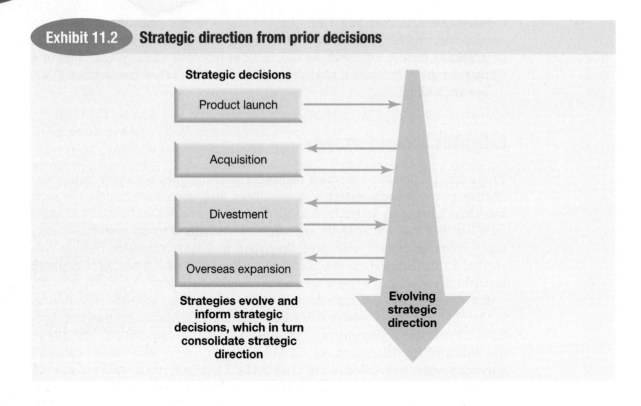

Exhibit 11.2   **Strategic direction from prior decisions**

In many ways this is to be expected. It would be strange and, arguably, dysfunctional for an organisation to change its strategy fundamentally very often. Moreover, if it has embarked on an overall strategic direction, it is to be expected that strategic decisions would be taken in line with that. So such a pattern is consistent with a view of strategy development as an intentional, considered and deliberate process. However, it is also possible to account for the same pattern as a persistent application of the familiar – organisations repeatedly taking decisions based on where they have come from, rather than a considered view of their future[12] or as the outcome of routines, activities and processes within an organisation leading to decisions that become the long-term direction – the strategy – of an organisation.[13] These cumulative decisions may then subsequently be more formally described, for example in annual reports and strategic plans, as the strategy of the organisation. This section explains the organisational processes that might account for such **emergent strategy** development.

Emergent strategy comes about through everyday routines, activities and processes in organisations leading to decisions that become the long-term direction of an organisation

11.3.1 Logical incrementalism

Logical incrementalism is the deliberate development of strategy by experimentation and learning from partial commitments

In a study of major multinational businesses, James Quinn[14] concluded that the strategy development processes he observed could best be described as logical incrementalism. **Logical incrementalism** is the development of strategy by experimentation and 'learning from partial commitments rather than through global formulations of total strategies'.[15] There are a number of reasons this is likely to be so:

- *Environmental uncertainty.* Managers realise that they cannot do away with the uncertainty of their environment by relying on analyses of historical data or predicting how it will change. Rather, they try to be sensitive to environmental signals by encouraging constant environmental scanning throughout the organisation.

- *Generalised views of strategy.* Managers have a generalised rather than specific view of where they want the organisation to be in the future and try to move towards this position incrementally. There is also a reluctance to specify precise objectives too early, as this might stifle ideas and prevent innovation and experimentation. Objectives may therefore be fairly general in nature.

- *Experimentation.* Managers may seek to develop a strong, secure, but flexible core business. They will then build on the experience gained in that business to inform decisions both about its development and experimentation with 'side bet' ventures. Commitment to strategic options may therefore be tentative in the early stages of strategy development. Such experiments are not the sole responsibility of top management. They emerge from what Quinn describes as 'subsystems', in the organisation. By this he means the groups of people involved in, for example, product development, product positioning, diversification, external relations, and so on.

- *Coordinating emergent strategies.* Top managers may then utilise a mix of *formal and informal* social and political processes (see section 11.3.4) to draw together an emerging pattern of strategies from these subsystems. These may then be formed into coherent statements of strategy for stakeholders (for example, shareholders, financial commentators, the media) that need to understand the organisation's strategy.

Quinn argues that, despite its emergent nature, logical incrementalism can be 'a conscious, purposeful, proactive, executive practice' to improve information available for decisions and build people's psychological identification with the development of strategy. In a sense, then, logical incrementalism encapsulates processes that bridge intention and emergence, in that they are deliberate and intended but rely on social processes within the organisation to sense the environment and experiments in subsystems to try out ideas.

This view of strategy making is similar to the descriptions that managers themselves often give of how strategies come about in their organisation. Illustration 11.2 provides some examples of managers explaining the strategy development process in their organisation as they see it. They see their job as 'strategists' as continually, proactively pursuing a strategic goal, countering competitive moves and adapting to their environment, whilst not 'rocking the boat' too much, so as to maintain efficiency and performance.

Arguably, developing strategies in such a way has considerable benefits. Continual testing and gradual strategy implementation provides improved quality of information for decision making, and enables the better sequencing of the elements of major decisions. Since change will be gradual, the possibility of creating and developing a commitment to change throughout the organisation is increased. Because the different parts, or 'subsystems', of the organisation are in a continual state of interplay, the managers of each can learn from each other about the feasibility of a course of action. Such processes also take account of the

Illustration 11.2

An incrementalist view of strategic management

Managers often see their job as managing adaptively: continually changing strategy to keep in line with the environment, whilst maintaining efficiency and keeping stakeholders happy.

- 'You know there is a simple analogy you can make. To move forward when you walk, you create an imbalance, you lean forward and you don't know what is going to happen. Fortunately, you put a foot ahead of you and you recover your balance. Well, that's what we're doing all the time, so it is never comfortable.'[1]

- 'I begin wide-ranging discussions with people inside and outside the corporation. From these a pattern eventually emerges. It's like fitting together a jigsaw puzzle. At first the vague outline of an approach appears like the sail of a ship in a puzzle. Then suddenly the rest of the puzzle becomes quite clear. You wonder why you didn't see it all along.'[2]

- 'We haven't stood still in the past and I can't see with our present set-up that we shall stand still in the future; but what I really mean is that it is a path of evolution rather than revolution. Some companies get a successful formula and stick to that rigidly because that is what they know – for example, [Company X] did not really adapt to change, so they had to take what was a revolution. We hopefully have changed gradually and that's what I think we should do. We are always looking for fresh openings without going off at a tangent.'[3]

- 'In our business you cannot know the future; it's changing so fast. That's why I employ some of the best brains in the industry. Their job is to keep at the forefront of what's happening and, through what they are working on, to help create that future. I don't give them a strategic plan to work to; my job is to discern a strategy from what they tell me and what they are doing. Of course they don't always agree – why would they, they can't *know* the future either – which means there's a good deal of debate, a good deal of trial and error and a good deal of judgement involved.'[4]

- 'The analogy of a chess game is useful in this context. The objective of chess is clear: to gain victory by capturing your opponent's king. Most players begin with a strategic move, that assumes a countermove by the opponent. If the countermove materialises, then the next move follows automatically, based on a previous winning strategy. However, the beauty of chess is the unpredictability of one's opponent's moves. To attempt to predict the outcome of chess is impossible, and therefore players limit themselves to working on possibilities and probabilities of moves that are not too far ahead.'[5]

Sources:
1. Quotes from interviews conducted by A. Bailey as part of a research project sponsored by the Economic and Social Research Council (Grant No.: R000235100).
2. Extract from J.B. Quinn, *Strategies for Change*, Irwin, 1980.
3. Extracts from G. Johnson, *Strategic Change and the Management Process*, Blackwell, 1987.
4. CEO of a hi-tech business in an interview with a co-author.
5. From a manager on an MBA course.

Questions

1 With reference to these explanations of strategy development, what are the main advantages of developing strategies incrementally?

2 Is incremental strategy development bound to result in strategic drift (see section 11.6.1)? How might this be avoided?

political nature of organisational life, since smaller changes are less likely to face the same degree of resistance as major changes. Moreover, the formulation of strategy in this way means that the implications of the strategy are continually being tested out. This continual readjustment makes sense if the environment is considered as a continually changing influence on the organisation.

11.3.2 Resource allocation processes

The resource allocation process (RAP) explanation of strategy development is that realised strategies emerge as a result of the way resources are allocated in organisations

The **resource allocation process** (RAP) explanation of strategy development is that realised strategies emerge as a result of the way resources are allocated in organisations.[16] This is sometimes known as the Bower–Burgelman explanation of strategy development after two American professors – Joe Bower and Robert Burgelman[17] – who identified similar processes in their different studies, as have others later.[18]

As with the logical incremental view of strategy development, the RAP explanation acknowledges that it is unrealistic to determine strategy in a top-down, prescriptive, detailed manner across an organisation, especially a large, complex organisation. A changing and uncertain environment together with the cognitive limits of managers to cope with this (see pages 33–39 in the Commentary) mean that strategy is better explained as the outcome of problems or issues being addressed as they arise. The RAP explanation then emphasises the formal and informal processes by which this is done, particularly:

● *Negotiation across organisational levels*. The nature of problems and their resolutions are typically the outcome of negotiation across levels of an organisation. Most obviously this could be between a corporate centre and business units but it might also be between a business and its operating units or functions. Such problems or issues usually start with a discrepancy. For example, this could be a discrepancy between where top management wish a corporation to be in terms of its share price; or at a business level a decline in market share or competitive position; or perhaps a shortfall in profits below corporate expectations. In any of these cases there is then likely to be a need to make sense of the significance of that discrepancy from one level (for example, the business level) to another (for example, corporate) and align expectations as to what needs to be resolved. The problem will then, most likely, be worked on at the level most appropriate to the problem. For example, if it is a market-related issue, by the marketing department in a business or a project team in that business. It is unlikely it would be dealt with in any detail by the chief executive or strategic planner in the business, let alone at corporate level. The point that needs emphasising here again is that a good deal of choice as to what to focus on and what choices to make may lie far down in an organisation's subsystems.

● The *influence of RAP* on the nature of the resolution of the problem. All organisations have within them systems, routines and standards for deciding upon proposed new ventures, products and services. These play a significant part on what sort of solutions to problems are advocated and those to which resources are allocated. To take a common example, many businesses have criteria for acceptability of new venture proposals based on measures of

Exhibit 11.3 **Strategy development through resource allocation processes**

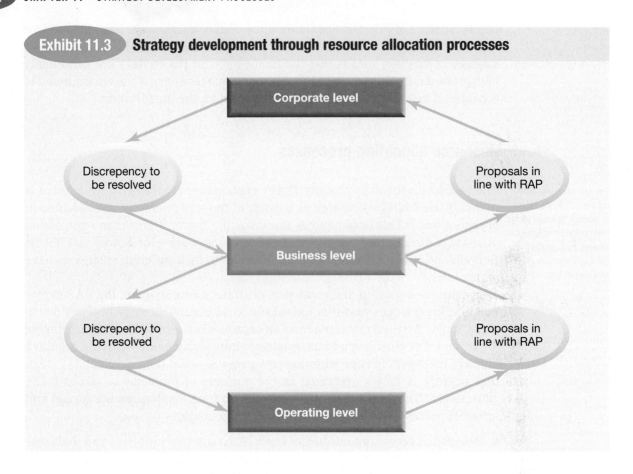

return (for example, return on capital employed). The level at which such returns are pitched will undoubtedly influence which new ideas are proposed; some will be seen as involving less capital resource or having the potential for greater returns than others. The same criterion will similarly affect which solutions are adopted. If different resource allocation criteria were to be used, different solutions would likely be advocated and different ones selected.

This RAP explanation of how strategies develop is summarised in Exhibit 11.3. The case example at the end of this chapter shows how this helps explain the major strategic changes at Intel in the 1980s. The top management of the firm were wedded to Intel as a memory company in the business of DRAMs – Dynamic Random Access Memories. Its major strategic switch to becoming a microprocessing company at that time did not come about because of top management direction, but because the internal resource allocation routines within the firm favoured projects with greater profit margins. This resulted in the emerging microprocessor business being allocated more resources and therefore a basis for future investment and growth greater than DRAMs.[19] However, as Illustration 11.3 shows, whilst localised processes may explain strategy development, they can lead to significant problems.

Finally it is worth noting that the explanations of RAP here bear a good deal of similarity to the developing role of strategic planning (see section 11.2.2) and

Illustration 11.3

European strategy at Viacom in the 1990s

Strategy processes at the business level may not be able to cope with corporate-wide issues.

After his takeover of the company in 1987, Sumner Redstone, as Chairman of Viacom, the US international media conglomerate, enlisted Frank Biondi as CEO. Under Biondi, Viacom grew steadily until the mid-1990s.

Biondi's corporate management approach was to cultivate a high-performance culture by providing divisions of the company with high levels of operating autonomy, reinforced by financial incentives linked to divisional results. This included them having responsibility for their strategy and the control of resources at the divisional level.

In the mid-1990s Viacom faced the task of rethinking its European strategy due to increasing global competition. Viacom's European divisions included Paramount and MTV/Nickelodeon and their major competitors in many of their markets at that time were businesses which were part of Rupert Murdoch's NewsCorp. NewsCorp was centrally run with a global vision. Murdoch, the central figure, employed a much more centralised management and interventionist style – he would take over temporary leadership of a division personally on occasions.

By late 1995, two separate strategic issues requiring major investment were being considered at Paramount and at MTV/Nickelodeon. Paramount wanted to move into what was then next-generation satellite-delivered programming services. Its preferred strategic option was to do this through a long-term partnership with the Kirch Group, which had such a service in place.

On the other hand, MTV/Nickelodeon was considering pursuing a wider market opening in Europe by creating locally tailored broadcasting channels. It believed this could allow it to build on its existing brand, but also accommodate the limited foreign language proficiency of young children in local markets. So the preferred strategy was to acquire localised content through equity-based partnerships with several companies wanting to launch satellite TV, rather than have an exclusive partnership with the Kirch Group.

These strategic issues were negotiated between the management teams of the two European divisions.

Although they wanted to collaborate to utilise the synergies they believed they had, they could not agree on the strategy to adopt. It was therefore decided that Paramount should take the lead in any negotiations with prospective media partners in Europe, while MTV/Nickelodeon would make clear its strategic preferences to Paramount. Biondi did not actively take part in these negotiations. The internal negotiations about the preferred strategy dragged on for the rest of that year, but no consensus was reached. This meant that the desired market developments in Europe were delayed, allowing competition to increase. This led to ever shorter time spans in which strategic issues had to be dealt with and the ultimate recognition that the devolved approach to corporate management was not working. Ultimately, in January 1996 Redstone released Biondi as CEO, assumed control himself and introduced a more centralised corporate strategic management style to improve the speed and efficiency of strategic decision making.

(Viacom later merged with CBS but by 2007 had demerged and was operating again as a separate company under the chairmanship of Sumner Redstone.)

Source: Based on T.R. Eisenmann and J.L. Bower 'The entrepreneurial M-form: a case study of strategic integration in a global media company', in J.L. Bower and C.G. Gilbert (eds), *From Resource Allocation to Strategy*, Oxford University Press, 2005, pp. 307–329.

Prepared by Michael Ubben, Lancaster University Management School.

Questions

1 How did Viacom's strategy development processes differ from the strategic planning approaches explained in Illustration 11.1?

2 Which of the corporate parenting approaches explained in Chapter 7 was being adopted by Biondi?

3 How might the problems that occurred at Viacom in 1995 have been avoided?

the way in which business or operating units within an organisation relate to the corporate centre. However, the RAP emphasis is much more on the processes within the subsystems driving an emergent strategy.

11.3.3 Organisational politics

The RAP explanation highlights the role of negotiation between organisational levels in strategy development. This signals the importance of organisational politics. Managers often suggest that the strategy being followed by their organisation is really the outcome of the bargaining and power politics that go on between important executives or between coalitions within the organisation and major stakeholders. These executives or coalitions are continually trying to position themselves such that their views prevail or that they control the resources in the organisation necessary for future success. For example, Motorola's inability to move fast enough from analogue to digital technology for mobile phones and its consequent loss of market dominance (see Illustration 5.1) was substantially the result of divisional 'warring tribes' across the company seeking to preserve their own interests.[20] The **political view**[21] of strategy development is, then, that strategies develop as the outcome of processes of bargaining and negotiation among powerful internal or external interest groups (or stakeholders). This is the world of boardroom battles often portrayed in film and TV dramas. Illustration 11.4 shows how the interests of different executive and non-executive directors of Vodafone in concert with various stakeholders hit the headlines as the company wrestled with its strategy development in 2006.

The political activity is often seen as an inevitable but negative influence on strategy development, getting in the way of thorough analysis and rational thinking. A political perspective on strategic management suggests that the rational and analytic processes often associated with developing strategy (see section 11.2.1) may not be as objective and dispassionate as they appear. Objectives that are set may reflect the ambitions of powerful people. Information used in strategic debate is not always politically neutral. Rather, information and data that are emphasised or de-emphasised can be a source of power for those who control what is seen to be important. Indeed one manager or coalition may exercise power over another because they control important sources of information. Powerful individuals and groups may also strongly influence the identification of key issues and the strategies eventually selected or the way they are selected.[22] Differing views may be pursued, not only on the basis of the extent to which they reflect environmental or competitive pressures, for example, but also because they have implications for the status or influence of different stakeholders.

None of this should be surprising. In approaching strategic problems, people may be operating within an overall organisational culture (see Chapter 4) but within this, they are likely to be differently influenced by at least:

● *Personal experience* from people's roles within the organisation.

● *Competition for resources and influence* between the different subsystems in the organisation and powerful people within them who are likely to be interested in preserving or enhancing the power of their positions.[23]

● *The relative influence of stakeholders* on different parts of the organisation. For example, a finance department may be especially sensitive to the influence of

The **political view** of strategy development is that strategies develop as the outcome of processes of bargaining and negotiation among powerful internal or external interest groups (or stakeholders)

Illustration 11.4

Boardroom battles at Vodafone

Political processes in organisations can influence the development of strategy.

Vodafone became a global player in the telecommunications industry under the guidance of Sir Christopher Gent, who had become the company's 'Life President'. However, following the takeover of the German company Mannesmann in 2000, Vodafone had seemed to lose its way. Some of the overseas acquisitions had not worked out, investors were calling for greater returns and commentators argued that the 'old guard' wedded to Gent's strategy had not embraced the convergence of technologies – broadband, information technology, TV and the Internet.

By mid-2006, Chief Executive Arun Sarin was known to be in discussions about the sale of Vodafone's controlling interest in its Japanese operation. There was talk that in the USA Verizon was interested in buying out Vodafone's 45 per cent share of Verizon Wireless. Sarin was also reported to be considering the sale of Arcor, Vodaphone's German fixed-line unit. In all this Sarin was portrayed as the 'shareholders' friend', trying to liquidate assets to improve dividends and fund expansion into broadband.

However, this had given rise to a major boardroom split between the supporters of Sarin and the old guard who supported the global development strategy of the Gent era. The *Financial Times* (6 March 2006) reported that Lord Maclaurin, Vodafone's Chairman, was 'losing patience with Mr Sarin'. The *Observer* (12 March 2006) reported that Maclaurin had sought to 'put the issue of Sarin's tenure . . . to a vote of the full board but after consultations with his non-executives it became clear that he could not carry a vote on this'.

Supporters of Sarin argued that he was trying to deal with strategic issues that should have been dealt with earlier.

It was also reported that there was pressure from investors for supporters of the old guard, including Lord Maclaurin, to retire earlier than planned and make way for a new chairman, Sir John Bond. One major investor was quoted in the *Observer* as saying that he was hoping that the arrival of Sir John Bond might help sort things out. He also added: 'I don't

know what Gent is still doing around. These positions always cause trouble. Do I think he should be there? No.' Indeed in March 2006 Sir Christopher resigned as Group Life President.

Investors also lobbied for the departure from the board of non-executive directors who were insufficiently independent, seen to be in either the Sarin or the old guard camp.

In all this, the *Observer* reported that Sarin had removed Peter Bamford, Chief Marketing Officer, who was seen as 'too pro-Gent and pro-Maclaurin' and added 'Sarin has tightened his grip; he has replaced 90% of the people at the top of the company over the last 12 months'.

In July 2006 when Sir John Bond arrived as the new Chairman he expressed support for Sarin but cautioned that his performance would be 'under constant review'. None the less, as Lord Maclaurin handed over to Sir John at the AGM, whilst admitting that the past six months had not been easy, he insisted that there had been 'no – repeat – no dissension on the board'.

By mid-2007 the reports of boardroom dissent were far less. What had emerged in the context of a flattening profit picture were reports of potential takeover or even the break-up of the group. The bases of such reports were, however, being dismissed by Sarin.

Sources: Daily Telegraph, 7 March (2006); *Financial Times*, 6, 8 March, 26 July (2006), 29 May, 1 June (2007); *Observer*, 12 March (2006).

Questions

1 Identify the key stakeholders, their views and their influence in the events of 2006.

2 Do you consider the reported events at Vodafone exceptional?

3 What strategy has Vodafone pursued since 2006? Does this suggest one or other of the rival camps prevailed?

financial institutions whilst a sales or marketing department will be strongly influenced by customers.[24]

● *Different access to information* or the salience of that information given their roles and functional affiliations.

In such circumstances emergent and incremental patterns of strategy development are likely. Emergent in the sense that it is this bargaining and negotiation that gives rise to strategy rather than carefully analysed, deliberate intent. Incremental for two reasons. First, if different views prevail in the organisation and different parties exercise their political muscle, compromise may be inevitable. Second, it is quite possible that it is from the pursuit of the current strategy that power has been gained by those wielding it. Indeed it might be very threatening to their power if significant changes in strategy were to occur. In such circumstances it is likely that a search for a compromise solution which accommodates different power bases may end up with a strategy which is an adaptation of what has gone before.

There are, however, alternative ways of considering the influence of political processes. Arguably, the conflict and tensions that manifest themselves in political activity, arising as they do from different expectations or interests, can be the source of new ideas (see the discussion on the 'ideas lens' in the commentaries) or challenges to old ways of doing things.[25] New ideas may be supported or opposed by different 'champions' who will battle over what is the best idea or the best way forward. Arguably, if such conflict and tensions did not exist, neither would innovation. The productive management of such tensions may be a learned competence or dynamic capability (see section 3.4.5) in some organisations that provides them with a basis for competitive advantage. Further, as Chapter 14 (section 14.4.5) shows, the exercise of power may be important in the management of strategic change.

All of this suggests that political activity has to be taken seriously as an influence on strategy development. Whatever thinking goes into a strategy will need to go hand in hand with activity to address the political processes at work. This is addressed in other parts of this book, in particular sections 4.4.1–4.4.2 and 14.4.5 as well as in the commentaries.

11.3.4 **Cultural processes**

Elsewhere in the book (see Chapter 5 in particular) the importance of culture has been discussed. Organisational culture is to do with the taken for granted in an organisation. That includes the basic assumptions and beliefs that are shared by members of an organisation (in this book termed the paradigm) and the taken-for-granted ways of doing things and structures that are encapsulated in the outer rings of the cultural web (see sections 5.4.5 and 5.4.6 and Exhibit 5.7). So a **cultural explanation of strategy development** is that it occurs as the outcome of the taken-for-granted assumptions and behaviours in organisations. The important thing to stress here is that this taken-for-grantedness works to define, or at least guide, how the people in an organisation view that organisation and its environment. It also tends to constrain what is seen as appropriate behaviour and activity. Some examples of this are given in Chapter 5 and in section 14.2. It

A cultural explanation of strategy development is that it occurs as the outcome of the taken-for-granted assumptions and behaviours in organisations is important to realise the impact of this on the emergent and incremental development of strategy, and the potential consequences.

In some respects this provides an underlying dimension to previous explanations of strategy development. The observed pattern of incremental strategy development can be explained in terms of, for example, deliberate logical incrementalism (see section 11.3.1). However, it can also be explained in terms of the outcome of the influence of organisational culture.[26] Similarly, the cultural web emphasises the strong influence of taken-for-granted organisational routines and power structures. Routines include the RAPs central to the RAP explanation of strategy development – and power structures are central to the political processes discussed above.

11.4 PATTERNS OF STRATEGY DEVELOPMENT

The discussion of different strategy development processes in sections 11.2 and 11.3 raises some further important general points:

- *Multiple strategy development processes.* There is a danger that the descriptions of processes above suggest that they are somehow discrete or mutually exclusive. They are not. Indeed, it is likely that there will be multiple processes at work in any organisation. As has already been suggested, the different processes explained here can be seen to exist within each other. For example, in practical terms, if a planning system exists in a large organisation, that organisation will also have RAP. Within these there will undoubtedly be some level of political activity; indeed the planning system itself may be used for negotiating purposes. Moreover, if there is a dominant mode of strategy development in an organisation, it is most likely that other processes will be evident too. Indeed, there is evidence that those organisations that employ multiple processes of strategy development may perform better than those that take more singular approaches.[27] It has to be recognised, therefore, that there is *no one right way* in which strategies are developed. The challenge is for managers to recognise the potential benefits of different processes of strategy development so as to build organisations capable of adapting and innovating within a changing environment, yet achieving the benefits of more formal processes of planning and analysis to help this where necessary.[28]

- *Contextual differences.* Processes of strategy development are likely to *differ over time* and in *different contexts*. An organisation that is going through rapid change, perhaps the result of environmental turbulence or the need for internal strategic change, will very likely have different strategy development processes from an organisation in a more steady state. The chapter-end case study for this chapter shows this for Intel from the 1980s through to the turn of the century. Different strategy development processes tended to be more pronounced at one stage in its development than another and, apparently, beneficially for the organisation.

Drawing together these two observations, Exhibit 11.4 shows some typical patterns of strategy development processes in different organisational contexts.[29]

Exhibit 11.4	**Some configurations of strategy development processes**

Dominant dimensions	Characteristics	Rather than	Typical contexts
Planning Incrementalism (Logical incrementalism)	Standardised planning procedures Systematic data collection and analyses Constant environmental scanning Ongoing adjustment of strategy Tentative commitment to strategy Step-by-step, small-scale change	Intrusive external environment Dominant individuals Political processes Power groups	Manufacturing and service sector organisations Stable or growing markets Mature markets Benign environments
Incremental Cultural Political	Bargaining, negotiation and compromise amongst conflicting interests of groups Groups with control over critical resources more likely to influence strategy Standardised 'ways of doing things' Routines and procedures embedded in organisational history Gradual adjustments to strategy	Deliberate, intentional process Well-defined procedures Analytical evaluation and planning Deliberate managerial intent	Professional service firms (e.g. consultancy or law firms) Unstable, turbulent environment New and growing markets
Imposed Political	Strategy is imposed by external forces (e.g. legislation, parent organisation) Freedom of choice severely restricted Political activity likely within organisation and between external agencies	Strategy determined within the organisation Planning systems impact on strategy development Influence on strategic direction mainly by managers within the organisation	Public sector organisations, larger manufacturing and financial service subsidiaries Threatening, declining, unstable and hostile environments

The findings above are based on a survey of perceptions of strategy development processes undertaken at Cranfield School of Management in the 1990s.

● *Perceptions of how strategies develop* will be seen differently by different people. For example, as Exhibit 11.5 shows, senior executives tend to see strategy development more in terms of intended, rational, analytic planned processes whereas middle managers see strategy development more as the result of cultural and political processes. Managers in public sector organisations tend to see strategy as externally imposed more than managers in commercial businesses, largely because their organisations are answerable to government bodies.[30] People who work in family businesses tend to see more evidence of the influence of powerful individuals, who may be the owners of the businesses. Illustration 11.6, the chapter's key debate, shows very different accounts of the strategy development for a highly successful strategy.

Exhibit 11.5	Managers' perceptions of strategy development processes

Perceptions that there exists:	Level in organisation		Environmental stability	
	CEO	Middle management	Higher	Lower
Precision of objectives	Yes	No	Yes	No
Detailed planning	Yes	No	Yes	No
Systematic analysis of environment	Yes	No	Yes	–
Careful evaluation of strategic options	Yes	No	–	–

These findings are based on a survey of perceptions of strategy development processes undertaken at Cranfield School of Management in the 1990s. The findings indicate statistically significant differences.

11.5 CHALLENGES FOR MANAGING STRATEGY DEVELOPMENT

The discussion in this chapter raises some important challenges and has implications for how managers manage the strategy development process.

11.5.1 Managing intended and realised strategy

The discussion so far in this chapter has drawn a distinction between intended and emergent strategy. It has also made the point that the different processes of strategy development are not mutually exclusive; organisations have multiple processes. A problem that managers face, then, is that it is not unusual for organisations to have an intended strategy, perhaps the result of a strategic planning process, but to be following a different strategy in reality, perhaps the outcome of political and cultural processes. We all experience this as customers of organisations that have stated strategies quite different from what we experience: government agencies that are there purportedly to serve our interests but act as bureaucratic officialdom; companies that claim they offer excellent customer service but operate call centres that frustrate customers and fail to solve problems, universities that claim excellence of teaching but are more concerned with their staff's research, or vice versa. Exhibit 11.6 shows this. There may well be an *intended strategy*, agreed by senior executives, based on careful analysis and expressed in a formal document explaining the intended strategy in a systematic way with the intention that this will be implemented (see route 1). However, much of what is intended follows route 2 and is *unrealised*; it does not come about in practice, or only partially so. There may be all sorts of reasons for this. The plans are unworkable; the environment changes after the plan has been drawn up and managers decide that the strategy, as planned, should not be put into effect; or people in the organisation or influential stakeholders do not go along

Exhibit 11.6 **Strategy development routes**

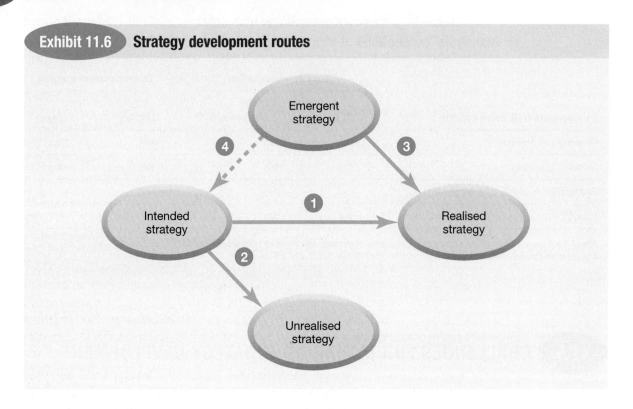

with the plan. (Also see the discussion of the drawbacks of planning systems in section 11.2.2) However, it could also be that the processes that give rise to emergent strategy give rise to a **realised strategy**: that is, the strategy actually being followed by an organisation in practice (route 3) rather than planned up front. There are at least three major implications here for strategists:

Realised strategy:
the strategy actually being followed by an organisation in practice

- *Awareness*. First, and most fundamental, have managers taken steps to check if the intended strategy and realised strategy are different? It should not be assumed that the top management of organisations are always close enough to customers or get sufficient feedback from those who are to understand the extent of difference between the intended and the realised.

- *The role of strategic planning*. It was pointed out in section 11.2.2 that strategic planning might not perform the role of formulating strategies so much as the useful role of coordinating the strategies that emerge within the organisation (route 4 in Exhibit 11.6). The danger is that this does little more than pull together the 'received wisdom' built up over time in the organisation such that the planning systems merely post-rationalise where the organisation has come from. If strategic planning systems are to be employed managers need to learn two key lessons:
  - They are not a substitute for other processes of strategy development. These other processes need to be managed too (see below).
  - There needs to be realistic expectations of the role of strategic planning. For example, is its primary role one of coordination of emergent strategies; or is the expectation that it will contribute proactively to the development of

strategy by, for example, encouraging the challenge of received wisdom and ways of doing things? If it is the latter, then the role of the strategic planner becomes more to do with internal consultancy than specialist analyst and coordinator.

● *The challenge of strategic drift*. One of the major strategic challenges facing managers was identified in Chapter 5 as the tendency of incremental strategy development to give rise to strategic drift (see section 5.1). The discussion in section 11.3 shows that incremental strategy development processes leading to the emergence of strategy is the natural outcome of the influence of organisational culture, individual and collective experience, political processes and prior decisions. This further highlights that strategy development processes in organisations need to encourage people in organisations to have the capacity and willingness to challenge and change their core assumptions and ways of doing things. This leads to the idea of the 'learning organisation' discussed in the next section. Desirable as this may be, the evidence is that it does not occur easily. It also emphasises the delicate balance that an organisation faces in developing its strategy. For example, it has internal cultural forces for inertia that tend to constrain strategy development, yet behaviours and routines within its culture that might potentially provide the capabilities for competitive advantage (see section 3.4.3).

● *Managing emergent strategy*. The processes of strategy development that give rise to emergent strategy may be rooted in organisational routines and culture, but they are not unmanageable. Indeed this is as much about managing strategy as is strategic planning. RAPs can be changed; political processes can be analysed and managed (see section 4.4.1 on stakeholder analysis); the challenge of the norms and routines of organisational culture can be encouraged (see section 11.5.1). Not least here is the management role of creating a clear vision directing future strategy.

11.5.2 The learning organisation

Traditionally, organisations have been seen as hierarchies and bureaucracies set up to achieve order and maintain control, as structures built for stability rather than change. A **learning organisation**, however, is one capable of continual regeneration from the variety of knowledge, experience and skills of individuals within a culture that encourages mutual questioning and challenge around a shared purpose or vision. It emphasises the potential capacity and capability of an organisations to regenerate itself from within, and in this way for dynamic strategies to emerge naturally.

The **learning organisation** is capable of continual regeneration from the variety of knowledge, experience and skills of individuals within a culture which encourages mutual questioning and challenge around a shared purpose or vision

Advocates of the learning organisation[31] point out that the collective knowledge of all the individuals in an organisation usually exceeds what the organisation itself 'knows' and is capable of doing; the formal structures of organisations typically stifle organisational knowledge and creativity. They argue that the aim of management should be to encourage processes that unlock the knowledge of individuals, and encourage the sharing of information and knowledge, so that every individual becomes sensitive to changes occurring around them and contributes to the identification of opportunities and required changes. This emphasises the importance of seeing organisations as *social networks*,[32] where the emphasis is not so much on hierarchies as on different interest groups that need to cooperate with each other and potentially learn from each other. So as ideas bubble up from below, the risk of their fizzling out because of lack of interest from other parts of the organisation is reduced.

The central tenets of organisational learning are:

- *Managers facilitate* rather than direct.
- *Information flows and relationships between people are lateral* as well as vertical.
- *Organisations are pluralistic,* where conflicting ideas and views are welcomed, surfaced and become the basis of debate.
- *Experimentation* is the norm, so ideas are tried out in action and in turn become part of the learning process.

All this relates to other concepts discussed in the book. It is akin to aspects of logical incrementalism described in section 11.3.1 and to insights from the ideas lens discussed in the commentaries. It also corresponds to what Gary Hamel calls 'resilient' organisations that continually reinvent themselves by refusing to take their success for granted and building the capability to imagine new business models.[33]

11.5.3 Strategy development in uncertain and complex conditions

Not all organisations face similar environments. They differ in their form and complexity; therefore different ways of thinking about strategy development and different processes for managing strategy may make sense in different circumstances. Exhibit 11.7 shows how organisations may seek to cope with conditions that are more or less stable or dynamic, and simple or complex:[34]

- In *simple/static* conditions, the environment is relatively straightforward to understand and is not undergoing significant change. Raw material suppliers and some mass manufacturing companies are examples, at least from the past. Technical processes may be fairly simple, and competition and markets remain the same over time. In such circumstances, if environmental change does occur, it may be predictable, so it could make sense to analyse the environment extensively on an historical basis as a means of trying to forecast likely future conditions. In situations of relatively low complexity, it may also be possible to identify some predictors of environmental influences. For example, in public services, demographic data such as birth rates might be used as lead indicators to determine the required provision of schooling, health care or social services. So in simple/static conditions, seeing strategy development in formal planning terms may make sense. It might also be tempting to rely on past experience and prior decisions since little is changing. There are, however, two problems. First, competitors in the same sort of environment may all end up following the same strategies, and this could be a recipe for high degrees of competition and low profits (see Chapter 6). Second, environmental conditions may change. Many organisations have found increasingly dynamic and/or complex conditions. When this happens it could well be that

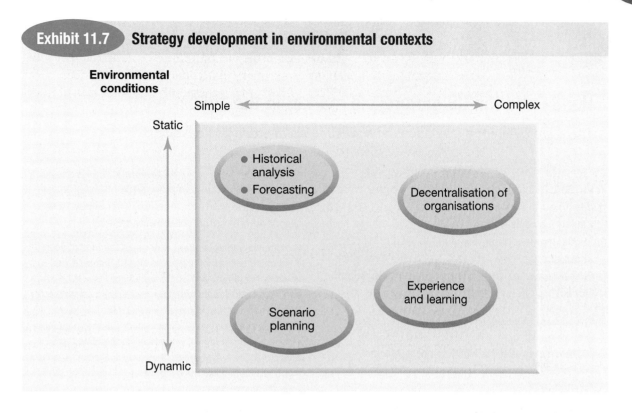

Exhibit 11.7   **Strategy development in environmental contexts**

they find difficulties in adjusting to those changed conditions because their strategy development processes are not suited to them.

- In *dynamic* conditions, managers need to consider the environment of the future, not just of the past. The degree of uncertainty therefore increases. They may employ structured ways of making sense of the future, such as *scenario planning*, discussed in Chapter 2 (see section 2.2.2), or they may rely more on encouraging and creating the organisational conditions necessary to encourage individuals and groups to be forward thinking, intuitive and challenging in their thinking about possible futures, approximating to *organisational learning* described above.

- In *complex* situations managers face an environment that is difficult to comprehend. This may be because of the knowledge complexity of an industry. Or it may be because of organisational complexity. The corporate centre of a big multinational firm with multiple business units, or a major public service such as a local government authority with many services, may exhibit such complexity because of its diversity, for example. Such organisations, of course, face dynamic conditions too, and therefore a combination of complexity and uncertainty. The electronics industry is in this situation. In such circumstances top management's need to recognise that the possibility of planning detailed strategies from the top is limited, arguably dangerous since specialists lower down in the organisation know more about the environment in which the organisation operates than they do. Top management's role may be more to do with setting overall strategic direction and coordinating and shaping emerging strategy from below. Insights from the ideas lens (see the commentaries) and, again, of organisational learning may be helpful here too.

Illustration 11.5

Honda and the US motorcycle market in the 1960s

There are different explanations of how successful strategies develop.

In 1984, Richard Pascale published a paper which described the success Honda had experienced with the launch of its motorcycles in the US market in the 1960s. It was a paper that has generated discussion about strategy development processes ever since. First he gave explanations provided by the Boston Consulting Group (BCG):

The success of the Japanese manufacturers originated with the growth of their domestic market during the 1950s. This resulted in a highly competitive cost position which the Japanese used as a springboard for penetration of world markets with small motorcycles in the early 1960s. . . . The basic philosophy of the Japanese manufacturers is that high volumes per model provide the potential for high productivity as a result of using capital intensive and highly automated techniques. Their market strategies are therefore directed towards developing these high model volumes, hence the careful attention that we have observed them giving to growth and market share.

Thus the BCG's account is a rational one based upon the deliberate building of a cost advantage based on volume.

Pascale's second version of events was based on interviews with the Japanese executives who launched the motorcycles in the USA:

In truth, we had no strategy other than the idea of seeing if we could sell something in the United States. It was a new frontier, a new challenge, and it fitted the 'success against all odds' culture that Mr. Honda had cultivated. We did not discuss profits or deadlines for breakeven. . . . We knew our products . . . were good but not far superior. Mr. Honda was especially confident of the 250cc and 305cc machines. The shape of the handlebar on these larger machines looked like the eyebrow of Buddha, which he felt was a strong selling point. . . . We configured our start-up inventory with 25 per cent of each of our four products – the 50cc Supercub and the 125cc, 250cc and 305cc machines. In dollar value terms, of course, the inventory was heavily weighted toward the larger bikes. . . . We were entirely in the dark the first year. Following Mr. Honda's and our own instincts, we had not attempted to move the 50cc Supercubs. . . . They seemed wholly unsuitable for the US market where everything was bigger and more luxurious. . . . We used the Honda 50s ourselves to ride around Los Angeles on errands. They attracted a lot of attention. But we still hesitated to push the 50cc bikes out of fear they might harm our image in a heavily macho market. But when

SUMMARY

This chapter has dealt with different ways in which strategy development occurs in organisations (see also Illustration 11.5). The main lessons of the chapter are as follows:

- It is important to distinguish between *intended* strategy – the desired strategic direction deliberately planned by managers – and *emergent strategy*, which may develop in a less deliberate way from the behaviours and activities inherent within an organisation.

- Most often the process of strategy development is described in terms of intended strategy as a result through *planning systems* carried out objectively and dispassionately. There are benefits and disbenefits of formal strategic planning systems. However, there is evidence to show that such formal systems are not an adequate explanation of strategy development as it occurs in practice.

key debate

the larger bikes started breaking, we had no choice. And surprisingly, the retailers who wanted to sell them weren't motorcycle dealers, they were sporting goods stores.

Two very different accounts, yet they describe the same market success. Since the publication of the paper, many writers on strategy have hotly debated what these accounts actually represent. For example, Henry Mintzberg observed: 'the conception of a novel strategy is a creative process (of synthesis), to which there are no formal techniques (analysis)'. He argued any formal planning was in the implementation of the strategy: 'strategy had to be conceived informally before it could be programmed formally'. He went on to add, 'While we run around being "rational", they use their common sense . . . they came to America prepared to *learn*.'

Michael Goold, the author of the original BCG report, defended it on the grounds that

its purpose was to discern what lay behind and accounted for Honda's success, in a way that would help others to think through what strategies would be likely to work. It tries to discern patterns in Honda's strategic decisions and actions, and to use these patterns in identifying what works well and badly.

Richard Rumelt concluded that

the 'design school' is right about the reality of forces like scaled economies, accumulated experience and

accumulative development of core competences over time . . . but my own experience is that coherent strategy based upon analyses and understandings of these forces is much more often imputed than actually observed.

And Pascale himself concluded that the serendipitous nature of Honda's strategy showed the importance of learning; that the real lessons in developing strategies were the importance of an organisation's agility and that this resides in its culture, rather than its analyses.

Source: This case example is based on R.T. Pascale, 'Perspectives on strategy: the real story behind Honda's success', *California Management Review*, vol. 26, no. 3 (Spring 1984), pp. 47–72; and H. Mintzberg, R.T. Pascale, M. Goold and R.P. Rumelt, 'The Honda effect revisited', *California Management Review*, vol. 38, no. 4 (1996), pp. 78–116.

Questions

1 Are the different accounts mutually exclusive?

2 Which of the different explanations of strategy development explained in the chapter do you discern in the Honda story?

3 Do you think Honda would have been more or less successful if it had adopted a more formalised strategic planning approach to the launch?

- Intended strategy may also come about on the basis of the direction of central *command or the vision of strategic leaders* and the *imposition of strategies* by external stakeholders.
- Strategies may emerge from within organisations. This may be explained in terms of:
  - How organisations may proactively try to cope through processes of *logical incrementalism*.
  - The *resource allocation processes* employed in the organisation that may favour some strategy projects over others.
  - The outcome of the bargaining associated with *political activity* resulting in a negotiated strategy.
  - The taken-for-granted elements of *organisational culture* favouring certain strategies.
- *Multiple processes of strategy development* are likely to be needed if organisations wish to encourage and facilitate the *challenge of taken-for-granted* assumptions and ways of doing things, create a *learning organisation* and cope with *increasingly dynamic and complex environments*.

Work assignments

*Denotes more advanced work assignments.   * Refers to a case study in the Text and Cases edition.*

11.1   Read the annual report of a company with which you are familiar as a customer (for example, a retailer or transport company). Identify the main characteristics of the intended strategy as explained in the annual report, and the characteristics of the realised strategy as you perceive it as a customer.

11.2   Using the different explanations in sections 11.3 and 11.4 characterise how strategies have developed in different organisations (for example, Intel, Ericsson*, Direct and Care*).

11.3 *   Planning systems exist in many different organisations. What role should planning play in a public sector organisation such as local government or the National Health Service and a multinational corporation such as the News Corporation*?

11.4 *   Incremental patterns of strategy development are common in organisations, and managers see advantages in this. However, there are also risks of strategic drift. Using the different explanations in sections 11.2 and 11.3, suggest how such drift might be avoided.

11.5   Suggest why different approaches to strategy development might be appropriate in different organisations such as a university, a fashion retailer, a diversified multinational corporation and high-technology company.

Integrative assignment

11.6 *   How does the concept of the 'learning organisation' (section 11.5.2) relate, not only to strategy development, but also to (a) that of strategic capabilities, dynamic capabilities and organisational knowledge (Chapter 3), (b) organisation culture (Chapter 5) and (c) strategic change (Chapter 14)? Bearing this in mind, what would be the challenges of developing a 'learning organisation' in a large international corporation?

An extensive range of additional materials, including audio summaries, weblinks to organisations featured in the text, definitions of key concepts and self-assessment questions, can be found on the *Exploring Corporate Strategy* Companion Website at **www.pearsoned.co.uk/ecs**

Recommended key readings

- A much quoted paper that describes different patterns of strategy development is H. Mintzberg and J.A. Waters, 'Of strategies, deliberate and emergent', *Strategic Management Journal*, vol. 6, no. 3 (1985), pp. 257–272.

- The changing role of strategic planning in the oil industry is explained by Rob Grant; see 'Strategic planning in a turbulent environment: evidence from the oil majors', *Strategic Management Journal*, vol. 24 (2003), pp. 491–517. Also see M. Mankins, 'Stop making plans, start making decisions', *Harvard Business Review*, January (2006), pp. 77–84.

- For an explanation of logical incrementalism, see J.B. Quinn, *Strategies for Change: Logical incrementalism*, Irwin, 1980; also summarised in J.B. Quinn and H. Mintzberg, *The Strategy Process*, 4th edition, Prentice Hall, (2003). Compare this with the different explanations of incremental change and the explanation of strategic drift by G. Johnson, 'Rethinking incrementalism', *Strategic Management Journal*, vol. 9, no. 1 (1988), pp. 75–91.

- How resource allocation processes develop strategies is explained in J.L. Bower and C.G. Gilbert, 'A revised model of the resource allocation process', in J.L. Bower and C.G. Gilbert (eds), *From Resource Allocation to Strategy*, Oxford University Press, 2005, pp. 439–455. The book also includes many case studies. A fascinating case study of the effects of resource allocation routines on the developing strategy of Intel is provided by Robert Burgelman in 'Fading memories: a process theory of strategic business exit in dynamic environments', *Administrative Science Quarterly*, vol. 39 (1994), pp. 34–56.

- Insights into the importance of multiple processes of strategy development can be found in S.L. Hart, 'An integrative framework for strategy-making processes', *Academy of Management Review*, vol. 17, no. 2 (1992), pp. 327–351.

References

1. Indeed there is some evidence that the social networks of leaders are related both to higher performance and to their personal reputation; see A. Mehra, A.L. Dixon, D. Brass and B. Robertson, 'The social network ties of group leaders: implications for group performance and leader reputation, *Organization Science*, vol. 17, no. 1 (2006), pp. 64–79.

2. For example, see W. Bennis and B. Nanus, *The Strategies for taking Charge*, Harper & Row, 1985; and J. Collins and J. Porras, *Built to Last: Successful Habits of Visionary Companies*, Harper Business, 2002.

3. The role of a command style in small businesses is discussed in D. Miller and I. Le Breton-Miller, 'Management insights from great and struggling family businesses', *Long Range Planning*, vol. 38 (2005), pp. 517–530. The quotes here are from p. 519.

4. In the 1970s and 1980s there were many books written on formal strategic planning approaches to strategy development. They are less common now but, for example, see N. Lake, *The Strategic Planning Workbook*, 2nd edition, Kogan Page, 2006; J.M. Bryson, *Strategic Planning for Public and Nonprofit Organizations: a guide to strengthening and sustaining organizational achievement*, 3rd edition, Jossey-Bass, 2005; and S. Haines, *The Systems Thinking Approach to Strategic Planning and Management*, St Lucie Press, 2000.

5. 'Strategic planning in a turbulent environment: evidence from the oil majors' is a study carried out by Rob Grant. See the *Strategic Management Journal*, vol. 24 (2003), pp. 491–517.

6. Again from Grant's research; see reference 5.

7. Many of these dangers are drawn from H. Mintzberg, *The Rise and Fall of Strategic Planning*, Prentice Hall, 1994.

8. Studies on the relationship between formal planning and financial performance are largely inconclusive. For example, see P. McKiernan and C. Morris, 'Strategic planning and financial performance in the UK SMEs: does formality matter?', *Journal of Management*, vol. 5 (1994), pp. S31–S42. Some studies have shown benefits in particular contexts. For example, it is argued that there are benefits to entrepreneurs setting up new ventures; see F. Delmar and S. Shane, 'Does business planning facilitate the development of new ventures?', *Strategic Management Journal*, vol. 24 (2003), pp. 1165–1185. And other studies actually show the benefits of strategic analysis and strategic thinking, rather than the benefits of formal planning systems; see C.C. Miller and L.B. Cardinal, 'Strategic planning and firm performance: a synthesis of more than two decades of research', *Academy of Management Journal*, vol. 37, no. 6 (1994), pp. 1649–1665.

9. T.J. Andersen, 'Integrating decentralized strategy making and strategic planning processes in dynamic environments', *Journal of Management Studies*, vol. 41, no. 8 (2004), pp. 1271–1299.

10. See reference 5.

11. See M. Mankins. 'Stop making plans, start making decisions', *Harvard Business Review*, January (2006), pp. 77–84.

12. See S. Elbanna, 'Strategic decision making: process perspectives', *International Journal of Management Reviews*, vol. 8, no. 1 (2006), pp. 1–20, for a useful explanation of

differences between deliberate, intended strategy development and incremental explanations. Also for a fuller discussion of different explanations of incremental strategic change see G. Johnson, 'Re-thinking incrementalism', *Strategic Management Journal*, vol. 9 (1988), pp. 75–91.

13. Two of the early extensive case studies showing how cultural and political processes give rise to the emergence of strategies are A. Pettigrew, *The Awakening Giant*, Blackwell, 1985; and G. Johnson, *Strategic Change and the Management Process*, Blackwell, 1987.

14. J.B. Quinn's research involved the examination of strategic change in companies and was published in *Strategies for Change*, Irwin, 1980. See also J.B. Quinn, 'Strategic change: logical incrementalism', in J.B. Quinn and H. Mintzberg, *The Strategy Process*, 4th edition, Prentice Hall, 2003.

15. See J.B. Quinn, *Strategies for Change*, reference 14, p. 58.

16. This definition is based on that on p. 349 of J.L. Bower and C.G. Gilbert, 'A revised model of the resource allocation process', in J.L. Bower and C.G. Gilbert (eds), *From Resource Allocation to Strategy*, Oxford University Press, 2005, pp. 439–455.

17. The original studies are J.L. Bower, *Managing the Resource Allocation Process: a Study of Corporate Planning and Investment*, Irwin, 1972; and R.A. Burgelman, 'A model of the interaction of strategic behaviour, corporate context and the concept of strategy', *Academy of Management Review*, vol. 81, no. 1 (1983), pp. 61–70; and 'A process model of internal corporate venturing in the diversified major firm', *Administrative Science Quarterly*, vol. 28 (1983), pp. 223–244.

18. For example, see T. Noda and J. Bower, 'Strategy as iterated processes of resource allocation', *Strategic Management Journal*, vol. 17 (1996), pp. 159–192.

19. The Intel case is also written up by Robert Burgelman, see *Strategy as Destiny: How strategy making shapes a company's future*, Free Press, 2002. Also see by Burgelamn, 'Fading memories: a process theory of strategic business exit in dynamic environments', *Administrative Science Quarterly*, vol. 39 (1994), pp. 34–56.

20. See S. Finkelstein, 'Why smart executives fail: four case histories of how people learn the wrong lessons from history', *Business History*, vol. 48, no. 2 (2006), pp. 153–170.

21. For political perspectives on management, see J.R. DeLuca. *Political Savvy: Systematic Approaches to Leadership Behind the Scenes*, 2nd edition, Evergreen Business Group, 1999; and G.J. Miller. *Managerial Dilemmas: The Political Economy of Hierarchy*, Cambridge University Press, 2006.

22. For a discussion and an explanatory model of this political perspective, see V.K. Narayanan and L. Fahey, 'The micro politics of strategy formulation', *Academy of Management Review*, vol. 7, no. 1 (1982), pp. 25–34.

23. For an example of how different political coalitions can influence, see S. Maitlis and T. Lawrence, 'Orchestral manoeuvres in the dark: understanding failure in organizational strategizing', *Journal of Management Studies*, vol. 40, no. 1 (2003), pp. 109–140.

24. This is sometimes referred to as a 'resource dependency view' of strategy development; for the original argument see J. Pfeffer and G.R. Salancik, *The External Control of Organisations: A Resource Dependence Perspective*, Harper & Row, 1978.

25. This is the argument advanced by J.M. Bartunek, D. Kolb and R. Lewicki, 'Bringing conflict out from behind the scenes: private informal, and nonrational dimensions of conflict in organizations', in D. Kolb and J. Bartunek (eds), *Hidden Conflict in Organizations: Uncovering Behind the Scenes Disputes*, Sage, 1992.

26. This is explained by Gerry Johnson more fully in 'Re-thinking incrementalism', reference 12.

27. See S. Hart and C. Banbury, 'How strategy making processes can make a difference', *Strategic management Journal*, vol. 15, no. 4 (1994), pp. 251–269.

28. This idea of a balance between analytic rigour and intuition and imagination is the theme of G. Szulanski and K. Amin, 'Learning to make strategy: balancing discipline and imagination', *Long Range Planning*, vol. 34 (2001), pp. 537–556.

29. For two approaches to analysing processes of strategy development see A. Bailey, K. Daniels and G. Johnson, 'Validation of a multi-dimensional measure of strategy development processes', *British Journal of Management*, vol. 11 (2000), pp. 151–162; and S.L. Hart, 'An integrative framework for strategy-making processes', *Academy of Management Review*, vol. 17, no. 2 (1992), pp. 327–351.

30. For a discussion of the differences between strategy development in the public and private sectors see N. Collier, F. Fishwick and G. Johnson, 'The processes of strategy development in the public sector', in G. Johnson and K. Scholes (eds), *Exploring Public Sector Strategy*, Pearson Education, 2001.

31. The concept of the learning organisation is explained in P. Senge, *The Fifth Discipline: The art and practice of the learning organisation*, Doubleday/Century, 1990. Also M. Crossan, H.W. Lane and R.E. White, 'An organizational learning framework; from intuition to institution', *Academy of Management Review*, vol. 24, no. 3 (1999), pp. 522–537. Also see J. Coopey, 'The learning organization, power, politics and ideology', *Management Learning*, vol. 26, no. 2 (1995), pp. 193–213.

32. The concept of the organisation as a set of social networks is discussed by, for example, M.S. Granovetter, 'The strength of weak ties', *American Journal of Sociology*, vol. 78, no. 6 (1973), pp. 1360–1380; and G.R. Carroll and A.C. Teo, 'On the social networks of managers', *Academy of Management Journal*, vol. 39, no. 2 (1996), pp. 421–440.

33. See G. Hamel and L. Valikangas, 'The quest for resilience', *Harvard Business Review*, September (2003), pp. 52–63.

34. R. Duncan's research, on which this classification is based, can be found in 'Characteristics of organisational environments and perceived environmental uncertainty', *Administrative Science Quarterly*, vol. 17, no. 3 (1972), pp. 313–327.

Strategy development at Intel*

Jill Shepherd, Segal Graduate School of Business
Simon Fraser University, Canada

Intel (an abbreviation of Integrated Electronics) is a digital company operating in, having arguably created, the semiconductor industry. Over 30 years the company has achieved strategic transformation twice.

Epoch I

Between 1968 and 1985, during which the CEO was mostly Gordon Moore, Intel was a memory company. Founded by Gordon Moore and Robert Noyce, Intel was the first company to specialise in integrated circuit memory products. Noyce co-invented the integrated circuit, whereas Moore, a physical chemist, saw the potential of metal–oxide–semiconductor (MOS) process technology as a way of mass producing semiconductors at low cost. Both managers left Fairchild Semiconductors, the subsidiary of Fairchild Camera and Instrument Corporation they had helped found. According to Noyce, senior management at Fairchild were unsupportive of innovation, perhaps because it had become too complex and big an organisation. In turn, Andy Grove joined Intel, thinking that the departure of Moore and Noyce left Fairchild fatally bereft of middle management. Their aim was not to transform the industry, but to make memory chips which did not compete directly with Fairchild and others because they were complex.

Two events were critical in these early days. First, the first Intel memory chip was static (SRAM), but was soon replaced by a dynamic (DRAM) chip. Second, the traditional strategic choice of second-sourcing manufacturing 'failed' as the chosen company could not deliver a new-generation manufacturing process. Intel was obliged to do all its own manufacturing, but also retained all the profits. This early success and

Photo: Courtesy of Intel Corporation

'luck', according to Gordon Moore, lasted nearly 20 years. Although this good fortune can be construed as luck, perhaps Intel was ahead of the silicon technology competence game – maybe without knowing it – and was expecting too much of its supplier.

Developing, manufacturing and marketing DRAM chips involved an approach to management which was structured, disciplined and controlled. Technical excellence was married with goals stipulated by senior management, which needed cross-functional discipline if they were to be reached on time. An ethos of top-down financial rigour was balanced by a culture in which those who knew what was needed to achieve the goals were never crowded out because they were junior. Knowledge was more powerful when associated with technical excellence than hierarchical position, creating an Intel ethos of constructive debate. Insofar as it existed, strategic

---

* Intel is one of the most researched companies, courtesy of a highly productive partnership between once CEO and subsequent Chairman of Intel, Andy Grove, and Robert Burgelman, a Professor of Management at Stanford University Graduate School of Business.

planning was fairly informal: ideas bubbled up from engineers and marketers which top management assessed and allocated funds to. Recruitment processes focused on hiring staff suited to the Intel culture, and rewards were associated with high performance.

Epoch II

Come the early 1980s, Intel moved towards a different era, courtesy of a more crowded marketplace. Over 10 years, the big earner, DRAM, lost market share from 83 per cent to 1.3 per cent and amounted to only 5 per cent of Intel's revenue, down from 90 per cent. Innovation moved towards the equipment manufacturers away from the chip suppliers and professional buyers sought much tougher deals. Competition had heated up with choices having to be made as to which technical areas to excel in.

At this time Intel made a decision to distance geographically its three main product development areas, DRAM, EPROM (its most profitable product in the mid-1980s) and microprocessors. In the case of microprocessors, the development of which had begun in Epoch I, the new basis of advantage increasingly became chip design rather than manufacturing process as it was in the other areas.

Over time DRAM lost manufacturing capacity within Intel to the unplanned microprocessor area. A rule, created by the first financial director and designed to maintain Intel as a technological leading-edge company, stipulated that manufacturing capacity was allocated in proportion to the profit margins achieved in the different product sectors. The emphasis within the DRAM group was on finding sophisticated technical solutions to DRAM's problems; it was, however, innovation in markets where innovation was no longer commercially viable. DRAM managers none the less fought to have manufacturing capacity assigned purely to DRAM, proposing that capacity be allocated on the basis of manufacturing cost. Senior management refused.

Once this decision was made to keep the resource allocation rule, the strategic freedom left to corporate managers to recover the founding businesses, SCRAM and DRAM, to which they were very attached, diminished as market share fell beyond what could be deemed worthwhile recovering. DRAM managers had to compete internally with the technological prowess

of the other product areas where morale and excitement were at high levels and innovation was happening in an increasingly dynamic market. And as microprocessors gradually became more profitable, manufacturing capacity and investment were increasingly allocated away from memory towards them. Eventually corporate managers realised that Intel would never be a player in the 64K DRAM chip game, despite having been the creator of the business. In 1985, top management came to realise they had to withdraw from the DRAM market. In 1986, Intel made a net loss of $173m (≈ €150m; £103m) and lost nearly a third of its workforce.

However, lingering resistance to the exit continued. Manufacturing personnel ignored implications of exiting from DRAM by trying to show they could compete in the marketplace externally, by explaining failure in terms of the strong dollar against the Japanese yen and battling with poor morale. Eventually Andy Grove, CEO from 1987, took the executive decision to withdraw from EPROM, leaving no doubt that microprocessors now represented Intel's future strategic direction. The subsequent exit from EPROM was rapidly executed. Staff associated with EPROM left and set up their own start-up.

The period pre and post the exiting of DRAM was turbulent. Although seemingly messy, it gave rise to a great deal of new thinking. A new link was created between manufacturing and technology, trying to rid the company of the rivalries established in the era of internal competition between DRAM and other technology areas and return to the era of collaboration. The approach to technology was also rethought and moved away from being so product based. Product definition and design as well as sales and marketing became more important, manufacturing less so. Corporate strategy came into line with market developments and middle management priorities; and formal strategic planning processes and corporate management's statements of strategy began to champion microprocessors.

That said, the potential of the PC was not recognised immediately. Indeed, a presentation made by a newly recruited manager on that potential failed to grab the attention of managers. Later Intel managers reflected this was because the presenter, although enthusiastic, appeared to be 'an amateur'. Had that same analytical content been presented by a 'smooth-talker', perhaps the importance of the PC market would have been taken on board sooner by corporate management.

By the mid-1990s the relatively informal processes of strategy development were becoming difficult in what had become a huge corporation. More formal strategic long-range plans were introduced where each business unit had a subcommittee which on a yearly basis developed a business plan to be submitted for approval to corporate. Whilst this added discipline, the problem was that these plans became repetitive and lacked the innovation and renewal that had driven Intel's success.

Epoch III

Intel's performance as a microprocessor company was financially spectacular. In 1998 Andy Grove became Chairman and Craig Barrett took over as CEO. Both were aware that, once again, Intel was facing new challenges. After 10 years of 30 per cent per annum compound growth, 1998 saw a slow-down. The era of the Internet had arrived and the company needed to broaden its horizons. Not only did Intel need to maintain its competence in design and product development alongside continuing manufacturing competence, but also it needed to understand more the needs of the user and develop competences in corporate venturing, allowing part or full ownership of companies with strategically important technologies. After a period of adhering strongly to its focus on microprocessors, it needed ways of regaining the entrepreneurial flourish of its former days. In any case, the business had become more complex, requiring as many chips as possible to be put along the whole value chain of the Internet moving it towards wireless and the digital home.

Barrett launched a series of seminars for Intel top management aimed at getting them to dream up new businesses and a New Business Group (NBG), with different processes and values, was founded with the brief to kickstart new internal business ventures. A framework was created to handle the interface between the NBG and the rest of the company to establish whether any proposed new business was not only strategically important externally but also built on, or required, the development of new competences internally.

The early years under Barrett saw a flourish of activity and new ventures. In the first two years these included: buying DEC's chip unit with rights to the zippy StrongARM processor, which Intel adopts for some mobile and networking products; dozens of new products in 1998, including routers and switches; the launch of the cheap Celeron chip; the establishment of a home-products group to develop web appliances and Internet-enabled TVs and set-top boxes; the acquisition of networking chipmaker Level One, specialising in chips that connect network cards to wiring; and of Dialogic, a maker of PC-based phone systems, giving Intel technology for the convergence of voice and data networks; and a home networking kit to send data over phone wiring in homes. The year of 1999 saw the launch of 13 networking chips and Intel's first web-hosting centre, with capacity for 10,000 servers and for serving hundreds of e-commerce companies; the acquisition of DSP Communications, a leader in wireless phone technology, and IPivot, a maker of gear for speeding up secure e-commerce transactions; and in 2000 the launch of seven server appliances, called the NetStructure family, to speed up and manage web traffic.

In 2002 efforts were directed at promoting wireless technology development through an investment fund which was extended in 2004 to fuel the advance of the Digital Age into people's homes making the transfer of photos, music, documents, films possible between various devices. The fund backed start-ups working in the area and was also aimed at expanding interest in the area, both technological and consumer oriented. Intel believed that PCs would be needed for storage in the digital home but saw its future in all kinds of semiconductors, not just those for PCs. For example, Intel invested in three companies: BridgeCo, which designs chips to link devices within the home; Entropic, which designed chips for networking over coaxial cable; and Musicmatch, selling software that records, organises and plays music. By how much digital appliances would complement or substitute for PCs remained to be seen, but by 2003 Intel had determined to establish itself as a leader in the design, marketing and selling of chips.

In 2004 it was announced that in 2005 Paul S. Otellini, who does not have the engineering background of Barrett, would take over from him as CEO, who would take over as Chairman, making Andy Grove Chairman Emeritus. *Business Week* commented:

In this new age of 'Think Intel Everywhere', not just inside the PC, Intel will face tough competition, as it enters the communication, entertainment and wireless sectors whilst also defending its flank from other microprocessor companies such as AMD. . . . Whilst remaining driven by innovation Barrett and Otellini have spent time trying to learn from past mistakes, to become more market savvy, forging closer relationship with customers to avoid designing products no one desires, becoming more cooperative and less arrogant whilst also investing in five new factories in 2005.

Sources:

R.A. Burgelman, *Strategy as Destiny: How strategy-making shapes a company's Future*, Free Press, 2002; R.A. Burgelman, 'Strategy as vector and the inertia of coevolutionary lock-in', *Administrative Science Quarterly*, vol. 47 (2002), pp. 325–358; *Business Week*, 13 March (2000), pp. 110–119.

Business Week, online (http://www.businessweek.com/technology/content/) (7 January 2004); O. Kharif, 'Intel bets big on the digital home', *Business Week*, 7 January (2004); *Business Week*, online (http://www.businessweek.com/technology/content/jan2004/tc2004017r7492rtc057.htm) (2 March 2004).

'What is CEO Craig Barrett up to? Hint: It's about much more than computers', *Business Week*, 8 March (2004), pp. 56–64.

Questions

1 Identify the different strategy development processes operating in Intel. How different/similar were these processes within and between the different epochs?

2 How effective were these different processes? What effect did these processes have on Intel's performance?

3 What were the tensions between processes within each epoch?

4 What proposals would you make as to the most appropriate strategy development processes that should exist as Intel moves into a more and more diversified business model?

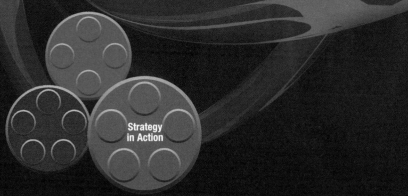

Organising for Success

LEARNING OUTCOMES

After reading this chapter you should be able to:

→ Identify key challenges in organising for success, including ensuring control, managing knowledge, coping with change and responding to internationalisation.

→ Analyse main structural types of organisations in terms of their strengths and weaknesses.

→ Recognise how important organisational processes (such as planning systems and performance targets) need to be designed to fit their circumstances.

→ Appreciate how internal and external relationships can integrate knowledge and resources within and between organisations.

→ Recognise how the three strands of structure, processes and relationships should reinforce each other in organisational configurations and the managerial dilemmas involved.

12.1   INTRODUCTION

Perhaps the most important resource of an organisation is its *people*. So the structural roles people play, the processes through which they interact and the relationships that they build are crucial to the success of strategy. These are all issues of 'organisational design'. Recalling Yahoo!'s 'Peanut Butter Manifesto' from Chapter 1, organisational design can be a critical issue in the success and failure of organisations. Yahoo! was failing partly because the business unit structure created overlapping responsibilities, organisational 'silos' were fragmenting necessary internal relationships, and organisational processes were not working well to hold managers accountable for performance.

Views about designing organisations are changing in today's world. Traditionally management scientists have emphasised formal structures.[1] This formal approach suited a top-down, command-and-control view of strategy, where managers at the top made the decisions and the rest of the organisation simply implemented them. The key debate in Illustration 12.6 questions whether formal structures can really adapt to strategy in this simple way. In a world where key knowledge is held by employees at all levels in the organisation, and where change is constant, relying on formal top-down structures may no longer be enough.

A fast-moving, knowledge-intensive world raises two issues for organisations. First, a static concept of formal structure is less and less appropriate. Organisations are constantly having to reorganise themselves in response to changing conditions. For this reason some authors suggest that we should use the *verb* 'organising' more than the *noun* 'organisation'.[2] Second, harnessing the valuable knowledge that lies throughout the organisation requires more than top-down formal hierarchies. Informal relationships and processes are vital to generating and sharing the in-depth knowledge that is now often fundamental to competitive advantage.

This chapter takes on board new thinking about organisational design both by emphasising change and by including informal processes and relationships alongside the formal. An important idea here is that formal structures and processes need to be aligned with informal processes and relationships into coherent *configurations*. An organisation's **configuration** consists of the structures, processes and relationships through which the organisation operates[3] – as shown in Exhibit 12.1. Configuring the organisation so that all these elements fit both together and with key strategic challenges is crucial to organisational success.

> An organisation's **configuration** consists of the structures, processes and relationships through which the organisation operates

Exhibit 12.1 shows the three strands of an organisation's configuration, locking together into a coherent 'virtuous circle'. These three strands provide the structure for the first parts of the chapter, addressing in turn:

● The *structural design* (describing formal roles, responsibilities and lines of reporting) in organisations. Structural design can deeply influence the sources of an organisation's advantage, particularly with regard to knowledge management; failure to adjust structures appropriately can fatally undermine strategy implementation. But good structure alone is not enough for success.

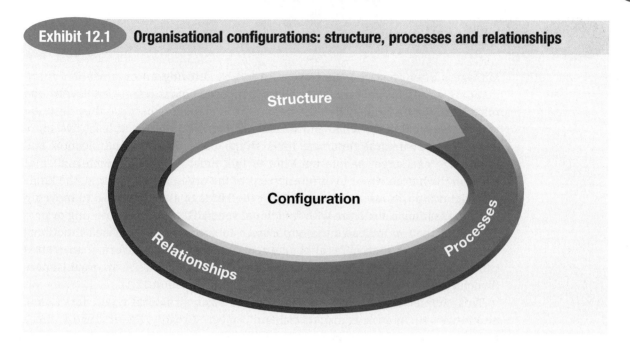

Exhibit 12.1 Organisational configurations: structure, processes and relationships

- The *processes* that drive and support people within and around an organisation. These processes too can have a major influence on success or failure, defining how strategies are made and controlled and the ways that managers and other employees interact and implement strategy in action.

- The *relationships* that connect people both within and outside the organisation, in particular:
  - relationships between organisational units and the centre (this relates to discussions in Chapter 7 about the role of corporate parents);
  - relationships outside the firm, including issues such as *outsourcing* (raised in Chapter 3) and *strategic alliances* (raised in Chapter 8).

The various structures, processes and relationships will be considered in the light of three key challenges for organisations in the twenty-first century:

- The *speed of change* and the increased levels of *uncertainty* in the business environment, as discussed in Chapter 2. As a result, organisations need to have flexible designs and be skilled at reorganising.

- The importance of *knowledge creation* and *knowledge sharing* as a fundamental ingredient of strategic success, as discussed in Chapter 3. Organisational designs should both foster concentrations of expertise and encourage people to share their knowledge.

- The rise of *internationalisation*, as discussed in Chapter 8. Organising for an international context has many challenges: communicating across wider geography, coordinating more diversity and building relationships across diverse cultures are some examples. Internationalisation also brings greater recognition of different kinds of organising around the world.

12.2   STRUCTURAL TYPES

Managers often describe their organisation by drawing an organisation chart, mapping out its formal structure. These structural charts define the 'levels' and roles in an organisation. They are important to managers because they describe who is responsible for what. But formal structures matter in at least two more ways. First, structural reporting lines shape patterns of communication and knowledge exchange: people tend not to talk much to people much higher or lower in the hierarchy, or in different parts of the organisation. Second, the kinds of structural positions at the top suggest the kinds of skills required to move up the organisation: a structure with functional specialists such as marketing or production at the top indicates the importance to success of specialised functional disciplines rather than general business experience. In short, formal structures can reveal a great deal about the role of knowledge and skills in an organisation. Structures can therefore be hotly debated (see Illustration 12.1).

This chapter begins with a review of five basic structural types: functional, multidivisional, matrix, transnational and project.[4] Broadly, the first two of these tend to emphasise one structural dimension over another, either functional specialisms or business units. The three that follow tend to mix structural dimensions more evenly, for instance trying to give product and geographical units equal weight. However, none of these structures is a universal solution to the challenges of organising. Rather, the right structure depends on the particular kinds of challenges each organisation faces.

Researchers propose a wide number of important challenges (sometimes called 'contingencies') shaping organisational structure, including organisational size, extent of diversification and type of technology.[5] This chapter will particularly focus on how the five structural types fit both the traditional challenge of control and the three new challenges of change, knowledge and internationalisation. This implies that the first step in organisational design is deciding what the key challenges facing the organisation actually are. As we shall see later, the configurational approach stresses that whatever structure is chosen should also be aligned with matching processes and relationships.

12.2.1   The functional structure

A functional structure is based on the primary activities that have to be undertaken by an organisation such as production, finance and accounting, marketing, human resources and research and development

Once an organisation grows beyond a very basic level of size and complexity, it has to start dividing up responsibilities. One fundamental kind of structure is the **functional structure**, which divides responsibilities according to the organisation's primary roles such as production, research and sales. Exhibit 12.2 represents a typical organisation chart for such a business. This structure is usually found in smaller companies, or those with narrow, rather than diverse, product ranges. Also, within a multidivisional structure (see below), the divisions themselves may be split up into functional departments (as in Exhibit 12.3 below).

Exhibit 12.2 also summarises the potential advantages and disadvantages of a functional structure. There are advantages in that it gives senior managers direct hands-on involvement in operations and allows greater operational control from the top. The functional structure provides a clear definition of roles and tasks,

KEY
CONCEPT

Structures

Illustration 12.1

Volkswagen: a case of centralisation

A new chief executive introduces a more centralised structure over this multi-brand giant.

In 2007, following the Porsche car company's building up of a controlling stake and the installation of a new chief executive, German car manufacturer Volkswagen announced a major reorganisation. For the previous few years, Volkswagen had been organised as two groups of brands under the main Volkswagen and Audi labels (see Figure 1), with technical and marketing expertise clustered around particular brands within these. Now the company was to be reorganised into two main groups, a mass market group (VW, Skoda, SEAT) and a more luxury market group (Audi, Bentley, Bugatti and Lamborghini). Volkswagen also had a large stake in truck company Scania. The company would be more centralised, with new corporate responsibilities for production, sales, distribution and R&D (see Figure 2). The new CEO, Martin Winterkorn, would also act as head of R&D and be directly responsible for the VW group of brands.

The stated aim of this more centralised structure was to increase synergies between the various brands. More centralised R&D would help ensure the sharing of engines and components, and

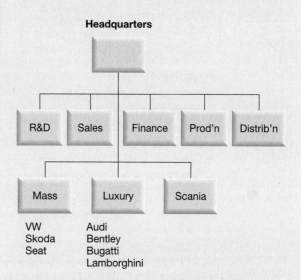

Figure 2 Volkswagen, January 2007 (simplifed)

centralisation of production would assist the optimisation of factory usage across the company. The departing head of the Volkswagen group took another view. He asserted that, in order to ensure cross-functional integration and motivation, expertise needed to identify closely with particular brands. According to him, the new structure mimicked the centralised Porsche structure, but Porsche was a much smaller company with just one main brand. Porsche's spokespersons responded by recalling that Porsche was the most profitable car company in the world, while Volkswagen was one of the least.

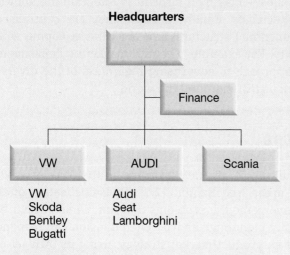

Figure 1 Volkswagen, November 2006 (simplified)

Questions

1 Which type of structure did the old decentralised structure resemble most and which type of structure is Volkswagen moving closer to?

2 What pros and cons can you see in the new Volkswagen structure?

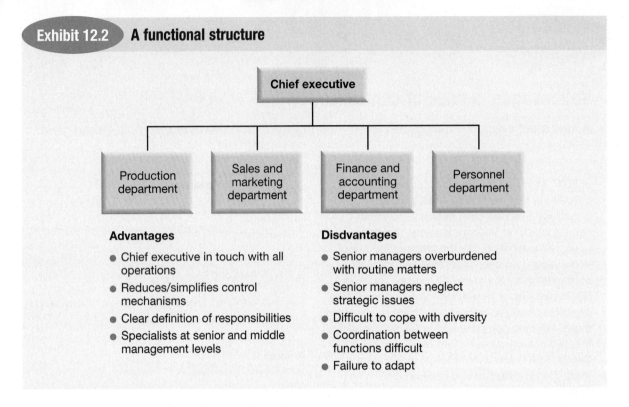

Exhibit 12.2   A functional structure

Advantages

- Chief executive in touch with all operations
- Reduces/simplifies control mechanisms
- Clear definition of responsibilities
- Specialists at senior and middle management levels

Disdvantages

- Senior managers overburdened with routine matters
- Senior managers neglect strategic issues
- Difficult to cope with diversity
- Coordination between functions difficult
- Failure to adapt

increasing accountability. Functional departments also provide concentrations of expertise, thus fostering knowledge development in areas of functional specialism.

However, there are disadvantages, particularly as organisations become larger or more diverse. Perhaps the major concern in a fast-moving world is that senior managers focus on their functional responsibilities, becoming overburdened with routine operations and too concerned with narrow functional interests. As a result, they find it hard either to take a strategic view of the organisation as a whole or to manage coordinated responses quickly. Thus functional organisations can be inflexible. Separate functional departments tend also to be inward looking – so-called 'functional silos' – making it difficult to integrate the knowledge of different functional specialists. Finally, because they are centralised around particular functions, functional structures are not good at coping with product or geographical diversity. For example, a central marketing department may try to impose a uniform approach to advertising regardless of the diverse needs of the organisation's various SBUs around the world.

12.2.2 The multidivisional structure

A multidivisional structure is built up of separate divisions on the basis of products, services or geographical areas

A **multidivisional structure** is built up of separate divisions on the basis of products, services or geographical areas (see Exhibit 12.3). Divisionalisation often comes about as an attempt to overcome the problems that functional structures have in dealing with the diversity mentioned above.[6] Each division can respond to the specific requirements of its product/market strategy, using its own set of functional departments. A similar situation exists in many public services, where the organisation is structured around *service departments* such as recreation, social services and education.

Exhibit 12.3   A multidivisional structure

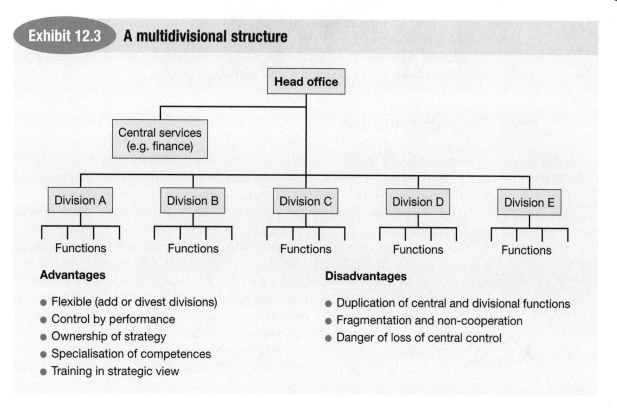

Advantages

- Flexible (add or divest divisions)
- Control by performance
- Ownership of strategy
- Specialisation of competences
- Training in strategic view

Disadvantages

- Duplication of central and divisional functions
- Fragmentation and non-cooperation
- Danger of loss of central control

There are several potential advantages to divisional structures. They are flexible in the sense that organisations can add, close or merge divisions as circumstances change. As self-standing business units, it is possible to control divisions from a distance by monitoring business performance. Divisional managers have greater personal ownership for their own divisional strategies. Geographical divisions – for example, a European division or a North American division – offer a means of managing internationally. There can be benefits of specialisation within a division, allowing competences to develop with a clearer focus on a particular product group, technology or customer group. Management responsibility for a whole divisional business is good training in taking a strategic view for managers expecting to go on to a main board position.

However, divisional structures can also have disadvantages of three main types. First, divisions can become so self-sufficient that they are *de facto* independent businesses, but duplicating the functions and costs of the corporate centre of the company. So it may make more sense to split the company into independent businesses, and demergers of this type have been very common. Second, divisionalisation tends to get in the way of cooperation and knowledge sharing between business units: divisions can quite literally divide. Expertise is fragmented and divisional performance targets provide poor incentives to collaborate with other divisions. Finally, divisions may become too autonomous, especially where joint ventures and partnership dilute ownership. In these cases, multidivisionals degenerate into *holding companies*, where the corporate centre effectively 'holds' the various businesses in a largely financial sense, exercising little control and adding very little value. Exhibit 12.3 summarises these potential advantages and disadvantages of a multidivisional structure.

Large and complex multidivisional companies often have a second tier of *subdivisions* within their main divisions. Treating smaller SBUs as subdivisions within a large division reduces the number of units that the corporate centre has to deal with directly. Subdivisions can also help complex organisations respond to contradictory pressures. For example, an organisation could have geographical subdivisions within a set of global product divisions.

12.2.3 The matrix structure

A **matrix structure** is a combination of structures which could take the form of product and geographical divisions or functional and divisional structures operating in tandem

A **matrix structure** combines different structural dimensions simultaneously, for example product divisions and geographical territories or product divisions and functional specialisms.[7] Exhibit 12.4 gives examples of such a structure.

Matrix structures have several advantages. They are effective at knowledge management because they allow separate areas of knowledge to be integrated across organisational boundaries. Particularly in professional service organisations, matrix organisation can be helpful in applying particular knowledge specialisms to different market or geographical segments. For example, to serve a particular client, a consulting firm may draw on people from groups with particular knowledge specialisms (for example, strategy or organisation design) and others grouped according to particular markets (industry sectors or geographical regions).[8] Exhibit 12.4 shows how a school might combine the separate knowledge of subject specialists to create programmes of study tailored differently to various age groups. Matrix organisations are flexible, because they allow different dimensions of the organisation to be mixed together. They are particularly attractive to organisations operating globally, because of the possible mix between local and global dimensions. For example, a global company may prefer geographically defined divisions as the operating units for local marketing (because of their specialist local knowledge of customers). But at the same time it may still want global product divisions responsible for the worldwide coordination of product development and manufacturing, taking advantage of economies of scale and specialisation.

However, because a matrix structure replaces formal lines of authority with (cross-matrix) relationships, this often brings problems. In particular, it will typically take *longer to reach decisions* because of bargaining between the managers of different dimensions. There may also be *conflict* because staff find themselves responsible to managers from two structural dimensions. In short, matrix organisations are hard to control.

As with any structure, but particularly with the matrix structure, the critical issue in practice is the way it actually works (that is, the processes and relationships). The key ingredient in a successful matrix structure can be senior managers good at sustaining collaborative relationships (across the matrix) and coping with the messiness and ambiguity which that can bring. It is for this reason that Christopher Bartlett and Sumantra Ghoshal describe the matrix as involving a 'state of mind' as much as a formal structure.[9]

12.2.4 The transnational structure

The **transnational structure** is a means of managing internationally which is particularly effective in exploiting knowledge across borders. The transnational

Exhibit 12.4   Two examples of matrix structures

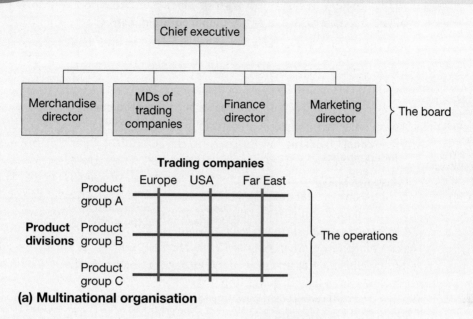

(a) Multinational organisation

(b) School

Advantages	Disadvantages
● Integrate knowledge	● Length of time to take decisions
● Flexible	● Unclear job and task responsibilities
● Allow dual dimensions	● Unclear cost and profit responsibilities
	● High degrees of conflict

A transnational structure combines the local responsiveness of the international subsidiary with the coordination advantages found in global product companies

structure seeks to obtain the best from the two extreme international strategies, the multidomestic strategy and the global strategy (see Chapter 8). As in Exhibit 12.5, a global strategy would typically be supported by global product divisions (for example, a worldwide cars division and a worldwide lorries division); a multidomestic strategy would be supported by local subsidiaries with a great deal of design, manufacturing and marketing autonomy for all products (for example, the local subsidiary responsible for both cars and lorries). In the exhibit, international divisions refer to stand-alone divisions tacked

Exhibit 12.5 **Multinational structures**

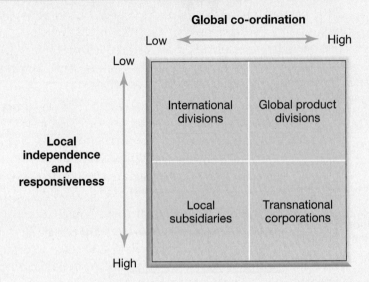

alongside the structures of the major home-based business, as is often the case with American corporations as they start to internationalise (for example, in North America having car and lorry divisions, while overseas both businesses would be handled by the international division). The transnational structure, however, attempts to achieve both high local responsiveness and high global coordination.

As Bartlett and Ghoshal describe it, the transnational is like a matrix but has two specific features: first, it responds specifically to the challenge of internationalisation; second, it tends to have more fixed responsibilities within its cross-cutting dimensions.[9] The transnational has the following detailed characteristics:

- Each national unit operates independently, but is a *source of ideas and capabilities* for the whole corporation. For example, in Unilever, the centre for innovation in hair-care products worldwide is in France.[9]

- National units achieve greater scale economies through *specialisation* on behalf of the whole corporation, or at least large regions. Unilever in Europe has replaced its web of small national food manufacturing units with a few specialised larger factories that export its products to other European countries.

- The *corporate centre* manages this global network by first establishing the role of each business unit, then sustaining the systems, relationships and culture to make the network of business units operate effectively. Unilever has established a system of 'forums' bringing managers together internationally to help them swap experience and coordinate their needs.

The success of a transnational corporation is dependent on the ability *simultaneously* to achieve global competences, local responsiveness and organisation-wide innovation and learning. This requires clarity as to boundaries, relationships and the roles that the various managers need to perform. For example:

- *Global business managers* have the overriding responsibility to further the company's global competitiveness, which will cross both national and functional boundaries. They must be the *product/market strategist*, the *architect* of the business resources and competences, the *driver of product innovation* and the *coordinator* of transnational transactions.

- *Country or area managers* have potentially a dual responsibility to other parts of the transnational. First, they must act as a *sensor* of local needs and feed these back to those responsible internationally for new products or services. Second, they should seek to *build* unique competences: that is, become a centre of excellence which allows them to be a *contributor* to the company as a whole, in manufacturing or research and development, for instance.

- *Functional managers* such as finance or IT have a major responsibility for ensuring worldwide innovation and learning across the various parts of the organisation. This requires the skill to recognise and spread best practice across the organisation. So they must be able to *scan* the organisation for best practice, *cross-pollinate* this best practice and be the *champion* of innovations.

- *Corporate (head office) managers* integrate these other roles and responsibilities. Not only are they the *leaders*, but they are also the *talent spotters* among business, country and functional managers, facilitating the interplay between them. For example, they must foster the processes of innovation and knowledge creation. They are responsible for the *development* of a strong management centre in the organisation.

There are some disadvantages to a transnational structure. It is very demanding of managers in terms of willingness to work not just at their immediate responsibilities but for the good of the transnational as a whole. Diffuse responsibilities also make for similar complexities and control problems to those of the matrix organisation. The Swiss–Swedish engineering giant ABB was often used as a model for the transnational during the 1990s, but at the beginning of this century the company restructured along clearer product divisional lines.[10] Strengthening the product divisions over the country managers was intended to reduce internal politics and simplify international coordination.

12.2.5   Project-based structures[10]

A project-based
structure is one where
teams are created,
undertake the work and
are then dissolved

Many organisations rely heavily on project teams with a finite life span. A **project-based structure** is one where teams are created, undertake the work (for example, internal or external contracts) and are then dissolved.[11] This can be particularly appropriate for organisations that deliver large and expensive goods or services (civil engineering, information systems, films) or those delivering time-limited events (conferences, sporting events or consulting engagements). The organisation structure is a constantly changing collection of project teams created, steered and glued together loosely by a small corporate group. Many organisations use such teams in a more ad hoc way to complement the 'main' structure. For example, *taskforces* are set up to make progress on new elements of strategy or to provide momentum where the regular structure of the organisation is not effective.

The project-based structure can be highly flexible, with projects being set up and dissolved as required. Because project teams should have clear tasks to achieve within a defined life, accountability and control are good. As project team members will typically be drawn from different departments within the firm, projects can be effective at knowledge exchange. Projects can also draw members internationally and, because project life spans are typically short, project teams may be more willing to work temporarily around the world. There are disadvantages, however. Without strong programme management providing overarching strategic control, organisations are prone to proliferate projects in an ill-coordinated fashion. The constant breaking up of project teams can also hinder the accumulation of knowledge over time or within specialisms.

Overall, project-based structures have been growing in importance because of their inherent flexibility. Such flexibility can be vital in a fast-moving world where individual knowledge and competences need to be redeployed and integrated quickly and in novel ways.

12.2.6 Choosing structures

At the beginning of this chapter we stressed the challenges of control, change, knowledge and internationalisation for organisational design today. From our discussion so far, it should be clear that functional, multidivisional, matrix, transnational and project structures each have their own advantages and disadvantages with regard to these four challenges. Organisational designers, therefore, have to choose structures according to the particular strategic challenges (or 'contingencies') they face.

Exhibit 12.6 summarises how the five basic structures meet the challenges of control, change, knowledge and inernationalisation introduced at the beginning of the chapter. No structure scores high across all four challenges. Organisational designers face choices. If they seek control, but are less concerned for flexibility in response to change or global reach, then they might prefer a functional structure. If they want to foster knowledge and flexibility on a global scale,

---

Exhibit 12.6   **Comparison of structures**

Challenge	Functional	Multidivisional	Matrix	Transnational	Project
Control	★★★	★★	★	★★	★★
Change	★	★★	★★★	★★★	★★★
Knowledge	★★	★	★★★	★★★	★★
Internationalisation	★	★★	★★★	★★★	★★

★ Stars indicate typical capacities to cope with each challenge, with three stars indicating high, two indicating medium and one indicating poor.

then they might consider a matrix or transnational structure. Structural choice depends on the strategic challenges the organisation faces.

In reality, few organisations adopt a structure that is just like one of the pure structural types discussed above. Structures often blend different types (see section 12.5) and have to be tailor-made to the particular mix of challenges facing the organisation. Michael Goold and Andrew Campbell provide *nine design tests* against which to check specific tailor-made structural solutions.[12] The first four tests stress fit with the key objectives and constraints of the organisation:

- *The Market-Advantage Test*. This test of fit with market strategy is fundamental, following Alfred Chandler's classic principle that 'structure follows strategy'.[13] For example, if coordination between two steps in a production process is important to market advantage, then they should probably be placed in the same structural unit.

- *The Parenting Advantage Test*. The structural design should fit the 'parenting' role of the corporate centre (see Chapter 7). For example, if the corporate centre aims to add value as a synergy manager, then it should design a structure that places important integrative specialisms, such as marketing or research, at the centre.

- *The People Test*. The structural design must fit the people available. It is dangerous to switch completely from a functional structure to a multidivisional structure if, as is likely, the organisation lacks managers with competence in running decentralised business units.

- *The Feasibility Test*. This is a catch-all category, indicating that the structure must fit legal, stakeholder, trade union or similar constraints. For example, after scandals involving biased research, investment banks are now required by financial regulators to separate their research and analysis departments from their deal-making departments.

Goold and Campbell then propose five tests based on good general design principles, as follows:

- *The Specialised Cultures Test*. This test reflects the value of bringing together specialists so that they can develop their expertise in close collaboration with each other. A structure fails if it breaks up important specialist cultures.

- *The Difficult Links Test*. This test asks whether a proposed structure will set up links between parts of the organisations that are important but bound to be strained. For example, extreme decentralisation to profit-accountable business units is likely to strain relationships with a central research and development department. Unless compensating mechanisms are put in place, this kind of structure is likely to fail.

- *The Redundant Hierarchy Test*. Any structural design should be checked in case it has too many layers of management, causing undue blockages and expense. Delayering in response to redundant hierarchies has been an important structural trend in recent years.

- *The Accountability Test*. This test stresses the importance of clear lines of accountability, ensuring the control and commitment of managers throughout the structure. Because of their dual lines of reporting, matrix structures are often accused of lacking clear accountability.

● *The Flexibility Test.* In a fast-moving world, an important test is the extent to which a design will allow for change in the future. For instance, divisional domains should be specified broadly enough to allow divisional managers to follow new opportunities as they emerge. As Kathleen Eisenhardt puts it, structures should also have enough 'modularity' (that is, standardisation) to allow easy 'patching' of one part of the organisation onto another part of the organisation, as market needs change.[14]

Goold and Campbell's nine tests provide a rigorous screen for effective structures. But even if the structural design passes these tests, the structure still needs to be matched to the other strands of the organisation's configuration, its processes and relationships. Each strand will have to reinforce the others. The following two sections introduce processes and relationships in turn.

12.3 PROCESSES

Structure is a key ingredient of organising for success. But within any structure, what makes organisations work are the formal and informal organisational processes.[15] These processes can be thought of as controls on the organisation's operations and can therefore help or hinder the translation of strategy into action.

Control processes can be subdivided in two ways. First, they tend to emphasise either control over inputs or control over outputs. Input control processes concern themselves with the *resources* consumed in the strategy, especially financial resources and human commitment. Output control processes focus on ensuring satisfactory *results*, for example the meeting of targets or achieving market competitiveness. The second subdivision is between direct and indirect controls. Direct controls involve *close supervision* or monitoring. Indirect controls are more *hands-off*, setting up the conditions whereby desired behaviours are achieved semi-automatically. How the six processes we shall consider emphasise either input or output controls or direct or indirect controls is summarised in Exhibit 12.7.

Organisations normally use a blend of these control processes, but some will dominate over others according to the strategic challenges. Again, capacities to cope with change, knowledge and internationalisation are important. As we shall

Exhibit 12.7 **Types of control processes**

	Input	Output
Direct	Direct supervision Planning processes	Performance targeting
Indirect	Cultural processes Self-control	Internal markets

see, input measures tend to require that the controllers have high levels of knowledge of what the controlled are supposed to do. In many knowledge-intensive organisations, especially those generating innovation and change, controllers rarely have a good understanding of what their expert employees are doing, and tend to rely more on output controls. At least they can know when a unit has made its revenue or profitability targets. Direct control relies heavily on the physical presence of management, although now surveillance through IT can substitute. For this reason, international organisations may make use of indirect controls for their geographically dispersed subsidiaries. On the other hand, direct control processes can be very effective for small organisations on a single site.

12.3.1 Direct supervision

Direct supervision is the direct control of strategic decisions by one or a few individuals

Direct supervision is the direct control of strategic decisions by one or a few individuals, typically focused on the effort put into the business by employees. It is a dominant process in small organisations. It can also exist in larger organisations where little change is occurring and if the complexity of the business is not too great for a small number of managers to control the strategy *in detail* from the centre. This is often found in family businesses and in parts of the public sector with a history of 'hands-on' political involvement (often where a single political party has dominated for a long period).

Direct supervision requires that the controllers thoroughly understand what is entailed by the jobs they supervise. They must be able to correct errors, but not cramp innovative experiments. Direct supervision is easiest on a single site, although long-distance monitoring (for instance, of trading strategies in banking) is now possible through electronic means. Direct supervision can also be effective during a *crisis*, when autocratic control through direct supervision may be necessary to achieve quick results. Turnaround managers are often autocratic in style.

12.3.2 Planning processes

Planning processes plan and control the allocation of resources and monitor their utilisation

Planning processes are the archetypal administrative control, where the successful implementation of strategies is achieved through processes that plan and control the allocation of resources and monitor their utilisation (see also Chapter 11). The focus is on controlling the organisation's inputs, particularly financial. A plan would cover all parts of the organisation and show clearly, in financial terms, the level of resources allocated to each area (whether that be functions, divisions or business units). It would also show the detailed ways in which this resource was to be used. This would usually take the form of a *budget*. For example, the marketing function may be allocated €5m (£3.45m) but will need to show how this will be spent, for example the proportions spent on staff, advertising, exhibitions and so on. These cost items would then be monitored regularly to measure actual spend against plan.

One strength of this planned approach to strategic control is the ability to monitor the implementation of strategy. The detailed way in which planning can support strategy varies:

- Planning can be achieved by *standardisation of work processes (such as product or service features)*. Sometimes these work processes are subject to a rigorous framework of assessment and review – for example, to meet externally audited quality standards (such as ISO 9000). In many service organisations such 'routinisation' has been achieved through IT systems leading to de-skilling of service delivery and significant reductions in cost. This can give competitive advantage where organisations are positioning on low price with commodity-like products or services. For example, the cost of transactions in Internet banking is a fraction of that of transactions made through branches.

- *Enterprise resource planning (ERP) systems,*[16] supplied by software specialists such as SAP or Oracle, use sophisticated IT to achieve planning-type control. These systems aim to integrate the entire business operations, including personnel, finance, manufacturing operations, warehousing, etc. This started with the use of EPOS (Electronic Point Of Sale) systems in retail outlets, which linked back into stock control. Further advantage may be gained if these systems can stretch more widely in the value system beyond the boundaries of the organisation into the supply and distribution chains – for example, in automatic ordering of supplies to avoid 'stockout'. E-commerce operations are taking the integrative capability further (this is discussed more fully in Chapter 9). Illustration 12.2 shows an example of enterprise resource planning.

- Centralised planning approaches often use a *formula* for controlling resource allocation within an organisation. For example, in the public services, budgets might be allocated on a per capita basis (for example, number of patients for doctors).

Planning processes work best in simple and stable conditions, where a budget or a formula can apply equally well to all the units in the organisation and where assumptions are likely to hold good for the whole of the budget or formula period. Where there is diversity in the needs of business units, standard budgets or formulae are likely to advantage some units, while handicapping others. Thus in the UK some argue that the government should no longer treat all hospitals and universities the same way: each has its own challenges and opportunities. Also budgets and formulae can be inflexible where changing circumstances contradict original assumptions. Organisations can be penalised unfairly for adverse changes in circumstances, or denied the resources to respond to opportunities unforeseen in the original budget.

Because of the dangers of insensitivity to diverse needs in the organisation, it is often helpful to involve those most directly involved in *bottom-up* planning. In 'bottom-up' planning, local business units at the 'bottom' of the organisation propose initial plans 'up' to the corporate headquarters. The role of the corporate headquarters is to set guidelines for these initial plans and review them when they arrive. Initial proposed plans are often incompatible both with other units' plans and with headquarters' expectations and resourcing capabilities. Incompatibilities are resolved through processes of *reconciliation*, typically involving bargaining and some revisiting of some of headquarters' original guidelines. There are sometimes several iterations of this proposal and review process and so, while it can take into account business unit needs better than simple central planning, bottom-up planning can be very time consuming and political.

Illustration 12.2

Enterprise resource planning (ERP) at Bharat Petroleum

ERP systems were at the heart of Bharat Petroleum's strategic transformation as it prepared for deregulation in the Indian oil industry.

Bharat Petroleum is one of India's top three refining and distribution companies. It has 4,854 gas stations, some 1,000 kerosene dealers and 1,828 liquid petroleum gas (LPG) distributors scattered all over the vast country that is India. Facing deregulation of its markets, and possibly partial privatisation, Bharat Petroleum embarked upon enterprise integration through the implementation of an SAP R/3 ERP system. The aim was to gain control over the company's operations through improved information in areas such as inventory and product despatch, all working to support better customer service and satisfaction. The new system was to cover 200 sites and include a wide range of processes from financial accounting, to personnel administration, quality management, maintenance, plant management and sales. The finance director projected cost savings alone of £5m (€7.5m) per year.

The implementation of the ERP system was not conceived simply as an information systems project. It built upon a previous delayering and restructuring of the company around six new strategic business units. The ERP implementation itself was named project ENTRANS, short for Enterprise Transformation. The head of the project team was not an information systems specialist, but a human resource professional. Only 10 members of the 60-person project team were from information systems. A project steering group, meeting at least monthly, oversaw the whole process, with the heads of all six strategic business units, finance, human resources and IT represented. The head of IT at Bharat Petroleum commented himself: 'The unique thing about Bharat Petroleum's ERP implementation is that, right from its conception, it has been a business initiative. We (IT) just performed the necessary catalytic role.'

Implementation was carried out with assistance from PricewaterhouseCoopers, 24 SAP consultants, a team of 70 in-house SAP qualified consultants and six full-time change coaches. All users were involved in training, focused on improving 'organisational learning' and Visionary Leadership and Planning Programmes. Bharat Petroleum's chairman declared there would be no reduction in the workforce as a direct result of ERP, even though lower staff costs were included in the benefits case.

Implementation was scheduled over 24 months, with pilots selected carefully on the basis of proximity to the project team (based in Mumbai), salience of the processes involved, and business and IT-readiness. Many initial teething problems were encountered. Informal processes were not always fully incorporated into the new SAP system, with awkward consequences. However, plant managers felt that ERP's formalisation of processes did eventually contribute greatly to increasing discipline amongst staff. In the year after completion of the implementation, Bharat Petroleum achieved 24 per cent sales growth. SAP itself rated Bharat Petroleum as in the top quartile of SAP ERP implementations.

Source: A. Teltumbde, A. Tripathy and A. Sahu, 'Bharat Petrolem Corporation Limited', *Vikalpa*, vol. 27, no. 3 (2002), pp. 45–58.

Questions

1 What is the significance of the ERP implementation not being headed by an information systems expert?

2 What possible dangers might there be in the formalisation and embedding of detailed business processes in an ERP system?

3 What should a company like Bharat Petroleum do with the large team of specialised in-house consultants and coaches once the ERP implementation project is completed?

12.3.3 **Cultural processes**

With rapid change, increasing complexity and the need to exploit knowledge, employee motivation is increasingly important to performance. Under these pressures, promoting *self-control* and personal motivation can be an effective means of control, influencing the quality of employee input without direct intervention. Many workers have naturally a strong degree of self-control and motivation that can help ensure appropriate kinds of performance for the strategy: for instance, musicians or doctors, who have strong commitment to craft or professional standards. However, craft or professional standards can also deviate from what the organisation's strategy demands, and some workers will shirk in any case. Here managers can use cultural processes to achieve appropriate kinds of performance.[17]

Cultural processes are concerned with organisational culture and the *standardisation of norms* (as discussed in Chapter 5). Control is indirect, internalised as employees become part of the culture. Control is exerted on the input of employees, as the culture defines norms of appropriate effort and initiative. Three processes are particularly important in shaping appropriate cultures: *recruitment*, the selection of appropriate staff in the first place; *socialisation*, the integration of new staff through training, induction and mentoring programmes, for example, but also through informal influences such as role models; and *reward*, in other words, recognising appropriate behaviour through pay, promotion or symbolic processes (for example, public praise). These cultural processes often meet subtle kinds of resistance by employees, for example cynicism and 'going-through-the-motions', and once instituted become hard to change as strategies evolve. Organisations have many cultural processes that are not within formal management control, such as peer group pressure not to respond to organisational strategies.

None the less, cultural processes are particularly important in organisations facing complex and dynamic environments. Sometime these positive cultural processes happen without deliberate management intervention. Collaborative cultures can foster 'communities of practice', in which expert practitioners inside or even outside the organisation share their knowledge to generate innovative solutions to problems on their own initiative.[18] These informal, self-starting communities range from the Xerox photocopying engineers who would exchange information about problems and solutions over breakfast gatherings at the start of the day, to the programmer networks which support the development of Linux 'freeware' internationally over the Internet.

12.3.4 **Performance targeting processes**

Performance targets relate to the *outputs* of an organisation (or part of an organisation), such as product quality, prices or profit

Performance targets focus on the *outputs* of an organisation (or part of an organisation), such as product quality, revenues or profits. These targets are often known as key performance indicators (KPIs). The performance of an organisation is judged, either internally or externally, on its ability to meet these targets. However, within specified boundaries, the organisation remains free on how targets should be achieved. This approach can be particularly appropriate in certain situations:

- *Within large businesses*, corporate centres may choose performance targets to control their business units without getting involved in the details of how they achieve them. These targets are often cascaded down the organisation as specific targets for sub-units, functions and even individuals.

- In *regulated markets*, such as privatised utilities in the UK and elsewhere, government-appointed regulators increasingly exercise control through agreed *performance indicators* (PIs), such as service or quality levels, as a means of ensuring 'competitive' performance.[19]

- In *the public services*, where control of resource inputs was the dominant approach historically, governments are attempting to move control processes towards outputs (such as quality of service) and, more importantly, towards outcomes (for example, patient mortality rates in health care, as previously seen in Illustration 4.7).

KEY CONCEPT

Balanced scorecards

Balanced scorecards combine both qualitative and quantitative measures, acknowledge the expectations of different stakeholders and relate an assessment of performance to choice of strategy

Many managers find it difficult to develop a useful set of targets. One reason for this is that any particular set of indicators is liable to give only a partial view of the overall picture. Also, some important indicators (such as customer satisfaction) tend to get neglected because they are hard to measure, leaving the focus on easily available data such as financial ratios. In the last decade or so, *balanced scorecards* have been increasingly used as a way of widening the scope of performance indicators.[20] **Balanced scorecards** combine both qualitative and quantitative measures, acknowledge the expectations of different stakeholders and relate an assessment of performance to choice of strategy (as shown in Exhibit 12.8

Exhibit 12.8 **The balanced scorecard: an example**

Financial perspective	
CSF*	**Measures**
Survival	Cash flow

Customer perspective	
CSF*	**Measures**
Customer service (standard products)	● Delivery time ● Maintenance response time

Internal perspective	
CSF*	**Measures**
IT systems development ● Features ● Cost	Performance per £ invested (vs. competitors)

Innovation and learning perspective	
CSF*	**Measures**
Service leadership	● Speed to market (new standards) ● Speed of imitation (robustness)

* CSF = critical success factor

Illustration 12.3

The balanced scorecard: Philips Electronics

Balanced scorecards attempt to reflect the interdependence of different performance factors – which together will determine success or failure.

Philips Electronics, with more than 250,000 employees in 150 countries, uses the balanced scorecard to manage its diverse product lines and divisions around the world. The company has identified four critical success factors (CSFs) for the organisation as a whole:

- competence (knowledge, technology, leadership and teamwork);
- processes (drivers for performance);
- customers (value propositions);
- financial (value, growth and productivity).

Philips uses these scorecard criteria at four levels: the strategy review; operations review; business unit; and the individual employee. Criteria at one level are cascaded down to more detailed criteria appropriate at each level. This helps employees understand how their day-to-day activities link ultimately to the corporate goals. At a business unit level, for example, the management team determine the local critical success factors and agree indicators for each. Targets are then set for each indicator based on the gap between present performance and desired performance for the current year plus two to four years into the future. These targets are derived from an analysis of the market and world-class performance. Targets must be specific, measurable, ambitious, realistic and time phased.

Examples of indicators at the business unit level include:

Financial
Economic profit
Income from operations
Working capital
Operational cash flow
Inventory turns

Processes
Percentage reduction in process cycle time
Number of engineering changes
Capacity utilisation
Order response time
Process capability

Customers
Rank in customer survey
Market share
Repeat order rate
Complaints
Brand index

Competence
Leadership competence
Percentage of patent-protected turnover
Training days per employee
Quality improvement team participation

Source: A. Gumbus and B. Lyons, 'The balanced scorecard at Philips Electronics', *Strategic Finance*, November (2002), pp. 45–49.

Questions

1 Imagine yourself as the chief executive of Philips Electronics and draw up a table that shows the various ways that the balanced scorecard could be used in managing your organisation.

2 Imagine yourself as an ordinary employee of Philips Electronics and list possible pros and cons of the balanced scorecard as applied to you individually.

3 What possible disadvantages or dangers might the balanced scorecard technique have for organisations?

and Illustration 12.3). Importantly, performance is linked not only to short-term outputs but also to the way in which processes are managed – for example, the processes of innovation and learning which are crucial to long-term success.

Exhibit 12.8 is an example of a balanced scorecard for a small start-up company supplying standard tools and light equipment to the engineering industry. The owner–manager's financial perspective was simply one of survival during this start-up period, requiring a positive cash flow (after the initial investments in plant, stock and premises). The strategy was to compete on customer service for both initial delivery and maintenance backup. This required core competences in order processing and maintenance scheduling underpinned by the company's IT system. These core competences were open to imitation, so, in turn, the ability to improve these service standards continuously was critical to success.

12.3.5 Market processes

Market processes
involve some formalised
system of 'contracting' for
resources

Market processes (or *internal markets*) can be brought inside organisations to control activities internally.[21] Here market processes typically involve some formalised system of 'contracting' for resources or inputs from other parts of an organisation and for supplying outputs to other parts of an organisation. Control focuses on outputs, for example revenues earned in successful competition for internal contracts. The control is indirect: rather than accepting detailed performance targets determined externally, units have simply to earn their keep in competitive internal markets.

Internal markets can be used in a variety of ways. There might be *competitive bidding*, perhaps through the creation of an internal investment bank at the corporate centre to support new initiatives. Also, a customer–supplier relationship may be established between a central service department, such as training or IT, and the operating units. Typically these internal markets are subject to considerable regulation. For example, the corporate centre might set rules for *transfer prices* between internal business units to prevent exploitative contract pricing, or insist on *service-level agreements* to ensure appropriate service by an essential internal supplier, such as IT, for the various units that depend on it.

Internal markets work well where complexity or rapid change makes impractical detailed direct or input controls. But internal markets can create problems as well. First, internal markets can increase bargaining between units, consuming important management time. Second, they may create a new bureaucracy monitoring all of the internal transfers of resources between units. Third, an overzealous use of market mechanisms can lead to dysfunctional competition and legalistic contracting, destroying cultures of collaboration and relationships. These have all been complaints made against the internal markets and semi-autonomous foundation hospitals introduced in the UK's National Health Service. On the other hand, their proponents claim that these market processes free a traditionally overcentralised health service to innovate and respond to local needs, while market disciplines maintain overall control. Illustration 12.4 shows internal markets being combined with other controls at successful investment bank Macquarie.

Illustration 12.4

Controlling investment bankers

Known as the 'Millionaire Factory', Macquarie's entrepreneurial bankers are pursuing deals all over the world.

Sydney-based Macquarie Bank is Australia's largest investment bank and its most successful division, the Infrastructure Group, is the largest operator of toll roads in the world. Its funds own Copenhagen Airport and Thames Water company and during 2006 it launched an audacious and ultimately unsuccessful bid for the London Stock Exchange. Despite this setback, 2006 was another record year for Macquarie. Its total staff has risen from under 5,000 in 2003 to just less than 10,000 in 2007; its international staff rose from less than a thousand to 3,200 in the same period.

The Chief Executive, Allan Moss, joined Macquarie in 1977, when it was still the subsidiary of British merchant bank Hill Samuel with about 50 employees. A Harvard MBA (he graduated in the top 5 per cent), Moss became chief executive in 1993 and listed the bank on the Australian Stock Exchange in 1995. According to the *Financial Times*, Moss has an image of a 'bumbling professor', spilling coffee and tripping over telephone cords. He does not travel overseas much, preferring to stay in Sydney, and he works short hours by investment banker standards, 8.30 a.m. to 7.30 p.m.

Moss describes the bank's culture as one of 'freedom within boundaries'. For him, Macquarie is a federation of businesses in which entrepreneurs can thrive: 'we provide the infrastructure, the capital, the brand and a controlled framework – and the staff provide the ideas'. The culture is very competitive internally, with colleagues pitching for 'mandates' (the responsibility for a bit of business) against each other. One former banker observed: 'Walking into Macquarie is like walking into a Turkish bazaar. Everyone has the same rug and they're all competing to sell the same rug.' In fact, though, the internal competition produces highly innovative ideas – for example, the proposal that the bank should provide financing for patients' operations, including cosmetic surgery such as breast implants. The rule of thumb guiding promotion to one of the coveted – and lucrative – 250 executive directorships has been generating an annual profit personally of A\$5m (£2.1m; €3m). The company receives 70,000 unsolicited CVs from would-be Macquarie bankers every year. All hires go through the same distinctive and rigorous psychological testing process.

Of course, there are some who doubt whether Macquarie's successful run can go on for ever. The *Financial Times* quotes one close observer of Macquarie: 'I am starting to detect some hubris at the bank. It has done so well it is inevitable. Allan [Moss] is loyal to those he trusts and only time will tell whether he is trusting his lieutenants a bit too much'.

Key sources: *Financial Times*, 17 December (2005); *Sydney Morning Herald*, 19 August (2006).

Questions

1 What control processes in this account are particularly important to Macquarie?

2 What threats are there to these processes?

12.4 RELATIONSHIPS

A key aspect of an organisation's configuration is the ability to integrate the knowledge and activities of different parts of an organisation (both horizontally and vertically) and with other organisations (particularly within the value chain, as discussed in Chapter 3). Structures and processes are an important part of this, as discussed in the previous sections. However, there are basic issues too around how both internal and external *relationships* are built and maintained, especially in ways that are fluid enough to respond to an uncertain environment. This section looks at the following issues (see Exhibit 12.9):

- Relating internally, especially with regard to where responsibility and authority for operational and strategic decisions should be vested inside an organisation.
- Relating externally, for example through outsourcing, alliances, networks and virtuality.

12.4.1 Relating internally

Relating to the centre

Devolution concerns the extent to which the centre of an organisation delegates decision making to units and managers lower down in the hierarchy

One of the important continuing debates in both public[22] and private sector organisations has been concerned with devolution. **Devolution** concerns the extent to which the centre of an organisation delegates decision making to units and managers lower down in the hierarchy.

Devolution is particularly effective where important knowledge is dispersed throughout the organisation and where responsiveness to the changing needs of different customer segments is important. In these conditions, top managers can be too remote from the 'sharp end' really to understand the organisation's resources and opportunities. In fast-moving markets, it is often better to place

Exhibit 12.9 **Relating internally and externally**

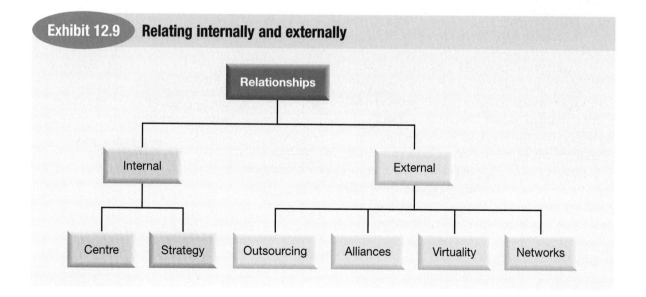

decision-making authority *close to the action* rather than force decisions up through slow and remote hierarchies.

Despite these reasons why increased devolution might make sense, it can become a 'fad' and simply a reaction to a previous era of overcentralisation. To avoid this risk the issue of centralisation vs. devolution needs to be seen as a *continuum* from highly centralised to highly devolved and not as a black or white choice.

Relating over strategy

Section 7.4 looked at the question of whether and in what ways a corporate parent can add value to its constituent business units or departments. An important determinant of organising for success is clarity around how responsibilities for strategic decision making are to be *divided* between the centre and the business units. Goold and Campbell[23] provide three *strategy styles* describing typical ways of dividing these responsibilities. The organisational processes and the way that relationships work are very different in each case.

Strategic planning style

In a **strategic planning style** of control, the relationship between the centre and the business units is one of a parent who is the *master planner* prescribing detailed roles for departments and business units

The **strategic planning style** (Exhibit 12.10) is the most centralised of the three styles. Here strategic planning refers not to planning in general but to a particular style of relationship between the centre and business units. The centre is the *master planner* prescribing detailed roles for departments and business units, whose role is confined to the operational delivery of the plan. In the extreme form of this style, the centre is expected to add value in most of the ways outlined in Exhibit 7.6. The centre orchestrates, coordinates and controls all of business unit activities through the extensive use of the formal planning and control

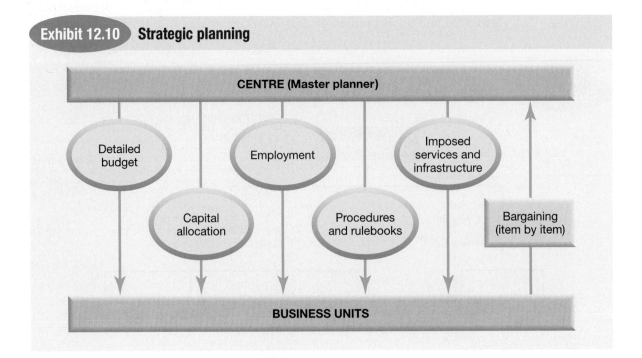

Exhibit 12.10 **Strategic planning**

systems (as discussed in section 12.3.2) shown in Exhibit 12.10. The centre also directly manages the infrastructure and provides many corporate services. This is the classic bureaucracy familiar to many managers in large public sector organisations.

The strategic planning style is well suited to the synergy manager or parental developer roles adopted by corporate centres, as discussed in section 6.4. It is particularly appropriate where corporate managers have a detailed working knowledge of each business unit and where business unit strategies are of a size or sensitivity that can have major ramifications for the corporate whole. Where the corporate centre does not have detailed working knowledge, the strategic planning style can be dysfunctional. Corporate managers may hold back the development of business areas that they do not understand or steer them in inappropriate directions. There are also the bureaucratic costs of centralisation and demotivating effects on business unit managers who may feel little personal commitment to strategies handed down from the centre. Goold and Campbell and others have found many private sector organisations abandoning this style.[24]

Financial control style

In the **financial control** style, the role of the centre is confined to setting financial targets, allocating resources, appraising performance and intervening to avert or correct poor performance

Financial control (Exhibit 12.11) is the most extreme form of devolution, dissolving the organisation into highly autonomous business units. The relationship between the centre and the business units is as a parent who is a *shareholder or banker* for those units. As the name suggests, the relationship is financial and there is little concern for the detailed product/market strategy of business units – even to the extent that they can compete openly with each other provided they deliver the financial results. They might even have authority to raise funds from outside the company. This style is typically managed through a holding company structure, as discussed in section 12.2.2, and is suited to the portfolio manager or restructurer roles of a corporate centre, as discussed in section 7.4.

In financial control the role of the centre is confined to setting financial targets, allocating resources, appraising performance and intervening in the case

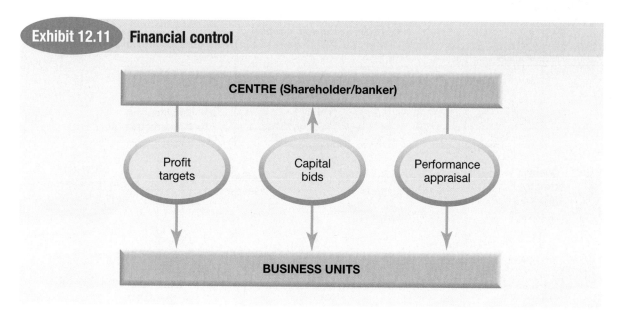

Exhibit 12.11 **Financial control**

of poor performance. Importantly, these interventions would usually be replacing business unit managers rather than dictating changes in strategy. So the dominant processes are performance targets as discussed in section 12.3.5. Business units managers are held strictly accountable for meeting these targets.

In the public sector, such extreme devolution is rarely found for reasons of political accountability: the minister is ultimately responsible. In the private sector, however, the style can be appropriate to organisations operating in stable markets with mature technologies and where there is only a short time lag between management decisions and the financial consequences: for example, organisations trading commodities or dealing with basic products. It is also appropriate where the diversity of business units is great – since the other two styles require some measure of relatedness between business units. A major concern with financial control can be the dominance of short-termism. No one has responsibility for fostering innovation and organisational learning. The business units are focused on meeting tough short-term targets set by a centre that does not have the resources or the competences to manage the knowledge creation and integration processes. So competence development can only really happen through acquisitions and alliances.

Strategic control style

The **strategic control style** is concerned with shaping the *behaviour* in business units and with shaping the *context* within which managers are operating

Strategic control (Exhibit 12.12) lies between the two extremes of the strategic planning and financial control styles and is the style most organisations operate. The relationship between the centre and the business units is one of a parent who behaves as a *strategic shaper*, influencing the *behaviour* in business units[25] and forming the *context* within which managers are operating. Like strategic planning, this is a style suited to the synergy manager or parental developer roles of a corporate centre as discussed in section 7.4. However, because it allows more

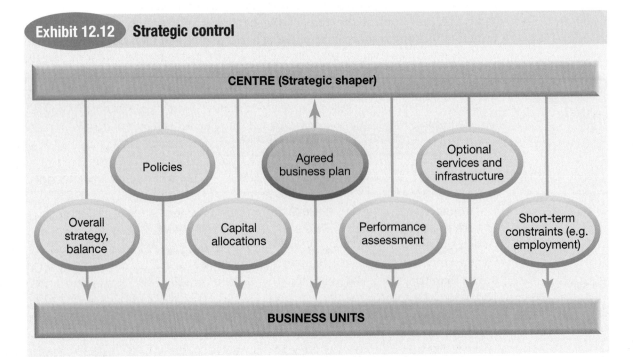

Exhibit 12.12 **Strategic control**

CENTRE (Strategic shaper)

Policies

Agreed business plan

Optional services and infrastructure

Overall strategy, balance

Capital allocations

Performance assessment

Short-term constraints (e.g. employment)

BUSINESS UNITS

discretion lower down, it is more suitable where the centre has little knowledge about business unit operations and business unit strategies are unlikely to make major impacts on the corporation as a whole. The centre would expect to add value by:

- Defining and shaping the *overall* strategy of the organisation.
- Deciding the *balance* of activities and the role of each business unit.
- Defining and controlling organisational *policies* (on employment, market coverage, interaction between units, etc.).
- Fostering *organisational learning* between units.
- Defining standards and assessing the *performance* of the separate business units and intervening to improve performance (that is, the processes of performance targeting discussed in section 12.3.5).

However, the centre does not fulfil these roles through an imposed master plan. Rather, strategic control is built through the processes of agreeing strategies with business units (perhaps through their business plans) – but within central boundaries and guidelines. Perhaps the biggest risk with this style is that the centre tries to shape strategy in these ways without being clear about the 'corporate logic' or having the competences actually to add value in these ways.

12.4.2 Relating externally

Organisations have important relationships outside their boundaries as well, for example with customers, suppliers, subcontractors and partners. This section will look at four of the most important such relationships, all of which have seen a good deal of change in recent years.

Outsourcing

In Chapter 3, outsourcing was presented as an important issue about strategic capability that arises from the concept of the value chain. Outsourcing occurs where organisations decide to buy in services or products that were previously produced in-house. For example, payroll, component manufacture, IT services and training are all common examples of outsourced activities. Two important principles were established when searching for candidates for outsourcing: first, that an outside supplier can provide better value for money than in-house provision; second, that core competences should not normally be outsourced since these activities critically underpin competitive advantage.

Many managers take on board these principles of outsourcing but do not pay enough attention to the organisational implications of outsourcing. For example, outsourcing requires managers to be much more competent at maintaining performance through their management of supplier (or distributor) *relationships* rather than through management control systems within their own organisation. This may take some considerable attention. For example, suppliers or distributors will need to be educated about the organisation's strategies, priorities and standards and how their work influences the final performance of the product or service. They need to be motivated to perform consistently to these required standards. It should be clear from section 12.3 that there are different processes by which this might be achieved. At one extreme, suppliers might be 'tied in' through enterprise resource planning systems. This might be possible and desirable where the requirements of the supplier are clear and unlikely to change quickly. At the other extreme, the relationship may be maintained through cultural processes and norms – for example, working with suppliers who know the company well and are tuned into the cultural norms. This would be important where suppliers are adding creative input to the product or service (such as designers) where the two-way interaction needs to be much more fluid. Between these extremes, market mechanisms could be used if a contractual approach to the relationship is felt to be appropriate – for example, for one-off projects or where there is a range of potential suppliers.

Strategic alliances

This issue of managing relationships with other organisations (or other parts of the same organisation) surfaced in Chapter 8 in the discussion about strategic alliances. The organisational concerns are similar to those with outsourcing except that a strategic alliance may be much more overtly relational in the way the alliance is constructed (as against the contractual nature of many supplier–customer relationships). Readers are referred to Exhibit 10.3, which shows the spectrum of strategic alliance types from loose networks to joint ventures. The important organisational issue is finding the balance between the best sources of specialist knowledge (which would suggest many members of an alliance) and the competence to integrate these strands of specialist knowledge to create a best value product or service to customers. The more members of an alliance, the more complex this integration task becomes and the more effort that needs to be put into the ingredients of successful alliances, as discussed in section 10.2.3 – such as trust. This will be discussed further below when considering networks and the ability of some organisations to achieve a nodal position in a network of multiple partners.

Networks[26]

Outsourcing, alliances and virtuality are particular cases of a general trend to rely on network relationships outside the organisation's boundaries. Taken together, they mean that more organisations have become dependent on internal and external networks to ensure success (see Illustration 12.5 for a public sector example). So *cooperation* has become a key aspect of organising for success. Other important networks include:

● *Teleworking*, where people carry out their work *independently* but remain connected to key corporate resources (such as databases and specialist advice) and to colleagues, suppliers and clients through the telecommunications and computing infrastructure. Since the exploitation of the Internet remains a major strategic issue for many organisations (see Chapter 9), new ways of organising will be essential. The Internet allows many formal structures to be dismantled and replaced with well-functioning networks supported by this information infrastructure.

Illustration 12.5

Developing school leaders through networks

The UK's National College for School Leadership is using networks rather than traditional bureaucratic structures for developing school head teachers.

In the 2000s, British schools were facing a leadership crisis. The demands upon school head teachers were increasing, both because of greater decentralisation of responsibilities to schools and evermore stringent performance requirements. But there was an acute shortage of appropriately trained teachers prepared to take on the job of school head.

Traditionally, city and town local education authorities (LEAs) had taken primary responsibility for developing head teachers in their particular areas. They had often worked in regional consortia and with local universities to develop appropriate training mechanisms. Typically LEAs had a concentration of relevant expertise in a variety of professional areas, which provided the basis for advice and development for schools in their areas. LEAs were also under the control of their democratically elected councils, and so accountable to local electorates. For the last two decades, however, LEA budgets and roles had been under steady attack as too costly and too bureaucratic. Budgets were nearly wholly devolved to schools and some schools were allowed to opt out of LEA control altogether. Meanwhile, universities, under pressure to perform more research, were increasingly reluctant to get involved in post-experience teacher training.

The year of 2002 saw the launch of a new National College of School Leadership (NCL). Based on the campus of Nottingham University, it was explicitly concerned to use networks rather than traditional structures to deliver training and development assistance for head teachers and future leaders. The NCL launched a Networked Learning Communities programme, designed to bring teachers together to exhange experience and develop themselves. New information technologies were enrolled as platforms for initiatives such as 'TalkingHeads' and 'VirtualHeads'. David Jackson, Director of the Networked Learning Communities programme, commented: 'The twentieth century

was the century during which we built large organisations (with silos and hierarchies) to do things for people. The twenty-first century is the one in which we help people to help one another.'

LEAs now had a new role: network brokers. Their task was to use their knowledge of local schools, other services and communities to bring the right people together in the appropriate networks. As the NCL put it: 'Networks offer the possibility of new patterns of leadership – more lateral and more distributed – they offer new possibilities for Local Authorities and schools to engage in co-leadership.' One LEA was quoted as commenting:

We are learning – quickly – that we need to look outside education if we are really going to make a differerence for the children in our schools. Working with social services, the police and health service is difficult. But the Local Authority is the only place where that can happen, so we're persevering.

David Jackson, the Director, was clear about the challenges for LEAs:

A local authority might previously have had a hundred schools and they've now got ten networks – what opportunities that creates! But it requires a massive change within themselves, their own modes of thinking, the way in which they design policy, generate incentives, hold people accountable, deploy resources. Everything requires change.

Sources: 'What does a Local Authority broker do?', National College for School Leadership; 'Cracking the concrete: David Jackson, in conversation with Madeline Church, reflects on how networks work across, around and within standard structures', National College for School Leadership.

Questions

1 What are the advantages of a networked learning model in this context? Are there any disadvantages?

2 Why might LEAs find it difficult to take on this new role of network broker?

● *Federations* of experts who voluntarily come together to integrate their expertise to create products or services. In the entertainment business, musicians, actors and other creative artists sometimes come together in this way as well as through the more formal processes of agents and contracts. Some organisations make their living by maintaining databases of resources (people) in the network and possibly facilitating social contact through organising networking events.

● *One-stop shops* are a solution to the problem of coordinating diverse network members so that the customer experiences a coherent, joined-up service. The one-stop shop creates a physical presence through which all customer enquiries are channelled (see Exhibit 12.13). The function of the one-stop shop is to put together a complete package of products or services from various network members. A 'turnkey' contractor (say, in civil engineering) might operate in this way – using its own expertise in project management and managing a network of suppliers, but not actually undertaking any of the detailed work itself. With the growth of e-commerce, the one-stop shop may, in fact, be *virtual* in the sense that clients enter via a 'gateway' (say a website) but the physical services or products that are being integrated into the customer's product or service are actually dispersed (in physical terms). The critical issue is that it feels joined up to the customer whose needs can be satisfied through this one gateway.

● In a *service network* the client may access all of the services of the network through any of the constituent members of the network. A well-functioning

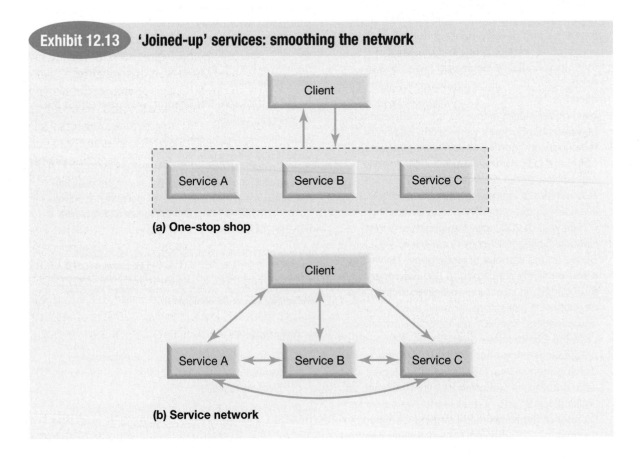

Exhibit 12.13 **'Joined-up' services: smoothing the network**

(a) One-stop shop

(b) Service network

service network may not be easy to achieve, since it requires all members of the network to be fully informed, capable and willing to 'cross-sell' other people's products and to act collaboratively. Above all else, it requires *trust and respect* between members of the network. Some service networks also have a one-start shop facility. For example, Best Western is an international network of independent hotels, where customers can receive information or make bookings at any hotel in the network or through central booking points. This facility has the clear advantage of encouraging travellers to 'book on' their next destination with Best Western.

It can be seen that coordination in a network is a crucial activity. It can also be well rewarded. Organisations that achieve a *nodal position* in the network, connecting many nodes in the network, are potentially highly valuable.[27] To achieve a nodal position, organisations should have three strengths:

- A *compelling vision* that legitimises the need for the network and entices in partners. In the public sector this may be a vision of politicians who then set up the network to deliver – for example, on drugs, crime and disorder, social exclusion, and so on.
- *Unique resources or core competences* to establish and hold the nodal position – such as a proprietary system as seen with technologies such as Apple's iTunes or the Windows computer operating system.
- *Networking skills* to sustain and develop the network.

Virtual organisation[28]

The logical extension of networking, outsourcing and alliances would be an organisation where in-house (owned) resources and activities are minimised and nearly all resources and activities reside outside the organisation. These so-called **virtual organisations** are held together not through formal structure and physical proximity of people, but by partnership, collaboration and networking. The important issue is that this organisation feels 'real' to clients and meets their needs at least as adequately as other organisations. It has been argued that such extreme forms of outsourcing are likely to result in serious strategic weakness in the long run, as the organisation becomes devoid of core competences and cut off from the learning which can exist through undertaking these activities in-house. This is now an important consideration in many industries such as civil engineering, publishing and specialist travel companies, all of which are highly dependent on outsourcing aspects of their business which hitherto were considered as core. The concern is whether short-term improvements are being achieved at the expense of securing a capacity for innovation. The danger of 'virtuality' is that knowledge creation and innovation only occur within the specialist 'boxes' represented by the activities of separate partners. There is no one who has the competence or authority to integrate these pockets of knowledge.

> Virtual organisations are held together not through formal structure and physical proximity of people, but by partnership, collaboration and networking

12.4.3 Configuration dilemmas

The beginning of this chapter stressed that successful organising requires fitting structure, processes and relationships to each other, all aligned to the key strategic challenges in a mutually reinforcing way. This mutual fit is described as an organisation's *configuration* (Exhibit 12.1). For example, the multidivisional structure lends itself to internal market processes (for example, divisions contracting with a central R&D function) and is compatible with certain strategy styles, particularly the financial control and strategic control styles. Project-based structures often rely on cultural processes to provide a common glue for fast-changing teams and can usually accommodate themselves to external relationships such as networks or virtual organising. Successful organisations thus tend to fall into a limited number of internally consistent patterns for integrating structures, processes and relationships.[29]

However, perfect fits across all three dimensions of the configuration can be hard to find. Sometimes, there are major trade-offs between optimising on one element and optimising on another. Managers face dilemmas in combining control with flexibility, for example. The chapter concludes by considering the most common practical dilemmas and the ways in which they can be addressed.[30]

Exhibit 12.14 summarises five key dilemmas in organising. Hierarchies are often necessary to ensure control and action, but they can sit uneasily with networks that foster knowledge exchange and innovation. Vertical accountability promotes maximum performance by subordinates, but can lead managers to maximise their own self-interest, at the expense of horizontal relationships. Empowerment of employees lower down the organisation gives scope for initiative, but over the long term can lead to incoherence. Centralisation might be needed for standardisation, but this can be at the cost of the initiative and flexibility fostered by devolution. Having the best practice on a particular element of the organisation, for instance financial controls, may actually be damaging if it does not fit with the needs of the organisation as a whole.

Exhibit 12.14   Some dilemmas in organising for success

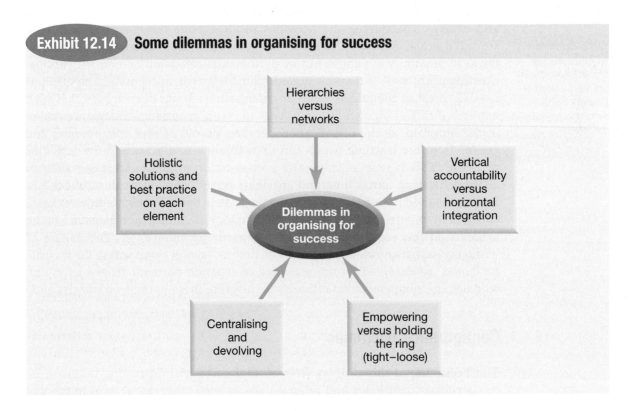

Managers should recognise that any organisational design is likely to face dilemmas of these kinds and is hard to optimise on all dimensions. However, they may be able to manage these dilemmas in three ways:

- By *subdividing* the organisation, so that the one part of the organisation is organised optimally according to one side of these dilemmas, while the rest responds to the other. Thus for example IBM created the PC in a specialised new venture division, kept separate from the traditional mainframe activities which were dominated by principles of hierarchy and vertical accountability highly antagonistic to radical innovation.[31]

- By *combining* different organising principles at the same time, for instance networks and traditional hierarchies. Managing simultaneously according to contradictory principles is obviously very demanding. However, it has been argued that organisations such as ABB and Unilever are now 'networked multidivisionals', combining network principles emphasising horizontal integration with divisional structures ensuring vertical accountability.[32]

- By *reorganising* frequently so that no one side of the dilemma can become too entrenched. The rate of major reorganisation for large UK companies increased from once every four years to once every three years in the last decade.[33] Given this pace of reorganising, many organisations are like pendulums, constantly swinging between centralisation and devolution, for example, without resting long on one side or another.[34]

A final dilemma arising from the interconnectedness of configurations is which element drives the others? The extent to which strategic elements drive structural elements is the subject of the key debate in Illustration 12.6.

SUMMARY

- Organising for success is about an organisation's configuration. This is built up of three related strands: structures, processes and relationships.

- Successful organising means responding to the key challenges facing the organisation. This chapter has stressed control, change, knowledge and internationalisation.

- There are many *structural types* (such as functional, divisional, matrix). Each structural type has its own strengths and weaknesses and responds differently to the challenges of control, change, knowledge and internationalisation.

- There are a range of different organisational *processes* to facilitate strategy. These processes can focus on either inputs or outputs and be direct or indirect.

- Relationships are also important to success. Internally, key issues are *centralisation versus devolution* and *strategy style*. Externally, there are choices around outsourcing, alliances, virtuality and networks which may help or hinder success.

- The separate organisational strands should come together to form a coherent *reinforcing cycle*. But these reinforcing cycles also raise tough dilemmas that can be managed by *subdividing*, *combining* and *reorganising*.

Illustration 12.6

key debate

Does structure follow strategy?

A key message of this chapter is that strategy and structure should fit together. But which determines which?

Alfred Chandler, Professor of Business History at Harvard Business School, proposes one of the fundamental rules of strategic management: 'unless structure follows strategy, inefficiency results'.[1] This logical sequence fits the 'design' lens for strategy, but does assume that structure is very much subordinate to strategy: structure can easily be fixed once the big strategic decisions are made. But some authors warn that this dangerously underestimates structure's role. Sometimes strategy follows structure.

Chandler's rule is based on the historical experience of companies like General Motors, Exxon and DuPont. DuPont, for example, was originally an explosives company. During the First World War, however, the company anticipated the peace by deliberately diversifying out of explosives into new civil markets such as plastics and paints. Yet the end of the war plunged DuPont into crisis. All its new businesses were loss making; only explosives still made money. The problem was not the diversification strategy, but the structure that DuPont used to manage the new civil businesses. DuPont had retained its old functional structure, so that responsibilities for the production and marketing of all the new businesses were still centralised on single functional heads. They could not cope with the increased diversity. The solution was not to abandon the diversification strategy; rather it was to adopt a new structure with decentralised divisions for each of the separate businesses. DuPont thrives today with a variant of this multidivisional structure.

D. Hall and M. Saias accept the importance of strategy for structure but warn that the causality can go the other way.[2] An organisation's existing structure very much determines the kinds of strategic opportunities that its management will see and want to grasp. For instance, it is easy for a company with a decentralised multidivisional structure to make acquisitions and divestments: all it has to do is add or subtract divisions, with few ramifications for the rest of the business. On the other hand, it can be very hard for the top managers of a decentralised multidivisional organisation to see opportunities for innovation and knowledge sharing within the operations of the divisions: they are too far away from the real business. In other words, structures can shape strategies.

T. Amburgey and T. Dacin tested the relative impact of strategy and structure on each other by analysing the strategic and structural changes of more than 200 American corporations over nearly 30 years.[3] They found that moves towards decentralised structures were often followed by moves towards increasingly diversified strategies: here, structure was determining strategy. Overall, however, increased diversification was twice as likely to be followed by structural decentralisation as the other way round. In other words, structure does follow strategy, but only most of the time.

Henry Mintzberg concludes that 'structure follows strategy as the left foot follows the right'.[4] In other words, strategy and structure are related reciprocally rather than just one way. Mintzberg warns that a simple 'design' approach to strategy and structure can be misleading. Structure is not always easy to fix after the big strategic decisions have been made. Strategists should check to see that their existing structures are not constraining the kinds of strategies that they consider.

Notes

1. A. Chandler, *Strategy and Structure: Chapters in the History of American Enterprise*, MIT Press, 1962, p. 314.
2. D.J. Hall and M.A. Saias, 'Strategy follows structure!', *Strategic Management Journal*, vol. 1, no. 2 (1980), pp. 149–163.
3. T. Amburgey and T. Dacin, 'As the left foot follows the right? The dynamics of strategic and structural change', *Academy of Management Journal*, vol. 37, no. 6 (1994), pp. 1427–1452.
4. H. Mintzberg, 'The Design School: reconsidering the basic premises of strategic management', *Strategic Management Journal*, vol. 11 (1990), pp. 171–195.

Question

Hall and Saias suggest that organisational structures can influence the kinds of strategies that management teams will pursue. What kinds of organisations might be particularly susceptible to structural constraints on their strategies?

Work assignments

*✱ Denotes more advanced work assignments.   * Refers to a case study in the Text and Cases edition.*

12.1   Go to the website of a large organisation you are familiar with and find its organisational chart (not all organisations provide these). Why is the organisation structured in this way?

12.2   Referring to section 12.2.2, on the multidivisional structure, consider the advantages and disadvantages of creating divisions along different lines – such as product, geography or technology – with respect to a large organisation you are familiar with or a case organisation such as SABMiller*, CRH* or News Corporation*.

12.3 ✱   Referring to Exhibit 12.9 on the balanced scorecard, write a short executive brief explaining how balanced scorecards could be a useful management process to monitor and control the performance of organisational units. Be sure you present an analysis of both the advantages and possible pitfalls of this approach.

12.4   As a middle manager with responsibilities for a small business unit, which 'strategy style' (section 12.4.1) would you prefer to work within? In what sorts of circumstances or corporate organisation would this style not work so well for you?

12.5   Explain the statement: 'when the organisational structure isn't working, it is just as likely to be the fault of the strategy as the fault of the structure'.

Integrative assignment

12.6   Take a recent merger or acquisition (see Chapter 10), ideally one involving two organisations of roughly equal size, and analyse how the deal has changed the acquiring or merged company's organisational structure. What do you conclude from the extent or lack of structural change for the strategy of the company going forward?

An extensive range of additional materials, including audio summaries, weblinks to organisations featured in the text, definitions of key concepts and self-assessment questions, can be found on the *Exploring Corporate Strategy* Companion Website at **www.pearsoned.co.uk/ecs**

Recommended key readings

- The best single coverage of this chapter's issues is in R. Daft, *Organisation Theory and Design*, 9th edition, South-Western, 2006.
- M. Goold and A. Campbell, *Designing Effective Organizations*, Jossey-Bass, 2002, provides a practical guide to organisational design issues.
- A review of contemporary issues and cases in organising is A. Pettigrew, R. Whittington, L. Melin, C. Sanchez-Runde, F. van den Bosch, W. Ruigrok and T. Numagami (eds), *Innovative Forms of*

Organizing, Sage, 2003. For a recent collection of relevant articles, see the special issue 'Learning to design organizations', ed. R. Dunbar and W. Starbuck, *Organization Science*, vol. 17 (2006), no. 2.

- Readers can gain useful insights into the financial aspects of strategy implementation, managing for value, expectation of stakeholders and strategic control in G. Arnold, *Corporate Financial Management*, 3rd edition, FT/Prentice Hall, 2005, Chapters 15 and 16.

References

1. Some of these early writings are to be found in D. Pugh, *Organisation Theory*, Penguin, 1984.

2. The point has been argued by R. Whittington and L. Melin, 'The challenge of organizing/strategizing', in A. Pettigrew, R. Whittington, L. Melin, C. Sanchez-Runde, F. van den Bosch, W. Ruigrok and T. Numagami (eds), *Innovative Forms of Organizing*, Sage, 2003; and also by R. Whittington, E. Molloy, M. Mayer and A. Smith, 'Practices of strategising/organising', *Long Range Planning*, vol. 39, no. 6 (2006), pp. 615–630.

3. This idea of configuration is similar to that of strategic architecture, as discussed by G. Hamel and C.K. Prahalad, *Competing for the Future*, Harvard Business School Press, 1994, chapter 10, and complementarities, as discussed by R. Whittington, A. Pettigrew, S. Peck, E. Fenton and M. Conyon, 'Change and complementarities in the new competitive landscape', *Organization Science*, vol. 10, no. 5 (1999), pp. 583–600.

4. A good review of new and old types can be found in G. Friesen, 'Organisation design for the 21st century', *Consulting to Management – C2M*, vol. 16, no. 3 (2005), pp. 32–51.

5. The view that organisations should fit their structures to key challenges ('contingencies') is associated with the long tradition of research on contingency theory: see L. Donaldson, *The Contingency Theory of Organizations*, Sage, 2001, or R. Whittington, 'Organisational structure', in *The Oxford Handbook of Strategy*, vol. II, Oxford University Press, 2003, chapter 28, for summaries.

6. This view of divisionalisation as a response to diversity was originally put forward by A.D. Chandler, *Strategy and Structure*, MIT Press, 1962. See R. Whittington and M. Mayer, *The European Corporation: Strategy, Structure and Social Science*, Oxford University Press, 2000, for a summary of Chandler's argument and the success of divisional organisations in contemporary Europe.

7. For a review of current experience with matrix structures, see S. Thomas and L. D'Annunzio, 'Challenges and strategies of matrix organisations: top-level and mid-level managers' perspectives', *Human Resource Planning*, vol. 28, no. 1 (2005), pp. 39–48.

8. For a discussion of matrix structures in knowledge-intensive R&D laboratory settings, see P. Rizova, 'Are you networked for successful innovation?', *Sloan Management Review*, vol. 47, no. 3 (2006), pp. 49–55.

9. Matrix structures are discussed by C. Bartlett and S. Ghoshal, 'Matrix management: not a structure, more a frame of mind', *Harvard Business Review*, vol. 68, no. 4 (1990), pp. 138–145.

10. The classic article on project-based organisations is by R. DeFillippi and M. Arthur, 'Paradox in project-based enterprise: the case of film-making', *California Management Review*, vol. 40, no. 2 (1998), pp. 125–145. For some difficulties, see M. Bresnen, A. Goussevskaia and J. Swann, 'Organizational routines, situated learning and processes of change in project-based organisations', *Project Management Journal*, vol. 36, no. 3 (2005), pp. 27–42.

11. For a discussion of more permanent team structures, see T. Mullern, 'Integrating the team-based structure in the business process: the case of Saab Training Systems', in A. Pettigrew and E. Fenton (eds), *The Innovating Organisation*, Sage, 2000.

12. M. Goold and A. Campbell, *Designing Effective Organisations*, Jossey-Bass, 2002. See also M. Goold and A. Campbell, 'Do you have a well-designed organisation?', *Harvard Business Review*, vol. 80, no. 3 (2002), pp. 117–224.

13. A.D. Chandler, *Strategy and Structure: Chapters in the History of American Enterprise*, MIT Press, 1962.

14. This practice of 'patching' parts of the organisation onto each other according to changing market needs is described in K. Eisenhardt and S. Brown, 'Patching: restitching business portfolios in dynamic markets', *Harvard Business Review*, vol. 25, no. 3 (1999), pp. 72–80.

15. The point has been argued by E. Fenton and A. Pettigrew, 'Theoretical perspectives on new forms of organising', in A. Pettigrew and E. Fenton (eds), *The Innovating Organisation*, Sage, 2000, chapter 1.

16. For readers who would like to read more about ERP the following are useful: P. Binngi, M. Sharma and J. Godia, 'Critical issues affecting an ERP implementation', *Information Systems Management*, vol. 16, no. 3 (1999), pp. 7–14; T. Grossman and J. Walsh, 'Avoiding the pitfalls of ERP system implementation', *Information Systems Management*, vol. 21, no. 2 (2004), pp. 38–42.

17. C. Casey, 'Come, join our family: discipline and integration in corporate organizational culture', *Human Relations*, vol. 52, no. 2 (1999), pp. 155–179; for an account of the socialisation of graduate trainees, see A.D. Brown and C. Coupland, 'Sounds of silence: graduate trainees, hegemony and resistance', *Organization Studies*, vol. 26, no. 7 (2005), pp. 1049–1070.

18. E.C. Wenger and W.M. Snyder, 'Communities of practice: the organized frontier', *Harvard Business Review*, vol. 78, no. 1 (2000), pp. 139–146.

19. D. Helm and T. Jenkinson, *Competition in Regulated Industries*, Clarendon Press, 1999, provides a number of in-depth case studies of competitive implications of deregulation. See also A. Lomi and E. Larsen, 'Learning without experience: strategic implications of deregulation and competition in the international electricity industry', *European Management Journal*, vol. 17, no. 2 (1999), pp. 151–164.

20. See R. Kaplan and D. Norton, 'The balanced scorecard: measures that drive performance', *Harvard Business Review*, vol. 70, no. 1 (1992), pp 71–79; for a recent development, see R. Kaplan and D. Norton, 'Having trouble with your strategy? Then map it', *Harvard Business Review*, vol. 78, no. 5 (2000), pp. 167–176; and R. Kaplan and D. Norton, *Alignment: How to Apply the Balanced Scorecard to Strategy*, Harvard Business School Press, 2006.

21. Companies like Royal Dutch Shell have been experimenting with internal markets to stimulate innovation. See G. Hamel, 'Bringing Silicon Valley inside', *Harvard Business Review*, vol. 77, no. 5 (1999), pp. 70–84. For a discussion of internal market challenges, see A. Vining, 'Internal market failure', *Journal of Management Studies*, vol. 40, no. 2 (2003), pp. 431–457.

22. For a discussion of these issues in the public sector context see K. Scholes, 'Strategy and structure in the public sector', in G. Johnson and K. Scholes (eds), *Exploring*

Public Sector Strategy, Financial Times/Prentice Hall, 2001, chapter 13; and T. Forbes, 'Devolution and control; within the UK public sector: National Health Service Trusts', ibid., chapter 16.

23. M. Goold and A. Campbell, *Strategies and Styles*, Blackwell, 1987.

24. See M. Goold, A. Campbell and K. Lucks, 'Strategics and styles revisited: strategic planning and financial control', *Long Range Planning*, vol. 26, no. 6 (1993), pp. 49–61; and R. Grant, 'Strategic planning in a turbulent environment: evidence from the oil majors', *Strategic Management Journal*, vol. 24, no. 6 (2003), pp. 491–517.

25. C. Bartlett and S. Ghoshal, 'Changing the role of top management: beyond strategy to purpose', *Harvard Business Review*, vol. 72, no. 6 (1994), pp. 79–88.

26. See W. Ruigrok, L. Achtenhagen, M. Wagner and J. Ruegg-Sturm, 'ABB: beyond the global matrix towards the network organisation', in A. Pettigrew and E. Fenton (eds), *The Innovating Organisation*, Sage, 2000, chapter 4. Also J.C. Jarillo, *Strategic Networks: Creating the borderless organisation*, Butterworth–Heinemann, 1993.

27. Y. Doz and G. Hamel, *Alliance Advantage*, Harvard Business School Press, 1998, p. 235.

28. Virtual organisations and the extensive use of subcontracting have been widely discussed. For example, W. Davidow and M. Malone, *The Virtual Corporation*, Harper Business, 1992. For a cautious view, see H. Chesborough and D. Teece, 'Organising for innovation: when is virtual virtuous?', *Harvard Business Review*, vol. 80, no. 2 (2002), pp. 127–136. See also Jarillo, reference 26.

29. H. Mintzberg describes common configurations in his classic *The Structuring of Organisations*, Prentice Hall, 1979.

30. A. Pettigrew and E. Fenton, 'Complexities and dualities in innovative forms of organising', in A. Pettigrew and E. Fenton (eds), *The Innovating Organisation*, Sage, 2000, chapter 10.

31. R.A. Burgelman, 'Managing the new venture division: implications for strategic management', *Strategic Management Journal*, vol. 6, no. 1 (1985), pp. 39–54.

32. R. Whittington and M. Mayer, *The European Corporation: Strategy, Structure and Social Science*, Oxford University Press, 2000; and Ruigrok *et al.*, reference 26.

33. R. Whittington and M. Mayer, *Organising for Success: A Report on Knowledge*, CIPD, 2002.

34. For an analysis of this process at a leading pharmaceutical firm, see S. Karim and W. Mitchell, 'Innovating through acquisition and internal development: a quarter-century of boundary evolution at Johnson & Johnson', *Long Range Planning*, vol. 37, no. 6 (2004), pp. 525–538.

Hurricane Katrina: human-made disaster?

Introduction

Early on Monday morning, 29 August 2005, Hurricane Katrina struck the southern American state of Louisiana, rushing quickly inland to the city of New Orleans. With wind speeds at 125 miles per hour (200 km/h), the levees (dykes) protecting the city collapsed in several places. Over the next few days, the world watched in horror as New Orleans and the surrounding areas struggled with chaos. Hurricane Katrina claimed 1,836 lives and left vivid images of bodies floating in the streets, families stranded on rooftops and 25,000 hungry and thirsty people trapped for days in the notorious Superdome. Six months after the hurricane, more than half of New Orleans' population had still not returned to the city.

Ultimately, of course, the destruction wrought by Hurricane Katrina had natural causes. But there is every sign that the damage and suffering were significantly increased by organisational failures. The disaster of Hurricane Katrina was partly a consequence of organisational design.

A new organisation

The government organisation ultimately responsible for coordinating the response to Katrina was the US Department of Homeland Security. This itself was a recent creation, a reaction to the terrorist attacks of September 11, 2001. One finding from investigations into the circumstances surrounding 9/11 was the difficulty of coordinating all the information regarding terrorist threats. For example, before the attacks, a flight training school had alerted local authorities about a student who only seemed interested in learning how to fly civil airliners, not about how to take off or land. But the information had not been passed on to the Federal Bureau of Investigations (FBI): the student went on to be one of the terrorist hijackers involved in 9/11.

Photo: Robert Galbraith/Reuters

The US government responded to 9/11 by placing terrorism as the highest priority. It believed that one way of improving coordination in response to potential terror threats was by centralising relevant government departments. Nine days after the 9/11 attack, President Bush appointed Pennsylvania Governor and decorated Vietnam veteran Tom Ridge to create and head a new department. The White House vetoed some of Tom Ridge's more radical proposals, so that both the Justice Department and the FBI remained independent. However, finally 22 departments were swept together in 2002 to create the new Department for Homeland Security (see Figure 1 for an organisational chart).

Involving more than 180,000 employees, this was the biggest reorganisation of the US government since the creation of the Pentagon in 1947. Amongst the major agencies that were gathered together under Tom Ridge's command were Customs, Immigration, Narcotics, the Coast Guard, the Secret Service and, most important here, the Federal Emergency Management Agency (FEMA). All were to unite in the fight against terrorism. As the head of the US Customs Service said: 'Terrorism is our highest priority, bar none. Ninety eight per cent of my attention . . . has been devoted to that one issue.' Tom Ridge anticipated turf battles between the

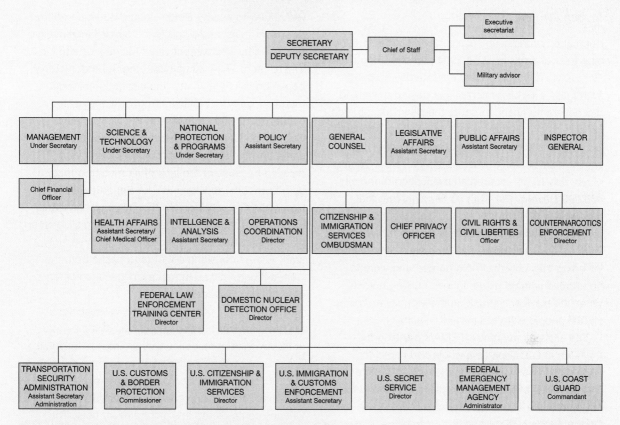

Figure 1 Department of Homeland Security organisation chart

Source: http://www.dhs.gov/xabout/structure/editorial_0644.shtm

newly amalgamated agencies but declared: 'The only turf we should be worried about protecting is the turf we stand on.'

FEMA, however, resisted the reorganisation. Responsible for responding to natural disasters such as hurricanes or earthquakes, FEMA had since 1993 been represented directly inside the President's Cabinet. Merger within the new Department of Homeland Security relegated FEMA to a mere internal division, with no direct Cabinet-level representation. FEMA's then head protested to the President's chief of staff: 'I told him it was a big mistake. The fact that FEMA could report to the President, any President – Democrat, Republican or independent – was what made the agency effective'. In the wake of 9/11, of course, this sounded like special pleading.

Within the new organisation, response to natural disasters had a low priority. In 2004, the Department drew up a list of 15 planning scenarios, doomsday events that could cause major fatalities. Twelve of these involved shadowy international terrorist groups, with plots involving mustard gas, sarin, nuclear weapons and anthrax, amongst other imaginative possibilities. One planning scenario did raise the threat of a hurricane flooding a nameless southern city and causing more than a thousand deaths. But terror attacks held the attention and these attracted the budgets.

Resources for protection against natural disasters began to get squeezed. Tom Ridge retired and was replaced by a new Secretary for Homeland Security, Michael Chertoff, a former judge. Various FEMA functions were stripped off and reallocated to other parts of the reorganisation. FEMA lost $80m (£44m; €64m) from its $550m operating budget. It struggled to get resources for rehearsing a response to a New Orleans hurricane scenario, and when it did do so, funds were denied for a follow-up. Between 2000 and 2005, the budget for the New Orleans Engineering Corps, responsible for the levees protecting the city, was cut by 44 per cent. Meanwhile, the Ohio Fire Service was able to get funds for bulletproof vests to protect their dogs in the event of terrorist attack.

Testing the new organisation

Hurricane Katrina gave several days' notice, forming over the Bahamas on 23 August and sweeping over Florida two days later. Early on Saturday morning, 27 August, a FEMA watch officer posted a warning of a severe hurricane threat to the New Orleans area, capable of causing thousands of fatalities. Michael Chertoff was at home that day, working on immigration issues. On Saturday night, New Orleans Mayor Ray Nagin ordered an evacuation of the city's 400,000 citizens. But, with no certainty that the hurricane would actually hit, and with what force, not everybody wanted to leave their homes for fear of looting. Moreover, many had no means of transport, including tragically many old people who were to be trapped without power in their nursing homes. When the hurricane struck on the Monday morning, 60,000 people were still in New Orleans.

The city was not ready. FEMA's planning for the state of Louisiana as a whole had called for 69 truckloads of water, 69 truckloads of ice and 34 truckloads of food to be in place. It planned for 400 buses and 800 drivers to ferry people to shelters. On the Sunday, FEMA had just 30 truckloads of water, 17 truckloads of ice and 15 truckloads of meals. FEMA had no buses in the state at all.

FEMA had got one officer into the city on the Sunday, but was otherwise not represented locally. When the flooding started, communications broke down. The various services had different communications systems, and the batteries on mobile devices soon ran down, with no power available to recharge. FEMA's high-tech communications wagon only reached New Orleans on the Friday (long after the world's journalists) and in the meantime Mayor Nagin's team had broken into an Office Depot store in order to steal functioning communications equipment. The sole FEMA officer on the ground had to bully his way onto one of the few helicopters available to confirm the broken levees on the first day. The Department of Homeland Security operations centre in Washington, guarding against panic responses, insisted on verification by a second source before passing the message up the chain, but no second source was available. Secretary Chertoff briefed President Bush about immigration issues on Monday morning, and made no mention of the hurricane.

The Department of Homeland Security struggled to cope over the following days. Michael Brown, FEMA's Head, flew to nearby Baton Rouge, but suffered from poor communications and found himself increasingly bypassed by Department Head Michael Chertoff in Washington. The evacuation of the Superdome only began on the Friday, after the instigation of food rationing, and the Washington operations centre overlooked 20,000 refugees at the New Orleans Convention Center for several days, thinking it the same building as the Superdome. Aircraft were delayed because of the lack of air marshals required by anti-terrorist regulations. The Department of Homeland Security insisted that all evacuees would have to be security screened before being allowed on planes, and then took eight hours to fly in security staff. A large consignment of food packs from the United Kingdom was turned away because of fears of Mad Cow Disease.

At a Thursday press conference in Washington, Michael Chertoff praised 'the genius of the people at FEMA' in their response to the disaster. 'I think it is a source of tremendous pride to me to work with the people who've pulled off this really exceptional response'. But television reports direct from New Orleans contradicted this picture every hour. The failure of FEMA, and of local agencies, was becoming very apparent. Facing heavy criticism, FEMA's head, Michael Brown, resigned on 13 September. Michael Chertoff kept his job.

Sources: C. Cooper and R. Block, *Disaster: Hurricane Katrina and the Failure of Homeland Security*, Times Books, 2006; and I. Daaddler and I. Destler, 'Advisors, Czars and Councils', *The National Interest*, 1 July (2002).

Questions

1 What was the 'strategy' of the Department of Homeland Security in the period immediately before Hurricane Katrina?

2 In the light of this strategy, what, if any, changes should be made to the Department's organizational structure after Hurricane Katrina?

3 Who was responsible for the organizational failures surrounding the response to Hurricane Katrina?

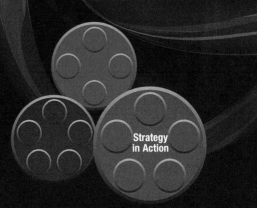

Strategy
in Action

13

Resourcing Strategies

LEARNING OUTCOMES

After reading this chapter you should be able to:

→ Analyse the resource management issues that are important to achieving strategic success in four key resource areas:
- The management of *people*. This includes the development of people's competences, the management of their behaviour and the appropriate organisational structures and processes.
- Access to and processing of *information* to build capabilities and change business models and/or management processes.
- The management of *finance* to create financial value, fund strategic developments and address the differing financial expectations of stakeholders.
- The management of *technology* to address changing competitive forces on an organisation and improve strategic capability.

→ Address the *integration* of resources and competences across resource areas to underpin the success of a strategy.

Photo: Horizon International Images Ltd/Alamy Images

13.1 INTRODUCTION

Most managers operate in a *part* of an organisation where their day-to-day work is dominated by issues that are specific to that function, department, division or project team. It should be clear from discussions earlier in this book that in all organisations, except the very smallest, this type of *specialisation* is usually a key factor underpinning success. Managers and individuals at this level will control resources, activities and business processes that are crucial to strategic success of the organisation as a whole. They are also likely to be the most knowledgeable about changes in parts of the business environment with which they interface. For example, HR specialists should understand the labour market, finance managers the money markets, R&D specialists the technological environment, and so on. So, many of the issues in the parts of an organisation have strategic implications. Therefore, these managers need to understand how the capabilities in 'their' resource area contributes to the overall success of organisational strategies and be capable of managing those resources (such as people, information, etc.) *strategically*.

This chapter will look at four key resource areas, people, information, finance and technology, and the ways in which they might underpin strategic success. In each case two related questions will be considered (see Exhibit 13.1):

● Are all of the different resource areas capable of *delivering* the organisation's business strategies? This will include the need for those managing resources to make sense of the business strategy and change capabilities and behaviours accordingly. For example, is the organisation using the appropriate mix of funding sources for the level of risk in its business strategies?

But also . . .

Exhibit 13.1 **Resourcing strategies**

● Are the business strategies of the organisation being shaped to *capitalise on the expertise* in each resource area? This requires senior managers to understand which business strategies might be made possible as a result of particular strengths in specific resource areas. For example, a particular expertise in IT can create better 'business models' than competitors. The resource-based view of strategy introduced in Chapter 3 is particularly concerned with this issue.

Resourcing strategies is concerned with the two-way relationship between overall business strategies and strategies in separate resource areas such as people, information, finance and technology

So, in summary, **resourcing strategies** is concerned with the two-way relationship between overall business strategies and strategies in separate resource areas such as people, information, finance and technology.

13.2 MANAGING PEOPLE[1]

The knowledge and experience of people can be the key factors influencing the success of strategies. So people-related issues should be a central concern and responsibility of most managers in organisations and are not confined to a specialist HR function. Creating a climate where people strive to achieve success is also a crucial role of any manager. Although formal HR systems and structures may be vitally important in supporting successful strategies, it is quite possible that they may hinder strategy if they are not tailored to the types of strategies being pursued. It is helpful to think about the people dimension of strategy as being concerned with three related issues (see Exhibit 13.2):

● people as a *resource* (which relates to Chapter 3);
● people and *behaviour* (which relates to Chapter 5);
● the need to *organise* people (which relates to Chapter 12).

13.2.1 People as a resource[2]

An important message from Chapter 3 of this book is that the possession of resources (including people) does not guarantee strategic success. Strategic capability is concerned with how these resources are deployed, managed, controlled and, in the case of people, motivated to create competences in those activities and business processes needed to run the business. This is a tough agenda in a rapidly changing world since the performance standards are constantly shifting in an upward direction. Much of this 'hard' side of HR management is concerned with these issues of performance management. So traditional HR activities can help underpin successful strategies in the following ways:

● *Audits* to assess HR requirements to support strategies and/or identify people-based core competences on which future strategies might be built.
● *Goal-setting and performance assessment* of individuals and teams. Most organisations will expect line managers to undertake these tasks, usually within a centrally designed appraisal scheme. This improves the chances of appraisals being linked to strategy. Also, there has been a move towards so-called 360° appraisals. These assess an individual's performance from multiple perspectives

Exhibit 13.2 **Strategy and people**

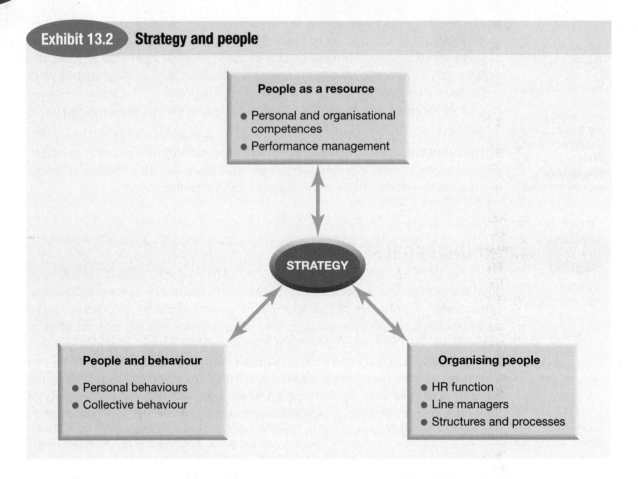

People as a resource
- Personal and organisational competences
- Performance management

STRATEGY

People and behaviour
- Personal behaviours
- Collective behaviour

Organising people
- HR function
- Line managers
- Structures and processes

– not just from the line manager but also from other parts of the organisation on which the work of the individual and/or his or her team impacts and even from external stakeholders. This is an attempt to assess the full impact of an employee's work on the success of strategy.

- In many organisations the planning of *rewards* has had to take on board the reality of more teamworking in delivering strategy. Highly geared individual incentives (often found in salesforces) may undermine this teamwork.

- *Recruitment and retention* are key ways of improving strategic capability. For example, many public sector organisations have needed to recruit and retain people with marketing and IT skills as they try to get closer to their customers and exploit IT. As organisations face faster changes, *succession planning* has had to be refocused away from preparing people for particular jobs to simply ensuring that a sufficiently large pool of talented individuals exists to meet future leadership requirements.[3] In some cases an organisation's strategy may require *uniquely competent individuals*, such as a top surgeon in a hospital, a criminal lawyer or a leading academic in a university. In contrast, some strategies might require *redeployment* and *redundancy* planning.

- Many *training and development* plans have reduced the use of formal programmes in favour of more coaching and mentoring to support self-development.

In order to put in place and execute HR strategies in all these areas, managers and HR professionals need to be familiar with the organisation's strategies, how these might be changing in the future and the implication to people's competences.[4] Many companies might attempt this alignment through formalised approaches to performance management – assisted by IT-based systems.[5]

However, it is not enough simply to adjust the performance management processes to support changing strategies. Managers need to be able and willing to envisage a future where the strategies and performance of the organisation are transformed by exploiting the performance management capabilities of the organisation better than their competitors. For example, a capability in mentoring and coaching could provide an environment that will attract creative people who like to be challenged and to learn. In turn, this creates a workforce that are much more able than competitors to 'think out of the box' and to produce innovative product features and new ways of competing in the market. This will require organisation structures and processes to support these behaviours, as explained in Chapter 12 and discussed further below.

13.2.2 People and behaviour[6]

People are not like other resources. They influence strategy both through their competence (section 13.2.1) and through their collective behaviour (culture) as discussed in Chapter 5. Chapter 14 will also emphasise that many of the problems of managing change result from a failure to understand, address and change culture. This 'soft' side of HR management is concerned with the behaviour of people – both individually and collectively. It is very often neglected in favour of the 'harder' issues discussed in the previous section. For example, these 'softer' issues might include:

- Understanding how they may need to change the *paradigm*[7] of the organisation as discussed in Chapter 5. This is particularly important when the business environment is changing quickly.

- Seeing their own role as people-oriented 'shapers of context'[8] and not just as 'business analysts'. This will require an understanding of how these 'softer' aspects of strategy help or hinder strategic success.

- Understanding *the relationship between behaviours and strategic choices*. This is crucial if managers are properly to prioritise their efforts in managing organisational behaviours. For example, there may be some strategies where an organisation's current culture gives unique advantage over other organisations. So culture is a core competence as discussed in Chapter 3.

- Being realistic about the *difficulty and time-scales* in achieving behaviour changes. Culture change is a long process of changing behaviours. The hard change tools (structures and systems) if used alone are unlikely to deliver, as seen in Chapter 14.

- Being able to vary their *style* of managing change with different circumstances, as will be discussed in Chapter 14. So a manager's relationship and leadership skills with both internal and external stakeholders are important. Also, *teams* in organisations must be capable of operating different styles simultaneously. Therefore, a manager's ability to build and maintain teams of different personality types is just as important as the mix of competences in those teams.[9]

Illustration 13.1 shows how important is the behaviour of front-line staff – particularly in service organisations. In this example their behaviour was clearly out of line with the stated business strategy of 'customer care'. So the intended strategy and the actual (realised) strategies were not the same. Fundamentally it is the day-to-day actions of managers that will shape and change the behaviour of front-line staff. But HR policies and frameworks can help with these softer-side issues. For example, in the high-technology sector the ability of staff and managers to build internal and external networks of personal contacts can be crucial in keeping at the leading edge of knowledge. These behaviours can be supported by 'hard-side' HR activities such as mentoring and rewards.[10]

13.2.3 Organising people[11]

Chapter 12 was concerned with the issues of organising for success with particular emphasis on how the balance of this agenda is changing in the twenty-first century. It is not the intention to repeat that detail here but to highlight some of the implications to how people might underpin strategic success.

The HR function

There are a number of important considerations concerning the HR function in organisations. The most challenging question is whether a specialist HR function is needed at all, or at least whether its traditional scale and functions are appropriate. In principle (and in practice in many organisations), people can be managed strategically without a specialist HR function. This may make sense for some HR issues – for example, the dismantling of across-company grades and pay scales as organisations globalise – to reflect the much greater diversity in the labour markets. But for other aspects the reverse might be true. For example, a major problem of highly devolved organisations is that managers at 'lower' levels are unfamiliar with corporate-level strategies, are extremely busy and may not have the professional HR knowledge.

If an HR function is felt to be valuable then the expectations as to its role must be clear and consistent with the discussion above. There are four broad roles that an HR function could fulfil in contributing to successful business strategies:[12]

- As a *service provider* (for example, undertaking recruitment or arranging training) to line managers who are carrying the strategic responsibility for the HR issues.
- As a *regulator* 'setting the rules' within which line managers operate, for example on pay and promotions.
- As an *advisor* on issues of HR strategy to line managers (ensuring that HR policies and practice are in line with the 'best practice').
- As a *change agent* moving the organisation forward.

The determinants of the most appropriate role for an HR function are the organisation's context.[13] The type of staff, the nature of the strategy and the broad structural arrangements in the organisation are all important. Of course it may prove difficult for the same HR specialists to operate in all of these roles

Illustration 13.1

Customer relations at KLM: The Reliable Airline

What people do in providing customer services needs to be aligned with an organisation's strategy.

Cityhopper Flight KL1481 was due to leave Amsterdam for Glasgow. As the time approached for boarding, passengers were informed that they would not be boarding that flight, though they were given no clear explanation as to why. They later found that it had been diverted to Leeds. They were, however, informed that there would be another aircraft departing at 21:30. It arrived at 21:00 and at 21:20 they began to board. This took 30 minutes. At 22:00 the pilot announced that this aircraft had a fault with the hydraulics. He went on to explain: 'We have had a bad day: five of our Cityhoppers have developed faults so we are short of planes.' Passengers wondered quite what this said about the maintenance standards of KLM. Some minutes later they were told that no replacement aircraft could be found and they would have to stay in Amsterdam that night. When they disembarked it became clear there would be further problems. Passengers were asked to move to a transfer desk where they would be informed of what would happen to them. When they arrived there were only five KLM ground staff and long queues developed. There was no announcement of what would happen the next day. One of the ground staff was heard to say that further of their colleagues would soon be arriving, so the back end of the queues moved to set up new lines. Additional staff did arrive but they could not deal with the passengers because their computer screens did not work. So whilst people queued, numerous ground staff stood around exchanging increasingly heated and acrimonious comments with passengers. One passenger was heard to say 'I'm being made to feel this is my fault!' Eventually a supervisor arrived. He also made no announcement to the passengers or engaged with them. After about 15 minutes he went away. It emerged, but was never announced, that KLM had

not laid on another flight to Glasgow, but was filling vacant seats on various other flights going to Scotland.

It was after midnight when the last passengers went on their way to hotels around the airport. Muttering passengers were heard to say they would never fly with KLM again.

The Director of Customer Relationship Management at KLM, commented:

We regret the problems encountered by our passengers on this particular flight. In this case, we certainly learnt that despite the fact that technical problems occur in our business, both to airplanes and computer systems, the number of ground handling staff was not sufficient to satisfy the needs of our customers at this particular moment. Consequently the attitude of our staff towards customers was not appropriate and communication was not managed properly.

We learn every day from our customers' negative travel experience by transforming this information into knowledge and action to prevent these things happening again to other passengers. Our product and services at all customer contact points, like for instance reservations, ground, transfer and inflight, is regularly monitored and measured by a set of standard survey and measurement tools. The process behind this information flow is organized in such a way that: the cause of the problem is notified; a correction is requested and implemented and the situation is monitored through regular surveys.

Questions

1 In what ways were KLM's HR policies and systems adequate or not to deliver the promise of The Reliable Airline?

2 How did the behaviour of front-line staff influence the actual service delivery?

3 What could be changed to improve the consistency of service delivery?

simultaneously. For example, they may feel a conflict between their role as a regulator whilst trying to advise or change a group of people in the organisation.

Middle (line) managers

It has been mentioned above that there has been a significant move towards line managers being centrally involved in managing people issues themselves. This has the clear advantage of more ownership and a better chance of blending people-related issues with business strategies. But there are also worries and research[14] confirms the concerns as to whether the circumstances in which line managers operate are conducive to their doing a good job on people management issues:

● Whether it is realistic to expect line managers to be *competent HR professionals*. Handled badly, this could be a formula for mediocrity. This same concern could equally be applied to other areas such as information management (discussed in section 13.3).

● The *short-term pressures* to meet targets do not help line managers in taking a more strategic view of people-related issues. Downsizing and de-layering have left the remaining managers too busy.

● Trade unions and professional associations have tended to *resist a dispersion of responsibility* for HR strategies. From a union's point of view it is much easier to deal with a single, centralised authority. Professional bodies may take a similar view.

● Managers may lack the *incentive* to take on more of the formal HR activities, either directly in their pay or grade or indirectly in their judgement as to which competences make them more marketable outside the company.

Despite these concerns it is important to recognise the crucial influence of middle managers on the day-to-day performance and behaviour of people in their organisation. The implication for top managers is not to bypass middle managers in the strategy development process, otherwise the changes may not stick with the people in the organisation.

Structures and processes

People may be held back from contributing to strategic success because the traditional structures and roles do not match future strategies. Also, as circumstances and strategies change, organisations may need to change the processes and relationships as discussed in Chapter 12.

Another challenge is whether some HR issues (for example, recruitment, training) should reside in the organisation or be bought in from specialist suppliers (for example, consultants). External agencies will have the advantage of a wider experience and knowledge of best practice but the disadvantage of being unfamiliar with the detailed circumstances of specific organisations.

13.2.4 Implications for managers

The various separate points about the relationship between business strategies and people have been brought together and summarised in the model shown in Exhibit 13.3:

Exhibit 13.3   Competitive advantage through people

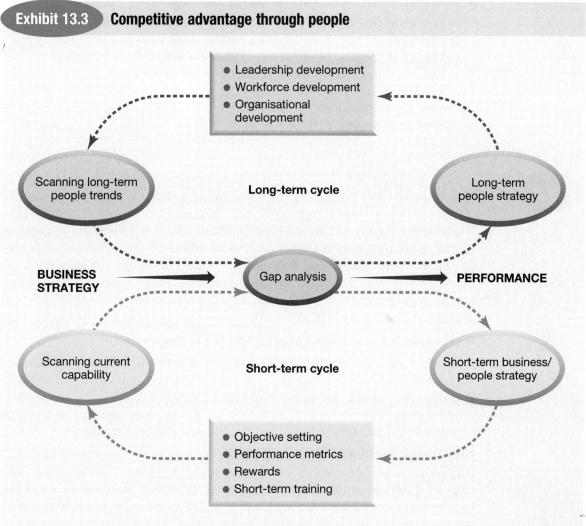

Source: Adapted from L. Gratton, V. Hope Hailey, P. Stiles and C. Truss, *Strategic Human Resource Management*, Oxford University Press, 1999, p. 185, Fig. 9.1. Copyright © 1999 Oxford University Press.

● There must be activities to ensure the *maintenance* of competitiveness. This is about ensuring that people are able to support the strategies of an organisation in the short term. For example, objective setting, performance appraisal, rewards and training.

● Simultaneously there must be activities to provide a *platform on which new strategies can be built* in the longer term. For example, leadership, culture, competences and organisation development. The management of these longer-term issues might create opportunities for significant *transformations* in strategy and competitiveness.

● These two 'cycles' of activities must be *linked*. Achieving short-term delivery goals must not be at the expense of longer-term capability. For example, using reward systems as the main tool to stimulate short-term success – say through individual bonus schemes – may compromise the ability to take more radical and strategic interventions, such as the creation of new roles and relationships to create a more innovative organisation.

- Those organisations that are *competent in managing these processes* are likely to gain competitive advantage.[15] Others run the risk of failing to deliver successful business strategies for one or more of the following reasons:
  - The *HR strategies* are out of line with the overall business strategy.
  - *People's competences and/or behaviours* are out of line with HR strategies and/or business strategies.
  - *Business strategies* are failing to capitalise on the strengths in an organisation's capabilities (Chapter 3) and/or culture (behaviours) (Chapter 5).

13.3 MANAGING INFORMATION[16]

Knowledge creation and information management should be issues at the front of managers' minds as potential sources of improved competitiveness, as discussed in Chapter 3. Within this wider agenda, considerations have naturally focused on IT and the extent to which it can transform competitiveness. This section will look at three main connections between information, IT developments and strategy (see Exhibit 13.4):

- information and *strategic capability* (linked to Chapter 3);
- information and changing *business models* within and across industries and sectors;
- information and *structures/management processes* (linked to Chapter 12).

13.3.1 Information and strategic capability

Chapter 3 explained the concept of strategic capability. Information strategies can have a profound influence on creating and destroying[17] the capabilities of an organisation and, hence, its competitive advantage. This will be demonstrated by

Exhibit 13.4 **Strategy and information**

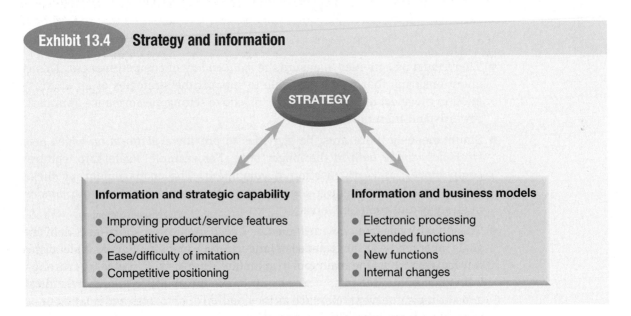

looking at examples of how information and IT might impact on three important 'elements' of a core capability as described in Chapter 3, namely: ensuring that products/services *are valued by customers, outperforming competitors* and making capabilities *difficult to imitate*. But wider availability of information will also accelerate the learning of competitors, so advantages gained through experience may be shorter-lived than hitherto. This will inevitably mean that organisations will need to revisit and redefine the basis on which they are competing more frequently, as discussed in Chapters 2 and 6.

Information and product/service features

The enhanced capabilities of IT already help organisations to provide product/service features that are valued by customers:

- *Lower prices* (through reduced costs) – particularly where the product is information, such as in financial services.
- Improved *pre-purchase information* (for example, website browsing, customer bulletin boards).
- *Easier and faster purchasing processes* (for example, online ordering) and delivery. This can allow customers to move closer to just-in-time with *their* business processes.
- *Shorter development times* for new features. These, in turn, might give purchasers advantage with *their* customers.
- *Product or service reliability* and diagnostics are being improved (for example, engine management systems in cars).
- *Personalised products* or services without price premium (for example, customising computer architecture for each purchaser).
- Improved *after-sales service*, for example automatic service reminders.

One of the most important implications for organisations producing or distributing physical products has been that competitive advantage is more likely to be achieved through service performance (for example, speed and reliability of delivery or maintenance) than in product features per se. So managers need to conceive of their business not as a product company with support services but as a service company which supplies a product. This has required a profound mindset shift for some managers when considering which competences are most crucial to competitive performance.

Information and competitive performance

If customers value some or all of these features listed above then competitors are likely to learn quickly how to provide those features. Therefore the threshold standards that need to be achieved to survive in a market will rise rapidly. So providers who are unable to deliver these higher standards will fall out of the market. Also Chapter 3 reminded readers that competitiveness and standards of performance are determined not just within a particular industry or sector. Customer expectations of service standards, for example on speed or reliability, become the universal benchmarks crossing all industries and public services.

The importance of market knowledge to competitiveness applies in all sectors of industry, commerce and the public services. This knowledge results from competences in analysing the subtle differences between customer needs in different parts of the market and building product or service features to meet these needs (as mentioned in Chapters 2 and 6). Most organisations have colossal amounts of raw data about these issues and the IT processing capacity to analyse the data (both of which are necessary). But they are not good at this data-mining process, which will convert data into market knowledge. **Data mining**[18] is the process of finding trends, patterns and connections in data in order to inform and improve competitive performance. For example, building up individual customer purchasing history as a basis for targeting promotional offers; identifying connected purchases (for instance, readers of particular newspapers or magazines have similar purchasing patterns for other goods and services); or simply finding underlying drivers of demand (such as demographic factors as discussed in Chapter 2). Data mining can also help with profitability analysis as a basis for creating priorities for customer retention. In financial services data mining can also help with credit risk assessment, customer attrition forecasts and detection of fraud.

Data mining is the process of finding trends, patterns and connections in data in order to inform and improve competitive performance

Information and imitation

Chapter 3 considered several reasons why resources or competences might be difficult to imitate. Information processing capability can have an influence on any/all of these:

● First, a resource or competence might be *rare*. When IT infrastructure costs were high this was a reason why a few larger organisations gained advantage over others through their IT infrastructure. Others could not afford the capital costs. On the whole, this is no longer true. IT is now pervasive even in very small companies.

● Capabilities may also be difficult to imitate because they are *complex*. The mastery of the hardware and standard software needed to build information systems used to be complex – now it is not. The current areas of complexity are more in data-mining activities (discussed above) and the activities which underpin speed to market. Managing relationships in the value network (see section 3.6.1) is an area where 'e-relationship management'[19] with customers can be particularly important (such as joining up all the different routes through which customers interface with a company).

● Capabilities may be hard to imitate because of *causal ambiguity* – competitors find it hard to understand the reasons why an organisation is successful. This is because the competences are *culturally embedded* in the way the organisation works and are not explicit. Many IT developments – particularly intelligent systems – are attempting to codify the tacit knowledge in organisations to make it explicit. For example, helplines use every customer query and its solution to build up progressively knowledge as to what can go wrong with a product and how it is solved. This ability to codify previously tacit knowledge removes barriers to imitation and undermines core capabilities. There is a danger in becoming overdependent on information systems and ignoring tacit knowledge simply because it is difficult to codify and build into the system. But this is the very reason why it is difficult to imitate and may be crucial to competitive advantage.

Information and competitive positioning

The strategic role of information in organisations will need to be different depending on the way in which the organisation is positioning its products or services in the market (as described by the strategy clock from Chapter 6 – Exhibit 6.2):

● *Routinisation* (positions 1 and 2 on the strategy clock) – where the role of information (usually IT systems) is to reduce drastically the cost of transactions with customers, suppliers or channels. For example, by moving the customer towards self-service (such as websites replacing face-to-face selling).

● *Mass customisation* (position 3 on the strategy clock) – where information systems can create more product features that customers value (as discussed above) at the same or lower price. This is a major battleground in many sectors at the present time – such as consumer electronics.

● *Customisation* (positions 4 and 5 on the strategy clock) – where information can be provided to customers in advance of any face-to-face or telephone contact (for example, through websites). Personal contact is then reserved for advising a much more knowledgeable potential customer.

It should be remembered that significant parts of the market in most sectors consist of customers who do not value the features that IT-based systems can offer. So targeting these *IT laggards* provides a continuing opportunity for those providers who are especially good at providing information in more traditional ways, for example personal face-to-face service.

13.3.2 Information and changing business models

A business model describes the structure of product, service and information flows and the roles of the participating parties

Information processing capability has provided the opportunity to transform the way in which organisations build their relationships with others in their value network (as discussed in section 3.6.1). This is concerned with how business models[20] have changed in both the private and public sectors. A **business model** describes the structure of product, service and information flows and the roles of the participating parties. This includes potential benefits and sources of revenue to each of the parties. The value network framework discussed in section 3.6.1 can be used to identify many traditional business models. For example, the linear supply chain from component manufacturers, to finished product assemblers, primary distributors, retailers and finally the consumer. Even in this case – where the product 'flows' in a linear fashion through the chain – information and other services may exist in branches of the chain. For example, market research and after-sales service may be undertaken by other parties from outside this linear chain. In more complex e-commerce models a critical question is how each 'player' in the value network receives revenue. For example, this could be from sale of a product/service, 'commission' or providing advertising space. Exhibit 13.5 shows how e-commerce models have emerged out of traditional business models based on the degree of *innovation* from traditional approaches and the *complexity* (mainly the level of integration of activities). Three main changes have occurred:

Exhibit 13.5	Changing business models

Degree of innovation

		Same as before	Extended	New
Degree of integration	Single function	E-shop E-procurement	E-auction Value chain services (e.g. payment systems, logistics) Trust services	Information brokerage (e.g. search engines)
	Integrated functions	E-mall	Third-party marketplace (e.g. web hosting)	Virtual communities Collaboration platforms Value chain integrator

Source: Adapted from P. Timmers, *Electronic Commerce*, Wiley, 2000, Chapter 3.

● *Electronic processes have replaced physical and paper-based processes*. For example, *e-shops* move marketing and 'display' to websites. *E-procurement* moves tendering, negotiation and purchasing processes to websites. In both cases the advantages are in reduced costs and wider choice. An *e-mall* takes the concept a little further by creating a collection of e-shops with a common umbrella – such as a brand. Nor is the public sector any different. Information gathering at scenes of crime is now aided by citizens and their digital camera/phones.

● Significant *extension of the functions* that traditional business models can offer. For example, sourcing or selling through *e-auctions* is both easy and cheap and can lead to significantly reduced purchasing costs or increased revenues. *Trust services* (such as supplier or customer certification or vetting) extend the types of information services available to members of trade associations. Other information functions in the value network can be provided more efficiently or effectively by *value chain service specialists* – such as payments or logistics. Some organisations see benefits in leaving a number of value activities to specialists who create *third-party marketplaces* and offer web-based marketing, branding, payment systems, logistics, and so on. This could be viewed as a complementary route to market rather than a complete replacement.

● Business models that are *transformational* in the sense that business can only be done this way electronically. Perhaps the most well-established example of transformational changes is the *information brokerage* role of companies like Yahoo! or Google with their search engines. *Virtual communities* can be sustained by IT – as Amazon tries to do in bringing authors, readers and publishers into dialogue on their website. Sometimes IT can provide a *collaboration platform*, for example, allowing customers and suppliers to work together on product design using specialist IT design tools. *Value chain integration* may be made possible through IT if separate activities can be knitted together by faster and more reliable information flows. For example, sales staff can discuss requirements with customers using both 'real-time' information about manufacturing capability, availability and production scheduling and also 'straight-through' information about the same issues in the supply chain. Frequently integration allows customers to change their specification and delivery schedules themselves – which then automatically reconfigures requirements back in the supply chain.

- In addition to these, there can also be important implications on how the internal 'business model' works. For example, better information can allow managers and external stakeholders to *bypass some of the traditional* **gatekeepers**, who gained power from their control of information. IT-based systems can create direct communication between the top and the bottom of an organisation and many chief executives use in-house websites for that purpose. The same issues also apply to the bypassing of unions as information conduits to employees. Also, externally, the salesforce are no longer the primary route through which customers gain their product knowledge or even place orders. Often their role has moved from 'closing deals' to relationship management and advice. In the public sector politicians are able to put in place two-way communication with their communities rather than relying on managers as the conduit and filter. There are already challenging implications for the whole way in which the political and service provision processes work.[21]

Gatekeepers are individuals or groups who gain power from their control of information

From a strategic point of view the important considerations of any of these e-commerce business models is the extent to which they are able to create better value for money for customers and/or suppliers as shown in Illustration 13.2.

13.3.3 Implications for managers[22]

There are some important implications of these previous discussions for managers and those responsible for information strategy in organisations:

- Managers need to realise that information processing capability can *transform* the organisation, not just fine-tune current strategies and processes. They need to move away from seeing information management as a support function and place it on a par with other business functions.

- At the same time information managers[23] need to understand the *full potential of IT* from their professional knowledge and external networks (that is, be the company benchmarker). They need to understand the limitations of formal information systems, which cannot replace certain types of knowledge (such as intuition) or knowledge sharing that depends on social contact. Information managers need to be involved in and credible on business strategy as part of the corporate team (and not sit on the sidelines) and to see new business opportunities that IT could open up. They also need to have the influencing skills to educate and persuade senior colleagues about these opportunities.

Illustration 13.2

The DIY craze extends to loans

IT can support new business models which allow new intermediaries to displace established players – like banks. But is it a better deal for the customers and suppliers?

An article in the *Financial Times* in November 2005 outlined the activities of a new Internet-based financial intermediary:

Zopa (www.zopa.com) seeks to bring together borrowers and lenders without requiring them to go through a bank or other financial institution. Zopa was launched earlier this year. Its business model is relatively simple. If you are looking to borrow money you post your details on Zopa's website indicating how much you want to borrow and over what period you are looking to pay the money back. Zopa will then analyse your financial situation, giving you a credit rating according to your perceived ability to continue meeting the loan repayments. It claims that by using this model not only can it give most borrowers a much more competitive rate for loans than they could get off the high street but that people who lend money via Zopa will also get a much better return than had they stuck their cash in a bank account. Of course there are risks. . . .

Under the Zopa model, the rate charged by the lender is exactly the same as the rate incurred by the borrower. In short, Zopa does not take a cut as an intermediary. The average interest rate [were better] for [both] borrowers and lenders [than through traditional banks]. . . .

I can hear you asking: 'So how does Zopa make its money?' Well it is looking to two main revenue streams. One is by selling payment protection insurance (PPI) to some borrowers. In the event that the borrower is unable to meet repayments because of illness or redundancy, this insurance will cover the loan repayments. And from next year, it will also start charging borrowers an upfront fee of 1 per cent of the value of the loan. There will be no fee charged to lenders. . . .

But for lenders, the risks are less clear cut. As a lender to Zopa you are taking on all the default risks of the borrower. So if the person you are lending to is unable to meet the loan repayments you risk losing out. Zopa seeks to minimise these risks in a number of ways. First, it conducts credit checks on its borrowers with three separate agencies. It also asks them an array of questions about their financial status.

Second, all loans are spread across 50 different borrowers with the same credit scores. So, in the event of one customer default, the maximum a lender could lose on a £5,000 [€7,250] loan is just £100. . . . In the event of a default, Zopa will also send out a debt collector on your behalf. The other risk is that Zopa itself goes under. Zopa insists that it has enough cash to see it through to profitability and, in the unlikely event that it did collapse, it has also set aside enough cash to continue acting as an intermediary.

This is of some comfort. But if you are lending via Zopa, you should be getting a much better return than you would from cash to compensate for these unknown risks.

Source: Robert Budden, *Financial Times*, 26 November 2005.

Questions

1 How has ZOPA changed the business model for both lending and borrowing compared with a traditional bank? (Refer to Exhibit 13.5.)

2 List the advantages and disadvantages for both lenders and borrowers of dealing with ZOPA instead of a bank.

3 How could the banks respond?

13.4 MANAGING FINANCE[24]

Finance and the way that it is managed can be a key determinant of strategic success. From a shareholder's point of view, what matters is the cash-generating capability of the business since this determines the ability to pay dividends in the short term and to reinvest for the future (which, in turn, should enable a future flow of dividend payments). In the public sector the equivalent issue is the need to deliver best value services within financial limits. There are three broad issues that organisations of all types face (see Exhibit 13.6):

● *Managing for value*, whether this is concerned with creating value for shareholders or ensuring the best use of public money, is an important consideration for, and responsibility of, all managers. However, the way in which finance is managed and controlled will have a major influence on this issue.

Exhibit 13.6 **Strategy and finance**

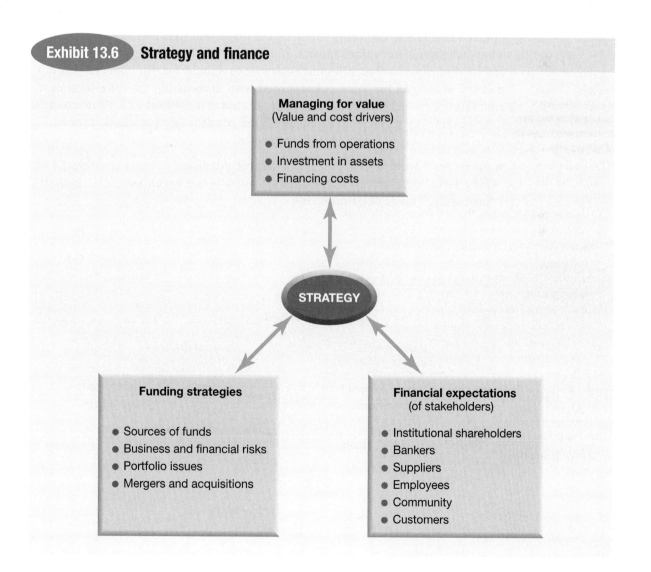

- *Funding* strategic developments is clearly important too: in particular, that the nature of the funding is appropriate for the type of strategy – and vice versa. This is also concerned with balancing business and financial risks.

- The *financial expectations* of stakeholders will vary – both between different stakeholders and in relation to different strategies. This should influence managers in both strategy development and implementation.

13.4.1 Managing for value[25]

There has been a continuing theme through this book that the long-term success of strategies is determined by the extent to which they deliver best value in the eyes of major stakeholders. Two examples of this are competitiveness in the marketplace (that is, value to customers) and the ability to provide value to shareholders (through the returns they receive in dividends and share price movement). In competitive markets these two issues are likely to be closely linked in the long term since the returns to shareholders are driven by market success. However, this broad connection between competitiveness and share-holder value needs exploring further. It is important that managers understand what 'managing for value' means and how it might be achieved.[26] This is a crucial contribution which financial strategies should make to overall business success. **Managing for value** is concerned with maximising the long-term cash-generating capability of an organisation. As shown in Exhibit 13.7, value creation is determined by three main financial issues: funds from operations, investment in (or disposal of) assets, and financing costs.

Managing for value is concerned with maximising the long-term cash-generating capability of an organisation

- *Funds from operations* are clearly a major contributor to value creation. In the long term, this concerns the extent to which the organisation is operating profitably. This is determined by:

Exhibit 13.7 **Financial aspects of value creation**

	DRIVERS	
	Value drivers (increase shareholder value)	**Cost drivers** (reduce shareholder value)
Operations	Revenue ⟨ Sales volume / Prices	Operational costs ⟨ Direct costs / Overheads
Investment	Disposal of fixed assets Reduction in current assets • stock • debtors	Capital investment (fixed assets) Reduction in current liabilities • creditors
Financing		Cost of capital ⟨ Equity / Loans

- Sales revenue – made up of sales volume and the prices that the organisation is able to maintain in its markets.
- 'Production' and selling costs – both made up of fixed and variable elements.
- Overhead or indirect costs.

● *Investment in assets* – the extent to which assets and working capital are being stretched is also a key consideration. This will affect value creation as follows:
  - The costs of capital investment or, in some cases, the disposal of redundant assets.
  - The management of the elements of working capital such as stock, debtors and creditors will increase or decrease shareholder value as indicated.

Some organisations have developed competences in supporting much higher levels of business from the same asset base than others.

● *Financing costs* – the mix of capital in the business – between debt (requiring interest payments) and equity will determine the cost of capital (and also the financial risk as seen in the next section).

The issues in the public sector are very similar. The problem for most public sector managers is that their financial responsibilities are usually confined to managing their budget (that is, the cash outflows of operations). They will usually be doing this with little understanding of the other financial issues from the diagram, which will be managed by the corporate financial function. There is a real need for managers to be much more familiar with the impact of their day-to-day management decisions on the wider financial health of the organisation. For example, the use of fixed assets or the incurring of bad debts.

Key value and cost drivers

It is not the intention in this book to discuss the detailed issues concerning the management of each of the separate items shown in Exhibit 13.7. From a business strategy point of view, the critical issue is to understand what are the **key value and cost drivers**. These are the factors that have the most influence on the cash generation capability of an organisation or, in the public service, on the ability to provide best value services. The value network concept (section 3.6.1) is important in helping managers understand how and where value may be created within an organisation and in the wider value network. Importantly, it is likely that costs and value creation are spread *unevenly* across the activities in the value chain and value network. So some activities are more crucial to value (or cost) creation than others. However, this will vary with the type of business and with the circumstances in which it is operating, as will be seen below.

Some examples illustrate the importance of this identification of key cost and value drivers:[27]

● *Sources of capital* are usually a major cost driver and will vary with source. So the relative cash outflows which result from servicing loans as against equity would be an important strategic consideration.

● *Capital expenditure* (capex) can be a major cash outflow that can destroy shareholder value unless it contributes to improving the revenues or reducing the costs elsewhere in Exhibit 13.7. In principle, the business cases for capex

Key value and cost drivers are the factors that have most influence on the cash generation cabability of an organisation

items should address this issue before expenditure is approved. Commonly the case for expenditure would relate to *enhanced product features* leading to increased sales and/or better prices; or *reduced costs* (for example, through increased labour productivity) or *decreased working capital* (for example, through stock reduction by streamlining production or distribution).

● The detailed *cost structure* of businesses varies considerably from sector to sector and hence the relative importance of specific cost items. For example, service organisations are generally more labour intensive than manufacturing – underlining the importance of wage levels. Retailers are concerned with stock turnover and sales volume per square metre – reflecting two major cost drivers.

● Sometimes the crucial cost or value drivers are *outside the organisation* (in the supply or distribution chain). The strategic implication is that organisations need to be competent in maintaining the performance of key suppliers or distributors. This means the ability to select, motivate and 'control' suppliers and distributors. It may also mean reconsideration as to whether any of these activities should be taken 'in-house' if they are so critically important to cost and value creation. This was discussed in Chapters 3 and 12 (outsourcing).

● The key cost and value drivers may change *over time*. For example, during the introduction of a new product, the key factor may be establishing *sales volume*; once established, *prices and unit costs* might be most important; during decline, improving cash flow through *stock and debtor reduction* may be essential to support the introduction of the next generation of products.

Overall, the message is that managers can benefit considerably from a detailed understanding of the value creation processes within their organisation and the wider value network – it can help them be more strategic in how they prioritise their efforts for performance improvement.

13.4.2 Funding strategy development

Sources of funds

Managers need to be familiar with the advantages and drawbacks of different sources of funds, which are well explained in standard financial texts.[28] Decisions on which sources to use will be influenced by the current financial situation of the organisation such as ownership (for example, whether the business is privately held or publicly quoted) and by the overall corporate goals and strategic priorities of the organisation. For example, there will be different financial needs if a business is seeking rapid growth by acquisition compared with if it is seeking to consolidate its past performance. A critical issue is the way in which financial strategies address the financial and business risks of different types of funding. This will now be discussed.

Balancing financial and business risks[29]

This section uses the growth/share matrix (see Exhibit 7.7) to illustrate how financial strategies need to vary for the different 'phases' of development of a business – see Exhibit 13.8.

Exhibit 13.8   **Balancing business and financial risk**

GROWTH (Stars)		LAUNCH (Question marks)	
Business risk:	High	Business risk:	Very high
Financial risk needs to be:	Low	Financial risk needs to be:	Very low
Funding by:	Equity (growth investors)	Funding by:	Equity (venture capital)
Dividends:	Nominal	Dividends:	Zero
MATURITY (Cash cows)		**DECLINE (Dogs)**	
Business risk:	Medium	Business risk:	Low
Financial risk can be:	Medium	Financial risk can be:	High
Funding by:	Debt and equity (retaining earnings)	Funding by:	Debt
Dividends:	High	Dividends:	Total

Source: Adapted from K. Ward, *Corporate Financial Strategy*, Butterworth–Heinemann, 1993, Fig. 2.7, p. 33.

The greater the risk to shareholders or lenders, the greater the return these investors will require. Therefore, from an organisation's point of view, the important issue is how it should balance the business risk with the financial risk to the organisation. As a generalisation, the greater the business risk, the lower should be the financial risk taken by the organisation, and the growth/share matrix is a convenient way of illustrating this:

- *Question marks* (or *problem children*)[30] are clearly high business risk. They are at the beginning of their life cycle and are not yet established in their markets; moreover, they are likely to require substantial investment. A stand-alone business in this situation might, for example, seek to finance such growth from specialists in this kind of investment, such as venture capitalists who, themselves, seek to offset risk by having a portfolio of such investments. Schemes for private investors (so-called 'business angels') have also become popular.

- In the case of *stars* the degree of business risk remains high in these high-growth situations even though relatively high market shares are being achieved. The market position here remains volatile and probably highly competitive. Since the main attractions to investors here are the product or business concept and the prospect of future earnings, equity capital is likely to be appropriate, say by public flotation.

- Businesses that operate in mature markets with high shares (*cash cows*) should be generating regular and substantial surpluses. Here the business risk is lower and the opportunity for retained earnings is high. In these circumstances, it may make sense to raise finance through debt capital as well as equity, since reliable returns can be used to service such debt. Provided increased debt (*gearing* or *leverage*) does not lead to an unacceptable level of risk, this cheaper debt funding will in fact increase the residual profits achieved by a company in these circumstances.

● If a business is in decline, in effect a *dog*, then equity finance will be difficult to attract. However, borrowing may be possible if secured against residual assets in the business. At this stage, it is likely that the emphasis in the business will be on cost cutting, and it could well be that the cash flows from such businesses are quite strong. These businesses may provide relatively low-risk investments.

Illustration 13.3 shows how funding sources need to match circumstances.

Funding a portfolio of businesses

At the corporate level in *diversified* companies there can be a problem in developing a financial strategy for a portfolio with a mix of businesses growing at different rates and in high- or low-share positions. The organisation needs to consider its *overall* risk/return position. For example, a company seeking to develop *new and innovative businesses* on a regular basis might, in effect, be acting as its own venture capitalist, accepting high risk at the business level and seeking to offset such risk by 'cash cows' in its portfolio. Public sector managers know this too. They need a steady core to their service where budgets are certain to be met, hence reducing the financial risk of the more speculative aspects of their service. Some companies may need to sell off businesses as they mature to raise capital for further investment in new ventures.

Funding mergers and acquisitions[31]

Section 10.2.2 looked at the advantages and pitfalls of developing strategy through mergers or acquisitions (M&A). In particular it raised some warnings about potential conflicts between long-term strategic reasons and shorter-term financial reasons for M&A activity. One key decision relates to the way in which a merger will be funded. Again some general principles are useful in tying financial and business strategies together:

● Payment by *cash* is likely to be attractive to the target business's shareholders and the shareholder control of the bidding business is not diluted by new shares. However, it may prove difficult for most bidding companies to raise enough cash. Of course the danger for cash-rich bidders is that they spend unwisely and build empires that lack strategic logic and are difficult to manage without loss of value in some of the acquired businesses.

● The issuing of *shares* may be attractive to the target company shareholders as they exchange their old shares for shares in the bidding company. This needs to be handled carefully so as not to depress share price before the conclusion of the deal. From a strategic point of view this is the option that keeps the capital structure of the merged company least changed and so the financial risk may be the least.

● A bidding company may issue *loan capital* to the target company shareholders. This may be attractive to them if they have some doubts about future financial

Illustration 13.3

Renewable energy

Changes in the business environment create new market opportunities. But who will fund the development of capacity?

Energy is the lifeblood of any developed economy, but alternatives to oil, gas and coal – so-called renewable energy sources such as wind and tide – have long been treated as a feeble joke, ring fenced for well-meaning but naive hair shirts and ethical investors. . . .

Not any more. The London estuary venture (a planned £1.5 billion [€2.2bn] construction of 270 turbines off the Kent coast) is the latest sign that clean energy is coming of age as a serious business. Yes, it's an Anglo-Danish minnow, Core, that has submitted the plans, but the people stumping up the cash are energy giants Shell and E.On.

'We're approaching the point of no return', says Peter Shortt, director of innovation and investment at the Carbon Trust, a quango that is busy investing £1–2 million chunks of venture capital in renewable energy projects. 'Once building work begins on these massive offshore wind farms, we'll have reached the tipping point, the next step of very significant development.' . . .

Wind is just one element. Pioneers of a range of forward-looking renewable energy technologies have propelled the recent surge in Alternative Investment Market (AIM) flotations. . . . Only a couple of years ago, just a handful of ethical banks and funds would take calls from renewable energy start-ups. Now the City's bluest-chip banks, private equity houses and venture capitalists, such as Fidelity, Fleming, Nikko, New Star and Cazenove, have woken up to the market's promise.

Just how big is that potential? The government's target is 10% of electricity from renewable sources by 2010 [but] . . . critics also say the sector would fall flat without government subsidies . . . running at £700 million a year.

To a sceptical eye, the renewables market looks built to flip – irresistible only to investors and entrepreneurs seeking a quick killing. But there are mega trends driving investment in this sector over the long term: soaring demand for electricity, rising oil prices and concerted efforts to reduce carbon dioxide emissions. . . . These factors have made alternative power sources more attractive, just as engineering advances have made clean energy technologies more efficient. . . . Of course, the large energy companies can't afford to write off their existing infrastructures of pipelines, tankers, refineries and transmission lines. Some are waiting until the last moment to adopt new technology, wringing the last drop of revenue from existing assets. While they do so, smaller companies will continue to thrive: early innovators such as Vestas Wind Systems of Denmark and Iberdrola of Spain now have global reach.

But the energy business is full of big incumbents. In the UK electricity market, for example, the 'big six' – British Gas, Powergen, npower, Scottish Power, Scottish and Southern, and EDF – carve up all but 0.5% of the pie. Will there be a change in the balance of power? Unlikely, as the smarter players are already shifting their centres of gravity. Jeroen van der Veer, Shell's chief executive, says it is pouring resources into whichever renewable energy source looks promising. 'The philosophy is pots on the fire: try everything, and by 2015 we have to make up our mind,' he told journalists in June.

Who can predict which energy source will be the future of Britain? Only the entrepreneurs and investors who are inventing it.

Source: Ian Wylie, 'New Power Generation', *Management Today*, December 2005, pp. 48–53. Reproduced from *Management Today* magazine with the permission of the copyright owner, Haymarket Business Publications Limited.

Question

Referring to section 13.4.2 and Exhibit 13.8, describe how you would try to balance the business and financial risks if you were:

● a new start-up renewables company;
● one of the 'big six' energy companies;
● the British government.

performance of the merged company. The bidding company shareholders avoid dilution of their control but the gearing is increased and hence the financial risk.

- External *loans* are often used by bidders to offer cash to target company shareholders. This has been the subject of much controversy as aggressive bids from individuals have been successful in purchasing publicly quoted companies and taking them private – but with high gearing. The Manchester United case study (in the Text and Cases edition) is a high-profile example of this.

13.4.3 The financial expectations of stakeholders

Section 13.4.1 looked at how business strategies might create or destroy value for shareholders of a business. The public sector equivalent is the extent to which politicians (as the owners or guardians of public money) would regard public money to have been well spent. But it was seen in Chapter 4 that the owners are not the only ones who have a stake in organisations. Other stakeholders will have financial expectations of organisations. The question is to what extent business strategies should address these other financial expectations and how they can be squared with creating value for the owners. For example:

- Chapter 4 made the point that *institutional shareholders* (such as asset managers of pension funds) are the ones who usually represent the interests of the real beneficiaries of a company's performance. This is the concept of the governance chain. So strategy is strongly influenced by the financial expectations of these intermediaries who can become the key players in major strategic changes – such as mergers or acquisitions. There is a continuing concern that managers are distorting the long-term strategies of their companies as they respond to the shorter-term pressures on earnings exerted by stock market analysts and institutional shareholders.[32]

- *Bankers* and other providers of interest-bearing loans are concerned about the *risk* attached to their loans and the competence with which this is managed. A consistently good track record in managing that risk could be regarded (in itself) as a reason for bankers to invest further with some companies and not others. The risk would be influenced by the capital structure of the company – particularly the gearing ratio (of debt to equity), which determines how sensitive the solvency of the company is to changes in its profit position. Interest cover is a similar measure that relates interest payments to profit.

- *Suppliers* and *employees* are likely to be concerned with good prices and wages but also the *liquidity* of the company, which is a measure of its ability to meet short-term commitments to creditors and wages. Bankers will share this concern because a deteriorating liquidity position may require correction through additional loans and the increased risk profile discussed above. Again, a track record in this area could be a competence underpinning good supplier relationships, resulting in discounts or improved credit.

- The *community* will be concerned about jobs but also with the *social cost* of an organisation's strategies, such as pollution or marketing. This is rarely accounted for in traditional financial analyses, but it is an issue of growing concern. Matters of business ethics and social responsibility were discussed in Chapter 4 (section 4.3). Failure to pay proper attention to these issues could be a source of strategic weakness.

● *Customers* are concerned about best value products or services. This assessment is rarely made in traditional financial analyses, the implication being that companies that survive profitably in a competitive environment *must* be providing value for money.

Overall, managers need to be conscious of the financial impact on various stakeholders of the strategies they are pursuing or planning to pursue. They also need to understand how the capability to meet these varied expectations could enable the success of some strategies whilst limiting the ability of an organisation to succeed with other strategies.

13.5 MANAGING TECHNOLOGY[33]

This section is about the relationship between technology and strategic success. As mentioned in Chapter 3, the technology itself may be easy to acquire by competitors so is not necessarily a source of advantage. The way in which the technology is exploited is where advantage may be created. Indeed Chapter 7 gave examples of how many innovations come about through the novel exploitation of both established and new technologies. The chapter will look at the following issues about the relationship between business and technology strategies and how technology can underpin strategic success (see Exhibit 13.9):

● how technology changes the *competitive situation*;
● technology and *strategic capability*;
● *organising* technology to achieve advantage.

13.5.1 Technology and the competitive situation

Competitive forces

In Chapter 2, the five forces framework was used as a checklist for understanding the competitive forces within an industry and how they might determine the competitive position of different organisations. Before making decisions about the technology strategy of an individual organisation it is important to understand the ways in which technology can have a significant impact on these forces – particularly in industries that are globalising,[34] as the following examples illustrate:

● *Barriers to entry* for potential new entrants may be lowered by reducing the economies of scale, for example in publishing, or the capital requirements for set-up, for example in computing. In some cases, barriers may be raised as technologies become more difficult to master and products more complex, for example in the aerospace industry.

Exhibit 13.9   **Strategy and technology**

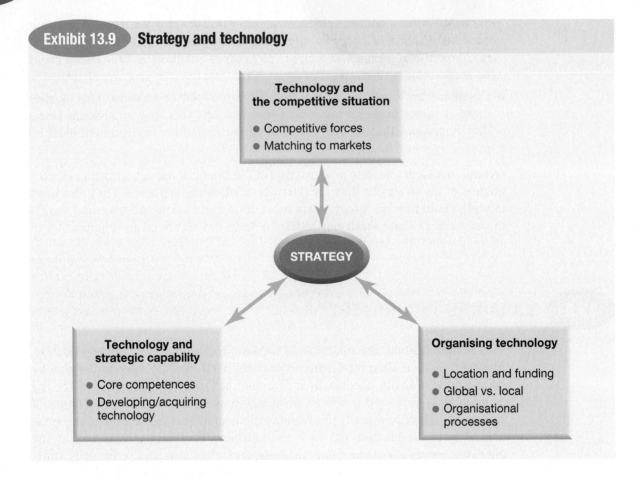

- *Substitution* may be made easier by technology at several levels. New products may displace old, for example DVDs for videotape. The need may be displaced, for example using video conferencing rather than travelling to meetings. Or technological developments in other sectors may 'steal' consumer demand through an array of exciting products, for example electronic goods displacing consumer spending on household durables such as kitchens and carpets. Sometimes technology can stop substitution, for example by tying the usage of one product to another – the 'debate' about Microsoft's success in tying software developments into the Windows operating system is an example.

- The *relative power of suppliers and buyers* can also be changed by technology. The Microsoft example applies here too since the issues raised in the court cases were about the extent to which Microsoft (as a supplier to most businesses and households) had unreasonably high levels of power over its customers. But technological developments can work in the favour of buyers by freeing them from a single source of supply. This often happens when international specifications and standards are agreed (say for steel).

- *Competitive rivalry* amongst organisations can be raised through this process of generic specifications or diminished if one firm develops a new product or process which it is able to patent. The level of competitive rivalry in generic pharmaceutical products as against ethical (proprietary) pharmaceutical products is markedly different.

The strategic issues raised for individual organisations through these examples are two-fold. First, some organisations may be technological leaders and trying to gain advantage in some of the ways outlined above. Second, other organisations may need to assess the likely impact on their competitive position of technological developments led by current or potential competitors.

Matching technology strategies to markets

The way in which technological developments can underpin competitiveness will vary depending on the nature of both the technology and the markets (see Exhibit 13.10):

● *Differentiated* strategies will be appropriate where both technologies and markets are mature. Product and service improvements are achieved by using existing technology to address a known customer requirement. Often this is concerned with improving quality – as the Japanese achieved with product reliability of automobiles. The danger is that this market looks attractive to imitators who might exploit technology to improve product features further or reduce cost.

● *Architectural* strategies work where existing technologies can be combined to create novel products or services or new applications. For example, glass and surface coating technologies have been used by glass companies to create a

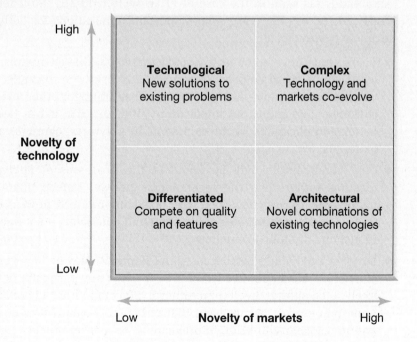

Exhibit 13.10   **Matching technology strategies to markets**

Source: J. Tidd, J. Bessant and K. Pavitt, *Managing Innovation: Integrating technological, market and organisational change*, 3rd edition, Wiley, 2005, Figure 7.1, p. 243.

range of new properties such as energy saving, reflective and self-cleaning glasses.

- *Technological* strategies apply new technologies to known customer needs. Products and services compete on the basis of enhanced performance against current products. Some big prizes in this category are the development of new 'wonder drugs' or even electrical energy storage devices to outperform massively the traditional battery in capacity, weight and price. The dangers here are imitation and high development costs. So the strategy usually requires technology protection (patents).

- *Complex* strategies are needed where both technologies and markets are novel and need to co-evolve. At the outset there are no clearly defined uses for the technology. So the critical issues here are understanding the processes of new product diffusion (as discussed in section 9.3). For example, there is a need for developers to work with early adopters to create new applications. The development of multimedia products and services is an ongoing example.

Illustration 13.4 shows how the choices of strategy may need to change as both technologies and markets change over time.

13.5.2 Technology and strategic capability

Core capabilities

Chapter 3 underlined the importance of identifying core capabilities as the basis of an organisation's competitive advantage. From a strategic point of view the importance of technology lies in the potential both to create and to destroy core capabilities (as seen in the case of IT in section 13.3.1). So if technology is to underpin success there are some important implications for both business and technology strategies:

- To tie future developments to a *single technology* that an organisation has mastered can be both inappropriate and unduly risky. For example, stainless steel was the wonder material of the 1960s, substituting for other materials in many consumer and industrial applications. But, in turn, it has been substituted in some applications by developments in polymers, ceramics and composite materials.

- Core competences may be found in the processes of *linking technologies* together rather than the technologies per se. Indeed, many advances in manufacturing are concerned with how computerised process control can be grafted to the technologies of the plant and machinery – not in being excellent in just one or other technology.

- *Dynamic capabilities* (as discussed in Chapter 3) may be important in a rapidly changing and competitive world. The fruits of any particular development are likely to be shorter-lived than hitherto. So competitive advantage needs to be underpinned by the processes that ensure a constant flow of improvements and in the ability to bring improvements to market quickly. This can lead to first-mover advantages. However, there is also evidence that in some circumstances commercial advantages of technological developments may accrue to 'fast-follower' companies rather than the pioneers.[35]

Illustration 13.4

Psion chief's warning to tech wannabes

The market will be the judge of the value of products from any technological development. So companies and entrepreneurs ignore it at their peril.

In an interview with the *Financial Times*, Sir David Potter, Founder and Chairman of Psion, the UK handheld computer company, warned that technology start-ups need to become more market savvy to survive. Sir David, one of the UK earliest academics-turned-entrepreneurs, having resigned from his tenure at Imperial College to found Psion in 1980, also wants the UK government to step up its efforts to encourage the transfer of technology from university laboratories to the commercial sector.

'Science does not translate itself into business just like that, it is far more complicated. We have in Britain a rather kind of fey belief that you have a nice idea in a laboratory and you get a market out of that. It doesn't happen like that,' he says. 'We need to be much closer to the market and not imagine that Cambridge or Imperial College are by themselves going to be able to spin out companies that are going to become world beaters.'

He says 10 or 12 national institutes should be set up, which would help in the exploitation of technology such as semiconductors or nanotechnology. With or without them, however, Sir David stressed the need for UK technology start-ups to become more adept at understanding the market.

'My first advice is follow the market above all. Don't think about your technology. If you've got skills and advantage in a particular area, work in that area but use the technology for the market not the other way around. Don't try and create the market from the technology,' he says.

Psion itself is a case in point. The company has managed to survive the brutal technology markets for 25 years mainly by reinventing itself many times. Psion, founded with less than £100,000 ($173,000; €145,000) of Sir David's own savings, began as publishers of other people's software, and gradually moved to writing its own. By 1983

it was the UK's leading developer in the nascent computer games market, thanks to a popular flight simulator game.

In a parallel universe, Psion might have gone on to become an Eidos or an Electronic Arts. But Sir David quickly decided that games were not really the market he wanted to be in.

'It could have been fun,' he mused. 'I would have probably had pink hair and a ponytail, God knows. But it wasn't really the culture of the company.'

Spotting a market opportunity, Sir David and his team moved into hardware and developed the world's first handheld computer – the Organiser – which was launched in 1986. Several golden years followed, in which Psion's iconic handhelds had the run of the market and easily saw off challenges with their rapid pace of innovation.

In the mid-1990s the market changed with the arrival of US rivals Palm and Compaq. Suddenly, it was not differentiation but scale that mattered, and Psion could no longer compete. In 2001 it was time for a strategic retreat. Psion took wide-scale job cuts and exited the consumer market, opting to focus on its more niche enterprise business.

While Sir David admits he has some regrets about the way things turned out, he says the important thing is that Psion is still here when many other companies have fallen by the wayside.

Source: Maija Palmer, *Financial Times*, 26 December 2005.

Questions

1 Trace the positioning of Psion on the technology/markets matrix (Exhibit 13.10) through the phases of its development.

2 Suggest how Psion might have followed a more successful path.

Exhibit 13.11	Developing or acquiring technology

Influencing factors

		Importance of the technology	Prior knowledge and reputation	Complexity	Willingness to take risk	Desire to lead or follow	Speed
Method	In-house	Key	High	Low/Medium	High	Lead	Slow
	Alliances	Threshold	Low	High	Medium	Follow	Medium
	Acquisition	Key or threshold	Very Low	High	Low	Follow	High

Source: Adapted from J. Tidd, J. Bessant and K. Pavitt, *Managing Innovation: Integrating technological, market and organisational change*, 2nd edition, Wiley, 2001, Table 8.6.

Developing or acquiring technology

Whether technology is developed 'in-house' or acquired externally can be a key determinant in the success or failure of strategies. This is a complex subject given that many different variables could influence these decisions.[36] However, for the purposes of illustrating the link between business and technology strategies a few general principles are useful (see Exhibit 13.11):

● *In-house development* may be favoured if the technology is key to competitive advantage and an organisation has expectations of gaining first-mover advantages. This will be feasible if the organisation already has a good knowledge of both the technology and the market opportunities and the complexity is not too great. This should be the case for *differentiated* strategies and possibly *architectural* strategies shown in Exhibit 13.10 above. It is also important that the organisation is willing to take commercial and financial risk.

● *Alliances* are likely to be appropriate for 'threshold' technologies rather than ones on which competitive advantage is to be built. For example, a manufacturer of branded drinks may seek a partner to improve bottling and distribution processes. These are both important activities but competitive advantage is concerned with the product itself and brand maintenance. Alliances might also be appropriate where there is an intention to follow and imitate rather than lead. This would be particularly the case where the complexity of product or market knowledge is beyond the current knowledge base – so organisational learning is an important objective (*complexity* strategies in Exhibit 13.10 above). Alliances also help to limit financial risk.

● *Acquisition of current players or rights* may be particularly appropriate if speed is important and there is no time for learning. It may also be essential if the level of complexity, in both technology and market application, is beyond current organisational knowledge (see *technological* and *complexity* strategies in Exhibit 13.10 above). It could be especially important where credibility of the technology is essential to business success – so the source of the technology matters. So production under licence of an established technology may be more successful than developing an alternative. Organisations acquiring technology need to have a good understanding of the technology needs of their product lines, an ability to identify and evaluate appropriate external technologies and the competence to negotiate an appropriate deal with the owners of the technology rights.[37]

The choice between in-house development, alliances and acquisition will also vary through the technology life cycle[38] as companies move from issues of product functionality and market share, through establishing industry-quality standards, to further developments in the technology. Long-term survivors may need to use all of these methods as they move through the life cycle.

13.5.3 Organising technology development

The location and funding of technology development

An important debate in many larger organisations is who within the organisation should be driving technology development and who should be funding it.[39] This is part of the wider strategic debate about how strategic responsibilities could be divided between the corporate centre and divisions/departments of an organisation as discussed above.

Exhibit 13.12 shows that different arrangements are likely to be suitable for different aspects of technology development. For example, at one extreme, new technologies are best assessed and funded corporately, whilst at the other, incremental product and process improvements are best undertaken and funded locally. Between these extremes, the commercialisation of new technologies is often best done locally but funded corporately since others will learn and benefit from the first moves. Experimentation with new technologies might

Exhibit 13.12   Funding and location of R&D

		Located at	
		Corporate	Divisional
Funded by	Corporate	Assessing new technologies	Commercialising new technologies
	Divisional	Exploratory development of new technologies	Incremental product or process improvements

Source: Adapted from J. Tidd, J. Bessant and K. Pavitt, *Managing Innovation: Integrating technological, market and organisation change*, 2nd edition, Wiley, 2001, Table 6.2.

remain corporate but be funded by divisions which see commercial potential in their arena.

These same principles might lead to conclusions that some technology development activities might be outsourced[40] where the technological expertise is inadequate in both divisions and the corporate centre but the particular technology development is crucial to securing current and future business. Also the different stages of development might be developed in different ways: for example, the ideas generation and early research might be undertaken internally whilst external organisations might be used to develop prototypes and/or undertake test marketing.[41]

Sometimes the technological expertise of an organisation might be greater than the current business can exploit – leading to considerations of spin-off of R&D (in whole or in part) to allow new commercial opportunities to be exploited (by licensing technology to third parties).

Global vs. local technology development

Another location decision for international organisations is where in the world it should locate R&D. The fact that major firms currently tend to locate smaller proportions of R&D overseas (compared with production) shows that this can be a difficult decision to make. The factors that managers need to consider when dispersing R&D away from the home base are:

● *Efficiency* losses – this includes slowness in dealing with problems.

● Loss of a *critical mass* of R&D staff at any location reducing the fostering of tacit knowledge by direct interaction. Also *proximity* to research and testing facilities may be lost.

● Increased difficulties in *integrating* R&D with production and marketing. Some large organisations also may have difficulties in integrating different technologies where they have created 'centres of excellence' in different locations for each technology.

● Dispersal may be needed because different *types of economy* require different technologies.[42]

These concerns tend to relate to an organisation's ability to launch major innovations – such as new products or processes. They are less problematic in terms of becoming or remaining part of a global knowledge network. Indeed scientists and technologists have always been good at this and IT developments are making the process easier.

Organisational processes

Chapter 12 underlined the importance of organisational processes in underpinning the success of strategies. This is particularly true in technology development where there are real dangers that an organisation's competence in technology fails to be exploited commercially. Since these processes are often difficult to manage, they may prove to be core competences that underpin competitive advantage, as mentioned above. Some of the following processes may be of crucial importance in achieving success through technology:

● *Scanning the business environment* (both technology and market developments) and spotting the opportunities for gaining advantage and the potential threats to current business. Related to this is the ability to select projects or developments that have a good strategic fit with the business. But this is not as easy as it sounds. It may mean giving preference to transformational technologies – which could be very challenging in terms of both competences and culture of the organisation.

● *Resourcing developments adequately*, but not over-generously, so as to ensure a good return for the investment. This is much easier to see in hindsight than in advance, but past experience, good benchmarking and a willingness to use appropriate approaches to investment appraisal[43] can help. This also includes the ability to monitor and review projects through their various stages – many organisations now use a **stage–gate process** to good effect.[44] This is a structured review process to assess progress on meeting product performance characteristics during the development process and ensuring that they are matched with market data. These processes must also include the ability to terminate and accelerate projects, to capture the learning from both successes and failures, and to disseminate results and best practice.

A **stage–gate process** is a structured review process to assess progress on meeting product performance characteristics during the development process and ensuring that they are matched with market data

Of course, behind these processes is a set of much more detailed activities which will determine their success or failure. This would include activities ranging from forecasting, concept testing and option screening to communication, negotiation and motivation.

13.5.4 Implications to managers[45]

The preceding sections were intended to underline the importance of 'aligning' business and technology strategies in organisations as a way of achieving strategic success. Successful organisations will be those where there is a strong commitment from senior management to innovation through technology and a business acumen based on an understanding of the business strategy and technology relationship.

There needs to be a creative climate where innovation is fostered, communication is extensive and there is a culture of a learning organisation. Structures and processes must facilitate the creation of this environment and provide a commitment to individual and team development. In particular, it must support key individuals who will champion and facilitate the exploitation of technology for strategic success.

13.6 INTEGRATING RESOURCES

The sections above have looked at how separate resource areas need to support an organisation's strategies and/or provide the basis on which new strategies can be built. However, there is a third issue that has only partly emerged from the consideration of the separate resource areas above. As discussed in Chapter 3, most organisational strategies not only require capabilities in separate resource

Exhibit 13.13   Resource integration in a new product launch

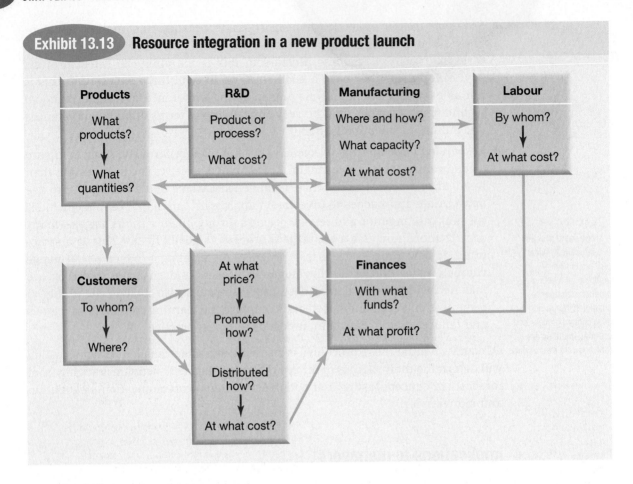

areas, but also require an ability to pull a range of resources and competences together – both inside the organisation and in the wider value network.[46] For example, Exhibit 13.13 shows some of the resources and activities that need to be integrated by an organisation hoping to gain competitive advantage through bringing new products to the market more quickly than competitors. Capability in new product launch requires an ability to integrate and coordinate the separate activities of R&D, manufacture, etc. – each of which, in turn, involves bringing together a complex mixture of resources. This can be a complex matter and, therefore, may be the basis of competitive advantage. Illustration 13.5 also shows how complex can be the resourcing and coordination for clearly prioritised strategies for governments and the public services – in that case, the reduction in anti-social behaviour. The key debate (Illustration 13.6) is a reminder of an important theme running through this chapter: that either too little or too much change of an organisation's resourcing strategies can create difficulties in delivering overall organisational strategic changes.

Illustration 13.5

Anti-social behaviour – nuisance neighbours

An important role of government is to improve the quality of life for its citizens. But this requires an ability to bring together and integrate many resources from both inside and outside government itself.

Together was a national campaign launched by the British government's Home Office in 2004. The focus of the campaign and subsequent action plans was anti-social behaviour (ASB). The government believed that

every citizen has a right to live their lives free from fear and distress and they, in turn, have a responsibility not to cause fear and distress to others . . . while it is a minority of people who persistently behave in a way that ruins the lives of those around them they have a disproportionate effect.

Commitments like this are easy for governments to make but notoriously difficult to deliver. The first step was a more detailed definition of what constituted ASB. The plan had four action areas: nuisance neighbours; begging; environmental crime; and putting victims and witnesses first. Government saw its role as bringing together resources and expertise from across government departments and external agencies to help 'practitioners' tackle these priority areas. For example, it developed and provided:

- The *Together Actionline* and website for help and advice.
- The *Together Academy* which ran training and conferences.
- New *money* to the already-established local *Crime and Disorder Partnerships* to help strengthen their response.
- *ASB Prosecutors* – a new national team in the Crown Prosecution Service.
- New *sentencing guidelines* for magistrates (courts) on ASB offences.

Of course a detailed action/resourcing plan had to be developed for each of the four priority areas (above). The plan to tackle *Nuisance Neighbours* centred round how families functioned and behaved:

At every stage in the development of a family this Government is committed to providing the help and intervention needed to make [families] strong. From improved ante-natal care, through 'Sure Start' and improved education, 'Parentline' and parenting classes the Government recognises the challenges of family life and the importance of support and help.

The plan then identified how government would contribute to sustaining stronger families:

- *Every Child Matters* – a commitment to ensuring that all children reach their potential. Resources to be increased for early years education, childcare, child poverty, supporting parents and raising school standards.
- *Behaviour Improvement Programme* – funds to improve behaviour and attendance at school in targeted areas.
- *Positive activities for young people* – a range of programmes to keep children off the streets.
- *Family and parenting policy* – including funding for the voluntary sector to support families in difficulty and direct help for 'perpetrators' to change their behaviour.
- *The Youth Justice Board* – including Youth Action Teams working to reduce the number of young people committing crimes and also preventing younger children being drawn into crime.
- *Nuisance noise and fireworks* – were to be tackled through advertising campaigns and new legislation about sale of fireworks.
- *Housing and benefits* – including licensing landlords and the withdrawal of state benefits for persistent offenders.

These initiatives were spread across several government departments (covering the key areas of: education, criminal justice, local government, environment, trade and industry, housing and benefits) which further raised the difficulties of a concerted government effort, not least because of the different priorities and cultures found in these separate departments.

Source: www.together.gov.uk. Reproduced under the terms of the Click-Use Licence.

Questions

1 Identify the key resources and activities that would contribute to a reduction in the 'nuisance neighbours' aspect of anti-social behaviour.

2 Show different ways in which these could be coordinated – giving the advantages and disadvantages of each approach.

Illustration 13.6

Resources or revolution

How far can an organisation go beyond its original resources in determining its strategy?

This chapter emphasises the importance of resources for supporting an organisation's strategy. For strategy guru Gary Hamel, Chairman of the international consulting firm Strategos, this reliance on resources can easily become too cautious. In the same way that Dorothy Leonard-Barton warns against 'core rigidities' (see Chapter 3), Hamel sees existing resources and markets as liable to trap organisations into a fatal conservatism. Incumbency, the sheer fact of already being in a market, is increasingly worthless. Hamel urges instead the importance of strategic 'revolutions', creating new markets and new business models.[1,2] We are now in an age when we need only be limited by our imaginations.

For Hamel, survival in the contemporary world of rapid technological change, shifting markets and global competition demands constant revolutionary innovation. Such innovation rarely comes from traditional strategy processes emphasising the 'fit' of resources to markets. As in his earlier work with C.K. Prahalad, Hamel emphasises 'stretch' over 'fit', and now 'revolutionaries' over 'planners'.

As an example, Hamel cites Pierre Omidyar, founder in 1995 of what rapidly became the world's premier Internet auction site, eBay. Omidyar's starting point was not the fit of resources to markets, but a desire to help his fiancée with her collection of Pez sweet dispensers. Starting on his own while retaining his day job, Omidyar had none of the resources of a traditional auction house. Far from fitting a market, he was creating a new kind of market. Traditional strategy processes would never have allowed eBay to happen.

A reminder of the importance of resources, however, comes from another of Hamel's exemplars of revolution, Enron. Enron is applauded by Hamel for its revolutionary capacity to create and trade in markets for gas, electricity, broadband and commodities. But it was inadequacies in unique and hard-to-imitate resources that contributed to Enron's ultimate failure. In the competitive markets that Enron created and traded in, Enron had few sources of sustainable advantage.[3] The result was losses that led to the largest bankruptcy in corporate history at that time. Here resources did matter.

Hamel points to an important truth about existing resources: they can constrain. At the same time,

however, building a strong resource base appears vital for sustained success. Even at eBay, Omidyar quickly brought in Harvard MBA Meg Whitman as Chief Executive Officer, who immediately invested in the managerial, measurement and infrastructural resources necessary to take it into the twenty-first century. It seems that David Teece's concept of 'dynamic capabilities',[4] the ability to develop and change competences (see Chapter 3), provides an essential bridge between the constraints of current resources and the unfettered but unsupported imagination of Gary Hamel's revolutionaries.

Notes

1. G. Hamel, *Leading the Revolution*, Harvard Business School Press, 2000.
2. G. Hamel and C.K. Prahalad, *Competing for the Future*, Harvard Business School Press, 1994.
3. S. Chatterjee, 'Enron's incremental descent into bankruptcy: a strategic and organisational analysis', *Long Range Planning*, vol. 36, no. 2 (2003), pp. 133–149.
4. D. Teece, G. Pisano and A. Shuen, 'Dynamic capabilities and strategic management', *Strategic Management Journal*, vol. 18, no. 7 (1997), pp. 509–533.

Questions

In his book *Leading the Revolution*, Gary Hamel notes that the current coffee bar fashion was created by Starbucks, a small Seattle coffee company founded in 1971, which only opened its first of more than 7,500 coffee bars in 1984. Hamel asks: why wasn't the coffee bar fashion launched by multi-billion-dollar multinational Nestlé, owner of Nescafé, the best-selling coffee in the world?

1 Compare the resources of Nestlé and Starbucks in the late 1980s and early 1990s (see www.nestle.com and www.starbucks.com). Why didn't Nestlé lead in the creation of the coffee bar fashion?

2 What implications does the failure of Nestlé have for other powerful incumbents in their present markets?

SUMMARY

- Understanding the relationship between resource management and strategic success is important. This is a two-way relationship. Resource management must support an organisation's business strategies. But the development of unique resources and core competences in parts of an organisation may provide the 'springboard' from which new business strategies are developed.

- The *'hard' side* of resource management – systems and procedures – is vitally important in enabling success. But in all resource areas the critical question is how these systems contribute to the creation and integration of knowledge. Only part of this knowledge can be captured in systems. Indeed, competitive advantage is more likely to be gained from knowledge that cannot be codified since it will be more difficult to imitate by competitors.

- Understanding the way in which *people* might underpin success concerns both the formal systems and procedures and the informal ways in which people behave. Also important are the ways in which people can be organised for success – the structures and processes discussed in Chapter 12.

- *Information* is a key resource which is of particular importance given the continuing advances in information technology. This increased ability to access and process information can build or destroy an organisation's core capabilities, so crucial to competitive advantage. IT has also spawned new business models – where traditional 'value networks' are reconfigured. This is a serious threat to some organisations and an opportunity for others.

- *Finance* is a resource of central importance in all organisations. It is particularly important to understand how business strategies might deliver financial value to shareholders or owners. Most strategic developments need funding which, in turn, creates risk. So the types of funding need to vary with strategy. Stakeholders other than owners have financial expectations that will also influence an organisation's business strategies.

- The final resource area considered in this chapter is *technology* development. This will affect the competitive forces on an organisation and also its strategic capability. So the ways that technology is developed, exploited, organised and funded will all influence the success or failure of strategy.

- Organisations need to be able to *integrate resources and competences across resource areas* to support current strategies or to develop new strategies. Capability in separate resource areas is not enough.

Work assignments

* Denotes more advanced work assignments.

13.1   Choose a strategic development for an organisation with which you are familiar and list the key human resource changes that will be needed to underpin success (refer to Exhibit 13.2 as a checklist).

13.2 * Write an executive report to your CEO advising on whether or not the HR function should be closed and the work devolved to middle (line) managers. Centre your arguments on the impact on the strategic performance of the organisation.

13.3 * (a) Choose an organisation which is shifting its generic competitive strategy from low price to differentiation (on the strategy clock). Describe how the information strategies will need to change to support this new strategy.
        (b) Choose an organisation which is attempting the opposite shift (differentiation to low price) and undertake the same analysis.

13.4   Find examples of all of the business models outlined in Exhibit 13.5. Explain in which sectors you feel each business model is most likely to have particular impact. Why?

13.5   Referring to Exhibit 13.7, give as many reasons as you can why profitable companies might be destroying shareholder value (with examples). Now repeat the exercise for organisations with poor levels of profitability that are none the less creating shareholder value (with examples).

13.6 * Write an executive report on how sources of funding need to be related to the nature of an industry and the types of strategies that an organisation is pursuing.

13.7 * By referring to Exhibit 13.11, write a report advising your CEO how technology should be acquired by your organisation. Remember to justify your conclusions.

13.8   Refer to the new product launch example in Exhibit 13.13. If you were project managing this launch, identify the specific ways in which you would ensure integration between the various resource areas. Remember to identify both 'hard' and 'soft' ways in which you would achieve this integration.

Integrative assignments

13.9   Using examples, discuss the proposition that 'IT is seen as the servant of current strategies and business models rather than as a way of revolutionising the way an organisation does business and gains advantage'. Support your answer by references to both the value network (Chapter 3) and culture (Chapter 5).

13.10 The knowledge of an organisation is dispersed throughout the major resource areas discussed in this chapter. So how does an organisation manage to integrate and gain advantage from this knowledge? Refer to Chapters 3 and 5 to support your answer.

An extensive range of additional materials, including audio summaries, weblinks to organisations featured in the text, definitions of key concepts and self-assessment questions, can be found on the *Exploring Corporate Strategy* Companion Website at **www.pearsoned.co.uk/ecs**

Recommended Key Readings

- A good general reference book on human resource management is L. Mullins, *Management and Organisational Behaviour*, 7th edition, FT/Prentice Hall, 2005.

- Three general books on information management are: P. Bocij, D. Chaffey, A. Greasley and S. Hickie, *Business Information Systems: Technology, Development and Management for the E-Business*, 3rd edition, FT/Prentice Hall, 2006 (particularly chapters 13 and 14); J. Ward and J. Peppard, *Strategic Planning for Information Systems*, 3rd edition, Wiley, 2002; D. Chaffey and S. Wood, *Business Information Management*, FT/Prentice Hall, 2005.

- Readers may wish to consult one or more standard texts on finance. For example, G. Arnold, *Corporate Financial Management*, 3rd edition, FT/Prentice Hall, 2005; P. Atrill, *Financial Management for Decision Makers*, 4th edition, FT/Prentice Hall, 2006.

- The relationship between technology and strategy is extensively discussed in J. Tidd, J. Bessant and K. Pavitt, *Managing Innovation: Integrating technological, market and organisational change*, 3rd edition, Wiley, 2005.

References

1. A good general reference book on human resource management is L. Mullins, *Management and Organisational Behaviour*, 7th edition, FT/Prentice Hall, 2005. Two useful papers are: J. Pfeffer and J. Veiga, 'Putting people first for organisational success', *Academy of Management Executive*, vol. 13, no. 2 (1999), pp. 37–50; and B. Becker and M. Huselid, 'Overview: strategic human resource management in five leading firms', *Human Resource Management*, vol. 38, no. 4 (1999), pp. 287–301.

2. See Mullins (chapters 19, 20 and 21), reference 1.

3. Developing future talent internally may be less risky than recruitment. See B. Groysberg, A. Nanda and N. Nohria, 'The risky business of hiring stars', *Harvard Business Review*, vol. 82, no. 5 (2004), pp. 92–100.

4. The importance of HR professionals understanding business strategy is emphasised in D. Ulrich and W. Brockbank, 'Higher knowledge for higher aspirations', *Human Resource Management*, vol. 44, no. 4 (2005), pp. 489–504.

5. See also D.D. Van Fleet, T.O. Peterson and E.W. Van Fleet, 'Closing the performance feedback gap with expert systems', *Academy of Management Executive*, vol. 19, no. 3 (2005), pp. 9–12.

6. See Mullins (chapters 4, 13 and 14), reference 1.

7. In this book we use the term 'paradigm' but 'mental models' is a similar concept. See J. Pfeffer, 'Changing mental models: HR's most important task', *Human Resource Management*, vol. 44, no. 2 (2005), pp. 123–128.

8. C. Bartlett and S. Ghoshal, 'Building competitive advantage through people', *Sloan Management Review*, vol. 43, no. 2 (2002), pp. 34–41.

9. The seminal work on this issue of balanced teams was R. Belbin, *Management Teams: Why they succeed or fail*, Heinemann, 1981.

10. See C. Collins and K. Clark, 'Strategic human resource practices, top management team social networks and firm performance: the role of human resource practices in creating organisational competitive advantage', *Academy of Management Journal*, vol. 46, no. 6 (2003), pp. 740–751.

11. See Mullins (chapters 6, 15 and 16), reference 1.

12. J. Storey, *Developments in the Management of Human Resources*, Blackwell, 1992, used this categorisation of the roles of HR functions. D. Ulrich, *Human Resource Champion*, Harvard Business School Press, 1997, presents a slightly different categorisation based on the two dimensions of change vs. maintenance *and* people vs. processes.

13. The following articles from the same volume of *Human Resource Management* discuss this issue: W.F. Cascio, 'From business partner to driving business success: the next step in the evolution of HR', *Human Resource Management*, vol. 44, no. 2 (2005), pp. 159–163; G. Armstrong, 'Differentiation through people: how can HR move beyond business partner?', *Human Resource Management*, vol. 44, no. 2 (2005), pp. 195–200; E.E. Lawler III, 'From human resource management to organisational effectiveness', *Human Resource Management*, vol. 44, no. 2 (2005), pp. 165–169.

14. For example, downsizing creates problems in this respect. See R. Thomas and D. Dunkerley, 'Careering downwards? Middle managers' experience in the downsized organisation', *British Journal of Management*, vol. 10 (1999), pp. 157–169.

15. See also J.M. Hiltrop, 'Creating HR capability in high-performance organisations', *Strategic Change*, vol. 14, no. 3 (2005), pp. 121–131.

16. Three good general books on information management are: P. Bocij, D. Chaffey, A. Greasley and S. Hickie, *Business Information Systems: Technology, Development and Management for the E-Business*, 3rd edition, FT/Prentice Hall, 2006 (particularly chapters 13 and 14); J. Ward and J. Peppard, *Strategic Planning for Information Systems*, 3rd edition, Wiley, 2002; D. Chaffey and S. Wood, *Business Information Management*, FT/Prentice Hall, 2005. P. Timmers, *Electronic Commerce*, Wiley, 2000, has been used as background on the issues of information management and the power of IT. Readers might also find the following to be useful: C. Prahalad

and M. Krishnan, 'The dynamic synchronisation of strategy and information technology', *Sloan Management Review*, vol. 43, no. 4 (2002), pp. 24–31; M. Porter, 'Strategy and the Internet', *Harvard Business Review*, vol. 79, no. 2 (2001), pp. 63–78; J. Brown and J. Hagel, 'Does IT matter?', *Harvard Business Review*, vol. 81, no. 7 (2003), pp. 109–112; G. Carr, 'IT doesn't matter', *Harvard Business Review*, vol. 81, no. 5 (2003), pp. 41–50.

17. The dangers IT can bring in destroying competitive advantage are discussed by N. Carr, 'The corrosion of IT advantage: strategy makes a comeback', *Journal of Business Strategy*, vol. 25, no. 5 (2004), pp. 10–15.

18. The details of how data mining is done in various sectors are discussed in: C. Carmen and B. Lewis, 'A basic primer on data mining', *Information Systems Management*, vol. 19, no. 4 (2002), pp. 56–60; J. Firestone, 'Mining for information gold', *Information Management Journal*, vol. 39, no. 5 (2005), pp. 47–52; J. Xu and H. Chen, 'Criminal network analysis and visualization', *Communications of the ACM*, vol. 48, no. 6 (2005), pp. 101–107; A. Hormozi, Amir M. and S. Giles, 'Data mining: a competitive weapon for banking and retail industries', *Information Systems Management*, vol. 21, no. 2 (2004), pp. 62–71.

19. The need to join up the different customer interfaces (such as salesforce, websites, call centres) is discussed in *Customer Essentials*, CBR Special Report, 1999, pp. 7–20.

20. See Timmers, reference 16, chapter 3. Also useful as background is N. Sheehan, 'Why old tools won't work in the "new" knowledge economy', *Journal of Business Strategy*, vol. 26, no. 4 (2005), pp. 53–60.

21. Governments have invested heavily in 'e-government' information systems. For the UK see 'Two years on: realizing the benefits from our investment in e-government', *Office of the Deputy Prime Minister*, March (2005). For the USA see J. Young, 'Oracle solutions transform state and local governments', *IDC*, September (2003).

22. Readers should find the following article useful: G. Rifkin and J. Kurtzman, 'Is your e-business plan radical enough?', *Sloan Management Review*, vol. 43, no. 3 (2002), pp. 91–95.

23. M. Vernon, 'The smartest CIOs', *Management Today*, May (2006), discusses the strategic contribution that CIOs should make.

24. Readers may wish to consult one or more standard texts on finance. For example: G. Arnold, *Corporate Financial Management*, 3rd edition, FT/Prentice Hall, 2005; and P. Atrill, *Financial Management for Decision Makers*, 4th edition, FT/Prentice Hall, 2006.

25. The seminal work on managing for shareholder value has been updated: A. Rappaport, *Creating Shareholder Value*, 2nd edition, Free Press, 1998. See also J. Barlow, R. Burgman and M. Molna, 'Managing for shareholder value: intangibles, future value and investment decisions', *Journal of Business Strategy*, vol. 25, no. 3 (2004), pp. 26–34. T. Grundy (with G. Johnson and K. Scholes), *Exploring Strategic Financial Management*, Prentice Hall, 1998, chapter 2, is also a useful reference on managing for value.

26. See J. Martin and W. Petty, 'Value based management', *Baylor Business Review*, vol. 19, no. 1 (2001), pp. 2–3, review the arguments briefly.

27. S. Williams, 'Delivering strategic business value', *Strategic Finance*, vol. 86, no. 2 (2004), pp. 41–48.

28. See P. Atrill, *Financial Management for Decision Makers*, 4th edition, FT/Prentice Hall, 2006, chapters 6 and 7; G. Arnold, *Corporate Financial Management*, 3rd edition, FT/Prentice Hall, 2005, Part IV.

29. For readers who wish to follow up the discussion in this section, see K. Ward, *Corporate Financial Strategy*, Butterworth–Heinemann, 1993, and T. Grundy and K. Ward (eds), *Developing Financial Strategies: A comprehensive model in strategic business finance*, Kogan Page, 1996.

30. There have been a great deal of research and publications around the funding of this start-up phase. For example: D. Champion, 'A stealthier way to raise money', *Harvard Business Review*, vol. 78, no. 5 (2000), pp. 18–19; Q. Mills, 'Who's to blame for the bubble?', *Harvard Business Review*, vol. 79, no. 5 (2001), pp. 22–23; H. Van Auken, 'Financing small technology-based companies: the relationship between familiarity with capital and ability to price and negotiate investment', *Journal of Small Business Management*, vol. 39, no. 3 (2001), pp. 240–258; M. Van Osnabrugge and R. Robinson, 'The influence of a venture capitalist's source of funds', *Venture Capital*, vol. 3, no. 1 (2001), pp. 25–39.

31. See Atrill, reference 24, pp. 474–478.

32. See A. Kennedy, *The End of Shareholder Value: corporations at the crossroads*, Perseus Publishing, 2000; and H. Collingwood, 'The earnings game', *Harvard Business Review*, vol. 79, no. 6 (2001), pp. 65–72.

33. The major source for this section is J. Tidd, J. Bessant and K. Pavitt, *Managing Innovation: Integrating technological, market and organisational change*, 3rd edition, Wiley, 2005. See also P.H. Antiniou and H.I. Ansoff, 'Strategic management of technology', *Technology Analysis and Strategic Management*, vol. 16, no. 2 (2004), pp. 275–291.

34. A useful international comparison of R&D strategies can be found in E. Roberts, 'Benchmarking global strategic management of technology', *Research Technology Management*, vol. 44, no. 2 (2001), pp. 25–36.

35. W. Boulding and M. Christen, 'First mover disadvantage', *Harvard Business Review*, vol. 79, no. 9 (2001), pp. 20–21.

36. J. Tidd, J. Bessant and K. Pavitt, *Managing Innovation: Integrating technological, market and organisational change*, 2nd edition, Wiley, 2001, p. 222; and J. Tidd and M. Trewhella, 'Organisational and technological antecedents for knowledge acquisition', *R&D Management*, vol. 27, no. 4 (1997), pp. 359–375.

37. For example, see G. Slowinski, S. Stanton, J. Tao, W. Miller and D. McConnell, 'Acquiring external technology', *Research Technology Management*, vol. 43, no. 5 (2002), pp. 29–35.

38. E. Roberts and W. Lui, 'Ally or acquire? How technology leaders decide', *Sloan Management Review*, vol. 43, no. 1 (2001), pp. 26–34.

39. R. Buderi, 'Funding central research', *Research Technology Management*, vol. 43, no. 4 (2000), pp. 18–25, gives some useful examples including Siemens, NEC, Hewlett Packard and IBM.

40. See C. Kimzey and S. Kurokawa, 'Technology outsourcing in the US and Japan', *Research Technology Management*', vol. 45, no. 4 (2002), pp. 36–42.

41. E. Kessler and P. Bierly, 'Internal vs. external learning in product development', *R & D Management*, vol. 30, no. 3 (2000), pp. 213–223.

42. R. Grieve, 'Appropriate technology in a globalising world', *International Journal of Technology Management and Sustainable Development*, vol. 3, no. 3 (2004), pp. 173–187.

43. A. Lloyd, 'Technology, innovation and competitive advantage; making a business process perspective part of investment appraisal', *International Journal of Innovation Management*, vol. 5, no. 3 (2001), pp. 351–376.

44. The stage-gate process is discussed in R. Thomas, *New Product Development: Managing and forecasting for strategic success*, Wiley, 1993; and R. Cooper, S. Edgett, J. Kleinschmidt and J. Elko, 'Optimising the stage-gate process: what best practice companies do', *Research Technology Management*, vol. 45, no. 5 (2002), pp. 21–26 and vol. 45, no. 6 (2002), pp. 43–49.

45. See Tidd *et al.*, reference 33, Part V, p. 465.

46. L. Gratton, 'Managing integration through cooperation', *Human Resource Management*, vol. 44, no. 2 (2005), pp. 151–158, underlines the importance of working cooperatively across both internal and external boundaries.

Video games

By the mid–2000s the development of computer-based video games had become a major international industry – dominated by companies in the UK, North America and Japan. But at the beginning of the industry (in the late 1980s) it was largely driven by individual developers writing programs in their bedrooms – it was a cottage industry. Then games cost as little as €6,000 (£4,100; $6,250) to develop and required just a couple of people – a programmer and an artist. By the end of the 1990s there were more than 300 games companies in the UK alone. However, by the mid–2000s new titles were costing €3m to develop, needing teams of 30 or more programmers, artists, sound engineers and producers. Many expected development costs to rise to perhaps €15m per new title. This clearly had a major impact on the structure of the industry and how games companies were funded. Firms needed to be big to survive. Many of the company founders chose to sell out to corporate organisations or go public through a share flotation. Some companies, such as Rock Star, had been founded in the UK but moved to the USA.

The *Irish Times* commented on the funding situation in the mid–2000s:

Currently with very few exceptions, the money to create best-selling games comes from the games' publishers: a small group of multinationals such as Vivendi and Electronic Arts, whose strength in the market comes from negotiating licensing deals with existing media properties (movie tie-ins such as *Spiderman*, sports stars, and arcade game adaptations), close relationships with console manufactures like Sony and Microsoft, and, most importantly, strong control over the distribution of the games. Almost all games are sold the old-fashioned way: in shops, shrink-wrapped and distributed via the publishers' marketing infrastructure.

Orbiting around these publishers are the developers and designers. Sometimes employed by the publishers, sometimes working in small independent outfits, they are beholden to the publishers for almost all of the up-front cost of producing a video game. A game doesn't get the green

Photo: Superstock/Alamy Images

light without a publishing deal; a game can't make it to the shops without that publisher footing the bill. As the average cost of developing a game has grown, the publishers' control over the game development process has grown tighter. Independent outfits are vanishing and the publishers are growing more conservative. . . .

Why the explosion in costs? Partly, it's a product of the increasing complexity of the modern games platform. Whether written for a PC or a games console, the hardware and creative input that underlies the modern fast-moving, endlessly detailed, cinematically scored, 3D action film, requires a great deal of money and management. But partly it's a product of the system. Four out of five games, it is said, don't make money. Publishers invest heavily in marketing and support a surprisingly old-fashioned way of shifting product: putting those boxes on shelves. Often . . . it's not the coders who see the money and it's not the games that benefit.

Even those who have made millions from their successful games are growing tired. Valve, the creators of (the 2004) hit game Half-Life 2, created an internet distribution system, Steam, rather than rely on publishers to ship their product. The release of Half-Life was delayed while its publisher, Vivendi, sued to prevent Steam from operating its distribution network, claiming breach of contract. At the other end of the development process, the world-famous British games developer Peter Molyneux spurned investment from publishers and turned to venture capitalists (VCs) to raise funds for his latest games.

At the 2005 Games Developers Conference (GDC) in San Francisco, it seemed that such attempts to escape the video games industry's studio system had popular support. 'Can we do any worse if we just trusted the creative folks entirely instead of the publishers?' asked industry veteran Warren Spector. It's hard to say whether the atmosphere at GDC will lead to developers striking out against their masters and starting their own, innovative distribution and investment approaches. Even if this is more than just fighting talk among peers, it may be nothing more than part of a long repeating cycle – at least, if the parallels with Hollywood continue. After all, the games publishers were once scrappy small companies, just as studios such as United Artists and Dreamworks began as breakaway companies run by the 'talent'. Will the money from Steam, which allows Valve to charge a monthly subscription to play its games, corrupt its coders as completely as developers believe the publishers have been corrupted? Will the VCs who funded Molyneux be as forgiving as publishers if his games don't make their return first time around? Maybe the world of video games is different.

Like most things in both the computing and entertainment sectors, the pace of change created threats to many but opportunities for others. In 2005 the publisher Electronic Arts signed a deal with Steven Spielberg the director of *Schindler's List*, *Saving Private Ryan*, *War of the Worlds* and many other Hollywood blockbusters to make three video games. Meanwhile the Screen Actors Guild (the largest union representing actors in the USA) was bargaining hard for increased fees for actors who provided voices for video game characters. The huge development costs were forcing publishers and games developers to look to new sources of gaming software – spawning the growth of new entrepreneurial businesses in places such as India. The advantages of outsourcing some or all of the development to India lie in the abundant creative talent and programming skills with much lower wages. This could amount to as much as 40 per cent reductions in development costs. But perhaps the key factor which underlies the popularity of video games with consumers is the capability of the hardware – whether that be consoles, computers or even mobile phones. The year of 2005 was an important one in the battle for dominance of the hardware market as reported by the *Financial Times*:

Sony and Microsoft are to unleash products capable of the same ferocious speed. . . . Machines packed with processing power and the ability to display high-definition moving images will soon be on sale for a few hundred dollars, to drive video games. Yet this is about far more than shooting aliens. The games business long ago outgrew its roots in the toy industry, but that could be nothing compared with the transition it is now facing. These high-performance boxes are weapons in a much bigger war: the struggle for dominance of all forms of home digital entertainment. 'The stakes for next-generation hardware leadership are enormous,' says Warren Jenson, chief financial officer of Electronic Arts, the biggest video games publisher. 'It's about owning the set-top box that may ultimately connect the living room to the internet.' . . .

In video game hardware, such periodic transitions to new generations of technology have historically marked big shifts in industry leadership. Atari gave way to Sega, which in turn surrendered leadership to Nintendo, before Sony rose to prominence. This time it is Microsoft that is eager to force the pace. Microsoft certainly understands the cost of being late. Its first Xbox arrived 18 months after [Sony's] PlayStation 2 and, despite winning accolades for its technical prowess, never made up lost ground with consumers or the developers whose games are essential to selling the hardware. . . . Just as, in a previous era, the minicomputer took over from the mainframe as the source of innovation in computing, only to give way to the PC, the games console is becoming the focus of breakthrough technology. Not that the PC is about to give up its role as the digital brain of the home. Some 64m PCs were sold for home use last year, according to IDC, the technology monitoring company, compared with about 24m games consoles. Yet, with power pouring into the consoles, the PC's role is set to be reduced – and the box most likely to be connected to the family television set is the games console.

The companies leading this latest charge into digital entertainment are well aware of what is at stake. For Sony, video games have been a rare and much-needed bright spot. In the four years since the PlayStation 2 hit its stride, the games business has on average contributed nearly 60 per cent of the company's operating profits. The losses that Microsoft has amassed from video games are even bigger than Sony's profits. Over the four years, the games business has produced $2.6bn [€2.1bn; £1.4bn] in operating earnings for Sony. In roughly the same period, Microsoft's home and entertainment division – essentially, its Xbox business – has lost $3.7bn. Yet for the software group, this was the cost to get into the game that is about to begin. Bill Gates, its chairman, acknowledged as much last week when he said: 'What we got this round – at some significant financial cost – was the opportunity to play again.'

Despite their wider ambitions, Microsoft and Sony are both aware that console sales will depend mainly on how successful they are at harnessing the power of their new digital workhorses to produce more compelling game-playing. It is not just about the heightened visual images promised by high-definition television or the ability to render sophisticated graphics in real time: with more computing power at their disposal, the artificial intelligence algorithms in the machines will be able to produce far more complex and unexpected interactions.

As more forms of media and entertainment go digital, however, these machines will also take on a broader role. Whether through a direct connection to the internet or through a home network that links them to a PC, they are designed to become the gateway through which you delve into your store of family photographs, listen to digital music or tap a library of films. The internet connection will make it easier for family members or friends to look at each others' pictures, share music or play together.

Sony . . . suggested that the (cell) chip could break down the technological barriers that have separated games from films, where animation and special effects are created using different technology. With the ability to render more lifelike images, the cell chip could turn out images that could be slotted equally well into games or movies. 'There's huge potential for the convergence of movies and games – and for something new that comes out of it,' Sony says.

'We're thinking holistically about the platforms,' says Dean Lester, head of Microsoft's Games for Windows group.

'In the past, publishers had to redesign the control systems, now they can build the game across the platforms.'

It adds up to Microsoft strengthening its games platform to appeal to publishers and win game franchises that will power the success of the console'.

Sources: *Sunday Times*, 12 October 2003; 'Developers of video games feel disillusioned' by D. O'Brien, *Irish Times*, 18 March 2005; *Financial Times* (US edition), 11 May 2005.

Questions

1 Identify how the 'business model' for the industry changed as information technology capability improved. Where might the next changes of business model be?

2 What were the human resource implications of the changing 'shape' of the games industry to the different 'players'?

3 Use Exhibit 13.8 to undertake a critique of the extent to which the financial strategies are appropriate for the industry.

Strategy in Action

14

Managing Strategic Change

LEARNING OUTCOMES

After reading this chapter you should be able to:

→ Identify the scope of a required strategic change.

→ Analyse how organisational context might affect the design of strategic change programmes.

→ Undertake a forcefield analysis to identify forces blocking and facilitating change.

→ Assess the impact of the role and management styles of change agents.

→ Assess the value of different levers for strategic change, including the management of organisational routines, political and symbolic processes and other change tactics.

→ Identify the pitfalls and problems of managing change programmes.

Photo: Panoramic Images/Robert Harding World Imagery

14.1 INTRODUCTION

This chapter is concerned with the management activities involved in changing strategies. Chapters 12 and 13 have addressed important issues to do with the structuring of organisations and the resourcing of strategies, both important in effecting strategic change. However, designing a structure and putting in place appropriate resources do not of themselves ensure that people will make a strategy happen. The major problem managers report in managing change is the tendency towards *inertia* and *resistance to change*;[1] people will tend to hold on to existing ways of doing things. As explained in Chapter 5 (section 5.1) this may lead to *strategic drift*. Discussion of the 'experience lens' in the Commentary at the end of the book and explanations of how strategies develop in Chapter 11 also emphasise the same tendency. Managing strategic change therefore poses a major challenge for managers. In addressing this challenge this chapter builds on three key premises:

- *Strategy matters*. It is important to remember that in managing strategic change much of what has been written in previous chapters should be seen as an essential precursor in identifying the need for and direction of strategic change. It will not be repeated in any detail here, but it is important to remember the need to understand:
  - Why strategic change is needed (discussed in Chapters 2, 3, 4 and 5).
  - The bases of the strategy in terms of strategic purpose, perhaps encapsulated in a statement of vision or mission (Chapter 4) and the basis of competitive advantage (Chapter 6).
  - The more specific strategy choices intended in terms of strategy directions and methods (Chapters 7 to 10).

- *Context matters*. The approach taken to managing strategic change needs to be *context dependent*. There is, therefore, no one 'right way' of managing strategic change. Managers need to consider how to balance different approaches according to the circumstances they face.

- *Multiple roles in managing strategic change*. Much of what is written on strategic change assumes that change happens in a *top-down* manner; that top managers put into effect the changes required. It is, of course, a major role of top managers to influence the strategic direction of the organisation. However, it is unrealistic to suppose they can control everything. There are many others in the organisation – middle managers and below – who play a major role in managing change. Indeed Chapter 11 (section 11.3) shows that strategies may emerge from lower down in the organisation.

Exhibit 14.1 provides a structure for the chapter. Section 14.2 begins by explaining important issues that need to be considered in *diagnosing the situation* an organisation faces when embarking on strategic change, in terms of the *types of change* required; the variety of *contextual and cultural factors* that need to be taken into account; and the *forces blocking or facilitating change*. Section 14.3 then discusses the management of strategic change in terms of the *styles of management* and the roles played by *strategic leaders* and other *change agents* in managing strategic change. Section 14.4 then goes on to review *levers for change*, including changes in *structure and control*, organisational *routines and systems*,

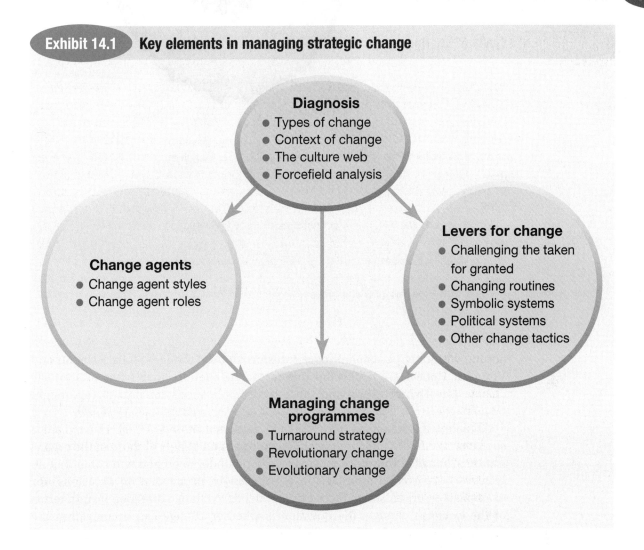

Exhibit 14.1   **Key elements in managing strategic change**

Diagnosis
- Types of change
- Context of change
- The culture web
- Forcefield analysis

Levers for change
- Challenging the taken for granted
- Changing routines
- Symbolic systems
- Political systems
- Other change tactics

Change agents
- Change agent styles
- Change agent roles

Managing change programmes
- Turnaround strategy
- Revolutionary change
- Evolutionary change

symbols, the role of *political activity*, and more specific *tactics*. Section 14. 5 draws all this together by considering how all this might take effect and what overall lessons can be drawn about *managing change programmes*.

14.2   DIAGNOSING THE CHANGE SITUATION

KEY CONCEPT

Types of strategic change

How change is managed will depend on the magnitude of the challenge faced in trying to effect strategic change. To understand this it is useful to consider the *type* of change required, the wider *context* in which change is to occur, the specific *blockages* to change that exist and forces that exist to *facilitate* the change process.

14.2.1   Types of strategic change

As was suggested in the discussion in Chapter 11, typically strategy development is *incremental* in nature. It builds on prior strategy; it is *adaptive* in the way it

Exhibit 14.2	Types of change

Extent of change

		Realignment	Transformation
Nature of change	Incremental	Adaptation	Evolution
	Big Bang	Reconstruction	Revolution

Source: Adapted from J. Balogun and V. Hope Hailey, *Exploring Strategic Change*, 2nd Edn, Prentice Hall, Pearson Education Ltd, 1999.

occurs, with only occasional more *transformational* changes. Julia Balogun and Veronica Hope Hailey[2] develop this further to identify four types of strategic change (see Exhibit 14.2), and these have implications for how change might be managed.

Arguably, it is beneficial for change in an organisation to be *incremental* since such change should build on the skills, routines and beliefs of those in the organisation. Change is therefore more likely to be understood and win commitment. However, a *big bang* approach to change might be needed on occasions, for example if an organisation faces crisis or needs to change direction fast. In terms of the *extent* of change, the question is whether change can occur within the current culture as a *realignment* of strategy. Or does it require culture change? This is more *transformational* change. Combining these two axes suggests four types of strategic change:

- *Adaptation* is change that can be accommodated within the current culture and occur incrementally. It is the most common form of change in organisations.

- *Reconstruction* is change that may be rapid and involve a good deal of upheaval in an organisation, but which does not fundamentally change the culture. It could be a *turnaround* situation where there is need for major structural changes or a major cost-cutting programme to deal with a decline in financial performance or difficult or changing market conditions. How this might be managed is discussed further in section 14.5.1.

- *Revolution* is change that requires rapid and major strategic but also culture change. This could be in circumstances where the strategy has been so bounded by the existing culture that, even when environmental or competitive pressures might require fundamental change, the organisation has failed to respond. This might have occurred over many years (see the discussion of strategic drift in section 5.1) and resulted in circumstances where pressures for change are extreme – for example, a takeover threatens the continued existence of a firm. How this might be managed is discussed further in section 14.5.2.

● *Evolution* is change in strategy that requires culture change, but over time. It may be that managers anticipate the need for transformational change. They may then be in a position of planned evolutionary change, with time in which to achieve it. Another way in which evolution can be explained is in terms the idea of the *learning organisation* (see section 11.5.2) where an organisation continually adjusts its strategy as the environment changes. How this might be managed is discussed further in section 14.5.3.

The sort of cultural analysis explained in section 5.4.6 can be useful as a means of considering whether the change envisaged could be accommodated within the bounds of the culture as it is, or whether it would require a really significant cultural shift. For example, a business may launch new products without requiring fundamental changes in the assumptions and beliefs of the organisation. On the other hand, some changes in strategy, even if they do not take the form of dramatic product changes, may require fundamental changes in core assumptions in the organisation. For example, the shift from a production focus for a manufacturer to a customer-led, service ethos may not entail product changes, but will very likely require significant culture change.

14.2.2 The importance of context

KEY CONCEPT

www.pearsoned.co.uk/ecs

Strategic change context

Managing change in a small entrepreneurial business, where a motivated team are driving change, would be quite different from trying to manage change in a major corporation, or perhaps a long-established public sector organisation, with set routines, formal structures and perhaps a great deal of resistance to change. Moreover, assuming that approaches to change are readily transferable between contexts is problematic. For example, many government departments in different parts of the world have sought to import change management practices from consultancies or by recruiting managers from commercial enterprises but with varying degrees of success.[3] Illustration 14.1 gives an example of the contextual issues faced in trying to manage change in the UK Ministry of Defence (MOD).[4]

Approaches to managing change therefore need to be differ according to context.[5] Balogun and Hope Hailey build on this point to highlight important contextual features that need to be taken into account in designing change programmes. Exhibit 14.3 summarises these.

Here are some examples of how the contextual features shown in Exhibit 14.3 might require different approaches to change:

● The *time* available for change could differ dramatically. A business facing immediate decline in turnover or profits from rapid changes in its markets has a quite different context for change compared with a business where the management may see the need for change coming in the future, perhaps years away, and have time to plan it carefully as a staged incremental process.

● The *scope* of change might differ in terms of either the *breadth* of change across an organisation or the *depth* of culture change required. The scope of change in an organisation such as the MOD in Illustration 14.1 is wholly different in terms of both breadth and depth and, in consequence, likely to be a much bigger challenge than, for example, adaptive change in a successful small business.

Illustration 14.1

The challenges of managing change in the UK Ministry of Defence

Understanding the challenge of managing strategic change requires an understanding of the context of change.

The UK Ministry of Defence (MOD) has found it difficult to make major changes. For example, in 2004, of the seven principles underpinning the recommendations of the Smart Procurement Initiative begun in 1998 only one was properly implemented and, of the other six, some hardly at all. Or, again, in 2000 the MOD established the Defence Logistics Organisation (DLO) to coordinate across the army, navy and air force. By 2005 it was accepted that this had stalled. Drawing on published studies and their own experience working with the MOD, Derrick Neal and Trevor Taylor, of the Defence Academy at Shrivenham, explain some of the reasons.

Size and complexity

The MOD comprises 300,000 people of whom 200,000 are military personnel. It also relies on a further 300,000 people in its supply chain. Moreover it comprises many parts so: 'Change initiated in one part of the system runs into resistance and difficulty from arrangements elsewhere, or has implications for other parts of the system that were not foreseen by the original change initiators.' It is also difficult to change all the systems simultaneously.

Empowerment

The MOD cannot decide overall defence strategy since that is decided by politicians. However, there is significant autonomy within the MOD. There are 13 top-level budget holders (TLBs), within each of which there is then further delegation of responsibility. The result is some 36 defence agencies and below them 120 'integrated project teams'. When the MOD centre tries to generate change, locally empowered leaders often produce their own version of change programmes. In 2003 it was found that there were 150 uncoordinated change initiatives under way within the DLO.

Personnel systems

The MOD employs both military staff and civilian staff. Military staff expect to move locations frequently.

Someone with 35 years of service is likely to have moved 20 times. Time horizons are therefore short within a 'can do' culture. Those who wish to make a quick impact do so by initiating change but moving on before initiatives are completed. However, follow-up is unlikely because 'you don't make your name by implementing another officer's change initiative'. The number of 'fast-track' civil servants who are likely to hold a series of jobs in quick succession is much more limited; most are not expected to move regularly. So time horizons are different for them.

The reluctance to invest for change

The MOD views change as a 'budget-neutral activity': that it is necessary to make savings in order to fund change, rather than fund change in order to make savings. For example, it was only after the stalled DLO initiative that the MOD recognised the need for investment in that change programme and obtained funding from the Treasury to try and address it.

The lack of urgency

There is no feeling of crisis. Paradoxically, for people who often find themselves at serious risk, they see the institutions that surround them as secure and fixed. The only signal of required change is from the Treasury's financial initiatives, which may be seen as a threat.

Source: Based on D. Neal and T. Taylor, 'Spinning on dimes: the challenges of introducing transformational change into the UK Ministry of Defence', *Strategic Change*, vol. 15 (2006), pp. 15–22.

Questions

1 Use the checklist of the change kaleidoscope in section 14.2.2 to identify the range of contextual issues that need to be taken into account in influencing change in the MOD.

2 What approach to change should be adopted to improve the MOD's ability to manage change?

Exhibit 14.3 Contextual features of strategic change programmes

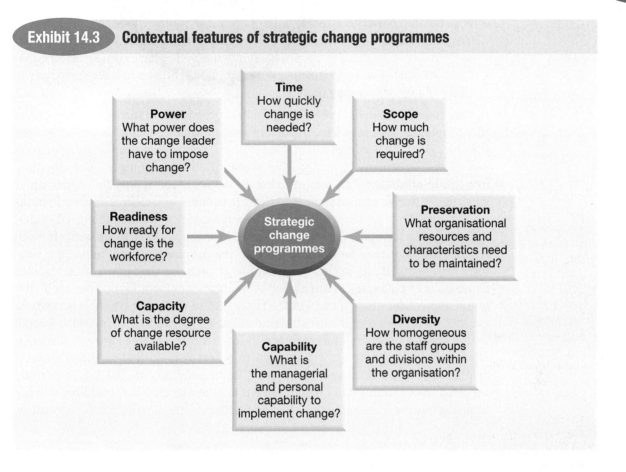

- *Preservation* of some aspects of an organisation may be needed: in particular, competences on which changes need to be based. Suppose, for example, that a computer software business needs to become more formally organised because of its successful growth. This could well upset technical experts who have been used to ready access to senior management, but it could be vital to preserve their expertise and motivation.

- A *diversity* of experience, views and opinions within an organisation may help the change process. However, if an organisation has followed a strategy for many decades, this may have led to a very homogeneous way of seeing the world. Change could be hampered by this. So gauging the nature and extent of diversity is important.

- Is there *capability* or experience of managing change in the organisation?[6] There may be managers who have managed change effectively in the past, or a workforce that have been used to and have accepted past changes, whilst another organisation may have little experience of change.

- *Capacity* for change in terms of available resources will also be significant. For example, change can be costly, not only in financial terms, but also in terms of management time.

- What is the *readiness* for change? Is there a felt need for change across the organisation, widespread resistance, or pockets or levels of resistance in some parts of the organisation and readiness in others?[7]

● Who has the *power* to effect change? Often it is assumed that the chief executive has such power, but in the face of resistance from below, or perhaps resistance from external stakeholders, this may not be the case. It may also be that the chief executive supposes that others in the organisation have the power to effect change when they do not.

This consideration of context needs to be borne in mind throughout the rest of this chapter. It also raises an important overarching question: *is one-off change possible?* Does the organisation in question have the capacity, capability, readiness and power structures to achieve the scope of change required? For example, in a study of attempts to manage change in hospitals[8] it was found that their governance and organisational structures prevented any clear authority to manage change. This, combined with the resource constraints they laboured under, meant that major one-off change initiatives were not likely to succeed. In such circumstances, it may be that the context needs to be changed before the strategic change itself can occur. For example, it could be that new managers with experience of managing change need to be introduced to enhance the capability and readiness for change and get the organisation to a point where it is ready to embark on a more significant strategic change programme. Or perhaps people with a greater diversity of experience in line with the future strategic direction need to be brought in. Or it may need to be recognised that in some contexts change has to be managed in stages. The researchers in the hospital study reported above found that change tended to take place by one initiative making limited progress, then stalling, followed by a later one making further advances.

14.2.3 Diagnosing the cultural context

Understanding the prevailing culture of an organisation can help inform the type of change needed, as well as an organisation's readiness for change. Chapter 5 introduced the cultural web (see section 5.4.6) as both a useful concept in explaining culture and a means of diagnosing the culture of an organisation. Illustration 5.4 showed the cultural web produced by managers and employees to analyse the prevailing culture for the Forestry Commission in the UK.[9] The collapse in world timber prices meant that alternative sources of income were needed. Additionally, the government's policy was to develop an emphasis on forestry for leisure and social inclusion, not just the production of timber. However, what emerged from the cultural web analysis was that the organisation's current culture (Illustration 5.4) raised problems over moving to such a future. Foresters saw themselves as *the* forestry experts, which translated into an attitude of 'FC knows best', a tendency to see the forests as 'theirs' and the public as a 'nuisance', getting in the way of efficient timber production. There was also an ingrained public sector ethos – a sense of contributing to society rather than working for commercial gain. The command and control style of management had led to a deference to senior management and there was the bureaucracy of a public sector organisation. It also took at least 50 years to grow trees: linked to this was a deep sense of tradition making the organisation conservative and slow to change.

As Illustration 14.2 shows, this analysis of the current culture can, however, be extended to consider changes that are needed if the desired future strategy is to

Illustration 14.2

The Forestry Commission of the future

The cultural web can be used to identify the desired culture of an organisation.

Stories
- Celebrating success – spreading good news about people and what they are doing
- Heroes who push boundaries
- Thanking and rewarding people
- Illustrating a sense of belonging
- The mistakes we learned from
- Success through empowerment and working in partnership

Symbols
- Diverse forest and people
- Of accessibility
- Accessible management
- Third-party endorsement
- Active sport and health symbols
- Icons of publications
- Open-plan working areas
- Two-tree logo on signs/clothing/vehicles

Rituals and routines
- People working inclusively
- Challenging the status quo
- Learning from mistakes
- Making time to talk
- Praise and recognition
- Resource and reward new ideas
- People regularly trying out new things
- Openness, honesty, mutual respect and trust in working relationships
- Flexible, adaptable, responsive

Paradigm
- **Inclusive**
- **Forests for the people**
- **Outward looking/forward thinking/innovative**
- **Strong work ethic, loyalty and commitment**
- **Focused on outcomes**
- **Valuing diversity**
- **Learning culture**

Power structures
- Less power distance between top/bottom of the hierarchy
- Greater autonomy and empowerment
- Internal networks – open, accessible, shared decision making
- External networks – partnerships and external funding
- Management encourage challenge of ideas

Control systems
- Communicating vision and plans, targets and milestones
- Measuring outcomes *not* processes
- Encourage debate/challenge rather than following the rules/allow for local action
- Two-way discussions about realistic forward job plans – expectations balanced with resources
- Common IT systems providing access to reliable and up-to-date guidance
- Improve rewards and recognition for innovation

Organisational structures
- Less hierarchical, networked organisation
- Flatter flexible, more organic structure
- Staff interchange across organisational boundaries
- Project working/working groups
- External partnerships
- Formal and informal networks
- Improved linkages at senior level
- Inclusive management style

Questions

1. How might the cultural web be used to help manage change?

2. What are likely problems in managing change indicated by the future web?

Source: Adapted from The Forestry Commission case study by Anne McCann.

be put into effect successfully. Together with an understanding of the context of the organisation, this can be used to inform discussions about what changes are required. If the Forestry Commission is to put more emphasis on social forestry or 'forests for the community', work with other organisations to do this and encourage its employees to embrace this mission, what would the culture be like? Illustration 14.2 shows the future cultural web envisaged by the same people in the Forestry Commission. Together with the understanding of the current culture (see Illustration 5.4) this helps identify what is problematic about the existing culture but also what might be added or introduced if change is to occur. It is useful in this respect, not least because it embraces the 'softer' aspects of culture, such as organisational symbols, but also political processes and the 'harder' aspects of organisations, such as operating routines, structures and control systems. What typically emerges from such an exercise is that all these aspects of an organisation's culture can be both important blockages and facilitators to change. In deciding which are blockages and which are facilitators a forcefield analysis can also help.

14.2.4 Forcefield analysis

A forcefield analysis provides a view of change problems that need to be tackled, by identifying forces for and against change

A **forcefield analysis** provides an initial view of change problems that need to be tackled, by identifying forces for and against change based on an understanding of the context of change – including the existing culture. It allows some key questions to be asked:

● What aspects of the current situation would block change, and how can these be overcome?

● What aspects of the current situation might aid change in the desired direction, and how might these be reinforced?

● What needs to be introduced or developed to aid change?

Exhibit 14.4 is a forcefield analysis for the Forestry Commission. Whilst the blockages identified constituted a significant problem, the forcefield analysis also identified aspects of the organisation and its culture that might facilitate change. The powerful support for change of the 'Director General', the commitment of employees to the organisation, the ethos of hard work and the potential flexibility, together with a desire from within the organisation to change the command and control culture, were all potentially positive. What was needed was to add to this: for example, widespread participation in the change programme could help achieve ownership of a clearly articulated future vision; and increased diversity of personnel together with a more organic management style could promote more innovation. It was, however, also clear that there were many blockages to be removed.

Changes in the structure, design and control systems of organisations have already been reviewed in Chapter 12. In the next two sections (14.3 and 14.4), different styles and roles in the change process and other levers for managing change are discussed.

Exhibit 14.4 **A forcefield analysis**

Pushing

- Hard work ethic that delivers results
- Commitment of employees
- Juggling priorities/potential flexibility
- Forestry know-how
- Encouragement/support of change from the top
- Feedback from staff survey – staff want changes in how they are treated

Additional

- Encouragement to work in new ways
- Increased diversity of staff
- Clear articulation of a vision for the future
- Participation in the change process
- Ownership of the future strategy
- Skills development

Resisting

- Traditional structure/ways of woking
- Bureaucracy
- Departmental silos
- Workloads/pressure of work
- Homogeneous workforce
- Conservative/risk averse/slow to change
- Blame culture
- Command and control management style
- Lack of ownership of the change – 'not invented here' syndrome
- Lack of local leadership/communication
- Deference to senior staff
- No past experience of change

14.3 CHANGE MANAGEMENT: STYLES AND ROLES

This section of the chapter is concerned with the role people play in managing strategic change and how they do it. It begins by considering the roles in strategic change played by *strategic leaders*, *middle managers*, *change teams* and the influence of *outsiders* such as consultants and external *stakeholders*. It then goes on to examine different *styles of managing change*.

14.3.1 Roles in managing change

> A **change agent** is the individual or group that effects strategic change in an organisation

When it comes to managing strategic change, there is too often an overemphasis on individuals at the top of an organisation. It is useful to think of *change agency* more broadly. A **change agent** is the individual or group that helps effect strategic change in an organisation. For example, the creator of a strategy may, or may not, be the change agent. He or she may need to rely on others to take a lead in effecting changes to strategy. It could be that a middle manager is a change agent in a particular context; or perhaps consultants, working together with managers from within the organisation.

> **Leadership** is the process of influencing an organisation (or group within an organisation) in its efforts towards achieving an aim or goal

Strategic leadership

The management of change is, however, often directly linked to the role of a strategic leader.[10] More generally, however, **leadership** is the process of influencing an organisation (or group within an organisation) in its efforts towards achieving an aim or goal.[11] So a leader is not necessarily someone at the top, but rather someone who is in a position to have influence in their organisation.

Leaders are often categorised in two ways:

- *Charismatic leaders*, who are mainly concerned with building a vision for the organisation and energising people to achieve it. The evidence suggests that these leaders have particularly beneficial impact on performance when the people who work for them see the organisation facing uncertainty.[12]

- *Instrumental or transactional leaders*,[13] who focus more on designing systems and controlling the organisation's activities.

However, ideally what is required is the ability to tailor the strategic leadership style to context and there is evidence[14] that the most successful strategic leaders are able to do just this. Indeed, with regard to the management of change, it would seem to be a problem if they cannot.[15] After all, some approaches are more to do with creating strategy or with control rather than the management of change, and might well lead to approaches to change not suited to the particular needs of the specific change context.

What is likely, however, is that those at the top of an organisation will be seen by others, not least those who work for them, but also other stakeholders and outside observers, as intimately associated with strategic change programmes when they occur. In this sense they are symbolically highly significant in the change process (see section 14.4.4 below on symbolic levers for change).

Middle managers

A top-down approach to managing strategy and strategic change sees middle managers as implementers of strategy. However, as chapter 15 (section 15.2.3) shows, they have multiple roles in relation to the management of strategy.[16] In the context of managing strategic change there are five roles they play:

- The *implementation and control* role. Here they are, indeed, the implementers of top management plans by making sure that resources are allocated and controlled appropriately, monitoring performance and behaviour of staff and, where necessary, explaining the strategy to those reporting to them.

- *'Sense making'* of strategy. Top management may set down a strategic direction, but how it is made sense of in specific contexts (for example, a region of a multinational or a functional department) may, intentionally or not, be left to middle managers. If misinterpretation of that intended strategy is to be avoided, it is therefore vital that middle managers understand and feel an ownership of it.

- *Reinterpretation and adjustment* of strategic responses as events unfold (for example, in terms of relationships with customers, suppliers, the workforce, and so on). This is a vital role for which middle managers are uniquely qualified because they are in day-to-day contact with such aspects of the organisation and its environment.

- A crucial *relevance bridge* between top management and members of the organisation at lower levels. They are in a position to translate change initiatives into a message that is locally relevant.

- *Advisors* to more senior management on what are likely to be blockages and requirements for change.

When it comes to strategic change, middle managers are therefore in a key 'mediating' role between those trying to direct from the top and the operating level. A number of researchers have made the point that, in this role, how they make sense of top-down strategy and how they talk about and explain it to others become critically important.[17] The key debate in Illustration 14.6 at the end of the chapter considers strategic change in relation to both a top-down perspective and some of the roles played by middle managers.

Outsiders

Whilst managers in the organisation have important roles to play, 'outsiders' can also be important. For example, these could include the following:

- A *new chief executive* from outside the organisation may be introduced into a business to enhance the capability for change. This is especially so in turnaround situations (see section 14.5.1). He or she changes the context for change by bringing a fresh perspective on the organisation, not bound by the constraints of the past, or the embedded routines that can prevent strategic change.

- *New management from outside the organisation* can also increase the diversity of ideas, help break down cultural barriers to change and increase the experience of and capability for change. However, their successful influence is likely to depend on how much explicit *visible backing* they have from the chief executive. Without such backing they may be seen as lacking authority and influence.

- *Consultants* are often used to help formulate strategy or to plan the change process. They are also increasingly used as facilitators of change processes: for example, in a coordinating capacity, as project planners for change programmes, as facilitators of project teams working on change, or of strategy workshops used to develop strategy and plan means of strategic change. The value of consultants is three-fold. First, they too do not inherit the cultural baggage of the organisation and can therefore bring a dispassionate view to the process. Second, as a result, they may ask questions and undertake analyses which challenge taken-for-granted ways of seeing or doing things. Third, they signal symbolically the importance of a change process, not least because their fees may be of a very high order.

- *Other stakeholders* may be key influencers of change. For example, government, investors, customers, suppliers and business analysts all have the potential to act as change agents on organisations.

14.3.2 Styles of managing change

Whoever the change agent is needs to consider the style of management they adopt. Different styles are likely to be more or less appropriate according to context. These styles are summarised in Exhibit 14.5.[18]

| Exhibit 14.5 | Styles of managing strategic change |

Style	Means/context	Benefits	Problems	Circumstances of effectiveness
Education	Group briefings assume internalisation of strategic logic and trust of top management	Overcoming lack of (or mis)information	Time consuming Direction or progress may be unclear	Incremental change or long-time horizontal transformational change
Collaboration	Involvement in setting the strategy agenda and/or resolving strategic issues by taskforces or groups	Increasing ownership of a decision or process May improve quality of decisions	Time consuming Solutions/outcome within existing paradigm	
Intervention	Change agent retains co-ordination/control: delegates elements of change	Process is guided/controlled but involvement takes place	Risk of perceived manipulation	Incremental or non-crisis transformational change
Direction	Use of authority to set direction and means of change	Clarity and speed	Risk of lack of acceptance and ill-conceived strategy	Transformational change
Coercion/edict	Explicit use of power through edict	May be successful in crises or state of confusion	Least successful unless crisis	Crisis, rapid transformational change or change in established autocratic cultures

Education involves the explanation of the reasons for and means of strategic change

- **Education** involves the explanation of the reasons for and means of strategic change. This might be appropriate when the problem in managing change is because of misinformation or lack of information and if there is adequate time to persuade people of the need for change. However, there are problems here. Assuming that reasoned argument in a top-down fashion will overcome perhaps years of embedded assumptions about what 'really matters' could be naive. Change may be more effective if those affected by it are involved in its development and planning.

Participation in the change process is the involvement of those who will be affected by strategic change in the change agenda

- **Participation** in the change process is the involvement of those affected by strategic change in the change agenda; for example, in the identification of strategic issues, the strategic decision-making process, the setting of priorities, the planning of strategic change or the drawing up of action plans. Such involvement can foster a more positive attitude to change; people see the constraints the organisation faces as less significant[19] and feel increased ownership of, and commitment to, a decision or change process. It may therefore be a way of building readiness and capability for change. However, there is the inevitable risk that solutions will be found from within the existing culture so anyone who takes this approach may need to retain the ability to intervene in the process.

Intervention is the coordination of and authority over processes of change by a change agent who delegates elements of the change process

- **Intervention** is the coordination of and authority over processes of change by a change agent who delegates *elements* of the change process. For example, particular stages of change, such as ideas generation, data collection, detailed planning, the development of rationales for change or the identification of critical success factors, may be delegated to project teams or taskforces (see section 15.4.2). Such teams may not take full responsibility for the change process, but become involved in it and see their work building towards it. The change agent retains responsibility for the change, ensures the monitoring of progress and that change is seen to occur.[20] An advantage is that it involves members of the organisation, not only in originating ideas, but also in the *partial implementation* of solutions, giving rise to commitment to the change.

Direction is the use of personal managerial authority to establish a clear strategy and how change will occur

- **Direction** involves the use of personal managerial authority to establish a clear strategy and how change will occur. It is top-down management of strategic change associated with a clear vision or strategic intent and may also be accompanied by similar clarity about critical success factors and priorities.

Coercion is the imposition of change or the issuing of edicts about change

- **Coercion** is direction in its most extreme form. It is the imposition of change or the issuing of edicts about change. This is the explicit use of power and may be necessary if the organisation is facing a crisis, for example.

There are some overall observations that can be made about the appropriateness of these different styles in different contexts:

- *Different styles for different stages*. Styles of managing change may need to differ according to stages in a change process. Clear direction may be vital to motivate a desire or create a *readiness* to change; participation or intervention can help in gaining wider commitment across the organisation and developing *capabilities* to identify blockages to change, plan and implement specific action programmes.

- *Time and scope*. Participative styles are most appropriate for incremental change within organisations, but where transformational change is required, directive approaches may be more appropriate. (It is worth noting that even where top management see themselves adopting participative styles, their subordinates may perceive this as directive and, indeed, may welcome such direction.)[21]

- *Power*. In organisations with *hierarchical power structures* a directive style may be common and it may be difficult to break away from it, not least because people expect it. On the other hand, in *'Flatter' power structures* (or an adhocracy, a more networked or learning organisation described elsewhere in this book), it is likely that collaboration and participation will be common and desirable.

- *Personality types*. Different styles suit different managers' personality types. However, those with the greatest *capability* to manage change may have the ability to adopt different styles in different circumstances (see section 14.3.2).

- *Styles of managing change are not mutually exclusive*. For example, clear direction on overall vision might aid a more collaborative approach to more detailed strategy development. Education and communication may be appropriate for some stakeholders, such as financial institutions; participation may be appropriate for groups in parts of the organisation where it is necessary to build *capability and readiness*; whereas if there are parts of the organisation where change has to happen fast, *timing* may demand a more directive style.

Illustration 14.3

Leadership styles for managing change

Successful top executives have different leadership styles.

Don't noodle

I have always been a pretty good listener, and I am quick to admit that I do not have all the answers. So I am going to listen. But shortly after I listen, the second piece is to pull the trigger. I have all the input, and here is what we are going to do. People need closure on a decision. If you listen and then noodle on it, people get confused, and that's not effective leadership.

Terry Lundgren, CEO of Federated Department Stores (Interviewed by Matthew Boyle, in *Fortune*, 12 December 2005, vol. 152, no. 12, pp. 126–127.)

Coach but don't coddle

My approach to leadership is to raise aspiration and then achieve great execution . . . communicate priorities clearly, simply and frequently . . . to a large degree our division leaders must define their own future. I play the role of coach; but coaching doesn't mean coddling. I expect our managers to make choices . . . to help managers make these strategic choices leaders must sometimes challenge deeply held assumptions. . . . Being a role model is vital . . . I know that I must be ready for moments of truth that alert the organisation to my commitment.

Allan G. Laffley, Chief Executive of Procter & Gamble (in *Leadership Excellence*, November 2006, vol. 23, no. 11, pp. 9–10)

Be dedicated

Sir Terry Leahy of Tesco has overseen one of the biggest retail transformations in the world. Yet he is 'disarmingly ordinary. . . . His speech is serious and straightforward. He's no showman . . . you are not confronted with some huge presence. . . . He talks only about Tesco; . . . it's like meeting a religious leader faithfully reciting a creed.' And strategically: 'He is a combination of the very smart – he's always seeing over the hill – and the very simple. . . . You give him a problem and he'll go off and work until he's solved it. His co-workers respect him for his decision-making but he doesn't make his moves on a whim. . . .

Everything is analysed, taken apart, discussed and put back together. . . . He's gathered around him senior managers who've been with him and the group for years. He's in charge but he's also collegiate.' He also likes to talk and listen to people in the stores: 'What makes Leahy different is the extraordinary degree to which he chats with junior staff and absorbs their views and the attention he pays to customers.'

Chris Blackhurst 'Sir Terry Leahy' *Management Today*, February 2004, p. 32. Reproduced from *Management Today* magazine with the permission of the copyright owner, Haymarket Business Publications Limited.

Build on the key influencers

William Bratton was the police commissioner of New York City responsible for the Zero Tolerance campaign that reduced crime in the city. Bratton's belief was that once 'the beliefs and energies of a critical mass of people are engaged, conversion to another idea will spread like an epidemic, bringing about fundamental change very quickly'. He put key managers face-to-face with detailed operational problems so that they could not evade reality and put them 'under a spotlight'. For example, he brought together senior policemen and required them to face questions from senior colleagues about the performance of their precinct and how it contributed to overall strategy. The aim was to introduce a 'culture of performance': to allow success to be applauded but to make it very clear that underperformance was not tolerated.

W.C. Kim and R. Mauborgne, 'Tipping point leadership', *Harvard Business Review*, April 2003, pp. 60–69.

Questions

1 What might be the benefits and problems of each of the leadership styles? In what circumstances?

2 Only some stakeholders are specifically mentioned in the examples. Does this mean that the style should be the same towards all stakehoders of the organisation?

Illustration 14.3 shows how chief executives may use different styles in different contexts.

14.4 LEVERS FOR MANAGING STRATEGIC CHANGE

The rest of the chapter examines different 'levers' for managing strategic change. Change agents need to consider which of these levers to emphasise according to the change context. On the basis of many years' study of corporate change programmes, Michael Beer and Nitin Nohria observe that, broadly, there are two approaches here that they describe as 'theory E and theory O':[22]

- *Theory E* is change based on the pursuit of economic value and is typically associated with the top-down, programmatic use of the 'hard' levers of change. The emphasis is on changes of structures and systems, financial incentives, often associated with portfolio changes, downsizing and consequent job layoffs.
- *Theory O* is change based on the development of organisational capability. The emphasis here is on culture change, learning and participation in change programmes and experimentation.

However, Beer and Nohria make the point that, stark as these alternatives seem to be, the use of change levers that combine both approaches may not only be required, but be beneficial. This might involve, for example:

- *Sequencing change* to start with theory E approaches and move on to theory O approaches.
- *Embracing both approaches* simultaneously and being explicit about it to people in the organisation and external stakeholders.
- *Combining direction from the top with participation from below.* By so doing the benefits of both clarity of overall strategic direction and potential upward spontaneity can be achieved.
- *Using incentives to reinforce change* rather than to drive change.

Some of the levers for change have already been discussed in Chapter 11 in relation to the effects of changes in structures and control systems of organisations. Here other possible change levers are discussed. In so doing it is worth noting that many of these correspond to the elements of the cultural web. The implication is that the forces that act to embed and protect current ways of doing things might also provide bases for change.

14.4.1 Challenging the taken for granted

One of the major challenges in achieving strategic change can be the need to change often long-standing mindsets or taken-for-granted assumptions – the paradigm (see section 5.4.6). There are different views on how this might be achieved.

One view is that sufficient evidence, perhaps in the form of careful strategic analysis, will itself serve to challenge and therefore change the paradigm.

However, where long-standing assumptions have persisted, they will be very resistant to change. People find ways of questioning, reconfiguring and reinterpreting such analysis to bring it in line with the existing paradigm. It may take much persistence to overcome this. Others argue that such taken-for-grantedness can be challenged by surfacing it analytically and encouraging people to question and challenge each other's assumptions and the received wisdom.[23] The idea is that making visible such assumptions means that they are more likely to be questioned. Scenario planning (see section 2.2.2) is similarly advocated as a way of overcoming individual biases and cultural assumptions by getting people to see possible different futures and the implications for their organisations.[24]

Others argue that senior managers in particular are often too far removed from the realities of their organisations and need to be brought face to face with them. They may rarely speak to customers directly or experience themselves the services offered by their own firms. A senior executive of a rail company explained that in the past senior executives in the organisation had always travelled first class or by chauffeur-driven car. Hardly any of them had ever travelled in a crowded railway carriage. He introduced a policy that all senior executives should travel economy class wherever possible.

14.4.2   Changing operational processes and routines

In the end, strategies are delivered through day-to-day processes and routines of the operations of the organisation. These might be formalised and codified or they might be less formal 'ways we do things around here'[25] which tend to persist over time and guide people's behaviour. As has been seen in the discussion in Chapters 3 and 6, it may be that such routines can be the basis of the organisation's core competences and therefore its competitive advantage. However, they can also be serious blockages to change; as Dorothy Leonard-Barton[26] points out, they can become 'core rigidities'. The relationship between strategic change and day-to-day processes and routines is therefore important to consider in a number of respects:

- *Planning operational change*. The planning of the implementation of an intended strategy requires the identification of the key changes in the routines of the organisation required to deliver that strategy. In effect, strategic change needs to be considered in terms of the re-engineering of organisational processes.[27] For example, in Shell Lubricants till 2002 seven people were involved in different aspects of order processing routines. In the search for improved efficiency and customer service, one person was given overall responsibility for an order, with the consequent reduction in order time of 75 per cent, reduction in order processing costs of 45 per cent and vastly improved customer satisfaction.[28]

- *Challenging operational assumptions*. Changing organisational processes and routines may also have the effect of challenging the often taken-for-granted assumptions underpinning them. This can be important because it may have the effect of getting people to question and challenge deep-rooted beliefs and assumptions in the organisation. Richard Pascale argues: 'It is easier to act your way into a better way of thinking than to think your way into a better way of acting';[29] in other words, that it is easier to change behaviour and by so doing change taken-for-granted assumptions than to try to change taken-for-granted assumptions as a way of changing behaviour. If this is so, the style of change employed (see section 14.3.2) needs to take this into account: it suggests that education and communication to persuade people to change may be less powerful than involving people in the activities of changing.

● *Operational-led change*. Operational change may not simply be the outcome of planned strategic change; it could be that opportunities for operational change can stimulate innovation and new strategic thinking. Michael Hammer[30] argues that managers do not consider changes at the operational level sufficiently radically. Typically they benchmark best practice against industry standards rather than looking for best practice wherever it can be found (see section 3.6.3). He gives the example of Taco Bell in the USA, which saved costs and improved the quality of its offering by re-examining its operational processes in terms of best practice in manufacturing instead of fast food operations.

● *Bottom-up changes to routines*. Even when changes in routines are not planned from the top, people do change them and this may result in wider strategic change. Martha Feldman[31] shows that, even where there are formalised (she calls them 'ostensive') routines in organisations, they themselves change as a result of how people actually carry them out (which she calls 'performative routines'). So, over time, the 'performative' can change the 'ostensive'. Other research shows that this may also occur more proactively through the bending of routines. Managers may deliberately '*bend* the rules of the game'. This could give rise to resistance, but persistent bending may eventually achieve enough support from different stakeholders such that new routines become acceptable. When sufficient questioning of the status quo is achieved, change agents may actively *subvert* existing ways of doing things so as to make clear a fundamental change from the past. This could, for example, be an approach adopted by middle managers in seeking to carry with them both more senior managers and people who work for them, both of whom may be resistant to change. It is an incremental, experimental process that is likely to suffer setbacks and require persistence and political acumen.

The overall lesson is that changes in routines may appear to be mundane, but they can have significant impact. Illustration 14.4 gives some examples of changes in routines linked to strategic change.

14.4.3 Symbolic processes[32]

Change levers are not always of an overt, formal nature: they may also be symbolic in nature. Chapter 5 (section 5.4.6) explained how the symbols of an organisation may help preserve the paradigm. Here the concern is their role in managing change. **Symbols** are objects, events, acts or people that convey, maintain or create meaning over and above their functional purpose. They may be everyday things which are nevertheless especially meaningful in the context of a particular situation or organisation. (In this sense the organisational processes and routines discussed above are also symbolic in nature.) Changing

Symbols are objects, events, acts or people that convey, maintain or creati meaning over and above their functional purpose

Illustration 14.4

Changes in routines and symbols

Changes in organisational routines and symbols can be a powerful signal of and stimulus for change.

Changes in routines

- A drug can only be promoted on launch on the basis of claims substantiated by clinical data, so how pharmaceutical firms conduct clinical trials is strategically important. The traditional approach has been to base extensive data collection on a scientific research protocol and then to write a report explaining why all this data had been collected: a highly time-consuming and costly process. Some firms changed their procedures to ensure that scientific tests addressed regulatory and medical need. They created ideal claims statements and drafted the report they would need. Only then did they create research protocols and data collection forms, specifying the data required from the trials to support the claims.

- In a retail business with an espoused strategy of customer care, the chief executive, on visiting stores, tended to ignore staff and customers alike: he seemed to be interested only in the financial information in the store manager's office. He was unaware of this until it was pointed out; his change in behaviour afterwards, insisting on talking to staff and customers on his visits, became a 'story' which spread around the company, substantially supporting the strategic direction of the firms.

Language that challenges and questions

- A chief executive facing a crisis addressed his board: 'I suggest we think of ourselves like bulls facing a choice: the abattoir or the bull ring. I've made up my mind: what about you?'

- When the new management team (Gordon Bethune as Chief Executive and Greg Brennemaan as Chief Operating Officer) took over ailing Continental Airlines they chose their language carefully. The future winning orientation was made clear consistently. The overall strategy was referred to as the 'Go forward plan', the marketing plan was 'Fly to win' and the financial plan 'Fund the future'. It was language reinforced in how Brennemaan explained the determination to succeed: 'Did you know there

are no rear view mirrors on an airplane? The runway behind is irrelevant.'

Source: J.M. Higgins and C. McCallaster, 'If you want strategic change don't forget your cultural artefacts', *Journal of Change Management*, vol. 4, no. 1 (2004), pp. 63–73.

Physical objects as symbols of change

- In a textile firm equipment associated with 'old ways of doing things' was taken into a yard at the rear of the factory and smashed up in front of the workforce.

- The head nurse of a recovery unit for patients who had been severely ill decided that, if nurses wore everyday clothes rather than nurses' uniforms, it would signal to patients that they were on the road to recovery and a normal life; and to nurses that they were concerned with rehabilitation. However, the decision had other implications for the nurses too. It blurred the status distinction between nurses and other non-professional members of staff. Nurses preferred to wear their uniforms. Whilst they recognised that uniforms signalled a medically fragile role of patients, they reinforced their separate and professional status as acute care workers.

Source: M.G. Pratt and E. Rafaeli, 'Organisational dress as a symbol of multi-layered social idealities', *Academy of Management Journal*, vol. 40, no. 4 (1997), pp. 862–898.

Questions

For an organisation with which you are familiar:

1 Identify at least five important routines, symbols or rituals in the organisation.

2 In what way could they be changed to support a different strategy? Be explicit as to how the symbols might relate to the new strategy.

3 Why are these potential levers for change often ignored by change agents?

symbols can help reshape beliefs and expectations because meaning becomes apparent in the day-to-day experiences people have of organisations, such as the symbols that surround them (for example, office layout and decor), the type of language and technology used and organisational rituals. Consider some examples:

- Many *rituals*[33] of organisations are concerned with effecting or consolidating change. Exhibit 14.6 identifies and gives examples of such rituals and suggests what role they might play in change processes.[34] New rituals can be introduced or old rituals done away with as ways of signalling or reinforcing change.

- Changes in *physical aspects* of the work environment are powerful symbols of change. Typical here is a change of location for the head office, relocation of personnel, changes in dress or uniforms, and alterations to offices or office space.

- The *behaviour of change agents*, particularly strategic leaders, is perhaps the most powerful symbol in relation to change. So having made pronouncements about the need for change, it is vital that the visible behaviour of change agents is in line with such change.

- The *language* used by change agents is also important. Either consciously or unconsciously, change agents may employ language and metaphor to galvanise change. Of course, there is also the danger that change agents do not realise this and, whilst espousing change, use language that signals adherence to the status quo, or personal reluctance to change.

Exhibit 14.6 Organisational rituals and culture change

Types of ritual	Role	Examples
Rites of passage	Consolidate and promote social roles and interaction	Induction programmes Training programmes
Rites of enhancement	Recognise effort benefiting organisation Similarly motivate others	Awards ceremonies Promotions
Rites of renewal	Reassure that something is being done Focus attention on issues	Appointment of consultants Project teams
Rites of integration	Encourage shared commitment Reassert rightness of norms	Christmas parties
Rites of conflict reduction	Reduce conflict and aggression	Negotiating committees
Rites of degradation	Publicly acknowledge problems Dissolve/weaken social or political roles	Firing top executives Demotion or 'passing over'
Rites of sense making	Sharing of interpretations and sense making	Rumours Surveys to evaluate new practices
Rites of challenge	'Throwing down the gauntlet'	New CEO's different behaviour
Rites of counter-challenge	Resistance to new ways of doing things	Grumbling Working to rule

Illustration 14.4 also gives some examples of such symbolic signalling of change. However, there is an important qualification to the idea that the manipulation of symbols can be a useful lever for managing change. The significance and meaning of symbols are dependent on how they are interpreted. So a change agent's intentions in the use of symbolic levers may not be interpreted as intended (see the nursing example in Illustration 14.4). So, whilst symbolic changes are important, their impact is difficult to predict.

14.4.4 Power and political processes[35]

Chapter 4 discussed the importance of understanding the political context in and around the organisation. There is also a need to consider the management of strategic change within this political context. This can be important because it may be necessary to build a political context for change (see section 14.2.2). It may also be important because, to effect change, powerful support may be required from individuals or groups. This may be the chief executive, a powerful member of the board or an influential outsider. Or, in managing strategic change, a reconfiguration of *power structures* may be necessary, especially if transformational change is required. Exhibit 14.7 shows some of the mechanisms associated with managing change from a political perspective:

- *Acquiring resources* or being identified with important resource areas or areas of expertise. In particular the ability to withdraw or allocate such resources can be a valuable tool in overcoming resistance or persuading others to accept change or build readiness for change.

- *Association with powerful stakeholder groups (elites)*, or their supporters, can help build a power base. Similarly, association with a change agent who is respected or visibly successful can help a manager overcome resistance to change. Or a change agent facing resistance to change may seek out and win over someone highly respected from within the very group resistant to change. It may also be necessary to *remove individuals or groups* resistant to change. Who these are can vary – from powerful individuals in senior positions to whole layers of resistance, perhaps in the form of senior executives in a threatened function or service.

- *Building alliances* and *networks* of contacts and sympathisers may be important in overcoming the resistance of more powerful groups. Attempting to convert the whole organisation to an acceptance of change is difficult, but there may be parts of the organisation, or individuals in it, more sympathetic to change than others, with whom a change agent might build support. He or she may also seek to marginalise those who are resistant to change. However, the danger is that powerful groups in the organisation may regard the building of such a team, or acts of marginalisation, as a threat to their own power, leading to further resistance to change. An analysis of power and interest using the stakeholder mapping (section 4.4.1) can, therefore, be useful to identify bases of alliance and likely resistance.

- *Symbolic change* is, again, potentially important. To build power, it may be necessary to identify initially with the very *symbols* which preserve and reinforce the paradigm – to work within the committee structures, become

Exhibit 14.7	Political mechanisms in organisations

| | Mechanisms | | | | |
Activity areas	Resources	Elites	Subsystems	Symbolic	Key problems
Building the power base	Control of resources Acquisition of/identification with expertise Acquisition of additional resources	Sponsorship by an elite Association with an elite	Alliance building Team building	Building on legitimation	Time required for building Perceived duality of ideals Perceived as threat by existing elites
Overcoming resistance	Withdrawal of resources Use of 'counter-intelligence'	Breakdown or division of elites Association with change agent Association with respected outsider	Foster momentum for change Sponsorship/reward of change agents	Attack or remove legitimation Foster confusion, conflict and questioning	Striking from too low a power base Potentially destructive: need for rapid rebuilding
Achieving compliance	Giving resources	Removal of resistant elites Need for visible 'change hero'	Partial implementation and collaboration Implantation of 'disciples' Support for 'Young Turks'	Applause/reward Reassurance Symbolic confirmation	Converting the body of the organisation Slipping back

identified with the organisational rituals or stories that exist, and so on. On the other hand, in breaking resistance to change, removing, challenging or changing rituals and symbols may be a very powerful means of achieving the questioning of what is taken for granted.

However, the political aspects of change management are also potentially hazardous. Exhibit 14.7 also summarises some of the problems. In overcoming resistance, the major problem may simply be the lack of power to undertake such activity. Trying to break down the status quo may become so destructive and take so long that the organisation cannot recover from it. If the process needs to take place, its replacement by some new set of beliefs and the implementation of a new strategy is vital and needs to be speedy. Further, as already identified, in implementing change, gaining the commitment of a few senior executives at the top of an organisation is one thing; it is quite another to convert the body of the organisation to an acceptance of significant change.

14.4.5 Change tactics

There are also more specific tactics of change which might be employed to facilitate the change process.

Timing

The importance of timing is often neglected in thinking about strategic change. But choosing the right time tactically to promote change is vital. For example:

● *Building on actual or perceived crisis* is especially useful the greater the degree of change needed. If there is a higher perceived risk in maintaining the status quo than in changing it, people are more likely to change. Indeed, it is said that some chief executives seek to elevate problems to achieve perceived crisis in order to galvanise change. For example, a threatened takeover may be used as a catalyst for strategic change.

● *Windows of opportunity* in change processes may exist. The arrival of a new chief executive, the introduction of a new, highly successful product, or the arrival of a major competitive threat on the scene may provide opportunities to make more significant changes than might normally be possible. Since change will be regarded nervously, it may also be important to choose the time for promoting such change to avoid unnecessary fear and nervousness. For example, if there is a need for the removal of executives, this may be best done before rather than during the change programme. In such a way, the change programme can be seen as a potential improvement for the future rather than as the cause of such losses.

● *The symbolic signalling of time frames* may be important. Change agents should avoid conflicting messages about the timing of change. For example, if rapid change is required, they should avoid the maintenance of procedures and signals that suggest long time horizons, such as maintaining long-established control and reward procedures or routines.

Visible short-term wins

A strategic change programme will require many detailed actions and tasks. It is important that some are seen to be successful quickly. This could take the form, for example, of a retail chain quickly developing a new store concept and demonstrating its success in the market; the effective breaking down of old ways of working and the demonstration of better ways; the speeding up of decisions by doing away with committees and introducing clearly defined job responsibilities; and so on. In themselves, these may not be especially significant aspects of a new strategy, but they may be visible indicators of a new approach associated with that strategy. The demonstration of such wins will therefore galvanise commitment to the strategy.

One reason given for the inability to change is that resources are not available to do so. This may be overcome if it is possible to identify 'hot spots' on which to focus resources and effort. For example, William Bratton, famously responsible for the Zero Tolerance policy of the New York Police Department, began by focusing resource and effort on narcotics-related crimes. Though associated with 50–70 per cent of all crimes, he found they only had 5 per cent of the resources allocated by NYPD to tackle them. Success in this field led to the roll-out of his policies into other areas and to gaining the resources to do so.[36]

14.5 MANAGING STRATEGIC CHANGE PROGRAMMES

There are then a variety of change levers that change agents may choose. Choosing the appropriate levers, rather than following a set formula for managing strategic change, is critically important. This will depend on the change context and the skills and styles of those managing change. For example, to take the extremes, if the need is to overcome resistance to achieve fast results, then the emphasis may have to be on achieving behavioural compliance to a change programme. On the other hand, if there is a need and the time to 'win hearts and minds' then there will need to be a focus on changing people's values and a much greater emphasis on their involvement in changing the culture of the organisation as Illustration 14.5 shows. However, it is likely that there will be, none the less, elements of both 'theory E' and 'theory O' in most change initiatives. Indeed, most successful change initiatives rely on multiple levers for change,[37] again as shown in Illustration 14.5.

This section first revisits three types of change identified in section 14.2.1 to consider which levers managers use in which contexts. It then suggests some general lessons about managing change programmes.

14.5.1 Strategy reconstruction and turnaround strategy

There are circumstances where the emphasis has to be on rapid reconstruction, in the absence of which a business could face closure, enter terminal decline or be taken over. This is commonly referred to as a **turnaround strategy**, where the emphasis is on speed of change and rapid cost reduction and/or revenue generation, and managers need to prioritise the things that give quick and significant improvements. Typically it is a situation where a directive approach to change (see section 14.3.1) is required. Some of the main elements of turnaround strategies are as follows:[38]

In a **turnaround strategy** the emphasis is on speed of change and rapid cost reduction and/or revenue generation

- *Crisis stabilisation*. The aim here is to regain control over the deteriorating position. This requires a short-term focus on cost reduction and/or revenue increase, typically involving some of the steps identified in Exhibit 14.8. There is nothing novel about these steps: many of them are good management practice. The differences are the speed at which they are carried out and the focus of managerial attention on them. The most successful turnaround strategies also focus on reducing direct operational costs and on productivity gains. Less effective approaches pay less attention to these and more on the reduction of overheads.[39]

    However, too often turnarounds are seen as no more than cost-cutting exercises when a wider alignment between causes of decline and solutions may be important. For example, where the business decline is principally a result of changes in the external environment it may be folly to expect that cost cutting alone can lead to renewed growth. Other elements of turnaround strategies are therefore important.

- *Management changes*. Changes in management may be required, especially at the top. This usually includes the introduction of a new chairman/woman or chief executive, as well as changes in the board, especially in marketing, sales

Illustration 14.5

ValuesJam at IBM

Changing strategy by 'values-based management'.

Sam Palmisano took over as Chief Executive of IBM in 2002 as successor to Lou Gerstner who was credited with the turnaround of IBM in the 1990s. Palmisano's challenge was very different from the challenge that faced Gerstner. As he explained, then there was 'a burning platform; in fact the whole place was in flames'. Now there was a need for a continuation of change but no burning platform: 'instead of galvanising people through fear of failure, you have to galvanise them through hope and aspiration.' Palmisano's answer to this was 'values-based management'. He believed it was impossible to manage a company as complex as IBM operating in 170 countries with almost 70 major product lines and dozens of customer segments by relying on structures and control systems. It had to be through values. But how to identify the core values and get people not only to believe them but to live them?

Palmisano's answer was based on a bottom-up reinvention of the values of IBM. In July 2003 over a three-day period over 50,000 employees took part in an intranet discussion on company values: the 'ValuesJam' (see Illustration 15.2). Much of what was posted was highly critical. IBM talked a lot about trust but spent endless time auditing people; no one questioned the views of senior executives; mistakes were not tolerated or seen as part of learning. It was uncomfortable criticism and some senior executives wanted to pull the plug on the exercise. But Palmisano not only insisted it continue, he joined in, posting his personal views and acknowledging problems.

The comments from ValuesJam were analysed and values statements produced: 'dedication to every client's success', 'innovation that matters – for our company and the world', 'trust and personal responsibility in all relationships'. As Palmisano observed, in many respects these values extended what IBM had already espoused in the past. The important point was that they were not being enacted. So the next step was to charge people with identifying where the values were not being delivered. This started with top management but was quickly rolled out to an online jam (see Illustration 15.2 also) for employees again. They identified example after example of IBM processes and routines which were contrary to the values.

Palmisano then turned his attention to instigating changes in those routines to bring them in line with the values. He changed the incentive scheme for managing directors of IBM businesses. This was already based on how clients scored their performance, but within a single year. It was changed to be based on a mix of a project profitability, annual targets and client satisfaction over the long term, not just a single year. Other changes appeared to be small scale: for example, the allocation of $5,000 (£2,800; €4,000) annually to line managers to use at their own discretion to generate business or develop client relationships – but multiplied by 22,000 managers across IBM, a significant commitment. Another example was pricing. Price setting in IBM was not client-friendly, especially if it involved products and services crossing IBM businesses. Palmisano insisted that the process be changed so that prices were delivered to the client seamlessly. This involved significant reworking of the IBM pricing routines to deliver what the clients were looking for.

Source: Based on Paul Hemp, 'Leading change when business is good', *Harvard Business Review*, vol. 82, no. 12 (2004), pp. 60–70.

Questions

1 Which levers for change described in the chapter are evident? Which others might have been used?

2 Compare Palmisano's approach to that of John Howie's at Faslane (see the case example).

3 Compare this values-based approach to a programme of revolutionary change or reconstruction.

| Exhibit 14.8 | Turnaround: revenue generation and cost reduction steps |

Increasing revenue	Reducing costs
● Ensure marketing mix tailored to key market segments	● Reduce labour costs and costs of senior management
● Review pricing strategy to maximise revenue	● Focus on productivity improvement
● Focus organisational activities on needs of target market sector customers	● Reduce marketing costs not focused on target market
● Exploit additional opportunities for revenue creation related to target market	● Tighten financial controls
● Invest funds from reduction of costs in new growth areas	● Tighten control on cash expenses
	● Establish competitive bidding for suppliers; defer creditor payments; speed up debtor payments
	● Reduce inventory
	● Eliminate non-profitable products/services

and finance, for three main reasons. First, because the old management may well be the ones that were in charge when the problems developed and be seen as the cause of them by key stakeholders. Second, because it may be necessary to bring in managers with experience of turnaround management. Third, because, if new managers come from outside the organisation, they may bring different approaches to the way the organisation has operated in the past.

● *Gaining stakeholder support*. Poor quality of information may have been provided to key stakeholders. In a turnaround situation it is vital that key stakeholders, perhaps the bank or key shareholder groups, and employees are kept clearly informed of the situation and improvements as they are being made.[40] It is also likely that a clear assessment of the power of different stakeholder groups (see section 4.4.1) will become vitally important in managing turnaround.

● *Clarifying the target market(s)*. Central to turnaround success is ensuring clarity on the target market or market segments most likely to generate cash and grow profits. A successful turnaround strategy involves getting closer to customers and improving the flow of marketing information, especially to senior levels of management, so as to focus revenue-generating activities on key market segments. Indeed, a reason for the poor performance of the organisation could be because it had this wrong in the first place.

● *Refocusing*. Clarifying the target market also provides the opportunity to discontinue or outsource products and services that are not targeted on those markets, eating up management time for little return or not making sufficient financial contribution.

● *Financial restructuring*. The financial structure of the organisation may need to be changed. This typically involves changing the existing capital structure, raising additional finance or renegotiating agreements with creditors, especially banks.

- *Prioritisation of critical improvement areas*. All of this requires the ability of management to prioritise those things that give quick and significant improvements.

14.5.2 Managing revolutionary strategic change

Revolutionary change differs from reconstruction in two ways that make managing change especially challenging. First, the need is for not only fast change but also cultural change. Second, it may be that the need for change is not as evident to people in the organisation as in a turnaround situation, or that they see reasons to deny the need for change. This situation may have come about as a result of many years of relative decline in a market, with people wedded to products or processes no longer valued by customers – the problem of strategic drift. Or it could be that the problems of the organisation are visible and understood by its members, but that people cannot see a way forward. Managing such change is likely to involve:

- *Clear strategic direction*. In these circumstances the need for the articulation of a clear strategic direction and decisive action in line with that direction are critical. So this is the type of change where individual CEOs who are seen to provide such direction are often credited with making a major difference. They may well also become the symbol of such change, within an organisation and externally.

- *Combining economic and symbolic levers*. Very likely some of the hard decisions outlined above for reconstruction (or turnaround) will be taken: for example, portfolio changes, greater market focus, top management changes and perhaps financial restructuring. However, often these are also employed to send major symbolic messages of change. In the newspaper industry, for example, Rupert Murdoch's decision in the 1970s to close his newspapers' offices in Fleet Street and move to purpose-built modern premises in Wapping is still regarded as the single most significant event in modernising not only his business, but the industry.

- *An outside perspective*. The introduction of new managers, often at a senior level, with different perspectives is common. For example, the reform of public sector organisations has seen the introduction of managers with private sector experience. Consultants may also be used to provide a dispassionate analysis of the need for change or facilitate the change process.

- *Multiple styles of change management*. Whilst a *directive style* of change management is likely to be evident, this may need to be accompanied by other styles. It may be supported by determined efforts to *educate* about the need for change and the use of an *intervention style* to involve people in aspects of change in which they have specific expertise or to overcome their resistance to change.

- *Working with the existing culture*. It may be possible to work with elements of the existing culture rather than attempt wholesale culture change. This involves identifying those aspects of culture that can be built upon and developed and those that have to be changed – in effect a forcefield approach (see section 14.2.4). For example, when Ed Zander became CEO at the ailing

Motorola in 2004 he built a change programme that emphasised much more innovation and market refocusing around the long-established values of quality and reliability.[41]

● *Monitoring change*. Revolutionary change is likely to require the setting and monitoring of unambiguous targets that people have to achieve. Often these will be linked to overall financial targets and in turn to improved returns to shareholders.

14.5.3 Managing evolutionary strategic change

Managing change as evolution involves transformational change, but incrementally. It can be thought of in two ways. The first is in terms of the creation of an organisation capable of continual change: of a learning organisation. The characteristics of this were described in section 11.5.2 and insights into how this might be achieved are best described in the ideas lens in the commentaries. Trying to achieve this in practice is a significant challenge for management, not least because it requires:

● *Empowering the organisation*. Rather than top-down management, there is the need here for people throughout the organisation to accept the responsibility for contributing strategic ideas, for innovating, and for accepting change as inevitable and desirable. Clearly, then, there is a need for a high level of participation in the change agenda.

● *A clear strategic vision*. It is the responsibility of top management to create the context within which new ideas can bubble up from below around a coherent view of long-term goals. This requires them to provide very clear guidelines – vision, mission or 'simple rules' – around which those ideas can cohere. In so doing, they need to find the balance between the clarity of such vision that allows people to see how they can contribute to future strategy whilst avoiding specifying that strategy in such detail as to constrain people's enthusiasm to contribute and innovate. (See the discussion on the ideas lens in the commentaries.)

● *Continual change and a commitment to experimentation* with regard to organisational processes throughout the organisation.

The second way of conceiving of strategic change as evolution is in terms of the movement from one strategy to a changed strategy but over time, perhaps many years. Here the principles that might guide managers are these:

● *Stages of transition*. Identifying interim stages in the change process is important. For example, in terms of the change context (see section 14.2.2) there may be insufficient readiness or an insufficient capacity to make major changes initially. It will therefore be important to establish these conditions before other major moves are taken.

● *Irreversible changes*. It may be possible to identify changes that can be made that, whilst not necessarily having immediate major impact, will have long-term and irreversible impacts. For example, in the early 1990s when KPMG was conceiving of the sort of strategy it needed into the new millennium, it established new criteria for the recruitment of university graduates and appointment to partnership. The time horizons for the effects of such changes to take effect were five to ten years. However, once made, the effects could not be reversed.

● *Sustained top management commitment*. The danger is that the momentum for change falters because people do not perceive consistent commitment to it from the top.

● *Winning hearts and minds*. Culture change is likely to be required in any transformational change. This may be more problematic than for revolutionary change because people may simply not recognise that there are problems with regard to the status quo. The need is for multiple levers for change to be used consistently: education and participation as styles of managing change to allow people to see the need for change and contribute to what that change should be; the signalling of the meaning of change in ways that people throughout the organisation understand both rationally and emotionally; and levers that signal and achieve improved economic performance.

14.5.4 Some overall lessons on the management of change programmes

This section draws together some of the overall lessons about the management of change programmes. First, there are lessons from understanding what can go wrong:[42]

● *Programme overload*. Change agents may recognise that change is not a one-off process; that it might require an ongoing series of initiatives, maybe over years. However, the risk is that these initiatives are seen by others as 'change rituals' signifying very little. There is also the risk that the original intention of the change programme becomes eroded by other events taking place, for example a redundancy programme.

● *Hijacked processes*. Well-meaning change efforts can be hijacked by others for different purposes. For example, in an insurance firm, the introduction of computerised telephone systems to improve customer service became a vehicle for reducing the number of personnel dealing with customer enquiries. The result was no improvement in service and a workforce highly sceptical about that and future change initiatives.

● *Reinvention*. Here the attempted change becomes reinterpreted according to the old culture. For example, an engineering company's intended strategy of adding value in customer terms was interpreted by the engineers within the firm as providing high levels of technical specification.

● *Disconnectedness*. People affected by change may not see the change programme connecting to their reality. Senior executives, as proponents of the change, might not be seen to be credible in terms of understanding the realities of change on the ground. Or perhaps new systems and initiatives introduced are seen as out of line with the intentions of the intended change.

● *Behavioural compliance*. There is the danger that people appear to comply with the changes being pursued in the change programme without actually 'buying into' them. Change agents may think they see change occurring, when all they see is superficial compliance.

Since 1994 the Boston Consulting Group[43] has used four key factors in managing strategic change programmes and the change teams associated with them. It claims the likelihood of success of such programmes is greatly increased if the following is in place:

- *Milestones for reviewing progress.* Change programmes should be formally reviewed by senior management at least bi-monthly against key tasks that need to be completed. The criteria against which such reviews will take place also need to be explicit and widely known.[44]

- *A high-'integrity' change team*, by which it means a team that have the skills, checked through the regular reviews, to execute the change programme. The selection of such a team, with the required mix of skills, is a key responsibility of senior management.

- *Visible commitment to change* by top management and consistency in how the change is explained. This needs to be accompanied by 'straight talking' about change with those who will be affected.

- *Time and effort for managing change*, which are needed by the change team responsible. It is the responsibility of top management to make sure they have sufficient time and resource to carry out their tasks.

Many of the problems and challenges of managing strategic change are reflected in Illustration 14.6, the key debate for this chapter.

SUMMARY

A recurrent theme in this chapter has been that approaches, styles and means of change need to be tailored to the context of that change. Bearing in mind this general point, this chapter has emphasised a number of key points:

- There are different *types of strategic change* which can be thought of in terms of the *extent* of culture change required and its *nature* – whether it can be achieved through incremental change or requires urgent action (the 'big bang' approach). Different approaches and means of managing change are likely to be required for different types of change.

- It is also important to diagnose wider aspects of organisational context such as *resources and skills that need to be preserved*, the degree of *homogeneity or diversity* in the organisation, the *capability, capacity and readiness* for change and the *power* to make change happen.

- The *cultural web* and *forcefield analysis* are useful as means of identifying blockages to change and potential levers for change.

- Change agents may need to adopt different *styles* of managing strategic change according to different contexts and in relation to the involvement and interest of different groups.

- *Levers for managing strategic change* need to be considered in terms of the type of change and context of change. Such levers include surfacing and *challenging the taken for granted*, the need to change *operational processes*, routines and *symbols*, the importance of *political processes*, and other change *tactics*.

Illustration 14.6
key debate

The management of change from top to bottom

Strategic change has always been seen as the responsibility of top management: but to what extent can top managers manage change?

John Kotter, one of the world's foremost authorities on leadership and change, argues that problems of strategic change arise because top executives fail to take the necessary steps to manage such changes. These include:

- Establishing a sense of urgency on the basis of market threats or opprortunities.

- Forming a powerful coalition of stakeholders for change.

- Creating and communicating a clear vision and strategy to direct the change and ensuring that the behaviour of the guiding coalition is in line with the vision.

- Removing obstacles to change, changing systems that undermine the vision and encouraging non-traditional ideas and activities.

- Creating short-term wins.

- Consolidating improvements but also continuing the process of change.

However, Julia Balogun studied a top management change initiative from the point of view of how middle managers interpreted it. She found that, whilst top managers believed they were being clear about the intended strategy, change actually took place by middle managers making sense of change initiatives in terms of their own *mental models* in relation to their *local responsibilities and conditions*, through discussion with their peers and on the basis of rumour. Top managers were inevitably too far removed from these dynamics and could not be expected to understand them in detail or intervene in specific ways. She argues that 'Senior managers can initiate and influence direction of change but not direct change.' They can:

- Monitor how people respond to change initiatives.

- Engage as much as possible with how people make sense of change and work with their reality, responding to their issues and interpretations.

- Live the changes they want others to adopt, especially avoiding inconsistencies between their actions, words and deeds.

- Focus on creating the understanding of higher-level principles rather than the details.

Hari Tsoukas and Robert Chia go further. They argue that change is an inherent property of organisations. Hierarchy and management control dampen that inherent change.

Change programmes trigger ongoing change: they provide the discursive resources for making certain things possible, although what exactly will happen remains uncertain when a change programme is initiated. It must first be experienced before the possibilities it opens up are appreciated and taken up (if they are taken up). Change programmes are . . . locally adapted, improvised and elaborated. . . . If this is accepted what is, then, the meaning of 'planned change'? . . . Change has been taken to mean that which occurs as a consequence of deliberate managerial action. In the view put forward here such a definition is limited. Although managers certainly aim at achieving established ways of thinking and acting through implementing particular plans, nonetheless, change in organisations occurs without necessarily intentional managerial action as a result of individuals trying to accommodate new experience and realise new possibilities. In the view suggested here, an excessive preoccupation with planned change risks failing to recognise the always ready changing texture of organisations. (pp. 578–579)

Sources: J. Kotter, 'Leading change: why transformation efforts fail', *Harvard Business Review*, March–April (1995), pp. 59–67; J. Balogun and G. Johnson, 'Organizational restructuring and middle manager sensemaking', *Academy of Management Journal*, vol. 47, no. 4 (2004), pp. 523–549; J. Balogun, 'Managing change: steering a course between intended strategies and unanticipated outcomes', *Long Range Planning*, vol. 39 (2006), pp. 29–49; H. Tsoukas and R. Chia, 'On organizational becoming: rethinking organizational change', *Organization Science*, vol. 13, no. 5 (2002), pp. 567–582.

Questions

1 What are the problems associated with top-down or bottom-up views of change management?

2 If your were a senior executive which approach would you take and in what circumstances?

3 Are the different views irreconcilable?

(You will find the perspectives on the management of strategy in the commentaries useful background reading.)

Work assignments

✳ *Denotes more advanced work assignments.* * *Refers to a case study in the Text and Cases edition.*

14.1 Drawing on section 14.2.2 assess the key contextual dimensions of an organisation (such as for the case example on Faslane) and consider how they should influence the design of a programme of strategic change.

14.2 ✳ Draw up a cultural web and use forcefield analysis to identify blockages and facilitators of change for an organisation (such as one for which you have considered the need for a change in strategic direction in a previous assignment). Redraw the web to represent what the organisation should aspire to given the new strategy. Using the cultural webs and forcefield analysis, identify what aspects of the changes can be managed by a change agent and how.

14.3 Compare and contrast the different styles of managing change of executives you have read about in the press or in this book (for example, John Howie at Faslane, Fergus Chambers at Direct and Care* and Stuart Rose at M&S*).

14.4 ✳ Consider a process of strategic change that you have been involved in or have observed. Map out the steps in the change process in the following terms: new rituals introduced or old rituals done away with, and the impact of these changes.

14.5 ✳ In the context of managing strategic change in a large corporation or public sector organisation, to what extent, and why, do you agree with Richard Pascale's argument that it is easier to act ourselves into a better way of thinking than it is to think ourselves into a better way of acting? (References 29 to 34 will be useful here.)

14.6 ✳ There are a number of books by renowned senior executives who have managed major changes in their organisation. Read one of these and note the levers and mechanisms for change employed by the change agent, using the approaches outlined in this chapter as a checklist. How effective do you think these were in the context that the change agent faced, and could other mechanisms have been used?

Integrative assignments

14.7 ✳ What would be the key issues for the corporate parent of a diversified organisation with a multidomestic international strategy (see Chapter 8) wishing to change to a more related portfolio? Consider this in terms of (a) the strategic capabilities that the parent might require (Chapters 3 and 7), (b) the implications for organising and controlling its subsidiaries (Chapter 12), (c) the likely blockages to such change and (d) how these might be overcome (Chapter 14).

An extensive range of additional materials, including audio summaries, weblinks to organisations featured in the text, definitions of key concepts and self-assessment questions, can be found on the *Exploring Corporate Strategy* Companion Website at www.pearsoned.co.uk/ecs

Recommended key readings

- J. Balogun, V. Hope Hailey (with G. Johnson and K. Scholes), *Exploring Strategic Change*, 3rd edition, Prentice Hall, 2007, builds on and extends many of the ideas in this chapter. In particular, it emphasises the importance of tailoring change programmes to organisational context and discusses more fully many of the change levers reviewed in this chapter.

- The paper by John Kotter, 'Leading change: why transformation efforts fail', *Harvard Business Review*, March–April (1995), pp. 59–67 (also see Illustration 14.6), provides a useful view of what a change programme might look like. An alternative but complementary perspective is provided by Julia Balogun, 'Managing change: steering a course between intended strategies and unanticipated outcomes', *Long Range Planning*, vol. 39 (2006), pp. 29–49.

- For an understanding of different approaches to managing change: M. Beer and N. Nohria, 'Cracking the code of change', *Harvard Business Review*, vol. 78, no. 3 (May–June 2000), pp. 133–141.

- Martha Feldman has written about how organisational routines may play a role in creating organisational inertia, but may also help explain organisational change. See M. Feldman, 'Resources in emerging structures and processes of change', *Organization Science,* vol. 15, no. 3 (2004), pp. 295–309; and M. Feldman and B. Pentland, 'Reconceptualizing organizational routines as a source of flexibility and change, *Administrative Science Quarterly*, vol. 48, no. 1 (2003), pp. 94–118.

- The study of change programmes by L.C. Harris and E. Ogbonna, 'The unintended consequences of culture interventions: a study of unexpected outcomes', *British Journal of Management*, vol. 13, no. 1 (2002), pp. 31–49, provides a valuable insight into the problems of managing change in organisations.

References

1. Many books and papers on strategic change build on the idea that the current state of the organisation is likely to be one of inertia or resistance to change, and that there is, then, a need to 'unfreeze' this situation. The dominance of this idea can be traced back to the work of K. Lewin; see 'Group decision and social change', in E.E. Maccoby, T.M. Newcomb and E.I. Hartley (eds), *Readings in Social Psychology*, Holt, Reinhart and Winston, 1958, pp. 197–211.

2. *Exploring Strategic Change* by J. Balogun and V. Hope Hailey, 3rd edition, Prentice Hall, 2007, is a sister text to this book; this part of the chapter draws on their chapter 3 on the context of strategic change.

3. For a discussion of the problems of importing change programmes from the private sector to the public sector, see F. Ostroff, 'Change management in government', *Harvard Business Review*, vol. 84, no. 5 (May 2006), pp. 141–147.

4. Based on D. Neal and T. Taylor, 'Spinning on dimes: the challenges of introducing transformational change into the UK Ministry of Defence', *Strategic Change*, vol. 15 (2006), pp. 15–22.

5. For an interesting example of how different contexts affect receptivity to change, see J. Newton, J. Graham, K. McLoughlin and A. Moore, 'Receptivity to change in a general medical practice', *British Journal of Management*, vol. 14, no. 2 (2003), pp. 143–153.

6. Prior experience of change is one of the key success factors in change highlighted by S. Miller, D. Wilson and D. Hickson, 'Beyond planning strategies for successfully implementing strategic change', *Long Range Planning*, vol. 37, no. 3 (2004), pp. 201–218.

7. The extent of readiness for change is another factor highlighted by Miller *et al.*; see reference 6.

8. See J.-L. Denis, L. Lamothe and A. Langley, 'The dynamics of collective change leadership and strategic change in pluralistic organizations', *Academy of Management Journal*, vol. 44, no. 4 (2001), pp. 809–837.

9. Approaches to how to use the cultural web for the purposes outlined here are dealt with in detail in the chapter, 'Mapping and re-mapping organisational culture', in V. Ambrosini with G. Johnson and K. Scholes (eds), *Exploring Techniques of Analysis and Evaluation in Strategic Management*, Prentice Hall, 1998, and the similar chapter in G. Johnson and K. Scholes (eds), *Exploring Public Sector Strategy*, Prentice Hall, 2000.

10. Indeed John Kotter defines leadership as being about the management of change: see J. Kotter, 'What leaders really do', *Harvard Business Review*, December (2001), pp. 85–96.

11. This definition of leadership is based on that offered by R.M. Stodgill, 'Leadership, membership and organization', *Psychological Bulletin*, vol. 47 (1950), pp. 1–14. For a more recent and more comprehensive discussion of leadership, see G.A. Yukl, *Leadership in Organizations*, 6th edition, Prentice Hall, 2005.

12. For this evidence see D.A. Waldman, G.G. Ramirez, R.J. House and P. Puranam, 'Does leadership matter? CEO leadership attributes and profitability under conditions of perceived environmental uncertainty', *Academy of Management Journal*, vol. 44, no. 1 (2001), pp. 134–143.

13. For fuller explanations of the distinction between charismatic and instrumental and transactional leadership see M.F.R. Kets de Vries, 'The leadership mystique',

Academy of Management Executive, vol. 8, no. 3 (1994), pp. 73–89, and the paper by Waldman *et al.*, reference 12.

14. The discussion on different approaches of strategic leaders and evidence for the effectiveness of the adoption of different approaches can be found in D. Goleman, 'Leadership that gets results', *Harvard Business Review*, vol. 78, no. 2 (March–April 2000), pp. 78–90; and C.M. Farkas and S. Wetlaufer, 'The ways chief executive officers lead', *Harvard Business Review*, vol. 74, no. 3 (May–June 1996), pp. 110–112.

15. A study that tracked successful leaders from one company who took up leadership positions in other companies found that many did not readily transfer to the new context. See B. Groysberg, A.N. McLean and N. Nohria, 'Are leaders portable?', *Harvard Business Review*, May (2006), pp. 92–100.

16. See S. Floyd and W. Wooldridge, *The Strategic Middle Manager: How to create and sustain competitive advantage*, Jossey-Bass, 1996.

17. See for example J. Balogun and G. Johnson, 'Organizational restructuring and middle manager sensemaking', *Academy of Management Journal*, vol. 47, no. 4 (2004), pp. 523–549; J. Balogun, 'Managing change: steering a course between intended strategies and unanticipated outcomes', *Long Range Planning*, vol. 39 (2006), pp. 29–49; J. Sillence and F. Mueller, 'Switching strategic perspective: the reframing of accounts of responsibility', *Organization Studies*, vol. 28, no. 2 (2007), pp. 155–176.

18. Different authors explain change styles in different ways. This section is based on the typologies used by J. Balogun and V. Hope Haley (see reference 2, section 2.4, pp. 31–36) and D. Dunphy and D. Stace, 'The strategic management of corporate change', *Human Relations*, vol. 46, no. 8 (1993), pp. 905–920. For an alternative framework see R. Caldwell, 'Models of change agency: a fourfold classification', *British Journal of Management*, vol. 14, no. 2 (2003), pp. 131–142.

19. For evidence of the effects of involvement in the strategy development process see N. Collier, F. Fishwick and S.W. Floyd, 'Managerial involvement and perceptions of strategy process', *Long Range Planning*, vol. 37, no. 1 (2004), pp. 67–83.

20. The intervention style is discussed more fully in P.C. Nutt, 'Identifying and appraising how managers install strategy', *Strategic Management Journal*, vol. 8, no. 1 (1987), pp. 1–14.

21. Evidence for this is provided by Dunphy and Stace, reference 18; see also Collier *et al.*, reference 19.

22. See M. Beer and N. Nohria, 'Cracking the code of change', *Harvard Business Review*, vol. 78, no. 3 (May–June 2000), pp. 133–141.

23. For an example of this approach see J.M. Mezias, P. Grinyer and W.D. Guth, 'Changing collective cognition: a process model for strategic change', *Long Range Planning*, vol. 34, no. 1 (2001), pp. 71–95. Also, for a systematic approach to strategy making and change based on such surfacing, see F. Ackermann and C. Eden with I. Brown, *The Practice of Making Strategy*, Sage, 2005.

24. For a discussion of the psychological context, thinking flaws, and the impact that these have for managers as they consider the future, see K. van der Heijden, R. Bradfield, G. Burt, G. Cairns and G. Wright, *The Sixth Sense: Accelerating organisational learning with scenarios*, Wiley, 2002, chapter 2.

25. T. Deal and A. Kennedy refer to 'the way we do things around here', in *Corporate Cultures: The rights and rituals of corporate life*, Addison-Wesley, 1984. Routines have, however, also become the focus of much discussion by researchers who take a resource-based view (see Chapter 3) because they are, arguably, the bases of organisational competences. See, for example, A.M. Knott, 'The organizational routines factor market paradox', *Strategic Management Journal*, vol. 24, no. 10 (2003), pp. 929–943.

26. For a full explanation of 'core rigidities' see D. Leonard-Barton, 'Core capabilities and core rigidities: a paradox in managing new product development', *Strategic Management Journal*, vol. 13, no. 5 (Summer 1992), pp. 111–125.

27. See M. Hammer and J. Champy, *Reengineering the Corporation: A manifesto for business revolution*, Harper Collins, 2004.

28. This example is given by Michael Hammer in 'Deep change: how operational innovation can transform your company', *Harvard Business Review*, vol. 82, no. 4 (April 2004), pp. 84–93.

29. This quote is on p. 135 of R. Pascale, M. Millemann and L. Gioja, 'Changing the way we change', *Harvard Business Review*, vol. 75, no. 6 (November–December 1997), pp. 126–139.

30. See reference 27.

31. Martha Feldman has written a number of papers about the relationship between routines and change. For example, see M. Feldman, 'Resources in emerging structures and processes of change', *Organization Science*, vol. 15, no. 3 (2004), pp. 295–309; and M. Feldman, and B. Pentland, 'Reconceptualizing organizational routines as a source of flexibility and change', *Administrative Science Quarterly*, vol. 48, no. 1 (2003), pp. 94–118.

32. For a fuller discussion of this theme, see G. Johnson, 'Managing strategic change: the role of symbolic action', *British Journal of Management*, vol. 1, no. 4 (1990), pp. 183–200. Also see J.M. Higgins and C. McCallaster, 'If you want strategic change don't forget your cultural artefacts', *Journal of Change Management*, vol. 4, no. 1 (2004), pp. 63–73.

33. For a discussion of the role of rituals in change, see D. Sims, S. Fineman and Y. Gabriel, *Organizing and Organizations: An introduction*, Sage, 1993.

34. See H.M. Trice and J.M. Beyer, 'Studying organisational cultures through rites and ceremonials', *Academy of Management Review*, vol. 9, no. 4 (1984), pp. 653–669; H.M. Trice and J.M. Beyer, 'Using six organisational rites to change culture', in R.H. Kilman, M.J. Saxton, R. Serpa and associates (eds), *Gaining Control of the Corporate Culture*, Jossey-Bass, 1985.

35. This discussion is based on observations of the role of political activities in organisations by, in particular, H. Mintzberg, *Power in and around Organisations*, Prentice Hall, 1983, and J. Pfeffer, *Power in Organisations*, Pitman, 1981. However, perhaps the most interesting book on political management remains Niccolo Machiavelli's sixteenth-century work, *The Prince* (available in Penguin Books, 2003). It is also the basis of a management book by Gerald Griffin, *Machiavelli on Management: Playing and winning the corporate power game*, Praeger, 1991.

36. For a fuller discussion of this approach by Bratton and other change agents, see W.C. Kim and R. Mauborgne,

'Tipping point leadership', *Harvard Business Review*, vol. 81, no. 4 (April 2003), pp. 60–69.

37. For a review of research that makes this point see D. Buchanan, L. Fitzgerald, D. Ketley, R. Gallop, J.L. Jones, S.S. Lamont, A. Neath and E. Whitby, 'No going back: a review of the literature on sustaining organizational change', *International Journal of Management Reviews*, vol. 7, no. 3 (2005), pp. 189–205.

38. Turnaround strategy is more extensively explained in D. Lovett and S. Slatter, *Corporate Turnaround*, Penguin Books, 1999; and P. Grinyer, D. Mayes and P. McKiernan, 'The Sharpbenders: achieving a sustained improvement in performance', *Long Range Planning*, vol. 23, no. 1 (1990), pp. 116–125. Also see V.L. Barker and I.M. Duhaime, 'Strategic change in the turnaround process: theory and empirical evidence', *Strategic Management Journal*, vol. 18, no. 1 (1997), pp. 13–38.

39. See the 'Sharpbenders' study, reference 38.

40. See K. Pajunen, 'Stakeholder influences in organizational survival', *Journal of Management Studies*, vol. 43, no. 6 (2006), pp. 1261–1288.

41. The value of working with aspects of the existing culture is a finding from the research of S. Finkelstein, C. Harvey and T. Lawton, documented in *Breakout Strategy*, McGraw-Hill, 2007.

42. The observations and examples here are largely based on L.C. Harris and E. Ogbonna, 'The unintended consequences of culture interventions: a study of unexpected outcomes', *British Journal of Management*, vol. 13, no. 1 (2002), pp. 31–49.

43. See H.L. Sirkin, P. Keenan and A. Jackson, 'The hard side of change management', *Harvard Business Review*, vol. 83, no. 10 (October 2005), pp. 109–118.

44. The monitoring of change programmes is discussed more fully in L. Gratton, V. Hope Hailey, P. Stiles and C. Truss, *Strategic Human Resource Management*, Oxford University Press, 1999.

Managing change at Faslane

Just 30 miles (48 km) west of Glasgow is HM Naval Base Clyde (Faslane), the home of the UK's nuclear submarines that carry the Trident weapon system. It is a Ministry of Defence (MOD) installation, but managed by private sector Babcock Naval Services (BNS), part of Babcock International. In 2006 John Howie, the Managing Director, was interviewed about the BNS change programme at Faslane.

John Howie's office overlooks the Gareloch on which the naval base is situated and where the ships and submarines are maintained. To the right are the berths for the Trident submarines, each 148 metres long, and the huge shiplift, a covered facility capable of lifting the 16,000 tonne submarines out of the water for maintenance. To the left are the base's offices, installations and accommodation for the sailors when they are not at sea. To the back of the offices are the barbed wire and heavily guarded perimeter fence. Over the peninsular is Coulport, also part of the base, where nuclear warheads are processed and loaded onto submarines.

John, how did BNS get involved at Faslane?

Faslane had been run entirely by the MOD and the Royal Navy. However, by 2000 the MOD had decided they needed to significantly reduce the cost and improve operational effectiveness of their naval bases and that in-house MOD management would find that difficult given the restrictions they operated under as part of a wider civil service. So they established partnering arrangements with industrial firms. By May 2002 we had signed a contract for a five year period to deliver £76 million [€110m; $136m] of cost savings without affecting the service provided to the Navy. A percentage of that saving would come to us as profit; the bulk would go to the customer as a cost reduction. Our profit was entirely a share of the savings, so no cost reduction, no profit; but the contract made sure we couldn't do that by prejudicing service levels.

From September 2002 over 1,700 civil service posts and nearly 300 Royal Navy personnel and civil servants were seconded to us. Overnight BNS went from being a company with 20 employees to 2,000. In addition there remained 1,000 other civil servants on site, security personnel, police and the MOD Guard Service, Royal Marines, together with the sailors, ships and the submarines. The population of Faslane and Coulport is about 7,500 people.

What was it like when you arrived?

The customer support ethos didn't feel right. Despite being a naval base, the staff saw buildings and infrastructure facilities as more important than supporting the Navy. The focus was from the waterfront inward rather than looking outwards to the ships and submarines. I think that was because the people who looked after the site were often civilians who had been here much longer than the navy people, who looked after ships and submarines and generally moved on after 2–3 years. The civilians were here long enough for them to build up empires. So the challenge was to become focused on delivering services to the customer, the Navy.

Moreover a public sector manager who's got wide ranging responsibilities and a fairly large budget has no incentive to reduce costs. They don't share in any benefits and were brought up in a system where, if they hadn't spent their budget, next year their budget would be cut. So we believed that a big opportunity might come from changing the mindset: to see their job isn't to spend the money allocated, but deliver the job with the minimum possible spend.

Another difficulty is that civil servants carry political accountability; every significant decision they make could be questioned by an elected politician. That makes people naturally much more conservative. You also end up with lots of layers in the organization; lots of people with limited autonomy or empowerment who focus on doing things within their own control. It tends to be procedural; its a 'handle turning' exercise.

With political accountability it's also important to demonstrate an audit path for the decision you made. So speedy decision making can be secondary to being able to be accountable for the decision and being able to demonstrate why you made it. All fairly bureaucratic and cumbersome. Some of that is understandable because it's driven by having nuclear weapons and nuclear reactors on site, but some of it is a legacy of 'take a simple process and then start building things round it'.

What of the management here before BNS?

Commodore John Borley had overall responsibility. He was put in charge at the point when this whole process started and was willing to change in a way some of his predecessors hadn't been. He'd come to the same conclusion about the need to change from being infrastructure focused to being naval focused. He saw in partnering the opportunity to better manage the people. And then there was the commodore's management team. They were a mix of people who either believed change was necessary and were willing to give partnering a try or people who were likely to be personally disadvantaged by partnering and were less supportive.

What of the workforce?

There was a perception that because of the base's role supporting the nuclear deterrent, they were ring fenced from radical changes. Their view was also that the base was doing a really good job and therefore why would you want to change that? There was no perception of financial pressure or need to save money. The base also has a 25–30 year role. There is no cliff edge. They'd been through a whole raft of MOD change, not least large scale outsourcing programmes. There was the feeling of flavour of the month change programmes. All very disruptive, not my day job, very much seen as negative. So the backdrop was a workforce forcibly transferred to a private company and fearful of what change by them would mean.

So how did you set about change?

We brought in people from Babcock who had lived through similar changes. What they didn't necessarily understand was how to run a naval base but the MOD transferred people to us who knew how to do that. Our job was to manage them differently.

The over-arching theme was to get visibility about how money was being spent whilst getting a focus back on things that matter to the customer. It meant looking carefully at structures and processes to figure out how they currently operated and ask how that could be done differently. For example, there was a process that required any change, such as a change of management structure, to be documented and passed through a series of review points. After all, in a nuclear naval base you have to be sure that changing something that's fundamental to safety can be done without unacceptable risk. At each stage of that process people were given a maximum of 14 days to review it; but of course everyone defaulted to looking at it on the thirteenth day. So the overall process took about 56 days. What became clear was a number of the review points weren't materially adding value; it was: 'I'm letting you look at this because you might be interested in it', not because involvement was critical. By taking those stages out you free up people's bureaucratic burden. You also don't give them 14 days to review it; you give them two days because they did it on the thirteenth and fourteenth day anyway. Now that 56 day process is six days. A simple example of process re-engineering.

All that sounds very mechanistic

It's not like that. We are an organisation that doesn't own any physical assets other than the people who walk through the gate every day. So change is very much about people. And with 2,000 people you get access to a whole raft of ideas and change initiatives that we would never have thought of because we had never worked in this environment. So part of it was about removing the shackles from people to come up with their own change ideas. But culturally that's a challenge when for many people there's no incentive to come up with a change when it might mean that people at the desk next to you get made redundant.

So how do you do it?

I'm not sure we entirely have yet. What became clear was that we had a management structure that wasn't right to deliver change. We had seven layers in it. It's now down to a maximum of four layers. We've reappointed all the jobs. We asked other companies who've been through large scale changes: 'what is the main lesson we should learn from what you did?' The answer was: 'Implement the management structural changes earlier than we did.' People tried to launch transformational change with the existing team, got two or three years into it, realised it wasn't working, and then changed the structure. We are doing it the other way round about. We implemented all the low level changes up front because they're easy. That allowed us to deliver £14 million of saving in the first year against a target of £3 million. But once you get into change which is more about transformation – about trying to deliver a strategy of being the best, most profitable organisation supporting the UK submarine fleet – we needed different skill sets. So we've changed the structure. The management team we had was about 250; it's now about half of that. Within 12 to 18 months that entire management team of 125 need to be change agents. At the moment it's about a dozen. However the signs are that the senior managers appointed will be better able to deal with the change challenge; they have enough knowledge of change in other environments.

The problem is that as we get away from the changes which are relatively mechanistic we get into changes that are much more complex in nature.

Such as?

Moving from 24 hour shifts to working day shift in some areas sounds like a simple thing to do, but when you've got a workforce and unions fearful of change, a management team without the skills to implement big change and people who just want the status quo maintained, it took far longer to deliver than it should have.

It also seems a difficult political situation

The first thing is to understand who you need to have as allies, such as the Naval Base Commander. Our success was intertwined. I have a parent company to satisfy, whilst Commodore Carolyn Stiat, the current Naval Base Commander, has to manage the relationships with the wider MOD and the Navy Board. Beyond that you have to look at the wider stakeholders. The commanding officers of the ships and submarines here: if they were saying 'we're getting a really bad service' we'd have struggled. Or if the security people thought we weren't interested in national security. And another key stakeholder was the local community. We did a lot of work up front with two local councils because the base represents 9.5% of all employment in the Dunbartonshire area and we've reduced by about 400 full time equivalent posts. Now some of those have been naval posts rather than people living locally. We've also been able to achieve about 98 reductions through voluntary redundancy, with attractive redundancy terms; so often people left without the need to be reliant on support from welfare services; even to set up businesses on their own. Fairly quickly the meetings with the council stopped because they became comfortable we were doing things the right way.

And are you on target in terms of the time frame you envisaged?

We discovered that getting through the evolutionary change took longer than we'd assumed, I suppose partly because we'd over-estimated the desire for change. It also took much more senior management involvement than we had assumed. Given that and a ten and a half year contract, there are two major milestones for me. One is getting to the end of the first five years having delivered against targets. We're now a year away from that but we will beat our target by some margin. The second is a more hazy 7–8 year time frame which is what the theorists say it takes to implement lasting cultural change: an organisation that's had the non-value-adding bureaucracy stripped away, team leaders managing people not paperwork, teams starting to get more responsibility to manage themselves. So instead of having somebody manage health and safety and training and the overtime allocation, people take responsibility in their own work teams to do that.

So, what has been achieved?

Year 1 the target was £3 million of savings, we delivered £14 million. Year 2 the target was £12 million, we delivered £16 million. By the end of Year 5 we had delivered around £100 million against our £76 million target. By the end of Year 10 we should have saved £280 million; that equates to a 38.2% reduction in annual running costs. By the end of Year 5 we had delivered over 20%. And the Navy's view was that the service they were receiving was better, attitude better, communication better, responsiveness better. So we have delivered cost reductions and service improvement.

Questions

1 In relation to sections 14.2.1 and 14.5, what is the type of change that is being pursued at Faslane?

2 Describe the change style of John Howie.

3 What levers for change are being used (see section 14.4)? What others might be used?

4 What problems of change may occur in the future?

5 Assess the effectiveness of the change programme.

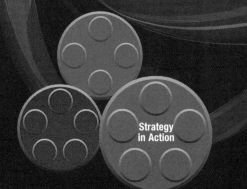

Strategy
in Action

15

The Practice of Strategy

LEARNING OUTCOMES

After reading this chapter you should be able to:

→ Identify key people involved in strategy making, including top management, strategy consultants, strategic planners and middle managers.

→ Assess which people should be included in strategy making for different kinds of issues.

→ Evaluate different approaches to strategising activity, including analysis, issue selling, decision-making and communications.

→ Recognise key elements in the various methodologies commonly used in strategising, including strategy workshops, projects, hypothesis testing and writing business cases and strategic plans.

Photo: Superstock/Alamy Images

15.1 INTRODUCTION

This final chapter is the place to examine how managers actually practice strategy, using the theoretical concepts, tools and techniques introduced earlier in the book. The concern here then is with the practicalities of strategy making – what managers do in making a strategy. Whereas Chapter 11 introduced the overall organisational process of strategy development, this chapter has a more detailed focus: it is about what gets done *inside* the process. The aim is to examine how people actually contribute to practical strategy making, whether as top managers, strategic planning specialists, strategy consultants or managers lower down the organisation. Strategic success is not simply about *having* a good strategy: that strategy has to be *made*, by the right people doing the right things in the right way.

The chapter has three core sections:

- *The strategists*. The chapter starts by looking at the various people involved in making strategy. It does not assume that strategy is made just by top management. As pointed out in Chapter 11, strategy is often emergent, and involves people from all over the organisation and often from outside. The key debate at the end of the chapter (Illustration 15.6) addresses the controversial involvement of external strategy consultants. Readers can ask themselves how they already fit into this set of strategists, or how they might in the future.

- *Strategising activities*. The chapter continues by considering the kinds of work and activity that strategists carry out in their strategy making. This includes not just the strategy analysis that has been central to a large part of this book, but also the managing of strategic issues over time, the realities of strategic decision making and the critical task of communicating strategic decisions throughout the organisation.

- *Strategising methodologies*. The final section covers some of the practical methodologies that managers use to carry out their strategising activities. This includes strategy workshops for formulating or communicating strategy; strategy projects and strategy consulting teams; hypothesis testing to guide strategy work; and the writing of strategic plans and business cases.

Exhibit 15.1 integrates these three sections in a *pyramid of practice*.[1] The pyramid highlights three questions that run through this chapter: *who* to include in strategy making; *what* to do in carrying out strategising activity; and *which* strategising methodologies to use in organising this strategising activity. The pyramid places strategists at the top. Placing strategists at the top in this way emphasises the role of managerial discretion and skill in strategy making. It is the strategists who choose and enact both the strategising activity and the strategy methodologies that are at the base of the pyramid. Strategists' choices and skill with regard to activity and methodologies can make a real difference to final outcomes. The rest of the chapter seeks to guide practising strategists through the key choices they may have to make in action.

Exhibit 15.1   **The pyramid of strategy practice**

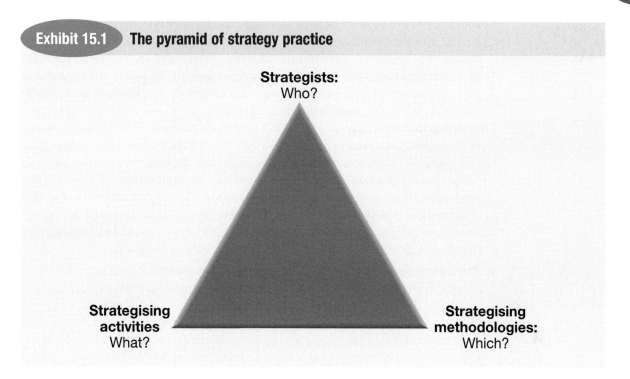

15.2   THE STRATEGISTS

This section introduces the different types of people involved in strategy. It starts at the top management level, but includes a much wider range of potential actors, from strategic planners and consultants to middle managers. One key issue is how middle managers can increase their influence in strategy making.[2]

15.2.1   Top managers and directors

The conventional view is that strategy is the business of top management. In this view, it is absolutely vital that top management are clearly separated from operational responsibilities, so that they can focus on overall strategy.[3] If top management are directly involved in operations such as sales or service delivery, they are liable to get distracted from long-term issues by day-to-day responsibilities and to represent the interests of their departments or business units rather than the interests of their organisation as a whole. In the private sector at least, top managers' job titles underline this strategic responsibility: company directors set direction; managers manage.

In reality, the top management role involves much more than setting direction. Also, different roles are played by different members of the top team, whether *chief executive officer*, the *top management team* or *non-executive directors*:

● The *chief executive officer* is often seen as the 'chief strategist', ultimately responsible for all strategic decisions. CEOs of large companies typically spend about one-third of their time on strategy.[4] Michael Porter stresses the value of a clear strategic leader, somebody capable of setting a disciplined approach to what fits and what does not fit the overall strategy.[5] In this view, the CEO (or managing director or equivalent top individual) owns the strategy and is accountable for its success or failure. The clarity of this individual responsibility can no doubt focus attention. However, there are dangers. First, centralising responsibility on the CEO can lead to excessive personalisation. Organisations respond to setbacks simply by changing their CEO, rather than examining deeply the internal sources of failure. Second, successful CEOs can become overconfident, seeing themselves as corporate heroes and launching strategic initiatives of ever-increasing ambition.[6] The overconfidence of heroic leaders often leads to spectacular failures. Jim Collins' research on 'great' American companies that outperformed their rivals over the long term found that their CEOs were typically modest, steady and long serving.[7]

● The *top management team*, often an organisation's executive directors, also share responsibility for strategy. Obviously they can bring additional experience and insight to the CEO. In theory, they should be able to challenge the CEO and increase strategic debate. In practice, the top management team are often constrained in at least three ways. First, except in the largest companies, top managers often carry operational responsibilities that either distract them or bias their strategic thinking: for example, the marketing director will have ongoing concerns about marketing, the production director about production, and so on. Second, top managers are also frequently appointed by the CEO: consequently, they may lack the independence for real challenge. Finally, top management teams, especially where their members have similar backgrounds and face strong leadership, often suffer from 'groupthink', the tendency to build strong consensus amongst team members and avoid internal conflict.[8] Top management teams can minimise groupthink by fostering diversity in membership (for example, differences in age, career tracks and gender) and by ensuring openness to outside views, for example those of non-executive directors.[9]

● *Non-executive directors* have no executive management responsibility within the organisation, and so in theory should be able to offer an external and objective view on strategy. Although this varies according to national corporate governance systems (see Chapter 4), in a public company the chairman/woman of the board is typically non-executive. He or she will normally be consulted closely by the CEO on strategy, as he or she will have a key role in liaising with investors. However, the ability of the chairman/woman and other non-executives in general to contribute substantially to strategy can be limited. Non-executives are typically part-time appointments. The predominant role for non-executive directors in strategy, therefore, is consultative, reviewing and challenging strategy proposals that come from the top management executive team. A key role for them also is to ensure that the organisation has a rigorous system in place for the making and renewing of strategy. It is therefore important that non-executives are authoritative and experienced individuals, that they have independence from the top management executive team and that they are properly briefed before board meetings.[10]

Top management capability in making strategy should not simply be assumed. Managers are often promoted to strategic roles for their success in dealing with operations or their professional skill in a particular functional specialism. These kinds of experience do not necessarily prepare them for the analytical and managerial tasks involved in making strategy. There are at least three important qualities senior managers need if they are to contribute effectively to high-level strategy making:

- *Mastery of analytical concepts and techniques*, as introduced in this book, is clearly important, and cannot be assumed, especially in arenas such as the public or not-for-profit sectors where strategy is still quite novel.[11] Sometimes an executive education course can help improve understanding of strategy concepts and techniques.

- *Social and influencing skills* are necessary if analysis is to be understood and accepted by senior colleagues. Again, senior managers are not equally effective in strategic discussions, but there are now many professional coaches who can help.[12]

- *Group acceptance as a player* in strategic discussions. Boards and senior executive teams are social groups like any other, where members have to win respect.[13] Clear and significant success in one's own particular sphere of responsibility is normally a precondition for being respected as a contributor to wider discussions of the organisation's strategy.

15.2.2 Strategic planners

> Strategic planners, sometimes known as corporate development managers or similar, are managers with a formal responsibility for contributing to the strategy process

Strategic planners, sometimes known as corporate development managers or similar, are managers with a formal responsibility for contributing to the strategy process (see Chapter 11). Although small companies very rarely have full-time strategic planners, they are common in large companies and increasingly widespread in the public and not-for-profit sectors. As in Illustration 15.1, organisations frequently advertise for strategic planning jobs. As in Illustration 15.1, organisations frequently advertise for strategic planning jobs. For this UK government Strategy Unit post, the specifications give a clear picture of the skills a strategic planner might be expected to have. The strategist is not only making strategy, but helping other departments to develop their own capabilities in strategy. Strategic thinking and analytical skills are clearly very important, but so too are the ability to communicate clearly to various audiences and to work well with teams. The strategist's role here is much more than back-office analysis.

Although the job in Illustration 15.1 is being advertised externally, strategic planners are often drawn from inside their own organisations. Internal strategic planners are likely to have an advantage in the important non-analytical parts of the job. As internal recruits, they bring to the planning role intuitive understanding of the business, networks with key people in the organisation and credibility with internal audiences. Moreover, an internal appointment to a strategic planning role can serve as a developmental stage for managers on track for top management roles.[14] Participating in strategy provides promising managers with exposure to senior management and gives them an overview of the organisation as a whole.

Strategic planners do not take strategic decisions themselves. However, they typically do have at least three important tasks:[15]

Illustration 15.1

Wanted: Team member for strategy unit

The following advertisement appeared on the UK Cabinet Office website. It gives an insight into the kind of work such strategic planners do and the skills and background required.

Job Description for a Team Member: Band A

About the Strategy Unit

The PMSU has three main roles:
- to carry out strategy reviews and provide policy advice in accordance with the Prime Minister's policy priorities;
- to support Government Departments in developing effective strategies and policies – including helping them to build their strategic capability; and
- to identify and effectively disseminate thinking on emerging issues and challenges facing the UK e.g. through occasional strategic audits.

Post holders will be members of small teams set up to address issues where innovative approaches and fresh thinking are necessary to ensure the achievement of the Government's objectives. Teams will be drawn from both inside and outside the Civil Service and work intensively on an issue, for periods ranging from 3–4 weeks to 3–4 months or longer depending on the task.

Candidates will need to have first rate policy or strategy experience, strong interpersonal skills, and the ability to write clearly and compellingly. Outstanding analytical and problem solving skills are absolutely essential to the role.

Essential competences for the SU

Strategic Thinking
1. Knowledge and understanding of government priorities
2. Knowledge of the wider policy environment, including political or institutional restraints
3. Ability to derive clear goals and strategies from a complex brief

Analysis and Use of Evidence
1. Knows and deploys a range of analytical tools
2. Uses a variety of tools in collecting and analysing evidence
3. Works in partnership with a wide range of analytical experts to achieve project goals
4. Ability to understand complex statistical data
5. Understands what constitutes good evidence

People Management
1. Able to develop individuals for high performance
2. Champions equality and diversity, and promotes best practice
3. Able to give good feedback that people can act on

Programme and Project Management
1. Can work with a team to develop a project plan
2. Anticipates, manages and monitors programme/project risks
3. Ensures effective communications with stakeholders

Specialist Professional Skills

Essential
1. Good quality qualifications or training in economics, social policy, operational research or similar
2. Excellent quantitative and qualitative analytical skills
3. Sector knowledge – an understanding of social policy is an advantage

Desirable
1. Experience in working in a think-tank or high profile management consultancy role or policy or analytical arm of a government department.

Source: Extracts from Strategy Unit Job Description for a Team Member: Band A from http://www.cabinetoffice.gov.uk/strategy/jobs/band_a.asp. Reproduced under the terms of the Click-Use Licence.

Questions

1 What would be the attractions of this job for you? What would be the disadvantages?

2 What relevant skills and experience do you already have, and what skills and experience would you still need to acquire before you were to apply for this job?

● *Information and analysis*. Strategic planners have the time, skills and resources to provide information and analysis for key decision makers. This might be in response to some 'trigger' event – such as a possible merger – or as part of a regular planning cycle. A background of good information and analysis can leave an organisation much better prepared to respond quickly and confidently even to unexpected events as they occur. Strategic planners can also package this information and analysis in formats that ensure clear communication of strategic decisions.

● *Managers of the strategy process*. Both for the headquarters and for business units, strategic planners can assist and guide other managers through their strategic planning cycles. Strategic planners can provide templates, analytical techniques and strategy training to support managers at business unit level having to make strategy for themselves. They can help CEOs design strategy processes according to their particular needs.

● *Special projects*. Strategic planners can be a useful resource to support top management on special projects, such as acquisitions or organisational change. Here strategic planners will typically work on project teams with middle managers from within the organisation and often with external consultants. Project management skills are likely to be important (see section 15.4.4).

15.2.3 Middle managers

As in section 15.2.1, a good deal of conventional management theory excludes middle managers from strategy making. Middle managers are seen as lacking an appropriately objective and long-term perspective, being too involved in operations.[16] In this view, middle managers just implement. Yet involving middle managers in the strategy formulation itself can provide at least two benefits. In the first place, middle manager involvement can lead to better strategic decisions, because middle managers have direct, up-to-date experience of the realities of the organisation and its market, unlike many top managers. In the second place, including middle managers in the original strategy formulation can improve implementation. Middle managers who have been involved in the original formulation process will be better at interpreting strategic intentions into action, have a stronger personal commitment to strategic goals, and communicate the strategy more effectively to their teams.[17]

Three trends are leading to increasing middle management involvement in strategy making nowadays.[18] First, many organisations are decentralising their organisational structures to increase accountability and responsiveness in fast-moving and competitive environments. As a result, strategic responsibilities are being thrust down the organisational hierarchy. Second, the rise of business education means that middle managers are now better trained and more confident in the strategy domain than they used to be. These higher-calibre middle managers are both more able and more eager to participate in strategy. Third, the shift away from a traditional manufacturing economy to one based more on professional services (such as design, consulting or finance) means that often the key sources of competitive advantage are no longer resources such as capital, which can be handed out from the headquarters, but the knowledge of people actually involved in the operations of the business. Middle managers at operational level can understand and influence these knowledge-based sources of competitive advantage much more effectively than remote top managers. For these three reasons, middle managers are increasingly involved in strategy formulation (see also the key debate in Chapter 11).

Even where middle managers are not formally involved in making strategy, they can increase their informal influence when they have:

● *Key organisational positions*. Middle managers responsible for strategically important parts of the organisation are in a strong position to exercise informal influence, because they are likely to have critical knowledge and their full-hearted commitment to the strategy is important. Not surprisingly, middle managers who are responsible for larger departments or business units typically have greater influence on strategic decisions.[19] Also, managers with outward-facing roles (for example, marketing) tend to have greater strategic influence than managers with inward-facing roles (such as quality or operations).[20] Middle managers seeking influence on strategy need to position themselves in the right organisational roles.

● *Access to organisational networks*. Middle managers may not have hierarchical power, but they can increase their influence by using their internal organisational networks. Drawing together information from network members can help provide an integrated perspective on what is happening in the organisation as a whole, something that otherwise can be difficult to get when occupying a specialised position in the middle of an organisation. Mobilising networks to raise issues and support proposals can also give more influence than any single middle manager can achieve on his or her own.[21] Strategically influential middle managers are therefore typically good networkers.

● *Access to the organisation's 'strategic conversation'*. Strategy making does not just happen in isolated, formal episodes, but is part of an ongoing strategic conversation amongst respected managers.[22] An organisation seeking to involve middle managers in its strategic conversations should cultivate an open strategic culture, for example by including middle managers in strategy workshops (see section 15.4.1) or having top management discuss strategy at management training events. Middle managers wanting to participate in these strategic conversations should: maximise opportunities to mix formally and informally with top managers; become at ease with the particular language used to discuss strategy in their organisation; familiarise themselves carefully with the key strategic issues; and develop their own personal contribution to these strategic issues.

In the public sector, senior management–middle management have their parallel in the formal divide between politicians and public officials. Just as directors are formally concerned with strategic 'direction', elected politicians were traditionally responsible for policy. Public officials, meanwhile, were supposed to do the implementation. However, three trends are challenging this division of roles. First, the rising importance of *specialised expertise* has effectively shifted influence to public officials who may have made their careers in particular areas, while politicians are typically generalists. Second, public sector reform in many countries has led to increased *externalisation of functions* to quasi-independent 'agencies' or 'QUANGOs' (Quasi-Autonomous Non-Governmental Organisations), which, within certain constraints, can make decisions on their own. Third, the same reform processes have changed *internal structures* within public organisations, with decentralisation of units and more 'executive' responsibility granted to public officials. All this is supported by the discourse of 'New Public Management', which encourages officials to be more enterprising and accountable. In short, strategy is increasingly part of the work of public officials too.[23]

15.2.4 Strategy consultants

External consultants are often used in the development of strategy in organisations. Leading consultancy firms that focus on strategy include Bain, the Boston Consulting Group, Monitor and McKinsey & Co.[24] Most of the large general consultancy firms also have operations that provide services in strategy development and analysis. There are also smaller 'boutique' consultancy firms and individual consultants who specialise in strategy.[25]

Consultants may play different roles in strategy development in organisations:[26]

- *Analysing, prioritising and generating options.* Strategic issues may have been identified by the executives, but there may be so many of them, or so much disagreement about them, that the organisation faces a lack of clarity on how to go forward. Consultants may analyse such issues afresh and bring an external eye to help prioritise them or generate options for executives to consider. This may, of course, involve challenging executives' preconceptions about their views of strategic issues.

- *Transferring knowledge.* Consultants play a role in disseminating views, insights and the conclusions drawn from their analysis within organisations in meetings and discussions and in disseminating knowledge between organisations. In effect they are the carriers of knowledge and best practice within and between their clients.

- *Promoting strategic decisions.* In doing all this, consultants may themselves substantially influence the decisions that organisations eventually take. A number of major consultancies have been criticised in the past for undue influence on the decisions made by their client organisation, leading to major problems. For example, leading strategy consulting firm McKinsey & Co. was heavily associated with Enron's controversial 'asset-lite' business model, and was also the proponent of SwissAir's failed 'Hunter' strategy of strategic alliances.[27]

- *Implementing strategic change.* Consultants play a significant role in project planning, coaching and training often associated with strategic change. This is an area that has seen considerable growth, not least because consultants were criticised for leaving organisations with consultancy reports recommending strategies, but taking little responsibility for actually making these happen.

The real value of strategy consultants is often controversial (see Illustration 15.6, the key debate on page 584). Enron was paying McKinsey & Co. $10m (£5.6m; €8m) a year before it collapsed. But consultants are often blamed for failures when in fact it is the client's poor management of the consulting process that is ultimately at fault. Many organisations select their consultants unsystematically; give poor initial project briefs; and fail to act on and learn from projects at the end. There are three key measures that client organisations can undertake to improve outcomes in strategy consulting:[28]

● *Professionalised purchasing of consulting services*, using specialists in the organisation's purchasing function, for instance. Instead of hiring consulting firms on the basis of personal relationships with key executives, as is often the case, introducing consultants can be treated like any other purchasing decision, following standard purchasing procedures. Professionalised purchasing can help ensure clear project briefs, a wide search for consulting suppliers, appropriate pricing, complementarity between different consulting projects and proper review at project end. The German engineering company Siemens has professionalised its consultancy purchasing, for example establishing a shortlist of just 10 preferred management consulting suppliers.

● *Developing supervisory skills* in order to manage portfolios of consulting projects. The German railway company Deutsche Bahn and automobile giant DaimlerChrysler both have central project offices that control and coordinate all consulting projects throughout their companies. As well as being involved in the initial purchasing decision, these central offices can impose systematic governance structures on projects, with clear responsibilities and reporting processes, as well as review and formal assessment at project end.

● *Partnering effectively* with consultants can improve both effectiveness in carrying out the project and knowledge transfer at the end of it. Where possible, project teams should include a mix of consultants and managers from the client organisation. Client organisation managers can provide inside information, guide on internal politics and, sometimes, enhance credibility and receptiveness. As partners in the project, client managers retain knowledge and experience when the consultants have gone and can help in the implementation of recommendations. Client managers should be ready to work to the demanding standards and schedules of strategy consulting firms.

15.2.5 Who to include in strategy?

KEY
CONCEPT
www.pearsoned.co.uk/ecs

Strategy
inclusion

There is, therefore, a potentially wide range of people to involve in any strategic issue: as well as the CEO and the top management team, non-executive directors, strategic planners, strategy consultants, middle managers and perhaps external stakeholders. This often raises practical dilemmas about who should be included on particular strategic issues. The paradox of strategy inclusion is that those with the most access to the CEO on strategy are often strategic planners and strategy consultants who have little responsibility for strategy implementation and little knowledge of business on the ground (see Exhibit 15.2). The middle managers who have both the knowledge and the implementation responsibility can have least access to the CEO in strategy discussions, either because they are too busy with operational realities or because they are seen as biased. Strategy is not necessarily being made by the right people.

However, there is no single correct answer about who should participate in strategy. McKinsey & Co research indicates that the people involved should vary according to the nature of the issue (see Exhibit 15.3).[29] Highly urgent issues, and those implying high strategic discontinuity (perhaps an acquisition opportunity), are often best approached by small special project teams, consisting of senior managers and perhaps planners and consultants. Issues which might imply

Exhibit 15.2   **The access/execution paradox**

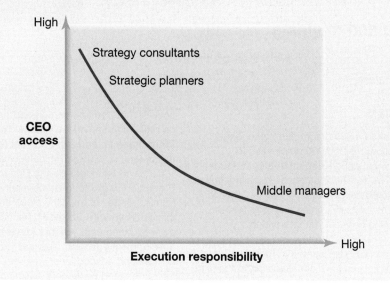

Exhibit 15.3   **Who to include in strategy making?**

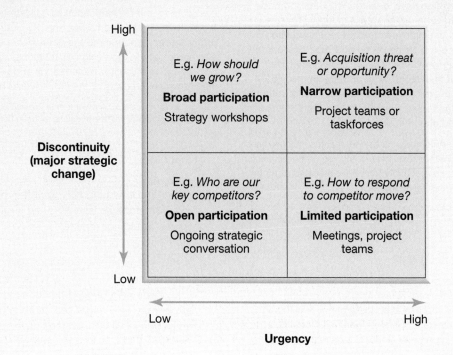

Illustration 15.2

Jamming and mapping

Participation in strategy making can be important in global businesses and developing enterprises alike.

Jamming at IBM

IBM has developed a $3m information technology platform that allows its 300,000 employees to participate in global debates about strategic issues (see Illustration 14.5). These debates are called 'jams' after the structured improvisation ('jamming') used in jazz music. Jams typically combine off-site face-to-face brainstorming sessions with 'threaded' discussions, theme-based forums and electronic idea-ratings organised through the corporate intranet site. All IBM employees have equal access to the jam sessions. IBM manager Mike Malloney explains: 'It's like jazz collaboration, with people building on other people's ideas in a structured format. Jams are a blend of technology and a kind of grassroots discussion of ideas'.

IBM has used jams to address managerial roles, post-merger integration, organisational barriers to innovation and revenue growth (informally dubbed the 'logjam') and the development of a new values statement (the 'ValuesJam'). The ValuesJam took place over three days, generating 2.3 million page views and over a million words of input. Tens of thousands of employee ideas were refined into 65 key ideas, using online voting and IBM's proprietory natural language analytical software ('jamalyzer'). A small team then set to work on refining these further into three overarching values based on innovation, the customer and trust. Chief Executive Sam Palmisano commented on the ValuesJam:

'Yes, the electronic argument was hot and contentious and messy. . . . We had done three or four big online jams before . . . Even so, none of those could have prepared us for the emotions unleashed by this topic'.

Sources: S.J. Palmisano, 'Leading change when business is good', *Harvard Business Review*, December (2004), p. 60–70; PR Newswire, 30 November (2005).

Mapping in Uganda

The International Trade Centre (ITC) in Geneva (www.intracen.org) is responsible for helping enterprises improve exports. In many developing countries where it operates there is little reliable published information available, development

activities can be fragmented and people tend to be reticent unknown individuals. The Ugandan fish processing and exporting sector provides one example of how these difficulties can be overcome.

ITC worked alongside the Uganda Export Promotion Board to facilitate meetings of stakeholders from all stages of the fish value network on a strategy for export growth. Stakeholders included enterprise owners, community leaders, government and development agencies, services providers such as transport, inspections, customs, banks, freight forwarders and packagers. Meeting in Kampala, they collaborated on a series of exercises to identify market opportunities, diagnose sector performance issues and organise development activity implementation.

They mapped the core stages of their value chains on large wall sheets from target markets back to sources of supply. Sector-wide issues and market requirements were broken down into value chain stage components and illustrated on these maps. The process surfaced tacit information and 'market realities' and stimulated new ideas for value addition, cost cutting and diversification (see Illustration 3.4). It also helped participants see 'the big picture opportunities', understand their mutual dependency and participate in the design of solutions, agree on the priorities to raise sector performance and who should implement which parts of the strategy and how.

Source: Ian Sayers, Senior Advisor for the Private Sector, Division of Trade Support Services, the International Trade Centre, Geneva.

Questions

1. Why was it important at IBM and in the Ugandan fishing industry to obtain wide input on strategic issues? What strategic issues would not require the same kind of input?

2. If you were a smaller company, without the information technology resources of IBM or the help of government agencies as in Uganda, how might you be able to get employee input into strategy development?

equal discontinuity, but for which there is more time (such as growth options), can benefit from the participation of a broader group of managers, perhaps through a strategy workshop (see section 15.4.1). For issues that are more routine, but which still require speedy response (such as competitors' pricing moves), only limited participation is probably required, involving perhaps meetings between the relevant marketing and operations managers. The most open kind of participation would be in the on-going 'strategic conversation' of managers throughout the organisation, regarding for example key competitors or the long-run evolution of the market.

The point from the McKinsey & Co. research is that there is no general rule about inclusion or exclusion in strategy making, but that there are criteria that can guide managers about who to include according to the nature of the strategic issues in hand. Managers should think carefully about who to include and they should make skilled use of different strategy-making methods, whether project teams or strategy workshops to enrol people who might have valuable contributions to make but who might otherwise be excluded from the normal process. Managers can use a variety of techniques to generate a more inclusive approach, as for example IBM has done with its 'strategy jam' and the International Trade Centre did in Uganda (Illustration 15.2). The public sector often uses the internet for public consultations and discussion forums regarding controversial policy issues: see for example www.communities.gov.uk/.

15.3 STRATEGISING

The previous section introduced the key strategists; this section concentrates on what people have to do in strategising. The section proceeds logically through these activities, starting with the initial strategy analysis, then proceeding through issue selling and decision making and concluding with communications about the chosen strategy. In practice, of course, these activities rarely follow this logical sequence: decisions are often made without great analysis; they are often reinterpreted in subsequent communications. There are, however, key choices to be made in how these strategising activities are conducted, particularly with regard to which managers trust in formal, analytical rationality.

15.3.1 Strategy analysis

A good deal of this book is concerned with strategy analysis, and indeed analysis is an important input into strategy making. However, as suggested in Chapter 11, strategy is often not the outcome of simple rational analysis. Analysis is frequently done in an ad hoc and incomplete fashion and not always followed through. The analysis activity itself may serve other functions than a simple input into subsequent decisions.

First of all, analysis in practice tends to be rough and ready. SWOT (Strengths, Weaknesses, Opportunities and Threats) analysis is the most widely used tool in strategy,[30] but even this simple tool is typically used in a way far from the technical ideal (see Chapter 3). One study found frequent deviations from textbook recommendations, by both managers and consultants.[31] For example, in practice SWOT analyses tend to produce unmanageably long lists of factors (strengths, weaknesses, opportunities and threats), often well over 50 or so. The result is these factors are rarely probed or refined; little substantive analysis is done to investigate them; and they are often not followed up systematically in subsequent strategic discussions. Technically, SWOT analyses should be more focused, prompt further investigation and lead to concrete actions on prioritised factors. If this experience with SWOT is typical, managers can often add value by more rigorous use of strategy's analytical tools.

However, criticism of poor analysis may sometimes be misplaced. There are both *cost* and *purpose* issues to consider. First of all, analysis is costly in terms of both resources and time. There are of course the costs of gathering information, particularly if using consultants. But with regard to time there is also the risk of 'paralysis by analysis', whereby managers spend too long perfecting their analyses, not enough time taking decisions and then acting upon them.[32] Managers have to judge how much analysis they really need: 'quick and dirty' may be good enough. Second, with regard to purpose, analysis is not always simply about providing the necessary information for good strategic decisions anyway.[33] The purposes of analysis can be quite different. Setting up a project to analyse an issue thoroughly may even be a deliberate form of *procrastination*, aimed at putting off a decision. Analysis can also be *symbolic*, for example to rationalise a decision after it has already effectively been made. Managers may be asked to analyse an issue in order to get their *buy-in* to decisions that they might otherwise resist. Analyses can also be *political*, to forward the agenda of a particular manager or part of the organisation.

The different purposes of strategy analysis have two key implications for managers:

- *Design the analysis according to the real purpose*. The range and quality of people involved, the time and budget allowed, and the subsequent communication of analysis results should all depend on underlying purpose, whether informational, political or symbolic. Prestigious strategy consulting firms are often useful for political and symbolic analyses. Involving a wide group of middle managers in the analysis may help with subsequent buy-in.

- *Invest appropriately in technical quality*. For many projects, improving the quality of the technical analysis will make a valuable addition to subsequent strategic decisions. On other occasions, insisting on technical perfection can be counter-productive. For example, a SWOT analysis that raises lots of issues may be a useful means of allowing managers to vent their own personal frustrations, before getting on with the real strategy work. It may sometimes be better to leave these issues on the table, rather than probing, challenging or even deleting them in a way that could unnecessarily alienate these managers for the following stages.

15.3.2 Strategic issue selling

Organisations typically face many strategic issues at any point in time. But in complex organisations these issues may not be appreciated to the same extent by all senior managers, or may not even be recognised by them at all. Some issues will be filtered out in the organisational hierarchy; others will be sidelined by more urgent pressures. Moreover, senior managers will rarely have sufficient time and resources to deal with all the issues that do actually reach them. In effect, strategic issues compete for top management attention. What gets top management attention is not necessarily the most important issues.[34]

Managers therefore have to 'sell' their particular strategic issues to top management and other important stakeholders. They cannot assume that issues get automatic attention, or that they will necessarily win support, however important they might be to them in particular. Managers need to consider at least four aspects in seeking attention and support for their **strategic issue selling**:

Strategic issue selling is the process of winning the attention and support of top management and other important stakeholders for strategic issues.

- *Issue packaging*. Care should be taken with how issues are packaged or framed. Clearly the strategic importance of the issue needs to be underlined, particularly by linking it to *critical strategic goals* or *performance metrics* for the organisation. The presentation of the issue should be consistent with the *cultural norms* of the organisation, but generally clarity and succinctness win over complexity and length. It usually helps if the issue is packaged with *potential solutions*. An issue can easily be parked as too difficult to address if no ways forward are offered at the same time.

- *Formal or informal channels*. Managers need to balance formal and informal channels of influence. Exhibit 15.4 indicates some *formal channels* for selling issues in a typical multidivisional organisation (based on General Electric).[35] Here formal channels are split between corporate, line and staff. On the corporate side, they include the annual business reviews that the CEO carries out with each divisional head, plus the annual strategy retreats (or workshops) of the top executive team. The line channel involves the regular line interaction of operational managers, divisional heads and the CEO and other executive directors. Finally, there are the various reporting systems to staff functions, including finance, human resources and strategic planning. Formal channels are of course not just for upward influence, but typically two-way: for example, strategic plans often iterate between divisions and corporate headquarters until a mutually satisfactory position is reached. Moreover, formal channels are rarely enough to sell strategic issues. *Informal channels* can be very important and often decisive in some organisational cultures. Informal channels might include ad hoc conversations with influential managers in corridors, on journeys or over meals or drinks.[36]

- *Sell alone or in coalitions*. Managers should consider whether to press their issue on their own or to assemble a *coalition of supporters*, preferably influential ones. A coalition adds credibility and weight to the issue. The ability to gather a coalition of supporters can be a good test of the issue's validity: if other managers are unpersuaded, then the CEO is unlikely to be persuaded either. But notice that enlisting supporters may involve compromises or reciprocal support of other issues, so blurring the clarity of the case being put forward.

- *Timing*. Managers should also time their issue selling carefully. A short-term performance crisis, or the period before the hand-over to a new top management team, are not good times to press long-term strategic issues.

Exhibit 15.4 **Formal channels for issue selling**

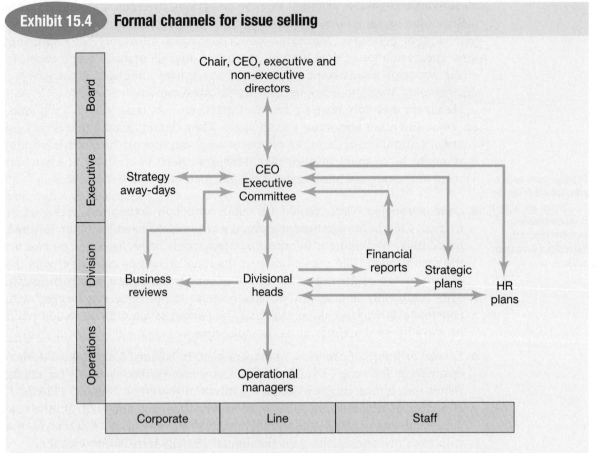

Source: Adapted from W. Ocasio and J. Joseph, 'An attention-based theory of strategy formulation: linking micro and macro perspectives in strategy processes', *Advances in Strategic Management*, vol. 22 (2005), pp. 39–62.

Selling an issue is only the start, of course. Even after an issue has been successfully sold, and actions and resources agreed, managers should make sure that attention is *sustained*.[37] Initial commitments in terms of top management attention and other resources need to be protected. As the strategic issue evolves over time, it may require more attention and resources than originally promised. Establishing at the outset a regular series of reviews and a set of relevant performance metrics will help keep top management attention focused on the issue and hopefully prepared to release more resources as required.

15.3.3 Strategic decision making

Strategic issues are ultimately decided upon in many ways. Success and failure are not always rational. Strategic decision making is also liable to several biases.[38] The notion of strategic issue selling points to the so-called *champion's bias*, the likelihood that people will exaggerate the case in favour of their particular proposal. Similarly, there is the *sunflower syndrome*, the tendency (like sunflowers following the sun) to follow the lead of the most senior person in the decision-making process, or to try to anticipate their view even before they have expressed it. Decision makers often hold exaggerated opinions of their competence, leading to over-optimistic decisions, especially where there is little data available. At the same time, they can be risk averse, being unduly deterred by substantial downsides, even when the chances of such downsides are very slight.

Just putting decisions in the hands of a team of managers, therefore, does not on its own guarantee rigorous and effective decision making. Katherine Eisenhardt's research on strategic decision making in fast-moving environments suggests four helpful guidelines for managers:[39]

- *Build multiple, simultaneous alternatives*. Having several alternatives on the table at the same time helps to encourage critical debate. This can help counter phenomena such as champion's bias and the sunflower syndrome. It is also faster than taking proposals sequentially, where alternatives are only sought out after a previous proposal has been examined and rejected. Examining multiple, simultaneous alternatives is a practice adopted by Barclays Bank, for example, where the rule is that proposals should never be presented in isolation, but always alongside at least two other alternatives.[40]

- *Track real-time information*. Eisenhardt's research found that fast decision makers do not cut back on the amount of information; they use a different type of information – real-time information. These managers prefer immediate information from current operations, rather than statistical trends and forecasts. They tend to spend a lot of time in face-to-face meetings, 'managing by wandering around' and reviewing the most up-to-date indicators, such as weekly and even daily measures of sales, cash, stocks or work-in-progress. In fast-moving environments especially, a quick decision may be better than a delayed decision, and trend data is liable to be rapidly outdated anyway.

- *Seek the views of trusted advisors*. Experienced managers in the organisation or sector can provide fast feedback on what is likely to work or not work based on their deep knowledge from the past. They can also ask tough questions given what they have seen before. The instincts of experienced managers are faster, and often both more reliable and more credible, than lengthy analysis undertaken by junior managers or consultants. Older middle managers whose careers have plateaued can be good people to listen to: not only do they have the experience, but they usually have less self-interest at stake.

- *Aim for consensus, but not at any cost*. Fast decision makers seek consensus amongst the decision-making team, but do not insist on it. Consensus can be too slow and often leads to mediocre choices based on the lowest common denominator. Fast decision makers recognise that debates cannot always be resolved to everybody's satisfaction. Eisenhardt's advice is that the CEO or other senior person should have the courage at a certain point simply to decide. Having had the chance to voice their position, the responsibility of other managers is to accept that decision as final and to get on with implementation.

However, it is easy to exaggerate both the importance and the effectiveness of decision making. Many decisions are not followed through with actions. Many strategies are emergent rather than consciously decided (see Chapter 11).[41]

Two widely held views about decision making are implicitly challenged so far. First, *intuition* is not always a bad thing.[42] Immersion in real-time information or the long experience of older middle managers can provide a strong 'gut-feel' for what should be done. This gut-feel can provide the basis for inspired hunches where there is little reliable data to be analysed anyway, for instance in the creation of radically new markets or products. Second, *conflict* in decision-making teams can be positively useful.[43] Conflict can expose champion's biases. It can challenge optimistic self-assessments of managerial competence. Conflict is fostered by having diverse managerial teams, with members prepared to be devil's advocates, challenging assumptions or easy consensus. But productive conflict needs careful management. Team members must accept decisions as final and share a fundamental mutual respect.

15.3.4 Communicating the strategy

Deciding strategy is only one step: strategic decisions need to be communicated. Managers have to consider which stakeholders to inform (see Chapter 4) and how they should tailor their messages to each. Shareholders, key customers and employees are likely to be particularly central, all with different needs. For every new strategy, there should be a communications strategy to match.

Employee communications are typically vital to ensure that the strategy is carried out in the first place. As in Chapter 5, strategies often drift away from original intentions. Unless people understand the strategy, then it is unlikely to be implemented. Everyday interactions of lower-level managers and ordinary staff can easily undermine an intended strategy. For instance, a new strategy of improved customer service will fail if managers do not hire, train and reward their staff consistently: old habits in the field will constantly spoil customer interactions. One example of an organisation seeking high understanding of strategy by all employees is the Volvo Group, where the target is that 90 per cent of employees will be aware of the company's strategic goals, tested by an annual attitude survey.[44]

In shaping a communications strategy for employees, four elements need to be considered in particular:[45]

- *Focus*. Communications should be focused on the key components of the strategy, avoiding unnecessary detail or complex language. CEO Jack Welch's famous statement that General Electric should be 'either Number One or Number Two' in all its markets is remembered precisely because of this clear focus on the importance of being a dominant player wherever the company competed.

- *Impact*. Communications should be impactful, with powerful and memorable words and visuals. For example, the United Kingdom's new community services strategy is powerfully titled 'Our health, our care, our say', in order to embody the inclusiveness and direct importance of the strategy for all citizens.[46] A strong 'story-line' can help by encapsulating the journey ahead and imagined new futures for the organisation and its customers. One struggling medical centre in New Mexico communicated its new strategy, and inspired its staff, with a story-line representing the organisation as 'The Raiders of the Lost Art', conveying a simultaneous sense of courage in adversity and recovery of old values.[47] Visual devices can be very important. Jeff Bezos at Amazon.com sketches a 'virtuous circle' to express how the growth strategy sets in motion a cycle in which lower costs produce improved customer experience, which in turn produces greater traffic, which would support a wider selection of goods, and so on.[48]

● *Media*. Choosing appropriate media to convey the new strategy is very important.[49] Mass media such as e-mails, voicemails, company newsletters, videos, intranets and senior manager blogs can ensure that all staff receive the same message promptly, helping to avoid damaging uncertainty and rumour mongering. However, face-to-face communications are important too in order to demonstrate the personal commitment of managers and allow for interaction with concerned staff. Thus senior managers may undertake *roadshows*, carrying their message directly to various groups of employees with conferences or workshops at different sites. They may also institute *cascades*, whereby each level of managers is tasked to convey the strategy message directly to the staff reporting to them, and these staff in turn are required to convey the message to their staff, and so on through the organisation.[50]

● *Employee engagement*. It is often helpful to engage employees directly in the strategy, so that they can see what it means for them personally and how their role will change. Interchanges through roadshows and cascades can help, but some organisations use imaginative means to create more active engagement. For example, one British public sector organisation invited all its staff to a day's conference introducing its new strategy, at which employees were invited to pin a photograph of themselves on a 'pledge wall', together with a hand-written promise to change at least one aspect of their work to fit the new strategy.[51] The same organisation also created a carpet depicting the strategic change journey, asking its employees to walk along the pathway to the envisioned future.

It is important to recognise that the process of communication is likely to change the strategy in various ways. Sense making by managers and staff typically involves reinterpretation; roadshows and cascades may raise new issues.[52] In a way, therefore, communications is not the end-point of a strategy-making process, but feeds into the identification of new strategic issues for the next round of strategising.

15.4 STRATEGY METHODOLOGIES

Strategists use a wide range of more or less standardised methodologies to organise and guide their strategising activity. The methodologies introduced here are not analytical concepts or techniques such as in most of the rest of the book, but approaches to managing the strategising process. This section, therefore, addresses which methodologies people might use in doing strategy activity. At the start of this process is often a strategy workshop. This can lead into a set of strategy projects. Projects are often driven by hypothesis testing techniques. Finally, strategising output typically has to fit the format of a business case or strategic plan. This section introduces key issues in each of these methodologies. While guidelines are offered, it should be clear that none of these methodologies offers an easy recipe for success.

15.4.1 Strategy workshops

Strategy workshops
(sometimes called
strategy retreats, away-
days or off-sites) usually
involve groups of
executives working
intensively for one or two
days, often away from the
office, on organisational
strategy

Strategy workshops (sometimes called strategy retreats, away-days or off-sites) are a common methodology for making strategy.[53] These workshops usually involve groups of executives working intensively for one or two days, often away from the office, on organisational strategy. These executives are typically senior managers in the organisation, although workshops can also be a valuable mechanism for involving a wider group of managers. Workshops are used typically to formulate or reconsider strategy, but are also used to address strategy implementation issues and to communicate strategic decisions to a larger audience. Workshops can be either ad hoc or part of the regular strategic planning process, and they may be stand-alone or designed as a series of events. As well as facilitating strategy making, workshops can have additional roles in team building and the personal development of individual participants. Illustration 15.3 demonstrates some of the purposes these strategy workshops can play.

Although strategy workshops can be a valuable part of an organisation's strategy-making activity, they are prone to at least two problems.[54] First, they are liable simply to reinforce managers' existing preconceptions. Especially when reduced to a routine part of the strategic planning cycle, and involving the usual group of senior managers, workshops may not be able to produce new ideas that radically challenge the status quo. Second, workshops can become detached from subsequent action. Precisely because they are separated from the ordinary routines of the organisation, it is difficult to translate workshop ideas and enthusiasm back into the workplace.

Strategy workshops need to be designed for the purpose they are intended to serve. Clarity of objectives is strongly correlated with perceived success.[55] Senior managers should discuss carefully what they want from the workshop, or workshop series beforehand, and design them accordingly. In designing workshops that seek to challenge existing strategy preconceptions, managers should consider:

● *Insisting on prior preparation*. Workshops are typically too short to allow much analysis during the workshop and data may be difficult and time consuming to access. It may be helpful to insist that participants bring key issues, analyses or data to the workshop, and present on them briefly as input to the workshop. Subsequent discussions are likely to be better grounded on firm facts, and awkward information is less easily dismissed.

● *Involving participants from outside the senior executive team*. It may be useful to invite non-executive directors who can be asked to bring an external and challenging view. Alternatively, promising middle managers can be included, as they may have a more direct understanding of issues on the ground and their participation could also be valuable for career development and management succession.

● *Involving outside consultants as facilitators*. Using consultants to chair and facilitate the workshop can free managers to concentrate on the discussion itself, help keep the discussion focused on the strategic issues and support all participants contributing equally to discussion. A consultant may be able to advise on workshop design, provide short stimulating exercises or analyses during the workshop and help with follow-up after the workshop. Such consultants need to be experienced, sensitive and not overbearing.

Illustration 15.3

Strategy workshops at ESB Power Generation

Strategy workshops may have a variety of purposes relating to strategy development and strategic change.

The managing director of ESB Power Generation, responsible for the running of power stations in Ireland, was concerned that impending deregulation and possible future privatisation would inevitably mean that the business would face a very different future. There would be pressure to reduce market share as well as costs, and the business could find itself in a competitive situation for the first time in its history. It was necessary to examine the future strategy of the business and he decided to do this through a series of strategy workshops involving different levels in the organisation.

Top team workshop

The process began with a two-day top team workshop which addressed a series of questions:

- What might be the key macro-environmental forces to affect the business in the next five years? Deregulation certainly, but that could take different forms. New technologies and raw material costs were also identified as major unknowns that could have significant impact.

- What form might future competition take? This was less likely to be local and more likely to be from the entry of power generators from other European Union countries.

- So what might the possible future scenarios be?

- What competitive advantage might the business have over possible new entrants and what strategic capabilities could these build on? Given the different types of power stations ESB had in Ireland, an advantage it should have was flexibility in its offering to the market compared with potential competitors.

- What were the strategic options to compete in a deregulated environment? The strategy would have to change significantly whichever scenario came about and more emphasis would have to be placed on the differential advantages ESB had and might further develop.

Workshops with middle managers

The next level of workshops spread the discussion to managers who reported to those in the top team, together with specialists from other functions. These reviewed the deliberations of the top team, going through the same process in order to establish whether they would come to similar conclusions. The managing director confirmed that the process was also about ensuring that they saw the need for change themselves and checking that they would be 'on board' with a very different strategy from the past.

Two such workshops were held and they did, indeed, endorse the strategy of the top team. They also examined just what a strategy emphasising flexibility would mean in terms of operational priorities in the various business functions.

Involvement throughout the organisation in planning change

There remained the problem of strategic change. Changing from a public sector utility to a competitive strategy of differentiation built on flexibility would require changes in the organisation from top to bottom. It was decided that these should be considered by means of workshops to consider the culture change necessary. The aim was to ensure that, not just the physical resources, but the people in the organisation and the way they dealt with customers and each other could deliver the flexibility that would be required. Workshops were held at levels varying from senior executives to supervisors in the production units to examine just what a culture of flexibility meant, the changes needed in detail and the priorities for action.

Questions

1 What frameworks of analysis might the different workshops have used to tackle the issues?

2 If you were a consultant facilitating the workshops what potential problems might you foresee for each level of workshop?

3 What benefits (or disadvantages) might such workshops have in comparison with other approaches to strategy development for such an organisation?

● *Breaking organisational routines.* A distinctive off-site location can help detach participants from day-to-day operational issues and symbolically affirm the occasion is not subject to the usual norms of executive team discussion. Clear rules about restricting use of mobile communication devices can be important to minimise distraction by ordinary operations. Ice-breaking and other apparently playful exercises – sometimes called 'serious play' – at the beginning of a workshop can help generate creativity and a willingness to challenge orthodoxies.[56]

In designing workshops that will be closely connected to subsequent action, managers should consider:

● *Making an agreed list of actions.* Plenty of time should be set aside at the end of the workshop schedule for a review of workshop outputs, and agreement on necessary actions to follow up.

● *Establishing project groups.* Workshops can build on the cohesion built around particular issues by commissioning groups of managers to work together on them and report back either to a regular executive meeting or to subsequent workshops.

● *Circulating agreed actions.* Circulating agreed actions widely in the organisation will increase the commitment of participants to follow through, as well as appeasing the curiosity or anxiety of those who were not included.

● *Making visible commitment by the top management.* The CEO or other senior manager needs to signal complete commitment throughout the event and afterwards, by both statements and actual behaviours. Senior managers need to be present throughout, undistracted by matters external to the workshop, supportive of all participants, and clear leaders in post-workshop actions.

There is no formula for success with strategy workshops. They typically bring together powerful people to discuss issues of crucial personal importance. Just because a workshop is held off-site in deliberately casual style does not mean that the usual organisational politics are entirely suspended.[57]

15.4.2 Strategy projects

Strategy projects involve teams of people assigned to work on particular strategic issues over a defined period of time

Both strategy making and strategy implementation are often organised in the form of projects or taskforces.[58] **Strategy projects** involve teams of people assigned to work on particular strategic issues over a defined period of time. Projects can be instituted in order to explore problems or opportunities as part of the strategy development process: for example, they might be charged to explore new opportunities in overseas markets. Alternatively they might be instituted to implement agreed elements of a strategy, for example an organisational restructuring or the negotiation of a joint venture. Translating a strategic plan or workshop into a set of projects is a good means of ensuring that intentions are turned into action. The projects can also include a wider group of managers in strategy activity.

Strategy projects should be managed like any other project. In particular they need:[59]

- *A clear brief or mandate.* The project's objectives should be agreed and carefully managed. These objectives are the measure of the project's success. 'Scope creep', by which additional objectives are added as the project goes on, is a common danger.

- *Top management commitment.* The continuing commitment of top management, especially the top management 'client' or 'sponsor', needs to be maintained. Top management agendas are frequently shifting, so communications should be regular.

- *Milestones and reviews.* The project should have from the outset clear milestones with an agreed schedule of intermediate achievements. These allow project review and adjustment where necessary, as well as a measure of ongoing success.

- *Appropriate resources.* The key resource is usually people. The right mix of skills needs to be in place, including project management skills, and effort should be invested in 'team building' at the outset. Strategy projects are often part-time commitments for managers, who have to continue with their 'day jobs'. Attention needs to be paid to managing the balance between managers' ordinary responsibilities and project duties: the first can easily derail the second.

Strategy projects are often organised as *programmes* and as *portfolios*. A programme contains a group of projects that address interrelated issues: for example, a set of projects examining new growth opportunities. The portfolio is an organisation's total set of projects, perhaps including several distinct programmes of projects. It is important that both programmes and overall portfolios have clear systems for governance, reporting and review. Projects can easily proliferate and compete. Programme managers should manage overlaps and redundancies, merging or ending projects that no longer have a distinct purpose because of changing circumstances. Senior management should have careful oversight of the whole portfolio, and again be ready to merge and end projects or even programmes, in order to prevent the 'initiative fatigue' that is often the result of project proliferation.

15.4.3 Hypothesis testing

Hypothesis testing is a methodology used particularly in strategy projects for setting priorities in investigating issues and options

Hypothesis testing

Strategy project teams are typically under pressure to deliver solutions to complex problems under tight time constraints. **Hypothesis testing** is an effective methodology for setting direction for a project, and is widely used by strategy consulting firms and members of strategy project teams.

Hypothesis testing in strategy is adapted from the hypothesis testing procedures of science.[60] It starts with a proposition about how things are (*the descriptive hypothesis*), and then seeks to test it with real-world data. For example, a descriptive hypothesis in strategy could be that being large scale in a particular industry is essential to profitability. To test it, a strategy project team would begin by gathering data on the size of organisations in the industry and correlate these with the organisations' profitability. Confirmation of this initial descriptive hypothesis (that small organisations are relatively unprofitable) would then lead

Illustration 15.4

Hypothesis testing at a bank

This outline of a consulting engagement for a large, diversified bank shows how the hypothesis testing process can shape a strategy project.

1 Defining the problem/question

The consultants' first step is to define the problem. As usual, the strategic problem has to do with the existence of a gap between what the client wants (here a certain level of profitability for a particular product) and what it has (declining profitability). In short, the consultants' problem is that the bank's profitability for this product is below target levels.

2 Develop a set of competing descriptive hypotheses about problem causes

The consultants gather some preliminary data and draw on their own experience to generate some possible descriptive hypotheses about the causes of the problem. Thus they know that some large national competitors are already exiting from this type of product; that profitability varies dramatically across competitors involved in this product; and that some specialised new entrants have taken significant market share. Three possible hypotheses emerge: that the industry structure is basically unattractive; that the bank lacks the right strategic capabilities; that the bank is targetting the wrong customer segments. The consultants use quick and dirty testing to reject the first two hypotheses: after all, some competitors are making profits and the bank has strong capabilities from long presence in this product area. Accordingly, the starting descriptive hypothesis is that the bank is targeting unprofitable customer segments.

3 Testing the starting descriptive hypothesis

The consultants next design a study to collect the data needed to support the descriptive hypothesis. They carry out a market segmentation analysis by customer group by doing interviews with customers across different geographies and income levels. They analyse the kinds of service different segments require and the fees they might pay. The consultants find that their data supports their starting hypothesis: the bank's branches are concentrated in locations which prosperous customers willing to pay higher fees for this product do not use. (Had they not been able to confirm their hypothesis, the consultants would have returned to the other two competing hypotheses, step 2.)

4 Develop prescriptive hypotheses

The consultants then develop prescriptive hypotheses about actions necessary to attract more profitable customer segments. One prescriptive hypothesis is that a better portfolio of branch locations will enhance profitability. The consultants carry out data gathering and analysis to support this hypothesis, for example comparing the profitability of branches in different kinds of locations. They find that the few branches that happen to be in the right locations do have higher profitability with this product.

5 Make recommendations to the client

The consultants prepare a set of preliminary recommendations based on the descriptive hypothesis and validated prescriptive hypotheses: one of these is that the branch locations need changing. These recommendations are checked for acceptability and feasability with key managers within the bank and adjusted according to feedback. Then the consultants make their formal presentation of final recommendations.

Source: Jeanne Liedtka, Darden School of Management, University of Virginia.

Questions

1 Select an important strategic issue facing an organisation that you are familiar with (or an organisation that is publicly in trouble or a case study organisation). Try generating a few descriptive hypotheses that address this issue. Use quick and dirty testing to select an initial descriptive hypothesis.

2 What data should you gather to confirm this descriptive hypothesis and how would you collect it? Should the descriptive hypothesis be confirmed, what possible prescriptive hypotheses follow?

to several *prescriptive hypotheses* about what a particular organisation should do. For a small-scale organisation in the industry, prescriptive hypotheses would centre on how to increase scale: one prescriptive hypothesis in this case would be that acquisitions were a good means to achieve the necessary scale; another would be that alliances were the right way. These prescriptive hypotheses might then become the subjects of further data testing.

This kind of hypothesis testing is ultimately about setting practical priorities in strategy work. Hypothesis testing in business (see Illustration 15.4) therefore differs from strict scientific procedure. The aim finally is to concentrate attention on a very limited set of promising hypotheses, not on the full set of all possibilities. Data is gathered in order to support favoured hypotheses, whereas in science the objective is formally to try to refute hypotheses. Business hypothesis testing aims to find a robust and satisfactory solution within time and resource constraints, not to find some ultimate scientific truth. Selecting the right hypotheses can be helped by applying *quick and dirty testing* (QDT). Quick and dirty testing relies on project teams' existing experience and easily accessed data in order to reject speedily unpromising hypotheses, before too much time is wasted on them.

15.4.4 Business cases and strategic plans

Strategising activities, such as workshops or projects, are typically orientated to creating an output in the form of a *business case* or *strategic plan*. Keeping this end goal in mind provides a structure for the strategising work: what needs to be produced shapes the strategising activities. A **business case** is usually focused around a particular proposal, perhaps an investment in new equipment. A **strategic plan**, of course, is more comprehensive, taking an overall view of the organisation's direction over a substantial period, usually three years and sometimes more (see Chapter 11). Many organisations have a standard template for making business cases or proposing a strategic plan, and where these exist, it is wise to work with that format. Where there is no standard template, it would be worth investigating recent successful business cases or plans within the organisation, and borrowing features from them. It is important that the business case or plan be consistent with the organisational culture, in terms of style, format and detail.

A **business case** provides the data and argument in support of a particular strategy proposal, for example investment in new equipment

A **strategic plan** provides the data and argument in support of a particular strategy for the whole organisation, over a substantial period of time

A project team intending to make a business case should aim to meet the following criteria:[61]

- *Focused on strategic needs*. The team should identify the organisation's overall strategy and relate its case closely to that, not just to any particular departmental needs. A business case should not look as if it is just an HR department or IT department project, for example. The focus should be on a few key issues, with clear priority normally given to those that are both strategically important and relatively easy to address.

- *Supported by key data*. The team will need to assemble appropriate data, with financial data demonstrating appropriate returns on any investment typically essential. However, qualitative data should not be neglected – for example, striking quotations from interviews with employees or key customers, or

Illustration 15.5

Planning to plan at the University Library of Notre Dame

A university library assesses its strategic planning process.

When the University of Notre Dame, Indiana, announced a campus-wide strategic planning inititative, the University's Library service launched its own strategic planning review. Specifically, the Library Director established a taskforce of four members to work for 10 weeks (alongside normal duties) in order to provide an initial assessment of the Library's own existing planning arrangements, which were thought to have been weak. This assessment would be the basis for the Library's own new strategic planning exercise.

The membership of the taskforce was as follows: the Director's own executive assistant, with 15 years' experience in the Library; the Library's budget officer; the business reference librarian, currently studying for a MBA; and the taskforce leader, a maths librarian who had joined the Library from a strategy consulting firm. The taskforce quickly established four stages to their work:

- Produce an operational definition of planning.

- Determine an appropriate planning framework for the Library and its existing materials.

- Evaluate the existing materials in the light of this framework and assess the coherence of the whole.

- Recommend a future planning process.

The taskforce soon arrived at an operational definition of strategic planning through a search of the business literature and professional resources. They then examined various published frameworks for planning, finally comparing five of them systematically on a blackboard. In the end, they settled on one of these frameworks, rather than trying to synthesise their own tailor-made variant. They next searched through the Library's own materials for anything relevant to planning, from presentations given by the Library Director

to formal vision and mission statements. Comparing against the chosen planning framework, the taskforce identified major gaps, such as the absence of any explicit statement about the Library's strategic planning process or anything that could be conceived of as an overall strategic plan. In evaluating these materials, the taskforce found that they were often inconsistent with each other, and light-weight with regard to implementation. In the end, the taskforce recommended that the Library create a completely new strategic plan, with library-wide input.

The last step for the taskforce was to present the findings and recommendations to the Library's senior management. The taskforce leader describes what went well and what went not so well in the presentation:

In a one hour session, we walked them through the four phases of work. We did well explaining . . . strategic planning and outlining a strategic planning framework. We should have taken more time to explain the definitions . . . this is a perpetual source of difficulty. Who can explain clearly the difference between a mission statement and a vision statement . . . ? Nevertheless we did well presenting our conclusions and recommendations and some in our audience were even enthusiastic about starting a thorough strategic planning process.

Within a year, the Library Director had developed a strategic plan, and won acceptance for it from the University's top management.

Source: J. Ladwig, 'Assess the state of your strategic plan', *Library Administration and Management*, vol. 19, no. 2 (2005), pp. 90–93.

Questions

1 What were the key strengths of the taskforce and the process they engaged in?

2 What could have gone wrong?

recent mini-cases of successes or failures in the organisation or at competitors. Some strategic benefits simply cannot be quantified, but are no less important for that: information on competitor moves can be persuasive here. The team should provide background information on the rigour and extent of the research behind the data.

- *Demonstrated solutions and actions*. As earlier, issues attached to solutions tend to get the most attention. The team should provide careful discussion of how proposals will be acted on, and who would be responsible. Possible barriers should be clearly identified. Also alternative scenarios should be recognised, especially downside risk. Implementation feasibility is critical.

- *Provide clear progress measures*. When seeking significant investments over time, it is reassuring to offer clear measures to allow regular progress monitoring. Proposing review mechanisms also adds credibility to the business case.

Many specific evaluation techniques for use in a business case are explained in Chapter 10.

Strategic plans have similar characteristics in terms of focus, data, actions and progress measures. Strategic plans are, however, more comprehensive, and they may be used for entrepreneurial start-ups, business units within a large organisation, or for an organisation as a whole (see also Illustration 15.5). Again formats vary, and it is important to follow one that fits the organisation's culture. However, a typical strategic plan has the following elements, which together should set a strategy team's working agenda:[62]

- *Mission, goals and objectives statement*. This is the point of the whole strategy, and the critical starting place. While it is the starting place, in practice a strategy team might iterate back to this in the light of other elements of the strategic plan. It is worth checking back with earlier statements that the organisation may have made to ensure consistency. See particularly Chapter 4.

- *Environmental analysis*. This should cover the whole of the environment, both macro trends and more focused issues to do with customers, suppliers and competitors. The team should not stop at the analysis, but draw clear strategic implications. See Chapter 2.

- *Organisational analysis*. This should include the strengths and weaknesses of the organisation and its products relative to its competitors and include a clear statement of competitive advantage. To avoid bias and reinforce credibility, the team might seek customer statements about organisational strengths and weaknesses. See Chapter 3.

- *Proposed strategy*. This should be clearly related to the environmental and organisational analyses and support the mission, goals and objectives. The team should offer a clear and realistic action timetable for implementation. Particularly useful here are Chapters 6 to 10.

- *Resources*. The team will need to provide a detailed analysis of the resources required, with options for acquiring them. Critical resources are financial, so the plan should include income statements, cash flows and balance sheets over the period of the plan. Other important resources might be human, particularly managers or people with particular skills. See particularly Chapter 13.

Illustration 15.6

key debate

What good are strategy consultants?

Strategy consultants are frequent participants in strategy making, and typically bring good analytical and project management skills. Why are they so controversial then?

There is no shortage of books criticising strategy consultants. Titles such as *Con Tricks*, *Dangerous Company* and *Rip Off!* provide the flavour. And there have been some spectacular failures. As in Section 15.2.4, McKinsey & Co. took a good deal of blame for the strategic mistakes of Enron and SwissAir.

The accusations made against strategy consultants are at least three-fold. First, they rely too much on inexperienced young staff fresh out of business school, who typically have the slimmest understanding of how client organisations and their markets really work. Second, they are accused of handing over strategy recommendations, and then walking away from implementation. Third, they are perceived as expensive, overpaid individually and always trying to sell on unnecessary extra projects. Clients end up paying for more advice than they really need, much of it unrealistic and unimplementable.

These accusations may be unfair. Most large strategy consulting firms are now organised on industry lines, so building up expertise in particular areas, and they increasingly recruit experienced managers from these industries. Most consultants also prefer to work in joint client–advisor teams, so that clients are involved in generating the recommendations that they will have to implement. Some consultanices, such as Bain, make a point of getting closely involved in implementation too. Finally, consultants are in a competitive market and their clients are typically sophisticated buyers, not easily fooled into buying advice they do not need: the fact that strategy consulting business increased in Europe from €3bn (£2.1bn; $3.8bn) in 1996 to €8bn in 2004 suggests there is plenty of real demand.

There are some successes too. Bain claims that, since 1980, its clients' stock prices have on average outperformed the Standard & Poors 500 large American companies index by four-to-one (www.bain.com). Some great corporate managers have originated in strategy consulting: Lou Gerstner, who turned around IBM, and Meg Whitman, leader of eBay, both started as McKinsey & Co. strategy consultants. And one of the world's most influential management books ever, *The Concept of the Corporation*, came from Peter Drucker's consulting assignment with General Motors during World War II.

There are clues to managing strategy consultants in the criticisms, however: for example, make sure to hire consultants with relevant experience; connect analysis to implementation; and keep a close eye on expenditure. James O'Shea and Charles Madigan close their book with a provocative quotation from Machiavelli's *The Prince*: 'Here is an infallible rule: a prince who is not himself wise cannot be wisely advised. . . . Good advice depends on the shrewdness of the prince who seeks it, and not the shrewdness of the prince on good advice.'

Sources: The European Federation of Management Consultancy Associations (www.feaco.org); J. O'Shea and C. Madigan, *Dangerous Company: Consulting Powerhouses and the Businesss they Save and Ruin*, Penguin, 1998; C.D. McKenna, *The World's Newest Profession: Management Consulting in the Twentieth Century*, Cambridge University Press, 2006.

Questions

1 What measures can a strategy consultant take to reassure a potential client of his or her effectiveness?

2 Are there any reasons to suspect that some people might want to exaggerate criticisms of strategy consultants' conduct?

SUMMARY

www.pearsoned.co.uk/ecs
AUDIO SUMMARY

- The practice of strategy involves critical choices about *who to involve* in strategy, *what to do* in strategising activity, and *which strategising methodologies* to use in order to guide this activity.

- Chief executive officers, senior managers, non-executive directors, strategic planners, strategy consultants and middle managers are frequently all involved in strategising. Middle manager involvement in strategy can suffer from the *CEO access/implementation responsibility paradox*, but the degree of appropriate involvement none the less should depend on the nature of the issue.

- Strategising activity involves *analysing, issue selling, decision making* and *communicating*. Managers should not expect these activities to be fully rational or logical and can valuably appeal to the non-rational characteristics of the people they work with.

- Practical methodologies to guide strategising activity include *strategy workshops*, *strategy projects, hypothesis testing* and creating *business cases* and *strategic plans*.

Work assignments

*✳ Denotes more advanced work assignments.   * Refers to a case study in the Text and Cases edition.*

15.1 Go to the careers or recruitment web page of one of the big strategy consultants (such as www.bain.com, www.bcg.com, www.mckinsey.com). What does this tell you about the nature of strategy consulting work? Would you like this work?

15.2 Go to the website of a large organisation (private or public sector) and assess the way it communicates its strategy to its audiences. With reference to section 15.3.4, how focused is the communication; how impactful is it; and how likely is it to engage employees?

15.3 If you had to design a strategy workshop, suggest who the participants in the workshop should be and what roles they should play in (a) the case where an organisation has to re-examine its fundamental strategy in the face of crisis; (b) the case where an organisation needs to gain commitment to a long-term, comprehensive programme of strategic change.

15.4 ✳ For any case study in the book, imagine yourself in the position of a strategy consultant and propose an initial descriptive hypothesis (section 15.4.3) and define the kinds of data that you would need to test it. What kinds of people would you want in your strategy project team (see sections 15.2.4 and 15.4.2)?

15.5 ✳ Go to a business plan archive (such as the University of Maryland's www.businessplanarchive.org or use a Google search). Select a business plan of interest to you and, in the light of section 15.4.4, assess its good points and its bad points.

Integrative assignment

15.6 For an organisation with which you are familiar, or one of the case organisations, write a strategic plan (for simplicity, you might choose to focus on an undiversified business or a business unit within a larger corporation). Where data is missing, make reasonable assumptions or propose ways of filling the gaps. Comment on whether and how you would provide different versions of this strategic plan for (a) investors; (b) employees.

An extensive range of additional materials, including audio summaries, weblinks to organisations featured in the text, definitions of key concepts and self-assessment questions, can be found on the *Exploring Corporate Strategy* Companion Website at **www.pearsoned.co.uk/ecs**

Recommended key readings

- For an overview of top management involvement in strategy, see P. Stiles and B. Taylor, *Boards at Work: How Directors View their Roles and Responsibilities*, Oxford University Press, 2001. For an overview of the middle management role, see S. Floyd and B. Wooldridge, *Building Strategy from the Middle*, Sage, 2000.

- Three journal special issues offer academic studies of strategy practice: the 'Micro strategy and strategizing', *Journal of Management Studies*, vol. 40, no. 1 (2003); 'Strategizing: the challenges of a practice perspective', *Human Relations*, vol. 60, no. 1

(2007); and 'The crafts of strategy', *Long Range Planning* (2008, forthcoming).

- A practical guide to strategising methodologies is provided by E. Rasiel and P.N. Friga, *The McKinsey Mind*, McGraw-Hill, 2001, which has much more general relevance than that particular consulting firm.

- P. Walcoff, *The Fast-Forward MBA in Business Planning for Growth*, Wiley, 1999, is a practical guide to writing a business or strategic plan, with plenty of models and templates.

References

1. A theoretical basis for this pyramid can be found in R. Whittington, 'Completing the practice turn in strategy research', *Organization Studies*, vol. 27, no. 5 (2006), pp. 613–634; and P. Jarzabkowski, J. Balogun and D. Seidl, 'Strategizing: the challenges of a practice perspective', *Human Relations*, vol. 60, no. 1 (2007), pp. 5–27.

2. A good review of the role of different managers in strategy according to evolving notions of strategic management is in T. O'Shannassy, 'Modern strategic management: balancing strategic thinking and strategic planning for internal and external stakeholders', *Singapore Management Review*, vol. 25, no. 1 (2003), pp. 53–67.

3. The classic statement is A. Chandler, *Strategy and Structure: Chapters in the History of American Enterprise*, MIT Press, 1962.

4. S. Kaplan and E. Beinhocker, 'The real value of strategic planning', *MIT Sloan Management Review*, Winter (2003), pp. 71–76.

5. M.E. Porter, 'What is strategy?', *Harvard Business Review*, November–December (1996), pp. 61–78.

6. M. Haywood and D. Hambrick, 'Explaining the premium paid for large acquisitions: evidence of CEO hubris', *Administrative Science Quarterly*, vol. 42, no. 1 (1977), pp. 103–128.

7. J. Collins, *Good to Great*, Random House, 2001.

8. I. Janis, *Victims of Groupthink: A Psychological Study of Foreign-Policy Decisions and Fiascoes*, Houghton Mifflin, 1972; R.S. Baron, 'So right it's wrong: groupthink and the ubiquitous nature of polarized group decision making', in Mark P. Zanna (ed.), *Advances in experimental social psychology*, vol. 37. pp. 219–253, Elsevier Academic Press, 2005.

9. C. Boone, W. Von Olffen, A. Van Witteloostuijn and B. De Brabander, 'The genesis of top management team diversity: selective turnover among top management teams in Dutch newspaper publishing', *Academy of Management Journal*, vol. 47, no. 5 (2004), pp. 633–656.

10. T. McNulty and A. Pettigrew, 'Strategists on the board', *Organization Studies*, vol. 20, no. 1 (1999), pp. 47–74; P. Stiles and B. Taylor, *Boards at Work: How Directors view their roles and responsibilities*, Oxford University Press, 2001.

11. For an insightful case of an orchestra CEO inadequacy with regard to strategy techniques, see S. Maitlis, 'Taking it from the top: how CEOS influence (and fail to influence) their boards', *Organization Studies*, vol. 25, no. 8 (2004), pp. 1275–1313.

12. For an in-depth analysis of a director failing to persuade his colleagues, see D. Samra-Fredericks, 'Strategizing as lived experience and strategists' everyday efforts to shape strategic direction', *Journal of Management Studies*, vol. 42, no. 1 (2003), pp. 1413–1442.

13. For an analysis of senior management teams as 'communities of practice' in which practitioners have to win legitimacy for full participation, see R. Whittington, 'Learning to Strategise', SKOPE Working Paper no. 23, University of Oxford, 2002.

14. R.M. Grant, 'Strategic planning in a turbulent environment: evidence from the oil majors', *Strategic Management Journal*, vol. 24, no. 6 (2003), pp. 491–517.

15. E. Beinhocker and S. Kaplan, 'Tired of strategic planning?', *McKinsey Quarterly*, special edition on Risk and Resilience (2002), pp. 49–57; S. Kaplan and E. Beinhocker, 'The real value of strategic planning', *MIT Sloan Management Review*, Winter (2003), pp. 71–76.

16. A. Chandler, *Strategy and Structure: Chapters in the History of American Enterprise*, MIT Press, 1962.

17. S. Floyd and B. Wooldridge, *Building Strategy from the Middle*, Sage, 2000.

18. G. Johnson, L. Melin and R. Whittington, 'Micro-strategy and strategising: towards an activity-based view', *Journal of Management Studies*, vol. 40, no. 1 (2003), pp. 3–22.

19. A. Watson and B. Wooldridge, 'Business unit manager influence on corporate-level strategy formulation', *Journal of Managerial Issues*, vol. 18, no. 2 (2005), pp. 147–161.

20. S. Floyd and B. Wooldridge, 'Middle management's strategic influence and organizational performance', *Journal of Management Studies*, vol. 34, no. 3 (1997), pp. 465–485.

21. S. Mantere, 'Strategic practices as enablers and disablers of championing activity', *Strategic Organization*, vol. 3, no. 2 (2005), pp. 157–184.

22. F. Westley, 'Middle managers and strategy: microdynamics of inclusion', *Strategic Management Journal*, vol. 11 (1990), pp. 337–351.

23. See D. Moyniham, 'Ambiguity in policy lessons: the agentification experience', *Public Administration*, vol. 84, no. 4 (2006), pp. 1029–1050; and L.S. Oakes, B. Townley and D.J. Cooper, 'Business planning as pedagogy: language and control in a changing institutional field', *Administrative Science Quarterly*, vol. 43, no. 2 (1997), pp. 257–292.

24. The websites of the leading strategy consultants are useful sources of information on strategy consulting and strategy in general, as well as strategy consulting careers: see www.mckinsey.com; www.bcg.com; www.bain.com; www.monitor.com.

25. The European Federation of Management Consultancies Associations website www.feaco.org is a useful source of information on trends in the strategy consulting industry generally. P. May and F. Czeniawska, *Management Consulting in Practice*, Kogan Page, 2005, provides many cases of consulting interventions, including strategy.

26. For theoretical discussion of advisers in strategy, see L. Arendt, R. Priem and H. Ndofor, 'A CEO-adviser model of strategic decision-making', *Journal of Management*, vol. 31, no. 5 (2005), pp. 680–699; an empirically-based study is M. Schwarz, 'Knowing in practice: how consultants work with clients to create, share and apply knowledge', *Academy of Management Best Papers Proceedings*, 2004.

27. C.D. McKenna, *The World's Newest Profession*, Cambridge University Press, 2006; R. Whittington, P. Jarzabkowski, M. Mayer, E. Mounoud, J. Nahapiet and L. Rouleau, 'Taking strategy seriously: responsibility and reform for an important social practice', *Journal of Management Inquiry*, vol. 12, no. 4 (2003), pp. 396–409.

28. S. Appelbaum, 'Critical success factors in the client-consulting relationship', *Journal of the American Academy of Business*, March (2004), pp. 184–191; M. Mohe, 'Generic strategies for managing consultants: insights from client companies in Germany', *Journal of Change Management*, vol. 5, no. 3 (2005), pp. 357–365.

29. E. Beinhocker and S. Kaplan, 'Tired of strategic planning?', *McKinsey Quarterly*, special edition on Risk and Resilience (2002), pp. 49–57: figure 2, p. 56.

30. G. Hodgkinson, R. Whittington, G. Johnson and M. Schwarz, 'The role of strategy workshops in strategy development processes: formality, communication, co-ordination and inclusion', *Long Range Planning*, vol. 30 (2006), pp. 479–496.

31. T. Hill and R. Westbrook, 'SWOT analysis: it's time for a product recall', *Long Range Planning*, vol. 30, no. 1 (1997), pp. 46–52. For a practical example of better usage, see R.G. Dyson, 'Strategic development and SWOT analysis at the University of Warwick', *European Journal of Operational Research*, vol. 15, no. 2 (2004), pp. 631–640.

32. A. Langley, 'Between paralysis by analysis and extinction by instinct', *Sloan Management Review*, vol. 36, no. 3 (1995), pp. 63–76.

33. A. Langley, 'In search of rationality: the purposes behind the use of formal analysis in organisations', *Administrative Science Quarterly*, vol. 34 (1989), pp. 598–631.

34. This draws on the attention-based view of the firm: see W. Ocasio and J. Joseph, 'An attention-based theory of strategy formulation: linking micro and macro perspectives in strategy processes', *Advances in Strategic Management*, vol. 22 (2005), pp. 39–62.

35. Ibid.

36. For an insightful analysis of the role of mealtimes and other informal moments to influence strategy, see A. Sturdy, M. Schwarz and A. Spicer, 'Guess who's coming to dinner? Structures and the use of liminality in strategic management consultancy', *Human Relations*, vol. 10, no. 7 (2006), pp. 929–960.

37. B. Yakis and R. Whittington, 'Sustaining strategic issues: five longitudinal cases in human resource management', Paper presented to the *Academy of Management*, Philadelphia, 2007.

38. D. Lovallo and O. Siboney, 'Distortions and deceptions in strategic decisions', *McKinsey Quarterly*, no. 1 (2006). A good review of decision-making biases is in G. Hodgkinson and P. Sparrow, *The Competent Organization*, Open University Press, 2002.

39. K.M. Eisenhardt, 'Speed and strategic choice: how managers accelerate decision making', *California Management Review*, Spring (1990), pp. 39–54.

40. M. Mankins, 'Stop wasting valuable time', *Harvard Business Review*, September (2004), pp. 58–65.

41. S. Elbanna, 'Strategic decision-making: process perspectives', *International Journal of Management Reviews*, vol. 8, no. 1 (2006), pp. 1–20.

42. C. Miller and R.D. Ireland, 'Intuition in strategic decision-making: friend or foe in the fast-paced 21st century?', *Academy of Management Executive*, vol. 21, no. 1 (2005), pp. 19–30.

43. K.M. Eisenhardt, J. Kahwajy and L.J. Bourgeois, 'Conflict and strategic choice: how top teams disagree', *California Management Review*, vol. 39, no. 2 (1997), pp. 42–62.

44. C. Nordblom, 'Involving middle managers in strategy at Volvo Group', *Strategic Communication Management*, vol. 10, no. 2 (2006), pp. 24–28.

45. This builds on M. Thatcher, 'Breathing life into business strategy', *Strategic Communication Management*, vol. 10, no. 2 (2006), pp. 14–18.

46. See http://www.cabinetoffice.gov.uk/strategy/work_areas/index.asp.

47. G. Adamson, J. Pine, T. van Steenhoven and J. Kroupa, 'How story-telling can drive strategic change', *Strategy and Leadership*, vol. 34, no. 1 (2006), pp. 36–41.

48. R.W. Keidel, 'Strategize on a napkin', *Strategy and Leadership*, vol. 33, no. 4 (2005), pp. 58–59.

49. R.H. Lengel and R.L. Daft, 'The selection of communication media as an executive skill', *Academy of Management Executive*, vol. 2, no. 3 (1988), pp. 225–232.

50. For examples of roadshows and cascades, see M. Thatcher, 'Breathing life into business strategy', *Strategic Communication Management*, vol. 10, no. 2 (2006), pp. 14–18.

51. R. Whittington, E. Molloy, M. Mayer and A. Smith, 'Practices of strategizing/organizing: broadening strategy work and skills', *Long Range Planning*, vol. 39 (2006), pp. 615–629.

52. On middle manager sense making, see J. Balogun and G. Johnson, 'Organizational restructuring and middle manager sensemaking', *Academy of Management Journal*, vol. 47, no. 4 (2004), pp. 523–540.

53. For a recent survey of strategy workshops in practice, see G. Hodgkinson, R. Whittington, G. Johnson and M. Schwarz, 'The role of strategy workshops in strategy development processes: formality, communication, coordination and inclusion', *Long Range Planning*, vol. 30 (2006), pp. 479–496.

54. C. Bowman, 'Strategy workshops and top-team commitment to strategic change', *Journal of Managerial Psychology*, vol. 10, no. 8 (1995), pp. 4–12; B. Frisch and L. Chandler, 'Off-sites that work', *Harvard Business Review*, vol. 84, no. 6 (2006), pp. 117–126.

55. G. Hodgkinson, R. Whittington, G. Johnson and M. Schwarz, 'The role of strategy workshops in strategy development processes: formality, communication, coordination and inclusion', *Long Range Planning*, vol. 30 (2006), pp. 479–496.

56. L. Heracleous and C. Jacobs, 'The serious business of play', *MIT Quarterly*, Fall (2005), pp. 19–20.

57. For a discussion of a failed strategy workshop from different points of view, see G. Hodgkinson and G. Wright, 'Confronting strategic inertia in a top management team: learning from failure', *Organization Studies*, vol. 23, no. 6 (2002), pp. 949–978; and R. Whittington, 'Completing the practice turn in strategy research', *Organization Studies*, vol. 27, no. 5 (2006), pp. 613–634.

58. P. Morris and A. Jamieson, 'Moving from corporate strategy to project strategy', *Project Management Journal*, vol. 36, no. 4 (2005), pp. 5–18. A comparative study of strategy project development teams is in F. Blackler, N. Crump and S. McDonald, 'Organizing processes in complex activity networks', *Organization*, vol. 72, no. 2 (2000), pp. 277–300. See also S. Paroutis and A. Pettigrew, 'Strategizing in the multi-business firm: strategy teams at multiple levels and over time', *Human Relations*, vol. 60, no. 1 (2007), pp. 99–135.

59. H. Sirkin, P. Keenan and A. Jackson, 'The hard side of change management', *Harvard Business Review*, October (2005), pp. 109–118; J. Kenny, 'Effective project management for strategic innovation and change in an organizational context', *Project Management Journal*, vol. 34, no. 1 (2003), pp. 43–53.

60. This section draws on E. Rasiel and P.N. Friga, *The McKinsey Mind*, McGraw-Hill, 2001; H. Courtney, *20/20 Foresight: Crafting Strategy in an Uncertain World*, Harvard Business School Press, 2001; and unpublished material from J. Liedtka, University of Virginia.

61. J. Walker, 'Is your business case compelling?', *Human Resource Planning*, vol. 25, no. 1 (2002), pp. 12–15; M. Pratt, 'Seven steps to a business case', *Computer World*, 10 October (2005), pp. 35–36.

62. Two practical books on creating strategic or business plans are P. Tiffany and S. Peterson, *Business Plans for Dummies*, IDG Books, 2004; and P. Walcoff, *The Fast-Forward MBA in Business Planning for Growth*, Wiley, 1999.

Ray Ozzie, software strategist

During 2005 and 2006, Ray Ozzie took an increasingly important strategic role at the computer software giant Microsoft, finally emerging as the company's Chief Software Architect. At the centre of Ozzie's new strategy was the endeavour to 'webify' Microsoft, widely perceived to have fallen behind Internet upstarts such as Google and Yahoo!. Developing this new strategy involved more than formulating a bold and challenging new vision for Microsoft. Ozzie faced difficult decisions even in the sheer practicalities of strategy making. Thus Ozzie had to design a top management strategy retreat; he had to find a way of maintaining the momentum after that retreat; and finally, he had to decide how best to communicate the key themes of the emerging new strategy.

Bill Gates (left) and Ray Ozzie (right)

Photo: Associated Press/PA Photos

Ozzie was regarded by many experts as a software genius. In 1984 he had founded Iris Associates, which five years later launched, under contract for the Lotus Development Corporation, the first commercial e-mail and collaboration software for major corporations, Lotus Notes. Lotus Development Corporation bought Iris for $84m (£47m; €67m) in 1994, and the next year computer giant IBM in turn bought Lotus. Three years later, Ozzie left IBM to found Groove Networks, another collaboration software company. In March 2005, Microsoft bought Groove Networks in order to integrate its collaboration features into the next generation of its Office products. Ozzie joined Microsoft as a new employee.

What Microsoft paid for Groove Networks was undisclosed, but it certainly made Ozzie an even wealthier man. In other respects, however, Ozzie's position was not so comfortable. Ozzie's starting position was as only one of three chief technology officers at Microsoft, a company with 70,000 employees. Initially he would be commuting weekly from his home in Boston on the East Coast to the Microsoft headquarters in Redmond on the West Coast. Besides, Groove Networks had been Ozzie's own show, and much smaller, with just

200 employees. As Ozzie said in an interview with MSNBC: 'The great thing about a small company is that you can put a lot of effort into one thing – but you can have limited impact. In a larger role, I'll probably have less focused impact, across a broader range of things.'

The company that Ozzie was joining did indeed operate across a broad range of products. It was responsible for the near universal Microsoft Windows operating system; for the equally pervasive Microsoft Office range of products; for the Xbox games business; for the MSN Internet portal; and for MSNBC cable television. Total turnover was $40bn and the company had $35bn cash reserves. The company was still dominated by Bill Gates, who had founded it in 1975 and boasted in 2005 that he had worked every single day in the intervening 30 years. In 2005, Gates was still the company's Chief Software Architect.

But by 2005 the company was apparently stagnating. Turnover and profits were still climbing, but the stock price had been stuck for several years. From a peak of nearly $60 a share, Microsoft had been fluctuating around $25 (see the figure). Microsoft's core business model relied on selling

Microsoft corporation
Price history – MSFT (9/11/1996 – 9/8/2006)

proprietary software direct either to users or to computer manufacturers for pre-installation on machines. This model was being challenged by free open-source software (such as Linux) and web-based companies whose software was free off the Internet and supported by advertising (such as Google or Yahoo!). Microsoft was widely perceived as yesterday's company.

Ozzie was not going into Microsoft blind. As a Fortune article describes, even before being hired, Ozzie had attended the March retreat of the company's top 110 or so executives, including Bill Gates. The two-day retreat was organised by Microsoft's CEO, Steve Ballmer, and took place at the luxurious Semiahmoo Resort, overlooking the Pacific and with a spa and two golf courses. According to Fortune, the retreat kicked off with a team-building exercise in which the executives broke into groups of six or seven. Each group was given a bag of parts for a battery-powered Mars rover. The goal: build the rover quickly, but with the fewest parts. Bill Gates' team won. On the second day, groups were assigned to breakout sessions in order to brainstorm various strategic issues. Gates, Ozzie and several other top

technologists were put in a group tasked with defining Microsoft's 'core' – the set of things Microsoft does uniquely well that could be used across all Microsoft's product lines. Ozzie recalled the breakout session: 'It was the first time I had a chance as an insider to see how people within the company relate to Bill.' When the group went into its appointed conference room, he told Fortune, 'they tended to just naturally fall with Bill at one end and other people around the sides. In some ways they were being deferential, and in some ways he was just one of the gang in a really lively peer discussion.'

The nature of Microsoft's core emerged as the key strategic issue from Semiahmoo. Ballmer, however, seemed unable to push the issue forward. The group of executives he had asked to arrange a larger event to develop the issue refused to organise it. They argued it was premature and likely to cause undue alarm to involve more people at that stage. The momentum from Semiahmoo seemed to have evaporated, until Ballmer turned to Ozzie to ask him to take forward the concept of the strategic core. Soon after, Ballmer asked Ozzie to take the lead with another top management retreat, to take place in June. As Ozzie commented to Fortune: 'I had more than a bit of anxiety, given I had never worked with these folks before'.

Ozzie worked closely with Gates, Ballmer and some other senior executives to design this second retreat. It would take place over one day at Robinswood House, a small hotel based on a nineteenth-century pioneer lodge close to Microsoft's headquarters. Just 15 senior executives were to attend; Gates was not invited. The Robinswood facilities were cramped and somewhat basic, with everybody sitting elbow to elbow in a small room. The room was cold and the food attracted complaints. Everybody had been circulated before the meeting with a 51-page memo from Ozzie with his diagnosis of the strategic challenge facing Microsoft.

Ozzie kicked off the retreat by restating the strategic challenge to Microsoft. Fortune reports that Ozzie maintained his usual genial and non-confrontational style, but no punches were pulled about Microsoft's past mistakes. Ozzie recalled how the group of senior managers then went through a 'cathartic exercise of venting about every negative thing' in the company's technical and organisational strategy of recent years. 'It was story after story after story.' For 14 hours, the senior Microsoft executives worked continuously debating the future of the company. The group's conclusion was that Microsoft needed major change. At the end of the debate, Ballmer demanded of his colleagues: 'If there are any concerns, you've got to say them now.' There was no dissent.

This time Ballmer and Ozzie worked hard to ensure follow-through. A series of weekly half-day meetings were scheduled for the executives who had been at the retreat, with strong pressure for attendance. Ozzie set the agenda for the meetings and for eight weeks the executives debated specific aspects of the new strategy in a conference room right next door to Ballmer's office. There was a good deal of controversy still, but progress was made. In mid-September, Ballmer announced a set of major organisational changes and promotions. Most significant was the merger of Windows and MSN to create a new Platform Products and Services group within Microsoft, firmly based on the web. Significant too was Ozzie's promotion to chief technology officer for Microsoft as a whole, and the movement of his office and staff to the high-security top-floor suite where Gates and Ballmer had their offices too.

The web strategy moved forward. In late October Bill Gates and Ray Ozzie each released important internal memos (soon leaked to the Internet). The Gates memo was dated Sunday 30 October, subject Internet Services Software and e-mailed to all Microsoft Executive Staff and Direct Reports and the Distinguished Engineers group. Gates recalled his memo of 10 years earlier, entitled the Internet Tidal Wave, which had launched a revolution within Microsoft to catch up with the first-generation Internet challenge. He then introduced the new issue of Internet software (or web-based) services. He attached Ozzie's own memo on which he commented: 'I feel sure we will look back on [this] as being as critical as the Internet Tidal Wave. Ray outlines the great things we and our partners can do using the Internet Services approach. The next sea change is upon us.'

Ozzie's own attached memo dated from the Friday before and was addressed to Executive Staff and Direct Reports. It was 5,000 words long, with the subject line 'The Internet Services Disruption'. The memo started positively, by asserting that Microsoft was in the midst of its most important new product

phase in its history, referring to the launch of the Xbox 360 and many other products. But it continued quickly to remind readers that the company was innovating at a time of great turbulence and change. This was not unprecedented, however. The memo continued by recalling that the company had needed to review its core strategy and direction roughly every five years throughout its history.

Ozzie recalled three previous changes, including the Internet Tidal Wave, on a five-year cycle going back to 1990. He then proposed the existence of a new business model, Internet-based software supported by advertising. He concluded the memo's introduction by insisting that everybody should reflect on the environmental change, on the company's strengths and weaknesses and on its leadership responsibilities. He warned that if his fellow employees did not reflect and respond quickly and decisively, the company as it stood was seriously at risk. He repeatedly used the word 'we' to underline the common challenge.

Ozzie's e-mail continued in detail. It contained criticism of Microsoft's past innovation leadership in the industry. It warned of more innovative competitors, specifically naming such companies as Google, Apple, Yahoo! and start-ups such as Flickr and Skype. The memo then proposed three key tenets driving fundamental shifts in the competitive landscape: the power of the advertising-supported economic model; the effectiveness of a new Internet download delivery model; and the demand for integrated user experiences that 'just work'. It developed new opportunities, in which the key repeated word was 'seamless', implying more integrated and user-friendly customer experiences across entertainment, communications and work applications. The memo also sketched key implications for all three Microsoft divisions.

The final parts of Ozzie's memo were particularly significant. In a section headed 'What's Different', Ozzie directly addressed possible sceptics amongst his audience. He acknowledged that many would just say that there was nothing very new in what he had said and that Microsoft had been trying similar things for many years, going back to the early 1990s. Some might say that this memo was no big deal.

Ozzie then specified four reasons why it would be different to last time. The first was simple. Invoking 'Bill' Gates and 'Steve' Ballmer by their first names, he insisted that the senior leadership was absolutely committed to the vision outlined in the memo. As evidence, he cited the recent reorganisation of the company into three divisions, including the creation of the new Platform Products and Services group.

The three other reasons highlighted the space opened up by the completion of the upcoming product launches, the technological opportunities now available and the competitive threat.

The memo continued with a final section headed 'Next Steps'. Here he specified a timetable by which division presidents would be assigning individual managers as 'scenario owners' to take forward various initiatives, to work together with Ozzie, to consult within Microsoft and finally to develop concrete new plans. Ozzie provided the address for an internal blog that he would keep, which would provide relevant documents and his own thoughts as they continued to develop. He also promised to experiment with various other ways to allow Microsoft employees to engage with him directly in the strategic conversation.

On 1 November, Bill Gates and Ray Ozzie jointly unveiled the new strategy to a press conference in San Francisco. In June 2006, Gates announced that he would be retiring from a full-time role in Microsoft, easing out over two years. Ozzie took over Gates' role as the company's Chief Software Architect. He had meanwhile bought himself an apartment near the Microsoft headquarters, overlooking Seattle harbour. His wife started commuting to him.

Main sources: D. Kirkpatrick and J.L. Yang, 'Microsoft's new brain', *Fortune*, 15 May (2006), pp. 52–63; 'Bill Gates: Internet Software Services', at http://blogs.zdnet.com/web2explorer/?page_id=53; 'Ray Ozzie: the Internet Services Disruption', at http://www.scripting.com/disruption/ozzie/TheInternetServicesDisruptio.htm; 'Microsoft to buy Groove Networks', MSNBC, 10 March (2005).

Questions

1 Why was the Semiahmoo retreat not successful in creating sustained momentum around the issue of Microsoft's 'core'?

2 Why was Ozzie more successful in creating follow-on action after the Robinswood retreat?

3 Comment on Ozzie's communications strategy with regard to the Internet Services Disruption.

Part III of the book has been concerned with strategy in action. Section 1.2 introduced the overall model to this book. The point that is made there is that strategic management should not necessarily be seen as a linear process: that, in effect, the activities and challenges raised in different parts of this book interact and inform each other. This is why the circles in Exhibit 1.3 overlap. However by necessity, the book is presented in a linear fashion and strategic management is often discussed in terms of strategy formulation followed by strategy implementation.

In this commentary the strategy lenses are used to explore this key issue further. Does it make sense to see strategic management as a process of formulating a strategy followed by a process of implementing a strategy?

Note that:

- There is no suggestion here that one of these lenses is better than another, but they do provide different insights into the problems faced and the ways managers cope with the challenge.
- If you have *not* read the Commentary following Chapter 1 that explans the four lenses, you should now do so.

Design lens

Building on the notion that thinking precedes organisational action, managing strategy is seen as a linear process. So, strategy is first formulated by top managers and then it is implemented through:

- Senior managers persuading people of the logic of the strategy.
- Project planning to ensure appropriate resourcing, timing and sequencing.
- Clear briefing of middle and junior managers.
- Establishing an appropriate organisational structure and control systems so that strategy implementation can be monitored. So 'structure follows strategy'.
- Senior managers as change agents identifying the style of change management required and the levers for managing change.

Experience lens

Strategies typically develop on the basis of experience and culture; current strategy informs and moulds future strategy. Moreover, control systems and resource allocation routines are likely to have become embedded and mould future strategy too. In effect 'strategy follows structure'. So the idea of implementation following formulation is misleading.

However, since it is likely that strategies will develop incrementally, strategic drift is likely over time and this may result in occasional periods of more top-down directed strategic change. At such times it is likely there will be a need to overcome cultural inertia and resistance to change (*unfreezing*). This may involve challenging the prevailing beliefs and assumptions of organisational culture.

Organisations are also political arenas so the management of change needs to be seen as a political process and managers need to be adept in such processes.

Commentary on Part III

Strategy in Action

Ideas lens

Strategies emerge as patterns of order from the ideas that bubble up from within and around an organisation. So, again, the division between strategy formulation and strategy implementation disappears.

It is top managers' role to identify the potential of new ideas and create the organisational context whereby these can be realised. In doing so, they need to bear in mind that:

- The greater the interaction within and across the boundaries of organisations, the more will new ideas and innovation come about. Formal structures and systems of control are unavoidable necessities, but can build barriers and boundaries.
- It may be helpful to change organisational structures in order to avoid relationships and routines becoming embedded and so as to encourage 'weak ties' which encourage new ideas.
- The need is not for cumbersome controls but a few key guiding principles or 'simple rules'.
- In dynamic environments there may be no need for *unfreezing* because the organisation is in a state of continual change.

Managers can usefully build structures and encourage organisational learning to promote all this, a role more important than trying to direct strategies in a top-down fashion.

Discourse lens

Strategy and its management are essentially about discourse – written and spoken. An implication is that the discourse of strategy is inevitably interpreted so the disconnect between intended strategy and how that is interpreted is likely to be higher than managers think.

A key lesson is that each stakeholder has their own identity and associated way of expressing that identity (their 'narrative'). The messages given to stakeholders about strategy may not be construed by them as intended; they will be 'rewritten' in terms of that narrative. It is important to manage strategic messages with stakeholders' identities and narratives in mind. So:

- The extent to which controls have the effect intended will depend on how congruent they are with the narratives of those affected. For example, challenging targets may work because people cannot afford not to comply, not because they like to be challenged.
- Managers need to consider carefully the nature of the discourse they employ, especially in managing the acceptance of the need for change and to ensure change initiatives, once under way, are not rejected.
- Discourse that is appropriate to the needs of stakeholders can have a powerful effect on getting strategies accepted and put into effect.

Glossary

Acceptability is concerned with the expected performance outcomes of a strategy and the extent to which these meet the expectations of stakeholders (p. 378)

An **acquisition** is where an organisation takes ownership of another organisation (p. 367)

Backward integration is development into activities concerned with the inputs into the company's current business (p. 271)

Balanced scorecards combine both qualitative and quantitative measures, acknowledge the expectations of different stakeholders and relate an assessment of performance to choice of strategy (p. 463)

Barriers to entry are factors that need to be overcome by new entrants if they are to compete successfully (p. 61)

Black holes are subsidiaries located in countries that are crucial for competitive success but with low-level resources or capabilities (p. 325)

A **business case** provides the data and argument in support of a particular strategy proposal, for example investment in new equipment (p. 600)

Business-level strategy is about how to compete successfully in particular markets (p. 7)

A **business model** describes the structure of product, service and information flows and the roles of the participating parties (p. 339, 499)

Buyers are the organisation's immediate customers, not necessarily the ultimate consumers (p. 62)

A **cash cow** is a business unit with a high market share in a mature market (p. 286)

A **change agent** is the individual or group that effects strategic change in an organisation (p. 544)

Coercion is the imposition of change or the issuing of edicts about change (p. 547)

Competences are the skills and abilities by which resources are deployed effectively through an organisation's activities and processes (p. 96)

Competitive rivals are organisations with similar products and services aimed at the same customer group (p. 64)

Competitive strategy is concerned with the basis on which a business unit might achieve competitive advantage in its market (p. 228)

Complementors are products or services for which customers are prepared to pay more if together than if they stand alone (p. 67)

An organisation's **configuration** consists of the structures, processes and relationships through which the organisation operates (p. 446)

Consolidation is where organisations focus defensively on their current markets with current products (p. 266)

Contributors are subsidiaries of international businesses with valuable internal resources but located in countries of lesser strategic significance, which none the less play key roles in a multinational organisation's competitive success (p. 324)

Convergence is where previously separate industries begin to overlap in terms of activities, technologies, products and customers (p. 67)

Core competences are the skills and abilities by which resources are deployed through an organisation's activities and processes such as to achieve competitive advantage in ways that others cannot imitate or obtain (p. 97)

Core values are the underlying principles that guide an organisation's strategy (p. 165)

Corporate governance is concerned with the structures and systems of control by which managers are held accountable to those who have a legitimate stake in an organisation (p. 135)

Corporate-level strategy is concerned with the overall purpose and scope of an organisation and how value will be added to the different parts (business units) of the organisation (p. 7)

The **corporate parent** refers to the levels of management above that of the business units, and therefore without direct interaction with buyers and competitors (p. 262)

Corporate social responsibility is concerned with the ways in which an organisation exceeds its minimum obligations to stakeholders specified through regulation (p. 148)

Critical success factors (CSFs) are those product features that are particularly valued by a group of customers and, therefore, where the organisation must excel to outperform competition (p. 79)

A **cultural explanation of strategy development** is that it occurs as the outcome of the taken-for-granted assumptions and behaviours in organisations (p. 426)

The **cultural web** shows the behavioural, physical and symbolic manifestations of a culture that inform and are informed by the taken-for-granted assumptions, or paradigm (p. 199)

Data mining is the process of finding trends, patterns and connections in data in order to inform and improve competitive performance (p. 498)

The **design lens** views strategy development as a logical process in which the forces and constraints on the organisation are analysed and evaluated analytically to establish clear strategic direction and a basis for the planned implementation of strategy (p. 30)

Devolution concerns the extent to which the centre of an organisation delegates decision making to units and managers lower down in the hierarchy (p. 467)

A **differentiation strategy** seeks to provide products or services that offer benefits that are different from those of competitors and that are widely valued by buyers (p. 233)

Diffusion is the process by which innovations spread amongst users, varying in pace and extent (p. 341)

Direct supervision is the direct control of strategic decisions by one or a few individuals (p. 459)

Direction is the use of personal managerial authority to establish a clear strategy and how change will occur (p. 547)

The **directional policy matrix** positions SBUs according to (i) how attractive the relevant market is in which they are operating, and (ii) the competitive strength of the SBU in that market (p. 287)

A **disruptive innovation** creates substantial growth by offering a new performance trajectory that, even if initially inferior to the performance of existing technologies, has the potential to become markedly superior (p. 349)

Diversification is defined as a strategy that takes an organisation away from both its existing markets and its existing products (p. 268)

Dogs are business units with a low share in static or declining markets (p. 286)

A **dominant strategy** is one that outperforms other strategies whatever rivals choose (p. 248)

Dynamic capabilities are an organisation's abilities to renew and recreate its strategic capabilities to meet the needs of a changing environment (p. 108)

Education as a style of managing change involves the explanation of the reasons for and means of strategic change (p. 546)

Emergent strategy comes about through everyday routines, activities and processes in organisations leading to decisions that become the long-term direction of an organisation (p. 418)

The **experience lens** views strategy development as the outcome of individual and collective experience of individuals and their taken-for-granted assumptions (p. 33)

A **failure strategy** is one that does not provide perceived value for money in terms of product features, price or both (p. 235)

Feasibility is concerned with whether an organisation has the capabilities to deliver a strategy (p. 390)

In the **financial control** style, the role of the centre is confined to setting financial targets, allocating resources, appraising performance and intervening to avert or correct poor performance (p. 469)

A **first-mover advantage** exists where an organisation is better off than its competitors as a result of being first to market with a new product, process or service (p. 346)

The **five forces framework** helps identify the attractiveness of an industry or sector in terms of competitive forces (p. 59)

A **focused differentiation** strategy seeks to provide high perceived product/service benefits justifying a substantial price premium, usually to a selected market segment (niche) (p. 234)

A **forcefield analysis** provides a view of change problems that need to be tackled, by identifying forces for and against change (p. 541)

Forward integration is development into activities which are concerned with a company's outputs (p. 272)

A **functional structure** is based on the primary activities that have to be undertaken by an organisation such as production, finance and accounting, marketing, human resources and research and development (p. 448)

Game theory is concerned with the interrelationships between the competitive moves of a set of competitors (p. 246)

The **global–local dilemma** relates to the extent to which products and services may be standardised across national boundaries or need to be adapted to meet the requirements of specific national markets (p. 312)

Global sourcing: purchasing services and components from the most appropriate suppliers around the world regardless of their location (p. 310)

Horizontal integration is development into activities which are complementary to present activities (p. 272)

A **hybrid strategy** seeks simultaneously to achieve differentiation and a price lower than that of competitors (p. 234)

Hypercompetition occurs where the frequency, boldness and aggressiveness of dynamic move-ments by competitors accelerate to create a condition of constant disequilibrium and change (p. 71)

Hypothesis testing is a methodology used particularly in strategy projects for setting priorities in investigating issues and options (p. 598)

The **ideas lens** sees strategy as emergent from the ideas that bubble up from the variety and diversity in and around organisations (p. 36)

Implementers are subsidiaries of international businesses that simply execute strategies developed elsewhere and may generate surplus financial resources to help fund initiatives elsewhere (p. 325)

An **industry** is a group of firms producing the same principal product or service (p. 59)

Innovation involves the conversion of new knowledge into a new product, process or service and the putting of this new product, process or service into use, either via the marketplace or by other processes of delivery (p. 335)

Intangible resources are non-physical assets such as information, reputation and knowledge (p. 95)

Intended strategy is an expression of a desired strategy as deliberately formulated or planned by managers (p. 411)

Intervention is the coordination of and authority over processes of change by a change agent who delegates elements of the change process (p. 547)

The **key drivers for change** are environmental factors that are likely to have a high impact on the success or failure of strategy (p. 56)

Key value and cost drivers are the factors that have most influence on the cash generation cabability of an organisation (p. 505)

Leadership is the process of influencing an organisation (or group within an organisation) in its efforts towards achieving an aim or goal (p. 544)

The **learning organisation** is capable of continual regeneration from the variety of knowledge, experience and skills of individuals within a culture which encourages mutual questioning and challenge around a shared purpose or vision (p. 431)

Legitimacy is concerned with meeting the expectations within an organisational field in terms of assumptions, behaviours and strategies (p. 196)

Logical incrementalism is the deliberate development of strategy by experimentation and learning from partial commitments (p. 418)

A **low-price strategy** seeks to achieve a lower price than competitors whilst trying to maintain similar perceived product or service benefits to those offered by competitors (p. 231)

Managing for value is concerned with maximising the long-term cash-generating capability of an organisation (p. 504)

Market development is where existing products are offered in new markets (p. 267)

Market penetration is where an organisation gains market share (p. 264)

Market processes involve some formalised system of 'contracting' for resources (p. 463)

A **market segment** is a group of customers who have similar needs that are different from customer needs in other parts of the market (p. 75)

A **matrix structure** is a combination of structures which could take the form of product and geographical divisions or functional and divisional structures operating in tandem (p. 452)

A **merger** is a mutually agreed decision for joint ownership between organisations (p. 367)

A **mission statement** aims to provide employees and stakeholders with clarity about the overall purpose and *raison d'être* of the organisation. (p. 166)

A **multidivisional structure** is built up of separate divisions on the basis of products, services or geographical areas (p. 450)

A **'no frills' strategy** combines a low price, low perceived product/service benefits and a focus on a price-sensitive market segment (p. 231)

Objectives are statements of specific outcomes that are to be achieved (p. 168)

Operational strategies are concerned with how the component parts of an organisation deliver effectively the corporate- and business-level strategies in terms of resources, processes and people (p. 8)

Organic development is where strategies are developed by building on and developing an organisation's own capabilities (p. 367)

Organisational culture is the 'basic *assumptions and beliefs* that are shared by members of an organisation, that operate unconsciously and define in a basic taken-for-granted fashion an organisation's view of itself and its environment' (p. 191)

Organisational knowledge is the collective experience accumulated through systems, routines and activities of sharing across the organisation (p. 109)

An **organisational field** is a community of organisations that interact more frequently with one another than with those outside the field and that have developed a shared meaning system (p. 194)

A **paradigm** is the set of assumptions held relatively in common and taken for granted in an organisation (p. 197)

The **parental developer** is a corporate parent seeking to employ its own competences as a parent to add value to its businesses and build parenting skills that are appropriate for its portfolio of business units (p. 282)

Participation in the change process is the involvement of those who will be affected by strategic change in the change agenda (p. 547)

Path dependency is where early events and decisions establish policy paths that have lasting effects on subsequent events and decisions (p. 187)

Performance targets relate to the *outputs* of an organisation (or part of an organisation), such as product quality, prices or profit (p. 462)

The **PESTEL framework** categorises environmental influences into six main types: political, economic, social, technological, environmental and legal (p. 55)

Planning processes plan and control the allocation of resources and monitor their utilisation (p. 459)

The **political view** of strategy development is that strategies develop as the outcome of processes of bargaining and negotiation among powerful internal or external interest groups (or stakeholders) (p. 424)

Porter's Diamond suggests that there are inherent reasons why some nations are more competitive than others, and why some industries within nations are more competitive than others (p. 308)

A **portfolio manager** is a corporate parent acting as an agent on behalf of financial markets and shareholders (p. 280)

Power is the ability of individuals or groups to persuade, induce or coerce others into following certain courses of action (p. 162)

Primary activities are directly concerned with the creation or delivery of a product or service (p. 110)

Product development is where organisations deliver modified or new products to existing markets (p. 267)

Profit pools refer to the different levels of profit available at different parts of the value network (p. 114)

A **project-based structure** is one where teams are created, undertake the work and are then dissolved (p. 455)

A **question mark** (or problem child) is a business unit in a growing market, but without a high market share (p. 285)

Realised strategy: the strategy actually being followed by an organisation in practice (p. 430)

A **recipe** is a set of assumptions, norms and routines held in common within an organisational field about organisational purposes and a 'shared wisdom' on how to manage organisations (p. 194)

Related diversification is corporate development beyond current products and markets, but within the capabilities or value network of the organisation (p. 271)

The **resource allocation process** (RAP) explanation of strategy development is that realised strategies emerge as a result of the way resources are allocated in organisations (p. 421)

The **resource-based view** of strategy: the competitive advantage and superior performance of an organisation is explained by the distinctiveness of its capabilities (p. 94)

Resourcing strategies is concerned with the two-way relationship between overall business strategies and strategies in separate resource areas such as people, information, finance and technology (p. 489)

Returns are the benefits which stakeholders are expected to receive from a strategy (p. 378)

Risk concerns the probability and consequences of the failure of a strategy (p. 387)

Rituals are activities or events that emphasise, highlight or reinforce what is especially important in a culture (p. 198)

Routines are 'the way we do things around here' on a day-to-day basis (p. 198)

Scenarios are detailed and plausible views of how the business environment of an organisation might develop in the future based on key drivers for change about which there is a high level of uncertainty (p. 57)

Social entrepreneurship involves individuals and groups who create independent organisations to mobilise ideas and resources to address social problems, typically earning revenues but on a not-for-profit basis (p. 356)

A **stage–gate process** is a structured review process to assess progress on meeting product performance characteristics during the development process and ensuring that they are matched with market data (p. 519)

Staged international expansion: firms initially use entry modes that allow them to maximise knowledge acquisition whilst minimising the exposure of their assets (p. 319)

Stakeholder mapping identifies stakeholder expectations and power and helps in understanding political priorities (p. 158)

Stakeholders are those individuals or groups who depend on an organisation to fulfil their own goals and on whom, in turn, the organisation depends (p. 134)

A **star** is a business unit which has a high market share in a growing market (p. 285)

A **strategic alliance** is where two or more organisations share resources and activities to pursue a strategy (p. 370)

A **strategic business unit** is a part of an organisation for which there is a distinct external market for goods or services that is different from another SBU (p. 7, 227)

Strategic capability is the resources and competences of an organisation needed for it to survive and prosper (p. 95)

Strategic choices involve understanding the underlying bases for future strategy at both the business unit and corporate levels and the options for developing strategy in terms of both the directions and methods of development (p. 14)

The **strategic control** style is concerned with shaping the *behaviour* in business units and with shaping the *context* within which managers are operating (p. 470)

The **strategic customer** is the person(s) at whom the strategy is primarily addressed because they have the most influence over which goods or services are purchased (p. 78)

Strategic drift is the tendency for strategies to develop incrementally on the basis of historical and cultural influences but fail to keep pace with a changing environment (p. 181)

A **strategic gap** is an opportunity in the competitive environment that is not being fully exploited by competitors (p. 81)

Strategic groups are organisations within an industry with similar strategic characteristics, following similar strategies or competing on similar bases (p. 73)

Strategic issue selling is the process of winning the attention and support of top management and other important stakeholders for strategic issues (p. 589)

Strategic leaders (in the context of international strategy) are subsidiaries that not only hold valuable resources and capabilities but are also located in countries that are crucial for competitive success (p. 324)

Strategic lock-in is where an organisation achieves a proprietary position in its industry; it becomes an industry standard (p. 239)

Strategic management includes understanding *the strategic position* of an organisation, *strategic choices* for the future and organising *strategy in action* (p. 12)

A **strategic method** is the *means* by which a strategy can be pursued (p. 366)

A **strategic plan** provides the data and argument in support of a particular strategy for the whole organisation, over a substantial period of time (p. 600)

Strategic planners, sometimes known as corporate development managers or similar, are managers with a formal responsibility for contributing to the strategy process (p. 579)

Strategic planning may take the form of systematised, step-by-step, chronological procedures to develop or coordinate an organisation's strategy (p. 412)

In a **strategic planning style** of control, the relationship between the centre and the business units is one of a parent who is the *master planner* prescribing detailed roles for departments and business units (p. 468)

The **strategic position** is concerned with the impact on strategy of the external environment, an organisation's strategic capability (resources and competences) and the expectations and influence of stakeholders (p. 13)

Strategy is the *direction* and *scope* of an organisation over the *long term*, which achieves *advantage* in a changing *environment* through its configuration of *resources and competences* with the aim of fulfilling *stakeholder expectations* (p. 3)

Strategy as discourse sees strategy development in terms of language as a 'resource' for managers by which strategy is communicated, explained and sustained and through which managers gain influence, power and establish their legitimacy and identity as strategists. (p. 42)

Strategy in action is concerned with ensuring that strategies are working in practice (p. 15)

The **strategy lenses** are four different ways of looking at the issues of strategy development for an organisation (p. 19)

Strategy projects involve teams of people assigned to work on particular strategic issues over a defined period of time (p. 597)

Strategy workshops (sometimes called strategy retreats, away-days or off-sites) usually involve groups of executives working intensively for one or two days, often away from the office, on organisational strategy (p. 594)

Substitutes can reduce demand for a particular 'class' of products as customers switch to the alternatives (p. 62)

Suitability is concerned with whether a strategy addresses the key issues relating to the strategic position of the organisation (p. 376)

Suppliers supply the organisation with what is required to produce the product or service, and include labour and sources of finance (p. 63)

Support activities help to improve the effectiveness or efficiency of primary activities (p. 111)

SWOT summarises the key issues from the business environment and the strategic capability of an organisation that are most likely to impact on strategy development (p. 120)

Symbols are objects, events, acts or people that convey, maintain or create meaning over and above their functional purpose (p. 201; 553)

Synergy refers to the benefits that are gained where activities or assets complement each other so that their combined effect is greater than the sum of the parts (p. 269)

The **synergy manager** is a corporate parent seeking to enhance value across business units by managing synergies across business units (p. 282)

Tangible resources are the physical assets of an organisation such as plant, labour and finance (p. 95)

Threshold capabilities are those capabilities needed for an organisation to meet the necessary requirements to compete in a given market (p. 97)

A **tipping point** is where demand for a product or service suddenly takes off, with explosive growth (p. 344)

A **transnational structure** combines the local responsiveness of the international subsidiary with the coordination advantages found in global product companies (p. 452)

In a **turnaround strategy** the emphasis is on speed of change and rapid cost reduction and/or revenue generation (p. 557)

Unique resources are those resources that critically underpin competitive advantage and that others cannot easily imitate or obtain (p. 97)

Unrelated diversification is the development of products or services beyond the current capabilities and value network (p. 273)

A **value chain** describes the categories of activities within and around an organisation, which together create a product or service (p. 110)

The **value network** is the set of interorganisational links and relationships that are necessary to create a product or service (p. 113)

Vertical integration is backward or forward integration into adjacent activities in the value network (p. 271)

Virtual organisations are held together not through formal structure and physical proximity of people, but by partnership, collaboration and networking (p. 475)

A **vision statement** is concerned with what the organisation aspires to be (p. 166)

Index of Names

General Index

Note: Page numbers in bold refer to definitions in the Glossary.